GUIDELINES FOR DETERMINING YOUR PURPOSE

1 What are the requirements of my writing project?

If I am writing to fulfill an assignment, do I understand that assignment? If I am writing on my own, do I have definite expectations of what I will accomplish?

2 As I proceed in this project, what do I need to know?

Do I have a good understanding of my subject, or do I need more information? Have I considered the possible audiences who might read my writing?

3 What hypothesis can I use as my working purpose?

How many different hypotheses can I formulate about my subject? Which of them seems to direct and control my information in the most effective manner?

4 What purpose have I discovered for this writing project?

Has my purpose changed as I learned more about my subject and audience? If so, in what ways? Have I discovered, by working with a hypothesis or hypotheses, what I want to do in my writing?

5 What is my thesis?

How can I state my main idea about my subject in a thesis sentence? Does my thesis limit the scope of my writing to what I can demonstrate in the available space? Does it focus my writing on one specific assertion? Does it make an exact statement about what my writing intends to do?

GUIDELINES FOR REVISING YOUR STYLE

1 What is my general impression of my writing?

Do I find my writing clear, unambiguous, and likely to engage my readers? Have I carried out my purpose at every level; that is, am I satisfied that the *how* of my writing—its attitude, organization, and language—conveys the *what* of my ideas?

2 What tone have I established in my writing?

Is my tone informative, affective, or a blend of both? How much distance have I maintained between myself and my readers? Is my tone appropriate for my subject and audience? Is it maintained consistently?

3 How can I characterize the overall style of my writing?

Have I written this essay in a moderate style, opting for more or less colloquialism or formality as my purpose requires? Does my purpose in fact require me to be overtly colloquial or formal?

4 Are my sentences well constructed and easy on the ear?

Have I written sentences varying in length and style so that they hold my readers' interest? Have I avoided the choppiness that comes from too many basic or loosely coordinated sentences? Have I avoided the density that comes from too many complicated sentences with multiple subordinate clauses?

5 Have I used words as effectively as possible?

Do the connotations and denotations of my words support my purpose? Have I avoided unnecessary formalities and slang? Is my language specific and, when appropriate, vivid? Have I inadvertently mixed metaphors? Have I used imagery successfully to *heighten* effects, not merely to strive after them?

WRITING WITH A PURPOSE

ELEVENTH
EDITION

WRITING WITH A PURPOSE

Joseph F. Trimmer
Ball State University

HOUGHTON MIFFLIN COMPANY   Boston   **Toronto**
Geneva, Illinois   Palo Alto   Princeton, New **Jersey**

Senior Sponsoring Editor: Dean Johnson
Project Editor: Helen Bronk
Senior Production/Design Coordinator: Sarah Ambrose
Senior Manufacturing Coordinator: Priscilla Bailey

Acknowledgments

Chapter 1

Gail Godwin, "Becoming a Writer." Copyright ©1979 by Gail Godwin. Reprinted by permission of John Hawkins & Associates, Inc.

Excerpt from "The Compositions of Mozart's Mind" from *Art, Mind, and Brain: A Cognitive Approach to Creativity* by Howard Gardner. Copyright ©1983 by Howard Gardner. Reprinted by permission of BasicBooks, a division of HarperCollins Publishers, Inc.

Chapter 2

"On Keeping a Notebook" from *Slouching Toward Bethlehem* by Joan Didion. Copyright ©1966, 1968 by Joan Didion. Reprinted by permission of Farrar, Straus and Giroux, Inc.

"The Five Rings" from *Information Anxiety* by Richard Saul Wurman. Copyright ©1989 by Richard Saul Wurman. Used by permission of Doubleday, a division of Bantam Doubleday Dell Publishing Group, Inc.

"Television and Reading" from *The Plug-in Drug,* Revised Edition by Marie Winn. Copyright ©1977, 1985 by Marie Winn Miller. Used by permission of Viking Penguin, a division of Penguin Books USA Inc.

Acknowledgments are continued on page 597, constituting an extension of the copyright page.

Cover Design: Marc English

Printed in the U.S.A.

Student Text ISBN: 0-395-43237-5

Examination Copy ISBN: 0-395-47367-5

Library of Congress Catalog Card Number: 94-76556

23456789-RM-98 97 96 95

Brief Contents

Note: See also complete Table of Contents on page vii.

Contents

4 | Revising   77

PART TWO   THE EXPRESSION OF IDEAS   103

5 | Common Methods of Development   104

15 | Writing the Research Paper   435

HANDBOOK OF GRAMMAR AND USAGE 479

Preface

Writing with a Purpose has always been distinguished by its emphasis on the role of purpose in the writing process, its comprehensive coverage of the materials and problems basic to the introductory writing course, and its effective use of examples and exercises to illustrate how writers make decisions that produce successful writing. The revisions embodied in the Eleventh Edition retain and reinforce these traditional features of the text, while also incorporating the best contemporary theory and practice in the teaching of writing. The result is a blend of familiar and new material invigorated by fresh approaches and examples and enlivened by student writing composed in different contexts and progressing through various stages of the writing process.

SPECIAL FEATURES

The two most dramatic additions to the Eleventh Edition are an anthology of *readings* and advice on *computers*.

Readings   Although *Writing with a Purpose* continues to include the work of professional writers and student writers throughout each chapter and in the brief selections at the end of each chapter, the Eleventh Edition features a new Part Three, "Readings with a Purpose," that provides student and professional essays arranged according to the common rhetorical strategies. The introduction to each strategy provides advice on *selecting your subject, analyzing your audience, determining your purpose, and using the strategy*. Each student essay is annotated to illustrate how the student has used the advice; each professional essay is followed by questions about how the writer has used the strategy; and each section concludes with **A Sampler of Other Essays** that refers readers to other selections in the text that use the same strategy.

Computers   In its last two editions, *Writing with a Purpose* has provided advice about computers and composition in its chapters on the research paper and in a special appendix on writing with a word processor. Advances in computer technology, however, demand that the text provide practical advice about "how to use your computer" at every stage of the writing process. In some chapters (e.g. Chapter 2, "Planning") the advice is placed strategically throughout the chapter. In other chapters (e.g. Chapter 3, "Drafting") the advice appears near the end of the chapter. In both cases, the advice is addressed to student writers who are learning the basic techniques of composing with a computer.

ORGANIZATION OF THE TEXT

Part One: The Writing Process

Part One, "The Writing Process," covers all aspects of composing from planning through revising. Chapter 1, which provides an overview of this process, details the variety of approaches writers use to complete their tasks and discusses those three activities common to every writing situation: selecting your subject, analyzing your audience, and determining your purpose. *Purpose* receives an expanded definition that is carefully reinforced throughout the text as the principal touchstone by which writers measure their progress through the writing process.

The remainder of Part One, enriched by new examples and exercises, focuses on the three stages of the writing process: planning, drafting, and revising. Chapter 2 offers multiple planning strategies to demonstrate how students can discover and evaluate their thinking in writing. Chapter 3 presents methods to arrange and assess the material discovered in planning to guide the creation of a discovery draft and then a more successful second draft. Chapter 4 defines the revising process, demonstrates methods for revising an essay, and provides an extended case study of revising from discovery draft to final draft. All the chapters in Part One are unified by recurring student writing-in-progress that illustrates a range of projects from expressive writing about personal experience to investigative writing about academic subjects.

Part Two: The Expression of Ideas

Part Two (Chapters 5 through 10) places the discrete skills of effective writing—methods of development, argument, paragraphs, sentences, diction, tone, and style—within the composing process. This is done partly through the use of quotations from personal interviews with professional writers who explain their own method for using the skill, and partly through the work of student writers who try to employ the skill in their own writing process. In particular, Chapter 5, "Common Methods of Development," and Chapter 6, "Argument," illustrate how a student writer works with the patterns of exposition and the structures of argument to plan, draft, and revise a compelling piece of writing.

The writing examples and exercises in each chapter have been selected to cluster around a different disciplinary theme to provide readers with the opportunity to discover provocative comparisons. Chapter 5 has a thematic emphasis on animal rights and environmental awareness, Chapter 6 on citizenship and contemporary social issues, Chapter 7 on families and ethnic groups, Chapter 8 on art and medicine, Chapter 9 on biology and the physical sciences, and Chapter 10 on travel and transportation.

Part Three: Readings With a Purpose

Part Three (Chapter 11) is an anthology of student and professional essays arranged in the same pattern of rhetorical strategies featured in Chapters 5 and 6 and corresponding to the sequence of writing assignments that conclude every chapter in the text:

1. Narration and description
2. Process analysis
3. Comparison and contrast
4. Division and classification
5. Definition
6. Causal analysis
7. Argument

Each section opens with some general observations about choosing your subject, audience, and purpose and ends with specific advice about using the strategy effectively. Each student essay is annotated, each professional essay is followed by questions, and each section directs readers to other essays in the text that have used the same strategy.

Part Four: Special Assignments

Part Four, "Special Assignments," demonstrates how the essay exam, the critical essay, and the research paper evolve from a writing process. Student writers, guided by the advice of professional writers, work through the special stages of each assignment. Chapter 12 illustrates how to evaluate exam questions, to abstract key concepts and phrases, and to use this material to develop ideas and reach conclusions to achieve successful essay exam answers. Chapter 13 demonstrates how the use of specific reading and writing strategies enables one student to compose a critical essay that integrates his personal response to a literary work with his understanding of the basic elements of literature.

Chapters 14 and 15 provide extensive analysis and illustrations of the many steps embedded in planning and writing the research paper. Chapter 14 demonstrates how to select a subject for research: how to use all the resources of the traditional and computerized library to select, assess, and analyze sources. Chapter 15 presents the methods by which information composed by other researchers can be incorporated into and help advance the student's own research paper. Special attention is given to the purpose and procedures of quoting, documenting, and listing sources. The whole range of planning and writing activities required to produce a successful research paper is illustrated by one student's progress through the process. Her paper, "The Recycling Controversy," is fully annotated so that readers can assess the decisions made during the writing process and the methods used to embody those discussions in an appropriate format.

Handbook of Grammar and Usage

The Handbook of Grammar and Usage provides a coherent coding system, clear explanations, and abundant exercises, making it a useful tool for classroom or individual review on a systematic basis or in response to occasional needs and questions.

ANCILLARIES

Accompanying the main text are a range of print and computer materials:

Print Ancillaries

▼ *Teaching with a Purpose* by Lolly Ockerstrom, Northeastern University. This Instructor's Resource Manual offers advice for each chapter on how to use the text in three classroom settings: conventional, collaborative, and computer-assisted. It also provides chapter synopses, suggested answers for exercises, commentary about readings, additional writing assignments, sample syllabi, and special sections on how teachers and students can use the writing center to expand and enrich classroom instruction.

▼ *Instructor's Support Package.* This envelope of duplicating masters contains supplemental exercises for the handbook section of the long edition of the text and three forms of a new 55-item diagnostic test.

Computer Ancillaries

▼ *Practical English Exercises and Review (PEER)* is an interactive software program for practice in sentence editing. It consists of 300 items eliciting five different kinds of responses from students.

▼ *Computerized Diagnostic Tests* are three forms of a 55-item diagnostic test.

Offered at Special Prices

▼ *Writing with a Purpose* and *The American Heritage Dictionary, Third College Edition.*

▼ *Writing with a Purpose* and *Fine Lines: Planning, Drafting, and Revising on the Computer.*

▼ *Fine Lines* by William H. Koon and Peter L. Royston. This innovative software program of seven modules is designed to help students in all stages of the writing process. The Drafting and Revising module contains an on-line handbook with MLA and APA documentation forms.

Please contact your regional sales office for additional information on these and other items.

ACKNOWLEDGMENTS

It is a pleasure to acknowledge those who have helped shape this edition of *Writing with a Purpose.*

For her help in composing the instructor's guide, *Teaching with a Purpose,* my thanks to Lolly Ockerstrom, Northeastern University. My continuing thanks go to Robert Perrin, Indiana State University, for his substantial work on the *Handbook of Grammar and Usage.*

For their extensive comments on the plans for the Eleventh Edition and for their criticism of the manuscript, I would like to thank the following people: Johnny Bennett, Fort Scott Community College (KS); Michael W. Connors, Yuba Community College (CA); Juanita B. Evans, Virginia State University; Jennie Wilson Harrison, North Harris College (TX); Johndan Johnson-Eilola, New Mexico Tech; Andrew Lamers, University of Kansas; Ollie O. Oviedo, Eastern New Mexico University; Peter Schenck, Northeast Iowa Community College; James R. Sodon, St. Louis Community College at Florissant Valley; Vera Solomon, University of Arkansas at Pine Bluff; Bruce Sonner, Corning Community College (NY); Howard Waters, Porterville College (CA).

For their willingness to talk at length about the craft they practice with such precision and intelligence, I would like to thank Calvin Trillin, John McPhee, Anna Quindlen, Bill Barich, Richard Selzer, Annie Dillard, and Patricia Hampl.

For their eagerness to participate in a variety of writing experiments, I would like to thank the students in my composition classes. In particular, I am indebted to the inventive, humorous and informative observations of the student authors whose writing gives this edition its unique voice: Wallace Armstrong, Robert Scheffel, Joanne Malbone, Amy Lindsay, Susan Reidenback, John Bedillion, Ellen Haack, Sarah S. Penning, Jane Graham, Matt Fisher, Lisa Widenhofer, Rob Sturma, Kris Modlin, Larry Bush, Sue Kirby, Yili Shi, Robin Jensen, Richard Gant, Julia Miller, and Jill Taraskiewicz.

Special thanks go to Dean Johnson whose faith in the abiding power of this book has helped generations of college students write with a purpose.

Joseph F. Trimmer

The Writing Process

PART ONE

1 | Toward Purposeful Writing

Some people find writing easy. They sit down and write, work until they are finished, and turn out a first draft that is so good that it is their final draft. Everyone has heard stories about students who dash off perfect term papers the night before the assignment is due. And many people know the story of how Jack Kerouac wrote his novel *On the Road*—composing it in fourteen days and typing it on a roll of Teletype paper to avoid changing pages. But such ease of composition is rare. Kerouac himself had been writing and rewriting his book for years before hammering out its final version. Most people—whether they are students writing papers, teachers researching articles, journalists assembling news stories, business people composing memos, or novelists—find writing hard work.

But writing is also *opportunity*. It allows you to express something about yourself, to explore and explain ideas, and to assess the claims of other people. By formulating and organizing ideas, and finding the right words to present them, you gain power. At times the task may seem overwhelming, but the rewards make the hard work worthwhile. As you come to see writing positively, as an opportunity for communication, you will develop the confidence you need to overcome its occasional frustrations.

You can gain this confidence by writing and learning from your own work and that of others. Experienced writers are one source of lessons that you may find helpful. Consider what Ernest Hemingway says about his early writing experiences in Paris in the 1920s.

> It was wonderful to walk down the long flights of stairs knowing that I'd had good luck working. I always worked until I had something done and I always stopped when I knew what was going to happen next . That way I could be sure of going on the next day. But sometimes when I was starting a new story and I could not get it going, I would sit in front of the fire and squeeze the peel of the little oranges into the edge of the flame and watch the sputter of blue that they made. I would stand and look out over the roofs of Paris and think, "Do not worry. You have always written before and you will write now. All you have to do is write one true sentence. Write the truest sentence that you know." So finally I would write one true sentence, and then go on from there. It was easy then because there was always one true sentence that I knew or had seen or had heard someone say. If I started to write elaborately, or like someone introducing or presenting something, I found that I could cut that scrollwork or ornament out and throw it away and start with

the first true simple declarative sentence I had written. Up in that room I decided that I would write one story about each thing that I knew about. I was trying to do this all the time I was writing, and it was good and severe discipline. (Ernest Hemingway, *A Moveable Feast*)

Hemingway's account contains some helpful pointers for all writers.

1. *Develop writing habits that work for you and trust in them.* Because they have written successfully before, experienced writers believe they will write successfully again. They put this belief at risk each time they write, for each new piece of writing will inevitably contain new challenges. At times their confidence may fluctuate, but they do not lose faith. They believe the habits that have worked before—composing in a special environment, maintaining a disciplined schedule, and using familiar tools—will work again.

2. *Understand the stages of the writing process.* Identifying the predictable stages of the writing process builds confidence. Experienced writers recognize the obstacles they encounter in each stage, the strategies that help them overcome those obstacles, and the signs that prompt them to repeat one or all of the stages. As they move forward from stage to stage, or backward to repeat a stage, they are confident that they are making progress because they are identifying and solving problems.

3. *Rely on three basic elements—subject, audience, and purpose—to guide you, whatever your writing task.* Experienced writers may talk from time to time about "inspiration" or "good luck," but they do not depend on such mysterious forces. Effective writing emerges from effective decision making, and effective decisions are made when writers focus on the constants in every writing situation: their subject, audience, and purpose.

One of the primary aims of this book is to offer you experience, and thereby confidence, in writing. In the following chapters, you will learn and practice writing strategies. This chapter will discuss the writer's environment and habits, the three-stage division of the writing process, and the central elements—subject, audience, and purpose—that shape each piece of writing.

THE WRITER'S ENVIRONMENT AND HABITS

Asked to describe their writing process, students usually begin by identifying their writing habits—the conditions and tools they believe they need whenever they write. Some of these habits are formed by chance. If you completed a good paper by secluding yourself in a quiet area of the library, inscribing neatly shaped words in a spiral notebook with a Number 2 lead pencil, then you may be convinced that you need isolation, silence, and simple tools to write successfully. If you produced a good paper seated at your desk at home, your fish tank humming in the background, banging out your sentences on your new word processor, you might believe that to write effectively you require a familiar environment, reassuring noises, and modern equipment. After a time, some writers look on their writing habits as rituals, procedures to be followed faithfully each time they write. They wear the same flannel shirt, choose the same background music, or again sharpen an entire box of pencils before they begin.

Although many writing habits are formed by chance and take on the nature of ritual, most come about almost unconsciously and conform to a writer's other personal habits. If, like Felix (the finicky character in Neil Simon's comedy *The Odd Couple*), you must have a carefully organized environment to accomplish any task—from brushing your teeth to preparing dinner—then you will no doubt develop precise writing habits. You will write regularly, at approximately the same time each day, and for almost the same period, in a serene atmosphere. On the other hand, if, like Oscar (Felix's opposite), you can tolerate disorder, then your writing habits are likely to reflect your preference for flexibility. Within reason and within the confines of your deadline, you will probably write in bursts of energy, at different hours of the day and night, for varying stretches of time, and in a number of different locations.

Most people fall somewhere in between these two extremes of working styles. You will probably experiment with several approaches before finding the environment and habits that work best for you. What matters is that you develop habits that enhance your concentration rather than interfere with it. If you try to write at an uncomfortable desk and chair where the light is too dim and the temperature too high, where friends or family members are likely to interrupt, you are sabotaging your chances for success. Find a comfortable, quiet, well-lit spot where you are as free as possible from internal and external distractions.

Consider, finally, that writing is both a *solitary* and a *social* act. At times you need isolation and silence to search for words that make meaning. At other times you need community and conversation to see if your words make sense. What matters is that you find the environment and habits that work best for you.

Exercise ———

1. What type of physical environment do you need to write effectively? What happens to you when you are forced to write in a "hostile" environment?

2. What kind of writing tools do you prefer? What happens when you have to write with "alien" tools?

3. How do your writing habits match other aspects of your life and personality? How do they differ?

4. What experiences or people helped you form your writing habits?

5. a. What steps have you taken to eliminate external distractions (noise, music, talking, wrong light or temperature, uncomfortable furniture, lack of adequate supplies) from your writing environment?

   b. What steps have you taken to eliminate internal distractions (hunger, fatigue, boredom, anxiety, daydreaming, restlessness) from your writing environment?

   c. What other steps could you take to enhance your ability to concentrate?

THE STAGES OF THE WRITING PROCESS

Whatever your writing environment and habits, they are simply the enabling conditions that allow you to enter and complete your writing process. They are the physical and psychological setting for the central action—the mental procedures you perform as you move through the stages of composition. The writing process may be divided into three stages: *planning, drafting,* and *revising.* They will be discussed briefly in this chapter and at greater length, with examples, in Chapters 2, 3, and 4.

Planning

Planning is a systematic process of developing your ideas and giving them shape. As the first stage in the writing process, *planning is a series of strategies designed to find and formulate information in writing.* When you begin a writing project, you need to discover what is possible within the confines of the assignment—to explore a variety of subjects and invent alternative ways to think and write about each subject. To create and shape your text, you need to consider all the ideas, however mundane or unsettling, that come to you. In Chapter 2 you will learn several planning strategies for generating information you can transform into a first draft.

Drafting

Drafting is a procedure for executing a preliminary sketch. As the second stage in the writing process, *drafting is a series of strategies designed to organize and develop a sustained piece of writing.* Once planning has enabled you to identify several subjects and gather information on those subjects from different perspectives, you need to select one subject, organize your information into meaningful clusters, and then discover the links that connect those clusters. In Chapter 3 you will learn how to use drafting techniques to produce a preliminary text. Chapters 5 through 10 will give you additional techniques for composing your preliminary draft.

Revising

Revising is a procedure for improving a work in progress. As the third and final stage in the writing process, *revising is a series of strategies designed to reexamine and reevaluate the choices that have created a piece of writing.* After you have completed your preliminary draft, you need to stand back from your text and decide whether to embark on *global revision*—a complete re-creation of the world of your writing—or to begin *local revision*—a concerted effort to perfect the smaller elements in your writing. In Chapter 4, you will learn how to use global revision to rethink, reenvision, and rewrite your work. In Chapters 7 through 10, you will learn strategies for making the small rearrangements and subtle refinements that will help you produce your most effective writing.

Working Within the Process

The division of the writing process into three stages is deceptive because it suggests that *planning, drafting,* and *revising* proceed in a linear sequence. According to this logic, you would complete all the activities in one stage and then move to the next. But writing is a complex mental activity that usually unfolds as a more flexible and "recursive" sequence of tasks. You may have to repeat the activities in one stage several times before you are ready to move on to the next, or you may have to loop back to an earlier stage before you can move forward again. For example, you may have to try a number of planning strategies until you generate enough information to work with. Or, in the middle of drafting, you may have to return to planning because you discover that the relationships you thought you saw in your material are not there after all. When you revise, you may find that your essay doesn't explain certain assumptions or illustrate important assertions, so that you must return to planning or drafting. Indeed, although planning, drafting, and revising can be seen as distinct activities, at any point in the writing process you are likely to be doing all three at once.

Experienced writers seem to perform within the process in different ways. Some spend an enormous amount of time planning every detail before they write; others prefer to dispense with planning and discover their direction in drafting or revising. The American humorist James Thurber once acknowledged that he and one of his collaborators worked quite differently when writing a play:

> Elliot Nugent . . . is a careful constructor. When we were working on *The Male Animal* together, he was constantly concerned with plotting the play. He could plot the thing from back to front—what was going to happen here, what sort of situation would end the first-act curtain and so forth. I can't work that way. Nugent would say, "Well, Thurber, we've got our problem, we've got all these people in the living room. Now what are we going to do with them?" I'd say that I didn't know and couldn't tell him until I'd sat down at my typewriter and found out. I don't believe the writer should know too much where he's going. (James Thurber, *Writers at Work: The Paris Review Interviews*)

Even experienced writers with established routines for producing a particular kind of work admit that each project inevitably presents new problems. Virginia Woolf planned, drafted, and revised some of her novels with great speed, but she was bewildered by her inability to repeat the process with other novels:

> . . . blundering on at *The Waves.* I write two pages of arrant nonsense, after straining; I write variations of every sentence; compromises; bad shots; possibilities; till my writing book is like a lunatic's dream. Then I trust to inspiration on re-reading; and pencil them into some sense. Still I am not satisfied . . . I press to my centre. I don't care if it all is scratched out . . . and then, if nothing comes of it—anyhow I have examined the possibilities. (Virginia Woolf, "Boxing Day" 1929, *A Writer's Diary*)

Writers often discover a whole set of new problems when they are asked to write in a different context. Those writers who feel comfortable telling stories about their personal experience, for example, may encounter unexpected twists and turns in their writing process when they are asked to describe the lives of other people, explain a historical event, or analyze the arguments in an intellectual controversy. Each context requires them to make adjustments in the way they typically uncover, assess, and assert information. Calvin Trillin, one of our most versatile writers, admits that he changes his writing process dramatically when he shifts from writing investigative reports to writing humorous essays or weekly columns.

> In my reporting pieces, I worry a lot about structure. Everything is there—in interviews, clippings, documents—but I don't know how to get it all in. I think that's why I do what we call around the house the vomit-out. I just start writing—to see how much I've got, how it might unfold, and what I've got to do to get through to the end. In my columns and humor pieces, I usually don't know the end or even the middle. I might start with a joke, but I don't know where it's going, so I fiddle along, polishing each paragraph, hoping something will tell me what to write next. (Personal interview)

This range of responses suggests that what appears to be a simple three-stage procedure may at times be a disorderly, contradictory procedure. But experienced writers know that disorder and contradiction are probably inevitable but temporary disturbances in the composition of most pieces of writing. Confusion occurs when you know too little about your writing project; contradiction occurs when you think too little about what you know. The secret to moving through temporary impasses is to keep your eye on the constants in every writing context.

MAKING DECISIONS IN THE WRITING PROCESS

As you write, you discover that you are constantly making decisions. Some of these decisions are complex, as when you are trying to shape ideas; others are simple, as when you are trying to select words. But each decision, large or small, affects every other decision you make so that you are continuously adjusting and readjusting your writing to make sure it is consistent, coherent, and clear. You can test the effectiveness of your decisions by measuring them against this dictum: in every writing situation, a writer is trying to communicate a *subject* to an *audience* for a *purpose.*

Initially, think of these three elements as *prompters,* ways to consider what you want to write about and how you want to write about it. Later, as you move through planning to drafting and revising, think of them as *touchstones,* ways to assess what you set out to accomplish. But mainly think of them as *guidelines,* ways to control every decision you make throughout the writing process, from formulating ideas to refining sentences.

SELECTING YOUR SUBJECT

Many student writers complain that their biggest problem is finding a subject. Sometimes that problem seems less complicated because the subject is named in the writing assignment. But assignments vary in how they are worded, what they assume, and what they expect. Suppose, for example, you are asked to discuss two characters in a play. This assignment does not identify a subject; it merely identifies an area in which a subject can be found. Another version of that assignment might ask you to compare and contrast the way two characters make compromises. This assignment identifies a more restricted subject but assumes you know how to work with a specific form (the comparison and contrast essay) and expects you to produce specific information (two ways of defining and dealing with compromise). In other words, the second assignment selects your subject but requires you to select and develop the subject matter of your essay.

At the end of this chapter (and every other chapter of this book) you will find a sampler of writing assignments. As you browse through each assignment, consider how the subject is defined and how you are expected to develop it. Also consider how you might respond to or reformulate each assignment in terms of your own experience. You may decide that none of the assignments strike your fancy but that part of one assignment or parts of several assignments suggest a subject that is worth pursuing.

Whether you are responding to an assignment or creating one, you need to take certain steps to find a suitable subject. First, select a subject you know or can learn something about. The more you know about a subject, the more likely you are to make it your own, shaping it to your own perspective. If, in addition, you select a subject, such as television, that is familiar to most of your readers, you will know that you share an area of common knowledge that allows you more freedom to explore *your* observations, ideas, and values. Second, select a subject you can restrict. A subject such as television is really a broad category that contains an unlimited supply of smaller, more specific subjects. The more you can restrict your subject, the more likely you are to control your investigation, identify vivid illustrations, and maintain a unified focus. The general category *television* can be divided into all sorts of subtopics, each of which can be restricted further into specific subjects.

▼ situation comedies—the portrayal of women

▼ quiz shows—the symbolism of set design

▼ detective series—the procedures for gathering evidence

▼ news broadcasts—the reliability of network and cable anchors

▼ home shopping networks—the categories of merchandise

▼ sports broadcasting—the language of play-by-play commentators

▼ music videos—the gestures of defiance

▼ soap operas—the strategies for resolving conflict

▼ cable television—the consequences of "channel surfing"

Although the subjects on the right could profit from further restriction, they illustrate why selecting a specific subject simplifies your writing task: it helps you focus on and form judgments about a concrete topic.

Finally, as you consider possible topics, ask yourself three questions: Is it significant? Is it interesting? Is it manageable? A significant subject need not be ponderous or solemn. In fact, many significant subjects grow out of ordinary observations rather than grandiose declarations. But you do need to decide whether a specific subject raises important issues (the reliability of television journalism) or appeals to the common experience of your readers (familiar methods of settling arguments). Similarly, an interesting subject need not be dazzling or spectacular, but it does need to capture your curiosity. If it bores you, it will surely bore your readers. You need to decide why a specific subject fascinates you (why you are attracted to quiz shows that give away money) and how you can make the subject more intriguing for your readers (how private detectives manipulate their friends in high places to gather evidence). A manageable subject is neither so limited that you can exhaust it in a few pages (the language of one sportscaster) nor so vast that lengthy articles or books would be required to discuss it adequately (the evolution of female stereotypes in situation comedies).

Ultimately you must develop your own methods for answering these questions each time you examine the choice of subjects available and as you consider your audience and purpose. When you compare subjects in the context of the complete writing situation, you will naturally prefer some to others. To decide which one will enable you to produce the most suitable subject, measure it against the criteria set forth in the following guidelines.

Guidelines for Selecting Your Subject

1. ***What do I know about my subject?***
   Do I know about my subject in some depth, or do I need to learn more about it? What are the sources of my knowledge—direct experience, observation, reading? How does my knowledge give me a special or unusual perspective on my subject?

2. ***What is the focus of my subject?***
   Is my subject too general? How can I restrict it to a more specific subject that I can develop in greater detail?

3. ***What is significant about my subject?***
   What issues of general importance does it raise? What fresh insight can I contribute to my readers' thinking on this issue?

4. ***What is interesting about my subject?***
   Why is this subject interesting to me? How can I interest my readers in it?

5. ***Is my subject manageable?***
   Can I write about my subject in a particular form, within a certain number of pages? Do I feel in control of my subject or confused by it? If my subject is too complicated or too simplistic, how can I make it more manageable?

"*You'll get it back once you articulate a coherent viewing policy.*"

Drawing by Mankoff; © 1992 The New Yorker Magazine, Inc.

ANALYZING YOUR AUDIENCE

Most inexperienced writers assume that their audience is their writing teacher. But writing teachers, like writing assignments, often vary in what they teach, what they assume, and what they expect. Such variation has often prompted inexperienced writers to define their writing tasks as "trying to figure out what the teacher wants." This definition is naive and smart at the same time. Superficially, it suggests that the sole purpose of any writing assignment is to satisfy another person's whims. On a deeper level, it suggests that when writers analyze the knowledge, assumptions, and expectations of their readers, they develop a clearer perception of their subject and purpose. To make this analysis truly effective, though, writers must remember that they are writing for multiple audiences, not a single person.

The most immediate audience is *you*. You write not only to convey your ideas to others but also to clarify them for yourself. To think of yourself as an audience, however, you must stop thinking like a writer and begin thinking like a reader. This change in perspective offers advantages, for you are the reader you know best. You are also a fairly representative reader because you share broad concerns and interests with other people. If you feel that your writing is clear, lively, and informed, other readers will probably feel that way, too. If you sense that your text is confused or incomplete, the rest of your audience is likely to be disappointed, too.

The main drawback to considering yourself as audience is your inclination to deceive yourself. You want every sentence and paragraph to be perfect, but you know how much time and energy you invested in composing them, and that effort may blur your judgment. You may accept bad writing from yourself even though you wouldn't accept it from someone else. For that reason you need a second audience. These readers—usually your friends, classmates, and teachers—are your most attentive audience. They help you choose your subject, coach you through various stages of the writing process, and counsel you about how to improve your sentences and paragraphs. As you write, you must certainly anticipate detailed advice from these readers. But you must remember that writing teachers and even peers are essentially collaborators and thus are not your ultimate audience. They know what you have considered, cut, and corrected. The more they help you, the more eager they are to commend your writing as it approaches their standards of acceptability.

Your most significant audience consists of readers who do not know how much time and energy you invested in your writing or care about how many choices you considered and rejected. These readers want writing that tells them something interesting or important, and they are put off by writing that is tedious or trivial. It is this wider audience that you (and your collaborators) must consider as you work through the writing process.

At times this audience may seem like a nebulous creature, and you may wonder how you can direct your writing to it if you do not know any of its distinguishing features. In those cases, it may be helpful to imagine a single significant reader—an attentive, sensible, reasonably informed person who will give you a sympathetic reading as long as you do not waste his or her time. Imagine an important person whom you respect and whose respect you want. This reader, specifically imagined though often termed the "general reader," the "universal reader," or the "common reader," is essentially a fiction, but a helpful fiction. Your writing will benefit from the objectivity and sincerity with which you address this reader.

Many times, however, especially as you learn more about your subject, you discover a real-world audience for your writing. More precisely, as you consider your subject in a specific context, you may identify a number of audiences, in which case you will ultimately have to choose among them. Suppose, for example, your knowledge of cable television suggests that "channel surfing" might make an interesting subject, but you are finding it difficult to focus this knowledge. You decide to identify your audience, and after some deliberation, you see that you have at least three possible audiences: (1) those who love channel surfing—remote-control freaks who relish the search for new possibilities; (2) those who hate channel surfing—viewers who despise the constant sampling of channels encouraged by the remote control; and (3) those who are indifferent to channel surfing—a group that has never explored the potential provided by the remote control or watched television with a channel surfer.

Now that you have identified your audience, analyze the distinctive features of each group. What do they know? What do they think they know?

What do they need to know? The more you know about each group, the more you will be able to direct your writing to their assumptions and expectations. If you use a remote control, you will have little difficulty analyzing the devotees and detractors of channel surfing. You have heard the addicts explain how moving across cable television's multiple channels enriches their viewing, creating a flow of provocative visual sensations. Similarly, you have heard critics assert that constant channel changing interferes with viewing, destroying the coherence of visual images.

At first you may have difficulty with the third group because these readers have no preconceptions about channel surfing either as a creative new form of television viewing or as a new development disrupting viewing behavior. In some ways, readers in the third group are like the "general reader"—thoughtful, discerning people who are willing to read about channel surfing if you can convince them that the subject is worth their attention.

As you consider addressing each of these audiences, you should be able to anticipate their interests. As you think about the addict, for example, you might describe how channel surfing produces effects similar to those produced by post-modern collages or hyperfiction. As you think about the critics, you might define problem-solving strategies psychiatrists suggest for working out more harmonious communal viewing. As you think about the neutral readers, you may decide that although they may have no interest in channel surfing, they may be intrigued by an analysis of the capacity to jump in and out of the stories broadcast on cable television.

Although this sort of audience analysis helps you visualize a group of readers, it does not help you decide which group is most suitable for your essay. If you target one group, you may fall into the trap of allowing its preferences to determine the direction of your writing. If you try to accommodate all three groups, you may waiver indecisively among them, so that your writing never finds any direction. Your decision about audience, like your decision about subject, has to be made in the context of the complete writing situation. Both decisions are ultimately related to your discovery of purpose—what you want to do in your essay. In the next several pages, you will learn how purpose guides your decisions in writing. But first, look at the following guidelines for analyzing your audience.

Guidelines for Analyzing Your Audience

1. **Who are the readers that will be most interested in my writing?**
    What is their probable age, gender, education, economic status, and social position? What values, assumptions, and prejudices characterize their general attitudes toward life?

2. **What do my readers know or think they know about my subject?**
    What is the probable source of their knowledge—direct experience observation, reading, rumor? Will my readers react positively or negatively toward my subject?

3. *Why will my readers read my writing?*
   If they know a great deal about my subject, what will they expect to learn from reading my essay? If they know only a few things about my subject, what will they expect to be told about it? Will they expect to be entertained, informed, or persuaded?

4. *How can I interest my readers in my subject?*
   If they are hostile toward it, how can I convince them to give my writing a fair reading? If they are sympathetic, how can I fulfill and enhance their expectations? If they are neutral, how can I catch and hold their attention?

5. *How can I help my readers read my writing?*
   What kind of organizational pattern will help them see its purpose? What kind of guideposts and transitional markers will they need to follow this pattern? What (and how many) examples will they need to understand my general statements?

DETERMINING YOUR PURPOSE

The central idea of this book is that writers write most effectively when they are "writing with a purpose." Inexperienced writers occasionally have difficulty writing with *a* purpose, because they see many purposes: to complete the assignment, to earn a good grade, to publish their writing. These "purposes" lie outside the writing situation, but they certainly influence the way you think about your purpose. If you want a good grade, you will define your purpose in terms of your teacher's writing assignment. If you want to publish your essay, you will define your purpose in terms of a given publisher's statement about its editorial policies.

When *purpose* is considered as an element inside the writing situation, the term has a specific meaning: *purpose is the overall design that governs what writers do in their writing.* Writers who have determined their purpose know what kind of information they need, how they want to organize and develop it, and why they think it is important. In effect, purpose directs and controls all the decisions writers make. It is both the *what* and the *how* of that process—that is, the specific subject the writer selects *and* the strategies, from creating an organization to refining the style, that the writer uses to communicate the subject most effectively.

The difficulty with this definition is that finding a purpose to guide you through the writing process *is* the purpose of the writing process. Writing is both a procedure of *discovering* what you know and a procedure for *demonstrating* what you know. For that reason, you must maintain a double vision of your purpose. You must think of it as a preliminary objective that helps illuminate the decisions you have to make. You must also think of it as a final assertion that helps you implement what you intend to do in your writing.

Forming a Working Purpose: The Hypothesis

As you begin writing, you start to acquire a general sense of your purpose. You make tentative decisions about your subject and audience, and you begin to formulate ideas about what you want to accomplish in a given context. Suppose again that you choose to write about channel surfing. You could approach this subject in many ways, but you have to start somewhere, so you decide to focus on its intent. This preliminary decision will help you gather and sort information, but as you assess it, you may see that you do not know what you want to do with it. You do not have a purpose; you only have a general notion that suggests a number of perspectives. Any one of these perspectives might provide an interesting angle from which to investigate your subject, and you can use any one of them to form a *hypothesis*—a working purpose.

Forming a hypothesis is a major step in determining your purpose. Sometimes you come to your writing certain of your hypothesis: you know from the outset what you want to prove and what you need to prove it. More often, you need to consider various possibilities; to convey something meaningful in your writing, something that bears your own mark, you need to keep an open mind and explore your options fully. Eventually, however, you must choose one hypothesis that you think most accurately says what you want to say about your subject and how you want to say it.

How do you know which hypothesis to choose? There is no easy answer to this question. The answer ultimately emerges from your temperament, experiences, and interests, and also from the requirements of the context—whether you are writing for yourself or on an assignment. Sometimes you can make the choice intuitively as you proceed: in thinking about your subject and audience, you see at once the perspective you want to adopt and how it will direct your writing. At other times you may find it helpful to write out various hypotheses and then consider their relative effectiveness. Which will be most interesting to write about? Which best expresses your way of looking at things? With which can you make the strongest case or most compelling assertions?

For example, as you look at the information you have gathered about the intent of channel surfing, you might see several hypotheses:

▼   Channel surfing enables viewers to create their own visual worlds.

▼   Channel surfing is caused by defects in viewer attention span.

▼   Channel surfing conflicts with communal viewing.

▼   Channel surfing will become a natural activity as cable television offers still more channels.

Any one of these or other hypotheses might guide you to the next stage of your writing. You must decide which one suits you best, and your decision must take into account the nature of your subject and intended audience.

Testing Your Hypothesis: The Discovery Draft

After you have chosen your hypothesis, you need to determine whether this preliminary statement of purpose really provides the direction and control you need to produce an effective piece of writing. You can test your hypothesis by writing a first, or *discovery*, draft. Sometimes your discovery draft demonstrates that your hypothesis works. More often, however, as you continue the writing process, you discover new information or unforeseen complications that cause you to modify your original hypothesis. In other cases, you discover that you simply cannot prove what your hypothesis suggested you might be able to prove.

Whatever you discover about your hypothesis, you must proceed in writing. If your discovery draft reveals that your hypothesis represents what you want to prove and needs only slight modification, then change your perspective somewhat or find the additional information so that you can modify it. If, on the other hand, your discovery draft demonstrates that your hypothesis lacks conviction or that you do not have (and suspect you cannot get) the information you need to make your case, then choose another hypothesis that reflects your intentions more accurately.

For example, if you choose the hypothesis that channel surfing is caused by defects in viewer attention span, you may realize in writing your discovery draft that even though you have gathered information that connects the invention of cable television with increased channel changing, you don't find the evidence overwhelming or particularly interesting. Because cable television offers viewers more choices, it comes as no surprise that this new form of technology has created a new form of viewing behavior. You see flaws in your reasoning, holes in your draft. If you remember a study that found most viewers of television coverage of a recent news event admitted they were addicted to Cable News Network (CNN), you have uncovered evidence that makes your hypothesis less compelling. You need to modify it or, more likely, find another hypothesis.

Purpose and Thesis

Whether you proceed with your original hypothesis, modify it, or choose another, you must eventually arrive at a final decision about your purpose. You make that decision during revision, when you know what you want to do and how you want to do it. Once you have established your purpose, you can make or refine other decisions—about your organization, examples, and style. One way to express your purpose is to state your thesis. A *thesis* is a sentence that usually appears in the first paragraph of your essay and states the main idea you are going to develop. Although the thesis is often called a purpose statement, thesis and purpose are not precisely the same thing. Your purpose is both contained in and larger than your thesis: it consists of all the strategies you will use to demonstrate your thesis in a sustained and successful piece of writing.

Your thesis makes a *restricted, unified,* and *precise* assertion about your subject—an assertion that can be developed in the amount of space you have, that treats only one idea, and that is open to only one interpretation. Devising a thesis from the information that you have about your subject and stating it well are key steps in the writing process; for that reason they will be discussed in more detail in Chapter 3. For now, remember that your thesis is stated after you have determined your purpose and that it expresses your main idea about your subject. For example, if you finally determine that you want to write about the way channel surfing destroys communal viewing, your thesis might be stated this way: "One viewer's innovative channel surfing denies other viewers the right to choose what programs to watch."

In certain situations you do not need to state your thesis explicitly. This does not mean that your writing will lack purpose, only that you do not need to compose a purpose statement. Narrating a story or describing an object, for example, does not usually require a stated thesis; the thesis is suggested, or implied.

In many ways the difference between a hypothesis (a working purpose) and a thesis (a final assertion) explains why you can speculate about your purpose *before* you write but can specify your purpose only *after* you have written. This connection between your writing process and your writing purpose requires you to pause frequently to consult the criteria set forth in the following guidelines.

Guidelines for Determining Your Purpose

1. **What are the requirements of my writing project?**
   If I am writing to fulfill an assignment, do I understand that assignment? If I writing on my own, do I have definite expectations of what I will accomplish?

2. **As I proceed in this project, what do I need to know?**
   Do I have a good understanding of my subject, or do I need more information? Have I considered the possible audiences who might read my writing?

3. **What hypothesis can I use as my working purpose?**
   How many different hypotheses can I formulate about my subject? Which of them seems to direct and control my information in the most effective manner?

4. **What purpose have I discovered for this writing project?**
   Has my purpose changed as I learned more about my subject and audience? If so, in what ways? Have I discovered, by working with a hypothesis or hypotheses, what I want to do in my writing?

5. **What is my thesis?**
   How can I state my main idea about my subject in a thesis sentence? Does my thesis limit the scope of my writing to what I can demonstrate in the available space? Does it focus my writing on one specific assertion? Does it make an exact statement about what my writing intends to do?

COORDINATING DECISIONS IN THE WRITING PROCESS

You need to understand how each of the three elements —subject, audience, and purpose—helps you measure your progress through the writing process. But you must not assume that these guidelines lock you into the fixed sequence of selecting your subject, analyzing your audience, and then determining your purpose. Subject, audience, and purpose are too interconnected to allow you to follow such a simple formula. Indeed, they resemble the elements in a complex chemical formula. You can isolate the elements in the formula, but you cannot understand what they create until you combine them. And each time you alter one element, however slightly, you change the character of the other elements, setting off another chain of relationships and a new formula. To make informed and purposeful decisions about your writing, therefore, you must not only understand the separate contributions of subject, audience, and purpose, but also learn to coordinate the complex and shifting relationships among them each time you write.

Exercise —————— Describe the concepts of subject, audience, and purpose implied in each original hypothesis, and then explain how each new decision will affect the three elements. Write a new hypothesis that reflects the changes.

1. *Original hypothesis:* Channel surfing has had an enormous influence on modern art.
   New decision: You decide to discuss forms of modern art, such as cubism, that emphasized multiple perspectives and that were created before the invention of television.

2. *Original hypothesis:* Channel surfing is the direct result of the availability of multiple choices on cable television.
   New decision: You decide to address your essay to someone trying to decide whether or not to subscribe to cable television.

3. *Original hypothesis:* Channel surfing increases our tolerance of different kinds of cultural experience.
   New decision: You decide to prove that channel surfing must be done privately because only one person can operate the remote control.

Becoming a Writer | Gail Godwin

In this brief excerpt from her essay "Becoming a Writer," novelist Gail God-win remembers the way she identified with her mother's work as a writer. She also remembers the importance of her grandmother's work as a reader. What does this selection suggest about how people choose role models? What makes her mother's work seem more interesting to Godwin than her grand-mother's work?

On weekend mornings my mother sat at the typewriter in a sunny break-   1
fast nook and wrote stories about women, young women like herself, who, after some difficulty necessary to the plot, got their men. In the adjoining kitchen, my grandmother washed the breakfast dishes and kept asking, "What do you two think you could eat for lunch?" My mother and I would groan in unison. Who could imagine lunch when we'd just finished breakfast? Besides, there were more important things to do than eat.

Already, at five, I had allied myself with the typewriter rather than the   2
stove. The person at the stove usually had the thankless task of fueling. Whereas, if you were faithful to your vision at the typewriter, by lunchtime you could make two more characters happy—even if you weren't so happy your-self. What is more, if you retyped your story neatly in the afternoon and sent it off in a manila envelope to New York, you'd get a check back for $100 within two or three weeks (300 words to the page, 16–17 pages, 2¢ a word: in 1942, $100 went a long way). Meanwhile, she at the stove ran our mundane life. Still new to the outrageous vulnerability of widowhood, she was glad to play Martha to my mother's Mary. In our manless little family, she also played mother and could be counted on to cook, sew on buttons, polish the piano, and give encouragement to creative endeavors. She was my mother's first reader, while the stories were still in their morning draft; "It moves a little slowly here," she'd say, or "I didn't understand why the girl did this." And the tempo would be stepped up, the heroine's ambiguous action sharpened in the after-noon draft; for if my grandmother didn't follow tempo and motive, how would all those other women who would buy the magazines?

The Compositions of Mozart's Mind | Howard Gardner

In this selection from *Art, Mind and Brain,* psychologist Howard Gardner examines Mozart's claim that he could hear an entire piece of music in his head at one time. How does Gardner interpret this claim? In what ways does Mozart's composing process resemble those of the other artists Gardner dis-

Godwin, Gail. "A Writing Woman." *Atlantic* October 1979: 84. Reprinted in *The Writer on Her Work.* Ed. Janet Sternburg. New York: Norton, 1980. 231–32.

cusses? Why does Gardner question artists' "introspective accounts" of their creative process?

Wolfgang Amadeus Mozart once described in a letter his manner of compos-   1
ing. It was most natural to compose, he said, when he was in a cheerful mood—traveling in a carriage or strolling after a hearty meal. "When and how my ideas come, I know not; nor can I force them," he explained. But the ideas he found to his liking were easily retained, and soon he was able to fashion an appealing piece of music out of their parts—"to make a good dish of it," as he put it. Mozart proceeded to characterize his activities in a most intriguing way:

All this fires my soul, and provided I am not disturbed, my subject enlarges itself, becomes methodized and defined, and the whole, though it be long, stands almost complete and finished in my mind, so that I can survey it, like a fine picture or a beautiful statue, at a glance. Nor do I hear in my imagination the parts *successively,* but I hear them, as it were all at once (*gleich alles zusammen*). What a delight this is I cannot tell!

The claim to hear an entire piece of music—which may take twenty or   2
thirty minutes to perform—in one's head at one moment in time when it has not even been composed seems incredible. Only because Mozart was one of the great geniuses—and perhaps the greatest prodigy—of all times has this letter been taken seriously at all (and some musicologists have in fact disputed its authenticity).

But even assuming that Mozart wrote the letter and that he was not exag-   3
gerating or boasting, the question arises of precisely *what* he meant? How can one hear something, as it were, in one's mind's ear? And how can one go on to contrive a composition entirely cerebrally and then, defying time, attend to it in its entirety in one's head at a single moment? We will never know the answers to these questions: Mozart has long been dead, and it is in any case unlikely that he could have amplified the comments made in the letter. For those interested in the creative process, however, it is worth our pondering what Mozart might have meant by this strange phrasing. And in the course of this "mental experiment," it should be possible to glimpse some of the concepts and some of the issues that are being pondered today by investigators of "mental representation"—by that growing tribe of researchers known as cognitive scientists.

To begin, it is worth recalling what else we know about Mozart's process of   4
composition, and considering how his procedures compare with other notable feats of creative activity. Beyond doubt Mozart composed with great ease and rapidity. There is no other way to account for the production of more than six hundred pieces of music, including forty-one symphonies and some forty-odd operas and masses, during barely three decades of creative life, except by invoking an extraordinary fluency. Mozart's colleagues and contemporaries confirm that he wrote with astonishing efficiency. As a biographer Alfred Einstein reported, "All witnesses of Mozart at work agree that he put a composition down on paper as one writes a letter, without allowing any disturbance or interruption

Gardner, Howard. "The Compositions of Mozart's Mind." *Art, Mind and Brain*. New York: Harper, 1982. 358–60.

to annoy him, the writing down, the 'fixing' was nothing more than that—the fixing of a completed work, a mechanical act." Yet, while confirming Mozart's own introspective account, observers and biographers have been quick to point out that Mozart was anything but careless or unduly hasty. Rather, when given an assignment, he thought about it for long periods of time, would try out various combinations on the piano, hum them to himself, and contemplate how to accommodate the musical idea (or theme) to the rules of counterpoint and to the peculiarities of particular texts, performers, and instruments.

There are on record other composers who produced works as rapidly, but there are also numerous contrasting cases. Like Mozart, Beethoven was a fluent and skillful improviser, but he composed only with much more overt difficulty. In addition to keeping a notebook replete with discarded themes and false starts, Beethoven would score a piece numerous times—revising, rejecting, crossing out in his impetuous and messy hand. While Mozart's rapidly produced scores seldom contained erased passages—and indeed were practically of "camera-ready" quality—Beethoven's sketchbooks chronicled painful, even tormented sieges of creation. Certainly Beethoven's agonies during the throes of creation—rather than Mozart's seemingly seamless composing activity— served as the model of the suffering romantic artist in his garret.   5

Accounts of creation in other media echo the same contrasts. For every fluent Mozart, Trollope, or Picasso, who poured forth works with unceasing fecundity, and for every Edgar Allan Poe who claimed to plot out his works with mathematical precision, one encounters reports of a Dostoevsky, who reworked his novels numerous times, a Thomas Mann, who struggled over three pages a day, or a Richard Wagner, who had to work himself up into a nearly psychotic frenzy before finally finding himself able to put pen to score.   6

One recourse in such a state of affairs is to discard such introspective accounts altogether. Alternatively, one can assume that these differences signal variations in personality, style, or introspective candor, rather than fundamental differences in approach to creation. As yet another possibility, individuals may intend different meanings by the same phrases. For example, the twentieth-century American composer Walter Piston once reported to a friend that a piece on which he had been working was almost completed. "Can I hear it then?" his friend asked. "Oh, no," Piston retorted, "I haven't yet selected the notes." Far from being ironic, Piston apparently meant that he had planned out the abstract structure of the piece—the number of movements, the principal shifts in orchestral color, the various forms to be employed, and so on—but had still to decide upon the specific vehicles with which to embody his musical conception.   7

Brandon's Clown | **Wallace Armstrong**

In this essay, Wallace Armstrong describes the process he followed as he completed his first commissioned painting. In what ways does the process of painting *Brandon's Clown* resemble the three-stage process of writing? How does Armstrong select the subject, analyze the audience, and determine the purpose of his painting? What is the subject, who is the audience, and what is the purpose of his essay?

F ew of those words of wisdom that are passed from father to son are fol-   1
lowed. Most are simply acknowledged and forgotten. My father's advice
about my adolescent love for painting was simple and direct: "Son, you have a
special talent. Be smart. Use it to make money." With his words guiding me, I
took my love to the marketplace. I began accepting commissions, painting fantasies for those who didn't have the skill or desire to paint their own.

Creating artwork for a client, I soon discovered, demands much more than   2
talent and a lust for money. A friend of mine in Art History 110 was offered
$175 to paint a mural in the lobby of her home-town bank. Her only direction
from the bank manager was to paint "something rural looking." Obviously,
rural looking can be anything from cows lapping at a sunlit pond to combines
ripping the heads from a field of golden wheat. Somewhere in that wide spec-
trum was the painting the manager wanted. Such flexibility forces the artist to
play mind reader or simply follow his own desires and hope the client likes the
result. A less common, perhaps even less desirable commission is the verbal
blueprint. The client knows exactly what he wants. "I want a portrait," he says,
"that makes me look like General Patton. I want two American flags in the
background and a Doberman at my side." Although there is some security in
knowing what the client expects, most artists aren't desperate enough to follow
such instructions.

Once the actual work begins, the question that most frequently plagues   3
the artist is "Why am I doing this?"—especially when the commission calls for
an uncharacteristic shift in creative expression. I am known on campus as "the
guy who paints screaming faces, " a tag I am quite happy with. I am proud of
the dark maelstroms of anxiety I can create on my canvas. For hours after leaving the easel, I will walk about with my shoulders stooped and head down,
frowning, lost in reflections on man's inability to overcome despair.

Naturally, my first commission was for a nursery painting. A young   4
mother expecting her first child wanted an oil painting to hang in a newly
remodeled nursery. Mutual friends had informed her that I was willing, able,
and cheap. My father's advice prompted me to take the job and I soon found
myself discussing infant tastes with the mother-to-be, a pleasant young woman
whose only exposure to art was probably the Sunday funnies.

"You know, something happy and cheery," she said between snatches of   5
dialogue on "General Hospital." "The usual stuff for a kid's room."

"Is there any kind of theme to your nursery?" I asked hesitantly.   6

"Well, it's blue." she said. "If it's a boy, we're going to call him Brandon.   7
Something like that would be nice."

I followed her finger to a baby stroller, decorated with circus animals.   8
"Oh," I said, as the room began to darken and spin. "I see."

For the next several weeks, I had nightmares of pink giraffes and smiling   9
zebras parading across my empty canvas. I spent hours hunched over my
sketchbook, filling page after page with oddly shaped animal skeletons. Before
long, the book looked like a Disneyland mortuary. The entire project seemed so
pointless that I was exhausted with frustration. How would I satisfy my cheerful client and remain true to my creative vision?

Resolved to compromise my pride for a buck, I began gathering my   10
paints, brushes and canvas with all the enthusiasm of the only girl in the
eighth grade not chosen for the pompom squad. I reviewed my sketches
hoping to find a subject and suddenly spotted a quick drawing I had made

of a clown. Eureka! The answer seemed obvious: a clown. Of course. Clowns had screaming faces, even though they concealed their real pain behind their painted masks. I would mask my true intentions by painting a clown with a slightly sorrowful expression lurking behind his grease paint. He would hold the strings of two balloons, suggesting comparisons to a man behind prison bars.

So I began to paint. Every morning before class, I ran to my studio to reap- 11 praise the work I had done the night before. The glistening, bright arts were so inviting. Algebra could wait. I picked out my favorite brush and dove back into the painting, detailing areas I had sketched before bedtime, making the highlights lighter and the shadows darker. Gradually, the clown's face began to emerge from the swirl of color. *Brandon's Clown* was my best work to date!

Feeling every bit like the proud parent myself, I carried the finished can- 12 vas home from my college studio to unveil it for my mother. As I held it up for her reaction, I was certain she would gush with glee and call the neighbors. But after a few moments of silence, she said, "It's so dark."

My defenses flew to Red Alert. "It's supposed to be dark. How can you 13 emphasize light and shadow without making it dark?"

Leaving Mom to her *Reader's Digest,* I drove to my client's house in hopes 14 of a better reception. Occasionally I glanced at the painting lying next to me on the seat. Perhaps it *was* a bit dark—for a nursery painting, that is. The expression on the clown's face suddenly seemed harsh and scolding. How could defenseless little Brandon lie in his crib and stare at this all day long?

"How do you like your painting, Mrs. Hobbs?" I asked meekly. For some 15 reason, the canvas which had seemed so perfect that morning in my studio now looked totally out of place in Brandon's nursery. A beautiful tiny wooden rocking horse swayed peacefully on the dresser top. An 8 × 10 hospital glossy of little Brandon, looking fresh and innocent, hung on the wall. And in the corner, nearly lost in the bundle of blankets, was Brandon himself, fast asleep and completely unaware of this ugly black thing that was about to disturb the harmony of his world.

"It's fine. Will you take a check?" his mother asked as she hung the paint- 16 ing right above Brandon's head.

As I left holding my first commission, I did not think about my father's 17 advice or my artistic reputation. I thought only of poor Brandon. I will not be surprised if, twenty years from now, a deranged young man stops me on the street and smashes a clown painting over my head. I probably deserve worse.

Writing Assignments

Narrate   **1.**   Make a list of your earliest memories of writing—e.g., learning to form your letters, drafting a letter to Santa Claus, composing your first report for school. Select the memory that had the most powerful effect on you. Then write the story, dramatizing the process and explaining what you learned.

Observe   **2.**   Describe the habits of someone who uses writing to conduct business. The person need not be a professional writer. For example, you might describe how a family friend drafts business letters or a former boss wrote up reports. Your purpose is to describe how writing works in the world beyond school.

Investigate   **3.**   Using the questions about writing habits on page 4, interview a classmate about his or her writing habits. After you have compiled your information, write an essay addressed to the rest of the class, explaining the rituals your partner believes he or she must perform to write successfully.

Collaborate   **4.**   Form a small writing group (three to four students), interview each other, focusing particularly on those problems that make writing difficult in each stage of the writing process. Then write a collaborative report for each member of the group, suggesting ways he or she might solve those problems.

Read   **5.**   Focus on the grandmother in Gail Godwin's "Becoming a Writer." Then construct a profile of your *first* reader. What qualities does the person possess? What do you want this reader to tell you? How do you take praise or criticism from such a reader? You may want to read the rest of Godwin's comments on "Becoming a Writer" in *The Writer on Her Work.* Ed. Janet Sternburg. New York: Norton, 1980. 231–55.

Respond   **6.**   Respond to Wallace Armstrong's "Brandon's Clown" by trying to remember some words of wisdom that your parents or trusted friend passed on to you as guidelines for giving your life a sense of purpose. Then describe an incident in which you tried to follow those guidelines.

Analyze   **7.**   Read a biographical sketch of your favorite painter, writer, musician, or movie star in a major reference dictionary. Then speculate on how aspects of their biography—family, education, work experience—may explain the style of their creative accomplishments.

Evaluate   **8.**   Make a list of the explanations Howard Gardner uses to interpret Mozart's claim that he could hear an entire piece of music in his head at one time. Then evaluate which of Gardner's explanations make the most sense. You may want to read Gardner's analysis of cognitive schemes in *Art, Mind and Brain.* New York: Harper, 1982: 358-68.

Argue   **9.**   Howard Gardner suggests that artists' comments about their creative process are open to question because of "variations in personality, style, or introspective candor." Compare your classmates' statements about their composing process with their actual practice. Use this information to prove that readers can usually—or rarely—believe writers' accounts of their writing process.

Argue **10.** Consider what you have learned in this chapter about the ways in which various professional writers work. Next consider the difference between the writing they do and the writing you have done as schoolwork. Then develop an argument in which you demonstrate in some detail why their advice *helps* or *hinders* the "school writer." You may want to document your argument with evidence from writing assignments you had to complete in courses other than English composition.

2 | Planning

As we saw in Chapter 1, Ernest Hemingway testified that when he had trouble starting a new story he would squeeze orange peels into the fire, gaze out the window, and worry about whether he would ever write again. Although they seem to have nothing to do with writing, activities like these are not a waste of time; some may even be necessary for writers to think their way into a writing project. Random thinking may seem pointless, but it often helps writers step away from the immediate problem they face and give it a chance to "cool down" so that they can think clearly again. Random thinking *is* a waste of time, however, if it encourages writers to wait for the perfect moment to begin working. Those who wait for the perfect moment usually do a lot of waiting and very little writing. Eventually, all writers must do what Hemingway recalls he did: give themselves a strong pep talk. "Stop worrying! Start writing!"

The best way to start writing is to begin planning. Inexperienced writers mistakenly regard planning as essentially a thinking activity. First, they think, they must plan inside their heads what they want to say and then they must copy these thoughts onto a piece of paper. Unfortunately, they discover that such planning usually produces two kinds of failure: (1) They cannot think through everything they want to say before they write, and (2) they cannot simply transfer their thinking into writing. Planning, in fact, is primarily a *writing* activity, as most experienced writers can testify. Although they admit that they do some planning before they write, these writers insist that they do their most productive planning after they have begun writing. For them, planning is not so much thinking *and* writing as it is *thinking-in-writing*. Read what poet William Stafford has to say about the relationship between thinking and writing:

> When I write, I like to have an interval before me when I am not likely to be interrupted. For me, this means usually the early morning, before others are awake. I get pen and paper, take a glance out the window (often it is dark out there), and wait. It is like fishing. But I do not wait very long, for there is always a nibble—and this is where receptivity comes in. To get started I will accept anything that occurs to me. Something always occurs, of course, to any of us. We can't keep from thinking. Maybe I have to settle for an immediate impression: it's cold, or hot, or dark, or bright, or in between! Or—well, the possibilities are endless. If I put down something, that thing will help the next thing come, and I'm off. If I let the process go on, things will occur to me that were not at all in my mind when I started. These things, odd or trivial as they may be,

are somehow connected. And if I let them string out, surprising things will happen. (William Stafford, "A Way of Writing," *Writing the Australian Crawl*)

STRATEGIES AND YOUR JOURNAL

As the first stage in the writing process, planning helps you uncover, explore, and evaluate a topic. Whether you are assigned a topic by your teacher or are free, like Stafford, to accept any topic that occurs to you, planning helps you locate and produce information in writing. An effective method to prompt your planning is to use one of several thinking-in-writing strategies discussed below. Used alone or in combination, these strategies help you identify familiar (or forgotten) information and create new information. These strategies are also flexible enough to use during other stages of the writing process. A strategy designed to get you started—such as listing—works equally well as a method for evaluating a draft or organizing a revision agenda.

Keeping a Journal on Your Computer

Use a separate disk for your journal. Create a file called "Journal." Then before or after each entry, record the date and a phrase indicating the focus of your writing and save it. Such a procedure will enable you to (1) store and locate each of your writing experiments; (2) reenter your experiments to add, delete, or rework your thinking in writing; (3) transfer chunks of your writing journal directly into a draft; and (4) print hard copies of your journal for your teacher and classmates.

A good place to experiment with these strategies is a writer's sourcebook or journal. Depending on your work habits or writing context, you can use anything from a looseleaf notebook to a computer disk for your journal. In this private, no-fault environment, you can write whatever you want. But try to avoid turning your journal into a diary that simply records the clutter of your daily schedule. Instead, use it to plan writing projects—the one due next week or the one you may want to try someday.

During planning, the writing you produce in your journal will read like "one step forward, two steps back." This movement is created by your attempt to answer two questions: (1) How much information can I *produce* about this topic in writing? (2) How much of this information can I *use* to shape an interesting piece of writing? You can answer the first question after you have worked with one or more thinking-in-writing strategies. You can answer the second by evaluating the information against the guidelines produced in Chapter 1 for selecting a subject, analyzing your audience, and determining your purpose.

Listing

Listing is a simple way to produce information in writing. If you are creating your own assignment, you can make a list of potential subjects. If you are responding to directions, you can list what you already know or need to know about the subject of the assignment. As you restrict your subject or identify its various subdivisions, you can make additional lists to help you recall more precise information. Begin by giving your list a title, a prompt that will evoke events, impressions, and ideas. Then, working down the page as quickly as possible, list any word or phrase that comes to mind. Don't stop to edit, organize, or evaluate the items in your list. Simply spill them down the page in whatever form they occur to you. Sometimes you will work in explosive bursts, producing ideas that instantly generate related ideas. At other times you will pause, probing for a new direction as you move from one isolated idea to another. Don't be discouraged by these occasional pauses or by the strange notions you jot down to keep the list going. The pauses may help you identify topics that require further consideration, and the strange notions may provoke unexpected insights into your subject.

In a sociology class, Robert Scheffel was asked to write a profile of a relative who had had an important influence on his life. Focusing on his relationship with his father, Robert selected the word *Dad* as a prompt and then produced the following list in his journal:

Dad

P.K.—preacher's kid, defensive, embarrassed, rebellious, special
friends' fathers had normal jobs—no explanations
worked at bank, factory—on weekends, slept late, played golf
Dad works at church—and at home
<u>Saturday</u> "Keep quiet! Dad's working on sermon"
Typing in study. No phone calls. Turn down T.V.
Skips lunch—dinner, glassy-eyed, distant
<u>Sunday Morning</u> —gone before breakfast—dress rehearsal
Mother checks our shoes, knots ties
Marches us to first pew—everybody looking
Organ, choir, congregation—processional
Dad in robe, carrying Bible—distinguished, important
Sunday voice—scripture, sermon (fidgety, sleepy)
Prayer—"Our Heavenly Father"—power, majesty
Heavenly father, my father—same words, same rules
Sunday afternoons—Sabbath—Keep it Holy
No football, no movies, no fun—goodie-two-shoes
Career day at school—doctor, lawyer, police chief
"What's your father do?"
"Nothing. He's a minister."

Evaluating Lists   After completing your list, examine your information carefully. What subject dominates your list? Can you identify other subjects or subjects you want to develop in greater detail? Circle and connect items that seem to go together. Pick a word or phrase and start another list. You may decide that you can use most of the information on your list, or you may

Listing on Your Computer

Type your prompt at the top of your screen and begin listing all the ideas, associations, and images that come to mind. To evaluate your list, review it, highlight promising items with an asterisk or in boldface, and insert additional ideas you forgot during your initial brainstorming. If you discover an image or cluster of words that provokes a new list, save the original one before creating and naming another list on a different or related subject.

discover that only a few fragments or sentences are worth pursuing. But one of those sentences may be what Hemingway called a "true sentence," a sentence that points the way to your subject, audience, and purpose.

Robert's list focuses immediately on his father's job. The initials *P.K.* evoke emotions he cannot easily explain. His friends' fathers have *normal* jobs, but his Dad's job is different. The weekend schedule clarifies that difference and suggests the possibility of a specific subject that is significant, interesting, and manageable. It also suggests at least three groups of readers ("normal" people, preachers' kids, and preachers) who might find the subject intriguing. But, most important, the list hints at several hypotheses about Robert's perception of his father's work that he may want to explore in greater detail, either through another list or through one of the other planning strategies described in this chapter. When he has collected enough information, he will sort through his sketchy hypotheses and select one to guide his writing during drafting.

Freewriting

Like listing, freewriting helps you write down as quickly as possible what you can remember. But freewriting encourages you to remember in coherent blocks and to write in phrases and sentences. Freewriting is *free*, however, because you don't have to worry about writing perfect sentences. You write in your journal for a sustained period of time (usually ten to fifteen minutes) without stopping. Under these conditions, you don't have time to reflect on where you are going, where you have been, or how anything looks. You certainly don't have time to correct misspelled words, cross out awkward phrases, or reread what you have written. Once you are finished, you will have time to look it over and identify useful ideas.

You can practice freewriting as an unfocused or focused activity. In unfocused freewriting, you simply begin writing, transcribing onto the page the first ideas that pop into your head and then allowing your mind to wander to other subjects. The chief advantage of this kind of writing is that it forces you to write *immediately*, bypassing the agony of selecting the perfect topic. Its chief disadvantage is that it often forces you to write about the *immediate*, the impulses and events that have just occurred. But while you are filling up the page, you may discover a provocative idea or forgotten episode that leads to a more complex or deeply textured pattern of ideas.

Joanne Malbone, for example, completed the following unfocused freewriting in her journal during the confusion of the first day of her writing class:

Here I go again. Summer's gone. September stomach back. Worry about clothes, teachers, grades. I mean how many times did I check and double-check my schedule, and then—wrong room, wrong class. Everybody's looking at blotches on my neck. Act like you're the only one who doesn't know. If you get lucky, finding this class—surprise, write an essay. Freewriting. Fat chance. First days are always a lie. I mean what do you people want? Solve the polynomial. Remember the <u>Maine</u>. Find the unknown. Never could figure out Bridgeman (Latin)—never learned to decline. My little revolt. He liked it—seemed to matter. Weird. Wonder if this matters? What are we supposed to be doing anyway? Why not "What I did on my summer vacation" or better yet "What I didn't do on my summer vacation"?

It is often difficult to evaluate unfocused freewriting because the sentences slide from subject to subject, never stopping long enough to develop. But you can underline words that seem significant or question phrases that seem suspicious. Does your writing have a common theme? Does one sentence or phrase evoke a particularly powerful memory? Answering these questions in your journal may help you select a subject for a focused freewriting exercise. Joanne, surprised that she remembered Mr. Bridgeman's Latin class, decided to reconstruct the episode suggested by the prompt "My little revolt":

My Little Revolt

"I'm a tough teacher. This is a tough class. Half of you will be gone in two weeks. The rest of you will love Latin." Tough love! Bridgeman paces behind desk like a caged panther. Knit shirts, no ties—pumps iron. Made Linda Thomas cry three days straight; then she was gone. Everybody got it. Even Tommy Hirschen, Latin ace. "Miss Reinhardt. Go to board. Decline <u>fēmina</u>." Stomach lurches. Don't cry in front of boys. Already sniffling—bad cold, no Kleenex. "Begin!" Nominative, genitive, dative . . . accusative? . . . Damn! Play with chalk. Read back of eraser. "Miss Reinhardt?" "I'm thinking." Thinking I need a Kleenex. Nose dripping, eyes watering. Should have stayed home. "Cease"—favorite word. Never "stop" or "that will be all" . . . . "Mr. Hirschen. Finish declining <u>fēmina</u>." Blotches on neck. Nose running all the way to desk. Ask Mary Keller for Kleenex—too loud. "Cease." Heart pounds. "What is it now, Miss Reinhardt?" "I need a Kleenex." Long sigh—"Is there a kind soul who can give Miss Reinhardt a Kleenex?" Book bags, purses, hands—six tissues. Don't look up. Stack them slowly in pile. Reshuffle them. Make him wait. Peel off top tissue and blow. Crumple in wad. Walk slowly toward his desk. He's still waiting. Drumming pencil. Drop wad in basket. Look him in the eye—"You can continue."

Turn around . . . Hirschen's mouth open. Keller's in shock. Note on my desk. "You're dead." Bell. "Miss Reinhardt. May I see you before you leave?" Class crunches out. Hirschen whispers, "Bridgeman kills." Don't cry no matter what. We're alone. He smiles . . . "Congratulations. I've been waiting a long time for somebody to do something like that." Like what? And that was it. Still can't figure it out. Never told anybody. Let 'em fight their own battles with Bridgeman. Never scared of him again. Never loved Latin. Tough luck, Bridgeman.

Evaluating Freewriting

Like Joanne, you will need to make a number of decisions about your subject, audience, and purpose, if you want to write a longer, more finished essay based on your freewriting. Reread both of Joanne's freewritings and then answer the following questions:

1. How does Joanne's decision to focus on her revolt restrict her subject? What does she find significant and interesting about this incident? What aspects has she managed effectively? What aspects need further development?

2. How might an assessment of her audience help Joanne transform her planning into a successful draft? What specific sections of her freewriting attract the sympathy of her readers? What additional information will they need to understand her revolt?

3. What is Joanne trying to prove about her subject? Is she attempting to prove more than one thing? Make a list of hypotheses she could use to clarify her intentions.

Freewriting on Your Computer

To experiment with unfocused freewriting, open a file and begin "fishing." For focused freewriting, type your prompt at the top of the screen and begin writing. After an initial session, review your work to find a focus, then move down the screen a few lines, type this focus as your new prompt, and begin another session. On occasion, try "invisible writing." Simply turn down the brightness control on your monitor, freewrite, and then turn up the brightness to review your work. Evaluate your freewriting by marking promising passages with asterisks or brackets. You may want to transfer them to your draft. You may also want to annotate such passages by hand on your hard copy.

Speculating

Speculating will help you produce different interpretations of a potential subject. The word *speculate* suggests an imaginative, hypothetical kind of seeing: you study your subject, mull over its possible meaning, and make several conjectures about its significance. Your subject might be an observed object (the reference room), a memory (your first trip to the public library), or something you read (a character in a book or play). As a thinking-in-writing strategy, speculating encourages you to expand your planning by seeing your subject from three different perspectives: [1]

---

[1] Based on the tagmemic theory of invention in Richard E. Young, Alton L. Becker, and Kenneth L. Pike, *Rhetoric: Discovery and Change.* New York: Harcourt, 1970.

▼ *Speculate about your subject as an object.*

This perspective suggests that you see your subject at rest, as a static object or scene that at a given moment has a fixed identity.

▼ *Speculate about your subject as an action.*

This perspective allows you to see your subject in motion, as a dynamic process that changes form as it progresses.

▼ *Speculate about your subject as a network.*

This perspective enables you to see your subject as a series of connections, as a complex system of relationships that extend and enhance its importance.

As you think about your subject from each of these perspectives, note your speculations in your journal. If one perspective does not produce provocative information, move on to the next. Write what you see and make guesses about what you don't see. Don't try to write perfect sentences: you are still *planning.* You are looking for something interesting and significant about your subject that you can reveal to an audience for a purpose.

Speculating both generates information (if you have at least some notion of your subject) and interprets information you have already collected. One assignment in Amy Lindsay's writing class called for her to observe a major meeting place on campus and compose its profile. Armed with her journal, she prowled around her normal haunts, looking for a suitable subject. She considered several possibilities—her dormitory lounge, the snack bar, the registration office—but settled on the library's reference room. Although she had been given the official library tour and had worked at the OPAC and EXAC[2] monitors, she had never really studied this room. Here are her speculations about a place where people constantly come and go, looking for information.

Reference Room as an Object

The Reference Room is on the main floor of the library. The entrance is marked by the new system (OPAC—monitors/printers) and the old system (card catalog). The whole room is cluttered with books and machines. Everything is intimidating. Bibliographies, dictionaries, indexes, EXAC—even the change and copy machines. At the center of the room is mission control. Three librarians manage the reference desk, waiting for questions. They stare at their monitors, answer the phone, and watch the traffic. Behind them are shelves of reference books, coded in mysterious numbers. There are signs everywhere—maps of the library, symbols for the Library of Congress classification system, instructions on how to operate data bases. This is supposed to be the

---

[2] Some libraries use different databases for periodicals, such as INFOTRAC, CARL/UNCOVER, Wilson Online, and MELVYL.

"yellow pages" for the library—the place where your fingers do the walking. But it's too much As a fixed object, it looks like a maze, a trap.

Reference Room as an Action

This must be the busiest room on campus. Students everywhere. Scowling at OPAC or EXAC monitors. Acting like they know what they are doing. Hunching over the copy machine as the light flashes under their book. Then the game begins. Reference desk to OPAC, OPAC to EXAC, EXAC to shelves, shelves to change machine, change machine to copy machine, copy machine to reference desk. Freeze. Now, start again. Around and around. "I just need three more sources." "Anybody change a five?" Most questions go to mission control. Stand in line, like a deli. "Next." "Where's microfiche?" Librarian with beard (Duffy) seems to know everything. Occasionally he'll go hunting in the stacks. A confused student tags along, looking at watch. This wasn't supposed to take so long. Student comes back alone. Duffy still searching. Student sits with girl at study table. Search rerouted. The computer data base becomes the computer dating base.

Reference Room as a Network

The Reference Room is the key to knowledge network. Everything connects, if you know how it works. So says Duffy. He stands at mission control—silent energy, stroking his beard, waiting for action. Loves the hunt. Other librarians ask him for leads when they're stumped. Faculty call him on phone. Shows students how to think. "Got anything on toxic waste?" "What about toxic waste?" "I just need some sources." The interrogation continues—patient, personable. Looking for clues. Ways to help student get started. "Let's begin at the beginning." (OED) "You need a better search word." (LOC Index) "Have you tried one of the other data bases?" (CD-ROM) Always thinking. Enthusiasm contagious. Students return carrying large books, computer printouts. Relieved. They've broken the code. Made connections. And a contact. Duffy made their day.

Evaluating Speculation   Amy's speculations have yielded a wealth of information about the reference room. Before she drafts an extended profile of this special place, she needs to reconsider her information in terms of her potential subject, audience, and purpose. Reexamine her speculation exercises, then write out your answers to the following questions. Your instructor may want you to discuss your answers in class.

1. How many specific subjects can you identify in the three speculations?
2. Which speculation produces the most interesting perspective on the reference room? How does that perspective define a significant and manageable subject?
3. What potential audience could Amy assume for her profile? What different audience does she assume in each of her speculations?
4. What hypotheses can you find in Amy's speculating exercises?
5. What purpose might Amy choose for writing an essay about the library reference room? Compose a thesis statement she could use to build an essay from.

Speculating on Your Computer

Speculate on your computer by composing a series of three focused freewritings. (Or create a three-column grid that will enable you to compose your speculations side by side.) Explore the information in each freewriting for connections that enlarge or enrich your subject. If your columns aren't evenly matched, save your file, review it at some later date, and push yourself to produce more information that will make your speculations more balanced. Such writing will allow you to hop around, adding, deleting, and annotating your planning. If you like this planning strategy, name and save the pattern so that you can call it up whenever you want to use it.

Interviewing

Interviewing someone is the most direct way to investigate a subject, but the process is never so simple or spontaneous as it appears on television. To use the strategy effectively, you must learn how to *prepare* for an interview, how to *manage* and *record* an interview, and how to *evaluate* the results.

How to Prepare for an Interview Begin by compiling a list of people who may know something about your subject. The list could include *experts* (people who have studied your subject), *participants* (people who have *lived* your subject), and *information brokers* (people who may know nothing about your subject but know how to put you in touch with people who do). Contact the people on your list and ask for an interview, stating in general terms what you are trying to find out and why you think they may be able to help. Ask to talk to them for a specific amount of time—no longer than an hour—and don't overstay your welcome. As you schedule your interviews, anticipate how your subjects may respond to your questions. Are they likely to be friendly, hostile, or merely puzzled when you arrive? Sometimes you can anticipate their attitudes because you know them or because you have heard them express their opinions on your subject. At other times you can anticipate their attitudes by imagining yourself in their position. How would you feel about being interviewed on this subject? What topics would you want to be asked about? What topics would you want to avoid? What questions would you have about the interviewer's motives and methods?

Next, ask yourself what you want to learn from each subject. To feel prepared and to avoid getting sidetracked, write out a list of questions in your journal following the journalist's formula: *who? what? where? when? why?* and *how?* Although these questions will help you organize what you want to learn, most interviews are dynamic, disorganized conversations. For that reason, you must remind yourself that your questions are likely to provoke surprising answers that will inspire new questions. The best interviewers prepare to discover things they need to know and plan to uncover things they had not expected to learn.

How to Manage and Record an Interview   Interviews can be formal occasions in which the interviewer acts like an attorney grilling witnesses and the interviewee acts like a jittery suspect. Or interviews can be informal occasions—pleasant and productive conversations among friends. Sometimes you cannot control the mood of an interview because the person you are talking to is suspicious before you arrive. But most of the time you can put yourself and your subject at ease by following a few basic tips:

▼ *Don't feel that you must apologize for your interview.* You may want to say something about how much you appreciate your subject's willingness to talk to you. Such remarks are part of the etiquette of interviewing. But someone who has agreed to be interviewed is probably flattered that you are there and has already made time for you in the day's schedule.

▼ *Tape recorders can supply a valuable record of your conversation, but they make some people uncomfortable.* Try your journal. Keep it out of sight as much as possible, and write in it as little as possible. When you do write, jot down words and phrases rather than complete sentences. Keep your eyes on the person you are talking to, not on your journal.

▼ *Begin your interview by talking about interesting and safe topics.* If you are conducting the interview in the subject's home or office, ask about some object or photograph you have noticed in the room. Even if you don't ask about these props, try to list them in your journal because they may help you interpret what your subject thinks is important in his or her life.

▼ *Don't tell your subject everything you want to know before your subject tells you what he or she knows.* You are trying to learn what other people think, not prove what you think. The best strategy is to encourage the interviewee to act like an expert: ask your subject to help you understand the topic at hand by answering your questions. And then LISTEN.

▼ *Use prepared questions only when the conversation drifts far away from the designated topic.* For the most part, allow the conversation to develop naturally. Before you end the interview, however, review your prepared questions as a final check.

▼ *Save two questions for the end of the interview:* (1) What should I have asked that I didn't ask? (2) Whom else do I need to interview (or what do I need to read) to understand the topic we've been discussing?

How to Evaluate an Interview   Once you have completed the interview, return to your room and immediately reconstruct the conversation. Describe the atmosphere of the room where the interview took place, the appearance of your subject, and the varying attitudes (eager, evasive, expansive) he or she displayed during the discussion. Transform your words and phrases into complete sentences. If your notes seem incomplete or if you want to be sure you are quoting your subject accurately, call the person to double-check your information. Such follow-up calls are not invitations to censor. People often want to revise what they said during an interview, but only you can decide whether their second thoughts should be yours. Your follow-up call is simply an effort to make the first version complete and accurate.

After you have reproduced the interview in writing, talk to yourself in your journal about what you learned. Did your subject provide useful answers to your prepared questions? What answers confirmed your assessment of his or her biases? What answers surprised you? What new questions did you ask? If you were to draft an essay based on this interview, could you identify a subject, anticipate an audience, and formulate a hypothesis? This last assessment suggests the degree to which even the most informal interview can propel you into further planning activities. Once you try to evaluate what other people have told you, you will discover that you are making lists of questions you should have asked, people you want to talk to next, and material you think you'd better read.

Susan Reidenbach decided to write about the set design in Arthur Miller's *Death of a Salesman* for a short research paper for her literature class. The university theater was scheduled to produce the play the next semester, and she decided to interview the theater's set designer.

10/25   Decided on my research paper—"Set Design in Arthur Miller's Death of a Salesman." Theater is producing it next semester. John knows the set designer—D. C. Schwanger. Says he's easy to talk to— real creative. Got an interview Thursday at 1:30. Wonder what he'll do with Salesman. Better think up some questions so I don't look dumb.

1. Who designed the original set for Salesman?

2. What kind of problems will you have to solve in designing the set?

3. Where will you find props for the play—trophy, tape recorder, flute?

4. When will you have to start building the set to complete it on time?

5. How will you create the set for the play—follow Miller's instructions or your own intuitions?

6. Why do some playwrights provide more information than others about the significance of the set?

10/28   Notes from Interview with D. C. Schwanger

Just back from Schwanger interview. First question blew my topic. Since Jo Mielziner's prize-winning design for the original production, nobody has done much with <u>Salesman</u>. Schwanger says all you need is three rooms for the house and open space (apron) for other scenes—restaurant, hotel, garden. He's more interested in sets he's designing for <u>Hedda Gabler</u> and <u>Waiting for Godot</u>. Need to write down what happened.

Sign above office door: "The Miracle Worker." Room filled with props (mostly swords), drawings of sets (<u>renderings</u>), awards (Outstanding Creative Achievement). Next to Schwanger's desk is a drafting table stacked with blueprints (<u>working drawings</u>). Sign behind the table: "It's a small world, but I wouldn't want to paint it." Behind his desk Schwanger looks small, unimpressive—until he starts talking about his work. Real dynamo.

Designing set for one play, building set for another, tinkering with another in performance—complicated schedule. Set designer has to be organized. Reads play, researches how other designers staged it, then looks at history books to see what a living room should look like in a specific time (<u>Hedda</u>). Next collaborates with director about initial ideas—sometimes there is disagreement, but director is always in charge. Next step, makes a rendering or scale model to illustrate things like space, mood, symbolism. Then the working drawings—15–20 pages of blueprints for each play. Designer has to be architect, historian, artist, draftsman, engineer, carpenter, plumber, electrician, upholsterer. Turns drawings over to shop foreman for construction but may have to change everything in rehearsal. Too much furniture. Lights change color of paint. Audience can't see props.

New challenge with every play. Historical plays like <u>Hedda</u> you have to be accurate. Modern plays like <u>Godot</u> you have to be creative. Strange—less set—i.e., <u>Godot</u>—frees you to be more creative with what you have—tree. Each play requires you to learn something new. With <u>Equus</u>, weld metal masks. With <u>Miracle Worker</u>, get water to the pump.

Schwanger blew my paper, but fired me up about the whole process. Volunteered to work for him next semester. I could still do <u>Salesman</u>, but I'd rather pick another play or maybe write about several plays that present different design problems. Wonder if I could write about the job of set designer and use different plays as examples? Audience doesn't know how complicated a job it is. Just sit there and watch the actors. Never think about plumbing or electricity unless it doesn't work. Maybe I could interview some other designers. Read textbooks or something by Mielziner.

Susan's interview produced much information on the world of set design. Her original topic, "Set Design in Arthur Miller's *Death of a Salesman*, " is still feasible, but it no longer seems interesting or significant. Read through her notes, and then try to answer these questions:

1. To what extent did Susan's list of questions *prepare* her for her interview?
2. How does she *manage* Schwanger's replies to her questions?
3. Why does the interview change the focus of Susan's research paper?
4. What kind of audience does she anticipate for the new essay she is planning?
5. What hypothesis is she beginning to formulate about this new subject?

Interviewing on Your Computer

Set up a file and write down your questions before you conduct your interview. Write up your interview notes or transcribe your interview tape into that file after the interview. Make a duplicate copy of the file so that you can speculate about or rearrange your subject's comments to reveal the patterns and themes that emerged during the interview. Although interviews are most successful face-to-face, the computer provides the option of an electronic interview. If you have access to your university's internal network (E-mail) or external network (Internet), send your questions to your subject on the network. Transfer his or her reply into the appropriate file. If the subject is accessible, transmit follow-up questions or begin an electronic conversation about the issues you are investigating.

Reading

Reading what other people have written about your subject is probably the most common strategy for gathering information for writing. But merely consuming other people's words will not help you compose your own. You must be a critical consumer—*selecting, analyzing,* and *evaluating* what you read for one purpose: to help you write. Chapters 14 and 15 will help you perform these activities according to the more formal requirements of the research paper: checking bibliographies, quoting evidence, documenting sources. In this chapter, you will use reading as an informal procedure for exploring different approaches to your subject.

The easiest way to keep track of your reading is to write about it in your journal. Think of reading as another form of interviewing—a way of talking to people who have already thought and written about your subject. So, just as you did in interviewing, start by making a list of material you want to read. Be sure to look for variety in your reading material: skim magazines in a bookstore; consult with a local expert on your subject; or talk to a reference librarian. Once you start reading, each selection will refer you to others; then your problem will be deciding when you have read enough. There is no way to make that decision—you can *always* read more—but usually you know that you have read enough when the same names, ideas, and issues begin to pop up in everything you read.

On most subjects, reading material falls into three broad categories: eyewitness accounts (printed in popular magazines), expert studies (documented in technical journals or official reports), and advocates' opinions (expressed in editorial or promotional pamphlets). Although these categories suggest the kind of material you need to read, they may not help you classify a specific selection. Indeed, many selections combine the features of all three categories. An editorial, for example, may cite personal anecdotes and statistical data to advance its argument. To sort out the material on your list, you need a set of questions to help you interpret what you are reading. These questions are similar to the guidelines you follow as you write, but in this case you are deciding how another writer, writing in a specific format and context, selects a subject, analyzes an audience, and determines a purpose.

1. Who is the author? What makes the author an expert on the subject? What might have formed the author's point of view?

2. Where and when was the article or book published? You may know little about the author, but you may know something about the point of view of the magazine (*Ms., Scientific American*) and whether the date of publication makes the information current and reliable.

3. What is the author's general subject? What is the restricted subject? What does this perspective contribute to your understanding of *your* subject? Does it confirm your perception, raise new and confusing questions, or lead you into detours and dead ends?

4 To whom is the writing addressed? What attitudes does the author assume in his or her audience? What knowledge does he or she expect these readers to possess or want to obtain?

5. What is the author's purpose? Does the author state a specific thesis or imply one? How does the thesis, stated or implied, control the direction of the writing?

These questions not only help you select the most intriguing reading material from your list, they also help you analyze and evaluate it. Keep your journal with you so you can write about your reading as you *preview, read,* and *review.*

▼ *Preview:* Before you read each selection, try to anticipate the kinds of information and the point of view you will find. Annotate each entry on your list, indicating what you expect to find when you read it.

▼ *Read:* As you read each selection, write a few notes in your journal. Comment on the major points, copy memorable sentences or important data, and write out short answers to your reading questions. You will also want to write any questions the author raises that you have not considered.

▼ *Review:* Put the material aside and write about the most vivid and thought-provoking things you remember. Thumb back through your reading notes. What did you discover that contributes to your view of the subject? Evaluate what the selection said and what it didn't say.

John follows this three-part procedure as he does his preliminary reading for a history essay on the Holocaust. He begins by skimming through some of the major studies—political explanations, personal accounts, historical analyses—but eventually decides to restrict his subject to the United States Holocaust Memorial Museum in Washington, D.C. Next, he compiles a short reading list, noting his expectations for each selection.

Reading List on Holocaust Memorial

Preview: 1. Kernan, Michael. "A New Monument to Remembering—with a Mission." Smithsonian 24 (April 1993): 50–62. Magazine features essays on history and museums. Lots of photos. PR for new museum? Credit line says author is a frequent contributor to magazine, "was a teenager during World War II, . . . and visited Auschwitz a few years ago with a friend who escaped the camp in 1943" (52). Expert on Holocaust? Expert on museums? Why set off "with a Mission"?

2. Wiesel, Elie. "For the Dead and the Living." The New Leader 76 (May 17–31, 1993): 13–14. Wiesel is a camp survivor, activist, winner of Nobel Prize, and chair of presidential commission that recommended building memorial. Credit line says essay was adapted from address at the dedication ceremonies (13). Cutting the ribbon? Ceremonial hype? "Look what we built!" 1st picture: The Hall of Witness—witness: noun or verb? 2nd picture: people watching film of woman talking. Caption: Testimony.

3. Gourevitch, Philip. "Behold Now Behemoth." Harper's 287 (July 1993): 55–62. Behemoth—Hebrew for "great beast." Phrase from Bible. Copy below title calls memorial "one more American theme park" (55). Disneyland? Essay in section on "criticism." Cultural editor of Jewish weekly newspaper. Why would he want to criticize Holocaust memorial?

Finally, John reads and reviews each selection, evaluating what the article contributes to his own planning.

Reading Notes

1. "A New Monument to Remembering—with a Mission"—Controversy—museum on morbid subject. Mall for museums on American accomplishments. History of project—Carter, Wiesel, Freed (architect) (51–53). Goes through

museum (tourist). Explains what he sees (54)—Holocaust victim card for each visitor. Gives name of real person—your age and gender. At different places in museum, insert card in computer and find out what's happening to you/person. Interactive. Elevator to top floor. Recording of "innocent" American soldier explaining the horrors he saw when he liberated camps. Exhibits on Nazi hate campaigns. Freight car; gas chamber door; 23,000 donated artifacts (4,000 shoes); photos of victims, murderers, liberators (55–59). Wall protects children from gruesome films. Eternal Flame. 24 computers to call up tapes of survivors telling their stories. Library for Holocaust scholarship. Information on dead and lost (60–61). "Hitler is gone, and we're still here" (62).

Review: Good description of the exhibits on each of the four floors. Acknowledges controversy—"museums deal in the beautiful" (60); American leaders <u>knew</u> what was going on in the camps. Writes mainly for the tourist. This is what you will see. This is why it is important. This is how the gimmicks—cards, computers—work. Mission—to make events visible, prevent events from becoming ordinary, prevent unspeakable from happening again. A museum should educate visitors!

Reading Notes

2. "For the Dead and the Living"—Celebrates nation's commitment (credits Carter) to build memorial. When asked about his vision of the museum, wrote one sentence—now inscribed on museum wall: "For the dead and the living, we must bear witness" (13). Story of mother's reaction to Jewish revolt in Warsaw ghetto. She didn't understand. One year later she was in a cattle car on her way to Auschwitz. Tells camp stories—SS officers using children for target practice. "As you look into the eyes of the killers and their victims, ask yourselves: How could the murderers do what they did and go on living? . . . Why was there no outcry, no public indignation? . . . Why was man's silence matched by God's?" (14). Museum is "not an answer but a question mark." Justifies museum by arguing "to forget would mean to kill the victims a second time" (14). Lesson of Holocaust. Right to be different. Hatred continues. Bloodshed in Bosnia has to be stopped.

Review: Wiesel was on the commission, but did not help design museum. Does not say much about museum, but he's at the dedication. His words are on building. Speech focuses on events, on racial hatred. Witness that it is still happening. American government did nothing then. Is doing nothing now. Twist. Dedicate building so that people will never forget. Already forgetting. "Ethnic cleansing." How did Clinton et al. react to Wiesel's talk? What did Clinton say?

Reading Notes

3. "Behold Now Behemoth"—Begins with stories about his parents (survivors) and his nightmares about Nazis. Switches to controversy over museum. Problem with two missions—1. memorialize victims, 2. preach ideals of American culture (Americanization of Holocaust) (55). Walk through museum is a walk through his nightmares. Dedication ceremony. Clinton's remarks ironic—inaction in Bosnia (56). Denouncing evil is not the same thing as doing good (57). Analyzes politics behind memorial. Carter (selling planes to Saudis); Wiesel (completes report, then resigns from commission); debates over Bosnia (57). Criticizes exhibits—gimmicks. Roles projected for visitors—victim, hero, bystander. Films of atrocities seen as "snuff films"—naked women led to execution (60). Why would anyone want to be here? What could they learn? "Violence and grotesque are central to American aesthetic" (61). Visitor as "voyeur of the prurient" (61). Elephant story—see the spectacle. Connection to Bible. The Lord said to Job, "Behold the Behemoth." Exposure to barbarism does not prevent it. ID cards—lives—pitched in litter bins outside museum (62). Just another show. The Air and Space Museum.

Review: Essay makes good contrast to Kernan's explanation of exhibits. Also gives political context for Wiesel's talk. Challenges American innocence. Reads exhibits as seducing rather than informing visitors. Exhibits of political and ethical madness do not "teach us anything about political and ethical sanity" (62). Barbarians learn from history, too. "First-ever plan for Holocaust museum was drawn up by Nazis . . . to serve as a triumphant memorial to [Jewish] annihilation" (62). Contrast to Wiesel—sees museum as "constantly recycling slaughter . . . Didn't these people suffer enough the first time their lives were taken from them?" (62). How can anyone answer such questions?

Evaluating Reading   John has come a long way since he decided to restrict his paper to the United States Holocaust Memorial Museum in Washington, D.C. His view of the subject has widened so that he doubts his ability to cover it. He is astonished at how much he (and his readers) will have to learn about the history of the Holocaust to understand the controversy prompted by the museum. But as he reads this material and searches for additional information, he discovers a working hypothesis: "The memorial to the victims of the Holocaust dramatizes racial hatred but does not help its visitors understand why this horror happened." When he composes his discovery draft, John will have to refine this hypothesis into a thesis.

Reading on Your Computer

Consult computer data bases in your library: OPAC for books and EXAC for periodicals. Use k= (keyword) to identify the topic you wish to locate (Holocaust) and then add other "descriptors" (United States Holocaust Memorial Museum) to refine your search. Browse through selections, noting title, author, kind of magazine, and (when available) abstract of entry. You can read the text of some sources directly off the computer screen and then transfer important passages into your journal or draft. Select promising readings, and type complete bibliographic information so that you can transfer it to "works cited" page. (See Chapters 14 and 15.) Below your citation, type "Preview," "Reading Notes," and "Review" and follow through with those procedures. Mark key ideas, direct quotations, and page numbers. Insert your own comments and questions. As you evaluate your reading notes, put an asterisk next to those quotations and paraphrases you may wish to transfer directly into your draft.

A FINAL WORD ABOUT PLANNING

The most important thing to learn about planning is to know when to stop. You probably know people who spend their lives making plans. If they have to study for a test, they make lists of what to study, map out a schedule for studying each item on the list, and then talk about their study plans to everyone else taking the test. Somewhere in the midst of all their planning, they lose sight of the project—the test. Planning as a part of the writing process has a specific and limited purpose: thinking-in-writing. Once you have completed this thinking, you must come to some conclusion about what you have written. You must make choices about your *subject, audience,* and *purpose.* And you must be willing to try out those choices in a fuller, more sustained piece of writing. You must begin drafting.

On Keeping a Journal

The following observations about keeping a journal were made by three important writers: Henry David Thoreau, nineteenth-century American philosopher and essayist; Virginia Woolf, twentieth-century British novelist and essayist; and Joan Didion, twentieth-century American novelist. How would you characterize the different ways these writers use their journals? Which writer's remarks seem to approximate best how you feel about keeping a journal?

Journal | Henry David Thoreau

To set down such choice experiences that my own writings may inspire me and at last I may make wholes of parts. Certainly it is a distinct profession to rescue from oblivion and to fix the sentiments and thoughts which visit all men more or less generally, that the contemplation of the unfinished picture may suggest its harmonious completion. Associate reverently and as much as you can with your loftiest thoughts. Each thought that is welcomed and recorded is a nest egg, by the side of which more will be laid. Thoughts accidentally thrown together become a frame in which more may be developed and exhibited. Perhaps this is the main value of a habit of writing, of keeping a journal—that so we remember our best hours and stimulate ourselves. My thoughts are my company. They have a certain individuality and separate existence, aye, personality. Having by chance recorded a few disconnected thoughts and then brought them into juxtaposition, they suggest a whole new field in which it was possible to labor and to think. Thought begat thought. (1852)

A Writer's Diary | Virginia Woolf

I have just re-read my year's diary and am much struck by the rapid haphazard gallop at which it swings along, sometimes indeed jerking almost intolerably over the cobbles. Still if it were not written rather faster than the fastest typewriting, if I stopped and took thought, it would never be written at all; and the advantage of the method is that it sweeps up accidentally several stray matters which I should exclude if I hesitated, but which are the diamonds of the dustheap. (January 20, 1919)

"On Keeping a Notebook" | Joan Didion

So the point of my keeping a notebook has never been, nor is it now, to have an accurate factual record of what I have been doing or thinking. That would be a different impulse entirely, an instinct for reality which I sometimes envy but do not possess. At no point have I ever been able successfully to keep a diary; my approach to daily life ranges from the grossly negligent to the merely absent, and on those few occasions when I have tried dutifully to record a day's events, boredom has so overcome me that the results are mysterious at best. What is this business about "shopping, typing piece, dinner with E, depressed"? Shopping for what? Typing what piece? Who is E? Was this "E" depressed, or was I depressed? Who cares? . . .

[1]

How it felt to me: that is getting closer to the truth about a notebook. I some-   2
times delude myself about why I keep a notebook, imagine that some thrifty
virtue derives from preserving everything observed. See enough and write it
down, I tell myself, and then some morning when the world seems drained of
wonder, some day when I am only going through the motions of doing what I
am supposed to do, which is write—on that bankrupt morning I will simply
open my notebook and there it will all be, a forgotten account with accumu-
lated interest, paid passage back to the world out there: . . . I imagine, in other
words, that the notebook is about other people. But of course it is not.

The Five Rings | **Richard Saul Wurman**

In this passage from *Information Anxiety* (1989), Richard Saul Wurman classifies five types of information. What type(s) of information are missing from
your planning? Why does the omission of this kind of information cause
information anxiety? How can you use one of the thinking-in-writing strategies described in this chapter to overcome this anxiety?

We are all surrounded by information that operates at varying degrees of   1
immediacy to our lives. These degrees can be roughly divided into five
rings, although what constitutes information on one level for one person may
operate on another level for someone else. The rings radiate out from the most
personal information that is essential for our physical survival to the most
abstract form of information that encompasses our personal myths, cultural
development, and sociological perspective.

The first ring is **internal** information—the messages that run our internal   2
systems and enable our bodies to function. Here, information takes the form of
cerebral messages. We have perhaps the least control over this level of information, but are the most affected by it.

The second ring is **conversational** information. It is the formal and infor-   3
mal exchanges and conversations that we have with the people around us, be
they friends, relatives, coworkers, strangers in checkout lines, or clients in business meetings. Conversation is a prominent source of information, although we
tend to play down or ignore its role, perhaps because of the informality of its
nature. Yet this is the source of information over which we have the most control, both as givers and receivers of information.

The third ring is **reference** information. This is where we turn for the   4
information that runs the systems of our world—science and technology—and,
more immediately, the reference materials to which we turn in our own lives.
Reference information can be anything from a textbook on quantum physics to
the telephone book or dictionary.

The fourth ring is **news** information. This encompasses current events—the   5
information that is transmitted via the media about people, places, and events
that may not directly affect our lives, but can influence our vision of the world.

The fifth ring is **cultural** information, the least quantifiable form. It encom-   6
passes history, philosophy, and the arts, any expression that represents an

---

Wurman, Richard Saul. *Information Anxiety.* New York: Doubleday, 1989. 42–45.

Drawing by Ed Fisher; © 1993 The New Yorker Magazine, Inc.

attempt to understand and come to terms with our civilization. Information garnered from other rings is incorporated here to build the body of information that determines our own attitudes and beliefs, as well as the nature of our society as a whole.

Although there are specific characteristics inherent to the transmission of information at each of these levels, their systems are remarkably similar and often they are fraught with the same problems and pitfalls. Within each is the potential for anxiety. And, cumulatively, the grappling with information at each of these levels can weigh us down and induce a state of helplessness. It can paralyze thinking and prevent learning.   **7**

Information anxiety can afflict us at any level and is as likely to result from too much as too little information.   **8**

There are several general situations likely to induce *information anxiety:* not understanding information; feeling overwhelmed by the amount of information to be understood; not knowing if certain information exists; not knowing where to find information; and, perhaps the most frustrating, knowing exactly where to find the information, but not having the key to access it. You are sitting in front of your computer which contains all of the spread sheets that will justify the money you are spending to develop a new product, but you can't remember the name of the file. The information remains just out of your grasp.   **9**

You are trying to describe yourself as a lover of wine, but you have no idea how to spell the word "oenophile." Now dictionaries are quite useful if you   **10** know how to spell, but if you can't remember how the word starts, you're in trouble. This is the nightmare of inaccessibility—trying to find something when you don't know what it is listed under. How do you ask for something if you don't know how to spell it or you don't know what it's called? This is *information anxiety*.

We are surrounded by reference materials, but without the ability to use   11
them, they are just another source of anxiety. I think of them as buddhas, sitting on my shelf with all that information and a knowing smile. It's a challenge for me to get access to them and to make them more accessible to others.

Television and Reading | Marie Winn

In this selection from *The Plug-In Drug* (1985), Marie Winn compares the process of watching television and reading books. How does she assess the process of *watching* and *reading* as a method for gathering information? How does her analysis of *reading* explain why it stimulates thinking-in-writing?

I t is not enough to compare television watching and reading from the view-   1
point of quality. Although the quality of the material available in each medium varies enormously, from junky books and shoddy programs to literary masterpieces and fine, thoughtful television shows, the *nature* of the two experiences is different and that difference significantly affects the impact of the material taken in.

Few people besides linguistics students and teachers of reading are aware   2
of the complex mental manipulations involved in the reading process. Shortly after learning to read, a person assimilates the process so completely that the words in books seem to acquire an existence almost equal to the objects or acts they represent. It requires a fresh look at a printed page to recognize that those symbols that we call letters of the alphabet are completely abstract shapes bearing no inherent "meaning" of their own. Look at an "o," for instance, or a "k." The "o" is a curved figure; the "k" is an intersection of three straight lines. Yet it is hard to divorce their familiar figures from their sounds, though there is nothing "o-ish" about an "o" or "k-ish" about a "k." A reader unfamiliar with the Russian alphabet will find it easy to look at the symbol "Ш," and see it as an abstract shape; a Russian reader will find it harder to detach that symbol from its sound, *shch*. And even when trying to consider "k" as an abstract symbol, we cannot see it without the feeling of a "k" sound somewhere between the throat and the ears, a silent pronunciation of the "k" that occurs the instant we see the letter.

That is the beginning of reading: we learn to transform abstract figures   3
into sounds, and groups of symbols into the combined sounds that make up the words of our language. As the mind transforms the abstract symbols into sounds and the sounds into words, it "hears" the words, as it were, and thereby invests them with meanings previously learned in the spoken language.

Winn, Marie. *The Plug-In Drug*. rev. ed. New York: Viking Penguin, 1985. 57–66.

Invariably, as the skill of reading develops, the meaning of each word begins to seem to dwell within those symbols that make up the word. The word "dog," for instance, comes to bear some relationship with the real animal. Indeed, the word "dog" seems to *be* a dog in a certain sense, to possess some of the qualities of a dog. But it is only as a result of a swift and complex series of mental activities that the word "dog" is transformed from a series of meaningless squiggles into an idea of something real. This process goes on smoothly and continuously as we read, and yet it becomes no less complex. The brain must carry out all the steps of decoding and investing with meaning each time we read; but it becomes more adept at it as the skill develops, so that we lose the sense of struggling with symbols and meanings that children have when they first learn to read.

But not merely does the mind *hear* words in the process of reading; it is **4** important to remember that reading involves images as well. For when the reader sees the word "dog" and understands the idea of "dog," an image representing a dog is conjured up as well. The precise nature of this "reading image" is little understood, nor is there agreement about what relation it bears to visual images taken in directly by the eyes. Nevertheless images necessarily color our reading, else we would perceive no meaning, merely empty words. The great difference between these "reading images" and the images we take in when viewing television is this: we *create* our own images when reading, based upon our own life experiences and reflecting our own individual needs, while we must accept what we receive when watching television images. This aspect of reading, which might be called "creative" in the narrow sense of the word, is present during all reading experiences, regardless of *what* is being read. When we read it is almost as if we were creating our own, small, inner television program. The result is a nourishing experience for the imagination. As Bruno Bettleheim notes, "Television captures the imagination but does not liberate it. A good book at once stimulates and frees the mind."

Television images do not go through a complex symbolic transformation. **5** The mind does not have to decode and manipulate during the television experience. Perhaps this is a reason why the visual images received directly from a television set are strong, stronger, it appears, than the images conjured up mentally while reading. But ultimately they satisfy less. A ten-year-old child reports on the effects of seeing television dramatizations of books he has previously read: "The TV people leave a stronger impression. Once you've seen a character on TV, he'll always look like that in your mind, even if you made a different picture of him in your mind before, when you read the book yourself." And yet, as the same child reports, "the thing about a book is that you have so much freedom. You can make each character look exactly the way you want him to look. You're more in control of things when you read a book than when you see something on TV."

It may be that television-bred children's reduced opportunities to indulge **6** in this "inner picture-making" accounts for the curious inability of so many children today to adjust to nonvisual experiences. This is commonly reported by experienced teachers who bridge the gap between the pretelevision and the television eras.

"When I read them a story without showing them pictures, the children **7** always complain—'I can't see.' Their attention flags," reports a first-grade teacher. "They'll begin to talk or wander off. I have to really work to develop their visualizing skills. I tell them that there's nothing to see, that the story is coming out of my mouth, and that they can make their own pictures in their 'mind's eye.' They get better at visualizing, with practice. But children never needed to learn how to visualize before television, it seems to me."

Viewing vs. Reading: Concentration

Because reading demands complex mental manipulations, a reader is required to concentrate far more than a television viewer. An audio expert notes that "with the electronic media it is openness [that counts]. Openness permits auditory and visual stimuli more direct access to the brain . . . someone who is taught to concentrate will fail to perceive many patterns of information conveyed by the electronic stimuli."

It may be that a predisposition toward concentration, acquired, perhaps, through one's reading experiences, makes one an inadequate television watcher. But it seems far more likely that the reverse situation obtains: that a predisposition toward "openness" (which may be understood to mean the opposite of focal concentration), acquired through years and years of television viewing, has influenced adversely viewers' ability to concentrate, to read, to write clearly—in short, to demonstrate any of the verbal skills a literate society requires.

Pace

A comparison between reading and viewing may be made in respect to the pace of each experience, and the relative control we have over that pace, for the pace may influence the ways we use the material received in each experience. In addition, the pace of each experience may determine how much it intrudes upon other aspects of our life.

When we read, clearly, we can control the pace. We may read as slowly or as rapidly as we can or wish to read. If we do not understand something, we may stop and reread it, or go in search of elucidation before continuing. If what we read is moving, we may put down the book for a few moments and cope with our emotions without fear of losing anything.

When we view, the pace of the television program cannot be controlled; only its beginning and end are within our control by clicking the knob on and off. We cannot slow down a delightful program or speed up a dreary one. We cannot "turn back" if a word or phrase is not understood. The program moves inexorably forward, and what is lost or misunderstood remains so.

Nor can we readily transform the material we see on television into a form that might suit our particular emotional needs, as we invariably do with material we read. The images move too quickly. We cannot use our own imagination to invest the people and events portrayed on television with the personal meanings that would help us understand and resolve relationships and conflicts in our own life; we are under the power of the imagination of the show's creators. In the television experience the eyes and ears are overwhelmed with the immediacy of sights and sounds. They flash from the television set just fast enough for the eyes and ears to take them in before moving on quickly to the new pictures and sounds . . . so as *not to lose the thread*.

Not to lose the thread . . . it is this need, occasioned by the irreversible direction and relentless velocity of the television experience, that not only limits the workings of the viewer's imagination, but also causes television to intrude into human affairs far more than reading experiences can ever do. If someone enters the room while we're watching television—a friend, a relative, a child, someone, perhaps, we have not seen for some time—we must continue to watch or else we'll lose the thread. The greetings must wait, for the television program will not. A book, of course, can be set aside, with a pang of regret, perhaps, but with no sense of permanent loss.

A grandparent describes a situation that is, by all reports, not uncommon: 15

"Sometimes when I come to visit the girls, I'll walk into their room and 16
they're watching a TV program. Well, I know they love me, but it makes me feel *bad* when I tell them hello, and they say, without even looking up, 'Wait a minute . . . we have to see the end of this program.' It hurts me to have them care more about that machine and those little pictures than about being glad to see me. I know that they probably can't help it, but still. . . . "

Can they help it? Ultimately, when we watch television our power to 17
release ourselves from viewing in order to attend to human demands that come up is not altogether a function of the pace of the program. After all, we might *choose* to operate according to human priorities, rather than electronic dictatorship. We might quickly decide "to hell with this program" and simply stop watching when a friend enters the room or a child needs attention.

We might . . . but the hypnotic power of television makes it difficult to shift 18
our attention away, makes us desperate not to lose the thread of the program.

Why Is It So Hard to Stop Watching?

A number of perceptual factors unique to the television experience may 19
play a role in making television more *fascinating* than any other vicarious experience, factors to do with the nature of the electronic images on the screen and the ways the eye takes them in.

Whereas in real life we perceive but a tiny part of the visual panorama 20
around us with the fovea, the sharp-focusing part of the eye, taking in the rest of the world with our fuzzy peripheral vision, when we watch television we take in the entire frame of an image with our sharp foveal vision. Let us say that the image on the television screen depicts a whole room or a mountain landscape; if we were there in real life, we would be able to perceive only a very small part of the room or the landscape clearly with any single glance. On television, however, we can see the entire picture sharply. Our peripheral vision is not involved in viewing that scene; indeed, as the eye focuses upon the television screen and takes it all in sharply, the mind blots out the peripheral world entirely. Since in real life the periphery distracts and diffuses our attention, this absence of periphery must serve to abnormally heighten our attention to the television image.

Another unique feature of the television image is the remarkable activity 21
of all contours on the television screen. While the normal contours of real-life objects and people are stationary, the electronic mechanism that creates images on a screen produces contours that are ever moving, although the viewer is hardly aware of the movement. Since the eye is drawn to fixate more strongly on moving than on stationary objects, one result of the activity of television contours is to make them more attention-binding.

Yet another consequence is to make the eye defocus slightly when fixing 22
its attention on the television screen. The reason is this: in viewing television the steadily changing visual activity of the contour causes the eye to have difficulties in fixating properly. Now in real life when the eye does not fixate properly a signal is sent to the visual center of the brain, which than takes corrective steps. Since improper fixation is normally the result of an eye tremor or some physical dysfunction of the viewer rather than of the thing being viewed, the

visual system will attempt to make corrections in the eye tremor or in some part of the viewer's visual system. However, in viewing television, it is the visual activity *at the contour of the image* that is causing the difficulties in fixation. Thus the visual system will have increasing difficulty in maintaining its normal fixation. Therefore it may be easier to give up striving for a perfect, focused fixation on a television picture and to accommodate by somewhat defocused fixation.

The sensory confusion that occurs as a result of the activity of television images is not unlike the state that occurs when the semicircular canals of the ears, which serve to maintain our balance and help the brain make the necessary adjustments to the body's movements, are confused by motion from external sources (as when one stands still and yet one's ear canals are moved this way and that by the motion of a car or ship or airplane). The unpleasant symptoms of seasickness or carsickness reflect this internal confusion.   23

The slight defocusing of the eyes while viewing television, while not as unpleasant as seasickness (it is barely perceptible, in fact), may nevertheless have subtle consequences that serve to make the television experience more dysfunctional for the organism than other experiences such as reading. Research shows that defocusing of the eye normally accompanies various fantasy and daydreaming states. Thus the material perceived on television may take on an air of unreality, a dreamlike quality. Moreover, similar visual-motor conflicts are frequently described as features of many drug experiences by users. This may very well be a reason for the trancelike nature of so many viewers' television experience, and may help to explain why the television image has so strong and hypnotic a fascination. It has even been suggested that "early experiences with electronic displays are predisposing to later enjoyment of psychoactive drugs which produce similar perceptual effects."   24

All these perceptual anomalies may conspire to fascinate viewers and glue them to the television set.   25

Of course there are variations in the attention-getting and attention-sustaining powers of television images, many of which depend on such factors as the amount of movement present on the screen at any given moment and the velocity of change from image to image. It is a bit chilling to consider that the producers of the most influential program for preschool children, *Sesame Street*, employed modern technology in the form of a "distractor" machine to test each segment of their program to ensure that it would capture and hold the child's attention to the highest degree possible. With the help of the "distractor," the makers of *Sesame Street* found that fast-paced cartoons and fast-moving stories were most effective in sustaining a child's attention. This attitude toward young children and their television experiences may well be compared to that revealed by Monica Sims of the BBC who states: "We're not trying to tie children to the television screen. If they go away and play halfway through our programs, that's fine."   26

The Basic Building Blocks

There is another difference between reading and television viewing that must affect the response to each experience. This is the relative acquaintance of readers and viewers with the fundamental elements of each medium. While the reader is familiar with the basic building blocks of the reading medium, the television viewer has little acquaintance with those of the television medium.   27

As we read, we have our own writing experience to fall back upon. Our understanding of what we read, and our feelings about it, are necessarily affected, and deepened, by our possession of writing as a means of communicating. As children begin to learn reading, they begin to acquire the rudiments of writing. That these two skills are always acquired together is important and not coincidental. As children learn to read words, they need to understand that a word is something they can write themselves, though their muscle control may temporarily prevent them from writing it clearly. That they wield such power over the words they are struggling to decipher makes the reading experience a satisfying one right from the start for children. **28**

A young child watching television enters a realm of materials completely beyond his control—and understanding. Though the images that appear on the screen may be reflections of familiar people and things, they appear as if by magic. Children cannot create similar images, nor even begin to understand how those flickering electronic shapes and forms come into being. They take on a far more powerless and ignorant role in front of the television set than in front of a book. **29**

There is no doubt that many young children have a confused relationship to the television medium. When a group of preschool children were asked, "How do kids get to be on your TV?" only 22 percent of them showed any real comprehension of the nature of the television images. When asked, "Where do the people and kids and things go when your TV is turned off?" only 20 percent of the three-year-olds showed the smallest glimmer of understanding. Although there was an increase in comprehension among the four-year-olds, the authors of the study note that "even among the older children the vast majority still did not grasp the nature of television pictures." **30**

Children's feelings of power and competence are nourished by another feature of the reading experience that does not obtain for television: the non-mechanical, easily accessible, and easily transportable nature of reading matter. Children can always count on a book for pleasure, though the television set may break down at a crucial moment. They may take a book with them wherever they go, to their room, to the park, to their friend's house, to school to read under the desk: they can *control* their use of books and reading materials. The television set is stuck in a certain place; it cannot be moved easily. It certainly cannot be casually transported from place to place by a child. Children must not only watch television wherever the set is located, but they must watch certain programs at certain times, and are powerless to change what comes out of the set and when it comes out. **31**

In this comparison of reading and television viewing a picture begins to emerge that quite confirms the commonly held notion that reading is somehow "better" than television viewing. Reading involves a complex form of mental activity, trains the mind in concentration skills, develops the powers of imagination and inner visualization; the flexibility of its pace lends itself to a better and deeper comprehension of the material communicated. Reading engrosses, but does not hypnotize or seduce the reader from his human responsibilities. Reading is a two-way process: the reader can also write; television viewing is a one-way street: the viewer cannot create television images. And books are ever available, ever controllable. Television controls. **32**

Writing Assignments

Narrate   **1.**   Find some photographs of a close relative in an old family album or, better yet, a letter or journal written when her or she was your age. In your journal, make a list of those features you find most familiar and most unsettling. Use this information to compose a narrative from your relative's perspective about "how it felt to be *me* at that age."

Observe   **2.**   Select a place in your old neighborhood that had an important influence on your life—a garden, a playground, a movie theater. Speculate on how this place functioned in your life as you were growing up. Then in an essay addressed to your writing class, compare the way this place used to be with the way it is now.

Investigate   **3.**   Interview someone on your campus or in your community who is involved in managing information—a reference librarian, a newspaper writer, an advertising designer. Ask your subject to describe the procedures he or she uses to discover, store, and reproduce information. Then write a profile of this information manager, focusing on the procedures he or she uses to overcome the anxieties certain types of information induce.

Collaborate   **4.**   Your writing group has been asked to design a museum to commemorate the history of the people (or a group of people) in your college community. Ask each member to list possible exhibits for the museum. Then ask each member to freewrite about one of these exhibits, focusing on ways it could be made interactive for visitors

Read   **5.**   Expand your planning in assignment 4 by assigning reading about the subjects of the various exhibits to each member of the group. Consult local histories, guidebooks, newspaper files, and the records of appropriate community organizations to widen and deepen your ability to plan the historical exhibits.

Respond   **6.**   Respond to Marie Winn's essay by diagnosing your own television-viewing habits. In your journal, keep a log of what you watch for a week, when you watch, and why you watch. Then write an essay for your student newspaper on "The Confessions of a Television Addict."

Analyze   **7.**   Analyze the strategies Marie Winn uses to create a special identity for her readers. In particular, notice the way she uses pronouns like "we" and "they" to distinguish between people who prefer to read and people who prefer to watch television.

Evaluate   **8.**   Evaluate the way Henry David Thoreau, Virginia Woolf, and Joan Didion use their journals. What kind of information does each writer save? How does each use this information as a resource for writing? Use your evaluation as the basis for an essay advising beginning writing students on the purposes of a journal. Use these three writers to illustrate your recommendations.

Argue   **9.**   As you consider drafting an essay on a specific subject, consult Richard Saul Wurman's "The Five Rings." Determine the kind of information that would be most persuasive to use in analyzing your subject. Then write a prospectus for your teacher, arguing the merits of using *one* of these rings as the *only* source of information for your essay.

Argue **10.**   Marie Winn's argument is that watching television is essentially a passive activity. In what ways could you make the same case for visiting an art museum, attending a musical performance, or listening to a lecture? Select one such activity, freewrite about it in your journal, and then compose an essay that demonstrates: (1) although X is usually considered an active procedure, it is really a passive process, or (2) although X might seem like a passive process, it demands intellectual activity.

3 | Drafting

Through drafting, you determine whether the information you discovered in planning can be shaped into successful writing. In Chapter 2, you learned to apply thinking-in-writing strategies to explore likely topics and to assess the potential of each topic by using the guidelines for selecting a subject, analyzing an audience, and determining a purpose. Now you will learn to work the most promising of these topics into a draft.

Although drafting requires you to make specific choices about your subject, audience, and purpose, you should resist the temptation to think of these choices as final. It's tempting to assume, when you are starting out in writing, that composing the first draft is virtually the last stage in the writing process. You might believe that a little quick repair work transforms a first draft into a final draft. Experienced writers, however, know that their first draft is only a very preliminary attempt at producing a sustained piece of writing. Planning allows them to examine possible topics; drafting enables them to experiment with possible arrangements of thoughts on a topic. They expect this experiment to lead to new discoveries, some of which emerge in the first draft but most of which will emerge in some subsequent draft. Experienced writers try several drafts. With each one, they come closer to what they want to say and how they want to say it.

In the following passage, May Sarton indirectly comments on the experienced writer's view of drafting when she compares the art of flower arranging to the art of writing:

> After breakfast I spend an hour or more arranging and rearranging seven or eight bunches of flowers for the house. There are flowers indoors here all the year around—in winter, bowls of narcissus, geraniums brought in from the windowboxes in the autumn, cut flowers from a local florist when all else fails. But from late May on I have a variety to play with, and the joy becomes arduous and complex. Arranging flowers is like writing in that it is an art of choice. Not everything can be used of the rich material that rushes forward demanding utterance. And just as one tries one word after another, puts a phrase together only to tear it apart, so one arranges flowers. It is engrossing work, and needs a fresh eye and a steady hand. When you think the thing is finished, it may suddenly topple over, or look too crowded after all, or a little meager. It needs one more note of bright pink, or it needs white. White in a bunch of flowers does a little of what black does in a painting, I have found. It acts as a catalyst for all the colors. After that first hour I have used

up my "seeing energy" for a while, just as, after three hours at my desk, the edge begins to go, the critical edge. (May Sarton, *Plant Dreaming Deep*)

You may be relieved to learn that drafting gives you additional opportunities to discover your subject, audience, and purpose, but you cannot lapse into inactivity. You must continue to exercise the "art of choice," evaluating your information, arranging and rearranging it, until you compose a coherent draft. The first section of this chapter presents three approaches to creating that draft: making a *scratch outline*, drafting a *hypothesis*, and composing a *discovery draft*. The second section of this chapter presents three strategies for measuring the success of that draft: constructing a *descriptive outline*, composing an *effective thesis*, and preparing a *formal outline*.

THE SCRATCH OUTLINE

To make a scratch outline you will need to study the information you created in planning. The scratch outline is not designed to impose a rigorous pattern on this material. Its main purpose is to get you started, to help you see how you might arrange the major portion (*body*) of your draft. Later, as you draft several hypotheses about this pattern, you will see how you might compose the opening section (*introduction*) that identifies your subject and explains why you are writing about it.

Begin by assembling whatever lists or reading notes you produced during planning. Then read through your material several times, looking for recurrent patterns and any unusual ideas or phrases. Use any system you like—marking key words, using numbers or circles—to identify the related information you discover. Once you have established these groups of information, connect and arrange them into a meaningful pattern, sketching the pattern onto another sheet of paper. Don't discard your planning materials: you may need to consult them again.

Sometimes you will discover that your planning has already evinced a simple pattern, such as Joanne Malbone's narration about Mr. Bridgeman's Latin class or Amy Lindsay's analysis of the activity in the reference room. More often, your information suggests several inconsistent methods of arrangement or none at all. Such confusion usually indicates that your information is too meager to work with (in which case you will have to do more planning) or that your information is too varied to work with (in which case you will have to make some tough choices). All the cherished items you found during planning will rush forward in drafting, "demanding utterance." But if you give everything equal attention, your essay is likely to "topple over." Some information may be significant enough to form a major division in your outline; other information may be less significant, useful only as minor subdivisions or illustrative examples. Still other information—wonderful, colorful, delightful information—may have to be eliminated because it does not fit into your scheme. As you arrange and rearrange various sections of your scratch outline, you may change your mind about the status of your information: you may want to condense or eliminate significant information or expand or reshape insignificant information. All the choices you make ultimately depend on one question: "What arrangement best enables me to communicate my *subject* to an *audience* for a *purpose*?"

Ellen Haack's assignment was to write an essay about *taste*—about how people decide what to eat, what to wear, what to read. During planning, she explored several ways to approach this assignment (the type of people she saw at the health food store, the problems she had selecting a necktie for a gift, and the kind of books she purchased for her personal library), but each time she tried out a thinking-in-writing strategy, she found herself thinking about her friend Barry and his habit of offering elaborate explanations for his choices. Ellen decided that Barry's behavior provided an interesting case study of "taste." Using *Barry* as her prompt, she produced the following list.

Barry

Drives me nuts

Type A—always busy, can't seem to relax

Discipline—routine, schedules, lists

Right way to do everything—always giving advice

Making granola—the right spoon, bowl

No junk food—Big Macs, doughnuts

Health nut—what's good for me

Salad bars, yogurt (?)

Sneaks ice cream—Heavenly Hash

Burns it off with exercise—but no jogging

Shin splints, tendons, new study

Rebounder—bounces to old time rock 'n' roll

Says he likes opera and ballet—improves his taste

Never listens, falls asleep—the sleep of the tasteless

Books—looks at diet books, buys classics

Impress himself, never reads—dust—"I'll get around to it someday"

Movies—Siskel and Ebert vs. <u>Revenge of the Nerds</u>

Always has his reasons—getting out of the house

Naps, wine, avoiding work

Good for me

Ellen is ready to begin drafting, but she needs to find a pattern in her information. Reading through her list, she begins to circle and number certain topics. She uses arrows to suggest how something from one part of her list belongs in another and question marks and asterisks to indicate problems she needs to solve or explore in greater detail.

Barry

1. Reasons
2. Food
3. Exercise
4. Culture

? Drives me nuts
1. Type A—always busy, can't seem to relax
1. Discipline—routine, schedules, lists
1. Right way to do everything—always giving advice
2. Making granola—the right spoon, bowl
2. No junk food—Big Macs, doughnuts
2. Health nut—what's good for me
2. Salad bars, yogurt (?)
2. Sneaks ice cream—Heavenly Hash
3. Burns it off with exercise—but no jogging
3. Shin splints, tendons, new study
3. Rebounder—bounces to old time rock 'n' roll
4. Says he likes opera and ballet—improves his taste
4. Never listens, falls asleep—the sleep of the tasteless
4. Books—looks at diet books, buys classics
4. Impress himself, never reads—dust—"I'll get around to it someday"
4. Movies—Siskel and Ebert vs. Revenge of the Nerds
1. Always has his reasons—getting out of the house
3. Naps, wine, avoiding work
1. Good for me

By circling and numbering, Ellen identifies and labels several information groups. Some groups evolve from the pattern of associations on the list (*food*); others form incomplete but potentially useful categories (*exercise*); still others are so cluttered that they will require additional planning to make them coherent (*culture*). Many of the items on Ellen's list could prompt the creation of new lists that relate to her assignment ("Type A," "sneaks ice cream," "sleep of the tasteless"). But Ellen decides that a phrase appearing intermittently throughout her list (*good for me*) provides the most promising topic for her first draft, one that might explain the concept of taste and pull together most of the information on her list. She continues her thinking-in-writing in a scratch outline.

Good for Me

1. Food
   you are what you eat
   health food—granola, complex carbohydrates
   junk food—Whoppers, doughnuts
   cancer—new studies—yogurt (?), salad bars (?)

"Guilty of flaunting it without having it. Sixty days."

Drawing by Lorenz; © 1990 The New Yorker Magazine, Inc.

2. Exercise
   keep in shape
   aerobics—jogging, swimming, rebounder (heart)
   isometrics—pumping iron, violent sports (competition, stress)
   serious injuries (shin splints), marathons—dehydration
3. Culture
   improve your mind
   novels, classics, history, philosophy
   romances, trash, junk magazines ("inquiring minds want to know")
   big tomes—fall asleep
   some reading better than none

Through her scratch outline, Ellen has discovered some new information ("you are what you eat," "pumping iron," "junk magazines") and has deleted other information that does not seem to fit into her plan ("movies," "wine," "opera"). Her outline has helped her restrict her subject to three categories of things *good for me*. Although still sketchy, they suggest an emerging pattern that is potentially significant, interesting, and manageable. Some potential audiences have also emerged: people interested in food, exercise, or culture, and people who define *taste* in terms of what is "good for me." Before she can convert this outline into an essay, however, Ellen needs to draft a preliminary hypothesis.

DRAFTING A HYPOTHESIS

A hypothesis states a possible purpose for your writing. Unlike the thesis, which formally asserts what you will prove in your essay, the hypothesis expresses a tentative purpose. You should certainly try to make your hypothesis restricted, unified, and precise, but you may discover that writing your first draft modifies rather than demonstrates your purpose. Once you have completed your first draft, in fact, you may decide to revise your purpose completely. The first draft is like a laboratory experiment: it gives you an opportunity to test one possible explanation (*hypothesis*) for the pattern you derived from your planning.

To draft a hypothesis, read through your scratch outline and then write out answers to these questions:

1. What do I want (what am I expected) to accomplish in this writing project?
2. What is my attitude toward the material I have gathered?
3. What hypotheses could I prove by writing about it?
4. Which hypothesis seems the most restricted, unified, and precise?

Your answers to the first two questions may be lengthy and provisional because you are trying to clarify your aims and analyze your assignment. You may not use this information in any direct way in your essay, but you may use it to determine your point of view toward your material and the ultimate effect you hope to achieve. Your answers to the second two questions should be simple and direct. These questions are designed to produce conditional theses, one of which you can use in your introduction to help keep your writing on track and to alert your readers to the main idea you are trying to develop.

When Ellen started to draft her hypothesis, she was confused about what she wanted to say about taste and what she wanted to prove about Barry's preoccupation with what is "good for me." Her answers to the first two questions exhibit her uncertainty, and her answers to the second two illustrate her attempt to resolve her confusion by proposing several provisional theses.

1. What do I want to accomplish with this project? I am supposed to be writing about taste. Why people prefer one thing over another. Or at least, the reasons people give for choosing one thing instead of another. Sounds pretty abstract. All I can think about is Barry. Drives me nuts with his explanations. Everything is either good or bad. I guess I wanted to show him that things aren't that simple. There are lots of Barrys in the world. Just like parents, always telling you what's good for you—body, mind, and soul. That's what I tried to do with my categories—<u>food</u>, <u>exercise</u>, and <u>culture</u>. It's not exact, but it might work. The interesting things in each group are the ones

that don't fit or that change. What used to be good for you now gives you cancer. Maybe I could make something out of that.

2. I think my attitude toward this material is weird. I started out thinking about Barry. He's so compulsive he's funny. Maybe not so funny. People who think things have to be good or bad are always changing their minds or cooking up new explanations. They could be devious, dangerous. How do other people react to the Barrys of the world? Maybe they're just like me. I mean I'm always trying to figure out whether <u>he's</u> good for me. I change my mind everyday—weird.

3. Possible hypotheses:

   a. Everybody wants to know what's "good for me."

   b. Most people try to divide the world into two categories—what's good for me and what's bad for me.

   c. The most interesting things in the world cannot be classified as absolutely good or bad.

4. I'm still not sure any of these will work, but if I had to pick one, I'd probably go with c.

As Ellen tries to draft her hypotheses, she struggles to clarify her subject, anticipate her readers, and define her purpose. She knows that this material is interesting and that she is raising significant issues that will appeal to most readers. Her scratch outline is simple enough to guide her through her first draft. As she tinkers with various ways to word her hypothesis, she feels confident enough to begin writing.

THE DISCOVERY DRAFT

Novelist Dorothy Canfield Fisher once compared writing the first draft to skiing down a slope she wasn't sure she was clever enough to manage. Although you have compiled a large body of information during planning, organized that information into a scratch outline, and drafted several hypotheses about its significance, you cannot stand at the top of the hill forever. You must push off and see if your preparation has made you clever enough to manage the long white slope of blank paper in front of you.

This first draft is called a *discovery draft* because you should expect as you write to discover something new about the subject, audience, and purpose of your essay. Some of what you discover will be disappointing. Sections of your essay that you felt certain were complete suddenly seem sketchy. Connections that you saw between sections disappear or appear in forms you had not anticipated. And individual sections may not prove useful because certain items cannot be developed in any detail or because these items duplicate others or detract from your working hypothesis.

Most discoveries—even negative ones—help you learn more about what you want to say and how you want to say it. As you convert notes into sentences and group sentences into paragraphs, your writing will talk to you—telling you things you had forgotten, making unexpected connections, pointing toward things you need to find out. Sections of your scratch outline will expand and contract before your eyes; your hypothesis may reshape itself into a more subtle statement. Your discovery draft gives you something to work with—a text, a core of information that you can rearrange or refine in a subsequent draft.

Ellen's discovery draft illustrates some of these changes as she struggles to say what she means.

Good for Me

1   Most people divide the world into two categories: (1) things that are good for me and (2) things that are bad for me. This system works as a general rule, but the most interesting things do not fit easily into one of the two categories.

2   First, there is food. Everybody knows that raw vegetables, whole grain cereals, and fresh fruit are nutritious, and that French fries, doughnuts, and Whoppers are junk. But what about yogurt? Most advertisements claim it is a health food, but a recent study points out that one 8-ounce serving of flavored yogurt contains 9 teaspoons of sugar. And what about salad bars? They are supposed to be good for you—better than a slab of red meat or a basket of deep-fried shrimp—but recent studies charge that dangerous chemicals are sprayed on salad bar vegetables to keep them looking good. What's supposed to be good for you might give you tooth decay or cancer.

3   Next, there is exercise. Doctors are always telling you to stay fit. Exercise, particularly aerobic exercise like jogging, is supposed to be good for you because it controls your weight, lowers your cholesterol, and strengthens the efficiency of your heart muscle. But there is a trade-off. Jogging can cause serious injuries such as sprained ankles, pulled tendons, and shin splints. And there is a recent study that says severe physical exertion may actually accelerate the causes of coronary heart disease. One doctor says "jog," another says "don't," and another says "it all depends." How can people know for certain whether jogging will be "good for me"?

4   Finally, there is reading. Teachers, parents, and politicians are always saying that reading improves your mind. But what kind of reading leads to improvement? Books that are supposed to help you—diet books, or pop-psychology books—don't really improve your

mind. They are stacked next to the candy near the cash register, and everybody knows they are trash. But some of the books that are supposed to be good for you—the classics—many people find too long and boring. If they can't finish the books that are supposed to be good for them, how can people improve their minds?

The world is really too complex for a simple good-for-me/bad-for-me system. Take ice cream, for example. On one level it is bad for me because it contains large amounts of sugar and cholesterol. On another level, however, it is really good for me. After a long day of dieting, exercising, and reading, what could be better for me than a few scoops of Heavenly Hash?   5

THE DESCRIPTIVE OUTLINE

A descriptive outline helps you assess what you have accomplished during drafting. In it you report what you have done with the discovery draft and speculate about how to compose your next draft.

To construct a descriptive outline, place your discovery draft on one side of your desk and some blank paper on the other. Do not look at your scratch outline; your objective is to make a new outline that describes your draft. Counting the introductory paragraph as *1*, number in sequence each paragraph, and then list those numbers on your blank piece of paper. For each number, write down as briefly as possible (a) what each paragraph *says*, and (b) what each paragraph *does.*

There is a subtle but significant difference between what a paragraph *says* and what it *does.* When you identify what a paragraph *says*, you are concerned with subject matter, with the major topic discussed in the paragraph. When you identify what a paragraph *does*, you are concerned with writing strategies, with the development of each paragraph and its function within the larger design of the essay. A paragraph can do many things: it can tell a story, describe a scene, list examples, compare evidence. You will learn more about what paragraphs can do individually and collectively in Chapters 5, 6, and 7. For the moment, use your own words to describe what each paragraph in your discovery draft *says* and *does.*

After you complete the descriptive outline, read through your discovery draft again. Then record your planning and drafting material. Now return to your descriptive outline. What kind of draft does it describe? Are you delighted or disappointed by what you see? Does the outline reveal an interesting progression of carefully developed ideas? Or does it show a fairly predictable pattern of underdeveloped notions?

All this rereading should force you to assess what you have already achieved and what you still need to do. Being as honest as you can, list at the bottom of your descriptive outline your conclusions about the effectiveness of your draft's introduction, working hypothesis, body, and closing. Ellen's conclusions show that she realizes that she could do a number of things to improve her essay. After you have examined her descriptive outline, reread her discovery draft on pages 61 and 62 and then study her conclusions.

1. a. People divide world into two categories.
   b. Introduces hypothesis: most interesting items don't fit easily into one of two categories.
2. a. Although most people know good from bad, some items cause confusion.
   b. Identifies two examples of food whose classification has been challenged by recent studies.
3. a. Although exercise is considered good for you, it can be dangerous.
   b. Compares benefits of exercise with possible risk factors.
4. a. Reading improves your mind—if you read.
   b. Compares not reading trash with not reading classics.
5. a. The world is too complex for a simple system of good/bad.
   b. Illustrates how ice cream can be both bad and good.

Conclusions

1. Everything goes wrong in first sentence when I replace <u>Barry</u> with <u>People</u>. Sounds more scholarly, but I'm not really interested anymore. Anybody can write about people; I want to write about Barry.
2. The hypothesis is probably all right. What does <u>interesting</u> mean? It would be more interesting if it introduced Barry's explanations.
3. Three sections—food, exercise, and reading—are really predictable. This is good. This is bad. Here's a problem. If I used Barry, I could include more examples under each category—or create some new categories—and show how Barry tries to deal with the problems.
4. The conclusion is good, but it doesn't sound like me. Heavenly Hash is really Barry talking.
5. Mainly, I need to get back to Barry and develop more examples from his point of view.

Ellen's descriptive outline has helped her identify what she has done right, what she has done wrong, and what she needs to do next. Her conclusions form an *agenda* for the next stage in the writing process—*revising.* But before Ellen revises her discovery draft, she decides to transform her hypothesis into an effective thesis and construct a formal outline.

COMPOSING AN EFFECTIVE THESIS

A thesis asserts the main idea you will develop in your writing. In a sense, it summarizes your ideas about your subject and suggests your point of view toward it. You cannot make such an assertion with any confidence until you understand your purpose. You will seldom succeed if you try to compose your thesis first and then write an essay that meets its specifications. It is more efficient to work by testing various hypotheses in drafts, selecting the one that best controls your material and refining it into a thesis.

An effective thesis, then, derives from and makes a compelling statement about your writing. But once you have selected a thesis, you must word it properly if it is to be effective.

Making Your Thesis Restricted, Unified, and Precise

Restricted, unified, and *precise* theses were defined in Chapter 1. The definitions are worth amplifying here, for the more fully your thesis reflects these qualities, the better it will control your writing in your remaining drafts.

To be *restricted,* a thesis must limit the scope of an essay to what can be discussed in detail in the space available. A thesis such as "The United States has serious pollution problems" might be suitable for a long magazine article, but using it for a three-page essay would force you to make statements so broad that your readers would find them superficial and uninformative. A better thesis about pollution might be one of the following:

▼ The government has not been sufficiently aggressive in enforcing the regulations that control the disposal of chemical wastes.

▼ In Toledo, industrial expansion has created severe air and water pollution.

▼ Widespread use of agricultural pesticides threatens the survival of certain species of wildlife.

A good thesis is *unified* if it expresses only one idea. The thesis "The use of drugs has increased significantly in the last fifteen years; hard drugs are admittedly dangerous, but there is considerable disagreement about marijuana" commits the writer to three topics: (1) the increase in drugs, (2) the dangerous effects of hard drugs, and (3) the controversy about marijuana. Each of these topics could form the thesis of a separate essay. To try to develop all three would almost surely result in an unfocused essay consisting of three unrelated, skimpy sections.

Lack of unity most often arises when a thesis contains two or more coordinate parts. The thesis "Compared with other languages, English has a relatively simple grammar, but its spelling is confusing" could lead to separate treatments of grammar and spelling. If you wanted to relate the two topics—for example, by contrasting the ease of learning grammar with the difficulty of learning spelling—the relationship has to be implied in your thesis: "In learning English, foreigners usually have less trouble with grammar than with spelling." If your chief interest is spelling, it would be safer to ignore grammar: "Foreigners have a hard time with English spelling." Sometimes one part of a two-part thesis can be embedded in the other: "The amateur ideal of the Olympic Games is being threatened; professionalism is on the increase" can be rewritten as "Increased professionalism threatens the amateur ideal of the Olympic Games."

Finally, a thesis is *precise* when it can have only one interpretation. The thesis "My home town is one of the most unusual in the state" does not indicate the content of your essay because *unusual* is vague and can mean many things. Readers will want to know in what way the town is unusual. If they have to read the whole essay to find out, the thesis does not help them. Moreover, because the wording is vague, the thesis does not help you see what you need to develop in your essay.

Words such as *unusual, inspiring,* and *interesting* are too vague for a thesis. So are metaphors. The thesis "Where instructors are concerned, all that glitters is not gold" may seem clever, but what does it mean? That the best scholars are not always the best teachers? That the instructors who are good classroom performers do not always help students master the subject? Or does it mean something else? The precise meaning of a thesis should be immediately clear. Metaphors may be effective in the text of your essay, but they can cause trouble in your thesis.

Throughout her drafting, Ellen has had difficulty composing an effective thesis. Her first hypothesis is imprecise because it relies on the vague word *interesting:* "The most interesting things in the world cannot be classified as absolutely good or bad." A second, even more imprecise version appears in the first paragraph of her discovery draft: "The system works as a general rule, but the most interesting things do not fit easily into one of the two categories." This version also suggests two subjects—a system and things that do not fit into it—that could destroy the unity of her essay. In her conclusions to her descriptive outline, Ellen recognizes the problem word and hints that she might be able to draft a more effective thesis if she restricted it to Barry's difficulties with explaining what is "good for me." This insight allows Ellen to restate her thesis. She might begin writing another draft immediately, but she decides instead to reevaluate and organize her material by constructing a formal outline.

Exercises ———— Some of the following statements would make acceptable theses; others, because they lack restriction, unity, or precision, would not. Explain your reasons for rejecting those that are unacceptable.

1. Foods with high fiber content are very important for your diet.

2. It's easy to see the beginning of things and harder to see the end.

3. Social historians agree that the American Dream is no more than the snows of yesteryear.

4. Although the average person thinks of gorillas as ferocious, chest-beating monsters, they are actually gentle creatures who live at peace with other animals.

5. Jane Fonda's workout tapes have enjoyed an enormous success, and they have proved that self-help videos are now a major consumer item.

PREPARING A FORMAL OUTLINE

A formal outline can serve as an additional writing tool, helping you to discover the need for more information and enabling you to organize a more precise design before you begin another draft. It breaks your topic into major units, marked by Roman numerals, and subdivides these into minor units, marked by capital letters; the next subdivision is marked by Arabic numerals; and a still smaller subdivision is marked by lower-case letters. One warning about this format: if you make any subdivision in your outline, you must have at least *two* subdivisions. You cannot divide something into only one part.

If it seems helpful, give your outline a title. Then begin to construct the formal outline by laying out the major, Roman numeral headings first; then break each Roman numeral heading into capital letter entries, and so on, completing each level of division before starting on the next lower level. This procedure keeps you in control of your outline: you will not distort your organization by developing some headings too much and others too little. As you work your way through each division, you may discover new structural patterns that will require you to revise all the headings in your outline. Such discoveries will help you prepare a consistent outline and compose a coherent draft.

When Ellen looks at her two previous outlines, she decides that she wants her formal outline to follow the same order. When she starts to work her way through each subdivision, however, she starts reclaiming information from her initial planning that applies directly to Barry. As a result, her organization—and outline—change dramatically. She drops one major division "exercise" and adds two new divisions ("movies" and "wine"). In the lower subdivisions, she rearranges information ("ice cream" is moved from the conclusion to the first major division) and develops new information (all the items on "movies" and "wine").

It is not always necessary to construct a formal outline to produce a new draft. Your discovery draft, descriptive outline, and reformulated thesis may give you all the direction you need. But Ellen's formal outline shows why it is such a powerful tool.

A MAN WITH ALL REASONS

<u>Thesis</u> : Barry admits that he has difficulty explaining what's "good for me."

   I. Barry has difficulty defending his eating habits

      A. He knows the foods that are nutritious

      B. He knows the foods that are junk

      C. He is attracted to foods that are both

         1. Yogurt has become a problem

         2. Ice cream presents a dilemma

  II. Barry has difficulty explaining his reading habits

    A. He knows how to select good books
       1. He reads reviews
       2. He talks to friends
       3. He consults lists
    B. He resists his fascination with self-help books
    C. He buys classics
       1. He believes in the value of owning such books
       2. He never reads them
III. Barry has difficulty justifying his choice of movies
    A. He attends critically acclaimed movies
    B. He also attends "junk" movies
    C. He contrives elaborate justifications to explain such inconsistency
IV. Barry has difficulty rationalizing his preference for wine
    A. Wine enhances his appetite
    B. Wine relaxes him
    C. Wine is served to French and Italian children
    D. Wine is a health risk
       1. Its high sugar content could induce diabetes
       2. Its high alcohol content could induce chemical dependency

Evaluating Outlines

Ellen can evaluate the usefulness of her formal outline as a stage in her writing process and as a completed product. For the first assessment, she compares her new outline with her previous writing on Barry's "good for me" justifications.

1. How much of the new outline derives from the original planning?
2. How many of the conclusions following the descriptive outline have been incorporated into the outline?
3. How effectively does the outline indicate possibilities for controlling *subject*, *audience*, and *purpose* in a final draft?

To make the *second* evaluation, Ellen considers the following criteria:

1. **Is the thesis satisfactory?** Because the thesis controls the whole outline, a faulty thesis invites trouble all along the way. A vigorous checking of the thesis is therefore the first and most important step in testing an outline.

    "Barry admits that he has difficulty explaining what's 'good for me'" is certainly more restricted, unified, and precise than Ellen's earlier hypotheses. It seems to control the whole outline, but does it say everything Ellen wants to say about her purpose? Ellen considers how she might open up her thesis to assert more about the information she is trying to present. She thinks, too, about why she feels this information is significant.

2. *Is the relationship among the parts clear and consistent?* In a good outline it should be clear how each main heading relates to the thesis and how each subdivision helps develop its main heading. If there is any doubt about the relation of any heading to the thesis, that heading is either poorly stated or indicates an inconsistency in the outline.

   Ellen's decision to focus on Barry's explanations has helped her establish a clearer connection among the four major divisions of her next draft.

3. *Does the order of the parts provide an effective progression?* Just as the sentences within each paragraph must follow a logical order, so must the parts of an outline. If any of the parts is out of order, the disorder will be magnified in the essay.

   Ellen's major divisions—*food, reading, movies,* and *wine* —suggest a progression different from the divisions of her earlier draft— *food, exercise,* and *reading.* She examines this new progression to determine if it is logical and then does the same with the material she has grouped under her capital letters and Arabic numerals.

4. *Is the outline complete?* This is not one question but two:
   a. Are all the major units of the subject represented?
   b. Is each major unit subdivided far enough to guide the development of the essay? The first question is especially important for essays that classify something or explain how something is done; all classes or steps must be included. The second question depends on the scope of the essay. For short papers, the outline may not need to go beyond the main headings. For longer papers, the outline needs to be developed in greater detail so that you can balance and control the information you group under each heading.

      Ellen's four major divisions do not represent every issue on which Barry has an opinion. She has omitted Barry's feeling about what kind of exercise is "good for me" to focus on the more interesting new subjects—movies and wine. She needs to consider whether these changes make her outline more or less complete. The other subdivisions will require the same consideration to ensure the completeness of her essay.

5. *Can each entry be developed in detail?* Each entry in the outline should be developed when the essay is written. There is no rigid rule about how much development each entry should receive. Sometimes a single entry will require two or three paragraphs; occasionally several minor entries may be dealt with in a single paragraph.

   In her discovery draft, Ellen devoted one paragraph to each of her three major divisions. She must consider whether her formal outline suggests the same coverage. The secondary divisions in Ellen's outline (those marked with capital letters) appeared singly as sentences in her discovery draft. Ellen must consider whether these, and the entries she marks with Arabic numerals, contain enough information to be developed into separate paragraphs or will remain single, supporting sentences.

Drafting on Your Computer

The fluid nature of composing on a computer counteracts the problems many writers have as they begin drafting. Make a scratch outline, print it out, and then begin composing those sections for which you feel you have enough information. For the moment skip those sections about which you feel uncertain.

Breaking up your draft into smaller composing units not only helps you get started, but it also helps you keep going when you hit a trouble spot. Try one of the following strategies: (1) place an asterisk in your text to mark the spot that is causing you trouble and then come back to it when you have found the information you need; (2) insert a bracketed note in your text, telling yourself what you need to find out; or (3) switch from drafting complete sentences and paragraphs to one of the planning strategies discussed in Chapter 2—that is, stop drafting and start listing, freewriting, or speculating about a particular section of your text—continue writing once you have worked your way through the problem.

You can also use the special features of your computer program to help you evaluate your draft. Create a split screen, composing your draft on one side and using the other to comment on your text or compose a descriptive outline. You can also split the screen horizontally. Use the bottom of the screen to draft alternative versions of the same passage after you have composed at the top.

In addition to using these strategies, you should always evaluate a hard copy of your draft. On a screen you can see only a small portion of your text (usually twenty-four lines) at a time. Triple-space your discovery draft, print it, and then read and annotate the complete text, marking those spots you want to develop, delete, or rearrange once you return to your computer.

A FINAL WORD ABOUT DRAFTING

The most important thing to learn about drafting is to expect frustration. You certainly know people who give up on a project if their effort fails to measure up. They think that additional effort is a punishment for failing to succeed on the first try. But writing, like any other valuable work, requires effort. For that reason, think of drafting as an opportunity rather than an ordeal. Remember May Sarton's comparison of arranging flowers and drafting a piece of writing. Both processes are arduous and complex, but they are also a joy. They require a fresh eye and a steady hand and, after a while, they use up your seeing energy. In Chapter 4, you will study strategies that will help you recover that energy. Revising helps you *see* your material *again*; it helps you find a catalyst to restore your creative ingenuity and critical edge.

Comforting Thoughts | Calvin Trillin

In this essay, Calvin Trillin speculates on several research studies that are supposed to comfort him. As he considers each hypothesis, he sounds like Barry, looking for reasons to justify his behavior. Construct a descriptive outline of his essay. Then reread Trillin's comments on page 7 about how he writes his humorous columns. To what extent does your descriptive outline conform to Trillin's description of his drafting process?

February 29, 1988

1   First I read about a study in Meriden, Connecticut, which indicated that talking to yourself is a perfectly legitimate way of getting comfort during a difficult time. Then I saw an item about research at Yale demonstrating that stress seems to be reduced in some people by exposing them to the aromas of certain desserts. Then I started talking to myself about desserts with aromas I find soothing. Then I felt a lot better. Isn't science grand?

2   I didn't feel perfect. One thing that was bothering me—this is what I decided after I was asked by myself, "Well, what seems to be the trouble, guy?"—was that the ten most popular methods of comforting yourself listed in the Meriden study didn't mention sniffing desserts, even though Yale, where all the sniffing research was going on, is only about twenty miles down the road. Does this mean that some of these scientists are so busy talking to themselves that they don't talk to each other? It got me so upset that I went to the back door of a baker in our neighborhood to sniff the aroma of chocolate chip cookies. I was talking to myself the whole time, of course.

3   "What the Yale people think," I said to myself, "is that a person's soothed by the smell of, say, chocolate chip cookies because it brings back pleasant memories, like the memory of his mother baking chocolate chip cookies."

4   "What if his mother always burned the chocolate chip cookies?" I replied.

5   "Are you talking about my mother?"

6   "Whose mother do you think I'm talking about?" I said. "We're the only one here."

7   "Were those cookies burnt?"

8   "What do you think all that black stuff was?"

9   "I thought that was the chocolate chips."

10 "No, she always forgot the chocolate chips."

11 I wasn't finding the conversation very comforting at all. I don't like to hear anyone make light of my mother's chocolate chip cookies, even me. I must have raised my voice, because the next thing I knew, the baker had come out to see what was going on.

12 Even though the Meriden study had shown that being with someone else was the most comforting thing of all—it finished ahead of listening to music and even watching TV—I saw right away that being with the baker wasn't going to be much more comforting than talking to myself. He said, "What are you, some kind of nut case, or what?"

Trillin, Calvin. *Enough's Enough (And Other Rules of Life)*. New York: Ticknor & Fields, 1990. 76–79.

I told him that I was engaging in two therapies that had been scientifically proven effective: sniffing chocolate chip cookies and talking to myself. He told me that I owed him two dollars and fifty cents. "For sniffing, we charge a buck and a quarter a dozen," he explained. 13

"How do you know I sniffed two dozen?" I asked. 14

"We got ways," he said. 15

I told him that according to the research done at Yale, certain odors caused the brain to produce alpha waves, which are associated with relaxation. I told him that in my case the odor of chocolate chip cookies—particularly slightly burnt chocolate chip cookies—was such an odor. I told him that he ought to be proud to confirm the scientific research done at one of the great universities of the English-speaking world. That alone, I told him, ought to be payment enough for whatever small part of the aroma of his chocolate chip cookies I had used up with my sniffing. 16

He thought about it for a moment. Then he said, "Take a walk, buddy." 17

I was happy to. As it happens, going for a walk finished tenth in the Meriden study, just behind recalling pleasant memories. Naturally, I talked to myself on the way. 18

"Maybe I can find someplace to smell what the Yale people call 'spiced apple,'" I said to myself. "They found that the smell of spiced apple is so effective that with some people it can stop panic attacks." 19

"But I don't know what spiced apple smells like," I replied. "Spiced with what?" 20

That was bothering me enough that my walk wasn't actually very soothing. I thought about bolstering it with some of the other activities on the list, but reading or watching TV seemed impractical. Prayer was also on the list, but praying for the aroma of spiced apple seemed frivolous. 21

I walked faster and faster. It occurred to me that I might be getting a panic attack. Desperately I tried to recall some pleasant memories. I recalled the time before I knew about the Meriden list, when I talked to myself only in private. I recalled the time before I knew about the Yale research and didn't have to worry about finding any spiced apple. Then I felt a lot better. I didn't feel perfect, but you can't always feel perfect. 22

A Man with All Reasons | Ellen Haack

Student Ellen Haack's final draft of her essay on "taste" focuses on Barry and his motives for choosing what he eats, reads, watches, and drinks. Compare this draft with her formal outline on pages 66 and 67. In what ways do the divisions of her outline identify the paragraphs in her essay?

Barry's in the kitchen making granola. His long, narrow frame moves deftly around the work area, pausing to scan the recipe book on the counter or search the shelves for the ingredients—wheat germ, bran, rolled oats, sunflower seeds, raisins, honey—he plans to mix in a large, gray earthenware bowl. While he works, he hums a vaguely recognizable version of "Blue Moon," drumming on the top of the counter or the edge of the bowl with a wooden spoon. He's happy. Making granola always has this effect on him. He doesn't 1 like to make granola—it's messy and time-consuming. He doesn't like to eat granola—it's too crunchy without milk and too mushy with it. But he likes to contemplate his reasons for eating granola—"it's good for me."

Barry moves through the world like he moves through the kitchen, carefully sorting everything into two categories: (1) things that are "good for me" and (2) things that are "not good for me." Although he is attracted to the simplicity of this system, he often has difficulty explaining what's "good for me."   2

Since he is a health nut, Barry seems most adept at sorting food. His first category includes nutritious foods such as raw vegetables, whole grains, and fish, while his second includes junk food such as French fries, doughnuts, and Whoppers. But not all food can be classified so easily. For example, Barry is currently in a quandary over yogurt. For years, he ranked it close to granola as a major "good for me." But recent reports on the sugar content of flavored yogurt have made its position shaky. Ice cream presents another dilemma. It contains too much sugar and cholesterol to be "good for me," but Barry loves it. Whenever he does something that is "good for me," he likes to reward himself with a large bowl of Heavenly Hash—which is obviously "not good for me."   3

Barry is also dedicated to improving his mind and is constantly looking for books that will be "good for me." He reads reviews, talks to his more literary friends, and consults an old mimeographed list of "150 Great Novels Every Well-Educated Person Should Read" that was given to him by his high school English teacher. Armed with such advice, he can work his way through a bookstore, sorting titles into his two categories. The cash register provides the ultimate test, however. He may be attracted to *Jane Fonda's Workout Book,* justifying his interest by saying that a strenuous exercise program would be "good for me." But despite his attraction to Jane and his dedication to health, he does not buy the book; exercise books are trash. Instead, he purchases *Milton Cross' Complete Stories of the Great Operas,* explaining that knowing more about opera would be "good for me." Unfortunately, the book gathers dust next to one of his other carefully chosen purchases, H. G. Wells' *The Outline of History.* Although he has never opened these books, he believes he will get around to them eventually because they are "good for me."   4

Movies present a similar difficulty. Barry believes that only critically acclaimed films about significant subjects are "good for me." Following the critics' advice, he went to see *My Dinner with Andre,* only to fall asleep during the first course. He blinked awake during the credits, saying the nap had been "good for me." On the other hand, he went to see *The Revenge of the Nerds,* knowing that the critics did not think it would be "good for me." He managed to stifle his laughter and maintain his disdain throughout the film. But walking to the car he announced that getting out of the house had been "good for me."   5

And finally there's wine. Barry assigns wine a high position in his ranking of things "good for me," and he has his reasons. Foremost among these is wine's appetite-enhancing properties. He is slightly underweight and views anything that encourages him to eat as "good for me." Wine is also a relaxant. Barry leans toward the Type A personality and so considers anything that helps him slow down as "good for me." And then there are the French and Italian children. He has read that French and Italian parents give even very young children wine on a regular basis. Parents couldn't possibly give their own children something that isn't good for them. He worries about wine, however, because sugar and alcohol are not "good for me."   6

Recently, as he was fretting about the onset of diabetes or alcoholism, he visited a friend in the hospital. When his friend's dinner tray arrived, he spotted a plastic glass of clear liquid between the Jello and the peas. 7

"Do they serve wine *here*?" he asked. 8

"Yeh, pretty nice, huh?" the friend replied, not realizing the cause of Barry's sudden elation. 9

"See, I told you it was good for me." 10

The Lean and Hungry Look | Suzanne Britt Jordan

Although "The Lean and Hungry Look" was originally published in *Newsweek* in 1978, the essay has been reprinted in many college anthologies because it conforms to a straightforward, logical pattern of organization. State Jordan's thesis and then construct a formal outline for her essay. What is her purpose in this essay? (Remember, purpose and thesis are not identical.)

Caesar was right. Thin people need watching. I've been watching them for most of my adult life, and I don't like what I see. When these narrow fellows spring at me, I quiver to my toes. Thin people come in all personalities, most of them menacing. You've got your "together" thin person, your mechanical thin person, your condescending thin person, your tsk-tsk thin person, your efficiency-expert thin person. All of them are dangerous. 1

In the first place, thin people aren't fun. They don't know how to goof off, at least in the best, fat sense of the word. They've always got to be a doing. Give them a coffee break, and they'll jog around the block. Supply them with a quiet evening at home, and they'll fix the screen door and lick S&H green stamps. They say things like "there aren't enough hours in the day." Fat people never say that. Fat people think the day is too damn long already. 2

Thin people make me tired. They've got speedy little metabolisms that cause them to bustle briskly. They're forever rubbing their bony hands together and eyeing new problems to "tackle." I like to surround myself with sluggish, inert, easygoing fat people, the kind who believe that if you clean it up today, it'll just get dirty again tomorrow. 3

Some people say the business about the jolly fat person is a myth, that all of us chubbies are neurotic, sick, sad people. I disagree. Fat people may not be chortling all day long, but they're a hell of a lot *nicer* than the wizened and shriveled. Thin people turn surly, mean and hard at a young age because they never learn the value of a hot-fudge sundae for easing tension. Thin people don't like gooey soft things because they themselves are neither gooey nor soft. They are crunchy and dull, like carrots. They go straight to the heart of the matter while fat people let things stay all blurry and hazy and vague, the way things actually are. Thin people want to face the truth. Fat people know there is no truth. One of my thin friends is always staring at complex, unsolvable problems and saying, 4

Jordan, Suzanne Britt. "The Lean and Hungry Look." *Newsweek* 9 Oct. 1978: 32–33.

"The key thing is . . . " Fat people never say that. They know there isn't any such thing as the key thing about anything.

Thin people believe in logic. Fat people see all sides. The sides fat people   5
see are rounded blobs, usually gray, always nebulous and truly not worth worrying about. But the thin person persists. "If you consume more calories than you burn, " says one of my thin friends, "you will gain weight. It's that simple." Fat people always grin when they hear statements like that. They know better.

Fat people realize that life is illogical and unfair. They know very well that   6
God is not in his heaven and all is not right with the world. If God was up there, fat people could have two doughnuts and a big orange drink anytime they wanted it.

Thin people have a long list of logical things they are always spouting off   7
to me. They hold up one finger at a time as they reel off these things, so I won't lose track. They speak slowly as if to a young child. The list is long and full of holes. It contains tidbits like "get a grip on yourself," "cigarettes kill," "cholesterol clogs," "fit as a fiddle," "ducks in a row," "organize" and "sound fiscal management." Phrases like that.

They think these 2,000-point plans lead to happiness. Fat people know   8
happiness is elusive at best and even if they could get the kind thin people talk about, they wouldn't want it. Wisely, fat people see that such programs are too dull, too hard, too off the mark. They are never better than a whole cheesecake.

Fat people know all about the mystery of life. They are the ones acquainted   9
with the night, with luck, with fate, with playing it by ear. One thin person I know once suggested that we arrange all the parts of a jigsaw puzzle into groups according to size, shape and color. He figured this would cut the time needed to complete the puzzle by at least 50 per cent. I said I wouldn't do it. One, I like to muddle through. Two, what good would it do to finish early? Three, the jigsaw puzzle isn't the important thing. The important thing is the fun of four people (one thin person included) sitting around a card table, working a jigsaw puzzle. My thin friend had no use for my list. Instead of joining us, he went outside and mulched the boxwoods. The three remaining fat people finished the puzzle and made chocolate, double-fudge brownies to celebrate.

The main problem with thin people is they oppress. Their good intentions,   10
bony torsos, tight ships, neat corners, cerebral machinations and pat solutions look like dark clouds over the loose, comfortable, spread-out, soft world of the fat. Long after fat people have removed their coats and shoes and put their feet up on the coffee table, thin people are still sitting on the edge of the sofa, looking neat as a pin, discussing rutabagas. Fat people are heavily into fits of laughter, slapping their thighs and whooping it up, while thin people are still politely waiting for the punch line.

Thin people are downers. They like math and morality and reasoned evaluation   11
of the limitations of human beings. They have their skinny little acts together. They expound, prognose, probe and prick.

Fat people are convivial. They will like you even if you're irregular and   12
have acne. They will come up with a good reason why you never wrote the great American novel. They will cry in your beer with you. They will put your name in the pot. They will let you off the hook. Fat people will gab, giggle, guffaw, gallumph, gyrate and gossip. They are generous, giving and gallant. They are gluttonous and goodly and great. What you want when you're down is soft and jiggly, not muscled and stable. Fat people know this. Fat people have plenty of room. Fat people will take you in.

Writing Assignments

Narrate **1.** Use the "Drives me nuts" note in the first item on Ellen Haack's list to start a list of your own. Try to remember a certain person (your roommate or boss) or policy (your parents' or teachers' rules) that drove you nuts. Then compose a narrative that focuses on one event that reveals the maddening inconsistency in the person's behavior or rules for your behavior.

Observe **2.** Select a public place where people are supposed to obey certain rules of etiquette—the checkout line at the grocery store, the traffic signals at a busy street corner, the ticket booth at the local theater. Observe people's behavior for an extended period, paying particular attention to their willingness to take turns or their readiness to break the rules. Then write a column for the local paper, using your observations to comment on the status of public courtesy.

Investigate **3.** Interview someone who collects *unusual* artifacts—old records, baseball cards, ceramic animals. Pose some of the following questions: What prompted you to start this collection? Where did you buy your first X? How have your organized your collection? Who has the best collection? Why do you think you collect X? Use your interview material to write a profile of this person and his or her collection.

Collaborate **4.** Your writing group has been asked to prepare a section of a student handbook on "stress." Interview one another about what causes you to feel stress, how stress affects you, and what you do to relieve it. Then expand your research by interviewing people at the health center, counseling center, and campus ministries about their experience helping stressed-out students. You may also read some self-help manuals or the appropriate sections in your psychology book. Pool your information and then write the section, offering new students advice about how to deal with stress.

Read **5.** Read several sources about *one* method of stress management—exercise, meditation, biofeedback. You may even want to test the method on yourself to see if it works. Then write a "how-to" essay in which you explain the benefits of this particular method in some detail.

Respond **6.** Respond to the "character" revealed in Calvin Trillin's column *or* described in Ellen Haack's essay. Imagine him as your roommate or date. Describe some of the difficulties you might have communicating with someone who talks to himself or is constantly explaining why something is "good for me."

Analyze **7.** Analyze the various outlines and drafts of Ellen Haack's essay. Which do you like better and why? Then go back to Ellen's original assignment—to write something on the issue of *taste*. Although the assignment is vague, it probably contains certain assumptions and expectations. Write an essay to Ellen explaining why her final essay does or does not satisfy those assumptions and expectations.

Evaluate **8.** Evaluate the differences Suzanne Britt Jordan sees between thin people and fat people. In particular, assess the evidence she uses to support her generalizations. You may want to cite exceptions to Jordan's assertions or modify her argument with other sorts of evidence. A health-science textbook for example, may offer some reasons why her attitude toward fat people may require revision.

Argue   9.   Although Suzanne Britt Jordan makes her comparison based on two physical types, much of her analysis deals with contrasting psychological types. Construct an argument that makes the case for the "thin people" in Jordan's analysis. Try to stay away from the predictable arguments for "thin people"—physical attractiveness, for example—and focus on the value of those psychological features Jordan dislikes.

Argue   10.   Write your own essay on the issue of *taste*—who has it, who doesn't and why. You may want to consider various kinds of taste—physical, aesthetic—or argue that one's taste (in food, books, or people) is a matter of education or social conditioning. Like Ellen Haack, you may want to select a case study (or two) to illustrate your thesis.

4 | Revising

Revising is the process of *seeing again*, of discovering a new vision for the writing you produced in planning and drafting. In a sense, you have been revising from the moment you began writing. As you experimented with thinking-in-writing strategies in planning, you revised your discussions about subject, audience, and purpose. As you tried to apply those decisions in drafting, you revised again when you saw a better thesis or a more effective outline. Now that you are ready to revise, you must try to gain a new perspective on writing you have already looked at several times. One thing is certain: you will not see much that is new if you think of revising as simply taking one last look.

Nothing identifies experienced writers more dramatically than the way they look at revision. For beginners, revision means *fixing* the first draft—rearranging a few phrases, substituting one word for another, correcting spelling and punctuation. For experienced writers, revision means *creating* the final draft—redefining their purpose, reshaping their draft, and reworking the transitions between and the connections among their examples. They know they have overlooked minor trouble spots, but before they begin polishing and proofreading they want to be sure they are looking at a final text.

Revision is a two-stage process. During the first stage (the focus of this chapter), you use various reading strategies to help you rethink, reorder, and rewrite substantial portions of your draft. When you are satisfied with this *global revision,* you can focus your attention on the second stage, *local revision,* and begin repairing individual paragraphs, sentences, and words. (Strategies for implementing local revision are presented in Chapters 7 through 10.) Work in this second stage may propel you back to the first stage, however, as your revision of individual parts may prompt you to revise a section or even the entirety of your essay.

Revision has been made easier by the wonders of word processing. But revision is more than a mechanical command. It is an intellectual choice that emerges from a creative attitude toward change. In the days before *delete* and *format,* novelist Eudora Welty expressed that attitude in her comments on revision:

> My ideal way to write . . . is to write the whole first draft through in one sitting, then work as long as it takes on revisions, and then write the final version all in one, so that in the end the whole thing amounts to one long

sustained effort. . . . [Using a typewriter] helps give me the feeling of making my work objective. I can correct better if I see it in typescript. After that, I revise with scissors and pins. Pasting is too slow, and you can't undo it, but with pins you can move things from anywhere to anywhere, and that's what I really love doing—putting things in their best and proper place, revealing things at the time when they matter most. Often I shift things from the very beginning to the very end. . . .

[Writing] is so much an inward thing that reading the proofs later can be a real shock. . . . [T]here's . . . a strange moment with every book when I move from the position of writer to the position of reader, and I suddenly see my words with the eyes of the cold public. It gives me a terrible sense of exposure, as if I'd gotten sunburned. (Eudora Welty, *Writers at Work: The Paris Review Interviews*)

LOOKING TO REVISE

Once you consider revising a creative rather than a cleaning-up activity, you will look at yourself, your readers, and your text with more objectivity.

How You Look at It

Revision is always hard work, especially since you have already invested considerable effort in your writing. But try to look objectively at what you have accomplished. Rethink, don't merely glance over, every aspect of your writing from your most abstract assumptions to your most concrete assertions. Do not fall in love with your words, no matter how clever or inspiring they seem. Your real concern is effectiveness, not eloquence. Like Welty, you should look forward to making changes—to achieving coherence and clarity—by moving "things from anywhere to anywhere . . . putting things in their best and proper place, revealing things at the time when they matter most."

How Someone Else Looks at It

When you are ready to revise, you may welcome the perspective of another reader—a teacher, editor, or friend. Your readers may ask about the larger elements in your writing (its subject, audience, or purpose) or its smaller elements (sentence structure, diction, or punctuation); they may talk about their general impression (whether your writing is interesting, funny, or dull). As you revise, you must consider all reactions to your work—even if they seem threatening or trivial. You must consider what your readers saw, why they liked or disliked what they saw, and how you might use *their* observations to strengthen *your* writing. Various readers may give you confusing or contradictory advice, making it difficult for you to decide what to do next. You will have to decide which readers you trust—and which of their recommendations you want to consider or resist. Remember, you are the *author* of your text and therefore must act as the final *authority* for deciding how it will be revised.

How It Looks

Once you start revising, your writing will often look unfamiliar. If you have neatly retyped your messy, handwritten draft, it may now look compact and complete, as if a clean page had somehow solved your writing problems. But you must look beneath this seductive surface to uncover problems that still require rethinking and rewriting.

If you have put your writing aside for a few days—or even a few hours—the mere passage of time will make your text look unfamiliar. You have been doing other things—talking, reading, thinking—while your writing has been incubating in your unconscious. Now, as you look at it again, you may see flaws that were not apparent before. Perhaps you have not restricted your subject, anticipated your audience, or defined your purpose effectively. This new perspective compels you to look for solutions that will make your writing stronger and sharper.

But mainly your writing will look unfamiliar when you revise because, like Welty, you have changed positions—from writer to reader. As a writer, your task was to create ideas; as a reader, your task is to judge the clarity of those ideas. And just as you used a set of guidelines for writing, so now you may use a set of guidelines for reading and revising what you have written.

READING TO REVISE

When you are reading to revise, you are still actively involved in the writing process. You are *not* proofreading. Proofreading presumes the existence of a completed manuscript. When you proofread, you are merely checking your writing one last time to prove that you have not mangled sentences, misplaced punctuation, or misspelled words. Reading to revise, by contrast, assumes the presence of an evolving manuscript. As you read, you are trying to identify the strengths and weaknesses of your subject. You are sharpening your perception of what your audience knows (what *is* on the page) and speculating about what your audience needs to know (what is *not* on the page). You are determining whether your purpose controls your essay and the connections among its parts.

Each of the following reading strategies suggests that you read your writing as though you were someone else—a fictitious person in a special situation who is "reading" for a particular reason. Each strategy will highlight a different facet of your work. Used jointly, they will lead to a complete revision.

Reading for Subject

Imagine you are seated in the waiting room of your dentist's office, flipping though several magazines, looking for something to read to pass the time. What subjects attract and sustain your attention? Now pick up your writing and skim through it as quickly as possible. Then put it aside and, maintaining your identity as an "impatient patient," jot down your general reactions using the following questions as a guide:

1. *Why was I attracted to this essay?* How did the title or the first few sentences—the lead—convince me that the essay was worth reading?

2. *What is the specific subject of the essay?* Did the essay focus on the subject immediately, or did I have to read a lot of preliminary material or prolonged digressions?

3. *What is significant about the subject?* Is it a subject I like reading about, one that I need to know about, or one I ought to think about?

4. *What makes the subject interesting*—the attitude of the writer, the nature of the subject, or the way the subject is presented?

5. *Does the essay seem the right length?* Is it long enough to answer all my questions yet short enough to keep my mind from wandering?

Reading for Audience

Now imagine you are seated in a large banquet hall listening to an after-dinner speech. You cannot avoid listening to the speech, so you decide to see how it's going over—how effectively the speaker has read the needs and expectations of the audience. One way to simulate this situation is to read your writing out loud to anyone who will listen—the important thing is to *hear* your writing. An excellent way to accomplish this objective is to read into a tape recorder; then, with your manuscript in hand, play back the "speech" with you as its audience. As you listen, use the following questions to identify passages that need revision. Stop the recorder each time your annotations become too detailed to keep up with the tape. Once you have copied down your comments, push *Play* and resume listening to your writing being read.

1. *What kinds of people does the speaker expect to find in the audience?* Does the speech acknowledge their values, assumptions, and prejudices?

2. *What role does the speaker invite the members of the audience to take (for example, that of dedicated, discerning people)?*

3. *What are the members of the audience likely to know about the subject of the speech?*

4. *Does the speaker ask questions that the audience would ask about the subject?* Does the speaker answer those questions when they need to be answered? Does the speaker anticipate challenging or hostile questions?

5. *Does the speaker help the audience focus on the subject and follow the development of the parts?* Where might the audience get bored, confused, or annoyed? Does the end echo and fulfill the promise of the beginning?

Reading for Purpose

Imagine you are seated in an attorney's office about to sign a contract that will have an enormous impact on your life. You must determine what the thesis of this contract promises and whether the various sections and subsections deliver on that promise. Read your writing slowly and deliberately, underlining your thesis and tracing its connection to each major topic in your essay. If there are sections that need to be rewritten, rearranged, or deleted, now is the time for renegotiation. The following guidelines will remind you of the purpose of the "contract" and call your attention to how that purpose is carried out in its various "clauses."

1. *Does the essay rest on hidden and undocumented assumptions?* How can these assumptions be introduced into the wording of the essay?

2. *What is the purpose of the essay?* Is that purpose expressed openly, or must it be inferred from the text?

3. *What is the thesis of the essay?* What specific promise does it make to its readers? Is the thesis sufficiently restricted, unified, and precise that it can be demonstrated?

4. *Does the body of the essay fulfill the promise of the thesis?* Is there a direct, logical, and dramatic connection among the various parts?

5. *Is each part of the essay sufficiently developed with evidence that is germane, reliable, and verifiable?* Does new evidence need to be introduced to clarify the thesis?

REVISION AGENDA

The detailed analysis produced by the reading-to-revise questions will help you compose a *revision agenda,* a plan for rethinking, rearranging, and rewriting the next draft of your essay.

▼ You may find that the subject, audience, and purpose are so intertwined that you cannot undertake three separate readings. For you, the easiest procedure may be to keep the three imaginary readers in your head simultaneously and, after one "combined" reading, to prepare a single revision agenda.

▼ You may prefer considering each element—subject, audience, and purpose—singly and thoroughly. If so, read through the text three times, answering the sets of questions that accompany each reading. After completing all three readings, prepare one revision agenda.

▼ A complex or difficult-to-formulate subject may invite three complete revisions. After you "read for subject," prepare a revision agenda and then a new draft. Use this text to "read for audience" and the text generated then to "read for purpose."

You will have to decide which procedure helps you produce the most effective agenda and the most polished revisions. You may discover, in fact, that each writing project you undertake requires its own procedure. If you have to write under pressure on a fairly straightforward subject, then you may be able to work with one revision agenda. If, on the other hand, you have time to allow a complex subject to evolve, then you may want to generate several revision agendas to identify and solve the problems in your writing.

Organize your revision agenda by asking yourself three questions:

1. What did I try to do in this draft?
2. What are its strengths and weaknesses?
3. What revisions do I want to make in my next draft?

Answer the third question by writing yourself prescriptions containing action verbs—for example, "Collapse section on . . . "; "Expand paragraph on . . . "; "Reword sentences in. . . ." Group the larger problems (subject, audience, purpose) at the top of the list and the smaller problems (style, mechanics, usage) at the bottom.

Remember, revision is an *intuitive* process: you may decide to relocate a paragraph or realign the parts of a sentence because a sudden impulse tells you it looks or sounds better. And revision is a *recursive* process: you are constantly stepping back from your writing to see the big picture, moving forward to touch up some detail, and stepping back again to see how the altered detail changes the composition of the whole. But revision is also a *logical* process. In any piece of writing, you will discover large problems of form and focus and smaller problems of syntax and usage. You may be tempted to fix the simple problems first and the more difficult problems later. But the logical way to proceed is to work on the difficult problems first, for in solving them you may eliminate the simple problems or at least discover an efficient method for dealing with them.

REVISING: A CASE STUDY

Early in their writing class, Sarah Penning and her classmates were challenged to write their final paper on how the economy had a direct impact on their lives. Some students explored the impact of a local business "down-sizing" or relocating. Other students wrote about the job skills they would need to succeed in a changing economy. Still others speculated on the products American business would have to create to keep the economy healthy in the next century.

But Sarah was in a dither. The standard topics sounded too much like those discussed on the nightly business report. None seemed to have a *direct impact* on her life. Then, one Sunday morning, as she was sorting through the inserts in the local paper, she saw her subject—COUPONS! They were everywhere. Where did they come from? Who used them? Why did people spend so much time designing, distributing, collecting, and trading them? And why—most of all—did the subject both fascinate and infuriate her? Amidst her colorful clutter on the kitchen counter, Sarah suspected she had uncovered a mystery worth exploring.

Sarah began by *planning*. She listed what she already knew about coupons, what she needed to know about them, and where she might go to confirm her suspicions and answer her questions. She interviewed shoppers, cashiers, store managers, and newspaper sales personnel. She read several articles in sales and marketing magazines. During *drafting*, however, Sarah decided to write about her personal experience with coupons. Using a scratch outline, she organized the experience under three chronological headings: *Buying Stuff, Checking Out, Saving Face.* She used the following hypothesis to begin her discovery draft: *Although I have become a skillful shopper, I would rather save my dignity than my money.*

NOT ME

(Discovery Draft)

Since I have moved out of the dorm into my apartment, I have learned that the secret to successful living is successful shopping. If I am going to save time for studying, then I must make my shopping trips effective. If I am going to save money for rent, I must make my shopping trips efficient. Although I have learned the strategies of a skillful shopper, I have also learned that at the checkout counter, I would rather save my dignity than my money.

Learning how to buy stuff at the supermarket is not hard. I think about what I want to eat, check the cabinets and refrigerator to see what I have, and then make a list. I go to the store after my eight o'clock class to avoid the crowds, and I go to the same store every time, so I know where things are. I grab an empty cart, cruise the aisles, compare prices, and check items off my list. I never pick up anything that's not on my list, unless it's absolutely necessary. My mother used to drive me crazy using these strategies, but I can see now that they save time and money.

The only flaw in my strategy is picking the right checkout counter. I seem to make the same mistake every time I go to the store. I round the last aisle and head toward the counters. Bingo! A register with only one person in line. I wheel behind a middle-aged mom unloading her cart and smile in a slightly superior way at the guy in the next line who has four people in front of him. My cashier begins sorting the woman's stuff and I congratulate myself on getting it right this time. I'll be putting my bags in the car before #5 gets out his wallet.

Then it happens. The cashier lets out a sigh. I try not to look, hoping the sigh doesn't mean what I think it means. But it always does. COUPONS! Mom is pulling them out of her purse and peeling them off her packages. When she begins sorting and stacking them, they slide off the counter and flutter into her cart, onto the floor, and under the gum rack. I look at my watch. Number 5 is checking out.

Mom and the cashier are on their hands and knees groping after the elusive coupons. Mom looks up for help, but I look at Number 5 pushing his cart through the electric door. Finally, they are standing again—Mom smiling like she won the lottery, the cashier smiling because she has to. Then they start over again. The cashier scans the groceries, scans the coupons, checks the expiration dates, and slides each coupon into her cash drawer. I see #5 pushing his empty cart back through the parking lot.

Mom stares at the tape as the cashier totals her bill, and then beams blissfully, "Saved five bucks!" Right, lady! And wasted twenty minutes of my time. As I start to unload my cart, a guy wheels in behind me with a sixpack of cokes, a bag of chips, some toothpaste, and a vaguely familiar smile. The cashier starts scanning my stuff. The moment arrives. Do I or don't I? I know there are coupons in my wallet. I could probably save some money. I watch Mom marching through the electric door, then glance at the smiling cashier in front of me and the happy guy behind me. No way! I'd rather save face than money. I pay up, bag my stuff, and head toward the parking lot—a few pennies poorer but my dignity intact.

Revision Agenda

1. <u>What did I want to do in this draft?</u>
   Tell a story about my personal experience with coupons.
2. <u>What are its strengths and weaknesses?</u>
   I like some parts of the story. Mom on her hands and knees. Number 5 pushing his cart through the parking lot. But the story doesn't focus on coupons. Why does mom use them and I don't? What's all that stuff about saving dignity? What does that mean? Most of the essay is about saving time.
3. <u>What revisions do I want to make in my next draft?</u>
   a. Cut personal stuff—my shopping skills.
   b. Focus on shoppers who use coupons.
   c. Classify them into different categories.
   d. Speculate about why each group uses them.
   e. Identify shoppers by the products in their cart.

Revising for Subject

Sarah's narrative about her supermarket excursion is an entertaining narrative, but she realizes that it focuses more on her shopping behavior than on coupons. She never deals with the issue of who uses them and why. She consults some of the notes she made during planning—her observations of shoppers, her interviews with cashiers and store personnel—and decides to broaden her subject. She writes a new hypothesis—"Depending on how much they participate in the system, coupon users can be classified into three categories"—and then tries to implement her revision agenda in a second draft.

HOW MUCH DO YOU SAVE?

(2nd Draft)

As you cruise the aisles in the supermarket, you will discover an interesting cultural phenomenon—COUPONS! Shoppers seem obsessed with these slippery little pieces of paper—saving, swapping, and spending them as if they were cash. To the casual observer, these shoppers form a cohesive economic community. But closer inspection reveals that not all coupon users are alike. Depending on how much they participate in the system, coupon users can be classified into three different categories.

The reluctant coupon user rarely uses coupons by choice. You can spot him rushing down the aisle searching for items on a list written in a circular feminine hand. His cart looks fuller than it should, given his list, because he has picked up a frozen pizza and some cookies on impulse. But he doesn't clip coupons. In fact, he protests that the whole system is a fraud and that only the misguided believe they can save by clipping. Despite such protests, he is not coupon clean. Somewhere—folded neatly in his wallet—he has a coupon for his favorite cereal or shaving cream. He will use it when he has to, but for now he scowls at the cashier as she peels a coupon off his pizza. Reluctantly, he pulls out a coupon for the box of Kleenex on his list. The cashier smiles patiently and tells him he doesn't understand—the coupon said he has to buy <u>two</u> boxes.

The occasional coupon user trades coupons when she remembers to sort through her stash before she comes to the store. You can spot her in the middle of an aisle, coupon in one hand, product in the other, mumbling. She's usually got it half right—coupon, cake mix—but "this won't work without frosting and sprinkles." She believes in the system, and when she remembers clips her own coupons—although most of those in her stash expired three months ago. She likes the idea of using coupons because it gives her an excuse to try new products.

Unfortunately, although she may save as much as a dollar or two on these occasional splurges, she is always surprised when the cashier rings up a total that is a few dollars higher than she expected.

Compulsive coupon users use coupons for every shopping occasion. You can spot them clustered in little groups by the special displays, comparing their portfolios where they arrange their coupons alphabetically by aisle. These people not only clip coupons; they also attend weekly coupon-club meetings, where they do some down-and-dirty swapping. You'll also hear them talking about driving from store to store, saving a few cents on Peter Pan here and a few cents on Pepto Bismol there. Their main concern is to make it to the cashier with a coupon for each item in their cart. They are less concerned about whether they actually need or want the items. In a few weeks, they will have trouble remembering why they bought a box of Tuna Helper Cheesy Noodles, but they will remember that they saved 55 cents.

Revision Agenda

1. <u>What did I want to do in this draft</u>?
   Classify three kinds of coupon users.

2. <u>What are its strengths and weaknesses</u>?
   Got to my subject—coupons and the people who use them. I liked describing people's behavior and purchases. "Nobody is coupon clean." But what do I do next? No conclusion. Still don't say what the coupon system is all about.

3. <u>What revisions do I want to make in my next draft</u>?
   a. Tell readers something about the coupon system.
   b. Look over notes from interview at newspaper.
   c. Reread articles on "double coupons" and "cashier coupons."
   d. Track delivery system—tell readers where coupons come from.
   e. Fix thesis so I can have a conclusion.

Revising for Audience

Sarah is beginning to know more about her subject. She is also beginning to recognize the difference between *recounting* her experience and *using* her experience to create a subject. But her major reaction to her second draft concerns her audience. She wants to separate herself from the shoppers in the store and tell her readers how the system works. Sarah thinks her interviews and reading will help her, in her next draft, to draw some conclusions about this system. This decision, made because she wants to enlighten her audience, also enlarges her subject and redefines her purpose.

THEY KNOW HOW TO GET TO US

(3rd Draft)

Coupons! What are they? Everywhere we look we see those shiny little slips of paper decorated with bright pictures, bar codes, and dotted lines. And whether we admit it or not, all of us have clipped or used a coupon at least once. None of us is coupon clean. But where do they come from? Once we start tracking them, we discover that they come to us through a complex delivery system.

A popular coupon distributor is the local newspaper, especially the Sunday edition. In fact, we probably spend as much time separating coupons from the newspaper as we do reading the news. Most of these colorful eye-catchers are called FSIs or Free Standing Inserts. The coupons or ads that are actually printed on the pages of the newspaper are called ROPs or Run of Press ads.

The difference between FSIs and ROPs suggests the complexity in the coupon system. Although ROPs are less detailed and less colorful, they cost more than FSIs because printing them supposedly replaces valuable news space. For that reason, most national companies bypass the cost and hassle of ROPs. Instead they print FSIs in bulk and pay local newspapers to insert them. Unfortunately newspapers must invest as much money in the machinery to insert FSIs as they do in the machinery to print the news. And they must also invest in storage space. Inserts start arriving in semis on Monday and must be stored on large flats until they are ready to be stuffed into Sunday's paper.

Another popular coupon distributor is the U.S. Postal Service. How many times have we opened our mailboxes, expecting an important letter, only to see a logjam of envelopes filled with coupons encouraging us to buy everything from birdseed to toilet paper? These envelopes used to be addressed to "Occupant," but direct mail companies are getting smarter. By purchasing mailing lists from our credit card companies, coupon distributors can chart our demographics, select an appropriate sample of coupons, and then insert them in an envelope addressed directly to us. Because these "manufacturer's coupons" have bar codes and expiration dates, they can be used in any store in America.

So, let's not forget the obvious. The most effective coupon distributor is the local supermarket. In-store coupons, coupons designed for a particular store, are stacked near the entrance doors where we pick up a shopping cart. In some stores, there are coupon machines at the end of each aisle. And in some areas of the country, stores use these devices to offer double coupons, where the value of a single coupon is doubled up to, but not exceeding one dollar.

Even if we avoid these temptations, we still see coupons everywhere. On the shelf where we reach for a box of cereal, some elf has left an unused coupon. The box we place in our cart often has a pull-off coupon on its side. And at the checkout register we discover the ultimate delivery system. The cashier smiles, says, "Thank you. Come again," and hands us our receipt. When we flip over the receipt, we discover a coupon printed on the tape—not just any coupon but a coupon for the product we just bought, or an invitation from its competitor to try it next time and save $1.00.

Home at last. Only mildly tainted by the system that seems to find us wherever we are, we pause for a snack. We open a box of cereal and start pouring. Surprise! Surprise! Mixed between the raisins and the bran is a COUPON!

Revision Agenda

1. <u>What did I try to do in this essay</u>?
   Track how different kinds of coupons are delivered to consumers.
2. <u>What are its strengths and weaknesses</u>?
   Good information on the delivery system—how coupons get to us. Good stuff from notes on machinery at newspaper and cash-register coupons. But I'm still not answering main question. Why? Why coupons? Why not cheaper prices, better commercials? Check interview notes on "the mix."
3. <u>What revisions do I want to make in my next draft</u>?
   a. Reduce information on delivery system to one section.
   b. Revise thesis to focus on <u>why</u> advertisers use coupons.
   c. Hook reader with opening—maybe use cereal bowl from last draft.
   d. Suggest ways to respond to system—now that you know, what are you supposed to do?
   e. Put people and products back into essay.
   f. Make sure paragraphs connect to thesis.

Revising for Purpose

Sarah's revisions are helping her discover her *purpose* for this project. She has written about her own experience with coupons, how others use coupons, and how coupons get to consumers, but she realizes that she still has not answered her fundamental question: Why do advertisers—given all the sophisticated strategies available in the American marketplace—use coupons? She suggests that her fascination with (and anger about) coupons is prompted by the feeling that the system controls what she buys.

She decides to revise her purpose so that she can demonstrate how coupons control consumer behavior. This revised purpose will allow her to use some of the information from her last draft, but will require her to present more significant and interesting information about why advertisers use coupons. Finally, she wants to hook her readers by planning some way to insert herself (and her mixed feelings about coupons) into her analysis of how to respond to the system.

THE COUPON CONSPIRACY

(4th Draft)

In the beginning, I'd be furious. I'd start to pour my 2% over my Raisin Bran and suddenly I'd spot one—another brightly colored coupon, folded in thirds, mixed with my raisins and bran. How did it get there? Why was it there? Was the competition so cutthroat that they expected me to eat their advertising? Slowly, I'd relent, unfolding the paper and beaming at my good fortune: a picture of Raisin Bran and an invitation to "Save $1.00." All right, I'd confess. I'm hooked, but I'm not hoodwinked. I've pushed my cart around the supermarket enough times to know that coupons are not gifts. Indeed, most skillful shoppers know that coupons are part of a complex conspiracy to control what they buy.

Coupons are actually part of a larger conspiracy advertisers call "the mix." To sell any product, advertisers concoct a mixture of strategies ranging from television commercials to highway billboards. But coupons play an important part in this conspiracy because they supply a valuable currency in the marketplace—information. If advertisers want to introduce a new product, increase the market share for an established product, or test the price range for a particular line of products, they flood the market with coupons. Some consumers buy. Some don't. Either way, advertisers study their reactions carefully, collecting information and projecting hypotheses about what sells.

Such studies have led to the careful design of coupons. They may be printed alone or marked by dotted lines at the bottom of a large ad, but they must resemble the size and shape of dollar bills to encourage consumers to think of them as money. They must also contain some basic information: (1) a colorful picture of the product to create brand recognition; (2) a simple headline to encourage savings and proclaim the amount saved; (3) an expiration date to set limits on their use; (4) a bar code for cashiers to scan and researchers to track; and (5) special information about the purchasing and redemption agreements to control and interpret the advertiser's purpose.

The subtle strategies of coupon design are matched by the elaborate systems of coupon distribution. Advertisers study the purchasing patterns of certain communities and neighborhoods to determine what kinds of coupons to insert into newspapers, stuff into mailboxes, or affix to products in the stores. In some areas of the country, there are coupon machines at the end of each aisle or cash register designed to print coupons on the back of receipts, encouraging consumers to buy the same product or one of its competitors the next time they shop.

Of course, advertisers have developed all sorts of theories about how to place and time coupon distribution. They are convinced that a coupon for Campbell's Chicken Noodle Soup is more tempting when placed next to a coupon for Ritz Crackers than next to a coupon for Puppy Chow. Their research also convinces them that a coupon for Taster's Choice Coffee produces a larger response if it is inserted in the Sunday paper rather than the Wednesday paper.

If shoppers think all this effort is the result of good will, well . . . they had better think again. If they clip a coupon to save a dollar on a new box of cereal, they should realize that <u>that</u> dollar has already been calculated into the four-dollar price. The dollar off looks terrific until the coupon expires. Then consumers must decide whether they like the new cereal well enough to pay the inflated price. If they discover a new coupon for an old standby, forty cents rather than thirty cents off a box of Kleenex, they had best check the redemption agreement where they will no doubt discover that the new coupon requires them to buy two boxes instead of one. And as long as they are checking, consumers should remember that the only price that matters is the one posted on the shelf. Supermarkets often raise the price on a particular product to cover the cost of handling its coupons.

Where does this leave me and my one-dollar coupon for Raisin Bran? I could pitch it, protest that the whole system is a fraud, and refuse to participate. But the coupon conspiracy is too pervasive. If I don't use my coupon, I'll simply pay an inflated price for Raisin Bran (and everything else I buy). I'm not that naive. On the other hand, I'm not nuts. I refuse to obsess about the conspiracy, calculating how I can use coupons to save pennies on every purchase. I don't have that kind of time and I'm not sure what I'd win if I could actually figure out a way to win. So . . . I guess I'll hang around the middle of the aisle, coupon in one hand, product in the other, at once fascinated by and furious at the fine mess they've got me in.

Revision Agenda

1. <u>What did I try to do in this draft</u>?
   Demonstrate how advertisers use coupons to control what consumers buy.

2. <u>What are its strengths and weaknesses</u>?
   I like the "inside" information about the coupon conspiracy—why and how advertisers use them. I also like the opening and closing paragraphs. Didn't think I'd turn out to be "the mumbler." Not sure about 3rd paragraph. List seems dull.

3. <u>What revisions do I want to make in my next draft</u>?
   a. I'm done. I never want to think about coupons again!
   b. If I must . . . Revise 3rd and 5th paragraphs.
   c. Decide if intro and conclusion match up.
   d. Add more "conspiratorial tone" to explanation.
   e. Question #1: Are advertisers really conspirators?
   f. Question #2: Does any other culture use coupons?

Post is a registered trademark of Kraft General Foods, Inc.

Exercises ————— Consider the following questions about Sarah's four revision agendas.

1. How does Sarah's *subject* change from her discovery draft to her final draft?

2. How does Sarah's concern about her *audience* affect her decision making.

3. What is Sarah's *purpose* for each draft? How does she try to embody that purpose in a thesis statement?

4. How effectively does Sarah follow Eudora Welty's notion of revising? For example, how does she move things around in her last draft? Which draft do you like best? Explain your answer.

Revising on Your Computer

The chief advantage of composing on a computer is the simplicity of revision. With a simple key command, you can delete words, rearrange sentences, and move paragraphs. But remember, substantial revision, unlike editing and proofreading, involves reseeing and reshaping the ideas and information in a draft. In Chapter 4, this process is called Global Revision. Chapters 7 through 10 illustrate the more restricted process of Local Revision, suggesting strategies for revising the paragraphs, sentences, diction, and style you see on your screen.

Global revision encourages you to think through the purpose of your planning and drafting in complete texts. Save and print each text. Assess its success in a revision agenda. Then compose the new text you prescribe. As you move on to the new text, reread your previous drafts and agendas to see if there is anything you can use or rework.

If you are uncertain about a draft, circulate your text among your peers. Pass out copies or send it via E-mail to the other members of your class (or writing group). Ask them to mark the sections they like and comment on the sections that surprise or confuse them. They can insert their comments beside or right into your text in bracketed capital letters, like this [CAN YOU ILLUSTRATE HOW THIS WOULD WORK?]. After they have read and annotated your text, ask them to compose their own revision agenda for your next draft.

A conference with your instructor will also help you to think about global revision. Send a copy of your text by E-mail first, so that he or she has time to think about the way you have defined your subject, audience, and purpose. Then schedule a conference so that the two of you can brainstorm about what you are attempting to discover and what you have already accomplished. Your instructor may decide to compose suggestions at a computer and then return them with your text or send them to you by E-mail.

No matter who initiates your revision, remember that global revision often requires a complete new text. Occasionally, modifying your thesis or repositioning certain examples will solve your problems. More often, you must start from scratch. Open a new file, reread all your notes and reader responses, and begin, again.

A FINAL WORD ABOUT REVISING

There is no final word about revising. You can revise endlessly, rearranging information, rewriting paragraphs, substituting new words. The more you look, the more you will see. But at some point, revising becomes rationalizing—an excuse for idle tinkering. The test of global revision is whether it produces significant improvement. Sometimes additional revision actually destroys good writing, replacing spontaneous, original insights with self-conscious, overwrought commentary. Like Sarah, you have to know when to say "I'm done." Strategies for local revision to help you polish and perfect your last draft are contained in Part Two.

New Products | **Andy Rooney**

In this brief essay, television commentator Andy Rooney asks if new products are necessarily better products. What evidence does Rooney use to distinguish between genuine innovation and cosmetic change? If the subject were writing rather than manufacturing, how would you characterize the difference between a *revised* text and a *changed* text?

1

M oney is not my game, so I don't often read the *Wall Street Journal,* but someone on the train I take got off at the stop before mine the other night and left the paper on the seat next to me, so I looked through it. The *Wall Street Journal* gives you sort of a digest of the news you get on television.

2

One small story in there said that the companies that make things are coming up with fewer new products this year than last. The paper suggested this was bad, but I thought it was good. You can carry freedom of choice too far in a grocery store, for example. I don't want all the big companies squeezing out all the little upstart companies, but I don't want to be faced with ten different brands of what is substantially the identical product, either.

3

Our kitchen sink got stopped up last Saturday and I went to the grocery store for a can of Drano. I don't know why Drano. I'm just familiar with what the can looks like, and I was surprised to find a whole shelf filled with products that were supposed to free a clogged sink. There were powders, liquids and pellets. They came in cans, tubes, bottles and plastic. All of them said that if they didn't work, call your plumber. That always makes me suspect that they probably won't work on my problem. I found myself wishing the grocer had taken it upon himself to test the products for me so that he could have become expert enough to narrow my choices to just two or three.

4

I ended up with a can of Drano, as always. I don't know whether any of those new, improved products were any better or not. I figured they were all more or less the same.

5

Genuine innovation is something we all like. That's what we mean by the line "Build a better mousetrap and the world will beat a path to your door."

6

The trouble is, too many big companies have been making the same old mousetrap and trying to get us to come to their door by painting it a different color or calling it the Official Mickey Mousetrap. That's not innovation, but that's what too often passes for a new product.

7

The automobile manufacturers of America are in trouble because we wanted something genuinely different and they gave us the same old mousetrap with electrically operated windows. The Japanese came up with some really new ideas in cars and people are buying them. When Volkswagen switched from the Bug to the Rabbit, the difference was more than new bumper stickers. You can tell a Saab from a Toyota, but you can't tell a Chevrolet from an Oldsmobile unless you own one.

8

Too many "new" products are coming from the sales departments of companies rather than from the engineering division. I hope Americans are tired of

Rooney, Andy. "New Products." *And More by Andy Rooney.* New York: Atheneum, 1982. 26–28.

being tricked. A lot of good U.S. companies spend big money on product development, on good design, on engineering or improved chemistry. They have good, serious professionals working to make real improvements, not cosmetic changes, but for all the effort that is put into making the product better, it is hardly ever as much money as is put into selling it.

It has always seemed to me that, over the long run, we do one thing about 9 as well or as poorly as we do something else in America. We have some national traits that show through our work no matter what our work is. Sometimes it's good, sometimes it isn't.

For instance, take two products as different as those produced by Detroit 10 and the television industry. Our cars and our television, for all my complaints, are in many ways the best in the world, but they both suffer from the same things. They're big, fluffy and tend to imitate the other products in their market. Two situation comedies on competing networks are apt to be as much alike as an Oldsmobile and a Chevrolet.

Putting the same product in a new package isn't what I call a new product. 11 When an advertisement tells me what I'm buying is "new and improved," I always wonder exactly what the improvement is and whether I was a sucker for having bought the product last year before they fixed whatever was wrong with it.

I don't care what the *Wall Street Journal* says, I like the idea of fewer new 12 products on the market. What we ought to do is keep making the old ones until we get them right.

Shopping on TV: Romance and Chat | **Walter Goodman**

In this commentary from the *New York Times,* critic Walter Goodman explores the strange world of television shopping. How does his description of "The Jewelry Showcase" explain the appeal of this kind of shopping? In what ways is it "safely impersonal" and "rewardingly personal"? What does Goodman say about how this "innovation" will revise the way consumers shop?

O n a snowbound Sunday my grazer stopped at the QVC (Quality, Value, 1 Convenience) network. I had often caught glimpses during channel hoppings of youngish women and men delivering conversational pitches for clothing, tools, necklaces, pots and pans, dolls, basketball cards and whatnot, but had quickly flicked away to "Nick at Nite" or other meat for the mind. But this time I resisted the remote and watched for an hour.

I had chanced upon "The Jewelry Showcase." A man in lightly rimmed 2 glasses, blue blazer, white shirt and necktie and matching pocket hanky was celebrating a sterling amethyst three-stone ring, one of the day's special values, reduced from the QVC price of $64.50 (which had been reduced from the retail price of $120) to only $53.82 plus a few dollars for shipping and handling, payable by credit card in installments. He was as clean-cut as the stones he was

Goodman, Walter. "Shopping on TV: Romance and Chat." *New York Times* 17 Mar. 1993: C15, 19.

showing; his cuticles, which spent a lot of time on screen while his scrubbed fingers displayed the ring, glinted like gems.

The selling was incessant, but the tone was easy. Like a PBS pitchman with-   3
out a superior attitude, he was asking us to join him in admiring the swell stuff he was letting us in on. Even when he said, "Don't wait. Get it right now," the sell sounded soft. More pressure came from the little box on the upper right of the screen that told how many of the rings had been sold (8,000 and rising), the bulletin that size 9 had just gone out of stock and the little box on the lower right that told how many minutes were left to take advantage of the special price.

But the salesman, whose name I missed, remained a relaxing presence.   4
Now and then, he tossed in bits of information, for instance that the amethyst was once considered good medicine for the digestive tract and the inner soul and that a product called Ammolite ($49.98) has something to do with a 70-million-year-old fossil. (He must have been reading from a prompter, but it didn't show.) After a few minutes of how pretty the stones were and how the colors did this and that, his voice became Wordzak: "Those diamonds really twinkle, don't they?"

He was your video gigolo, and it was easy to imagine a woman alone with   5
her set on a Sunday afternoon being eased into taking a plunge on $53.82 plus shipping and handling (possibly not a bad buy if you wanted an amethyst, which few of those 8,000-odd customers could have known they wanted until they tuned in), as second best to taking home this pleasant fellow himself. There was even the possibility of getting to chat briefly with the host, who, for fans, is by now a celebrity, like everybody else on the tube.

Yes, this is interactive television, and every few minutes a viewer-shopper   6
comes on the line. The conversation often begins with the seller asking, "What are you shopping for today?" and then congratulating the buyer on her good luck in being able to get whatever it is. There is some small talk—"Is purple a color you wear well?—but the chat is never allowed to drift far from the merchandise being moved. (Can our host be operating on commission?) Many callers announce that they watch for hours at a sitting and are congratulated and urged to stay with it because there's so much still to come.

A few standard gimmicks are applied to keep less dedicated consumers   7
from deserting between the items that excite them. The particularly fortunate caller may get to play a word game: Julie was asked to name a plant that could be construed from the letters a-s-t-c-c-u. She replied unhesitatingly "cactus," adding that she is married to a high school biology teacher, and won $75.

Also, if certain digits on your special QVC card, attainable just by calling   8
an 800 number that keeps appearing on the bottom of the screen, match the four-digit Lucky Number that is announced frequently, you win a little something and qualify for the big $1,000 shopping-spree drawing, the prize to be applied to QVC goods.

The show-biz consumerism ("the enjoyable way to shop") being pioneered   9
by operations like QVC and its main competitor, the Home Shopping Network, is only a beginning. The business will no doubt grow and take on new forms until stores with premises become fossils like Ammolite. The appeals are manifest and manifold beyond giving millions something to do as well as to watch.

The operation makes acquisitiveness seem wholesome. It is at once safely   10
impersonal and rewardingly personal; there is even a touch of romance as the young man caresses the jewel of the moment. There is status in learning that one is a collector of collectibles instead of a mere knoodler of knickknacks.

There may be a feeling of community among the people who call in to share their love of porcelain dolls, their acquaintance with tools or utensils, their tastes in casual outfits, and there must be reassurance in knowing that one will be wearing what, as the figures on the screen keep certifying, thousands of other people are wearing. It's as democratic as an electronic town hall, and it's all so easy, not to mention, discounted.

Tomorrow at 3 P.M., QVC offers something new, "the spiritual hour," fea-   11
turing Bibles and other devotional artifacts. You might want to tune in if there's another blizzard.

Packaged Deception | Marya Mannes

In the early 1960s, Marya Mannes gave the following testimony before the Congressional Subcommittee on Antitrust and Monopoly, arguing that American manufacturers use a variety of confusing packages to deceive consumers. How does Mannes demonstrate this deception exists? Why does she think legislation is necessary to correct these practices? In the thirty years since she gave this talk, how have manufacturers changed their behavior? What new forms of deception have they packaged?

I am a writer and a housewife. As a writer I sell words and ideas. They are not   1
packaged. The buyer can see exactly what they are and pay what he thinks they are worth. As a housewife I buy what is sold to me. It is packaged. I buy it on faith. That is why, these days, the word consumer is sometimes spelled s-u-c-k-e-r.

And that is why I stand before you here not as a writer but as a sucker, one   2
of millions who wonder why so much money drains out of the foodbag and the handbag every week, and who then forget about it.

Now, I have always believed that the majority of people were too good to   3
be smart. Ever since we bartered a beaver pelt for ten eggs, we have assumed that the eggs were fresh and the pelt was supple, for how else can decent business be transacted? Except for the relation between man and wife, nothing is more intimate than the relation between the buyer and the seller; and there would be neither marriage nor commerce if the fundamental basis of both were not trust. Without trust, a civilized society cannot endure. When the people who are too smart to be good fool the people who are too good to be smart, then society begins to crumble. I think this is what is happening now, and I believe it must be stopped before our integrity as Americans is chiseled away as fast as our dollars are.

What am I talking about? I am talking about certain practices in the market   4
which manage to evade the spirit of the law while adhering by an eyelash to the letter of the law. I am talking about what happens when a housewife like myself goes to buy food for her family, and how she spends her money doing it.

And I am talking about the many small deceptions, most of them deliberate,   5
which make a rational buying choice—the basis of free enterprise—meaningless. You can only choose when you know what you are choosing, and the plain

Mannes, Marya. "Packaged Deception." *But Will It Sell?* Philadelphia: Lippincott, 1964. 36–42.

truth is that much of the time we don't. That great American institution, the supermarkets, those gleaming palaces of convenience and bounty, have come to be the greatest exercise in planned confusion since the bazaars of Samarkand. If you don't believe me, climb into my pushcart and come around with me, shelf by shelf.

Need some applesauce for the baby? Pick up a few of Brand A's new jars. They look just like the old ones. They cost the same. But do you know that the new jar has only seven and a half ounces of applesauce while the old one had seven and three-quarters ounces? No? You mean you didn't *look* at that fine print with your glasses? Now, how about some breakfast food? Well, Brand B's old box contained six biscuits and weighed six ounces, but when you open the new box which is exactly the same size, you'll find only five ounces of biscuits—a drop in contents of about sixteen per cent. Oh sure, they tell you what's inside the jar or box, but you need a slide rule to figure out the difference. And what housewife with a kid inside the cart and one at her heels can spare the time?   6

This is confusion number one: to make you think you're getting the same value in the same box at the same price when you're actually getting less. If you complain, the manufacturers say that they're saving you a price raise by reducing the contents. Can you beat it?   7

Confusion number two is in sizes. Know the difference between Giant and Jumbo? Between two-ounce and a *big* two-ounce? Between a quart and a *full* quart? What's a *tall* 24-inch? What does Extra Long mean? Who's kidding who? And what's the matter with simple sizes, like a pint or two pints or a quart or two quarts? I'll tell you what's the matter. They're too easy to figure. You might know what you were getting. And that goes for the Economy Size too. What economy? If you stop to figure it out, half the time the price per unit remains exactly the same regardless of size, and you save nothing. It just seems economical to us suckers.   8

Now, let's stop at detergents, where the Giant sizes are. Well, with a box of Brand C, *Giant* means three pounds, five and one-half ounces, but with Brand D, *Giant* means three pounds one and one-fourth ounces; but both boxes look the same size and cost the same price—77 cents. Are the ingredients of the one so superior to the ingredients in the other that four ounces don't matter? And how do you know it, anyway?   9

Let's move next door to the all-purpose liquid cleaners. With 69 cents you can buy one quart of Brand E, or 1 pint, 12 fluid ounces of Brand F. The shapes are slightly different, but they look the same size. Do you know where the four ounces go? Do you care?   10

Want some soap pads? Well, you can buy a box of Brand G or a box of Brand H for 13 cents, but unless you turn the box upside down and use your bifocals, you won't know that there are only four pads of Brand G compared to five pads of Brand H. Care about one less pad? Half the time, the quantity of such products is printed in very small type or in a color that merges in the background. Sometimes it's even printed *underneath* the flap, and you can't see it until you open it. Do you see it even then?   11

Now, you would think that if packages were different sizes, they'd contain different amounts, but that's because you're congenitally dumb. Brand I, a table salt, is in a box one inch taller than Brand J, another table salt, but each has exactly one pound and ten ounces in them. And how are you to know if the first box is slightly thinner than the second one. Where was your tape measure?   12

Then there are the simple devices of not really filling the box or bottle. You **13** open up a cereal, say, and you find an inch or more space on the top—slack-filled, it's called. Or the liquid in a bottle has an inch or more empty space about it. And there's the business of using paper to wrap around crackers or soap and fill the loose space. The manufacturers will, of course, claim these are necessary for safe handling and so forth. But we're paying enough for outer space not to have to pay for inner space, too.

There's another good gimmick to confuse you: funny shapes of bottles that **14** make any real estimate of contents impossible.

Then there are all those lovely phrases like the New, the Improved, the **15** Activated, the Super, and so forth. Don't they give you the impression that you are getting a better product, justifying a higher price? Well, half the time you aren't. These words are like the bells the scientists ring to make dogs salivate. You see the word "new" and you reach for it.

For now, you see, there is no salesman anymore to tell you what you are **16** getting. In supermarkets, the *package* is the salesman. The more space he takes up on the shelf (*that's* the reason for Giant and Jumbo, *not* economy), the louder his letters scream at you, the sooner you'll notice him. But while he shouts "Buy me!" he also talks double talk out of the side of his mouth. And while you put *him* in your cart, he picks *your* pocket.

Why? Because you're dumb? Because you're gullible? Because you're care- **17** less? Some of us are all of these. But most of us are simply too busy or too tired or too harassed to take a computer, a slide rule, and an M.I.T. graduate to market and figure out what we're buying. And the makers of the goods we buy know this. In fact, they know far more about us than we know about them. They have spent millions of dollars studying us—the consumer. They know what colors and what sizes and what shapes and what words we go for. Compared to them the Big Brother in George Orwell's *1984*, who knows all and sees all, is a piker. The Big Brothers in our society today are not government dictators: they are the sellers and their brainwashing handmaidens, the behavioral scientists. Together, and under the banner of free choice and open competition, they have made us believe that we are getting what we pay for. Their purpose is that innocent goal of free enterprise—to make an extra buck. But when their profit becomes our loss, how innocent is that goal? And what is our loss?

Not much, you may say. An ounce here, a cent there, and what real differ- **18** ence does it make? Most of us have learned to accept the added charges of packaging and advertising and distribution along with the product. But must we pay for deception too?

Just take one figure—baby foods again. Remember the brand where you **19** paid the same price as you used to but got a quarter ounce less food? Well, if your baby ate four jars of this applesauce or carrot puree a day, he would eat twenty-four pounds less food per year—without your knowing it. Do you care? Does it matter?

Maybe it doesn't. We are a spoiled and lazy and wasteful people; our **20** pay checks were never higher and so what—that's the way business is done. A little less applesauce, a few less crackers, a few more pennies here and there: who cares?

But it isn't a question of applesauce. It's a question of morality. Little **21** deceptions of single consumers can add up to a mighty deception of a whole people. You may only lose a penny here and there, but the loss in dollars

sustained daily by American consumers who pay for more than they get is estimated to be greater than the staggering amount we forfeit to crime and corruption. But it's not sensational. It doesn't hit the headlines. And who is going to
bring it to your attention? The press which depends on advertising? Television
which owes its existence to products? The makers of the products? As Eliza
Doolittle said in *Pygmalion,* "Not bloody likely!"

Only those whose prime concern is people and not profit can tell us the   22
score: organizations like the Consumers Union and those agencies of government who regulate the pure and basic world of weights and measures and law
and justice, so that the exchange of goods is a transaction of trust.

But we, the public, have got to want to know the score. If we don't care,   23
nobody else will care. Dishonest practices, because they succeed, will drive out
honest practices, because they don't. In the end our condition depends entirely
on us. And I think at last we may be beginning to realize it.

The murmur of rebellion against these widespread deceptions and confu-   24
sions in packaging is swelling daily. People *are* bringing their slide rules to
market, they *are* taking a good look at what the package says and what it holds,
they *are* beginning to write protests to the manufacturers who manipulate
them. But still not enough.

We hear day in and day out of the revolutions that are sweeping the   25
world. I think we are ripe for one here. And when you hear the testimony that
follows in this chamber, I believe you will think we are ripe for one too—a revolution of the American consumer against the manipulation of his mind and
money by practices of packaging and labeling that empty his purse and his
market basket while he is looking the other way.

So far the manufacturers guilty of these deceptions are not the majority;   26
yet among them are some of the most respected brand names in the business.
They will, of course, deny deliberate deception and produce any number of
reasons that they consider both valid and legal for packaging and labeling as
they do. But the evidence stands and the confusion mounts.

Ladies and gentlemen—Consumers—we *are* being kidded. In the days of   27
McCarthy, Elmer Davis said of those who tried to confuse our thinking, "Don't
let them scare you." Today I would like to say of those who try to confuse our
buying and our values, "Don't let them kid you."

And I kid you not.   28

Writing Assignments

Narrate   **1.**   Compile a list of sales ventures you have encountered—for example, selling door-to-door, shopping for a special present, negotiating the terms of a warranty. Select one that raised your expectations. Then write a narrative that reveals how your experience caused you to revise your expectations.

Observe   **2.**   Visit a shopping mall or large discount store. Find a store or a particular section of a store where you can observe shoppers. Then write an essay in which you describe the behavior of three kinds of shoppers: reluctant, recreational, and relentless.

Investigate   **3.**   Interview someone at your campus newspaper about his or her experience selling ad space to local merchants. What kind of merchants purchase ads in a college newspaper? How do they determine the timing and placement of those ads? Use your interview information to write a feature revealing how local merchants try to affect how students spend their money.

Collaborate   **4.**   Convert your writing group into a coupon club for a month. Develop an investment strategy for collecting, trading, and redeeming coupons. Keep a record of what you save. Then write a guide for students on how to use coupons effectively.

Read   **5.**   Search the business journals in your library for articles directed toward readers who want to work in some unusual form of marketing—infomercials or telephone sales, for example. Read one article carefully. Write a brief analysis of its projected audience. Then speculate about a completely different audience—for example, consumer advocates who want to eliminate such marketing strategies. Revise the information in the article so that you can present it effectively to this new audience.

Respond   **6.**   Look through mail-order catalogues for products that support or refute Andy Rooney's claim that "too many companies have been making the same old mousetrap." Then write a letter to Rooney presenting your findings as evidence that he is correct or that the products you have found are indeed better.

Analyze   **7.**   Establish the purpose of Walter Goodman's essay, "Shopping on TV: Romance and Chat." What is his attitude toward the jewelry salesman? What assumptions does he make about those viewers he imagines are watching? Compose a "revision agenda" that would enable Goodman to revise his conclusions about the purpose of shopping on TV.

Evaluate   **8.**   Consult your responses to the exercises on page 92. Then write an essay reassessing the strengths and weaknesses of one of Sarah Penning's four essays on coupons. Begin by revising her assessment of the essay's strengths and weaknesses. Then compose a new set of directions for how she might improve her essay.

Argue   **9.**   Take Marya Mannes' side in the argument about deceptive packaging. Identify some recent legal cases supporting her claim that consumers cannot trust manufacturers. Then present your evidence to argue for a consumers' revolution.

Argue **10.**   Revise Marya Mannes' argument: argue that creative deception is essential to the free-enterprise system. Support your claim with examples of successful advertising campaigns. Or, if you want to take on Mannes directly, demonstrate how she herself has *packaged* her testimony *deceptively* to sell her argument to the Congressional Subcommittee on Antitrust and Monopoly.

5 | Common Methods of Development

In Part One you learned how working through the stages of the writing process enables you to discover your subject, audience, and purpose. You also learned how these discoveries suggest various structures for shaping your writing. Once Joanne Malbone decided to write about Mr. Bridgeman, she began telling a story about her "little revolt" in his Latin class. Once Ellen Haack decided to explain Barry's preoccupation with "what's good for me, " she began to think of illustrative examples that would engage her audience. And once Sarah decided to write about the "coupon conspiracy," she reformulated her purpose to demonstrate how advertisers use coupons to control what consumers buy. In each case, the method of development—the structure of the writing—emerged from the material the writer discovered in planning, drafting, and revising.

In Part Two you will learn how and when to use various structures to express your ideas more effectively. Nonfiction writer John McPhee asserts that "everything in writing is a structure within a structure within a structure down to the simple sentence, which, of course, is also a structure" (personal interview). As you work your way through particular writing assignments, you need to decide whether to impose a structure on your information or look for a structure within your information.

McPhee explains that selecting a method (or methods) of developing his writing is probably the most important decision he makes, but one he can make only after immersing himself in the writing process:

> The structure of a piece of writing arises from within the material I have collected. When I go out to gather information on a subject, I am observing, asking questions, constantly scribbling notes. Then I go to the library, read, and make more notes. I end up with this great pile of miscellaneous notes that don't reveal their important relationships. It's at this point that I go over my notes again and again, looking for a couple of things that might illuminate each other. When I find them, I think, "Well, that makes sense. I could put these two things side by side." So I put them there. Once these two go together, gradually, slowly, the other segments work themselves out until I have a beginning, middle, and end. It's sort of the way the structure of some kind of mineral might get itself together. (Personal interview)

Like McPhee, you will uncover various patterns for developing your ideas throughout the writing process. In *planning,* these patterns often emerge as answers to the basic questions you might ask about any body of information: *What is it? How does it work? Why does it matter?* These questions are like the different lenses you attach to your camera: each lens gives you a different picture of your subject. If you decide to write about women artists, for example, you might formulate a series of questions such as: Why are comparatively few women ranked among the world's great artists? What historical forces may have discouraged women from becoming artists? Who is in charge of the "ranking" process and how does it work? Do the ways women look at the world differ from the ways men look at it, and if so, what implications does this difference have for women's art and its reception? As you can see, each question not only shifts your perspective on your subject, but also suggests a different method for developing your information about it.

If planning gives you the opportunity to envision your subject from a variety of perspectives, then *drafting* encourages you to develop the pattern (or patterns) that appears to you most effective for demonstrating your purpose. In some writing projects, a pattern may seem to emerge naturally from your planning. If you decide to write about your observation of a game of lacrosse, your choice seems obvious: to tell what happened. In attempting this, however, you may need to answer other questions about this unfamiliar sport: What do the field and equipment look like? How is it played? How is it similar to or different from other sports? Developing this new information may require you to develop new patterns that challenge your ability to advance your purpose without distorting your structure.

Logically, this judgment is made best during *revising*. As you look over your draft, you will need to make two decisions. First, you must decide whether individual segments or patterns of information develop or distort your original structure. The history of lacrosse—its creation by Iroquois Indians, its discovery by French explorers, and its development by Canadians—is an interesting body of information, but it may need to be reshaped, relocated, or even eliminated in revision to preserve the purpose of your original design: to tell what happened. Second, you must decide whether your original design, often mirroring the method by which you discovered the structure of your essay, is still the best method for presenting your information to your audience. Instead of using this organic structure, telling what happened, you may decide that you can best express your ideas by choosing a more formal structure, comparing lacrosse to games with which your readers are already familiar, such as soccer or hockey.

Whatever you decide, you need to understand each pattern's purpose, strategies, and effect if you are going to use it successfully to develop a paragraph, a section of your essay, or your whole essay. The remainder of this chapter presents and analyzes the most common methods of development, except for building arguments, which, because of its complexity, is given extended explanation in Chapter 6.

WHAT HAPPENED? *Narration*

Narration tells a story to make a point. It can be used in an anecdotal, abbreviated way to introduce or illustrate a complicated subject or in an extended way to provide a detailed, personal account of "what happened." An effective narrative has a *plot*—a meaningful and dramatic sequence of action—that may or may not follow the order in which events actually occurred and usually focuses on some tension or conflict within the writer, between the writer and others, or between the writer and the environment.

A narrative depends on pace to effect its purpose. *Pace* means the speed at which events are narrated. Sometimes you need to slow the pace to describe one aspect of an event in great detail; at other times several related events can be quickly summarized in a few sentences. By making such decisions about pace, you control the development of your narrative to dramatize its purpose for your readers.

A narrative requires the selection of a *point of view,* that is, establishing the person and position of the narrator. If you tell the story as "I" or "we," you are writing in the *first person;* if you recount what "he," "she," or "they" did, you are writing in the *third person.* In addition to identity, *person* refers to the attitude and personality of the narrator. *Position* is the narrator's closeness to the action in both space and time: the narrator may be a participant or an observer and may be telling the story as it happens, shortly thereafter, or much later.

In the following passage, Francine duPlessix Gray narrates a scene that illustrates what happens when tourists invade an animal habitat.

Introduces context and intended conflict.

Driving one evening through Amboseli, at the foot of Kilimanjaro, we see twenty-one minibuses gathered near a clearing to observe three cheetahs stalking. The first cheetah curtly moves through the thicket toward a small herd of impalas, occasionally twitching her ears as a signal for her companions to move on. There is an exaggerated stylishness about these animal's features—extravagantly long, elegant forelegs, outlandishly small, heavily marked faces. These most endangered animals of East Africa—champion runners but unskilled at camouflage, their temperament as open as the plains they frequent—seem only too willing to be movie stars, and cock their heads photogenically toward the tourists.

Climax of narrative produces reversal of action.

After we have watched them for several minutes the cheetahs have approached to about a hundred and fifty yards of their prey, coming close to the distance from which they make their famous sixty-mile-per-hour dash for the kill. But as they reach the critical moment minibuses start crashing about them; tourists lean on the open rooftops of their vehicles, cameras poised, and urge their drivers to get the closest possible view of the kill. Startled by the commotion, the impalas race about in circles and cough out their warning message, the baboons' terrierlike barking comes sloughing off the trees. The cheetahs must know better than we that they have lost their chance for dinner, but they go on stalking for a few minutes, as if to finish their pose. And then, amid the clicking of some fifty cameras, the head scout abruptly turns away from the impalas. The three cheetahs slink off into the plain. Their fragile rib cages seem terribly thin in the dusk, the black markings of their cheeks—like rivulets of black tears—seem to express their frustrated hunger.

Concludes by establishing point of narrative.

We are going to kill these animals with sentiment. Having slain and trapped wild creatures for food, domesticated them for our amusement, and hunted them for sport, we are now decimating them by our fantasies of wilderness. How curious that photographic "shooting" is becoming deadlier to game than the ancient pastime of sport shooting. How regrettable that the tourists' most intrusive drivers tend to be Africans. The ancient code of hunting is past, a new etiquette of viewing has yet to be elaborated if the animals are to survive. I turn to Big Hunter, who, along with two other European drivers, respectfully kept his vehicle still during the cheetahs' attempted hunt. "Looking at game may become more dangerous to them than hunting," I say. "Worse than that," he remarks laconically, "it's so bloody rude to the animals." (Francine duPlessix Gray, "On Safari")

Like Gray, Jane Graham wants to write about a journey to an animal habitat, her first whale watch. Although she was only at sea for a few hours, she was overwhelmed by events, information, and insights. She decides that one way to explore her ideas is to transcribe the sequence of events in a narrative.

1. How does Jane establish the position and attitude of the narrator?

2. What conflicts does she introduce to characterize her narrative?

3. How does the conclusion resolve conflicts and confirm the purpose of the narrative?

Vicarious experience

It was mist upon mist. The Portuguese Princess plowed out of Provincetown harbor toward Stellwagen Bank where the humpbacks had been feeding for several months. I was seated forward, so that the gasoline fumes would not combine with the rolling swell to make me sick. Nothing was going to spoil this long-anticipated adventure. My insistence chased away the mist, and we chugged along in the hot sun for about an hour. Some people tried to talk above the sound of the engine: "I've watched all the Cousteau specials." "Have you seen the skeletons at the Museum of Natural History?" Others checked their camera lenses or scanned the horizon through binoculars. "Thar she blows!" yelled our tour guide. "Off the port bow. There!" I followed his finger, straining to see what he saw in the dark blue sea. Nothing. Then, suddenly, against the skyline, I saw it. A definite vertical spray. Then a pause. Then another. A whale. At last, a whale.

Exercises ———

1. Freewrite in your journal about an experience in which you intruded on some group's privacy. How did you disrupt its behavior? How did you feel? What alternative did you consider before you intruded?

2. List the events that contributed to your achievement of a long-anticipated goal. Then draft a narrative in which you help your readers appreciate the conflicts, large and small, you had to overcome to reach your goal.

WHAT DOES IT LOOK LIKE? *Description*

Description presents a verbal portrait of a person, place, or thing. It can be used to enrich other forms of writing or as a dominant strategy for developing a picture of a subject. A successful description does not depend solely on visual effects, however, but attempts to identify the subject's significant features by evoking all the senses. Impressions and observations are arranged in an appropriate pattern designed to capture both detail and wholeness. Specific, vivid detail makes your readers see what you see, and arranging those details in an appropriate sequence helps your readers understand why your subject is interesting and significant. Description is not merely a catalogue of facts or a collection of ornaments; like narration, it must make a point.

In the following passage from "The Courage of Turtles," Edward Hoagland describes the unique physical behavior of turtles:

Evokes senses.

Arranges details in sequence.

Extends significance of description.

> Turtles cough, burp, whistle, grunt and hiss, and produce social judgments. They put their heads together amicably enough, but then one drives the other back with the suddenness of two dogs who have been conversing in tones too low for an onlooker to hear. They pee in fear when they're first caught, but exercise both pluck and optimism in trying to escape, walking for hundreds of yards within the confines of their pen, carrying the weight of that cumbersome box on legs which are cruelly positioned for walking. They don't feel that the contest is unfair; they keep plugging, rolling like sailorly souls—a bobbing, infirm gait, a brave, sea-legged momentum—stopping occasionally to study the lay of the land. For me, anyway, they manage to contain the rest of the animal world. They can stretch out their necks like a giraffe, or loom underwater like an apocryphal hippo. They browse on lettuce thrown on the water like a cow moose which is partly submerged. They have a penguin's alertness, combined with a build like a Brontosaurus when they rise up on tiptoe. Then they hunch and ponderously lunge like a grizzly going forward. (Edward Hoagland, "The Courage of Turtles")

Jane saw and photographed so many whales on her voyage that she has trouble sorting out her impressions. She decides that a description of a whale will concentrate and enrich her narrative. She describes the last whale she saw—the one that saw her.

How does Jane introduce the point of her description?

What senses does she evoke?

How does she arrange details to create a dominant impression?

The biologist hushed us. A finback, the world's second largest whale, had been spotted swimming toward the boat. He was way off course from the usual pattern of his species. Finbacks are shy, solitary creatures, and, because they are still hunted, usually stay clear of boats. The boat, its engine cut, rolled on four-foot swells. The smell of oil and gas hung in the air, making my head ache and my throat tighten as I tried to swallow. Soon, we saw him—a sea-green monolith, silhouetted several feet beneath the water. His color was uneven. The small distinguishing dorsal fin was speckled with white and gray spots. He was silent. We were silent. He swam purposefully toward the boat. Then under. More silence. I crossed to the other side in time to see his huge greenish head explode through the surface. One watery eye looked back at me before he arched his body and sounded. We did not see him again, but we knew we had seen something rare.

Exercises ——— 1. Look up a description of some mythical beast—a dragon, griffin, or unicorn—in an encyclopedia. Then describe your own impressions of one of these beasts. You may want to describe the way such beasts have been portrayed in film.

2. Interview people who have extensive contacts with animals—veterinarians, zookeepers, park rangers. For them, what animal "contains the rest of the animal world"? How would they describe it?

HOW DO YOU DO IT? *Process Analysis*

A *process* is a sequence of actions or changes that bring about a result. The development of the human embryo from conception to birth is one process; the procedure by which citizens of the United States elect the president is another. To *analyze* a process effectively, you must know it thoroughly or learn as much as you can about it, and then you must divide it into steps or stages. A careful division will help you see the best way to describe the process: several small steps may be combined into one large step; certain steps may be suspended while others are completed; still other steps may require special emphasis so that they are not overlooked or reversed. After you have established an effective pattern of steps, you must explain each step, acknowledging how it connects to the next and what special knowledge or tools will be needed to complete it.

You must also make a careful assessment of your audience to determine whether you want to provide them with information about *how something works or happens* or to give them instructions on *how to do something*. In the first case, your readers may be interested in the stages and operation of a particular process even though they have no direct involvement in it. In the second case, they will want to know enough about the process so they can actually perform it.

In the following selection, humorist H. Allen Smith asks an expert, "Mr. Buttolph," to analyze the proper process for killing a wasp.

Introduces need for "campaign."

Describes "necessary" tools and strategies.

Analyzes steps—and advises additional steps.

"Don't ever think," Mr. Buttolph explained, "that you can handle a wasp the way you handle a fly. You've got to plan a campaign—figure out just exactly how you're going to proceed against him, and hope he doesn't get you while you're mapping your plans. Keep your eye on him, *but don't let him know you're looking at him.* Quietly assemble your equipment. A rubber fly swatter. Thick gloves. Put a hat on. Turn your shirt collar up and button it. Keep a ball peen hammer handy. Then go after him—but don't do directly at him. Sidle up to him. Pretend you're just walking in his direction by accident. Say something to throw him off guard, like 'Now, I wonder what I did with those glasses.' Watch him out of the corner of your eye, and if he starts to wiggle or flap his legs ease away from him, back off, and wait a while. Give him a chance to settle down. Go outdoors and practice with the rubber swatter. Drive a tack into a wall and stand off and swat at it—develop your aim, because that's important. God help you if you ever swing at a wasp and miss him. Now, go back in and locate him again and see what sort of a mood he's in. If he's at ease, sidle up to him and when you're sure of your position, when you're certain that you've got the proper range, bust him one as hard as you can. If he falls to the floor, jump on him, stomp him—even then he may get up off the floor and stab you. Hit him with the hammer. Don't take your eye off him. No matter that he's lying there like a corpse. He may be playing possum. Get a newspaper and wrap him up in it and then set fire to it. After that it *may* be that he won't bother you again." (H. Allen Smith, "How to Kill a Wasp")

One of the real dangers Jane faced when she went on the whale watch was her susceptibility to seasickness. She had been at sea enough and sick enough to qualify as an expert on the illness. In her draft, she composes a section in which she provides instructions about how to avoid the whale-watcher's curse.

1. How does Jane establish the need for an effective procedure?

2. What are the stages in the prevention process?

3. What is the effect of not following the process?

A person who suffers from motion sickness and loves whale watching has a problem. Whales do not fit under microscopes. They must be watched at sea, atop rolling four-foot swells. I have solved this problem by developing a procedure to combat the sickness that attacks me when "I go down to the sea in boats." Several hours before boarding, I eat a mild meal: toast, tea, mashed potatoes. An hour later, I take two Dramamine tablets. Then, I dress warmly, knowing that I will not be able to go below when I get cold. When I board the ship, I stay away from the engine, which spews gas and oil fumes into the air. Once underway, I stand forward, always to windward, so that I can feel the cold, salty breeze on my face. When we finally encounter some whales, I try to avoid looking too quickly from whale to whale. Finally, on the way back to port, I avoid the green tourist who has not taken these precautions. The next "Thar she blows" might be her.

Exercises ———

1. Map the steps in a familiar process. Divide the process into major stages and then smaller steps. Consult with an expert to see if you have overlooked some hidden steps or failed to provide the appropriate cautions.

2. Analyze a process that confuses, intimidates, or terrifies most people. Use your personal experience to demystify the process: "I did this and survived to tell the tale. So can you."

HOW IS IT SIMILAR OR DIFFERENT? *Comparison*

A *comparison* systematically analyzes and evaluates the similarities of two or more things. (A *contrast* is a comparison that emphasizes differences rather than similarities.) An effective comparison demonstrates one of three general purposes: (1) two things thought to be different are shown to be quite similar; (2) two things thought to be similar are shown to be quite different; or (3) two things, although comparable, are shown to be not equal (that is, one is shown to be better than the other). To demonstrate one of these purposes, you will need to develop your comparison according to either the divided (A + B) pattern or the alternating (A/B + A/B) pattern.

The Divided Pattern of Comparison: *A + B*

The *divided pattern*, the most common of the two strategies, divides the comparison into two sections, the first devoted to a discussion of A and the second to a discussion of B. Linking the examples in A to those in B —for example, by making three points about A and three similar points about B —unifies the two contrasting parts. The points should be in the same sequence and, where possible, paired points should be treated in the same amount of space. Although such exact pairings are not always necessary, in working out your purpose you should demonstrate that A + B are inextricably bound.

The two main parts of an A + B comparison should develop cumulatively. A simple description of two unlike houses, for example, becomes a contrast only when its thesis points out the significance of the differences. In some cases, as when one side of the contrast is so well known to readers that it need not be stated, the comparison is *implied*. If you are contrasting American football (A) with English rugby (B) for an American audience, the details of A are already in the mind of your audience and need only be mentioned in passing to explain the significant details of B.

From an interview with Richard, the marine biologist on the *Portuguese Princess,* and from her reading, Jane gathers information on two of the world's largest creatures—the diplodocus and the blue whale. Then she develops this information in a divided pattern that contrasts their enormous size with their gentle behavior.

Thesis contrasts perception with reality.

A. Diplodocus

1. Enormous size

2. Small brain

3. Gentle behavior

4. Eating habits

The creatures that seem to threaten man most with their size and power have often been quite gentle. They have banded together to care for their young, to protect one another, and to provide each other with company. Consider the big, dumb diplodocus—his huge body laboring with a slow, steady drumbeat through the prehistoric forest. Although his body was enormous, his brain was small, so small that it did not generate enough power to control his weighty tail. He needed a separate ganglion to control that end of his body. His size promised danger, but Big D spent most of his day grazing harmlessly on vegetation with his pals. When a meat-eating enemy approached, he lumbered into knee-deep water and munched on a soggy plant.

Similarly, the blue whale, the largest creature ever to exist, is as gentle as a golden retriever. One hundred feet long, he glides soundlessly through the ocean, his enormous head concealing his fifteen-pound brain. Like Big D, Big Blue was once a pack animal, but his numbers have been so depleted by hunters that he is rarely seen alone, much less in groups. He feeds on krill and other microscopic marine life. Instead of teeth, he has baleen, long strands of tissue that hang from his upper jaw. He sifts his food through this tissue by swimming, mouth open, through tons of water When he closes his mouth, the water strains back through the baleen, and he swallows the remaining food in gigantic gulps.

The Alternating Pattern of Comparison: *A/B + A/B*

The *alternating pattern* develops your material through matched pairs of *A* and *B*, expressed either in the same paragraph or in the same sentence. The divided pattern is perhaps easier to organize and control, particularly in short essays, but unless you connect the two subjects with a clear thesis, you may discover that you have written two separate essays. The alternating pattern requires you to organize your material more precisely than the divided pattern, especially in a longer essay, but the pattern is often more interesting and accessible for your reader because the point-by-point development can be written in balanced sentences that reinforce the comparison with every pair of matched details. Gretel Ehrlich uses the alternating pattern in the following passage to compare the romanticized conception (*A*) and the real character (*B*) of the American cowboy:

How does Ehrlich use the Marlboro man to introduce the two terms in her comparison?

When I'm in New York but feeling lonely for Wyoming I look for the Marlboro ads in the subway. What I'm aching to see is horseflesh, the glint of a spur, a line of distant mountains, brimming creeks, and a reminder of the ranchers and cowboys I've ridden with for the last eight years. But the men I see in those posters with their stern, humorless looks remind me of no one I know here. In our hellbent earnestness to romanticize the cowboy we've ironically disesteemed his true character. If he's "strong and silent" it's because there's probably no one to talk to. If he "rides away into the sunset" it's because he's been on horseback since four in the morning moving cattle and he's trying, fifteen hours later, to get home to his family. If he's "a rugged individualist" he's also part of a team: ranch work is teamwork and even the glorified open-range cowboys of the 1880s rode up and down the Chisholm Trail in the company of twenty or thirty other riders. Instead of the macho, trigger-happy man our culture has perversely wanted him to be, the cowboy is more apt to be convivial, quirky, and softhearted. To be "tough" on a ranch has nothing to do with conquests and displays of power. More often than not, circumstances—like the colt he's riding or an unexpected blizzard—are overpowering him. It's not toughness but "toughing it out" that counts. In other

How does she use parallel sentence structure to contrast A and B?

...does the comparison of cowboys with rocks contribute to her thesis?

words, this macho, cultural artifact the cowboy has become is simply a man who possesses resilience, patience, and an instinct for survival. "Cowboys are just like a pile of rocks—everything happens to them. They get climbed on, kicked, rained and snowed on, scuffed up by wind. Their job is 'just to take it,'" one old timer told me. (Gretel Ehrlich, *The Solace of Open Spaces*)

Exercises ———

1. Speculate in your journal on some of the similarities you have observed between two apparently different activities—eating and sleeping, talking and listening, reading and running. Arrange the points of your comparison in a list and then freewrite about the specific advantages and disadvantages of presenting your information according to one of the two patterns.

2. Read through several popular magazines looking for common comparisons between people and animals: the lawyer is as sly as a fox, the doctor is as busy as a beaver, the tennis player moves like a gazelle, the two political candidates are in a real dogfight, and so on. Develop an extended comparison to show how the comparison to animals may elevate or demean the true character of the two subjects.

WHAT KIND OF SUBDIVISION DOES IT CONTAIN? *Classification*

Classification organizes information into groups and categories. An effective classification begins by defining a subject and then dividing it into major categories based on a common trait. The categories are then arranged in a sequence that shows that the division is *consistent* (the same principle is used to classify each category), *complete* (no major categories are omitted), and *significant* (categories and subcategories are arranged in an order that demonstrates some purpose).

Classification, like comparison, builds on your readers' expectations for precision, balance, and order. Call your readers' attention to the principle you have used to classify each category, or clearly imply it, and devote approximately the same amount of space to each category. Finally, arrange your categories and subpoints clearly and logically so that your reader is able to follow your system.

In the following excerpts Desmond Morris employs these strategies to establish three kinds of territories people define and defend:

Establishes three kinds of territory.

A territory is defended space. In the broadest sense, there are three kinds of human territory: tribal, family and personal. . . .

Arranges categories in logical sequence (largest to smallest).

First: the Tribal Territory. We evolved as tribal animals, living in comparatively small groups, probably of less than a hundred, and we existed like that for millions of years. It is our basic social unit, a group in which everyone knows everyone else. Essentially, the tribal territory consisted of a home base surrounded by extended hunting grounds. Any neighbouring tribe intruding on our social space would be repelled and driven away. As these early tribes swelled into agricultural super-tribes, and eventually into industrial nations, their territorial defence systems became increasingly elaborate. The tiny, ancient home base of the hunting tribe became the great capital city, the primitive war-paint became the flags, emblems, uniforms and regalia of the specialized military, and the war-chants became national anthems, marching songs and bugle calls. Territorial boundary-lines hardened into fixed borders, often conspicuously patrolled and punctuated with defensive structures—forts and lookout posts, checkpoints and great walls, and, today, customs barriers. . . .

Second: the Family Territory. Essentially, the family is a breeding unit and the family territory is a breeding ground. At the centre of this space, there is the nest—the bedroom—where, tucked up in bed, we feel at our most territorially secure. In a typical house the bedroom is upstairs, where a safe nest should be. This puts it farther away from the entrance hall, the area where contact is made, intermittently, with the outside world. The less private reception rooms, where intruders are allowed access, are the next line of defence. Beyond them, outside the walls of the building, there is often a symbolic remnant of the ancient feeding grounds—a garden. Its symbolism often extends to the plants and animals it contains, which cease to be nutritional and become merely decorative—flowers and pets. But like a true territorial space it has a conspicuously displayed boundary-line, the garden fence, wall, or railings. . . .

Presents the same kind of information to distinguish each territory.

Third: the Personal Space. If a man enters a waiting-room and sits at one end of a long row of empty chairs, it is possible to predict where the next man to enter will seat himself. He will not sit next to the first man, nor will he sit at the far end, right away from him. He will choose a position about halfway between these two points. The next man to enter will take the largest gap left, and sit roughly in the middle of that, and so on, until eventually the latest newcomer will be forced to select a seat that places him right next to one of the already seated men. Similar patterns can be observed in cinemas, public urinals, aeroplanes, trains and buses. This is a reflection of the fact that we all carry with us, everywhere we go, a portable territory called Personal Space. If people move inside this space, we feel threatened. If they keep too far outside it, we feel rejected. (Desmond Morris, "Territorial Behaviour," *Manwatching*)

Jane was fascinated by the many types of whales. The books she read emphasized their physical differences, and Richard, who had studied many individual whales, helped her understand their behavioral idiosyncrasies. During planning, Jane tries to combine her sources to classify whales according to their "personalities."

1. How does Jane attempt to establish the completeness of her classification?

2. How does she avoid the apparent contradiction in her system?

3. What is significant about the sequence in which she presents her categories?

Although there are over one hundred kinds of whales in the world (and even more names to designate each kind), most whales can be classified into three major categories. The gregarious whales are outgoing, curious, and friendly toward people. This category includes extroverts, like the humpback, who have baleen and feed off microscopic marine life, and acrobats, like the porpoises, who have teeth and eat small fish. The aggressive whales are formidable, ornery, and dangerous. This category includes killer whales, who hunt in packs, stalking all sorts of marine life from penguins to baby blue whales, and sperm whales, who hunt alone, devouring such impressive prey as octopi, and who have been known to ram ships. The shy whales are solitary, enigmatic, and unpredictable. This category includes whales like the finback, who seem indifferent to other whales as well as to people, and the blue whale, who has been hunted to near-extinction by those eager to kill the world's largest creature.

Exercises ————

1. Interview friends or family members about their behavior in certain types of territory—tribal, family, personal. What special techniques have they discovered for claiming and defending space with "signals rather than fists"?

2. Read about an established method for classifying information, such as categories for rating films or the procedure for naming plants. Then devise a principle that will enable you to simplify and streamline the system.

HOW WOULD YOU CHARACTERIZE IT? *Definition*

Definition provides a necessary explanation of a word or concept. The explanation may be a simple substitution of a familiar for an unfamiliar word, as when you substitute *cancer* for *carcinoma*. It may be the addition of a phrase, as when you follow *vintage* with "the yield of wine or grapes from a particular vineyard or district during one season." It may be a single sentence: "In the theater, a *prompter* is a person who provides cues for the actors or singers on stage." Or a definition may consist of one or more paragraphs, or even a whole essay, in which you explain your subject, such as *tradition* or *excellence*, in some depth.

Definitions may be short, stipulative, or extended. *Short* definitions, like the definition of *carcinoma, vintage,* and *prompter,* provide brief explanations similar to those in your dictionary. *Stipulative* definitions specify the exact meaning or sense of a word as you intend to use it in your writing. Some words may have favorable or unfavorable connotations, depending on the audience. In a political election, for example, a candidate, on being called *liberal,* might reply, "Yes, I am a liberal, but only in the true sense of the word. It originally meant *free,* and I believe in the freedom of individuals to think, speak, and act according to their consciences." The candidate is emphasizing one meaning and excluding others. Such definitions enable your readers to see the purpose of your words. The definition of *purpose* on page 13 is another example of a stipulative definition.

Extended definitions, usually long pieces of writing, explain a writer's view of a subject, sometimes using short or stipulative definitions but going far beyond both. The writer adds to, modifies, and illustrates the basic definition. Any pattern of development may be used: comparison of a word's synonym, for example, or an analysis of changes in its meaning. Cultural geographer Yi-Fu Tuan combines different strategies in his extended definition of *fear*.

What is fear? It is a complex feeling of which two strains, alarm and anxiety, are clearly distinguishable. Alarm is triggered by an obtrusive event in the environment, and an animal's instinctive response is to combat it or run. Anxiety, on the other hand, is a diffuse sense of dread and presupposes an ability to anticipate. It commonly occurs when an animal is in a strange and disorienting milieu, separated from the supportive objects and figures of its home ground. Anxiety is a presentiment of danger when nothing in the immediate surroundings can be pinpointed as dangerous. The need for decisive action is checked by the lack of any specific circumventable threat.

Alarm and anxiety are exhibited in all higher animals. Human beings have much in common with other primates both in the causes of these sensations and in their subsequent behavioral response. Where humans differ from other species, the reason lies in their greater emotional range and superior mind.

Emotional range is a gauge of the nervous system's complexity and hence, indirectly, of the mind. A jellyfish's repertoire of emotions is very limited compared with that of a complex animal like the rabbit, and the rabbit's range of feeling is narrow compared with that of a human being. An animal perhaps knows anger and sadness, but can it be wistful or melancholic? It shows alarm and signs of anxiety, but does it stand in dread of humiliation, of being shamed by its peers? A capacity for shame and guilt adds greatly to the scope of human fear. Can an animal living in its natural setting experience the macabre and the uncanny? Awareness of preternatural evil, unique to the human species, enables a person to see and live in phantasmagorical worlds of witches, ghosts, and monsters; these figures embody a weight of dread unknown to other animals. Fear of betrayal by a relative or friend is very different from fear of an enemy outside the familiar circle. Imagination adds immeasurably to the kinds and intensity of fear in the human world. (Yi-Fu Tuan, *Landscapes of Fear*)

During Jane's whale-watching experience, she encountered many unusual words. She had heard some of them before (*breeching, spouting*) but did not appreciate their true significance until she saw the actions they identified. Others she heard for the first time on the *Portuguese Princess* (*krill, baleen*), grasping their meaning as Richard explained them. But one term, *gam*, was used without explanation. In reviewing her notes, she found the word popped up again, prompting her to research and meditate on its meaning in the following definition:

When Herman Melville used the word <u>gam</u> in <u>Moby Dick</u>, he was certain he was the first writer to define it: "you might wear out your index finger running up and down the columns of dictionaries and never find the word." But he was equally certain that the word needed an official definition because it "has now for many years been in constant use among fifteen thousand true born Yankees" (Herman Melville, "The Gam," <u>Moby Dick</u>). Perhaps because of Melville, the word now appears in most dictionaries. <u>Gam</u>, like its equally unusual synonyms <u>pod</u> and <u>school</u>, refers to a herd of whales. By extension, <u>gam</u> refers to a meeting of two or more whaling ships at sea. Its precise origin is unknown, but some speculate that the word derives from <u>gammon</u>, a little-used word for talk or chatter. And that's what whales and whalers do when they <u>gam</u>. They socialize. Whales seem to enjoy each other's company as they feed. And whalers, once they meet at sea, stop the hunt, visit between ships, and settle down to food and conversation.

3. How do her closing examples extend the definition?

Exercises —— —

1. Select a common word, such as *stress,* that seems to have many subtle meanings. Freewrite a few simple definitions: "Stress is . . ." Next, try a few negative definitions: "Stress is not . . ." Then look up the word in a dictionary to determine its precise meaning.
2. Select an unusual word that puzzled you when you first heard or read it. Interview several "authorities" about what the word might mean. Check the word in several dictionaries (especially a historical dictionary such as the *Oxford English Dictionary*). Then prepare your own extended definition.

WHY DID IT HAPPEN? *Causal Analysis*

Causal analysis, like process analysis, details a sequence of steps that produce a result. But rather than describing these steps, causal analysis examines them for *causes* and *effects.* Such an analysis can be developed in three ways: by describing an action or event and then demonstrating the effect; by describing an action or event and then determining its cause; or by examining two related actions or events and proving a cause-and-effect connection between them.

In each case, you must be careful not to exaggerate or oversimplify the cause-and-effect relationship. You may mistake coincidence for cause, or you may identify one cause as *the* direct cause when any number of complex causes (working independently or in combination) could have produced the same effect. In the following passage Alan Devoe analyzes the many causes of hibernation:

Suggests possible causes

1. cold

2. diminishing food supply

3. increased darkness

4. silence

The season of hibernating begins quite early for some of the creatures of outdoors. It is not alone the cold which causes it; there are a multiplicity of other factors—diminishing food supply; increased darkness as the fall days shorten; silence—frequently decisive. Any or all of these may be the signal for entrance into the Long Sleep, depending upon the habits and make-up of the particular creature. Among the skunks, it is usually the coming of the cold that sends them, torpid, to their root-lined underground burrows; but many other mammals (for instance, ground squirrels) begin to grow drowsy when the fall sun is still warm on their furry backs and the food supply is not at all diminished. This ground-squirrel kind of hibernating, independent of the weather and the

Supplies another cause

5. instinctual behavior presents new effect for investigators.

food supply, may be an old race habit, an instinctual behavior pattern like the unaccountable migrations of certain birds. Weather, food, inheritance, darkness—all of these obscurely play their parts in bringing on the annual subsidence into what one biologist has called "the little death." Investigation of the causes will need a good many years before they can be understood, for in captivity, where observation is more easy than in the wild, the hibernators often do not sleep at all. (Alan Devoe, *Lives Around Us*)

Her first whale watch had a profound effect on Jane, and as she read more about whale watching, she realized that many other people had had similarly significant experiences. In fact, she speculates that whale watching has produced three important effects.

1. How does Jane account for the origin of whale watching?

2. What have been the three main effects of this popularity?

3. Why is the third effect potentially the most important?

Since its inception over a decade ago, whale watching has become a major industry. It began as a scientific enterprise as marine biologists, concerned about extinction, attempted to chart the feeding and migrating patterns of whales. The biologists soon became so adept at sighting whales and so enthusiastic about what they saw that they offered the experience to the public, producing three significant effects. First, whale watching has become an enormously popular recreational experience. The exhilarating voyage out to sea, the spectacular acrobatics of the whales, and the sensation of seeing something extraordinary rivals the best rides at Disneyland. Second, whale watching has increased public awareness about preservation. Once people have seen the power, grace, and agility of whales, they can never again be indifferent to their wholesale slaughter. Third, whale watching in America has become so profitable that entrepreneurs are trying to convince the nations that still hunt whales, such as Japan and the Soviet Union, that there is more money to be made in watching whales than in killing them.

Exercises ———

1. Analyze the possible causes for one of your common problems, such as occasional insomnia or headaches. Read a general reference work, such as *The Columbia Medical Encyclopedia,* to identify some probable causes. Then interview others who are afflicted by the same problem to see how they explain its causes.

2. Speculate on the possible effects that some dramatic change might have on your life. For example, how would one of the following events affect your life?
   a. Purchasing an expensive camera.
   b. Studying in another country (such as Kenya or New Zealand) for a semester.
   c. Acquiring a new pet.
   d. Working in a zoo.

Exploring Methods of Development on Your Computer

Use your subject as a prompt to explore various methods of discovering and arranging information in your draft. Begin with the question (What is it? How do you do it? Why did it happen?) that got you started, and develop your writing according to the method it suggests (definition, process analysis, causal analysis). Save this first draft, and then study it for questions your readers might have about various aspects of your subject (What does it look like? How is it similar or different? What kind of subdivision does it contain?). Mark the passages that prompt these questions. Then move down the screen and draft your answer to each question by using the appropriate pattern (description, comparison, classification). Insert each block of new information into the draft at the spot where you marked the question. Determine whether this additional text—or some revised version of it—helps or detours your readers. Another way to use this new material is to print all your answers, shuffle them, and then read them several times as different texts. If one of these answers seems to reshape the purpose of your essay, compose another draft, using the new method to develop a dominant plan for your essay. Use other portions of your new material to answer your readers' questions about your subject.

Animals in Transit | Peter Singer

In this passage from *Animal Liberation,* animal rights activist Peter Singer explains how animals react to being transported across the country in trucks. What is the dominant pattern in this passage? What other patterns does Singer use to develop his explanation? How does his explanation make you react to the last sentence in the passage?

A nimals placed in a truck for the first time in their lives are likely to be   1
frightened, especially if they have been handled hastily and roughly by the men loading the truck. The motion of the truck is also a new experience, and one which may make them ill. After one or two days in the truck without food or water they are desperately thirsty and hungry. Normally cattle eat frequently thoughout the day; their special stomachs require a constant intake of food if the rumen is to function properly. If the journey is in winter, subzero winds can result in severe chill; in summer the heat and sun may add to the dehydration caused by the lack of water. It is difficult for us to imagine what this combination of fear, travel sickness, thirst, near-starvation, exhaustion, and possibly severe chill feels like to the animals. In the case of young calves who may have gone through the stress of weaning and castration only a few days earlier, the effect is still worse. Veterinary experts recommend that, simply in order to improve their prospects of surviving, young calves should be weaned, castrated, and vaccinated at least thirty days prior to being transported. This gives them a chance to recover from one stressful experience before being subjected to another. These recommendations, however, are not always followed.

Although the animals cannot describe their experiences, the reactions of   2
their bodies tell us something. There are two main reactions: "shrinkage" and "shipping fever." All animals lose weight during transportation. Some of this weight loss is due to dehydration and the emptying of the intestinal tract. This loss is easily regained; but more lasting losses are also the rule. For an eight-hundred-pound steer to lose seventy pounds, or 9 percent of his weight, on a single trip is not unusual; and it may take more than three weeks for the animal to recover the loss. This "shrink," as it is known in the trade, is regarded by researchers as an indication of the stress to which the animal has been subjected. Shrink is, of course, a worry to the meat industry, since animals are sold by the pound.

"Shipping fever," a form of pneumonia that strikes cattle after they have   3
been transported, is the other major indicator of stress in transportation. Shipping fever is associated with a virus that healthy cattle have no difficulty in resisting; severe stress, however, weakens their resistance.

Shrinkage and susceptibility to fever are indications that the animals have   4
been subjected to extreme stress; but the animals who shrink and get shipping fever are the ones who survive. Others die before reaching their destination, or arrive with broken limbs or other injuries. In 1986, USDA inspectors condemned over 7,400 cattle, 3,100 calves, and 5,500 pigs because they were dead

Singer, Peter. *Animal Liberation.* 2nd ed. New York: Random, 1990. 148–50.

"I'd like to hear less talk about animal rights and more talk about animal responsibilities."

Drawing by Lorenz; © 1990 The New Yorker Magazine, Inc.

or seriously injured before they reached the slaughterhouse, while 570,000 cattle, 57,000 calves, and 643,000 pigs were injured severely enough for parts of their bodies to be condemned.

Animals who die in transit do not die easy deaths. They freeze to death in winter and collapse from thirst and heat exhaustion in summer. They die, lying unattended in stockyards, from injuries sustained in falling off a slippery loading ramp. They suffocate when other animals pile on top of them in overcrowded, badly loaded trucks. They die from thirst or starve when careless stockmen forget to give them food or water. And they die from the sheer stress of the whole terrifying experience. The animal that you may be having for dinner tonight did not die in any of these ways; but these deaths are and always have been part of the overall process that provides people with their meat. 5

Watching Whales | Jane Graham

Jane Graham's final essay incorporates much of the writing she developed during planning and drafting. Read her essay and then review her experiments with various patterns throughout the chapter. What patterns has she reshaped, relocated, or eliminated during revising? Is the dominant structure of her essay the most effective method for accomplishing her purpose? Explain your answer.

The problem with whales is that they don't fit under a microscope. As a small girl, I walked around and around the large skeleton of a blue whale on the first floor of the American Museum of Natural History, trying to compare its size to the skeletons of the brontosaurus and diplodocus I had seen on the fourth floor. Like those creatures from another time, whales challenged and held my imagination. I could never see enough of them. The drawings in textbooks outlined their shape but reduced their enormous size to a few inches. The photographs in magazines suggested their magnificence but usually focused on their parts—the head rising to breech, the tail arching to dive. Last summer, hoping to see more, I booked passage on the *Portuguese Princess* out of Provincetown, Massachusetts, for my first whale watch.

A motley crowd assembled on MacMillan Pier in the early morning mist. Seasoned whale watchers checked their binoculars, cameras, and lens cases. Casual tourists chased after wayward children, counted their supply of Dramamine, and looked anxiously at the *Princess* as it creaked and groaned against its moorings. Various members of the crew, dressed in T-shirts and cutoffs, peered into the engine hole or studied the sighting charts stacked on the elevated table behind the wheel house. The haunting sounds of whale songs were piped through the mist by the boat's loud-speaker system. Soon, Richard, a marine biologist, dressed like the crew but wearing a Red Sox cap, walked out of the mist and jumped aboard. He checked the charts for a few minutes and then picked up a clipboard to call the seventy names on his new manifest.

I crossed the gangplank and took a position forward, away from the engine, knowing that the combination of gasoline fumes and rolling seas could make me sick. The engine sputtered to life, drowning out the whale songs and the nervous chatter of passengers. As the *Princess* plowed out of the harbor, I looked back to watch Provincetown disappear. The streets crowded with gawking summer people blurred, and the silhouette of the old fishing village—shacks resting on huge pilings, seagulls diving behind weathered boats—lingered briefly on the horizon.

"We're headed for Stellwagen Bank," Richard announced from his perch behind the wheel house. "This is an area of shallow water and undersea crags that attracts microscopic marine life, plankton, and krill, the staple diet of many whales, especially the humpbacks. Humpbacks are baleen whales. They do not hunt, kill, and devour. Instead of teeth, they have baleen, long strands of tissue that hang from their upper jaws. They sift their food through this tissue by swimming, mouth open, through tons of water. When they close their mouths, the water strains back through the baleen, and they swallow the remaining food in gigantic gulps."

The mist had cleared, the sun burned my neck, and a cold, salty spray occasionally splashed my face as the *Princess* headed into the wind for the next half hour. The passengers talked, gestured and looked for signs. "I've watched all the Cousteau specials," a New Hampshire bride was telling me when Richard yelled, "Thar she blows! Off the port bow! There!" We followed his finger, focusing binoculars, twisting telephoto lenses, straining to see what he had seen in the dark blue swells. Against the skyline, I saw it. A definite vertical spray. Then a pause. Then another.

I was actually seeing two sprays, one from each of the whale's spouts or nostrils. Whales are mammals and so, like us, cannot breathe under water. They store air in their lungs before they dive and then "blow" it out their spouts when they surface. This whale was diving and blowing steadily, heading away from Stellwagen Bank. Richard tried to identify its flukes, the large flippers at the end of its tail. The patterns and notches on a whale's flukes are like fingerprints, enabling expert whale watchers to identify individual whales. But this whale, swimming intently toward some destination, was too far away for even Richard to see its colors.

The *Princess* churned on for another thirty minutes. Suddenly, the captain killed the engine. "We're here." And so were they. As we drifted, several sets of feeding humpbacks swam into view. A mother, her calf beside her, dived, surfaced, and waved her flukes in a perfect vertical before diving again. Her calf, eager to imitate, tried the same maneuver over and over, but his tail and flukes flopped sideways at the last minute like a sloppy cartwheel. At our stern, an obstreperous male leaped totally out of the water and then fell sideways with an impressive clap. I could see his huge, vulnerable underbelly and the white undersides of his long flippers. When he burst out of the water, he held his flippers at a slight angle to his side. As he descended, he moved them gracefully away from his body like the arms of a ballerina finishing a pirouette.

After an hour of dashing around the deck, elbowing my way to the rail, and snapping pictures of everything I could see, I thought I had seen enough. Other excursion boats and private craft had slowly encircled the feeding whales. Shortwave radios crackled: "Look to the west. A male is breeching." "Over to the south. Two bachelors are gamming." "In the center. The mother and calf are resting." The noise prompted thoughts of other messages delivered on distant seas: "Finback, south, southwest. Lower the boats. Aim the harpoon." Richard had apparently seen enough as well. The engine erupted, and the *Princess* began to turn. I looked forward, trying to sort it all out—the graceful, powerful gentleness of the whales; the curious, careless intrusiveness of the whale watchers. Why couldn't we simply watch? Why did people have to hunt, kill, and destroy?

The engine stopped. Richard's voice came over the loud-speaker in an excited, controlled whisper. "There's a finback heading toward us. He's way off course. Finbacks are shy and solitary. They're still hunted and so usually stay clear of boats. If we're quiet, we may see something rare." Seventy watchers became still. The *Princess* rolled on four-foot swells. Soon we saw him—a sea-green monolith, his huge bulk silhouetted several feet beneath the surface. His distinguishing fin was mottled in patterns of white and gray. He was swimming purposefully toward us. We were obviously in his path, but not in his way. He was silent. We were silent. Closer, closer, and then under. More silence. I rushed to the other side. His green head exploded through the surface twenty feet away. One large, watery eye looked back at me before he arched his body into the sea. He swam in a straight line for a couple of hundred yards, blew, and then sounded.

Although we watched eagerly for him to surface again, we looked in vain. Soon we began to look at one another. We smiled, but we did not talk. Neither did Richard. No explanation was necessary. We had watched a whale. A whale had watched us. Finally, the engine coughed, and the *Portuguese Princess* resumed her journey back to Provincetown.

Grizzly | John McPhee

Reread John McPhee's comments on how he organizes his writing (page 104) then read this passage from *Coming into the Country*. As you read this selection, identify McPhee's predominant pattern and the way he employs other patterns to enhance his purpose. Which pattern seems to emerge naturally from the material? Which pattern seems to be imposed on the material?

We passed first through stands of fireweed, and then over ground that was   1
wine-red with the leaves of bearberries. There were curlewberries, too,
which put a deep-purple stain on the hand. We kicked at some wolf scat, old
as winter. It was woolly and white and filled with the hair of a snowshoe hare.
Nearby was a rich inventory of caribou pellets and, in increasing quantity as we
moved downhill, blueberries—an outspreading acreage of blueberries. Fedeler
stopped walking. He touched my arm. He had in an instant become even more
alert than he usually was, and obviously apprehensive. His gaze followed straight
on down our intended course. What he saw there I saw now. It appeared to me to
be a hill of fur. "Big boar grizzly," Fedeler said in a near-whisper. The bear was
about a hundred steps away, in the blueberries, grazing. The head was down, the
hump high. The immensity of muscle seemed to vibrate slowly—to expand and
contract, with the grazing. Not berries alone but whole bushes were going into
the bear. He was big for a barren-ground grizzly. The brown bears of Arctic
Alaska (or grizzlies; they are no longer thought to be different) do not grow to the
size they will reach on more ample diets elsewhere. The barren-ground grizzly
will rarely grow larger than six hundred pounds.

"What if he got too close?" I said.   2
Fedeler said, "We'd be in real trouble."   3
"You can't outrun them," Hession said.   4

A grizzly, no slower than a racing horse, is about half again as fast as the   5
fastest human being. Watching the great mound of weight in the blueberries,
with a fifty-five-inch waist and a neck more than thirty inches around, I had difficulty imagining that he could move with such speed, but I believed it, and was
without impulse to test the proposition. Fortunately, a light southerly wind was
coming up the Salmon valley. On its way to us, it passed the bear. The wind was
relieving, coming into our faces, for had it been moving the other way, the bear
would not have been placidly grazing. There is an old adage that when a pine
needle drops in the forest the eagle will see it fall; the deer will hear it when it
hits the ground; the bear will smell it. If the boar grizzly were to catch our scent,
he might stand on his hind legs, the better to try to see. Although he could hear
well and had an extraordinary sense of smell, his eyesight was not much better
than what was required to see a blueberry inches away. For this reason, a grizzly
stands and squints, attempting to bring the middle distance into focus, and the
gesture is often misunderstood as a sign of anger and forthcoming attack. If the
bear were getting ready to attack, he would be on four feet, head low, ears
cocked, the hair above his hump muscle standing on end. As if that message
were not clear enough, he would also chop his jaws. His teeth would make a
sound that would carry like the ringing of an axe.

One could predict, but not with certainty, what a grizzly would do. Odds   6
were very great that one touch of man scent would cause him to stop his activity,
pause in a moment of absorbed and alert curiosity, and then move, at a not
undignified pace, in a direction other than the one from which the scent was
coming. That is what would happen almost every time, but there was, to be sure,
no guarantee. The forest Eskimos fear and revere the grizzly. They know that certain individual bears not only will fail to avoid a person who comes into their
country but will approach and even stalk the trespasser. It is potentially inaccurate to extrapolate the behavior of any one bear from the behavior of most, since

McPhee, John. *Coming into the Country*. New York: Farrar. 1976. 58–65.

they are both intelligent and independent and will do what they choose to do according to mood, experience, whim. A grizzly that has ever been wounded by a bullet will not forget it, and will probably know that it was a human being who sent the bullet. At sight of a human, such a bear will be likely to charge. Grizzlies hide food sometimes—a caribou calf, say, under a pile of scraped-up moss—and a person the bear might otherwise ignore might suddenly not be ignored if the person were inadvertently to step into the line between the food cache and the bear. A sow grizzly with cubs, of course, will charge anything that suggests danger to the cubs, even if the cubs are nearly as big as she is. They stay with their mother two and a half years. . . .

If a wolf kills a caribou, and a grizzly comes along while the wolf is feeding   7
on the kill, the wolf puts its tail between its legs and hurries away. A black bear will run from a grizzly, too. Grizzlies sometimes kill and eat black bears. The grizzly takes what he happens upon. He is an opportunistic eater. The predominance of the grizzly in his terrain is challenged by nothing but men and ravens. To frustrate ravens from stealing his food, he will lie down and sleep on top of a carcass, occasionally swatting the birds as if they were big black flies. He prefers a vegetable diet. He can pulp a moosehead with a single blow, but he is not lusting always to kill, and when he moves through his country he can be something munificent, going into copses of willow among unfleeing moose and their calves, touching nothing, letting it all breathe as before. He may, though, get the head of a cow moose between his legs and rake her flanks with the five-inch knives that protrude from the ends of his paws. Opportunistic. He removes and eats her entrails. He likes porcupines, too, and when one turns and presents to him a pygal bouquet of quills, he will leap into the air, land on the other side, chuck the fretful porpentine beneath the chin, flip it over, and with a swift ventral incision, neatly remove its body from its skin, leaving something like a sea urchin behind him on the ground. He is nothing if not athletic. Before he dens, or just after he emerges, if his mountains are covered with snow he will climb to the brink of some impossible schuss, sit down on his butt, and shove off. Thirty-two, sixty-four, ninety-six feet per second, he plummets down the mountainside, spray snow flying to either side, as he approaches collision with boulders and trees. Just short of catastrophe, still going at bonecrushing speed, he flips to his feet and walks sedately onward as if his ride had not occurred.

His population density is thin on the Arctic barren ground. He needs for   8
his forage at least fifty and perhaps a hundred square miles that are all his own—sixty-four thousand acres, his home range. Within it, he will move, typically, eight miles a summer day, doing his travelling through the twilight hours of the dead of night. To scratch his belly he walks over a tree—where forest exists. The tree bends beneath him as he passes. He forages in the morning, generally; and he rests a great deal, particularly after he eats. He rests fourteen hours a day. If he becomes hot in the sun, he lies down in a pool in the river. He sleeps on the tundra—restlessly tossing and turning, forever changing position. What he could be worrying about I cannot imagine.

His fur blends so well into the tundra colors that sometimes it is hard to see   9
him. Fortunately, we could see well enough the one in front of us, or we would have walked right to him. He caused a considerable revision of our travel plans. Not wholly prepared to follow the advice of Andy Russell, I asked Fedeler what one should do if a bear were to charge. He said, "Take off your pack and throw it into the bear's path, then crawl away, and hope the pack will distract the bear. But there is no good thing to do, really. It's just not a situation to be in."

Writing Assignments

Narrate   **1.**   Freewrite in your journal about your memories of a specific animal you remember from books (*The Black Stallion*), films (*Gorillas in the Mist*), or television ("The Muppets"). List those features that encouraged you to identify with the animal. Then write a narrative that records your adventures with this imaginary companion.

Observe   **2.**   Keep a log in which you list the various ways people respond to your pet or to an animal you know. In particular, describe the tone of voice, body language, and emotional temperament that signals whether people are frightened or relaxed by the presence of an animal. Then write an essay in which you classify the types of responses you have observed.

Investigate   **3.**   Interview faculty and students who work with laboratory animals. You may want to contrast those who simply observe animal responses with those who dissect animals. Develop your interview notes into a profile that documents the use of laboratory animals on your campus.

Collaborate   **4.**   Most universities have a formal policy governing the use of animals in laboratory experiments. Your writing group has been asked to revise that policy. Read the policy carefully, then ask members of your group to conduct more interviews (with faculty researchers and animal rights advocates) and to read more documents (policies from other research institutions and criticism from activists like Peter Singer). Then revise or defend your university's policy.

Read   **5.**   Read some articles and books on the history (and philosophy) of zoos (e.g., H. Hediger, *Man and Animal in the Zoo*, or Virginia McKenna *et al.*, eds., *Beyond the Bars*). Visit a zoo in your area. Talk to attendants and visitors. Finally, write an analysis, based on personal experience and historical documentation, that speculates on the causes and effects of zoos in our culture.

Respond   **6.**   Respond to Peter Singer's analysis of the "process that provides people with their meat." You may want to interview ranchers who raise cattle or doctors who recommend vegetarian diets. In either case, you are looking for information that will help you understand your attitude toward eating meat.

Analyze   **7.**   Analyze the way Jane Graham expands, contrasts, or relocates her experiments with the common patterns of development in her essay. Jane's essay seems to be driven by a narrative question: What happened. What other questions emerge as the result of her attempt to tell what happened? How do those questions affect Jane's overall purpose? You may want to alter this assignment by using one of Jane's experiments as a prompt to write a longer essay of your own.

Evaluate   **8.**   Compare and contrast the attitudes expressed by Jane Graham and Francine duPlessix Gray toward animal watching. What motivates each of them to watch? Why does Gray (and her guide) object to the watching? Why does Jane (and her guide) savor it? Evaluate each writer's perspective in relation to each other or write an essay suggesting a third.

Argue 9. Compare John McPhee's comments on structure (page 104) and his commentary on the grizzly bear. Then argue that McPhee's comments do or do not help explain the method(s) of development he uses in the selection.

Argue 10. Using the information gathered from your reading or experience, argue for or against a "wilderness ethic" that forbids people from studying, managing, and altering the behavior of animals.

6 | **Argument**

Argument, in a sense, underlies all writing. In expressing your ideas, no matter what method or combination of methods you use, you are "arguing" some point about your subject. In Chapter 5, for example, each of Jane Graham's writing ventures attempts to demonstrate a certain thesis: whales can be understood best when seen at sea; whales may seem threatening but are really gentle; whale watching has helped increase public support for whale preservation. Jane uses these informal arguments to advance her primary purpose—explaining her impressions of a whale watch.

Formal arguments, too, commonly employ expository patterns to convey information. But because their primary purpose is to convince others—to accept a proposal, to challenge a situation, to support some cause—formal arguments must be developed according to rules of evidence and logical reasoning. These demands may seem formidable, but in many ways they are simply extensions of what you have learned about those elements that govern the writing process.

You begin composing an argument by planning, by investigating a variety of sources so that you can discover a subject. Next, you organize your argument into a draft so that it most effectively and fully expresses your subject to persuade your audience. Finally, you examine your text to revise those features that obscure the clarity or weaken the credibility of your purpose.

As you move through these stages, you will expand your appreciation of other arguments (particularly those of the opposition), develop your authority to present those features of your argument that matter most, and increase your understanding of those aspects of your argument or your opponent's argument that might be negotiated or that might never be resolved.

INVESTIGATING THE ARGUMENT: *Planning*

In planning an argument, you *select a subject, collect and use evidence,* and *consider the opposition.*

Selecting a Subject

Not every subject can be treated in a formal argument. Common sense tells you that there is no point in arguing about *facts*. You may like to argue about when the Red Sox last won the World Series or how many times Katharine Hepburn has won an Oscar, but such trivial disputes can be settled quickly by looking up the correct answer in an almanac. You may like to argue that chocolate chocolate chip is the best flavor of ice cream in the world or that all politicians are corrupt—but these assertions are merely *opinions,* based on preference (or prejudice) rather than evidence.

A formal argument must focus on a subject that can be debated. Such subjects are open to interpretation because opposing opinions can be supported with evidence and the audience is free to consider both claims and to choose sides.

As you think about possible subjects for an argument, review "Guidelines for Selecting Your Subject" in Chapter 1 (page 9). Your subject should be one you know something about, consider interesting and significant, and can restrict to a manageable size. When you develop your subject into an argument, you will need to view it as a controversy with at least two contending sides. What you know about a subject (or what you can find out about it) will lead you to take a side. But to convince your readers that yours is the right side (or at least the better side), you will need to support your position.

Exercise ———— Matt Fisher is an older student who, after working for several years in a factory, has returned to college to study pre-law. In his business-law course, he is asked to write an argument about a controversy in the work place. Read his list of potential subjects and identify those that are (a) facts, (b) opinions, or (c) open to debate. Explain your choices.

1. Unions have ruined free enterprise in America.

2. Random drug testing is an invasion of privacy.

3. The cost of health care for alcoholics and their families is double that for nonalcoholics and their families.

4. Workers on the day shift are more conscientious than those on the night shift.

5. Less than 10 percent of the upper management of America's major corporations belongs to a minority group.

Collecting and Using Evidence

Once you have selected a subject, start gathering evidence. You might begin by making lists or freewriting in your journal. Such activities help you identify what you already know (or think you know) about your subject, but eventually you will need to expand and deepen your knowledge by conducting some research. Anna Quindlen, a columnist for the *New York Times,* suggests that an effective investigation requires several planning strategies:

> I begin by reading, reading, reading. I have to understand my subject before I interview people, otherwise I won't understand the terms they use or the

issues they raise. Also, I have to understand where they're coming from. You need to watch out for those red flags, those people on one side of an argument who distort issues by making highly inflammatory statements. Sometimes you can catch their bias when you ask other people to comment on their remarks. So much of reporting is bouncing from one person to another, trying to get all sides of the story. You never get it all. You simply run out of time. (Personal interview)

Whatever planning strategy you use, follow Quindlen's advice and collect information from all sides of the issue, not just your side. The most common kinds of evidence are *facts*, *judgments*, and *testimony*.

Facts   Facts are a valuable ally in building an argument because they cannot be debated. It is a fact that the stock marked crashed on October 29, 1929. It is a fact that the Dow Jones Industrial Average first exceeded 3000 on April 17, 1991. But not all facts are so clear-cut, and some statements that look like facts may not be facts. A stock analyst who announces a company's projected earnings for the next five years is making an estimate, not a statement of fact.

Judgments   Judgments are conclusions inferred from facts. Unlike opinions, judgments lend credibility to an argument because they result from careful reasoning. A doctor considering a patient's symptoms reaches a tentative diagnosis of either tuberculosis or a tumor. If a laboratory test eliminates tuberculosis, then the patient probably has a tumor that is either malignant or benign, questions that can be settled by surgery. The doctor's judgment emerges from the following chain of reasoning:

1. *The patient's symptoms are caused by tuberculosis or a tumor.*
   This diagnosis is based on knowledge of the symptoms of or facts about the two conditions.

2. *The patient does not have tuberculosis.*
   This is a judgment based on the results of a laboratory test that produces certain factual information.

3. *The patient has a tumor.*
   This judgment is inferred from the facts of statements 1 and 2.

4. *The patient does not have cancer.*
   This judgment is determined after surgery, which reveals the fact that the tumor is benign.

Testimony   Testimony affirms or asserts facts. A person who has had direct experience (an *eyewitness*) or who has developed expertise in a subject (an *expert witness*) can provide testimony based on fact, judgment, or both. An eyewitness is asked to report facts, as when an observer reports seeing a man drown in strong current. An expert witness is asked to study facts and render a judgment, as when a coroner reports that an autopsy has shown that the victim did not drown but died of a heart attack.

Both kinds of testimony can constitute powerful evidence. Eyewitness testimony provides authenticity. Expert testimony provides authority. Each has its limitations, however. An eyewitness is not always trustworthy; eyewitness testimony can be distorted by faulty observation or biased opinion. An expert witness is not infallible or always unbiased; expert testimony, though often difficult for the nonexpert to challenge, can be disputed by other experts employing a different method of investigation. Each type of testimony can be abused. An eyewitness account of an event may be convincing, but it should not be used to draw parallels to unrelated events. And expert credentials in one field, whatever eminence they convey, do not automatically carry over to other (even related) fields.

Using the Evidence   Evaluate your evidence by determining whether it is *pertinent, verifiable,* and *reliable.* A stock analyst who uses the success of the polio vaccine as a reason for investing in a drug company researching a vaccine for the common cold is not presenting evidence *pertinent* to the argument. A historian who claims that Amelia Earhart's flying ability was impaired by Alzheimer's disease is using an argument that is not *verifiable.* And an attorney who builds a case on the eyewitness testimony of a person who has been arrested several times for public intoxication is not using the most *reliable* evidence (see "Evaluating Sources," Chapter 14).

As you collect your evidence, be careful to identify and record its source. Your readers will want to know where you found the information important to your argument. If you cannot identify your source, your reader may question your knowledgeability. If your information comes from dubious sources, your readers may doubt your credibility. Identify information from printed and other sources in the text of your paper (see "Documenting Sources," Chapter 15).

Exercises ——— Matt has decided to write about drug testing in the work place. During his last year at the factory, the subject became a hot issue in contract negotiations: management proposed random drug testing on the job; the union opposed all forms of drug testing. As he investigated the subject, Matt gathered evidence from many sources. Examine these items from his notes to determine for each: (1) whether it is a fact, a judgment, or eyewitness or expert testimony, and (2) whether it is likely to be *pertinent, verifiable,* and *reliable* evidence.

1. "According to the Research Triangle Institute, a respected North Carolina business-sponsored research organization, drug abuse cost the United States economy $60 billion in 1983, or nearly 30% more than the $47 billion estimated for 1980."
   Castro, Janice. "Battling the Enemy Within." *Time* 17 March 1986:53

2. "Right now, if the foreman doesn't like somebody, he can ask him to take a drug test—claiming probable cause. That makes the guy look suspicious. Even though Fred's test came back clean, everybody said, 'Well, there must be something in it.' That's not fair."
   Factory worker. Personal interview. 10 November 1986.

3. "Employers have always had rules to govern the work place. You can't be late or absent without just cause. There are some capital offenses that are just cause for firing. You can't be intoxicated on the job. Your work is impaired, you jeopardize your co-workers, and you destroy the reliability of the company's product. Testing for drug abuse is just another way to ensure safety in the work place."
   Chief counsel at local factory. Personal interview. 15 November 1986.

4. The Centers for Disease Control reports that in the thirteen laboratories they studied, there was "up to 67% error rate in false positive identification of drugs."
   Hansen, Hugh J. "Crisis in Drug Testing." *Journal of American Medical Association* April 1985: 2382.

5. "An estimated 45% of the Fortune 500 corporations will be involved in drug testing next year."
   Chapman, Fern Schumer: "The Ruckus Over Medical Testing." *Fortune* 19 August 1985: 58

6. "Drug abuse is hard to detect. There's no odor. People seem to act normally. Management wants to use this urine test as a cheap way to see if they have a problem. What if they do? Are they going to invest in a rehabilitation program or just fire people?"
   Local union leader. Personal interview. 12 November 1986.

7. "It costs over $10,000 to hire and train even an entry level employee. For the average employee this cost exceeds $25,000. Before I terminate an employee for drug abuse I need to be confident that he or she is really a drug abuser. I can't afford to fire a productive employee on the basis of a test that isn't much better than flipping a coin."
   Maltby, Lewis L. "An Employer's Perspective." *The Drug Testing Debate: Remedy or Reaction.* Washington, D.C.: American Civil Liberties Union, 1986. 4.

Considering the Opposition

If you have selected a debatable subject and collected a broad range of evidence, you have discovered that controversies are tricky. You may remain convinced that your side is the right side; you may be tempted, given your discovery of new information, to change sides; or you may feel confused as you try to balance the evidence on both sides of the debate. To complete your investigation and test your original position (or to write your way out of your current confusion), you must give serious consideration to the opposition.

Assume the identity of your opposition and draft an argument entitled "Their Side." This planning exercise will enable you to understand the important evidence that makes your opponents' position credible—evidence that you may have to concede when you present your side of the argument. The exercise will also help you to uncover the weak spots in their argument—points that you will have to disguise when you write "Their Side," but points that you can dispute when you write "My Side." And finally, this exercise will encourage you to identify the points, often overlooked in the heat of argument, on which both sides agree.

If you are going to compose an effective "Their Side," you have to be *knowledgeable* and *fair*. You must present your opponents' best arguments in such a way that they would recognize it as a thorough and accurate statement of their position. If you set up a "straw man," presenting your opponents' weakest evidence in the most unfavorable light with the intention of knocking it down, the exercise will not be useful to you. Knowledge of your opponents' best arguments and a sincere effort to avoid bias will help you avoid an unfair, unproductive effort. Common signs of such unfairness are *distortion, slanting,* and *quoting out of context.*

Distortion   You distort your evidence if you intentionally exaggerate your opponents' views. Councilwoman Jones supports Planned Parenthood because the agency provides valuable information on birth control. Councilman Smith distorts his opponent's position by claiming that support for Planned Parenthood is an endorsement of an extreme form of birth control, such as abortion.

Slanting   If you select facts favorable to your position and suppress those unfavorable to it, you are slanting the evidence. A business executive who says there can be no real poverty in a country where the average annual income is $10,000 ignores two facts: (1) the average includes incomes of $1 million or more, and (2) a great many incomes fall far below the average.

Quoting Out of Context   If you remove words deliberately (or carelessly) from their original context and reuse them in a new context that changes their meaning, you are quoting out of context. In reviewing a play, a critic writes: "The plot is fascinating in a strange way: you keep waiting for something to happen, but nothing does. The characters never come close to greatness, and the few witty lines are out of place among the predictable dialogue." An advertisement based on this review quotes out of context if it reads: "Fascinating plot . . . characters close to greatness . . . witty lines."

Exercises ——— When Matt Fisher began his investigation, he was opposed to drug testing in the work place. As a former factory worker, he resisted management's inclination to establish arbitrary rules to control employees. As a pre-law student, he was sensitive to policies that disregarded the rights of the individual. But as he collected more research on drug testing, he tried to assess the power of the opposition by drafting a "Their Side" argument. Discuss whether *those in favor of drug testing* would see Matt's presentation of their position as knowledgeable and fair: (1) What types of evidence does he present? (2) Does this evidence seem to be the best evidence—most *pertinent, verifiable, reliable*? (3) In what sections of the essay might Matt be accused of misrepresenting the opposing position?

Their Side

On January 4, 1987, an Amtrak train traveling north of Balti-   1
more collided with three Conrail engines, causing the worst accident in Amtrak's history. Sixteen passengers were killed, 170 were in-jured, and five locomotives from the two trains were destroyed. Investigators have since discovered that the crew operating the Conrail engines had been using marijuana.

The Amtrak disaster near Baltimore is not an isolated example.   2
Every day news stories report truck drivers in drug-related accidents, air-traffic controllers impaired on the job by drug abuse, and assembly-line workers selling and using drugs in the work place. Dr. Howard Franbrel, medical director at Rockwell, estimates that "20% to 25% of the workers at the plant responsible for the final assembly of the space shuttle were high on drugs, alcohol or both" (Castro 53). The Research Triangle Institute in North Carolina reports that "drug abuse cost the United States economy $60 billion in 1983, or nearly 30% more than the $47 billion estimated for 1980" (Castro 53).

Employers have an obligation to protect the safety of workers,   3
the efficiency of the work place, and the reliability of their products. Workers on drugs are less productive, more likely to harm them-selves or their co-workers, and more likely to steal from their com-pany. Because they are more susceptible to illness, they drive up the premiums of health insurance. And because their errors create flawed products or unreliable services, they increase the probability of lawsuits and the cost of liability insurance.

Fortunately there is a solution to this growing problem: drug   4
testing. Drug testing, particularly urine analysis, is now being used by a large number of corporations to protect the safety of their em-ployees and the investment of their stockholders. An estimated 45%

of Fortune 500 companies will be involved in drug testing by next year (Chapman 57).

There are three basic methods of drug testing currently in use: pre-screening, probable-cause testing, and random/massive testing. Most employers require a physical examination for all job applicants. The additional cost of a pre-employment urine analysis is minimal and well worth the expense since employers can thus identify drug users before they are hired, trained, and become a problem.

The probable-cause method is used when a worker's performance provides sufficient reason to justify a test. Drug abuse is more difficult to detect than alcohol abuse: there is no obvious smell, slurred speech, or red eyes. But there are signs of possible drug abuse: excessive absenteeism, inconsistent work performance, deterioration of personal appearance, severe financial problems, and increased trips to the restroom.

In random or massive testing any part or all of the work force is tested to spot abusers. This is the most costly and controversial of the three methods. Weekly or monthly testing of an entire work force is an enormous investment, but given the pervasiveness of drugs in our society such an investment may prevent a costly accident. There are those who argue that without probable cause, such testing is an invasion of workers' privacy. But if workers are drug free, then requiring such a test is no more an invasion of privacy than requiring protective masks or helmets. If workers are users, then they need to be placed in a rehabilitation program before they endanger themselves or their co-workers.

Employers are in business to make money. To do so, they need a dependable work force. In 1982, an Illinois Central Gulf freight train carrying hazardous chemicals derailed at Livingston, Louisiana, because the engineer, affected by drugs, had fallen asleep. In 1984, a spectacular rear-end collision of two trains near Newcastle, Wyoming, occurred while six of the twelve crew members were using drugs. In July 1984, two Amtrak trains collided in Queens, killing one and injuring 125; traces of marijuana and cocaine were later found in the urine of the track-signal operator. To prevent disasters like these and the one near Baltimore, American industry must adopt a more aggressive drug-testing program.

ORGANIZING THE ARGUMENT: *Drafting*

Once you have completed your preliminary investigation, you need to develop, organize, and draft your argument, following the procedures you learned in Chapters 3, 4, and 5. Anna Quindlen points out that organizing an effective argument is terribly important and terribly difficult:

> Structure is a slippery subject. I usually like to lead with an anecdote, particularly if I can use a quote that works like a punch in the stomach. Also, up front, in what I call my *nut paragraph,* I like to spell out the issues I've discovered. "Where are we going? Where have we been? Have we gone too far?" Then I'll get into an "on the one hand, on the other hand" pattern where I present the sides in the debate. But in a true controversy, the debate is taking place on so many levels—emotional, ethical, social—that I can't choose sides. I switch back and forth and usually wind up somewhere in the middle. (Personal interview)

The final shape of an argument depends, as Quindlen suggests, on a series of interrelated decisions. To make *informed* decisions, you need to *analyze the audience, arrange the evidence,* and *monitor the appeals*

Analyzing the Audience

In the preceding chapters you learned that knowing your audience helps you discover and demonstrate your purpose. This is particularly true in argument because you are attempting to convince your audience to believe in your purpose. To do this, you must assess what potential audiences are likely to know about your subject, what they believe is important in the controversy, and what kind of evidence will influence their judgment.

As Quindlen points out, arguments take place in a context that contains "many levels—emotional, ethical, social." To help you clarify this context and to sort out how your readers might be affected by it, use the advice below in conjunction with "Guidelines for Analyzing Your Audience" in Chapter 1 (pages 12–13).

Identify Specific Readers   You need to identify the specific groups of readers who form the potential audience for your argument. Some may seem in the thick of things—friendly or hostile to your position. Others may seem on the edge—skeptical about any proposal or merely uncommitted. Unfortunately, the sides in controversies are rarely that clear-cut, and your potential audience usually contains many people with uncertain or conflicting views. Identify these specific groups of potential readers for your argument. Then acknowledge their conflicting opinions and anticipate their various objections to your draft.

Identify with Your Readers   The "Their Side" exercise helped you see the debate from the perspective of your opponent. Now, as you identify other readers who have only partial or passing interest in the controversy, place yourself in those positions and assess the issues from those viewpoints. Who are the "friendlies"? What do they know? Who are the skeptics? What makes them resist? Who are the uncommitted? What will make them decide? Such imaginative identification helps you establish the points of conflict and areas of agreement among the various readers in your audience.

Establish Your Identify for Your Readers   In drafting your argument, you inevitably establish an identity (or a *persona*) that reveals to your readers your attitude toward your subject. You should be alert to strategies that strengthen your bond with your readers and avoid tactics that distance you from them. As the "Their Side" exercise helped demonstrate, the most effective arguments consider all sides of a controversy. In arguing, your identity should be that of a "reasonable citizen" who follows a balanced discussion with a thoughtfully rendered judgment. You must consider your readers, too, to be reasonable citizens. However indignant you are about the situation you are writing about, you cannot be indignant with your readers—not if you want their agreement. You can concede or refute certain points, but you cannot flatter or talk down to your readers, or neglect to provide logical proof of your argument—not if you want their respect. You are trying to establish a partnership of mutual inquiry. Anything that distorts your identity in that partnership will destroy your credibility.

Provide Your Readers with Appropriate Evidence   If you respect your readers, you will not ask them to accept unsupported assertions. A business executive would not ask her partners to accept her unsupported word that investing in another company will be profitable. She would provide detailed evidence for their review and would address the particular concerns (management, labor, debt, productivity, competition) of individual partners with appropriate evidence. She may believe the investment is sound, but if she wants to convince her partners, she must supply the right kind of evidence. As a writer of argument, you have an obligation to spell out in detail why you think your readers should accept your conclusion. And you must provide the specific kinds of evidence your readers will find compelling.

Draft an Argument Your Readers Can Read   You are asking your readers to agree with you, so make their job as easy as possible. Highly complex arguments, technical terminology, abstract diction, confusing statistics—all these obstructive elements make communication difficult. You want to convince your readers that you are knowledgeable, but you do not want to clutter your argument with arcane or unnecessary information that confuses and annoys them. Anticipate your readers' needs and try to fulfill them to obtain the response you seek.

Exercise ———   As Matt thinks about drafting his argument about drug testing in the work place, he identifies the following specific readers as potential members of his audience. Examine his list. Has he overlooked any group that has a stake in the controversy? Identify readers who might belong to more than one group. Then discuss how each group of readers might see the issue.

Employer   Health insurance claims agent
Worker (drug free)   Potential employer
Worker (abuser)   Stockholder
Drug rehabilitation counselor   Liability insurance executive
Medical laboratory analyst   American Civil Liberties Union
Union negotiator   representative
Company attorney   Consumer
Competitors (other employers)

Arranging the Evidence

Because every controversy creates its own problems and possibilities, no one method of arrangement will always work best. Sometimes you may even have to combine methods to make your case. To make an informed decision you need to consider how you might adapt your evidence to the three common methods of arrangement: *induction, deduction,* and *accommodation.*

Induction   Often called the scientific method, induction begins by presenting specific evidence and then moves to a general conclusion. This arrangement reflects the history of your investigation. You began your research with a hypothesis about what you wanted to find out and where you needed to look. You collected a cross section of examples until a pattern emerged. At this point, you made what scientists call an "inductive leap": you determined that although you had not collected every example, you had examined enough examples to risk proposing a probable conclusion.

To incorporate this arrangement into a draft, begin by posing the question that prompted your research:

Question   Why is our company losing so many valuable computer operators to other companies?

Then arrange your individual pieces of evidence in such a way that they help your readers see the pattern you discovered. You need not list all the false leads or blind alleys you encountered along the way, unless they changed your perspective or confirmed your judgment.

Evidence   1. Most computer operators are women who have preschool children (Provide examples.)

2. A nearby day-care center used by employees has closed because it lost federal funding. (Provide examples.)

3. Other day-care centers in the area are inconvenient and under-staffed. (Provide examples.)

4. Other companies provide on-site day care for children of employees. (Provide examples.)

5. On-site day care is beneficial to the emotional well-being of both preschool children and their mothers, because of the possibility of contact during the workday.

Conclusion   Finally, present the conclusion that seems warranted by the evidence you have presented.

Therefore, our company needs to provide on-site day care to retain valuable employees.

Deduction   Usually identified with classical reasoning, deduction begins with a general statement or *major premise* that, when restricted by a *minor premise*, leads to a specific conclusion. Unlike induction, which in theory makes an assertion only in its conclusion, deduction does make initial assertions (based on evidence) from which a conclusion is derived.

To use this organization in your draft, consider the pattern of this three-step syllogism.

Major premise   Retention of computer operators who have preschool children is promoted by on-site day care.

Minor premise   Our company wants to retain computer operators who have preschool children.

Conclusion   Our company should establish on-site day-care centers.

To gain your audience's acceptance of your major and minor premises, you must support each assertion with specific evidence. Demonstrate that retaining computer operators who have preschool children is promoted by on-site day-care centers and that "our company" wants to retain computer operators who have preschool children. If your readers accept your premises, then they are logically committed to accepting your conclusion.

Accommodation   Sometimes called "nonthreatening argument," accommodation arranges evidence so that all parties believe their position has received a fair hearing. Induction reveals how a chain of evidence leads to a conclusion. Deduction demonstrates why certain premises demand a single conclusion. Although both procedures work effectively in specific situations, they occasionally defeat your purpose. Readers may feel trapped by the relentless march of your argument; though unable to refute your logic, they are still unwilling to listen to reason. Accommodation takes your audience's hesitations into account. Instead of trying to win the argument, you try to improve communication and increase understanding.

To employ this strategy, begin by composing an objective description of the controversy: women computer operators who have preschool children are leaving the company. Then draft a complete and accurate statement of the contending positions, supplying the evidence that makes each position credible.

Corporation board   We need a qualified work force, but we are not in business to provide social services. (Provide evidence.)

Fellow workers   We understand their problem, but providing an on-site day-care
(Single, male, etc.)   center is giving expensive, preferential treatment to a small segment of the work force. (Provide evidence.)

Competitors   We need better computer operators if we are going to compete, and we will provide what is necessary to hire them. (Provide evidence.)

Next, show where and why you and the various parties agree: the corporation should not be in the day-care business; providing a center is preferential treatment; women computer operators have the right to market their skills in a competitive market. Then present your own opinion, explaining where it differs from other positions and why it deserves serious consideration: we have invested a large amount of money in training our work force; child care is an appropriate investment in view of the long-term contribution these people will make to the corporation. Finally, present a proposal that might resolve the issue in a way that recognizes the interests of all concerned: suggest that the corporation help fund the nearby day-care center that was previously supported by government money.

Exercise ———— Matt Fisher decides to make a scratch outline to organize his evidence *against* drug testing. What method of arrangement does he use? What sections of his outline suggest the potential for combining several methods?

Drug Testing in the Work Place

I. Drug testing is unreliable
   Cheap screening tests
   Lab error—"sink tests" (dumping samples)
   "Black market" for urine samples
   "Chain of custody" for urine samples
   Cross-reactivity—false positives from other chemicals
   Expensive confirmatory tests
II. Drug testing is counterproductive
   Decline in workers' morale
   Potential for discrimination

       Constant surveillance—time-consuming

       Worker paranoia—worry about behavior, possibility of false
         positives

       Supervisors play cop—loss of rapport, cooperation with workers

       Status of productive but rehabilitated worker?

       Class bias—rehabilitate executive; fire janitor

III. Drug testing is an invasion of employees' privacy

       Presumption of guilt

       Humiliating test—objective observer

       Confidentiality of test result—liability?

       Control lifestyle outside work place

       Dangerous precedent—genetic testing for future health risks (long-
         term illness, insurance premiums)

Monitoring the Appeals

In organizing your draft, you must keep track of how you are using the three basic appeals of argument: the *emotional* appeal, the *ethical* appeal, and the *logical* appeal. These three appeals are rarely fully separate; they all weave in and out of virtually every argument. But to control their effects to your advantage, you must know when and why you are using them.

The Emotional Appeal   Readers feel as well as think, and to be thoroughly convinced they must be emotionally as well as intellectually engaged by your argument. Some people think that the emotional appeal is suspect; because it relies on the feelings, instincts, and opinions of readers, they link it to the devious manipulations of advertising or politics. The emotional appeal is often used to stampede an audience into thoughtless action, but such abuses do not negate its value. The emotional appeal should never replace more rational appeals, but it can be an effective strategy for convincing your readers that they need to pay attention to your arguments.

    The greatest strength of the emotional appeal is also its greatest weakness. Dramatic examples, presented in concrete images and connotative language, personalize a problem and produce powerful emotions. Some examples produce predictable emotions: an abandoned puppy or a lonely old woman evokes pity; a senseless accident or recurring incompetence evokes anger; a smiling family or a heroic deed evokes delight. Some examples, however, produce unpredictable results, and their dramatic presentation often works against your purpose. It would be difficult to predict, for instance, how all your readers would respond to a working mother's fears for and guilt about her preschool child in day care. Some might pity her, others might disdain her inability to solve her problems. Because controversial issues attract a range of passions, use the emotional appeal with care.

The Ethical Appeal   The character (or *ethos*) of the writer, not the writer's morality, is the basis of the ethical appeal. It suggests that the writer is someone to be trusted, a claim that emerges from a demonstration of competence as an authority on the subject under discussion. Readers trust a writer such as Anna Quindlen and are inclined to agree with her arguments because she has established a reputation for informed, reasonable, and reliable writing about controversial subjects.

You can incorporate the ethical appeal into your argument either by citing authorities, such as Quindlen, who have conducted thorough investigations of your subject, or by following the example of authorities in your competent treatment of evidence. There are two potential dangers with the ethical appeal. First, you cannot win the trust of your readers by citing as an authority in one field someone who is an authority in another. Lee Iacocca is an established authority on building cars, but he should not be cited as an authority on nuclear disarmament. And second, you cannot convince your readers that you are knowledgeable if you present your argument exclusively in personal terms. Your own experience in trying to find reliable, convenient day-care services may make your argument for providing on-site day care more forceful, but you need to consider the experience of other people to establish your ethical appeal.

The Logical Appeal   The rational methods used to develop an argument constitute a logical appeal. Some people think that the forceful use of logic, like the precise use of facts, makes an argument absolutely true. But controversies contain many truths, no one of which can be graded simply true or false. By using the logical appeal, you acknowledge that arguments are conducted in a world of probability, not certainty; by offering a series of reasonable observations and conclusions, you establish the most reliable case.

The logical appeal is widely used and accepted in argument. Establishing the relationships that bind your evidence to your proposition engages your readers' reasoning power, and an appeal to their intelligence and common sense is likely to win their assent. But the logical appeal is not infallible. Its limit is in acknowledging limits: How much evidence is enough? There is no simple answer to this question. The amount of evidence required to convince fellow workers that your company should provide on-site day care may not be sufficient to persuade the company's board of directors. On the other hand, too much evidence, however methodically analyzed, may win the argument but lose your audience. Without emotional or ethical appeal, your "reasonable" presentation may be put aside in favor of more urgent issues. Accurate and cogent reasoning is the basis for any sound argument, but the logical appeal, like the emotional and ethical appeals, must be monitored carefully during drafting to make sure it is accomplishing your purpose.

Exercise ———   In his ongoing investigation of drug testing in the work place, Matt Fisher has collected a great deal of evidence, considered the position of his opponents, and analyzed the claims of his various readers. Now he wants to turn off these other voices and rediscover his own: he is ready to write "My Side" of the argument. As you read his discovery draft, identify the various appeals he has used to accomplish his purpose. Note the places that were probably strengthened by his decision to write "Their Side" first. Finally, point to the sections that would have been weaker had he written "My Side" first.

My Side

The increased public awareness of drug abuse in our society has [1] created a sense of public alarm about the potential dangers of drug abuse in the work place. Although such concern is justifiable, particularly when it affects the safety of workers and consumers, most companies are trying to solve this complex problem with a simple urine test. Whether it is used to weed out job applicants or identify suspected abusers on the job, urine testing is a misguided attempt to find a quick fix. The test is not only unreliable and counterproductive, it is a serious invasion of workers' privacy.

The biggest argument for urine testing is that it is a cheap and [2] efficient way to spot abusers. It is certainly cheap. Many test kits cost less than ten dollars. But they are hardly reliable. In order to perform an effective drug test, urine samples must be taken according to strict procedures, to guarantee the right kind of sample and to protect against sample switching from the rapidly developing "black market" for clean urine. When the test is taken at the job site, this "chain of custody" is often broken, increasing the opportunity for error and fraud.

The laboratories that analyze these samples are also suspect. [3] Many of them have been set up to make a fast buck off the high demand for drug testing. The Centers for Disease Control discovered that in the thirteen laboratories they studied, there was "up to 67% error rate in false positive identification of drugs" (Hansen 2382.) Some of these labs reported false negatives 100% of the time when they tested for certain drugs. Dr. Joe Boone, chief of CDC's clinical chemistry and toxicology section, reports that "if these labs would have dumped the samples down the sink and tossed a coin, they would have come up with the same reliability in their test results" (Chapman 57).

To even approach reliability, an initial urine screening needs to [4] be checked by a second, more expensive "confirmatory test." This test attempts to offset the problem of "cross-reactivity." According to

David Greenblatt, chief of clinical pharmacy at Tufts New England Medical Center, "many chemicals in the body, such as caffeine, cough syrup, or antiasthmatic medication can throw off findings" (Chapman 59). Employers who do not invest in a confirmatory testing procedure will never know whether job applicants or employees who tested positive were abusing drugs or following a doctor's orders.

Questions about the reliability of drug testing contribute to a   5
decline in workers' morale. Rather than ensuring productivity, urine testing has created a climate of paranoia. Workers distrust the motives of their employers and worry about the potential for discrimination. If they become too emotional, make too many trips to the restroom, or behave in any way that is viewed as suspicious, they could be asked to take a urine test. Even if the results are negative, they are "on record" as former suspects. Supervisors, who should focus their attention on workers' productivity, are not responsible for worker surveillance. They may know little about the symptoms of drug abuse, but they are expected to look for telltale signs. By playing super-cop, they destroy their rapport with their workers.

A more serious threat to workers' morale emerges from the   6
debate about the purpose of drug testing. Does the company want to pacify its stockholders, protect its workers, or identify abusers? More to the point, what is the fate of those who are identified as abusers? Are they replaced or rehabilitated? If the latter, who pays for the rehabilitation? Workers' morale is certainly not bolstered by rumors that executives are counseled in rehabilitation programs paid for by company insurance, whereas workers are quickly fired.

The most significant objection to urine testing, particularly   7
random/massive testing, is that it is an invasion of workers' privacy. The test may seem simple enough, like other tests in a routine physical, but the legal and ethical consequences are hardly routine. First, the institution of the test raises serious concerns regarding an employer's right to control an employee's activities off duty. Second, the test presumes the guilt of all workers until the "results" establish their innocence. Third, these highly debatable results may ruin the career of a valuable employee who has no way

to appeal a decision or reform his or her behavior. And finally, such testing sets a dangerous precedent. There is already significant corporate support for genetic testing—a test that determines an employee's predisposition toward such "costly" diseases as diabetes and cancer (Chapman 60).

There is reason for the public to be alarmed about drug abuse in   8 the work place, but the evidence on urine testing suggests that the public should be equally alarmed about the abuse of drug testing in the work place.

ELIMINATING FALLACIES: *Revising*

Once you have organized your argument, reexamine your draft to see if it accomplishes your purpose. Revision, as you learned in Chapter 4, can mean *global revision* —the rethinking, reordering, and rewriting of your text—or *local revision* often necessitated by a small problem: a faulty thesis, an undeveloped paragraph, or an unclear sentence. In argument, many local problems are the result of errors in reasoning known as *fallacies*. Some fallacies are unintentional, created in the haste of composition. Others are intentional, created to deceive readers. In either case, they oversimplify or distort evidence, thus making an argument unreliable. Read the following list as a guide to finding and eliminating fallacies from your writing during revision, or to detecting them in the writing of others.

▼ *Faulty analogy* attempts to argue that because two things are alike in some ways they are alike in all ways. Attending school may be analogous to working at a factory in that both require long hours to complete specific tasks for a supervisor. School work and factory work are not the same, however. An analogy can be useful in helping your readers understand how something complex or unknown is similar to something simple and familiar, but such illustrations should not be confused with proof. Arguments by analogy are particularly suspect when an insignificant resemblance is proposed as evidence for a more relevant (but unsupportable) comparison.

▼ *Hasty generalizations* are conclusions drawn from inadequate or atypical evidence. Suppose there are twelve women and ten men in your section of business law. On the final exam, the four highest scores are made by men and the four lowest scores by women. On the basis of the evidence, you conclude that women are unqualified for business law. There is no justification for that generalization because twelve women in one section are not typical of all women, and twelve is hardly an adequate sample to justify such a sweeping conclusion. To avoid hasty generalizations, make sure you provide sufficient and appropriate evidence to support your conclusions.

▼   *Post hoc, ergo propter hoc* (Latin for "after this, therefore because of this") asserts that one event caused another because it preceded it. Lowering the drinking age in your state should not be claimed as the direct cause of the increased crime rate. The first event may have contributed in some way to the other, but the two events may also be merely coincidental. Because direct cause-and-effect relationships are difficult to establish, do not overstate your claims for events that may have many plausible explanations.

▼   *Begging the question* occurs when part of what has to be proved is assumed to be true. When a lawyer seeks to use as evidence the results of a polygraph test because such tests verify the truth, he begs the question: Are polygraph tests reliable? Sometimes begging the question can produce a *circular argument* that restates in different words what you are trying to prove: "Polygraph tests do not provide reliable evidence because their results cannot be trusted." As you revise, check each of your claims to make sure you advance your argument with evidence; do not assume a claim is credible because you have used "new and improved" language.

▼   *Either-or* states a position in such categorical terms—either *A* or *B*—that it ignores (or denies) the possibility of other alternatives. An economist who argues that "the United States must either adopt a new industrial policy or face financial ruin" does not see (or prefers not to see) that there are many possible ways to solve our economic difficulties and that financial ruin does not inevitably follow from the failure to adopt one policy. If you have conducted a thorough investigation, you know that there are more than two sides to the issue.

▼   *Ad hominem* (Latin for "to the man") distorts an argument by attacking the character of the opponent to arouse the emotions or prejudices of the audience. This strategy attempts to discredit an opponent by using labels (or stereotypes) with highly unfavorable connotations: "Senator Hoover is an avowed feminist. Her antidiscrimination bill just expresses her radical political views." As you have seen, an expert witness's trustworthiness is always on trial. If Senator Hoover's opinions are not supported by evidence, then her credibility should be discounted. But as long as she presents evidence for her case, you should resist calling her names and address her argument.

▼   *Red herring* is a smoked fish that has a reddish color and strong odor. A hunter may drag a red herring across a trail to distract the hounds and trick them into following a new scent. In argument, a *red herring* is an unrelated issue introduced to divert attention from the real issue: "As long as we are discussing whether women should receive equal pay, we should also discuss whether women still want to retain preferred treatment on social occasions, as when men open doors for them and pay for their meals. It seems to me that women want equal and preferred treatment at the same time." Such diversions confuse the issue by introducing irrelevancies. Economic equality and social courtesy are two different issues.

Exercises ———   1. In checking through his planning notes and preliminary drafts, Matt
Fisher found several assertions that looked like fallacies. In the following
list, identify the probable fallacies and then discuss how they might be
revised to avoid oversimplifying or distorting the evidence.
   a. Every Monday morning he shows up at work looking tired and acting
      moody. He must be using drugs on the weekend.
   b. We must face the problem of drug abuse with an aggressive testing
      program or face the possibility of a serious industrial accident.
   c. The union leadership is against drug testing. But most of those guys
      dress like back-alley thugs. What else would you expect from people
      who look like they belong on "Miami Vice"?
   d. Requiring urine tests is no more an invasion of workers' privacy than
      requiring protective masks or helmets.
   e. What would happen if the executive vice president were arrested for
      drunk driving? Executives often have drinks when they conduct busi-
      ness over long lunches.
   f. Several corporations have started talking about genetic testing. In a
      few years, all workers in the United States will be tested to see if they
      have a predisposition toward "costly" diseases like diabetes or cancer.
   g. Drug testing violates workers' civil rights by invading their privacy.
2. Review Matt's two drafts, "Their Side" (pages 134–136) and "My Side"
   (pages 143–145), examining each for fallacies. Speculate on how Matt could
   eliminate those fallacies and make the same point in a more reliable and
   effective way.

The Gun Controversy

The following ads present the opposing sides in the gun controversy. What arguments does the National Rifle Association present for its position? What arguments does Handgun Control present for its position? How does the photograph in each ad enhance the power of the argument?

REP. ALBERTO GUTMAN: Florida Legislator, Businessman, Husband, Member of the National Rifle Association.

"Being from a country that was once a democracy and turned communist, I really feel I know what the right to bear arms is all about. In Cuba, where I was born, the first thing the communist government did was take away everybody's firearms, leaving them defenseless and intimidated with fear. That's why our constitutional right to bear arms is so important to our country's survival.

"As a legislator I have to deal with reality. And the reality is that gun control does not work. It actually eliminates the rights of the law-abiding citizen, not the criminal. Criminals will always have guns, and they won't follow gun control laws anyway. I would like to see tougher laws on criminals as opposed to tougher laws on legitimate gun owners. We need to attack the problem of crime at its roots, instead of blaming crime on gun ownership and citizens who use them lawfully.

"It's a big responsibility that we face retaining the right to bear arms. That's why I joined the NRA. The NRA is instrumental in protecting these freedoms. It helps train and educate people, supporting legislation that benefits not only those who bear arms but all citizens of the United States. The NRA helps keep America free." **I'm the NRA.**

The NRA's lobbying organization, the Institute for Legislative Action, is the nation's largest and most influential protector of the constitutional right to keep and bear arms. At every level of government and through local grassroots efforts, the Institute guards against infringement upon the freedoms of law-abiding gun owners. If you would like to join the NRA or want more information about our programs and benefits, write J. Warren Cassidy, Executive Vice President, P.O. Box 37484, Dept. AG-15, Washington, D.C. 20013.

Paid for by the members of the National Rifle Association of America. Copyright 1986.

Reprinted by the permission of the National Rifle Association of America.

—Mrs. James S. Brady—

"A $29 handgun shattered my family's life."

"Seven years ago, John Hinckley pulled a $29 revolver from his pocket and opened fire on a Washington street. He shot the President. He also shot my husband.

I'm not asking for your sympathy. I'm asking for your help.

I've learned from my own experience that, alone, there's only so much you can do to stop handgun violence. But that together, we can confront the mightiest gun lobby—the N.R.A.—and win.

I've only to look at my husband Jim to remember that awful day... the unending TV coverage of the handgun firing over and over... the nightmare panic and fear.

It's an absolute miracle nobody was killed. After all, twenty thousand Americans are killed by handguns every year. Thousands more—men, women, even children—are maimed for life.

Like me, I know you support *stronger* handgun control laws. So does the vast majority of Americans. But the National Rifle Association can spend so much in elections that Congress is afraid to pass an effective national handgun law.

It's time to change that. Before it's too late for another family like mine... a family like yours.

I joined Handgun Control, Inc. because they're willing to take on the N.R.A. Right now we're campaigning for a national waiting period and background check on handgun purchases.

If such simple, basic measures had been on the books seven years ago, John Hinckley would never have walked out of that Texas pawnshop with the handgun which came within an inch of killing Ronald Reagan. He lied on his purchase application. Given time, the police could have caught the lie and put him in jail.

Of course, John Hinckley's not the only one. Police report that thousands of known criminals buy handguns right over the counter in this country. We have to stop them.

So, please, pick up a pen. Write me to find out how you can help. And support our work with a generous contribution.

It's time we kept handguns out of the wrong hands. It's time to break the National Rifle Association's grip on Congress and start making our cities and neighborhoods safe again.

Thank you and God bless you."

"Don't let it happen to you."

Dear Sarah,

It's time to break the N.R.A.'s grip on Congress once and for all. Here's my contribution to Handgun Control, Inc., the million-strong nonprofit citizens' group you help direct:

☐ $15   ☐ $29   ☐ $35   ☐ $50   ☐ $100 or $_____ .
☐ Tell me more about how I can help.

NAME _____

ADDRESS _____

CITY _____ STATE _____ ZIP _____

HANDGUN CONTROL

1400 K Street, N.W., Washington, D.C. 20005, (202) 898-0792.

Contributions to Handgun Control, Inc. are not tax deductible.

The Penalty of Death | H. L. Mencken

One of America's most prolific journalists, H. L. Mencken was never bashful about taking a stand on an issue. In fact, he published six volumes of essays, aptly titled *Prejudices* (1919–1927). In this essay, Mencken tries to refute the two common arguments against capital punishment. How carefully does he present "Their Side" of the argument? In what ways does Mencken use the emotional, ethical, or logical appeals? Identify specific places where he over-simplifies or distorts evidence.

Of the arguments against capital punishment that issue from uplifters, two are commonly heard most often, to wit: 1

1. That hanging a man (or frying him or gassing him) is a dreadful business, degrading to those who have to do it and revolting to those who have to witness it.

2. That it is useless, for it does not deter others from the same crime.

The first of these arguments, it seems to me, is plainly too weak to need serious refutation. All it says, in brief, is that the work of the hangman is unpleasant. Granted. But suppose it is? It may be quite necessary to society for all that. There are, indeed, many other jobs that are unpleasant, and yet no one thinks of abolishing them—that of the plumber, that of the soldier, that of the garbage-man, that of the priest hearing confessions, that of the sand-hog, and so on. Moreover, what evidence is there that any actual hangman complains of his work? I have heard none. On the contrary, I have known many who delighted in their ancient art, and practised it proudly. 2

In the second argument of the abolitionists there is rather more force, but even here, I believe, the ground under them is shaky. Their fundamental error consists in assuming that the whole aim of punishing criminals is to deter other (potential) criminals—that we hang or electrocute A simply in order to so alarm B that he will not kill C. This, I believe, is an assumption which confuses a part with the whole. Deterrence, obviously, is *one* of the aims of punishment, but it is surely not the only one. On the contrary, there are at least half a dozen, and some are probably quite as important. At least one of them, practically considered, is *more* important. Commonly, it is described as revenge, but revenge is really not the word for it. I borrow a better term from the late Aristotle: *katharsis*. *Katharsis*, so used, means a salubrious discharge of emotions, a healthy letting off of steam. A schoolboy, disliking his teacher, deposits a tack upon the pedagogical chair; the teacher jumps and the boy laughs. This is *katharsis*. What I contend is that one of the prime objects of all judicial punishments is to afford the same grateful relief (*a*) to the immediate victims of the criminal punished, and (*b*) to the general body of moral and timorous men. 3

These persons, and particularly the first group, are concerned only indirectly with deterring other criminals. The thing they crave primarily is the satisfaction of seeing the criminal actually before them suffer as he made them suffer. What they want is the peace of mind that goes with the feeling that 4

Mencken, H. L. *A Mencken Chrestomathy*. New York: Knopf, 1954. 118–21.

accounts are squared. Until they get that satisfaction they are in a state of emotional tension, and hence unhappy. The instant they get it they are comfortable. I do not argue that this yearning is noble; I simply argue that it is almost universal among human beings. In the face of injuries that are unimportant and can be borne without damage it may yield to higher impulses; that is to say, it may yield to what is called Christian charity. But when the injury is serious Christianity is adjourned, and even saints reach for their sidearms. It is plainly asking too much of human nature to expect it to conquer so natural an impulse. A keeps a store and has a bookkeeper, B. B steals $700, employs it in playing at dice or bingo, and is cleaned out. What is A to do? Let B go? If he does so he will be unable to sleep at night. The sense of injury, of injustice, of frustration will haunt him like pruritus. So he turns B over to the police, and they hustle B to prison. Thereafter A can sleep. More, he has pleasant dreams. He pictures B chained to the wall of a dungeon a hundred feet underground, devoured by rats and scorpions. It is so agreeable that it makes him forget his $700. He has got his *katharsis*.

The same thing precisely takes place on a larger scale when there is a   5
crime which destroys a whole community's sense of security. Every law-abiding citizen feels menaced and frustrated until the criminals have been struck down—until the communal capacity to get even with them, and more than even, has been dramatically demonstrated. Here, manifestly, the business of deterring others is no more than an afterthought. The main thing is to destroy the concrete scoundrels whose act has alarmed everyone, and thus made everyone unhappy. Until they are brought to book that unhappiness continues; when the law has been executed upon them there is a sigh of relief. In other words, there is *katharsis*.

I know of no public demand for the death penalty for ordinary crimes,   6
even for ordinary homicides. Its infliction would shock all men of normal decency of feeling. But for crimes involving the deliberate and inexcusable taking of human life, by men openly defiant of all civilized order—for such crimes it seems, to nine men out of ten, a just and proper punishment. Any lesser penalty leaves them feeling that the criminal has got the better of society—that he is free to add insult to injury by laughing. That feeling can be dissipated only by a recourse to *katharsis*, the invention of the aforesaid Aristotle. It is more effectively and economically achieved, as human nature now is, by wafting the criminal to realms of bliss.

The real objection to capital punishment doesn't lie against the actual exter-   7
mination of the condemned, but against our brutal American habit of putting it off so long. After all, every one of us must die soon or late, and a murderer, it must be assumed, is one who makes that sad fact the cornerstone of his metaphysic. But it is one thing to die, and quite another thing to lie for long months and even years under the shadow of death. No sane man would choose such a finish. All of us, despite the Prayer Book, long for a swift and unexpected end. Unhappily, a murderer, under the irrational American system, is tortured for what, to him, must seem a whole series of eternities. For months on end he sits in prison while his lawyers carry on their idiotic buffoonery with writs, injunctions, mandamuses, and appeals. In order to get his money (or that of his friends) they have to feed him with hope. Now and then, by the imbecility of a judge or some trick of juridic science, they actually justify it. But let us say that, his money all gone, they finally throw up their hands. Their client is now ready for the rope or the chair. But he must still wait for months before it fetches him.

That wait, I believe, is horribly cruel. I have seen more than one man sit-   8
ting in the death-house, and I don't want to see any more. Worse, it is wholly
useless. Why should he wait at all? Why not hang him the day after the last
court dissipates his last hope? Why torture him as not even cannibals would
torture their victims? The common answer is that he must have time to make
his peace with God. But how long does that take? It may be accomplished, I
believe, in two hours quite as comfortably as in two years. There are, indeed,
no temporal limitations upon God. He could forgive a whole herd of murderers
in a millionth of a second. More, it has been done.

Execution | **Anna Quindlen**

Reread Anna Quindlen's comments on the difficulties she encounters when
she tries to organize an argument on a controversial subject (page 136). Then
read her essay on the emotionally charged issue of capital punishment. How
does she present the evidence for the contending positions? How does she
introduce and support her own opinions? Which argument on this issue is
more effective—Mencken's dismissal of the opposition or Quindlen's attempt
to accommodate the opposing positions? Explain your answer.

Ted Bundy and I go back a long way, to a time when there was a series of   1
unsolved murders in Washington State known only as the Ted murders.
Like a lot of reporters, I'm something of a crime buff. But the Washington Ted
murders—and the ones that followed in Utah, Colorado, and finally in Florida,
where Ted Bundy was convicted and sentenced to die—fascinated me because I
could see myself as one of the victims. I looked at the studio photographs of
young women with long hair, pierced ears, easy smiles, and I read the descriptions: polite, friendly, quick to help, eager to please. I thought about being
approached by a handsome young man asking for help, and I knew if I had
been in the wrong place at the wrong time I would have been a goner. By the
time Ted finished up in Florida, law enforcement authorities suspected he had
murdered dozens of young women. He and the death penalty seemed made
for each other.

The death penalty and I, on the other hand, seem to have nothing in com-   2
mon. But Ted Bundy has made me think about it all over again, now that the
outlines of my sixties liberalism have been filled in with a decade as a reporter
covering some of the worst back alleys in New York City and three years as a
mother who, like most, would lay down her life for her kids. Simply put, I am
opposed to the death penalty. I would tell that to any judge or lawyer under-
taking the voir dire of jury candidates in a state in which the death penalty can
be imposed. That is why I would be excused from such a jury. In a rational,
completely cerebral way, I think the killing of one human being as punishment
for the killing of another makes no sense and is inherently immoral.

But whenever my response to an important subject is rational and com-   3
pletely cerebral, I know there is something wrong with it—and so it is here. I

Quindlen, Anna. *Thinking Out Loud*. New York: Random, 1988. 220–23.

have always been governed by my gut, and my gut says I am hypocritical about the death penalty. That is, I do not in theory think that Ted Bundy, or others like him, should be put to death. But if my daughter had been the one clubbed to death as she slept in a Tallahassee sorority house, and if the bite mark left in her buttocks has been one of the prime pieces of evidence against the young man charged with her murder, I would with the greatest pleasure kill him myself.

The State of Florida will not permit the parents of Bundy's victims to do that, and, in a way, that is the problem with an emotional response to capital punishment. The only reason for a death penalty is to exact retribution. Is there anyone who really thinks that it is a deterrent, that there are considerable numbers of criminals out there who think twice about committing crimes because of the sentence involved? The ones I have met in my professional duties have either sneered at the justice system, where they can exchange one charge for another with more ease than they could return a shirt to a clothing store, or they have simply believed that it is the other guy who will get caught, get convicted, get the stiffest sentence. Of course, the death penalty would act as a deterrent by eliminating recidivism, but then so would life without parole, albeit at greater taxpayer expense.   4

I don't believe deterrence is what most proponents seek from the death penalty anyhow. Our most profound emotional response is to want criminals to suffer as their victims did. When a man is accused of throwing a child from a high-rise terrace, my emotional—some might say hysterical—response is that he should be given an opportunity to see how endless the seconds are from the thirty-first story to the ground. In a civilized society that will never happen. And so what many people want from the death penalty, they will never get.   5

Death is death, you may say, and you would be right. But anyone who has seen someone die suddenly of a heart attack and someone else slip slowly into the clutches of cancer knows that there are gradations of dying.   6

I watched a television reenactment one night of a execution by lethal injection. It was well done; it was horrible. The methodical approach, people standing around the gurney waiting, made it more awful. One moment there was a man in a prone position; the next moment that man was gone. On another night I watched a television movie about a little boy named Adam Walsh, who disappeared from a shopping center in Florida. There was a reenactment of Adam's parents coming to New York, where they appeared on morning talk shows begging for their son's return, and in their hotel room, where they received a call from the police saying that Adam had just been found: not all of Adam, actually, just his severed head, discovered in the waters of a Florida canal. There is nothing anyone could do that is bad enough for an adult who took a six-year-old boy away from his parents, perhaps tortured, then murdered him and cut off his head. Nothing at all. Lethal injection? The electric chair? Bah.   7

And so I come back to the position that the death penalty is wrong, not only because it consists of stooping to the level of the killers, but also because it is not what it seems. Just before one of Ted Bundy's execution dates was postponed pending further appeals, the father of his last known victim, a twelve-year-old girl, said what almost every father in his situation must feel. "I wish they'd bring him back to Lake City," said Tom Leach of the town where Kimberly Leach lived and died, "and let us all have at him." But the death penalty   8 does not let us all have at him in the way Mr. Leach seems to mean. What he wants is for something as horrifying as what happened to his child to happen to Ted Bundy. And that is impossible.

Drug Abuse in the Work Place | Matt Fisher

When Matt Fisher finished his "My Side" draft, he knew that he had only presented one side of a complex argument. Combining "Their Side" with "My Side," he composed this final draft of his argument. Compare Matt's three drafts. Which one is the most convincing? Does everyone in your writing group agree? What "emotional, ethical, social" issues influence your choice?

I n the last decade drug abuse has reached epidemic proportions in our country—destroying the lives of our young people, exhausting the energies of our legal system, and eroding our fundamental values. Nowhere is the problem more alarming than in the work place, where drug abuse costs the American economy in excess of $60 billion a year. All of us—employers, workers, and consumers—want to cure this plague that threatens the health of our culture. Unfortunately, there is as much controversy about the cure as there is about the disease.

Employers, rightfully concerned about the investments of their stockholders, the safety of their workers, and the credibility of their goods and services, favor various forms of urine testing to identify drug abusers. Many employers now include a urine test as part of the routine preemployment physical. Such a test allows them to spot abusers before they are hired, trained, and become problems. Other employers use urine testing when a worker's behavior suggests that drug abuse is a reasonable explanation for impaired performance. Such testing enables employers to restore the productivity of their work force and to encourage rehabilitation of abusers. Employers whose workers' tasks directly affect the safety of fellow workers or consumers, or whose workers are engaged in sensitive security positions, may employ massive or random testing to guarantee the integrity of the work place.

Workers are concerned about protecting the integrity of the work place, but they are equally concerned about protecting their own integrity. The initial urine test now being administered by most employers is highly unreliable. False results (positive and negative) can be produced by careless procedures in taking the sample or by inaccurate procedures in testing the sample. In fact, the Centers for Disease Control reported that in the thirteen laboratories they studied, there was "up to 67% error rate in false positive identification[s]" (Hansen 2382). The reliability of these tests is compromised by the problem of "cross-reactivity"—chemicals in the body such as caffeine or cough syrup that can corrupt the results.

If urine testing is judged unreliable, workers are justifiably concerned about the potential for discrimination. Uninformed supervisors may misread their behavior and ask for a drug test. If the results are falsely positive, they are uncertain about their right to appeal. If the results are negative, they are uncertain about their status as "former suspects." And if the results are positive, they are uncertain of their fate. Is the employer interested in replacing or rehabilitating employees?

This question is at the heart of the controversy. Putting aside the issues of efficiency, reliability, and discrimination, and the most serious issue of invasion of workers' privacy, all of us need to be clear about the purpose of drug testing. Employers need a reliable work force; workers want a safe environment; and consumers expect dependable goods and services. But is drug testing the best way to satisfy these needs and expectations?

Pre-employment drug screening does not guarantee that workers have never used drugs or, once employed, will not become drug abusers. It simply provides highly questionable evidence about one sample of a worker's urine. Testing for probable cause may prevent or determine the cause of some accidents, but it does not solve the larger problem of ensuring a drug-free work place. And massive or random testing of a large work force (like the testing of "suspicious workers") may identify a few abusers, but it could also discredit innocent employees. The whole procedure, rather than increasing productivity, destroys the mutual trust between employer and workers so essential to quality performance.

In order to solve the complex problem of drug abuse in the work place, we need more than a simple urine test. What we need is a comprehensive drug policy developed by all those concerned. Under such a policy, drug testing might still be used, but employers would make a concerted effort to establish and monitor the credentials of urinalysis laboratories. They would also spell out in detail the purpose and procedures of all drug testing. Job applicants would be told in advance that drug screening is required and informed about the results. Workers on the job would help establish the specific criteria for impairment. If they fail to meet those criteria and then fail the test, they would have the right to ask for a series of confimatory tests. In all cases, especially those that involved massive or random testing, the employer would protect the confidentiality of test results and provide an agreed-upon counseling procedure for those who do not pass.

More important than mere drug testing, however, is an enlightened employee assistance program. Such a program would have as its primary goals the well-being and long-term productivity of employees. For example, employers would be more concerned about obtaining detailed references about an applicant's qualifications and work history than in collecting a urine sample. On the job, workers and supervisors would be given extensive educational programs about the causes and consequences of drug abuse. If detailed medical examinations confirm drug abuse, workers would be given sick leave and assigned to a designated drug treatment program. For those who refuse treatment or who become multiple offenders, a predetermined administrative action is justified. But for those who enter rehabilitation, the prospects are good. Companies that provide such treatment report a 70% to 75% success record (Castro 57).

Lewis L. Maltby, Vice President, Drexelbrook Controls, Inc., describes the kind of consensus policy that should cure drug abuse in the work place: "We can attack drug abuse with drug testing. It's quick, it's easy, and it's cheap. It just doesn't work. It gives us inaccurate and irrelevant information and undermines the trust of good employees who resent being ordered to pee in a bottle when they've done nothing wrong. Or, we can take the time to learn about our employees, watch their job performance, and help them when it starts to slip. It's time-consuming, difficult, and expensive. But it works. Not just in preventing work-place drug abuse, but in creating a committed and productive work place" (Maltby 4).

Writing Assignments

Narrate **1.** Select an occasion when you (or one of your fellow workers) felt as though your civil rights were abused by an employer's policy. Write a narrative about that occasion in a way that your readers will understand why the events influenced you to select "My Side" in the controversy.

Observe **2.** Study the ads about the gun controversy. Then write an essay in which you compare how each ad uses the person's testimony and photograph to make the three appeals: emotional, ethical, and logical.

Investigate **3.** Interview someone who has to make arguments in public for a living—a lawyer who has to make a case to jurors, a minister who has to preach to a congregation, a college president who has to address alumni groups, a professor who has to present lectures to other scholars. Ask about the special "tricks of the trade" that he or she has discovered work in difficult situations. Then write a profile about the person entitled "Speaking My Mind and Getting My Way."

Collaborate **4.** Your writing group has been asked to draft a letter to the newspaper editor about a controversial campus practice such as library fees, preferential parking, or distribution of birth-control information. An initial poll reveals that your group is undecided or perhaps even strongly divided about the issue. Discuss ways to reach accommodation so that you can collaborate on a text whose purpose is to increase your audience's understanding of the issue.

Read **5.** Locate and read an article about the effectiveness of HIV testing. Use the information in this article to argue for or against HIV testing as a condition of employment.

Respond **6.** Examine your emotional response to H. L. Mencken's argument for capital punishment. How do various features of his tone and language encourage you to accept or reject his argument? What personal experiences or beliefs make you more likely to agree or disagree with his position? Present your analysis in progress; that is, trace your emotional reactions as you read through each section of Mencken's essay. How did you feel when he said X? What did you think when he said Y?

Analyze **7.** Analyze the types of evidence that Anna Quindlen uses in her essay, "Execution." Identify what is fact, judgment, eyewitness testimony, and expert testimony. Sort out the kinds of evidence that make it difficult for Quindlen to decide where she stands on the issue. Then analyze which argument—H. L. Mencken's or Quindlen's—is more effective. Explain the reasons for your decision.

Evaluate **8.** Evaluate each of Matt Fisher's drafts. Then write him a letter to convince him which of the three he should place in his writing portfolio for final assessment. Reread Anna Quindlen's advice on pages 129–130 and page 136. Which one of Matt's essays raises "red flags" or leads with a "punch in the stomach"? Which one will Matt's teacher prefer? Which one will Matt's fellow workers prefer? Your purpose is to convince him to submit his "best" argument. Your problem is to define which of these essays is the "best" argument.

Argue   9.   Select an issue that is currently provoking heated discussion on the editorial page of your community newspaper but about which you have no strong opinion. Collect editorials and letters to the editor that represent the range of disagreement on the issue. Interview the local people who are involved in the controversy or who are reporting on it for the local paper. After you have completed your investigation, compose an historical analysis in which you explain how the issue became an issue.

Argue   10.   Write an essay for the college alumni magazine in which you argue that a current university decision is not in the spirit of your school's stated educational mission. Do your homework so that you know why the university made its decision and why the decision is in conflict with the school's educational mission. As you think through what you want to say and how you want to say it, remember that you are appealing to the best interests of the alumni, the students, the faculty, the university administration, and the person who made the decision you are contesting.

7 Paragraphs: Units of Development

A paragraph is a set of related sentences that express or develop a topic. A paragraph is usually part of an extended piece of writing, although in some situations you may need only one paragraph to fulfill your purpose. In narration or description, a new paragraph usually signals a shift in time, scene, or speaker. In exposition or argument, a new paragraph adds information or announces another point supporting your thesis. This chapter discusses two kinds of paragraphs: *topical paragraphs,* those that develop a topic or idea; and *special paragraphs,* those that introduce or conclude a piece of writing or provide a transition between major parts.

Paragraphs serve several purposes for you and your readers. You can use them to divide your subject into manageable units of information: by grouping ideas into paragraphs, you show the relationship of ideas to one another and their significance to your overall purpose. You can also use paragraphs to control emphasis: by placing a paragraph in a particular position, you demonstrate the relative importance of an idea in your essay. Finally, you can use paragraphs to establish rhythm: by interrupting a series of long paragraphs with a short paragraph, or creating a series of brief paragraphs, you fix and vary cadence in your writing.

Readers use your paragraphs to grasp key points and follow your reasoning. Extended, uninterrupted passages tax their attention. They expect and need to see the regularly spaced indentations that signal a new paragraph. This visual cue tells them that they have completed one topic and are about to take up another. Because the new paragraph promises new information, they refocus their attention to see how this change alters or advances your essay.

Like so many other writing procedures, making paragraphs depends on your subject, your audience, your purpose—and your own composing process. Some writers like to plan every detail of a project before they begin, assigning each subdivision of their subject to a specific paragraph. Such a procedure usually produces a blueprint for an orderly essay, but it may box the writer into a pattern that forces connections and discourages discoveries. Other writers prefer a more open-ended procedure. They know what they want to accomplish but realize that when they start writing they will discover ideas and associations that will call for paragraphs they could not have anticipated. Bill Barich, a regular contributor to the *New Yorker,* admits that he prefers this more organic approach to creating paragraphs:

When I am planning an essay or a piece of reporting, I usually have a sense of the beginning and ending, but my paragraphs tend to arrange themselves during the writing. The process is instinctive and often surprising. I have general ideas grouped together in my notes—facts and information I want to include. But I don't know where I will put them until the piece begins to unfold. Information gathers around a center and becomes a paragraph. It's a thought unit, an energy unit. When the energy runs out, I move on, establishing a rhythm that tells me how much information I can use in the next paragraph.

This sounds a little disorderly, but for me a piece becomes lifeless if I know from the beginning what goes where. I am less interested in getting the information in the right place the first time through than I am in finding the rhythm that will carry the information. I like the structure to be organic, to flow naturally. Once I have finished writing, I can check for things like sequence and fullness of statement. Maybe there is something in my notes that I can insert in a phrase or use in a new paragraph. I may push myself to shorten everything, just to see what that does to the energy of the work. I'll shift, compress, and strip away extraneous material, hoping that what remains is diamond bright. (Personal interview)

Whether you chart every paragraph before you write or form paragraphs intuitively as you compose, once you have made them you must be sure, as Barich suggests, that they meet certain criteria. The following pages discuss the four characteristics of effective topical paragraphs, the primary functions of special paragraphs, and strategies for revising paragraphs.

THE REQUIREMENTS OF TOPICAL PARAGRAPHS

An effective topical paragraph must meet four requirements. First, it must discuss one topic only—that is, its statements and illustrations must display a *unity* of subject matter, often expressed in a topic sentence. Second, it must say all that your readers need to know about the topic; it must be *complete* enough to do what it is intended to do. Third, the sentences within the paragraph must exhibit an *order* that your readers can recognize and follow. Fourth, the sentences within the paragraph must display *coherence*, allowing readers to move easily from one sentence to the next without feeling that there are gaps in the sequence of your ideas.

Unity

Paragraph unity requires the considered development of the idea in your paragraph. To achieve this, each sentence must show a clear connection to the topic. In the following paragraph, the first sentence introduces Middletown, the topic the paragraph intends to develop.

(1) Middletown is not an actual place but an assortment of principles—the democratic ideal, the golden mean, the common citizen—central to our sense

of the American experience. (2) We have located it in a middle landscape, somewhere between the desolation of the wilderness and the debauchery of the city, and we have envisioned it as a middle-sized community, large enough to provide everything its citizens want and small enough to preserve everything they need. (3) Our culture contains many Middletowns. (4) Although their names change—Winesburg, Main Street, Mayberry—their image remains the same. (5) Their courthouse squares, tree-lined streets, and warm-hearted people represent our desire for stability in a century of bewildering change.

Notice that each succeeding sentence casts light on the topic; all the sentences together focus on the distinguishing characteristics of Middletown. This close relationship among individual sentences gives the paragraph unity.

Any sentence that digresses or drifts away from the topic blurs the focus of the paragraph and obscures your purpose. Consider the following paragraph.

(1) The legend of the Old South has a certain timeless beauty. (2) On the veranda of stately mansions, courtly gentlemen and charming ladies talked quietly of family, land, and cotton. (3) Even the slaves, who worked the fields, were said to be content. (4) The poor whites were barely visible until the vigilante movement after the Civil War. (5) They formed secret societies such as the Klan to terrorize the black community and to acquire political power. (6) Political power led to economic power, and by the turn of the century the poor whites were no longer poor.

The first three sentences deal with the legend of the Old South, and the reader assumes that this "timeless beauty" will be the topic for the rest of the paragraph. In sentence 4, however, the writer shifts to poor whites, a topic that is "barely visible" in the legend. The remaining sentences build on the allusion to the vigilante movement and shift the focus of the paragraph to the Ku Klux Klan and its use of violence to acquire political and economic power. Most readers can follow this digression, but as they proceed past the first few sentences they become less sure about the main topic of the paragraph and more certain that the paragraph lacks unity.

Exercise ———— Read the following paragraph, checking for unity by marking shifts in focus. Each sentence should clearly refer to the topic of Oregon as an ideal place to live. Suggest revisions where you think they are needed.

(1) With its seaside beaches, snowcapped mountains, and extensive forests, Oregon is an ideal place to live. (2) Its magnificent forests alone, covering more than 30 million acres, make it a natural paradise. (3) The National Park Service protects 17 million acres in national forests, but the rest is used for Oregon's lumber industry. (4) Loggers "harvest" trees with chain saws and then send their "crop" to the mill on trucks. (5) Many sawmills that used to employ 100 or more people are now closed because of the decline in the lumber business. (6) But loggers are not like steelworkers. (7) They don't go on relief and wait for their factory to reopen. (8) Self-reliant, eccentric, and impatient, loggers simply move to other parts of the country to look for work.

The Topic Sentence

A *topic sentence* is a statement that presents the main idea to be developed in the paragraph. It is often a single sentence, although sometimes you will need two sentences to state the topic. By beginning a paragraph with a topic sentence, you immediately tell your readers what main idea you are going to develop. In turn, they expect that the remaining sentences in your paragraph will elaborate on that idea. The following example shows how an opening topic sentence controls a paragraph.

> There is no simple formula for describing the intricate logic of the Pawnee people's lives. One thing is clear—that no one is caught within the social code. Against the backdrop of his natural environment, each individual stands as his own person. The Old World design for the human personality does not apply to this New World Man. The Pawnee child was born into a community from the beginning, and he never acquired the notion that he was closed in "within four walls." He was literally trained to feel that the world around him was his home—*kahuraru,* the universe, meaning literally the inside land, and that his house was a small model of it. The infinite cosmos was his constant source of strength and his ultimate progenitor, and there was no reason why he should hesitate to set out alone and explore the wide world, even though years should pass before he returned. Not only was he not confined within four walls but he was not closed in with a permanent group of people. The special concern of his mother did not mean that he was so closely embedded with her emotionally that he was not able to move about. (Gene Weltfish, *The Lost Universe)*

Gene Weltfish begins his paragraph with a simple declarative sentence: "There is no simple formula for describing the intricate logic of the Pawnee people's lives." His purpose is to explain the complexity of that logic, and the remaining sentences in the paragraph advance that purpose by showing how the Pawnees imagined the universe and their place in it.

Not all topical paragraphs begin with topic sentences. If you begin composing and don't discover the main point of your paragraph until you reach the end, you must decide whether to move the topic sentence to the beginning, place it somewhere else, or leave it where you found it—at the end. In most cases, you will probably want to place it at the beginning to cue your readers about the significance of the sentences to come. On a few occasions, you may want to place it in midparagraph, where it serves as a commentary on the sentences that come before or after it.

In the following paragraph, Richard Rodriguez uses his first sentence to make a flat statement of fact: two nuns come to visit. He uses his second sentence to explain the reason for their visit: they suggest that the family speak English more often. But he defers his actual statement of topic until the third sentence, where he confirms the significance of the preceding sentences and points a direction for the rest of the paragraph.

> I remember when, 20 years ago, two grammar-school nuns visited my childhood home. They had come to suggest—with more tact than was necessary, because my parents accepted without question the church's authority—that

we make a greater effort to speak as much English around the house as possible. The nuns realized that my brothers and I led solitary lives largely because we were barely able to comprehend English in a school where we were the only Spanish-speaking students. My mother and father complied as best they could. Heroically, they gave up speaking to us in Spanish—the language that formed so much of the family's sense of intimacy in an alien world—and began to speak a broken English. Instead of Spanish sounds, I began hearing sounds that were new, harder, less friendly. More important, I was encouraged to respond in English. (Richard Rodriguez, "On Becoming a Chicano," *Saturday Review*)

Sometimes you will want readers to follow the path that led to your discovery. On such occasions, build your paragraph toward a topic sentence that provides an appropriate conclusion. Ralph Ellison uses this technique skillfully in the following paragraph.

To live in Harlem is to dwell in the very bowels of the city; it is to pass a labyrinthine existence among streets that explode monotonously skyward with the spires and crosses of churches and clutter under foot with garbage and decay. Harlem is a ruin—many of its ordinary aspects (its crimes, its casual violence, its crumbling buildings with littered area-ways, ill-smelling halls and vermin-invaded rooms) are indistinguishable from the distorted images that appear in dreams, and which, like muggers haunting a lonely hall, quiver in the waking mind with hidden and threatening significance. Yet this is no dream but the reality of well over four hundred thousand Americans; a reality which for many defines and colors the world. Overcrowded and exploited politically and economically, Harlem is the scene and symbol of the Negro's perpetual alienation in the land of his birth. (Ralph Ellison, "Harlem Is Nowhere," *Shadow and Act*)

Not every paragraph needs a topic sentence. Sometimes your readers will be able to infer your purpose from the way you express your thoughts. On such occasions a topic sentence would be gratuitous, out of place. In the following paragraph, for example, E. B. White, one of America's master stylists, evokes a summer place without composing a formal topic sentence.

Summertime, oh, summertime, pattern of life indelible, the fade-proof lake, the woods unshatterable, the pasture with the sweetfern and the juniper forever and ever, summer without end; this was the background, and the life along the shore was the design, the cottages with their innocent and tranquil design, their tiny docks with the flagpole and the American flag floating against the white clouds in the blue sky, the little paths over the roots of the trees leading from camp to camp and the paths leading back to the outhouses and can of lime for sprinkling, and at the souvenir counters at the store, the miniature birch-bark canoes and the postcards that showed things looking a little better than they looked. This was the American family at play, escaping the city heat, wondering whether the newcomers in the camp at the head of the cove were "common" or "nice," wondering whether it was true that the people who drove up for Sunday dinner at the farmhouse were turned away because there wasn't enough chicken. (E. B. White, "Once More to the Lake," *Essays of E. B. White*)

As a rule, you should reserve paragraphs without topic sentences for special occasions. When used for effect, they can be powerful and memorable, but you risk misleading your readers and yourself if you routinely decline to write topic sentences.

Remember, your readers are most disoriented and most alert at the beginning of a paragraph. They look to your first sentences for help. They expect that you will tell them how to interpret the new group of sentences they are about to read. Although you don't have to place your topic sentence at the beginning of a paragraph, or even use a topic sentence, be aware that your readers will scrutinize your first sentence for a clue to the unity of your paragraph. If that opening sentence does not declare the topic of your paragraph, it must at least point your readers toward the sentence or group of sentences that does identify or evoke the main topic.

Completeness

Completeness, the second major requirement of an effective paragraph, is relative. The amount of explanation an idea requires depends on the amount your readers need. You must decide this based on your knowledge of your subject and of your audience. Too much information can overwhelm readers, too little can annoy them. Inexperienced writers tend to supply too little detail. Consider this example.

> American Sign Language is a language unto itself. It has its own rules that determine the meaning and significance of each gesture. Experts familiar with these rules can use their hands to communicate extremely complex thoughts.

If that is all the writer is going to say about American Sign Language, this paragraph is incomplete for most readers because the first two sentences merely state the topic. This paragraph would only "satisfy" readers who were already familiar with the intricacies of American Sign Language—but such readers would not even need this brief paragraph. For those who do need it, the writer must provide further explanation:

> American Sign Language—ASL—is a language unto itself, with its own syntax and grammar. Adjectives follow nouns, as in Romance languages. In sign, one says "house blue," establishing a picture of what is being described and then embellishing on that. Many sign language "sentences" begin with a time element and then proceed with what happened, thereby conjugating the verbs. The movement of the shoulders, the speed of the hands, the facial expression, the number of repetitions of a sign, combine with the actual signs to give meaning to the language. Signing is precise. The casual gestures hearing people make when talking have no meaning in sign language. Hearing people who do learn sign usually practice "signed English," a word-for-word coding of English into signs, but that translation sorely limits the language. In some hands, signing is an art equal to an actor's rendering of Shakespeare. It is not just swoops and swirls but an enormous variety of expression, just as a great actor's delivery is completely different from some ham's idea of haughty speeches. (Lou Ann Walker, *A Loss for Words*)

Detailed information is necessary to make the meaning of the short paragraph clear. Of course, you can begin with a short paragraph if your purpose is to state the idea and then develop the topic in greater detail in a subsequent paragraph. In that case, the second paragraph would complete the first.

Here is another example of an incomplete paragraph:

> A child understands far more than we suspect. She may not understand words too well, but she senses what they mean by how they are spoken.

If the writers stops there, the reader is left with only a topic sentence and a brief statement that barely begins to develop the main idea. The reader needs to know how a child can "sense" the meaning of words she does not understand. The complete version of the paragraph supplies the answer:

> There is also a sense in which a child understands far more than we suspect. Because a child doesn't understand words too well (and also because his nervous system is not yet deadened by years spent as a lawyer, accountant, advertising executive, or professor of philosophy), a child attends not only to what we say but to everything about us as we say it—tone of voice, gesture, facial expression, bodily tensions, and so on. A child attends to a conversation between grown-ups with the same amazing absorption. Indeed, a child listening is, I hope, like a good psychiatrist listening—or like a good semanticist listening—because she watches not only the words but also the nonverbal events to which words bear, in all too many cases, so uncertain a relationship. Therefore a child is in some matters quite difficult to fool, especially on the subject of one's true attitude toward her. For this reason many parents, without knowing it, are to a greater or lesser degree in the situation of the worried mother who said to the psychiatrist to whom she brought her child, "I tell her a dozen times a day that I love her, but the brat still hates me. Why, doctor?" (S. I. Hayakawa, "Words and Children," *Through the Conversation Barrier*)

The additions to the paragraph clarify the process children use to understand words: they pay attention to tone of voice, gestures, facial expressions, and so on. The final example illustrates that children see beyond the words we use and understand what we really mean.

These examples demonstrate that you need to spell out the implications of a topic sentence with facts, illustrations, explanations—whatever is needed. Unless you give your readers the necessary information, they will have difficulty grasping your purpose. You can easily flesh out incomplete paragraphs once you realize that every generalization must be developed with supporting details.

Exercises ——— The following paragraphs are incomplete. Complete them by adding several examples or a sustained illustration from your own experience.

1. You cannot and should not try to eliminate all anger from your life. If you react mildly to everything, you will often suppress your true feelings. You must learn to recognize situations where expressing anger is counterproductive.

2. Most families have a private set of signs that enable them to communicate with one another without having to say a word. Family members use these signs in public to warn each other about a potential problem.

Order

The third requirement of effective paragraphs is consistent *order.* You saw in the paragraph on the Old South (page 161) that when sentences point in various directions readers are likely to have trouble following the writer's line of reasoning.

Order in a paragraph is like organization in an essay, but because paragraphs are smaller in scope, it may be easier to consider order as *direction of movement.* Four directional patterns in expository paragraphs are from *general to particular,* from *particular to general,* from *whole to parts,* and from *question to answer* or *effect to cause.*

General to Particular   A common pattern in expository paragraphs moves from a general statement, often a topic sentence, to specific explanations or illustrations of that statement. The purpose of the paragraph is to help the reader understand the general statement. That meaning becomes increasingly clear as the paragraph progresses. You saw this kind of clarification in the paragraphs on American Sign Language and children's ability to make sense of nonverbal language. Here is another example.

> It is easy to produce examples of the many ways in which Americans attempt to minimize, circumvent, or deny the interdependence upon which all human societies are based. We seek a private house, a private means of transportation, a private garden, a private laundry, self-service stores, and do-it-yourself skills of every kind. An enormous technology seems to have set itself the task of making it unnecessary for one human being ever to ask anything of another in the course of going about his daily business. Even within the family Americans are unique in their feeling that each member should have a separate room, and even a separate telephone, television, and car, when economically possible. We seek more and more privacy, and feel more and more alienated and lonely when we get it. What accidental contacts we do have, furthermore, seem more intrusive, not only because they are unsought but because they are unconnected with any familiar pattern of interdependence. (Philip Slater, *The Pursuit of Loneliness*)

Particular to General   A particular-to-general pattern reverses the preceding pattern. It begins with specific information and leads to a general conclusion, as in this example.

> We look at old family photographs in which we stand next to black, boxy Fords and are wearing period costumes, and we do not gaze fascinated

> because there we are young again, or there we are standing, as we never will
> again in life, next to our mother. We stare and drift because there we are . . .
> historical. It is the dress, the black car that dazzle us now and draw us
> beyond our mother's bright arms which once caught us. We reach into the
> attractive impersonality of something more significant than ourselves.
> (Patricia Hampl, *A Romantic Education*)

Had Hampl chosen, she could have followed a general-to-particular order by beginning with her last sentence and then illustrating its significance with details about family photographs.

The direction of movement within an individual paragraph is often determined by the direction of movement within an extended passage. As Bill Barich points out, paragraphs develop a rhythm for carrying various kinds of information. In the paragraphs that precede the quoted example, Hampl uses several general-to-particular patterns to discuss the search for a family past. In the example, she reverses the order to emphasize the particulars—family photographs. She returns to the general-to-particular order in the next paragraph, when she explores the impersonality of history.

Whole to Parts Sometimes the purpose of a paragraph is to show the parts or divisions of a topic, as in this example.

> There are medium friends, and pretty good friends, and very good friends
> indeed, and these friendships are defined by their level of intimacy. And
> what we'll reveal at each of these levels of intimacy is calibrated with care.
> We might tell a medium friend, for example, that yesterday we had a fight
> with our husband. And we might tell a pretty good friend that this fight with
> our husband made us so mad that we slept on the couch. And we might tell a
> very good friend that the reason we got so mad in that fight that we slept on
> the couch had something to do with that girl who works in his office. But it's
> only to our very best friends that we're willing to tell all, to tell what's going
> on with that girl in his office. (Judith Viorst, "Friends, Good Friends—and
> Such Good Friends," *Redbook*)

This order is also called *partitive* or *enumerative*. The opening statement announces the divisions of the topic, often indicating their number; the rest of the paragraph identifies and defines each of the parts. The partitive or enumerative paragraph is often used in argument, either to introduce the issues to be considered or to summarize a discussion. In exposition, it is used to introduce the categories to be analyzed. Such paragraphs are usually less detailed than Viorst's paragraph because succeeding paragraphs supply information about the categories.

Question to Answer, Effect to Cause A paragraph may begin with a question and give the answer or with an effect and explain the cause. Such a paragraph may have no specific topic sentence beyond the opening question or statement of the effect. This paragraph begins with a question which it proceeds to answer.

So what are we to do, those of us whose habit and pleasure and doom is our tendency, as a Georgia lady put it, to "fly off at every other whipstitch"? Think in terms of movable feasts, for a start. Live here, wherever here may be, as if we were going to belong here for the rest of our lives. Learn to hallow whatever ground we happen to stand on or land on. Like medieval knights who took their tapestries along on Crusades, like modern Afghanis with their yurts, we must pack such totems and icons as we can to make short-term quarters feel like home. Pillows, small rugs, watercolors can dispel much of the chilling anonymity of a sublet apartment or motel room. When we can, we should live in rooms with stoves or fireplaces or anyway candlelight. The ancient saying still is true: Extinguished hearth, extinguished family. Round tables help, too, and as a friend of mine once put it, so do "too many comfortable chairs, with surfaces to put feet on, arranged so as to encourage a maximum of eye-contact." Such rooms inspire good talk, of which good clans can never have enough. (Jane Howard, *Families*)

The next paragraph begins with an effect and then considers some of the causes of that effect.

There is something very wrong with an institution that so often disintegrates at the very point it is supposed to be the most useful. It is obviously absurd that we should marry, have children, get divorced, and then start the whole thing over in an even more difficult and complicated way. The "reconstituted" families of remarriage give statistical stability to the big picture. But the clue to what is wrong with the big picture lies in the "transition period to new family life," which is likely to be three or four years when a woman is caring for very small children. Nearly half the children born today will spend a significant part of their lives in a single-parent home. Raising a child or—worse—children, alone, is the wrong way to do it. It is too hard, not on the children—if recent studies mean anything—but on the mother. Of American women divorced and separated, only 4 percent receive alimony, and only 23 percent with children receive child support. Women earn, on the average, fifty-nine cents for every dollar men earn. And of all female-headed families, 41.8 percent live below the poverty level. (Jane O'Reilly, "But Who Will Take Care of the Children?")

Summary of Main Orders of Movement Within Paragraphs

1. *General to particular*
   Opening general statement or topic sentence followed by illustration or details of explanation or proof. The paragraph may conclude with a restatement of the topic sentence.

2. *Particular to general*
   From a series of detailed statements to a conclusion drawn from them. If there is a topic sentence, it occurs at or near the end of the paragraph.

3. *Whole to parts*
   Paragraph begins with an introductory statement about the number of parts and then explains each part: often a first, second, third order.

> **4. Question to answer, or effect to cause**
> Paragraph begins with question or effect, then answers the question or shows the cause.

Coherence

A paragraph is coherent when the sentences are woven together in such a way that readers move easily from one sentence to the next and read the paragraph as an integrated discussion rather than as a series of separate sentences.

If you have a sense of purpose when you begin writing, then you are not likely to have trouble with coherence. Lack of coherence often results if you think about your topic one sentence at a time: you write one sentence, stop, think a minute, write a second sentence, stop, and continue in a series of spurts and pauses. Paragraphs written in this way are likely to lack coherence because your ideas do not flow from one sentence to the next and continuity is lost.

A paragraph can exhibit unity, completeness, and order but still lack coherence. The writer of the following paragraph is composing a paper to describe the ordeals of the immigration experience. Here he tries to illustrate the processing procedure at Ellis Island in New York Harbor, the official place of entry for most European immigrants from 1892 until 1943.

The immigrants were herded off the boat onto Ellis Island. Inspectors talking in a strange language pushed them into a building where metal railings divided them into lines. They waited as the doctors examined them for diseases and defects. Some were separated from their families and sent to other parts of the building. The rest moved on to the next test. They were asked about their relatives, their politics, their work, their money. The questions were confusing, and they were never sure they gave the right answers.

Although this paragraph moves in an orderly sequence, it requires revision. Consider the following points:

▼ What is the purpose of the paragraph? You know from the description of the paper that the writer wants to describe the ordeal of immigration. The information does illustrate this experience, but its significance would be clearer if the paragraph possessed a topic sentence that bound the individual sentences together. Without such a sentence, a reader may not see the writer's purpose in describing the activity on Ellis Island.

▼ What is the relationship between this paragraph and the one that preceded it? The reader is told that the immigrants were on a boat, but there is no introductory statement that explains the transition from boat to island.

▼ Although the repetition of *they* provides some coherence, the sentence structure becomes monotonous, emphasizing the paragraph's disjointedness.

Now consider this revised version.

Although the immigrants endured many physical hardships during the crossing, they were not prepared for the psychological ordeal of Ellis Island. They had come so far, and now they realized that they could be sent back. Inspectors shouting strange words herded them into a massive building where metal railings divided them into lines. There they waited in silent humiliation as one doctor after another poked at their bodies, looking for diseases and defects. Occasional screams followed family members who were pulled out of line and led off to another part of the building. The rest moved on to the next test. Interpreters asked them about their relatives, their politics, their work, their money. Every question seemed like a trap. If they told the truth, they might be turned away. If they lied, they might be caught. If they said nothing, they might be marked dumb and sent back where they came from.

The revision was improved in the following ways:

▼ The topic sentence states the purpose of the paragraph, gives significance to all the details that follow, and connects this paragraph to preceding paragraphs.

▼ The more detailed and evocative explanation of the psychological ordeal of the inspection process helps bind the sentences together more effectively than in the unsatisfactory version, where sentences were connected only by a common subject.

▼ The concluding sentences dramatize the anxiety of those waiting for clearance and sum up the content of the whole paragraph.

This contrast of the original and revised paragraphs shows how an unsatisfactory piece of writing can better express the main idea by providing the links that reveal the relationship among the sentences. Other connective devices that increase paragraph coherence are *pronouns, contrast, repetitive structure,* and *transitional markers.*

Coherence Through Pronoun Reference   Because it refers to an antecedent, a pronoun points back (or forward) to create a simple, natural connection. Notice in the following paragraph how the pronoun *they* links the whole paragraph to the antecedent *emigrants.* Pronoun repetition reinforces the purpose of this paragraph: to illustrate that emigrants "shared certain characteristics."

Looking for lost baggage, Ellis Island, 1905. © Lewis Hine from the collection of Walter and Naomi Rosenblum.

Most of the emigrants shared certain characteristics as a group: they were men and women who had already made one or more moves before in a restless search for better lands. They were children of parents who themselves had moved to new lands. If ever a people could be said to have been "prepared" for the adventure of the Overland Trail, it would have to be these men and women. They possessed the assortment of skills needed to make the journey and to start again. They had owned land before, had cleared land before, and were prepared to clear and own land again. And they were young. Most of the population that moved across half the continent were between sixteen and thirty-five years of age. (Lillian Schlissel, *Women's Diaries of Westward Journey*)

Coherence Through Contrasted Elements When a topic sentence calls for a comparison or contrast, the pairing of the contrasted elements enhances coherence. In the following paragraph, the middle sentences illustrate the contrast between the lives of generals Grant and Lee—a contrast that is announced in the topic sentence and summarized in the concluding sentence.

> So Grant and Lee were in complete contrast, representing two diametrically opposed elements in American life. Grant was the modern man emerging; beyond him, ready to come on the stage, was the great age of steel and machinery, of crowded cities and a restless, burgeoning vitality. Lee might have ridden down from the old age of chivalry, lance in hand, silken banner fluttering over his head. Each man was the perfect champion of his cause, drawing both his strengths and his weaknesses from the people he led. (Bruce Catton, "Grant and Lee: A Study in Contrasts," *The American Story*)

Coherence Through Repetitive Structure   Purposeless repetition should be avoided, but deliberate repetition of key words, phrases, or sentence patterns can make sentences flow into a coherent paragraph. In the following example, every sentence after the first has the same structure and the same opening words, "There is nothing." This kind of repetition (discussed as *parallel structure* in Chapter 8) ties the sentences together in a coherent development of the topic sentence.

> America, the richest and most powerful nation in the world, can well lead the way in this revolution of values. There is nothing to prevent us from paying adequate wages to schoolteachers, social workers and other servants of the public to insure that we have the best available personnel in these positions which are charged with the responsibility of guiding our future generations. There is nothing but a lack of social vision to prevent us from paying an adequate wage to every American citizen whether he be a hospital worker, laundry worker, maid or day laborer. There is nothing except shortsightedness to prevent us from guaranteeing an annual minimum—and *livable* income for every American family. There is nothing, except a tragic death wish, to prevent us from reordering our priorities so the pursuit of peace will take precedence over the pursuit of war. There is nothing to keep us from remolding a recalcitrant status quo with bruised hands until we have fashioned it into brotherhood. (Martin Luther King, Jr., *Where Do We Go from Here: Chaos or Community?*)

Coherence Through Transitional Markers   *Transitional markers* are words or phrases often placed at or near the beginning of a sentence or clause to signal the relationship between the new sentence or clause and the one before it. The most common markers are the conjunctions *and, or, nor, but,* and *for.* Others—sometimes called *transitional connectives*—indicate the direction a new sentence is about to take and prepare the reader for what is to follow. The most common transitional connectives are used as follows:

▼ *To introduce an illustration:* for example, for instance, to illustrate

▼ *To add another phrase of the same idea:* second, in the second place, then, furthermore, next, moreover, in addition, similarly, again, also, finally

▼ *To point out a contrast or qualification:* on the other hand, nevertheless, despite this fact, on the contrary, still, however, conversely, instead

▼ *To indicate a conclusion or result:* therefore, in conclusion, to sum up, consequently, as a result, accordingly, in other words

Coherence Through Connection Between Paragraphs

Coherence is necessary not only within a paragraph but also between the paragraphs of an essay, so that your readers can see how each paragraph is related to those that precede or follow it. The following passage begins with an assertion. At the end of the first paragraph, the writer notes a change, thus providing the transitional link to the next paragraphs and giving coherence to the whole passage.

Those of us who grew up in the fifties believed in the permanence of our American-history textbooks. To us as children, those texts were the truth of things: they were American history. It was not just that we read them before we understood that not everything that is printed is the truth, or the whole truth. It was that they, much more than other books, had the demeanor and trappings of authority. They were weighty volumes. They spoke in measured cadences: imperturbable, humorless, and as distant as Chinese emperors. Our teachers treated them with respect, and we paid them abject homage by memorizing a chapter a week. But now the textbook histories have changed, some of them to such an extent that an adult would find them unrecognizable.

One current junior-high-school American history begins with a story about a Negro cowboy called George McJunkin. It appears that when McJunkin was riding down a lonely trail in New Mexico one cold spring morning in 1925 he discovered a mound containing bones and stone implements, which scientists later proved belonged to an Indian civilization ten thousand years old. The book goes on to say that scientists now believe there were people in the Americas at least twenty thousand years ago. It discusses the Aztec, Mayan, and Incan civilizations and the meaning of the word "culture" before introducing the European explorers.

Another history text—this one for the fifth grade—begins with the story of how Henry B. Gonzalez, who is a member of Congress from Texas, learned about his own nationality. When he was ten years old, his teacher told him he was an American because he was born in the United States. His grandmother, however, said, "The cat was born in the oven. Does that make him bread?" After reporting that Mr. Gonzalez eventually went to college and law school, the book explains that "the melting pot idea hasn't worked out as some thought it would," and that now "some people say that the people of the United States are more like a salad bowl than a melting pot." (Frances FitzGerald, *America Revised*)

Exercise ———— Read the following passage excerpted from "The Crazy Life," Bill Barich's article on youth gangs in Los Angeles. The passage is presented without its original paragraphing. Reread Barich's comments on paragraphing (page 160); review the four requirements of effective topical paragraphs; and then discuss how you would break this passage into manageable units.

The landmark work in the sociology of gangs is Frederic M. Thrasher's "The Gang," which was published in 1927. Thrasher was a founder of the Chicago school, a methodology that stressed the importance of interviews and direct observation. In pursuing his study, he observed more than a thousand Illinois gangs before arriving at his well-known theory that gangs are largely a phenomenon of immigrant communities. According to Thrasher, they represent an ethnic group in transition, waiting out its adolescence until it can be assimilated into the mainstream. The underlying assumption is that the attractions of a so-called "normal" life—a job, a family, a house in the suburbs—far outweigh the attractions of a life of crime. Over the years, Thrasher's ideas would be repeated, with variations, in many other studies, monographs, and books, and they still echo in current sociological theory, coloring the way youth-gang members are perceived, making them seem distant, opposite, always somewhat less than human. In Los Angeles County, there are Hispanic youth gangs whose histories go back almost a century, involving three and sometimes four generations of men. There are black gangs of such size, sophistication, and economic well-being that they put many small corporations to shame. There are gangs of Chinese teen-agers who run gambling emporiums as skillfully as old Vegas hands. When immigrants, legal or illegal, come to Southern California, their children form gangs—Korean, Vietnamese, Filipino, Honduran, Salvadoran, Nicaraguan, Guatemalan. There are Somoan gangs in Los Angeles County, and gangs from Tonga, and they feud with each other just as their ancestors did on the islands. Increasingly, in affluent suburban towns, there are gangs of white teen-agers, kids from decent homes, who—the saying goes—"have everything," and still take to the streets. (Bill Barich, "The Crazy Life," *The New Yorker*)

SPECIAL PARAGRAPHS

So far in this chapter you have examined topical paragraphs, the main paragraphs in an essay that develop your topic or some aspect of it. Special paragraphs are used to *introduce* or *conclude* an essay and to *mark transitions* from one unit to another.

Introductory Paragraphs

Readers want to know what you are writing about and whether they will find your subject interesting and significant. Your introductory paragraph leads into your essay, giving your readers a preview. Most introductions contain attention-getting statements that engage the readers' interest or statements that suggest the organization or indicate the scope, focus, or thesis of your essay. Notice how Bill Barich blends these in his introductory paragraph to "The Crazy Life."

The first time I met Manuel Velazquez, he greeted me awkwardly, unable to shake hands. He had cut himself on a broken bottle while crawling around in a tunnel to read a new graffito, and a doctor at a local clinic had sewed him up with seventeen stitches and then wrapped the wound in cotton, gauze, and tape. Manuel was stoical about his injury, seeing it as an unfortunate but perhaps necessary consequence of his job, which is to keep teen-age gang members in the San Fernando Valley, in California, from killing one another in wars. In Los Angeles County, of which the valley is a part, there are an estimated fifty thousand youth-gang members, and about three hundred of them are expected to be murdered this year. In the old days of youth-gang warfare, the days of "Blackboard Jungle" and "West Side Story," a boy might arm himself with a knife or a homemade zip gun, but now in times of trouble he has access to .357 magnum pistols, hunting rifles with pinpoint scopes, and Uzi semi-automatics from Israel. (Bill Barich, "The Crazy Life," *The New Yorker*)

You can utilize many strategies in your introductory paragraph to suggest your intentions. The writers whose essays you have examined in previous chapters have used the following techniques.

Direct Statement   Matt Fisher uses direct statement to introduce two of his essays on drug abuse in the work place. In one version, he begins with a general statement about the effect of drug abuse, restricts this statement to drug abuse in the work place, and then offers further clarification (see Chapter 6, page 154):

> In the last decade drug abuse has reached epidemic proportions in our country—destroying the lives of our young people, exhausting the energies of our legal system, and eroding our fundamental values. Nowhere is the problem more alarming than in the work place, where drug abuse costs the American economy in excess of $60 billion a year. All of us—employers, workers, and consumers—want to cure this plague that threatens the health of our culture. Unfortunately, there is as much controversy about the cure as there is about the disease.

In his "My Side" essay Matt begins with three statements about the problem of drug abuse in the work place (see Chapter 6, page 143). These narrow the focus of the paragraph but build toward a direct statement of his thesis—that drug testing is unreliable, counterproductive, and an invasion of workers' privacy.

> The increased public awareness of drug abuse in our society has created a sense of public alarm about the potential dangers of drug abuse in the work place. Although such concern is justifiable, particularly when it affects the safety of workers and consumers, most companies are trying to solve this complex problem with a simple urine test. Whether it is used to weed out job applicants or identify suspected abusers on the job, urine testing is a misguided attempt to find a quick fix. The test is not only unreliable and counterproductive, it is a serious invasion of workers' privacy.

Factual Information   In his first essay, "Their Side," Matt attempts to establish an objective tone by engaging his readers' interest with the *facts* of the dramatic train wreck (see Chapter 6, page 134).

On January 4, 1987, an Amtrak train traveling north of Baltimore collided with three Conrail engines, causing the worst accident in Amtrak's history. Sixteen passengers were killed, 170 were injured, and five locomotives from the two trains were destroyed. Investigators have since discovered that the crew operating the Conrail engines had been using marijuana.

Quotation   Wallace Armstrong uses his father's "words of wisdom" to set up his essay about painting *Brandon's Clown* (see Chapter 1, page 21). The quotation guides the reader through the narration and serves as an ironic commentary on Wally's subject and purpose:

> Few of those words of wisdom that are passed from father to son are followed. Most are simply acknowledged and forgotten. My father's advice about my adolescent love for painting was simple and direct: "Son, you have a special talent. Be smart. Use it to make money." With his words guiding me, I took my love to the marketplace. I began accepting commissions, painting fantasies for those who didn't have the skill or desire to paint their own.

Dramatic Episode   Ellen Haack's description of Barry making granola dramatizes the unique features of Barry's personality (see Chapter 3, pages 71–72). She concludes the episode with his infamous words, "it's good for me"— words with which Barry, as the reader soon discovers, justifies everything:

> Barry's in the kitchen making granola. His long, narrow frame moves deftly around the work area, pausing to scan the recipe book on the counter or search the shelves for the ingredients—wheat germ, bran, rolled oats, sunflower seeds, raisins, honey—he plans to mix in a large, gray earthenware bowl. While he works, he hums a vaguely recognizable version of "Blue Moon," drumming on the top of the counter or the edge of the bowl with a wooden spoon. He's happy. Making granola always has this effect on him. He doesn't like to make granola—it's messy and time-consuming. He doesn't like to eat granola—it's too crunchy without milk and too mushy with it. But he likes to contemplate his reasons for eating granola—"it's good for me."

Anecdote   After her attention-getting first sentence, Jane Graham uses an anecdote about her trip to the American Museum of Natural History to introduce her reasons for her whale-watching trip (see Chapter 5, page 121). The purpose of her allusions to textbooks and magazines is to arouse the curiosity of her readers, making them want to "see more":

> The problem with whales is that they don't fit under a microscope. As a small girl, I walked around and around the large skeleton of a blue whale on the first floor of the American Museum of Natural History, trying to compare its size to the skeletons of the brontosaurus and diplodocus I had seen on the fourth floor. Like those creatures from another time, whales challenged and held my imagination. I could never see enough of them. The drawings in textbooks outlined their shape but reduced their enormous size to a few inches. The photographs in magazines suggested their magnificence but usu-

ally focused on their parts—the head rising to breech, the tail arching to dive. Last summer, hoping to see more, I booked passage on the *Portuguese Princess* out of Provincetown, Massachusetts, for my first whale watch.

Transitional Paragraphs

A transitional paragraph signals a change in content. It tells your readers that they have finished one main unit and are moving to the next, or it tells them that they are moving from a general explanation to specific examples or applications. A transitional paragraph is often as brief as one sentence:

> So much for the parents. We come now to the children.

> Let us see how this theory works in practice.

> And this brings us to the final ordeal of the crossing: Ellis Island.

> A few examples will make this explanation clear.

Sometimes you will need to supplement such signals with a concise summary of what has been covered or with a suggestion of what is to come, as Howard Gardner did in this paragraph from "The Compositions of Mozart's Mind" (see Chapter 1, page 20).

> Accounts of creation in other media echo the same contrasts. For every fluent Mozart, Trollope, or Picasso, who poured forth works with unceasing fecundity, and for every Edgar Allan Poe, who claimed to plot out his works with mathematical precision, one encounters reports of a Dostoevsky, who reworked his novels numerous times, a Thomas Mann, who struggled over three pages a day, or a Richard Wagner, who had to work himself up into a nearly psychotic frenzy before finally finding himself able to put pen to score.

Concluding Paragraphs

Not every essay needs a concluding paragraph. If you have adequately demonstrated your thesis, nothing more is necessary. You do not need to add a paragraph that mechanically restates the obvious: "Thus I have shown. . . ."

A good concluding paragraph does not necessarily sum up the ideas in an essay. Bill Barich concludes "The Crazy Life" with a quotation from Manuel, the man he introduced at the beginning of the essay. This paragraph echoes the introduction, but it also opens up the essay by suggesting that Manuel will always have more work to do.

> "You can't get depressed about it," he said. "You know, with the people on my team, I tell them they have to make their job fun—even though it's a crummy job. It's got lots of negatives, but lots of positives, too. Once you start an input into somebody's life, you begin to influence them, you break the monotony. Some kids, they don't know any other kind of life. What we do, it's like throwing a wrench inside an engine. It screws up the structure. Suddenly, you're a part of their lives. That's good to feel. Sometimes it's like I can almost control what's going on. It's like having a sixth sense. Like seeing into the future and controlling it. That's when you know you're doing your job." (Bill Barich, "The Crazy Life," *The New Yorker*)

An effective concluding paragraph leaves the reader with a sense of completeness, a conviction that the point has been made, that nothing else needs to be said; it contributes something significant to the essay that could not have been accomplished by a "Thus I have shown . . ." conclusion.

The following examples, taken from essays in previous chapters, show various strategies for concluding paragraphs.

Restatement and Recommendation   Andy Rooney summarizes the main points he has made about advertising and emphasizes the need to perfect existing products instead of increasing the number of new products (see Chapter 4, page 95):

> Putting the same product in a new package isn't what I call a new product. When an advertisement tells me what I'm buying is "new and improved," I always wonder exactly what the improvement is and whether I was a sucker for having bought the product last year before they fixed whatever was wrong with it.
>
> I don't care what the *Wall Street Journal* says, I like the idea of fewer new products on the market. What we ought to do is keep making the old ones until we get them right.

Prediction   Wallace Armstrong begins his conclusion by drawing on the information he has discussed in other paragraphs—his father's advice, his artistic reputation. But he ends by predicting that in twenty years Brandon may pay him back for his creation (see Chapter 1, page 22):

> As I left holding my first commission, I did not think about my father's advice or my artistic reputation. I thought only of poor Brandon. I will not be surprised if, twenty years from now, a deranged young man stops me on the street and smashes a clown painting over my head. I probably deserve worse.

Resolution   Jane Graham presents a chronological wind-up to her narrative and a final, climactic insight into her experience (see Chapter 5, page 123):

> Although we watched eagerly for him to surface again, we looked in vain. Soon we began to look at one another. We smiled, but we did not talk. Neither did Richard. No explanation was necessary. We had watched a whale. A whale had watched us. Finally, the engine coughed, and the *Portuguese Princess* resumed her journey back to Provincetown.

Quotation   Sometimes a single line of dialogue makes an effective ending, especially when the words resonate like Ellen Haack's (see Chapter 3, page 73):

> "See, I told you it was good for me."

At other times, a carefully chosen quotation from an expert can strengthen the authority of your conclusion. Matt Fisher uses this strategy to make his final points about drug testing in the work place (see Chapter 6, pages 155–156):

> Lewis L. Maltby, Vice President, Drexelbrook Controls, Inc., describes the kind of consensus policy that should cure drug abuse in the work place: "We

can attack drug abuse with drug testing. It's quick, it's easy, and it's cheap. It just doesn't work. It gives us inaccurate and irrelevant information and undermines the trust of good employees who resent being ordered to pee in a bottle when they've done nothing wrong. Or, we can take the time to learn about our employees, watch their job performance, and help them when it starts to slip. It's time consuming, difficult, and expensive. But it works. Not just in preventing work-place drug abuse, but in creating a committed and productive work place" (Maltby 4).

REVISING TOPICAL PARAGRAPHS

As you learned in Chapter 4, there are two types of revision: global revision, employed while you are still creating your final draft, and local revision, in which you fine-tune your final draft. Local revision of paragraphs ensures that each paragraph in your essay not only works externally, to advance the purpose of your essay, but also works internally, to create a sensible sequence of thought. The discussion of topical paragraphs in this chapter has shown you some ways to think about local revision, especially in the case of the paragraph about Ellis Island (pages 169–170). To identify problems in your own paragraphs, you must view your paragraphs as your readers will. In other words, after you have refined your subject, audience, and purpose through global revision, and after you have established a reasonably firm organization, you must give your work a sentence-by-sentence reading, concentrating on the relation of sentences to each other and to the topic sentence.

One helpful technique in such close reading is creating a descriptive outline (see Chapter 3, pages 62–63). As you recall, in a descriptive outline you describe what each paragraph in an essay says (that is, its main idea) and does (that is, how the paragraph supports the main idea). You should be able to state succinctly the main idea of every topical paragraph you write. If in reading a paragraph you find that you cannot succinctly state its main idea, you probably need to reconsider your topic sentence—or create one in the first place. If you find that you cannot determine what a paragraph does, the problem may be that it does nothing: it may fail to support the topic sentence or fail to relate any particular meaning.

You need then to consider the paragraph's internal qualities: unity, completeness, order, and coherence. A paragraph that does not exhibit each of these qualities will not effectively advance your purpose. It will leave questions unanswered, details unsupported, transitions incomplete; and your readers will receive less from your writing than you intended. You must question both the meaning and function of each sentence in your paragraph and the overall effect of all the sentences.

In the following example a writer reports a series of impressions:

(1) On Bourbon Street in the French Quarter of New Orleans there are a 50-cent peepshow and a theater that shows pornographic movies. (2) Pictures painted by talented artists are for sale in a shop down the street. (3) Canned

music blares through doors held partly open by hustlers of strip joints. (4) There is a concert hall with no doors and no admission fee, where the crowd is entertained by jazz musicians. (5) In some places there are "dancing girls" who just walk across the stage and do "bumps" in what is supposed to be a dancer routine. (6) Sometimes there is a young woman who dances gracefully. (7) She has mastered the techniques that the better burlesques made popular in earlier years.

This paragraph does not lack detail; it is a series of details that try to capture the confusion of Bourbon Street. But the paragraph is all detail and no pattern: it has no unifying idea, no recognizable order, and no semblance of coherence.

The details in the paragraph fall into two groups: sentences 1, 3, and 5 show an unfavorable impression of Bourbon Street; sentences 2, 4, 6, and 7 suggest a more favorable impression. By classifying the details in this way, you can discern that the writer probably intends to contrast the two impressions. This purpose, stated in a topic sentence, is: "Bourbon Street in the French Quarter of New Orleans is a contrast of vulgarity and art." With that topic sentence as the controlling idea of the paragraph, you can revise its order in one of two ways:

▼   Use an *A+B* contrast in which all the details suggesting vulgarity (*A*) are placed in the first half of the paragraph and all those suggesting art (*B*) are placed in the second half, with a transitional marker (*but* or *on the other hand*) to mark the change.

▼   Use an *A/B +A/B* contrast in which matched details of vulgarity and art alternate within each sentence.

For this paragraph, the second arrangement is better because it is truer to the frequent contrasts the writer is trying to describe. Here is a revised version:

Bourbon Street in the French Quarter of New Orleans is a contrast of vulgarity and art. Just a few doors down the street from a 50-cent peepshow and a theater that presents pornographic movies is a shop displaying and selling paintings by talented artists. At strip joints canned music blares out from doors kept ajar by hustlers seeking to entice passers-by; yet not far away is a concert hall with no admission fee, where musicians play first-rate jazz. Even the "dancing girls" offer a sharp contrast: most limit themselves to a slow walk across the stage, interrupted by exaggerated "bumps"; but a few gracefully demonstrate the techniques that once made burlesque at its best an art form.

REVISING SPECIAL PARAGRAPHS

Because introductory, transitional, and concluding paragraphs are used for special purposes, they require a somewhat different approach in revision. In judging how well they do what they are meant to do, you should focus less on method than on effect.

Be sure that your introductory paragraph clearly states the thesis you intend to develop and that the thesis is advantageously positioned within the paragraph. Or, if you have used an attention-getting device, you need to look carefully at this "hook" to see that it entices rather than confuses your readers.

Check to see that your opening paragraph fits your final draft. An introductory paragraph written before the final draft was completed may no longer be appropriate. Does your opening seem misleading, flat, or simply uninspiring? View it with an open mind, and do not hesitate to revise it completely if your other revisions make a different opening necessary.

As you revise, pay particular attention to transitional paragraphs, the structural seams of your essay. Significant revisions elsewhere may require you to revise your transitional paragraphs or to delete them and use a concluding sentence or an opening phrase in existing paragraphs. Or you may discover that changes in your essay require you to add a transitional paragraph to clarify the movement from one unit to another. Such decisions require you to reexamine the connections between your ideas to be certain that you have chosen the most effective strategy for communicating those connections to your readers.

When you revise a concluding paragraph, consider whether your essay needs a formal conclusion. You do not want to belabor the obvious. If your conclusion merely repeats what you have already said, delete it. If you decide that your essay does need a conclusion, consider the impression you want to leave in closing. You will sometimes discover that other revisions—both global and local—have weakened the effectiveness of your original conclusion. After revising the other parts of your essay, you will know what you must do to round off your work effectively, perhaps even memorably.

Exercises ———— Identify the problems in the following paragraphs and then revise each paragraph.

1. The front porch was once a doorsill. It became a square platform large enough to hold two chairs. It lengthened and began to expand around the sides of the house. At one time, it was long and narrow, just wide enough for a row of chairs. People sat there watching and talking about their neighbors. Porches were a status symbol of economic prosperity and social prominence. Architects complained that they were too ornate. Cars created dust and fumes, so families went inside. The car also gave young lovers more privacy than the porch swing. Air conditioning made it unnecessary to go outside for air. People built backyard patios so the family could have some privacy.

2. It is unusual for one family to live in the same community for more than two generations. The average American family moves once every five years. Americans want to look for their roots. Many have complex ties to different parts of the world and are proud of their heritage. It's hard to trace the effects of immigration. Most families are scattered all over the country. Parents or grandparents who used to bring everyone together for Christmas spend December in trailer parks in Florida.

3. The Gateway Arch in St. Louis is a 630-foot stainless-steel arch. It marks the most prominent point of embarkation for those who traveled into the new territories. A Museum of Westward Expansion, near the arch, commemorates the frontier experience. Inside the steel structure is a contraption like a Ferris wheel that travels to the apex of the arch. The small windows provide

a thirty-mile view in any direction. On the Mississippi River, tied to a dock near the arch, is a fast-food restaurant designed to look like a riverboat.

4. The people whose ancestors built the Great Wall of China made one of the most widely acclaimed contributions to American history. Over thirteen thousand Chinese built the western half of the transcontinental railroad. Digging tunnels through mountains and track beds across desserts, they laid 10 miles of track a day. On May 10, 1869, when a golden spike was driven at Promontory Point, Utah, no Chinese were visible. Americans resented the strength and skill of the "little yellow men." Anti-Chinese resentment was so high that Congress passed a series of Exclusion Acts that prohibited Chinese immigration. These laws were repealed in 1943, and Chinese were admitted under a strict quota system.

Composing Paragraphs on Your Computer

The size of your computer screen limits the amount of text you can see at one time. To evaluate all the paragraphs in your essay, you will have to print out your entire text and read the hard copy. You can make a quick check on your screen, however, by marking the first sentence in every paragraph and transferring it to another file on your computer. This new file should then contain an outline of your essay. Read this sequence of sentences to determine if it organizes and advances the purpose of your text in a logical and coherent way.

Next, return to your original text and evaluate each individual paragraph. If a paragraph needs additional development, add appropriate examples to make it *complete*. If a sentence distracts from your purpose or destroys the *unity* of your paragraph, delete it. If other sentences are out of *order*, use the cut-and-paste feature of your word-processing program to move them to a logical position. You can also use the copy-and-paste feature to compare the original passage with the new one you have created.

After you have checked individual paragraphs, reread the hard copy to assess the visual and dramatic features of your paragraphs. If your introduction seems too long, condense it so that your readers can easily locate your subject and purpose. If you need to add a transitional paragraph, or a transitional marker within a paragraph, do so at the appropriate spot. If your concluding paragraphs seem undramatic, delete them and compose another ending. If you want to change your emphasis, mark your paragraphs and move them to another place in your text.

Family: The One Social Glue | Ellen Goodman

In her syndicated newspaper column, Ellen Goodman takes occasion to comment on a variety of social issues. In this column her subject is the American family, the "only place where we remember we're all related." How do you account for the difference in length between Goodman's and Barich's paragraphs? How do the size and sequence of Goodman's paragraphs contribute to her purpose?

They are going home for Thanksgiving, traveling through the clogged   1
arteries of airports and highways, bearing bridge chairs and serving plates, Port-a-Cribs and pies. They are going home to rooms that resound with old arguments and interruptions, to piano benches filled with small cousins, to dining-room tables stretched out to the last leaf.

They no longer migrate over the river and through the woods straight into   2
that Norman Rockwell poster: Freedom from Want. No, Thanksgiving isn't just a feast, but a reunion. It's no longer a celebration of food (which is plentiful in America) but of family (which is scarce).

Now families are so dispersed that it's easier to bring in the crops than the   3
cousins. Now it's not so remarkable that we have a turkey to feed the family. It's more remarkable that there's enough family around to warrant a turkey.

For most of the year, we are a nation of individuals, all wrapped in sepa-   4
rate cellophane packages like lamb chops in the meat department of a city supermarket. Increasingly we live with decreasing numbers. We create a new category like Single Householder, and fill it to the top of the Census Bureau reports.

For most of the year, we are segregated along generation lines into retire-   5
ment villages and singles complexes, young married subdivisions and college dormitories, all exclusive clubs whose membership is defined by age.

Even when we don't live in age ghettos, we often think that way. Those   6
who worried about a generation gap in the sixties worry about a generation war in the seventies. They see a community torn by warring rights: the Elderly Rights vs. the Middle-Aged Rights vs. the Children Rights. All competing for a piece of the pie.

This year, the Elderly Rights fought against mandatory retirement while   7
the Younger Rights fought for job openings. The Children Rights worried about money to keep their schools open, while the Elderly Rights worried about the rising cost of real estate taxes.

The retired generation lobbied for a increase in Social Security payments,   8
while the working generation lobbied for a decrease in Social Security taxes. The elderly wanted health care and the children wanted day care and the middle-aged were tired of taking care. They wanted the right to lead their own lives.

Goodman, Ellen. *Close to Home.* New York: Simon, 1979. 150–51.

At times it seemed as if the nation had splintered into peer pressure groups, panthers of all ages. People who cried, not "Me First" but, rather, "My Generation First." **9**

But now they have come home for Thanksgiving. Even the Rights are a family who come together, not to fight for their piece of the pie this day, but to share it. **10**

The family—as extended as that dining-room table—may be the one social glue strong enough to withstand the centrifuge of special interests which send us spinning away from each other. There, in the family, the Elderly Rights are also grandparents and the Children Rights are also nieces and nephews. There, the old are our parents and the young are our children. There, we care about each other's lives. There, self-interest includes concern for the future of the next generation. Because they are ours. **11**

Our families are not just the people (if I may massacre Robert Frost) who, "when you have to go there, they have to let you in." They are the people who maintain an unreasonable interest in each other. They are the natural peacemakers in the generation war. **12**

"Home" is the only place in society where we now connect along the ages, like discs along the spine of society. The only place where we remember that we're all related. And that's not a bad idea to go home to. **13**

Black Men and Public Space | Brent Staples

In this essay, which first appeared in *Ms.* magazine, Brent Staples analyzes the effects his appearance creates in a public environment. What kind of strategies does he use in his introductory paragraph to attract his readers' attention? How does he arrange and develop the topical paragraphs in the body of his essay? How does his concluding paragraph echo his introductory paragraph while suggesting new dimensions to his purpose?

My first victim was a woman—white, well dressed, probably in her early twenties. I came upon her late one evening on a deserted street in Hyde Park, a relatively affluent neighborhood in an otherwise mean, impoverished section of Chicago. As I swung onto the avenue behind her, there seemed to be a discreet, uninflammatory distance between us. Not so. She cast back a worried glance. To her, the youngish black man—a broad six feet two inches with a beard and billowing hair, both hands shoved into the pockets of a bulky military jacket—seemed menacingly close. After a few more quick glimpses, she picked up her pace and was soon running in earnest. Within seconds she disappeared into a cross street. **1**

That was more than a decade ago, I was twenty-two years old, a graduate student newly arrived at the University of Chicago. It was in the echo of that terrified woman's footfalls that I first began to know the unwieldy inheritance I'd come into—the ability to alter public space in ugly ways. It was clear that she **2**

Staples, Brent. "Black Men and Public Space." *Ms.* September 1986: 54, 88.

thought herself the quarry of a mugger, a rapist or worse. Suffering a bout of insomnia, however, I was stalking sleep, not defenseless wayfarers. As a softy who is scarcely able to take a knife to a raw chicken—let along hold one to a person's throat—I was surprised, embarrassed, and dismayed all at once. Her flight made me feel like an accomplice in tyranny. It also made it clear that I was indistinguishable from the muggers who occasionally seeped into the area from the surrounding ghetto. That first encounter, and those that followed, signified that a vast, unnerving gulf lay between nighttime pedestrians—particularly women—and me. And I soon gathered that being perceived as dangerous is a hazard in itself. I only needed to turn a corner into a dicey situation, or crowd some frightened, armed person in a foyer somewhere, or make an errant move after being pulled over by a policeman. Where fear and weapons meet—and they often do in urban America—there is always the possibility of death.

In that first year, my first away from my hometown, I was to become   3
thoroughly familiar with the language of fear. At dark, shadowy intersections, I could cross in front of a car stopped at a traffic light and elicit the *thunk, thunk, thunk, thunk* of the driver—black, white, male, or female—hammering down the door locks. On less traveled streets after dark, I grew accustomed to but never comfortable with people crossing to the other side of the street rather than pass me. Then there were the standard unpleasantries with policemen, doormen, bouncers, cabdrivers, and others whose business it is to screen out troublesome individuals *before* there is any nastiness.

I moved to New York nearly two years ago and I have remained an avid   4
night walker. In central Manhattan, the near-constant crowd cover minimizes tense one-on-one street encounters. Elsewhere—in SoHo, for example, where sidewalks are narrow and tightly spaced buildings shut out the sky—things can get very taut indeed.

After dark, on the warrenlike streets of Brooklyn where I live, I often see   5
women who fear the worst from me. They seem to have set their faces on neutral, and with their purse straps strung across their chests bandolier-style, they forge ahead as though bracing themselves against being tackled. I understand, of course, that the danger they perceive is not a hallucination. Women are particularly vulnerable to street violence, and young black males are drastically overrepresented among the perpetrators of that violence. Yet these truths are no solace against the kind of alienation that comes of being ever the suspect, a fearsome entity with whom pedestrians avoid making eye contact.

It is not altogether clear to me how I reached the ripe old age of twenty-   6
two without being conscious of the lethality nighttime pedestrians attributed to me. Perhaps it was because in Chester, Pennsylvania, the small, angry industrial town where I came of age in the 1960s, I was scarcely noticeable against a backdrop of gang warfare, street knifings, and murders. I grew up one of the good boys, had perhaps a half-dozen fistfights. In retrospect, my shyness of combat has clear sources.

As a boy, I saw countless tough guys locked away; I have since buried sev-   7
eral, too. They were babies, really—a teenage cousin, a brother of twenty-two, a childhood friend in his mid-twenties—all gone down in episodes of bravado played out in the streets. I came to doubt the virtues of intimidation early on. I chose, perhaps unconsciously, to remain a shadow—timid, but a survivor.

The fearsomeness mistakenly attributed to me in public places often has a   8
perilous flavor. The most frightening of these confusions occurred in the late 1970s and early 1980s, when I worked as a journalist in Chicago. One day,

rushing into the office of a magazine I was writing for with a deadline story in hand, I was mistaken for a burglar. The office manager called security and, with an ad hoc posse, pursued me through the labyrinthine halls, nearly to my editor's door. I had no way of proving who I was. I could only move briskly toward the company of someone who knew me.

Another time I was on assignment for a local paper and killing time before   9
an interview. I entered a jewelry store on the city's affluent Near North Side. The proprietor excused herself and returned with an enormous red Doberman pinscher straining at the end of a leash. She stood, the dog extended toward me, silent to my questions, her eyes bulging nearly out of her head. I took a cursory look around, nodded, and bade her good night.

Relatively speaking, however, I never fared as badly as another black male   10
journalist. He went to nearby Waukegan, Illinois, a couple of summers ago to work on a story about a murderer who was born there. Mistaking the reporter for the killer, police officers hauled him from his car at gunpoint and but for his press credentials would probably have tried to book him. Such episodes are not uncommon. Black men trade tales like this all the time.

Over the years, I learned to smother the rage I felt at so often being taken   11
for a criminal. Not to do so would surely have led to madness. I now take precautions to make myself less threatening. I move about with care, particularly late in the evening. I give a wide berth to nervous people on subway platforms during the wee hours, particularly when I have exchanged business clothes for jeans. If I happen to be entering a building behind some people who appear skittish, I may walk by, letting them clear the lobby before I return, so as not to seem to be following them. I have been calm and extremely congenial on those rare occasions when I've been pulled over by the police.

And on late-evening constitutionals I employ what has proved to be an   12
excellent tension-reducing measure: I whistle melodies from Beethoven and Vivaldi and the more popular classical composers. Even steely New Yorkers hunching toward nighttime destinations seem to relax, and occasionally they even join in the tune. Virtually everybody seems to sense that a mugger wouldn't be warbling bright, sunny selections from Vivaldi's *Four Seasons*. It is my equivalent of the cowbell that hikers wear when they know they are in bear country.

La Frontera | **Bill Barich**

In this opening section of a much longer essay, Bill Barich describes the movement across the "most heavily travelled border in the world." Reread his comments on composing paragraphs on page 160. Then examine the *unity, completeness, order,* and *coherence* of his paragraphs. How do the size and sequence of his paragraphs contribute to his purpose?

The most heavily travelled border in the world is a strip of scrubby California desert that runs for fifteen miles between the United States and Mexico, starting at the Pacific Ocean and ending at a thriving yet isolated spot called Otay Mesa. A chain-link fence follows the border for much of its course,   1

Barich, Bill. "La Frontera." *The New Yorker* 17 Dec. 1990: 72–74.

but it is torn in many places and trampled in many others, and in some places it has fallen down. Where the fence is still standing, you find litter on both sides of it which illegal aliens have left behind—beer and soda cans, cigarette packs, diapers, syringes, candy wrappers, and even comic-book *novelas* that feature cautionary tales about the perils of a trip to *El Norte.* These *novelas* tell of dishonest employers, horrible living conditions, and the corruptive power of American dollars. In their most dramatic stories, families come apart, brothers murder brothers, and lovers' hearts are broken beyond mending. The stories offer a liberal blend of truth and fiction, but that is an accurate reflection of the border, where nothing is ever absolute.

Between the ocean and the mesa, the only town of any size is San Ysidro, [2] California, just across from Tijuana. About forty-three million people pass through its legal port of entry every year, in vehicles, on bicycles, and on foot, but nobody knows for certain how many undocumented migrants slip illegally over *la frontera.* An educated guess would be about five thousand every day. They come primarily from Mexico and Central America, and they carry their most precious belongings with them in knapsacks or plastic supermarket bags. The Border Patrol, in its San Diego Sector—a territory roughly as big as Connecticut—apprehends about a third of them, logging almost fifteen hundred arrests every twenty-four hours, but the others drift on to Los Angeles or San Francisco or Sacramento, or to farms in the great Central Valley, staying with relatives and friends while they look for work. If they fail to be hired anywhere, they go farther north, to Oregon and Washington, ready to pick fruit or to gut salmon in a packing-house, willing to do anything to earn their keep.

Like many border towns, San Ysidro is conducive to paranoia. Set in the [3] midst of sagebrush and dry, brown mountains covered with chaparral, it has the harmless look of an ordinary suburb, but this is deceptive and does not hold up under close inspection. For instance, there is a blood bank on the edge of its largest mall, and all day you can watch donors come out the door with balls of cotton pressed to their forearms, bound for a shopping spree at a nearby K mart before going home to Tijuana. The sky above San Ysidro is often full of ravens and buzzards, and skulls of small animals turn up in its playgrounds. Its population is mostly Hispanic, but more and more Anglos—retired people, and people who commute to San Diego—are buying property in the tile-roofed housing tracts that are devouring the last farms and ranches, and they get very angry the first time some illegal aliens dash through their back yards, trampling the shrubbery and pausing to drink from garden hoses.

The Border Patrol is the uniformed arm of the Immigration and Naturali- [4] zation Service, and it is supposed to control the flow of uninvited foreigners into the States. In California, as in Texas, its stations are understaffed and underfunded, and are asked to perform a nearly impossible task. In the San Diego Sector, agents must police all of San Diego County, as well as substantial parts of Orange and Riverside Counties, scouring not only the canyons and the backwoods but also the teeming barrios in cities, where aliens frequently seek shelter. Although the sector captures more illegal aliens than any other sector in the country—more than four hundred and seventy thousand in fiscal year 1990, almost half the United States total—this record does little for the morale of the agents, since there is no real penalty imposed on those who are apprehended, unless they have some contraband or resist arrest. Mexicans are given a brief interview, then returned to Tijuana, sometimes so quickly that they get caught crossing again on the same night.

The law isn't the only obstacle that the Border Patrol faces in dispatching its duty. It used to be easy for agents to spot new arrivals because they dressed like field hands and looked dirty and frightened, but now the aliens disguise themselves in clothes fresh off the rack, relying on such items as bluejeans, Reeboks, and L.A. Dodgers caps for protective coloration. The business of providing goods and services to migrants has grown enormously, forming a closed economy worth millions, and they have an elaborate network of support, which often involves extended families and functions in the manner of an underground railroad. Then, too, illegal aliens are always testing agents by devising new tricks for sneaking into California. On a hot summer day, they like to put on bathing suits and wander up the coast, or they dive from a boat and swim to shore. They wade through raw sewage in the Tijuana River and slip into Imperial Beach, just north of San Ysidro. They jam themselves into car trunks and into boxcars, and they ride across the border spread-eagled on top of freight trains. The boldest ones merely sprint through the backed-up traffic at the port of entry, defying the Border Patrol to chase them.   5

Once illegal aliens get by this first line of defense, they can relax and blend into the crowd of legal Hispanics in San Ysidro. They treat the town as a sort of flea market, making connections and buying Stateside necessities, usually on the sly. If they require fake documents—anything from birth certificates to green cards—they seek out a dealer in such papers and begin negotiations. A high-quality document might cost more than a thousand dollars. Only an expert can detect that it's a forgery, while a so-called "fifty-footer" looks bad even at that distance and can be bought without much haggling. If migrants have some pesos to be laundered, they speak to the fellows hanging around the pay phones by the United States Customs gate. Those phones, supplied by half a dozen different companies, are the conduit through which a fortune in drug profits—from the sale of cocaine, marijuana, and methamphetamines—is annually rerouted. The men who smuggle in aliens use the phones, too, arranging transportation for their customers. The smugglers are known as *coyotes,* on account of their predatory habits, and they flourish on the border, where expediency is the rule of thumb.   6

In San Ysidro, there are also safe houses, where, for a price, a migrant can hole up for a while. The safe houses look like the houses around them, but everybody on a given block can point them out. As it happens, secrecy tends to play a very limited role in illegal immigration. Anyone who wants to see how openly aliens cross the border, even in broad daylight, can take a drive on Dairy Mart Road, which winds from the outskirts of town through beanfields, pastures, and fallow land scattered with junked farm machinery. On any morning or afternoon, in any season, you'll have to brake to a halt as people streak by in front of your car, speeding from one hiding place to another. For the most part, they are young men in their late teens and early twenties, and they never seem the slightest bit afraid. They emerge from arroyos, from stands of bamboo and pampas grass, from copses of trees, and from vacant buildings. One morning as I cruised on Dairy Mart Road, I counted twenty-two people in a two-hour period.   7

The action at night is even more spectacular, and it occurs on a much larger scale. At dusk, you start hearing sirens and whistles all over San Ysidro, as if several robberies were in progress, and then comes the chopping sound of helicopter blades slashing up the clouds. Step outside your motel room and   8 you notice beams from above shining down on a Carl's, Jr., restaurant, on kids in baseball uniforms and elderly folks out for an evening stroll. Sometimes a beam illuminates a drainage ditch, and a human form scampers away, like a rabbit rousted from its burrow. It's disconcerting to find normal life going on in what appears to be a suburban war zone. If you walk to a weedy field near the blood bank, you can look toward the concrete levee of the Tijuana River, where, in the glare of I.N.S. floodlights and in full view of the Border Patrol, more than five hundred people will be congregated in little bands, waiting for an opportune moment to begin their journey to the United States.

Writing Assignments

Narrate   **1.**   Your family, like most, probably has a relative about whom you like to tell stories. Freewrite about this person without stopping to divide your information into paragraphs. Then reread your material to determine how you might group and sequence your information into paragraphs that present a coherent biographical sketch of your family's favorite hero or villain.

Observe   **2.**   Examine old pictures in a family photograph album. Select a photograph taken during a significant or revealing occasion. Reread Patricia Hampl's comments on old family photographs on pages 166–167, then write a letter to a member of your family describing the photograph and your interest in this historical moment.

Investigate   **3.**   Interview a student or someone in your university's office of student affairs who is concerned with the status of minority students on your campus. Inquire about the social, intellectual, and emotional difficulties specific minority students face as they acquire an education with students (and faculty) from the dominant culture. Then write a profile for your student newspaper on "A Day in the Life" of a minority student on your campus.

Collaborate   **4.**   Your writing group has been asked to compile a group portrait that describes its ethnic diversity. Pair up with a member of your group. Interview one another. Then talk to relatives to explore your family's ethnic history. When did the first member of your family immigrate to the United States? What advantages or difficulties did members of your family face because of their ethnicity? Is your family in touch or out of touch with its ethnic heritage? Use such questions to collect information that can be transformed into topical paragraphs. Then write a collaborative portrait of your group in which you select a similar sequence of paragraphs to present the biographical profile for each member of your group.

Read   **5.**   Select a cultural group you are unfamiliar with—for example, Amish, Lithuanian, or Zuni—and then read several articles about how that group has been treated in the United States. Draft several topic sentences that advance an explanation for this treatment. Then compose an essay by developing those sentences into topical paragraphs. Experiment with each paragraph by placing the topic sentence in a different position.

Respond   **6.**   Respond to Brent Staples's essay, "Black Men and Public Space," by writing an opinion column for your daily newspaper in which you describe experiences you may have had in being stereotyped as a member of a group. You may have been ignored, belittled, or mistreated because of your ethnicity, sex, age, accent or dialect, style of dress, physical characteristics, or home town. Reserve some of your paragraphs, as Staples does, for revealing the strategies you have developed for dealing with this stereotyping.

Analyze   **7.**   Compare and contrast the paragraphs by Ellen Goodman and Bill Barich. The most obvious difference, size, can be explained by the context for their essays—a short newspaper column (Goodman) and a long magazine feature (Barich). You may want to analyze the effectiveness of these conventions. For example, are Goodman's paragraphs *complete?* Are Barich's paragraphs *unified?* You may also want to consider the appropriateness of form and purpose—short paragraphs about the social fragmentation (Goodman); long paragraphs about social crowding (Barich). Write an analysis explaining these concepts, using examples from these sources.

Evaluate **8.** Reread the paragraphs on the status of the American family in this chapter (Philip Slater, page 166; Jane Howard, page 168; Jane O'Reilly, page 168). Reexamine Ellen Goodman's argument about the stresses and strengths within the American family. Then argue that (a) the power of the American family was always more an ideal than a reality, (b) the American family is breaking up beneath the forces of contemporary culture, or (c) the contemporary American family, though changed in character, is as strong as it ever was.

Argue **9.** Reread the paragraphs on Ellis Island on pages 169 and 170. You may want to read additional material on immigration in the 1890s. (Some good sources are Oscar Handlin's *Uprooted: The Epic Story of the Great Migrations That Made the American People* and Wilson Tifft and Thomas Dunne's *Ellis Island*.) Reread Bill Barich's description of *La Frontera*. You may want to read the whole essay (*The New Yorker* 17 December 1990: 72–92). Then argue either that (a) there is no real difference between the way immigrant groups were treated at Ellis Island and the way they are treated along the Mexican border, or (b) specific issues—economic, social, legal—account for contemporary attitudes toward those who want to cross America's borders.

Argue **10.** Examine your university catalogue and reading lists for courses. What opportunities are available in your college curriculum for studying the history and culture of various ethnic groups? Use this information to compose an open letter to the faculty and administration, arguing either that (a) such opportunities already exist, but students need better advice about why they should study such material, or (b) such opportunities do *not* exist in the current curriculum, but faculty can enrich existing courses or create new ones that would meet this need.

8 | Sentences: Patterns of Expression

As you saw in Chapter 7, the sentences in a well-written paragraph are not isolated statements; they exist in complex interrelationships with each other. Although traditionally called units of composition, sentences are units chiefly in the grammatical sense that each sentence has its own subject and predicate and is not part of another sentence. Beyond these basic attributes, however, sentences vary widely in style—and therefore in the effect they create. By varying the arrangements of words, phrases, and clauses in sentences, writers reveal emphasis, shade meaning, and create various kinds of movement in their writing.

Richard Selzer, surgeon and writer, composes sentences in two stages:

The *first* propels me across the page with an armful of language. It's like the technique of the abstract painter. He will make a brush stroke on a bare canvas. That stroke leads to another and the combination to a third until the canvas is done and he realizes what he has made. The *second* is the fully conscious tinkering that goes on. The artist is always blacking out parts of his canvas and correcting small details until the painting is done in his mind. So one of my essays isn't finished until I cross out half of it and revise its individual parts. I try to respond to the marvellous elasticity of the language by constantly opening up or compressing my sentences. When I am done, they possess a distinctive rhythm and resonance. I can pick them out immediately on any page of prose. They're like my signature. (Personal interview)

This chapter will take a close look at how writers such as Selzer express their purpose by expanding, combining, and revising their sentences.

EXPANDING AND COMBINING SENTENCES

Like a brush stroke, a basic sentence moves across the page in a simple line. It consists of a subject and a predicate. The predicate may be a complete verb or a verb that needs something to complete it. For example, the sentence "The doctor smiled" consists of the subject *doctor* and the complete verb *smiled*. But in the following two sentences the verb requires completion:

The doctor + *examined* + the patient. [Subject, verb, and object]

The doctor + *was* + courteous. [Subject, verb, and complement]

A *basic sentence,* then, is a main clause consisting of subject and verb and any object or complement required to complete the verb.

Any element in a basic sentence may be modified by adjectives, adverb phrases, or clauses that describe or limit the words being modified. Or the whole main clause rather than one of its elements may be modified. For example, in the sentence "If you can't do it, I'll ask Dr. Helena," the introductory *if* clause modifies the whole main clause and is called a *sentence modifier.*

In the following examples the basic sentence is underscored; the modifiers are italicized and are connected by arrows to the words they modify.

Many students *enrolled in the pre-med curriculum* find *organic* chemistry *extremely* difficult.

To prepare for a test they study *for hours* with *incredible* concentration.

Some, *recognizing their limitations in math,* hire *private* tutors *to help them prepare for each exam.*

Others study alone, *because they are driven to master the material in seclusion.*

If their study habits predict how they will behave as doctors, some will consult with colleagues, while others will insist on making their own diagnosis.

As these examples show, modifiers may be single words or phrases (*many, private, for hours*) or subordinate clauses (*because they are driven to master the material in seclusion*). The modifiers may come before, after, or within the main clause. In the last two sentences, the subordinate clauses modify the whole main clause and are therefore sentence modifiers.

Exercise ——— Distinguish between basic sentences and modifying words or phrases in the following passage from Richard Selzer's "An Absence of Windows." First underline the basic sentence, then circle the modifiers.

(1) Part of my surgical training was spent in a rural hospital in eastern Connecticut. (2) The building was situated on the slope of a modest hill. (3) Behind it, cows grazed in a pasture. (4) The operating theater occupied the fourth, the ultimate floor, wherefrom high windows looked down upon the scene. (5) To glance up from our work and see lovely cattle about theirs, calmed the frenzy of the most temperamental of prima donnas. (6) Intuition tells me that our patients had fewer wound infections and made speedier recoveries than those operated upon in the airless sealed boxes where we now strive. (7) Certainly the surgeons were of gentler stripe.

Expanding Sentences by Modification

In effective writing, details communicate specific information and hold the reader's interest. Any sentence can be enriched by modification. Notice how much detail is added by the italicized modifiers in the following sentences.

> My father kept his own books, *in a desk calendar that recorded in his fine Spencerian handwriting the names of the patients he had seen each day, each name followed by the amount he charged, and that number followed by the amount received.* (Lewis Thomas, "Amity Street," *The Youngest Science: Notes of a Medicine Watcher*)

> I debated whether I should major in zoology *so early in the term before I knew whether my high-school science courses had prepared me for the difficult challenges of the college curriculum.*

> The drug companies, *usually operating through private physicians with access to the prisons,* can obtain healthy human subjects *living in conditions that are difficult, if not impossible, to duplicate elsewhere.* (Jessica Mitford, *Kind and Unusual Punishment*)

> In this portion of the chart, *after all the histories are taken, after the chest has been thumped and the spleen has been fingered, after the white cells have been counted and the potassium surveyed,* the doctor can be *seen to abandon the position of recorder and assume that of* natural scientist. (Gerald Weissman, "The Chart of the Novel," *The Woods Hole Cantata: Essays on Science and Society*)

In sentences like these, the effect comes not from the main clause, which provides no details, but from the specific information provided by the modifiers. You can easily see that this is so by isolating the main clauses from the modifiers:

> My father kept his own books.

> I debated whether I should major in zoology.

> The drug companies can obtain healthy human subjects.

> In this portion of the chart, the doctor can be natural scientist.

Effective modifiers such as the ones shown in the full sentences above have two qualities. First, they are not tacked on as afterthoughts but are essential parts of the writers' purposes. A significant portion of Thomas's recollection of his father's books focuses on the shape of the handwriting and the pattern of the accounts; the student's debate about majoring in zoology is occasioned by her doubts about her high-school preparation in science; Weissman's description of a doctor's writing process is based on the details he has to record. In each case the modifying details are necessary to express the writer's complete thought.

Second, effective modification is grounded in observation or experience. Weissman knows from experience how to keep a patient's chart. Mitford has researched her subject and knows about the doctor's cooperation and the conditions that made prisoners ideal subjects for experiments. In each example, the writer has used modification to get his or her observations into the sentences.

Suppose you were asked to expand these three sentences by modification:

I am uncomfortable in my doctor's office.

My doctor always seems impatient.

Doctors study the human body.

To complete the assignment, you need to know the context in which the writer is working and his or her purpose for composing the sentences. Without that knowledge, asking you to expand them is asking you to supply a context and purpose. By drawing on your own experience, you can describe why doctors' offices make you uncomfortable, what makes your doctor appear impatient, and how doctors study the human body. You might expand the first sentence this way:

I am uncomfortable in my doctor's office because while I sit in the posh chairs of the waiting room, I imagine that my body is being secretly afflicted with all sorts of life-threatening diseases.

Exercises ———— Drawing on your own experience, expand the following basic sentences to make them fuller expressions of the ideas they suggest to you.

1. My doctor always seems impatient.
2. I don't like to read reports about medical studies.
3. I always get sick on vacations.
4. Doctors study the human body.
5. I don't know if an ache is a symptom or something that will just go away.

Combining Sentences by Coordination

Coordination is combining or joining similar elements into pairs or series. As in the following pairs of examples, sentences can be combined by using a common subject or predicate and compounding the remaining element:

Medical technology contributes to the high cost of health care. Medical liability insurance is also extremely expensive.

Compound subject/
Common predicate
Medical technology and medical liability insurance both contribute to the high cost of health care.

Doctors must complete their charts under pressure. They also must carefully think through their comments and notations.

Compound predicate/
Common subject
Doctors completing their charts must carefully think through their comments and notations and must write under pressure.

Exercises ———— By combining parts through coordination, compress the sentences in each group into a single sentence.

1. Coronary heart disease is the major cause of death in this country. Cancer also causes many deaths.

2. My doctor warned me about trying to lose weight too fast.
   My coach reminded me of the danger involved.
   My mother told me the same thing.

3. The first documented case of AIDS within the United States occurred in 1977.
   The AIDS crisis continues to grow.
   The number of newspaper and magazine articles on AIDS has declined in the last few years.

4. Breakfast cereals contain fiber.
   Oat bran may reduce cholesterol.
   Advertisers stress the health benefits of their products.

5. The cost of running shoes is escalating.
   Most people are very selective about the kind of running shoes they buy.

Using Parallel Structure

When two or more coordinate elements have the same form, they are said to have *parallel structure*. Such structures may be unnoticed in any sentence, but when the parallelism is conspicuous, the whole sentence may be called a *parallel sentence*. Thus, "He was without a job, without money, without opportunity, and without hope" is a parallel sentence in which the four phrases have the same form (they all start with *without*) and the same grammatical function (they all complete the verb *was*).

Consider these contrasted sentences:

I am in favor of equal economic rights for women. Women should be able to compete with men for jobs for which they are both qualified. The pay should be the same for the same jobs. There should be the same oppor-	I am in favor of equal economic rights for women: the right to compete with men for jobs for which they are both qualified, the right to get the same pay for the same job, and the right to equal opportunities for

Both versions assert the same three rights. The version on the left advances the assertions in four sentences, each using a different subject. The version on the right states all three rights in one sentence and focuses the reader's attention by the repetition of the phrase "the right to." The parallel structure of the second version gives it the unity, coherence, and emphasis that the first version lacks.

Parallel elements may be single words, phrases, clauses, or sentences (contributing to a paragraph with parallel structure); they may act as subjects, objects, verbs, or adverbial or adjectival modifiers. But for elements in a pair or a series to be parallel, all members must have the same form and serve the same grammatical function. You cannot coordinate nouns with adjectives, verbs with infinitives, or phrases with clauses. Any attempt to do so disrupts parallelism, disappoints your readers, and produces awkwardness.

In each of the following sentences, the italicized element disrupts parallelism by switching from one grammatical form to another:

The children were laughing, squealing, and *danced.* [To restore parallelism, *danced* should be changed to *dancing.*]

My two ambitions are to become a doctor and *having* enough money to give my children a good education. [Parallelism requires that *to become* must be matched with *to have.*]

My parents taught me such things as honesty, faith, *to be fair,* and *having patience.* [Parallelism with the two nouns would be sustained by replacing the infinitive and participial phrases with the nouns *fairness* and *patience.*]

The following diagrams show the similarity in form and function of various parallel structures:

Parallel predicates

He

walked past the information desk,

followed the signs to obstetrics,

selected a seat in the waiting room, and

watched the other expectant fathers pace the floor.

Prepositional phrases **in a series**

Fat people know all about the mystery of life. They are the ones acquainted

with the night,

with luck,

with fate,

with playing it by ear.

(Suzanne Britt Jordan)

Participial phrases **in a series**

This was the American family at play

escaping the city heat,

wondering whether the newcomers in the camp at the head of the cove were "common" or "nice,"

wondering whether it was true that the people who drove up for Sunday dinner at the farmhouse were turned away because there wasn't enough chicken.

(E. B. White)

Exercises ———— 1. Identify and diagram the parallel elements in the following sentences.
a. We hold these truths to be self-evident: that all men are created equal, that they are endowed by their Creator with certain unalienable Rights. . . .
b. Berton Roueche's narratives of "medical detection" are full of patients with unusual symptoms, of laboratory technicians with specialized knowledge, and of doctors with extraordinary diagnostic powers.

2. The following are lists of the distinguishing characteristics of people who exhibit Type A and Type B behaviors. Organize the items into parallel lists, and then write a parallel sentence coordinating the information in the two series.

Type A behavior	*Type B behavior*
Obsessed with deadlines	Evokes serenity in others
Intense need to win at all costs	Enjoys creating images and metaphors
Conversation dominated by numbers	Secure sense of self-esteem
Harshly critical of others	Rarely wears a watch

3. List characteristics of the brain suggested by the following list for the computer. Then compose a parallel sentence contrasting the advantages of the brain with those of the computer as a "thinking machine."

Computer	*Brain*
Circuits	
Blank disk	
Storage	
Program	

When parallelism is extended through a paragraph, each sentence becomes an element in a series. An example of a series of parallel sentences appears on page 172 in the paragraph by Martin Luther King, Jr., in which each sentence begins with the phrase "There is nothing." Such deliberate repetition binds individual sentences into a coherent paragraph. Consider the features of conspicuous parallelism in the following paragraph.

H. G. Wells continues to be a biographer's dream and book reviewer's waltz. His life stretches very nearly from Appomattox to Hiroshima. He was one of the world's great storytellers, the father of modern science fiction, an autobiographic novelist of scandalous proportions, a proselytizer for world peace through brain power, an unsurpassed popular historian, a journalist and inexhaustible pamphleteer, the friend and worthy adversary of great men and the lover of numerous and intelligent women. (R. Z. Sheppard, *Time*)

Combining Sentences by Subordination

Subordination reduces one sentence to a subordinate clause or to a phrase that becomes part of another sentence. Consider the following basic sentences.

We left early. We had work to do.

The second of these sentences may be embedded in the first as a subordinate clause.

We left early *because we had work to do.*

In the next example, a basic sentence is reduced to a phrase.

The man was evidently in great pain. He was taken to a hospital.

The man, *evidently in great pain,* was taken to the hospital.

As these examples show, when two sentences are combined by subordination, the information in one sentence is embedded in the other. Using subordination, a writer can pack a great deal of information into a sentence and still emphasize what is most important. This does not mean that short, basic sentences are always inappropriate. Often they are useful to create variety and achieve emphasis. But consistent use of basic sentences in a sustained piece of writing can make the writing seem repetitive and dull.

In the following example, a complex sentence is created through the subordination of four basic sentences.

1. Last weekend I saw a science fiction film.
2. Three friends went with me.
3. The film focused on the experiments of a mad doctor.
4. He altered his patients' lives by manipulating their dreams.

Last weekend three friends and I saw a science fiction film in which a mad doctor altered his patients' lives by manipulating their dreams.

The original four sentences contain 32 words. Using subordination to embed sentences 2, 3, and 4 in sentence 1 creates a denser sentence in which the same information is expressed economically, in 24 words, and the monotony of the original sentences is eliminated.

Exercises —— Practice creating denser sentences through subordination by reducing each of the following sets of sentences to a single sentence without omitting any of the information.

1. Scientists use guinea pigs in their laboratory experiments.
   They inject them with a disease.
   They observe their behavior.
   They dissect them.
   They examine the effect of the disease on their organs.
2. Michelangelo studied anatomy.
   He dissected cadavers.
   Such gruesome work helped him understand human bones and muscles.
   His sculpture celebrates the human body.
3. X-rays can penetrate the human body.
   They produce images on photographic film.
   Shadows on the picture reveal changes in body tissue.

4. The early history of medicine is filled with guesswork.
   Doctors did not know what caused disease.
   They developed cures through trial and error.
   Most of the cures did not work.
   Cures that worked were considered magical.

5. People went to spas to restore their health.
   Most spas were located in beautiful settings.
   They featured special mineral waters.
   The waters were supposed to purge the body of disease.
   These watering spots developed into vacation resorts.

Combining for a Purpose

When you combine basic sentences into denser structures through coordination and subordination, you should choose the sentence pattern that best suits your purpose. If you are writing a paper on the latest developments in frozen foods for a nutrition class, you might collect the following information.

1. Frozen food has long been part of the American way of life.

2. Frozen dinners once consisted of such dull items as lima beans, gooey potatoes, and mystery meat.

3. Currently available frozen-dinner entrées include beef bourguignon with glazed carrots, asparagus crepes with Mornay sauce, and vegetarian lasagna.

4. Some frozen-food companies have even developed gourmet dietetic dinners.

5. Americans have fast-paced, busy lifestyles these days.

6. They are also more concerned than before about eating healthful, interesting, and balanced meals.

Strung together in this order, these sentences have little meaning. They trace a sequence, to be sure, but what is significant about that sequence and what are its implications? The answer, of course, depends on your purpose. If you have a purpose, you can combine the sentences through coordination or subordination to achieve focus and establish relationships among the facts.

For example, if you want to propose a cause-and-effect relationship between the change in American lifestyles and the change in frozen food, you can reduce sentence 1 to a subordinate clause and embed it in sentence 2.

> Frozen dinners, long part of the American way of life, once consisted of such dull items as lima beans, gooey potatoes, and mystery meat.

Through a similar process you can combine sentences 5 with 6 and 3 with 4.

> To satisfy busy Americans' concern for healthy, interesting, and balanced meals, today's frozen-food companies have developed more sophisticated

fare: beef bourguignon with glazed carrots, asparagus crepes with Mornay sauce, vegetarian lasagna, and even gourmet dietetic dinners.

With a coordinating conjunction you can combine the two sentences into one.

Frozen dinners, long part of the American way of life, once consisted of such dull items as lima beans, gooey potatoes, and mystery meat, but to satisfy busy Americans' concern for healthy, interesting, and balanced meals, today's food companies have developed more sophisticated fare: beef bourguignon with glazed carrots, asparagus crepes with Mornay sauce, vegetarian lasagna, and even gourmet dietetic dinners.

If you want to say that those who once found frozen dinners unappetizing now have a reason to try them, you can combine the original sentences for this purpose.

Busy Americans once identified frozen dinners with such dull items as lima beans, gooey potatoes, and mystery meat, but today those same consumers are tempted by a new variety of healthy, interesting, and balanced frozen meals: beef bourguignon with glazed carrots, asparagus crepes with Mornay sauce, vegetarian lasagna, and even gourmet dietetic dinners.

The last version focuses on the customer rather than on the company, but the focus is still achieved by subordination and coordination.

The three devices you have been studying—modification, coordination, and subordination—allow you to combine and present information in complex sentences. Organizing ideas into an effective form is just as important in a sentence as it is in a paragraph or essay. In a series of simple sentences, each idea is stated separately; the statements lack coherence, and relationships among the ideas are not clear. Moreover, such sentences lack emphasis; all information appears to be of equal importance. By subordinating the less important to the more important, or by showing the equality of ideas through coordination, you can revise such sentences so that they have variety, clarity, and emphasis.

Exercises ———— For each of the following clusters, combine as many of the items as you need (you may not need or want to use them all) into a sentence that fulfills each of the two purposes specified. Combine any remaining items into a second, supporting sentence.

Cluster A

1. Clothes reveal an individual's personality and attitudes.
2. Clothes like blue jeans and T-shirts make a statement.
3. Dark blue suits and white laboratory jackets also make a statement.
4. Certain occasions, situations, or jobs require appropriate attire.
5. "Appropriate" attire is often formal: a dress, suit, tie.
6. People should be free to dress as they please.
7. In many professional situations, people judge others by their appearance.

Purpose 1   You want to assert that people should be free to dress as they please.

Purpose 2   You want to argue that people should dress appropriately in professional situations.

Cluster B
1. Hospitals are often the setting for television soap operas.
2. Characters spend more time discussing their personal problems than their professional responsibilities.
3. Doctors are seen making rounds; nurses are seen keeping charts.
4. Soap operas rarely show medical procedures.
5. Characters conveniently develop illnesses to complicate the plot.
6. Doctors use vague medical terminology to discuss cases.

Purpose 1   You want to demonstrate that soap operas treat the topic of illness superficially.

Purpose 2   You want to illustrate that soap operas use hospitals as a convenient setting for dramatic conflict.

Cluster C
1. Many of today's sports injuries are treated with arthroscopic surgery.
2. Major surgery requires doctors to cut through the muscle to find the damaged area.
3. Such surgery requires many months of rehabilitation.
4. An arthroscopic surgeon punctures the muscle with a catheter carrying a microscopic television camera and another catheter carrying appropriate surgical tools.
5. He locates the injury with the camera and uses the tool to repair it.
6. Players can often return to action within several weeks.
7. Any injury requires sufficient recuperation.
8. Reinjury of damaged areas can result in disability.

Purpose 1   You want to argue that arthroscopic surgery is a major medical breakthrough.

Purpose 2   You want to suggest that the availability of arthroscopic surgery can give players a false sense of security.

TYPES OF SENTENCES AND THEIR EFFECTS

In this section you will learn to use to good effect three important sentence types: the *balanced* sentence, the *periodic* sentence, and the *cumulative* sentence.

The Balanced Sentence

In a balanced sentence, two coordinate but contrasting structures are set off against each other like the weights on a balanced scale. In each of the following sentences the underlined parts balance each other:

<u>Many are called</u> but <u>few are chosen</u> . (Matthew 22:14)

<u>I came to bury Caesar</u>, not <u>to praise him</u> . (William Shakespeare, *Julius Caesar*)

<u>Where I used to suture the tissue of the body together</u>, <u>now I suture words together</u> . (Richard Selzer)

When you read a balanced sentence aloud, you tend to pause between the balanced parts. That pause is often marked by a coordinating conjunction (*but, or, nor, yet, and*), sometimes by *not* (as in the second sentence), and sometimes by punctuation alone (as in the third sentence). Whatever the marker, it serves as a fulcrum, the point at which the contrasted parts balance against each other, as the following diagram illustrates:

but

| When a man dies on shore, his body remains with his friends, and the "mourners go about the streets," | when a man falls overboard at sea and is lost, there is a suddenness in the event . . . which gives it an air of awful mystery. |

(Richard Henry Dana)

The balanced structure points up the contrast in thought. It is effective when two subjects are to be contrasted within the same sentence.

Exercises ——— Compose a sentence about each item in each pair. Then combine the two sentences into a balanced sentence.

jogging—swimming	pain—stress
doctors—dentists	painting—photograph
smokers—nonsmokers	mural—miniature

Periodic and Cumulative Sentences

A *periodic* sentence builds to a climactic statement in its final main clause. The writer withholds the main idea until the end of the sentence. Here is an example:

Just before I went away to college, my father took me aside, as I had expected, and said, as I had not expected, "Now, Son, if a strange woman comes up to you on a street corner and offers to take your watch around the corner and have it engraved, don't do it." (Eric Lax)

The father's remarks lead up to the advice given in the final main clause—"don't do it"—which provides a climax, like the punch line of a joke. All the rest of the sentence has been a preparation for that statement.

Cumulative sentences, also called *loose sentences,* reverse the order of periodic sentences. Instead of withholding the main idea until the last clause, the writer states it immediately and then adds examples and details. Compare the style and effect of the cumulative and periodic sentences in these two examples.

I fought migraine then, ignored the warnings it sent, went to school and later to work in spite of it, sat through lectures in Middle English and presentations to advertisers with involuntary tears running down the right side of my face, threw up in washrooms, stumbled home by instinct, emptied ice trays onto my bed and tried to freeze the pain in my right temple, wished only for a neurosurgeon who would do a lobotomy on house call, and cussed my imagination. (Joan Didion, "In Bed," *The White Album*)

For doctors, who confront death when they go to work in the morning as routinely as other people deal with balance sheets and computer print outs, and for me, to whom a chest x-ray or a blood test will never again be a simple routine procedure, it is particularly important to face the fact of death squarely, to talk about it with one another. (Alice Trillin, "Of Dragons and Garden Peas: A Cancer Patient Talks to Doctors," *The New England Journal of Medicine*)

Both writers could have reversed the order of their sentences. Didion could have listed her agonies first, building to her main clause, "I fought migraine." But by announcing her struggle first and then providing the details, she exhausts the main idea and forces her reader to experience some of the exhaustion she feels. Similarly, Trillin could have begun with a clause that states her main idea—that doctors and patients talk squarely to each other about death—and then added the details to illustrate her assertion. But by suspending her assertion until she establishes the contrasting perspectives of doctors and patients, she gains the reader's sympathy and interest. In each example the style and effect of the sentence advance the writer's purpose.

Exercise ———   Write a periodic sentence describing the most frustrating, fulfilling, or comic day you have had recently. Use your opening clauses to build suspense and reveal your final assertion in the last clause. Then reverse this order and write a cumulative sentence. Make your assertion first and then accumulate detailed examples. Which pattern is more effective? Explain your answer.

REVISING SENTENCES

You have been examining the structure of different types of sentences and techniques for increasing the density of sentences through modification, coordination, and subordination. The process of shaping ideas into sentences is a learning process, and as you grope toward a satisfactory statement of your meaning, you will try out different sentence structures, revising your sentences while you write them. But in this section you will be trying, through local revision, to make your sentences more effective expressions of the ideas you intend them to convey, to improve sentences that have already been written—to "tinker," as Richard Selzer suggests, with your completed draft—by revising for *clarity, emphasis, economy,* and *variety.*

Revising for Clarity

This section is concerned only with revising confusing sentence structure, even though lack of clarity can also result from faulty grammar or punctuation, misleading pronoun reference, or vague or ambiguous wording. Unclear sentence structure sometimes occurs when a writer tries to pack too much information into one sentence. The following sentence illustrates this problem:

> Last month while I was visiting the federal buildings in Washington on a guided tour, we went to the National Art Gallery, where we had been for an hour when the rest of the group was ready to move on to the Treasury Building and I told a friend with the group that I wanted to stay in the Art Gallery a while longer and I would rejoin the group about a half an hour later, but I never did, even though I moved more quickly than I wanted to from room to room, not having seen after about four more hours all that I wanted to see.

As written, this sentence of 108 words consists of three main clauses and eight subordinate clauses. This involved structure is hard going for both writer and reader. The goal of revision should be to simplify the structure by reducing the number of clauses. This can be done by (1) distributing the clauses into two or more sentences, or (2) omitting material irrelevant to the writer's purpose.

Here is a revision that employs the first strategy:

> While I was visiting the National Art Gallery with a tour group last month, I decided to stay longer when the group left after an hour, and so I told a friend that I would rejoin the group at the Treasury Building in about half an hour. I moved from room to room much more quickly than I wanted to, but after four more hours I had not seen all I wanted to see. I never did rejoin the tour group that day.

This revision distributes all the original material into three sentences and makes the passage easier to read. In addition, the revision uses 25 fewer words, a reduction of over 23 percent.

Here is a revision that employs the second strategy, cutting the original drastically by leaving out irrelevant material.

> While visiting the National Art Gallery with a tour group last month, I stayed four hours after the group left. Even then I did not see all that I wanted to.

This version reduces the original eleven clauses to four and compresses the 108-word sentence to 31 words in two sentences.

Both revisions are clearer than the original. The first revision is minor, since it makes little change in content. The second is major, since it both selects and reorganizes the content. In addition to these revisions, others are possible. Try a few variations to see which you prefer.

Notice that the revisions above reduce the amount of information in the original sentence. This may seem to contradict what was said earlier about combining sentences to increase their density. But in fact there is no contradiction. Some sentences should be combined to achieve greater density; others should be separated into several sentences to achieve greater clarity. The decision to combine or to separate, to enrich or to simplify, depends on your material and your best judgment about your audience and purpose.

Exercises ——— Simplify the structure of the following sentences to make them easier to read.

1. For centuries artists have known that the paint that they keep in their studios and that they allow to collect on their clothing, and that they are constantly touching and breathing, so that it penetrates their skin and gets into their bloodstream, contains lead, which can poison them, causing them to have convulsive cramps, fatigue, and making them look sickly by comparison to the portraits of the healthy subjects they paint.

2. In the movies, artists are often portrayed as tormented and anguished people who live in poverty and squalor that causes them to contract all sorts of strange diseases that make them suffer so that they become more sensitive than normal people, which enables them to create beautiful art in the midst of their illness, even though they have to die for their art and only become famous once they are dead.

3. One of the conceptions not founded in fact that many people have about abstract painters is that they don't possess the skills necessary to draw a landscape or a face. In fact, most abstract painters have developed the ability to be extremely adept at drawing objects and people with photographic accuracy. Instead of painting such realistic portraits, however, they design thickly woven textures of paint that enable them to create more universal symbols that express aspects of all human experience. Some of these symbols are called "biomorphic" because they appear to resemble organic forms or fragments of human anatomy sandwiched into densely packed spatial landscapes. These symbols are often interpreted to express the abstract painter's sense of fragmentation in modern society.

Revising for Emphasis

Emphasis reflects your purpose and helps you convey that purpose to your readers. Among the numerous ways available to express any idea, the most effective are those that underscore your purpose—that best achieve the effect you have in mind. You can create purposeful emphasis by means of *emphatic word order, emphatic repetition, climactic order,* and *emphatic voice.*

Emphatic Word Order　To employ emphatic word order, you must know what you want to emphasize and which positions in a sentence provide the most emphasis. In an English sentence the positions of greatest emphasis are the beginning and the end. The most important material should be placed in those positions; less important material, in midsentence. Unimportant details piled up at the end of a sentence get more emphasis than they deserve and make your readers feel that the sentence is "running out of gas."

Notice the difference between the following statements.

Unemphatic order	*Emphatic order*
From 1904 to 1914, Americans built the fifty-mile Panama Canal, which caused over five thousand workers to die of malaria in the jungles of Central America.	Over five thousand workers died of malaria in the jungles of Central America when Americans labored from 1904 to 1914 to build the fifty-mile Panama Canal.

The most important information in this sentence is that over five thousand workers died of malaria to build a fifty-mile canal—about one hundred workers per mile. The version on the left puts the number of deaths and the size of the canal in the least important position, lessening the impact. The version on the right puts this information where it will get the most emphasis, relegating the less important information to the middle of the statement.

Exercises ——— Revise the order of each sentence to emphasize the points you think most important.

1. It is entirely possible that longevity depends on the luck of your genes, I sometimes think.

2. A proposal that has caused much discussion about our national health policy is the one about insurance for catastrophic illness that is now before Congress.

3. Dr. Albert Schweitzer, even when he was ninety, worked in his clinic all day and played his piano at night because he believed that a sense of purpose and creativity was the best medicine for any illness he might have.

4. Thomas Eakins, in his painting *The Gross Clinic* (page 208), reveals his extensive knowledge of anatomy by portraying Samuel Gross, the famous surgeon, standing next to the operating table with a scalpel in his hand, lecturing to his students as his assistant probes the patient's open wound.

5. One of America's leading authors and child psychiatrists, Robert Coles, learned about sickness when he was a medical student from the stories he heard from the patients he met as he went on rounds with poet and physician William Carlos Williams.

Emphatic Repetition   Unintentional repetition generally weakens a sentence, as the following examples show:

The disappointing results were all the more disappointing because we were sure that the experiment would be a success, and so were disappointed in the results.

Thomas Eakins (1844–1916), *The Gross Clinic,* oil on canvas (1875). From the Jefferson
Medical College of Thomas Jefferson University, Philadelphia.

The writer who wrote the novel that won the award for the best novel of the
year did not attend the awards ceremony.

Deliberate repetition, by contrast, can produce a desired emphasis. You have
seen how the repetition of words can help unify a paragraph and how the use
of parallel and balanced structures creates coherence. The following examples
show the effective use of deliberate repetition:

If we *write* about our scientific *observations,* our *observations* inevitably color
our *writing*. (Leigh Hafrey, "Write About What You Know: Big Bang or Gre-
cian Urn")

And this hell was simply, that he had never in his life owned anything— *not
his* wife, *not his* house, *not his* child—which could *not,* at any instant, be taken
from him by the power of white people. (James Baldwin)

Paul Gauguin (1848–1903), *Where Do We Come From? What Are We? Where Are We Going?*, oil on canvas (1897). Tompkins Collection. Courtesy Museum of Fine Arts, Boston.

Climactic Order   Climactic word order achieves emphasis by building to a major idea. The effect of a periodic sentence depends on climactic order, but climax may be used in other sentences as well. The following example contrasts anticlimactic and climactic order. Study both versions of the sentence to determine what changes were made in revision.

Anticlimactic order	*Climactic order*
Paul Gauguin, near the end of his life, painted *Where Do We Come From? What Are We? Where Are We Going?* in the hopes of glimpsing the life we live from infancy to our last years.	Near the end of his life, in the hopes of glimpsing the life we live from infancy to our last years, Paul Gauguin painted *Where Do We Come From? What Are We? Where Are We Going?*

Emphatic Voice   Although it is commonplace that writers should use verbs in the active rather than passive voice, this sound advice is worth repeating. The active voice creates natural, vigorous sentences; the passive voice encourages awkward shifts in structure and anemic, evasive wordiness.

Weak passive	*More emphatic active voice*
Fantasies of the self are created by modern artists.	Modern artists create fantasies of the self.
Real people afflicted by real diseases have been helped by medical science.	Medical science helps real people afflicted by real diseases.

Exercises ——— Revise the following sentences by changing passive verbs to the active voice.

1. Changing the criteria for what people consider ugly has been proposed by critics as the goal of much modern art.

2. It must surely be recognized by the American Hospital Association that such costs cannot be afforded by many families.

3. The critic said that the winners in the photographic competition would be announced by her within three days.

4. Once the danger was gone, the safety precautions that had been so carefully observed by us were abandoned.

But in some cases, the passive voice may provide greater emphasis than the active voice. Passive constructions can be used to bypass a sentence's grammatical subject in order to emphasize a more important element, such as a significant action or object of an action. For example:

Active voice	*Passive voice*
A person may not smoke in the museum.	Smoking is prohibited in the museum.
The doctor performed the emergency surgery under battery-operated lights.	The emergency surgery was performed under battery-operated lights.

Choosing active or passive voice is like any other choice you make in the writing process. You must judge by results: which form provides the emphasis you want? But to avoid the awkward or ungrammatical sentences that can result from misuse of the passive, use the active voice unless the passive advances your purpose more effectively.

Revising for Economy

Economical prose achieves an equivalence between the number of words used and the amount of meaning they convey. A sentence is not economical because it is short, or wordy because it is long. Consider these two statements:

I should like to make it entirely clear to one and all that neither I nor any of my associates or fellow workers had anything at all to do in any way, shape, or form with this illicit and legally unjustifiable act that has been committed.	I want to make it clear to everyone that neither I nor any of my associates had anything to do with this illegal act.

The version on the left takes 46 words to say what is more clearly said on the right in 24. The 22 additional words do not add significant information: they merely make reading more difficult and annoy the reader with useless repetition.

Now contrast the following statements:

His defense is not believable.

His defense is not believable: at points it is contradicted by the unanimous testimony of other witnesses, and it offers no proof that that testimony is false; it ignores significant facts about which there can be no dispute, or evades them by saying that he does not recollect them; it contains inconsistencies that he is unable to resolve, even when specifically asked to do so.

The version on the right contains over twelve times more words than the one on the left, and its greater length is justified by the greater information it provides. Both versions express the same judgment, but the second presents the reasons for that judgment. If the writer believes these reasons must be stated, it would be foolish to omit them simply to compose a shorter sentence. Decisions about economy must always be made in relation to meaning and purpose.

Wordiness—the failure to achieve economy—is a common writing problem. Essays can be wordy because of scanty planning (corrected through global revision) or a monotonous style (corrected through better use of coordination and subordination). To eliminate wordiness *within* a sentence entails local revision. The two most common methods are deleting useless words and phrases and substituting more economical expressions for wordy ones.

Cutting Out Useless Words and Phrases

~~It seems unnecessary to point out that~~ the purpose of chemistry lab is to give students ~~the kind of~~ practical experience ~~they need~~ in testing chemical formulas.

~~I would say in response to your question that~~ the task of the art teacher is to help students ~~develop the ability~~ to understand the function of shape, line, color, and light.

Picasso ~~was an artist who~~ took ~~everyday~~ common objects such as a ~~bicycle~~ seat and the handlebars of an old bicycle and ~~through the process of his imagination~~ transformed them into ~~a work of art called~~ Bull's Head.

Substituting an Economical Expression for a Wordy One

Contemporary researchers in
~~The forward looking thinking of those working in the area of~~ coronary
emphasize
artery disease ~~tends to place a great deal of emphasis on~~ the potential of laser technology.

an international

The Armory Show, ~~a famous~~ exhibition of painting and sculpture ~~that~~

~~brought together the works of artists from throughout the world and dis-~~
held
~~played them~~ in the Armory of the 69th Regiment in New York City in
introduced
1913, ~~enabled~~ the American public to ~~see for the first time artistic move-~~

~~ments such as~~ Cubism and Expressionism.

Over   *ago*   *argued that*
~~It has been more than~~ thirty years ~~since~~ C. P. Snow ~~presented his argu-~~
our
~~ment that the~~ world ~~we live in~~ is divided into *two cultures*—one ~~of these~~
dedicated to   *to*
~~cultures was preoccupied with~~ the humanities; the other ~~was interested~~
~~only in~~ the sciences.

Exercises ———   Eliminate wordiness in the following sentences.

1. As far as the average citizen is concerned, it is probable that most people are not greatly concerned with the latest critical reaction to the new fads in the world of art.

2. When we studied the parts of the human face, which we did in our art class, I discovered that I knew most of the parts that were discussed in the textbook.

3. Concerning the question of whether there are more gifted men artists than women artists, it seems to me that the answer is variable depending on how one interprets the word *gifted*.

4. When, after much careful and painstaking study of the many and various problems involved, the administrators in charge of the different phases of the operation of the hospital made the decision to build a rehabilitation center for patients with all sorts of disabilities, a completely new staff of doctors, nurses, and physical therapists had to be hired.

5. Many doctors, after trying many different methods of relaxing, have discovered that taking up a pleasurable pastime or hobby such as painting calms them down and reduces the amount of stress in their lives.

Revising for Variety

Variety is a characteristic not of single sentences but of a succession of sentences, and it is best seen in a paragraph. But variety is achieved through modification, coordination, subordination, and changes in word order, as shown in the following example:

1. Maxwell Perkins was born in 1884 and died in 1947.

2. He worked for Charles Scribner's Sons for thirty-seven years.

3. He was the head editor for Scribner's for the last twenty of those thirty-seven years.

4. He was almost certainly the most important American editor in the first half of the twentieth century.

5. He worked closely with Thomas Wolfe, F. Scott Fitzgerald, and Ernest Hemingway.

6. He also worked closely with a number of other well-known writers.

The sentences are of similar length (10, 9, 15, 17, 11, and 11 words, respectively) and structure (subject + predicate). Their lack of variety becomes monotonous. Now contrast the same passage revised for variety:

> Maxwell Perkins (1884-1947), head editor of Charles Scribner's Sons for the last twenty of his thirty-seven years with that company, was almost certainly the most important American editor in the first half of the twentieth century. Among the many well-known writers with whom he worked closely were Thomas Wolfe, F. Scott Fitzgerald, and Ernest Hemingway.

The revision combines the original into two sentences of 37 and 18 words, respectively, and results in greater economy (57 words instead of 73), greater density, and more variety. The following operations produced the revision.

▼ Sentences 1, 2, 3, and 4 of the original were combined into a new sentence by: (a) making *Maxwell Perkins* the subject of the new sentence; (b) placing his dates in parentheses; (c) reducing sentences 2 and 3 to a phrase in apposition with the subject of the new sentence; and (d) making sentence 4 the complement of the new sentence.

▼ Sentences 5 and 6 of the original were combined into a new sentence by: (a) having them share a common verb, *were;* and (b) making sentence 6 the subject of *were* and sentence 5 the complement.

Exercises ——— Consider the possible revisions listed after this paragraph about Nathaniel Hawthorne's story "The Birthmark." Decide which of those procedures you want to use to revise the paragraph. You do not need to use them all; just use those that will give you the best paragraph.

> (1) Nathaniel Hawthorne's "The Birthmark" is one of his most famous short stories. (2) It is essentially a story about the limits of science and human perfectibility. (3) Aylmer has conducted many previous experiments in the attempt to improve nature, but all of them have failed. (4) Even so, he decides to perfect his wife Georgiana's beauty by removing a tiny birthmark on her cheek. (5) At the beginning of his experiment, Aylmer is confident he will succeed. (6) He secludes Georgiana in a private chamber. (7) Then he doctors her with strange medicines concocted in his laboratory. (8) He soon discovers that the birthmark is stronger than he thought. (9) He tries to avoid another

failure by giving Georgiana an extremely powerful potion. (10) At the climax of the story, Aylmer sees his experiment succeed. (11) Unfortunately, it does so at a price. (12) Georgiana loses her birthmark. (13) She also loses her life.

Consider these revisions:

▼ Combine 1 and 2 by omitting everything after *is* in 1 and adding everything after *essentially* in 2. Write the revised sentence.

▼ Reduce most of 3 to a subordinate clause, "whose previous attempts to improve nature have failed," and insert it after *Aylmer* in 3 and before *decides* in 4. Write the revised sentence.

▼ Leave 5 as it is.

▼ Combine 6, 7, and 8 into a parallel structure using *but* to separate 7 and 8. Write the revised sentence.

▼ Change the pattern of 9 by beginning the sentence with an introductory phrase, "To avoid another failure," and converting "by giving" to "he decides to give." Write the revised sentence.

▼ Join 10 and 11 by adding a dash after *succeed* and then inserting the phrase "at a price." Write the revised sentence.

▼ Combine 12 and 13 with coordinating conjunction *and*. Write the revised sentence.

Using any of those revised sentences, or any revisions of your own, rewrite the complete paragraph.

THREE PIECES OF ADVICE ON SENTENCE VARIETY

1. *Don't overdo it.* It is neither necessary nor effective to give every sentence a different structure. Within a paragraph, try to have *some* variety in the pattern of your sentences. Most of your sentences will probably be basic sentences containing about 20 words. Individual sentences will range from 10 words or less to 30 words or more and will include balanced, periodic, or cumulative structures.

2. *Postpone revising for variety until you have written your first draft.* As Richard Selzer suggests, the process of *tinkering,* of opening up and compressing sentences, takes place after you have a number of sentences on the page. As you rework your completed sentences, read them aloud, listening for the variations in sound and rhythm that Selzer says are essential to effective writing. You can even *see* recurring structures in sentences, just as Bill Barich sees unvaried patterns in paragraphs, by noticing that they all occupy about the same number of lines.

3. *Be aware of the effect that sentence length has on your readers.* In general, long sentences slow down reading, and short ones speed it up. Short sentences

are often effective as topic sentences because they state the general idea simply; longer sentences are often needed to develop the idea. Short sentences are excellent for communicating a series of actions, emotions, or impressions; longer sentences are more appropriate for analysis and explanation. Short sentences are closer to the rhythms of speech and are therefore suitable when you want to adopt an intimate tone and a conversational style. The more formal the tone and style, the more likely you are to use long and complex sentences.

Keep in mind that these statements are relative to the particular material and perspective you are trying to present to your readers. As in all writing, your choices should reflect your purpose.

Composing Sentences on Your Computer

The computer enables you to expand, combine, and delete sentences with great speed. Indeed, you can compose them almost as fast as you can think them. If you are stuck in an individual sentence, compose other versions of it, one after another. Determine which one works best and delete the others. You can also use the cut-and-paste feature of your word-processing program to rearrange the order of parts of sentences. For example, you can mark a subordinate clause at the beginning of a sentence and move it to the end to achieve more variety.

The editing feature of your word-processing program may also call your attention to sentences that appear wordy. As you look at these sentences, you may determine that, although they are long, they fulfill your purpose. A computer editor does not know your subject, audience, and purpose—much less the context for each sentence. It simply compares your sentences to standard formulas and points out those that seem different. But this does give you the opportunity to reexamine your sentences to see if they are concise and cogent and contribute to your overall purpose.

Excerpts from a Painter's Studio Notes | Pam Smith

In these excerpts from her "studio notes," Pam Smith comments on her creative process in progress. What kind of sentences does she use to describe different stages of her process? How might her sentences be compared to brush strokes?

June 1981

When confusion visits me these days, I tell myself it is the blur of growth. 1

Suggestion is too coy for the real meaning of a painting. I struggle with 2
whether my images are complete or incomplete, not with what they may suggest.

July 1981

It is color, color, color that moves me. 3

I am an ambassador for the color green, a spy for the color red, and a sur- 4
geon sent to insert the color blue.

In private life, I am white's lover. And gray's. 5

No painting I have ever painted has ended up being the same painting I 6
started.

Some days, I feel like I'm a dictionary in reverse, cataloguing all the pos- 7
sible meanings, and then coming up with a word.

I'm concerned about showing my work. I feel this is forced on me, to 8
"prove" my serious intentions. But when I finish a painting, I am only interested in what I am going to paint next.

I had a dream last night. I kept saying in this dream, "I am in love with a 9
green painting." Then I would paint it. This happened over and over, each time
the painting was different and beautiful.

October 1981

The point of a painting is not to say, "This way, and only this way." That's 10
fascism. The point of a painting is, "There's something extra here because it is
done this way."

My paintings these days are renegades. Such unruly things. Each painting is 11
its own world. I try to rework a problem from another painting, and I end up getting a completely different painting. These paintings slip away from my understanding, like baffling children, they elude me. I listen for them to speak to me.

Some days, in my studio, I feel like a plumber who's always fixing leaks. 12
Which is to say, I don't approach a canvas with solemn ceremony, I squint and
gyrate in front of a canvas, to see what needs to be fixed.

Smith, Pam. "Powerful Red Dogs: Excerpts from a Painter's Studio Notes." *Georgia Review 34*
(Spring/Summer 1990): 184–86.

Art is adjustment.   13

November 1982

My new paintings are pretty good. They may even be still lifes and land-   14
scapes, it's possible.

Some of these new paintings are all gray, some of them have new color.   15
They are sassy. I love that.   16
You can look in, but some of them just roar off the wall.   17
I think it's wonderful, because the painting goes from being a view of   18
something, a canvas window with a set scene, to BEING something.

When I paint, my colors are a shape and a placement. I paint their bound-   19
aries. Just this much I paint. Here. And how.

Sometimes I enhance the boundaries by painting them as lines. Sometimes   20
I let the boundaries be where two areas bump into each other.

The way to become an artist is to apprentice yourself and make a thou-   21
sand stupid mistakes from the heart.

When I paint, the world is malleable. It is up to some definition the paint   22
and I work out.

February 1983

I started a new painting today. Large, silky, sexy, lush geometry. I am   23
doing this painting from a casual sketch in an old notebook. I have lifted the
bones of the sketch intact and put it on the canvas, but painting this painting is
a battle between chaos and control.

There is such texture to this experience, the painting comes into and out of 24
focus all the time. Possibilities flash by, and each one of them dictates a completely different painting. Literally every stroke affects this large painting. I
understand the original image which spawned the sketch, but I want to do
more to it. I simultaneously curse myself for not having planned the whole
painting out beforehand, and feel exhilarated by the discoveries that are made.

I believe that a painting reveals itself. It reveals itself while it is being   25
painted.

I believe the motion of my right hand, drawing or painting, is another   26
form of thought.

The Painter's Eye | Diane Ackerman

In this selection from her book *A Natural History of the Senses*, Diane Ackerman analyzes the relationship between defective vision and innovative painting. What kinds of sentences appear in the passages she quotes from Maurice
Merleau-Ponty? What kinds of sentences appear in the passages she quotes
from Patrick Trevor-Roper? How would you compare Ackerman's sentences
to those of the art critics she quotes?

Ackerman, Diane. "The Painter's Eye." *A Natural History of the Senses*. New York: Vintage, 1990.
267–70.

In his later years, Cézanne suffered a famous paroxysm of doubt about his genius. Could his art have been only an eccentricity of his vision, not imagination and talent guarded by a vigilant esthetic? In his excellent essay on Cézanne in *Sense and Nonsense,* Maurice Merleau-Ponty says: "As he grew old, he wondered whether the novelty of his painting might not come from trouble with his eyes, whether his whole life had not been based upon an accident of the body." Cézanne anxiously considered each brush stroke, striving for the fullest sense of the world, as Merleau-Ponty describes so well:

> We *see* the depth, the smoothness, the softness, the hardness of objects; Cézanne even claimed that we see their odor. If the painter is to express the world, the arrangement of his colors must carry with it this invisible whole, or else his picture will only hint at things and will not give them in the imperious unity, the presence, the insurpassable plenitude which is for us the definition of the real. That is why each brush stroke must satisfy an infinite number of conditions. Cézanne sometimes pondered for hours at a time before putting down a certain stroke, for, as Bernard said, each stroke must "contain the air, the light, the object, the composition, the character, the outline, and the style." Expressing what *exists* is an endless task.

Opening up wide to the fullness of life, Cézanne felt himself to be the conduit where nature and humanity met—"The landscape thinks itself in me . . . I am its consciousness"—and would work on all the different sections of a painting at the same time, as if in that way he could capture the many angles, half-truths, and reflections a scene held, and fuse them into one conglomerate version. "He considered himself powerless," Merleau-Ponty writes, "because he was not omnipotent, because he was not God and wanted nevertheless to portray the world, to change it completely into a spectacle, to make *visible* how the world *touches* us." When one thinks of the masses of color and shape in his paintings, perhaps it won't come as a surprise to learn that Cézanne was myopic, although he refused glasses, reputedly crying "Take those vulgar things away!" He also suffered from diabetes, which may have resulted in some retinal damage, and in time he developed cataracts (a clouding of the clear lens). Huysmans once captiously described him as "An artist with a diseased retina, who, exasperated by a defective vision, discovered the basis of a new art." Born into a different universe than most people, Cézanne painted the world his slightly askew eyes saw, but the random chance of that possibility gnawed at him. The sculptor Giacometti, on the other hand, whose long, stretched-out figures look as consciously distorted as one could wish, once confessed amiably: "All the critics spoke about the metaphysical content or the poetic message of my work. But for me it is nothing of the sort. It is a purely optical exercise. I try to represent a head as I see it."

Quite a lot has been learned in recent years about the vision problems of certain artists, whose eyeglasses and medical records have survived. Van Gogh's "Irises" sold at Christie's in 1988 for forty-nine million dollars, which would surely have amused him, since he sold only one painting during his lifetime. Though he was known for cutting off his ear, van Gogh also hit himself with a club, went to many church services each Sunday, slept on a board, had bizarre religious hullucinations, drank kerosene, and ate paint. Some researchers now feel that a few of van Gogh's stylistic quirks (coronas around streetlamps, for instance) may not have been intentional distortions at all but the result of illness, or, indeed, of poisoning from the paint thinners and resins he used, which could have damaged his eyes so that he saw halo effects around light sources. According to Patrick Trevor-Roper, whose *The World Through Blunted Sight* investigates the vision problems of painters and poets, some of the possible diagnoses for van Gogh's depression "have included cerebral tumour, syphilis, magnesium deficiency, temporal lobe epilepsy, poisoning by digitalis (given as a treatment for epilepsy, which could have provoked the yellow vision), and glaucoma (some self-portraits show a dilated right pupil, and he depicted coloured haloes around lights)." Most recently, a scientist speaking before a meeting of neurologists in Boston added Geschwind's syndrome, a personality disorder that sometimes accompanies epilepsy. Van Gogh's own doctor said of him: "Genius and lunacy are well known next-door neighbors." Many of those ailments could have affected his vision. But equally important, the most brilliant pigments used to include toxic heavy metals like copper, cadmium, and mercury. Fumes and poisons could easily get into food, since painters frequently worked and lived in the same rooms. When the eighteenth-century animal painter George Stubbs went on his honeymoon, he stayed in a two-room cottage, in one room of which he hung up the decaying carcass of a horse, which in free moments he studiously dissected. Renoir was a heavy smoker, and he probably didn't bother to wash his hands before he rolled a cigarette; paint from his fingers undoubtedly rubbed onto the paper. Two Danish internists, studying the relationship between arthritis and heavy metals, have compared the color choices in paintings by Renoir, Peter Paul Rubens, and Raoul Dufy (all rheumatoid arthritis sufferers), with those of their contemporaries. When Renoir chose his bright reds, oranges, and blues, he was also choosing big doses of aluminum, mercury, and cobalt. In fact, up to 60 percent of the colors Renoir preferred contained dangerous metals, twice the amount used by such contemporaries of his as Claude Monet or Edgar Degas, who often painted with darker pigments made from safer iron compounds.

According to Trevor-Roper, there is a myopic personality that artists, mathematicians, and bookish people tend to share. They have "an interior life different from others," a different personality, because only the close-up world is visually available to them. The imagery in their work tends to pivot around things that "can be viewed at very close range," and they're more introverted. Of Degas's myopia, for example, he says:

> As time passed he was often reduced to painting in pastel rather than oil as being an easier medium for his failing sight. Later, he discovered that by using photographs of the models or horses he sought to depict, he was able to bring these comfortably within his limited focal range. And finally he fell back increasingly on sculpture where at least he could be sure that his sense of touch would always remain true, saying, 'I must learn a blind man's trade now,' although he had always in fact had an interest in modelling.

Trevor-Roper points out that the mechanism which causes shortsightedness (an elongated eye) affects perception of color as well (reds will appear more starkly defined); cataracts, especially, may affect color, blurring and reddening simultaneously. Consider Turner, whose later paintings Mark Twain once described as "like a ginger cat having a fit in a bowl of tomatoes." Or Renoir's "increasing fascination for reds." Or Monet, who developed such severe cataracts that he had to label his tubes of paint and arrange colors carefully on his palette. After a cataract operation, Monet is reported by friends to have been surprised by all the blueness in the world, and to have been appalled by the strange colors in his recent work, which he anxiously retouched.

One theory about artistic creation is that extraordinary artists come into this world with a different way of seeing. That doesn't explain genius, of course, which has so much to do with risk, anger, a blazing emotional furnace, a sense of esthetic decorum, a savage wistfulness, lidless curiosity, and many other qualities, including a willingness to be fully available to life, to pause over both its general patterns and its ravishing details. As the robustly sensuous painter Georgia O'Keeffe once said: "In a way, nobody sees a flower really, it is so small, we haven't time—and to see takes time, like to have a friend takes time." What kind of novel vision do artists bring into the world with them, long before they develop an inner vision? That question disturbed Cézanne, as it has other artists—as if it made any difference to how and what he would end up painting. When all is said and done, it's as Merleau-Ponty says: *This work to be done called for this life.*

The Knife | **Richard Selzer**

In this selection, Richard Selzer uses a language of poetic intensity to describe the steps of a surgical process. Review his comments on composing sentences on page 192. In the selection here, what kinds of sentences does Selzer use to create a "distinctive rhythm and resonance"? When does he use short sentences? When does he build long sentences? How do such sentences contribute to his purpose?

One holds the knife as one holds the bow of a cello or a tulip—by the stem. Not palmed nor gripped nor grasped, but lightly, with the tips of the fingers. The knife is not for pressing. It is for drawing across the field of skin. Like a slender fish, it waits, at the ready, then, go! It darts, followed by a fine wake of red. The flesh parts, falling away to yellow globules of fat. Even now, after so many times, I still marvel at its power—cold, gleaming, silent. More, I am still struck with a kind of dread that it is I in whose hand the blade travels, that my hand is its vehicle, that yet again this terrible steel-bellied thing and I have conspired for a most unnatural purpose, the laying open of the body of a human being.

A stillness settles in my heart and is carried to my hand. It is the quietude of resolve layered over fear. And it is this resolve that lowers us, my knife and me, deeper and deeper into the person beneath. It is an entry into the body that is nothing like a caress; still, it is among the gentlest of acts. Then stroke and stroke again, and we are joined by other instruments, hemostats and forceps, until the wound blooms with strange flowers whose looped handles fall to the sides in steely array.

There is sound, the tight click of clamps fixing teeth into severed blood vessels, the snuffle and gargle of the suction machine clearing the field of blood

Selzer, Richard. *Mortal Lessons*. New York: Simon, 1976. 92–97.

for the next stroke, the litany of monosyllables with which one prays his way down and in: *clamp, sponge, suture, tie, cut.* And there is color. The green of the cloth, the white of the sponges, the red and yellow of the body. Beneath the fat lies the fascia, the tough fibrous sheet encasing the muscles. It must be sliced and the red beef of the muscles separated. Now there are retractors to hold apart the wound. Hands move together, part, weave. We are fully engaged, like children absorbed in a game or the craftsmen of some place like Damascus.

Deeper still. The peritoneum, pink and gleaming and membranous, bulges into the wound. It is grasped with forceps, and opened. For the first time we can see into the cavity of the abdomen. Such a primitive place. One expects to find drawings of buffalo on the walls. The sense of trespassing is keener now, heightened by the world's light illuminating the organs, their secret colors revealed—maroon and salmon and yellow. The vista is sweetly vulnerable at this moment, a kind of welcoming. An arc of the liver shines high and on the right, like a dark sun. It laps over the pink sweep of the stomach, from whose lower border the gauzy omentum is draped, and through which veil one sees, sinuous, slow as just-fed snakes, the indolent coils of the intestine. **4**

You turn aside to wash your gloves. It is a ritual cleansing. One enters this temple doubly washed. Here is man as microcosm, representing in all his parts the earth, perhaps the universe. **5**

I must confess that the priestliness of my profession has ever been impressed on me. In the beginning there are vows, taken with all solemnity. Then there is the endless harsh novitiate of training, much fatigue, much sacrifice. At last one emerges as celebrant, standing close to the truth lying curtained in the Ark of the body. Not surplice and cassock but mask and gown are your regalia. You hold no chalice, but a knife. There is no wine, no wafer. There are only the facts of blood and flesh. **6**

And if the surgeon is like a poet, then the scars you have made on countless bodies are like verses into the fashioning of which you have poured your soul. I think that if years later I were to see the trace from an old incision of mine, I should know it at once, as one recognizes his pet expressions. **7**

But mostly you are a traveler in a dangerous country, advancing into the moist and jungly cleft your hands have made. Eyes and ears are shuttered from the land you left behind; mind empties itself of all other thought. You are the root of groping fingers. It is a fine hour for the fingers, their sense of touch so enhanced. The blind must know this feeling. Oh, there is risk everywhere. One goes lightly. The spleen. No! No! Do not touch the spleen that lurks below the left leaf of the diaphragm, a manta ray in a coral cave, its bloody tongue protruding. One poke and it might rupture, exploding with sudden hemorrhage. The filmy omentum must not be torn, the intestine scraped or denuded. The hand finds the liver, palms it, fingers running along its sharp lower edge, admiring. Here are the twin mounds of the kidneys, the apron of the omentum hanging in front of the intestinal coils. One lifts it aside and the fingers dip among the loops, searching, mapping territory, establishing boundaries. Deeper still, and the womb is touched, then held like a small muscular bottle— the womb and its earlike appendages, the ovaries. How they do nestle in the cup of a man's hand, their power all dormant. They are frailty itself. **8**

There is a hush in the room. Speech stops. The hands of the others, assistants and nurses, are still. Only the voice of the patient's respiration remains. It is the rhythm of a quiet sea, the sound of waiting. Then you speak, slowly, the terse entries of a Himalayan climber reporting back. **9**

"The stomach is okay. Greater curvature clean. No sign of ulcer. Pylorus, duodenum fine. Now comes the gallbladder. No stones. Right kidney, left, all right. Liver . . . uh-oh."   10

Your speech lowers to a whisper, falters, stops for a long, long moment, then picks up again at the end of a sigh that comes through your mask like a last exhalation.   11

"Three big hard ones in the left lobe, one on the right. Metastatic deposits. Bad, bad. Where's the primary? Got to be coming from somewhere."   12

The arm shifts direction and the fingers drop lower and lower into the pelvis—the body impaled now upon the arm of the surgeon to the hilt of the elbow.   13

"Here it is."   14

The voice goes flat, all business now.   15

"Tumor in the sigmoid colon, wrapped all around it, pretty tight. We'll take out a sleeve of the bowel. No colostomy. Not that, anyway. But, God, there's a lot of it down there. Here, you take a feel."   16

You step back from the table, and lean into a sterile basin of water, resting on stiff arms, while the others locate the cancer.   17

Writing Assignments

Narrate   **1.**   Compose a freewriting exercise about your most memorable experience with illness. Follow Richard Selzer's advice and simply make one "brush stroke" after another until you have painted a fairly complete portrait of the experience. Then expand and combine your sentences to turn your freewriting into a finished essay.

Observe   **2.**   Visit your local art museum or look through one of the oversized art books in your library. Select a particular painting that "speaks to you." *Study* the way the painter arranges the subject for your observation. Then write a letter to a close friend describing the painting and speculating about why it has had such a powerful impact on you.

Investigate   **3.**   Visit the studio of a local artist or the studios in your university's art department. Ask for permission to observe a painter at work. Watch the way he or she uses different techniques—applying paint with fingers, brushes, spray devises, or palette knives—to "compose" the painting. Ask a few questions, but encourage the painter to talk about his or her work as it is being created. You may have to visit the studio several times to see the project through to completion. Then write a "biography of the painting" to introduce it to the students in your writing group.

Collaborate   **4.**   Your writing group has been asked to draft a program for an exhibit of student paintings. Assign each member of your group to write the copy for one painter. Study previous programs to see how many and what kinds of sentences have been used to describe the painters and their work. Decide if you want to *expand* or *modify* that pattern. Then interview the student painters, study their work, design the layout for the program, and collaborate on creating the final copy.

Read   **5.**   Read selections from some of Richard Selzer's other books about surgery, *Rituals of Surgery* (1974), *Confessions of a Knife* (1979), and *Letters to a Young Doctor* (1982). Compose a series of sentences on the reasons why you *would* or *would not* want to become a surgeon. After you have compared one set of reasons with the other, subordinate one group to the other in an essay entitled "I Want to Be a Surgeon" or "I Don't Want to Be a Surgeon."

Respond   **6.**   Select a painting by one of the artists described in Diane Ackerman's "The Painter's Eye." How do you respond to its design and color? How do you respond to it knowing that the painter may have had defective vision? Draft an essay explaining how the painting's success depends on the painter's "inner eye" rather than his or her eyesight.

Analyze   **7.**   Analyze the sentences in Pam Smith's "Excerpts from a Painter's Studio Notes." Reread Richard Selzer's comparison of sentences and brush strokes on page 192. Then write an essay, citing specific sentences from Smith's "studio notes," to demonstrate the appropriateness of Selzer's comparison of painting and writing.

Evaluate   8.   Richard Selzer uses many comparisons in "The Knife" to illustrate the process he is describing. Analyze each of these comparisons—the surgeon is like a priest, a poet, a traveler in a dangerous country. Then select one—for example, the artistry of the surgeon is similar to the artistry of the writer—and evaluate the points of the comparison that Selzer leaves out, the points that suggest that the two processes are radically different.

Argue   9.   You have been asked by a friend or your employer to select a painting by a local artist to be hung in a special location. Visit local galleries or art shows, looking for the *right* painting. Consider your immediate audience (the person who asked you to select the painting), your ultimate audience (the people who will see the painting), and the context (where the painting will be hung). Compose a series of sentences (or reasons) why you think a particular painting is the *right* painting. Then write a letter recommending your choice to your friend or employer. (You may want to reread Wallace Armstrong's "Brandon's Clown" in Chapter 1 to remind yourself of how such purchases affect the painter.)

Argue   10.   As an experiment in revising sentences, work with the following sentences by expanding, modifying, or combining them into an effective argument. Add other sentences to fill out your portrait and fulfill your purpose.
a. Surgeons are revered as medical priests.
b. They are cloaked and masked in green vestments.
c. They have acquired a secret knowledge.
d. They are given absolute authority over life and death.
e. They cut the human body with special tools.
f. They eliminate disease.
g. They stitch the body together.
h. They wash their hands after the ritual.
i. The people they restore to health view the process as a miracle.

9 | Diction: The Choice of Words

As you think your way through a sentence, you inevitably search for the best words to convey your thoughts. Sometimes, especially when you are quite clear about what you want to say, the words come so easily that you are hardly aware of choosing them. At other times, especially when you are trying to discover what you want to say, you find yourself scratching out one choice after another as you search for the exact word to express your meaning. Such revisions are not necessarily a sign of indecision. The best writers worry constantly about diction—the selection and use of words for effective communication. Perhaps they are the best writers partly because they take pains to choose the best word.

Words are not right or wrong in themselves. What makes a particular word right is the effect it creates in the context of your sentence or paragraph. Annie Dillard, celebrated for her evocative descriptions of nature, explains how she chooses words.

> I learn words by learning worlds. Any writer does that out of simple curiosity. When I choose words, I think about their effect—of course I like to create a rich prose surface that pommels the reader with verbs and images. I think of them as jabs. Jab, jab, jab, left. Jab, jab, jab, right. That's the vigor I want. (Personal interview)

To create vigor in your writing and to advance your purpose, you must, like Dillard, learn the words that represent the "worlds" you want to write about and learn to use words for their effect. You must learn the denotations and connotations of words.

DENOTATION AND CONNOTATION

The most familiar use of words is to name things—plants, people, oceans, stars. When words are used in this way, the things they refer to are called their *denotations*. The word *molecule* most commonly denotes small structures of atoms. The denotation of *Mars* is the fourth planet from the sun. The denotation is a word's explicit meaning.

But some words acquire connotations as well as denotations. A connotation is an *implicit* meaning, an implied or suggested attitude that is not stated outright. When you label theories about life on Mars "improbable" or "preposterous," you

Wordsmiths

Drawing by W. B. Park; © 1988 The New Yorker Magazine, Inc.

are not only describing them, you are also expressing, and inviting your readers to share, an attitude toward them.

In each of these sentences, the writer implies a different attitude toward similar events.

My wife asked me why I was *slashing* the shrubbery. I told her I was merely *pruning* it.

The difference between *childish pranks* and acts of *vandalism* depends on whose child does the mischief.

Although most bathers thought the high surf looked *threatening*, a few thought it looked *challenging*.

When our team of scientists traveled across the crater to *collect samples*, they encountered another team *stealing evidence*.

The contrast in each example is not between denotations and connotations but between favorable and unfavorable connotations. *Slashing* and *pruning* refer to similar actions; but the first implies destructive recklessness, and the second suggests careful cutting.

The words you choose should support your purpose. If you wish to report objectively, select words that suggest a neutral attitude: *collect samples* not *stealing evidence*. If you wish to convey a tolerant or approving attitude, use words that invite a tolerant or approving response: *pruning, childish pranks, challenging.* If you wish to suggest disapproval, select words with unfavorable connotations: *slashing, act of vandalism, threatening.*

Exercises ——— In the following sentences the blank may be filled with any of the words in parentheses, but each choice creates different connotations. Discuss how each choice affects the writer's intention and the reader's interpretation of the sentence.

1. The roses _____ the trellis. (climbed, adorned, strangled)
2. She was a _____ reader. (compulsive, critical, perceptive)
3. The children were _____. (sleepy, exhausted, weary)
4. The reef _____ beneath the surface. (appeared, loomed, glimmered)
5. The comet _____ across the night sky. (shot, blinked, blazed)

THREE QUALITIES OF EFFECTIVE DICTION

Choice of diction is always made with reference to a particular sentence and to the total context of your writing. For this reason no dictionary or thesaurus will give you *the* right word. A dictionary presents a word's various meanings, and a thesaurus provides a list of synonyms, words with slightly varying meanings. You must decide which word and meaning meet your needs. To make this decision, consider the qualities of effective diction: *appropriateness, specificity,* and *imagery.*

Appropriateness

Words are appropriate when they are suited to your subject, audience, and purpose. Imagine an astronomer reporting the discovery of a new star to a convention of scientists and then to the viewers of a morning television show. The subject is the same, but the audience and purpose are so different that the speaker alters the content, style, and language of the report. Choices to accommodate audience and purpose affect not only diction, the subject of this chapter, but tone and style, the subjects of the next chapter. Diction, tone, and style are alike in requiring you to make important decisions about the degree of formality appropriate for a given context. Jeans and a T-Shirt are not appropriate for a formal dance; an evening gown or tuxedo is conspicuously inappropriate for the classroom; in the same way, some words inappropriate in some situations are perfectly acceptable in others. The best way to understand this distinction is to consider four types of words: *learned, popular, colloquial,* and *slang.*

Learned and Popular Words
Most words in English, as in other languages, are common to the speech of educated and uneducated speakers alike.

These words are the basic elements of everyday communication. They are called *popular words* because they belong to the whole populace.

By contrast, there are words that you read more often than you hear, write more often than you speak—words used more widely by educated than by uneducated people, and more likely to be used on formal than on informal occasions. Such words are called *learned words.*

The following list contrasts pairs of popular and learned words that have similar denotations.

Popular	*Learned*	*Popular*	*Learned*
agree ——————— concur		help ——————— succor	
begin ——————— commence		make easy——— facilitate	
clear——————— lucid		secret——————— esoteric	
disagree ——— remonstrate		think ——————— cogitate	
end——————————— terminate		wordy ——————— verbose	

Colloquialisms   The term *colloquial* is defined by the *American Heritage Dictionary* as "characteristic of or appropriate to the spoken language or writing that seeks its effect; informal in diction or style of expression." Colloquialisms are not "incorrect" or "bad" English. They are the kinds of words people, educated and uneducated alike, use when they are speaking together informally. Their deliberate use in writing conveys the impression of direct and intimate conversation. To achieve this effect you might use contractions *(don't, wasn't, hasn't)* or clipped words *(taxi, phone).* Other typical colloquialisms are:

awfully *(for* very)	fix *(for* predicament)	movie *(for* film)
back of *(for* behind)	it's me	over with *(for* completed)
cute	kind of *(for* somewhat)	peeve *(for* annoy)
exam	a lot of; lots of	plenty *(as an adverb)*
expect *(for* suppose)	mad *(for* angry)	sure *(for* certainly)

Slang   The *Oxford English Dictionary* defines slang as "language of a highly colloquial type." Notice that the adjective used is *colloquial,* not *vulgar* or *incorrect.* Slang is used by everyone. The appropriateness of slang, however, depends on the occasion. A college president would probably avoid slang in a public speech but might use it at an informal gathering.

Slang satisfies a desire for novelty of expression. It is often borrowed from the vocabularies of particular occupations or activities: *input* (computer technology), *on the beam* (aerial navigation), *behind the eight ball* (pool), *dunk* (basketball). Some slang words are from the "insider" languages of those who commit crimes or take drugs: *sting, torch, grass, stoned.* Much slang is borrowed from the popular vocabulary and given new meanings: *flipped, split, cool, soul, rap, high, trip, wheels, vibes, bread.* Some slang proves so imaginative and useful that it becomes part of the popular vocabulary, but quickly becomes dated, obscure, and loses its impact.

The scale below shows the four types of diction within the range of formality.

Learned   Popular   Colloquial   Slang

←————————————————————————————————→

Most formal   *Least formal*

In most of your writing, words from the middle of this scale will be appropriate. Unfortunately, some inexperienced writers think that formality is a virtue and that big, fancy words are more impressive than short, common ones. If writers cannot maintain an appropriate level of formality, their diction becomes strained and inconsistent.

The following passage provides a humorous illustration of such inconsistency. In this scene from George Bernard Shaw's play *Pygmalion* (from which the musical *My Fair Lady* was created), Liza Doolittle, a cockney flower girl who is being taught by Professor Higgins to speak like a lady, meets her first test at a small party at the home of Mrs. Higgins, the professor's mother. Notice the contrast between Liza's first speech and her last.

Mrs. Higgins: Will it rain, do you think?

Liza: The shallow depression in the west of these islands is likely to move slowly in an easterly direction. There are no indications of any great change in the barometrical situation.

Freddy: Ha! Ha! How awfully funny!

Liza: What is wrong with that, young man? I bet I got it right.

Freddy: Killing!

Mrs. Eynsford Hill: I'm sure I hope it won't turn cold. There's so much influenza about. It runs right through our whole family regularly every spring.

Liza: My aunt died of influenza: so they said. . . . But it's my belief they done the old woman in. . . . Why should *she* die of influenza? She come through diphtheria right enough the year before. I saw her with my own eyes. Fairly blue with it, she was. They all thought she was dead; but my father he kept ladling gin down her throat 'til she came to so sudden that she bit the bowl off the spoon. . . . What call would a woman with that strength in her have to die of influenza? What become of her new straw hat that should have come to me? Somebody pinched it; and what I say is, them as pinched it done her in.

The obvious switch from formal to highly colloquial speech is justified by Shaw's purpose, which is to show Liza in a transitional stage at which she cannot yet consistently maintain the pose of being a well-educated young woman. Liza does not see that her learned comment on the weather is inappropriate in this situation, and therefore has no idea why Freddy is laughing. When the subject changed to influenza, she forgets she is supposed to be a lady and reverts to her natural speech—which is much more expressive and colorful than her phony formality. Her inconsistency is amusing, as Shaw meant it to be.

But in the compositions of inexperienced writers, most inconsistencies are not intended for humorous effect. They slip in when the writer is not in control of *how* to say *what* he or she wants to say. The writer may start off like Liza, hoping to make a good impression, but the writer's natural voice asserts itself and the result is neither formal nor informal diction but an embarrassing mixture. Try to choose words consistently appropriate to your purpose throughout the writing process, and, of course, in revision, stay alert for unintentional shifts in diction.

Exercise —————— The following paragraph does not maintain a consistent level of diction. Identify the words and phrases that seem too formal or too informal. Then rewrite the paragraph, substituting more appropriate diction to make the language of the paragraph consistent.

> In my perusal of the morning paper, I often pause to take a gander at my horoscope. This stuff is supposed to be figured out on a chart of the heavens, which manifests the positions of the sun, moon, and the signs of the zodiac at the honest to goodness time and location of your birth. These configurations are then juxtaposed to the twelve hours of the celestial sphere. The signs are presumed to hold sway over certain parts of the body, and the houses are supposed to tell you what's happening in the various conditions of life. The degree of influence attributed to these houses depends on a bunch of factors. Sometimes my horoscope predicts the orb of my daily activities with confounding accuracy. But most of the time it's just hogwash.

Specificity

General and *specific* are opposite terms. Words are general when they refer not to individual things but to groups or classes: *mother, flowers, hurricane.* Words are specific when they refer to individual persons, objects, or events: *Joe's mother, the flowers in the vase near the window, Hurricane Bob.* A general term may be made more specific with a modifier that restricts the reference to a particular member of the group or class.

Specific and *general* are also relative terms: a word may seem specific in one context and general in another, as the diagram shows.

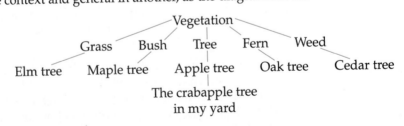

Most general	Vegetation
Less general	Grass Bush Tree Fern Weed
Still less general	Elm tree Maple tree Apple tree Oak tree Cedar tree
Specific	The crabapple tree in my yard

Exercises —————— For each set of terms, show the gradation from general to specific. Place the most general term at the left and the most specific at the right, as in this example:

matter, food, fruit, citrus fruit, orange

1. Labrador retriever, quadruped, bird dog, animal, dog
2. protons, molecule, electrons, atom, nucleus
3. bush, rosebush, plant, decorative bush, Tropicana rosebush
4. Jupiter, Milky Way, sun, solar system, galaxy
5. Scientist, chemist, Marie Curie, Nobel Prize winner

Your context determines whether a specific or a general word is required. Some purposes require generalities. A president's inaugural address, for example, does not deal with specifics; it states general policies and intentions. The best policy is to be as specific as the situation permits. Notice how the specific language in the examples on the right communicates meaning that is not conveyed by the general diction on the left.

A drop of water contains particles.	A drop of water contains microscopic strands of algae and multicellular aquatic organisms.
Saturn has rings.	Saturn is surrounded by a vast swarm of meteoric fragments revolving in various orbits.

The term *concrete* is used to describe some kinds of specific diction. *Concrete* is the opposite of *abstract*. Concrete words refer to particular things or qualities that can be perceived by your senses: details of appearance, sounds, smells, textures, tastes. Abstract words refer to qualities shared by many people or things: newness, width, size, shape, value, joy, anger. Abstract qualities cannot be perceived directly by observation; they are concepts that you infer from what you see.

In the following paragraph, Annie Dillard uses concrete, sensory detail to illustrate her abstract opening sentence. The image of successive flocks of red-winged blackbirds materializing from the dense, green foliage of the Osage orange tree remains in the mind in a way impossible for concepts such as *nature* or *revelation*.

For nature does reveal as well as conceal; now-you-don't-see-it, now-you-do. For a week this September migrating red-winged blackbirds were feeding heavily down by Tinker Creek at the back of the house. One day I went out to investigate the racket; I walked up to a tree, an Osage orange, and a hundred birds flew away. They simply materialized out of the tree. I saw a tree, then a whisk of color, then a tree again. I walked closer and another hundred blackbirds took flight. Not a branch, not a twig budged: the birds were apparently weightless as well as invisible. Or, it was as if the leaves of the Osage orange had been freed from a spell in the form of red-winged blackbirds; they flew from the tree, caught my eye in the sky, and vanished. When I looked again at the tree, the leaves had reassembled as if nothing had happened. Finally I walked directly to the trunk of the tree and a final hundred, the real diehards, appeared, spread, and vanished. How could so many hide in the tree without my seeing them? The Osage orange, unruffled, looked just as it had looked from the house, when three hundred red-winged blackbirds cried from its crown. I looked upstream where they flew, and they were gone. Searching, I couldn't spot one. I wandered upstream to force them to play their hand, but they'd crossed the creek and scattered. One show to a customer. These appearances catch at my throat; they are the free gifts, the bright coppers at the roots of trees. (Annie Dillard, "Sight into Insight," *Pilgrim at Tinker Creek*)

Words that refer to sensory experiences—to what you see, hear, touch, taste, and smell—call up sensory images (particularly when they are embedded in strong verbs) and create the "rich prose surface" Dillard uses to "jab" her reader. The following is a list of additional examples (some words fit into more than one sensory category):

Touch   chill, clammy, cold, grainy, gritty, jarring, knobby, moist, numb, rough, smooth, sting, tingle

Taste   bland, bitter, brackish, metallic, minty, peppery, salty, sour, spicy, sweet

Smell   acrid, fetid, greasy, musky, musty, pungent, putrid, rancid, rank, reek, stench

Sound   bellow, blare, buzz, chime, clang, clatter, clink, crackle, crash, creak, gurgle, hiss, hum, murmur, pop, purr, rattle, rustle, screech, snap, squeak, whine, whisper

Sight   blaze, bleary, bloody, chalky, dappled, ebony, flame, flicker, florid, foggy, gaudy, glare, glitter, glossy, grimy, haze, inky, leaden, muddy, pallid, sallow, shadow, smudged, streak, tawny

Exercises ———

1. Read the following passage and note the words or phrases that seem most concrete. Then copy the passage over without those words or phrases. In what ways is the meaning of the second version diminished?

A single knoll rises out of the plain in Oklahoma, north and west of the Wichita Range. For my people, the Kiowas, it is an old landmark, and they gave it the name Rainy Mountain. The hardest weather in the world is there. Winter brings blizzards, hot tornadic winds arise in the spring, and in summer the prairie is an anvil's edge. The grass turns brittle and brown, and it cracks beneath your feet. There are green belts along the rivers and creeks, linear groves of hickory and pecan, willow and witch hazel. At a distance in July or August the steaming foliage seems almost to writhe in fire. Great green and yellow grasshoppers are everywhere in the tall grass, popping up like corn to sting the flesh, and tortoises crawl about on the red earth, going nowhere in plenty of time. Loneliness is an aspect of the land. All things in the plain are isolate; there is no confusion of objects in the eye, but *one* hill or *one* tree or *one* man. To look upon that landscape in the early morning, with the sun at your back, is to lose the sense of proportion. Your imagination comes to life, and this, you think, is where Creation was begun. (N. Scott Momaday, "The Way to Rainy Mountain")

2. The following contrasted statements deal with the same subject. From each pair, choose the statement that you think is more concrete. Explain the specific reasons for your choice.

In the past, girls in rural communities had no facilities for bathing except those offered by some neighboring stream. In such circumstances a bathing suit was not always a necessity, but if one was worn it was likely to consist of nothing more than some discarded article of clothing tailored to fit the occasion.

Forty years ago, if the farmer's daughter went swimming she swam in the crick below the pasture, and if she wore a bathing suit, which was not as customary as you may think, it was likely to be a pair of her brother's outgrown overalls trimmed with scissors as her discretion might suggest.

Suddenly I felt something on the biceps of my right arm—a queer light touch, clinging for an instant, and then the smooth glide of its body. I could feel the muscles of the snake's body slowly contract and relax. At last I saw a flat, V-shaped head, with two glistening, black, protruding buttons. A thin, pointed, sickening yellow tongue slipped out, then in, accompanied by a sound like that of escaping steam.

Suddenly I felt the snake moving over my arm. I felt the contraction of its muscles as it moved. Then I saw its ugly head and its evil-looking eyes. All the time its tongue keep moving in and out, making a kind of hissing noise.

Imagery

Imagery has two general meanings when applied to diction: the images or pictures that concrete words sometimes suggest and figures of speech such as similes and metaphors. The first meaning includes the pictorial quality of phrases such as *an anvil's edge, green belts, popping up like corn.* In this section you will learn about the second meaning—the use of figurative language.

The chief element in all figures of speech is an imaginative comparison in which dissimilar things are described as having a meaningful similarity. The writer, by thus linking the unfamiliar with the familiar, creates a context in which the reader may more easily or clearly understand a new aspect of the subject or new information and ideas. Here is an example:

The moon was a ghostly galleon tossed upon cloudy seas. (Alfred Noyes)

The line of poetry compares the moon to a sailing ship. Now in most ways the moon is quite unlike a ship. But as the poet watches it alternately emerging from behind the clouds and disappearing into them again, he thinks of a ship alternately emerging and disappearing from view as it rides the troughs and crests of the waves. In his imagination the moon is being tossed by the clouds as a ship is tossed by the waves.

The most commonly used figures of speech are *simile, metaphor, analogy, personification,* and *allusion.* Each figure makes a comparison, but each has its own characteristic form and use.

Simile   A simile compares two things—*A* and *B*—by asserting that one is like the other. A simile usually contains the word *like, as,* or *so* and is used to transfer to *A* the qualities or feelings associated with *B.* Thus, when Annie Dillard in "Total Eclipse" describes a solar eclipse, she imagines that the sky *(A)*— or more precisely the moon—functions like the lens cover *(B)* on a camera, covering the lens and shutting out all the light:

> The sky snapped over the sun like a lens cover.

Here are some other similes:

> Insects in the first frosts of autumn all run down like little clocks. (Loren Eiseley, "How Flowers Changed the World," *The Star Thrower*)

> When, as you approach, [the iguanas] swish away, there is a flash of azure, green and purple over the stones, the colour seems to be standing behind them in the air, like a comet's luminous tail. (Isak Dinesen, *Out of Africa*)

> Floating on one's back is like riding between two skies. (Edward Hoagland, "Summer Pond")

> Laverne wasn't too bad a dancer, but the other one, old Marty . . . was like dragging the Statue of Liberty around the floor. (J. D. Salinger, *Catcher in the Rye*)

Metaphor   A metaphor compares two things by identifying one with the other. It does not say that *A* is like *B* but instead states that *A* is *B.* Lewis Thomas is using metaphor when he suggests that the sky encloses the earth just as a membrane surrounds an organ or cell.

> Aloft, floating free beneath the moist, gleaming membrane of bright blue sky, is the rising earth, the only exuberant thing in this part of the cosmos. (Lewis Thomas, "The World's Biggest Membrane," *The Lives of a Cell*)

Here are other metaphors:

> Time is but a stream I go a-fishing in. (Henry David Thoreau, *Walden*)

> Suddenly the whole room broke into a sea of shouting, as they saw me rise. Waves of rejoicing swept the place. (Langston Hughes, *The Big Sea*)

> Each rich nation is a lifeboat full of comparatively rich people. In the ocean outside each lifeboat swim the poor of the world who want to get in, or at best to share some of the wealth. (Garrett Hardin, "Lifeboat Ethics: The Case Against Helping the Poor")

Many words and phrases no longer thought of as figures of speech were originally metaphors or similes. "At bay" originally described a hunted animal cornered by pursuers and forced to turn and fight the baying hounds. "Crestfallen" first described a cock that had been humbled in a cockfight. Many other expressions can be analyzed as metaphors even though you no longer think of them as figures of speech—expressions such as the "mouth" of a river, the "face" of a clock, the "brow" of a hill. Such expressions are often called, metaphorically, *dead* or *frozen metaphors.* They are so common in the language that it is hard to write a paragraph without them, but you should try to avoid those (such as "rosy red," "dirt cheap," and "face the music") that have become clichés.

Analogy   An analogy is an extended metaphor that, through several sentences or paragraphs, explains an abstract idea or seeks to persuade readers that because two things are alike, a conclusion drawn from one suggests a similar conclusion can be drawn from the other. In the following passage, Robert Jastrow uses analogy to explain the shape of our galaxy:

> The Galaxy is flattened by its rotating motion into the shape of a disk whose thickness is roughly one-fifth of its diameter. Most of the stars in the Galaxy are in this disk, although some are located outside it. A relatively small, spherical cluster of stars, called the nucleus of the Galaxy, bulges out of the disk at the center. The center structure resembles a double sombrero with the gigantic nucleus as the crown and the disk as the brim. The sun is located in the brim of the sombrero about three-fifths of the way out from the center of the edge. When we look into the sky in the direction of the disk we see so many stars that they are not visible as separate points of light, but blend together into a luminous band stretching across the sky. This band is called the Milky Way. (Robert Jastrow. The Size of Things," *Red Giants and White Dwarfs)*

Personification   Personification is a figure of speech by which inanimate objects or abstractions are given human or animal characteristics. Thus winds are said to "roar" or "bite"; flames "eat hungrily" at a burning house and may even "devour" it; a tree may "bow" before a gale or in fair weather "stretch" its branches; truth or virtue emerges "triumphant"; and justice is "blind." In these examples, the writer imagines a resemblance between the acts observed and the actions of an animal or person.

Such implied comparisons are often effective, but they should be used with restraint. If they seem exaggerated ("the waves roared their threat to the listening clouds while the palm trees nodded their approval"), your reader is likely to reject them as far-fetched or as an unsuccessful attempt to be "literary."

Allusion   An allusion is a comparison between a historical, literary, or mythological event or person and the subject under discussion. When a scientific discovery is said to possess Copernican significance, it is being associated with Copernicus's theory that revolutionized the way we saw the universe (the Earth rotating around the sun rather than the sun rotating around the Earth). Or when a film is called another *Star Wars*, it is being likened to one of the most extraordinary films ever made about outer space.

A successful allusion provides a flash of wit or insight and gives your readers the pleasure of recognition. But you must be reasonably sure that an allusion is suited to your audience; if your readers do not recognize or understand the allusion, they will be confused and not appreciate its effect. Calling writing a research paper a "Sisyphean task" is amusing only if your audience remembers that Sisyphus was condemned forever to roll a huge stone up a steep hill in Hades, only to have it roll back down just as it neared the top.

Exercises ———

1. In the following selections, underline effective examples of specificity and imagery.

When wild ducks or wild geese migrate in their season, a strange tide rises in the territories over which they sweep. As if magnetized by the great triangular flight, the barnyard fowl leap a foot or two into the air and try to fly . . . and a vestige of savagery quickens their blood. All the ducks on the farm are transformed for an instant into migrant birds, and into those hard little heads, till now filled with humble images of pools and worms and barnyards, there swims a sense of continental expanse, of the breadth of seas and the salt taste of the ocean wind. The duck totters to the right and left in its wire enclosure, gripped by a sudden passion to perform the impossible and a sudden love whose object is a mystery. (Antoine de Saint Exupéry, *Wind, Sand and Stars*)

The word is terracide. As in homicide, or genocide. Except it's terra. Land.

It is not committed with guns and knives, but with great, relentless bulldozers and thundering dump trucks, with giant shovels like mythological creatures, their girded necks lifting massive steel mouths high above the tallest trees. And with dynamite. They cut and blast and rip apart mountains to reach the minerals inside, and when they have finished there is nothing left but naked hills, ugly monuments to waste, stripped of everything that once held them in place, cut off from the top and sides and dug out from the inside and then left, restless, to slide down on houses and wash off into rivers and streams, rendering the land unlivable and the water for miles downstream undrinkable.

Terracide. Or, if you prefer, strip-mining. (Skip Rozin, "People of the Ruined Hills," *Audubon*)

"On nights like that," Raymond Chandler once wrote about the Santa Ana, "every booze party ends in a fight. Meek little wives feel the edge of the carving knife and study their husbands' necks. Anything can happen." That was the kind of wind it was. I did not know then that there was any basis for the effect it had on all of us, but it turns out to be another of those cases in which science bears out folk wisdom. The Santa Ana, which is named for one of the canyons it rushes through, is a *foehn* wind, like the *foehn* of Austria and Switzerland and the *hamsin* of Israel. There are a number of persistent malevolent winds, perhaps the best known of which are the mistral of France and the Mediterranean sirocco, but a *foehn* wind has distinct characteristics: it occurs on the leeward slope of a mountain range and, although the air begins as a cold mass, it is warmed as it comes down the mountain and appears finally as a hot dry wind. Whenever and wherever a *foehn* blows, doctors hear about headaches and nausea and allergies, about "nervousness," about "depression." In Los Angeles some teachers do not attempt to conduct formal classes during a Santa Ana, because the children become unmanageable. In Switzerland the suicide rate goes up during the *foehn*, and in the courts of some Swiss cantons the wind is considered a mitigating circumstance for crime. Surgeons are said to watch the wind, because blood does not clot normally during a *foehn*. A few years ago an Israeli physicist discovered that not only during such winds, but for the ten or twelve hours which precede them, the air carries an unusually high ratio of positive to negative ions. No one seems to know exactly why that should be; some talk about friction and others suggest solar disturbances. In any case the positive ions are there, and what an excess of positive ions does, in the simplest terms, is make people unhappy. One cannot get much more mechanistic than that. (Joan Didion, "Los Angeles Notebook," *Slouching Towards Bethlehem*)

2. Evaluate the effectiveness of the following figures of speech from the student writing used in previous chapters. Discuss how each figure contributes to the writer's purpose.

a. Wallace Armstrong, "Brandon's Clown" (Chapter 1):

Before long, the book looked like a Disneyland mortuary.

b. Jane Graham, "Watching Whales" (Chapter 5):

When he burst out of the water, he held his flippers at a slight angle to his side. As he descended, he moved them gracefully away from his body like the arms of a ballerina finishing a pirouette.

c. Matt Fisher, "Drug Abuse in the Work Place" (Chapter 6):

All of us—employers, workers, consumers—want to cure this plague that threatens the health of our culture.

REVISING DICTION

In considering the qualities of effective diction, you evaluated ways of expressing ideas, and your evaluation included a great deal of revision. In this stage of local revision, you need to change your emphasis from expressing yourself effectively to rooting out the ineffective. Work through your text slowly, looking for words that don't fully express your purpose. Four major weaknesses to watch for are *vagueness*, *jargon*, *triteness*, and *ineffective imagery*.

Eliminating Vagueness

Words are vague when, in context, they do not convey a single, specific meaning to your readers. Consider this sentence:

I could tell by the funny look on her face that she was mad.

Funny and *mad* can have quite specific meanings, but not in that sentence. What does *funny* mean here—a purposeful attempt to provoke laughter? What does *mad* mean—"insane," as it might in another sentence? Certainly not. "Angry," then, or "annoyed" or irritated" or "offended"? A reader cannot be sure. The writer can remove doubt by using more specific diction.

I could tell by the *way her face stiffened* that she was *offended*.

Words like *funny* and *mad* belong to a group called *utility words*. Such words, as their name implies, are useful. In ordinary conversation, which does not usually permit or require deliberate choice and offers little chance for revision, utility words are common and often pass unnoticed. In writing, they may be adequate if the context limits them to a single, clear interpretation. But because their meaning is often left vague, they should be used with caution. The following is a list of some of the most common utility words:

affair	funny	marvelous	regular
awful	gadget	matter	silly
business	glamorous	nature	situation
cute	goods	neat	stuff
fantastic	gorgeous	nice	terrible
fierce	great	outfit	terrific
fine	line	peculiar	weird
freak	lovely	pretty	wonderful

Usually the simplest way to clarify a vague utility word or phrase is to substitute a specific word or phrase, as in the following examples:

puzzling
It was a ~~peculiar~~ statement.

alarming
The news is ~~terrible~~.

clear, sunny, and in the low 80s.
The weather will be ~~fantastic~~.

Vagueness is not limited to unclear utility words. Any word or phrase that is more general than the intended meaning should be revised. The substitutions in these sentences make the information more specific.

Annie Dillard's "Total Eclipse."
The class was discussing ~~an essay~~.

how this winter's storms eroded the sand dunes on Cape Cod.
Professor Jones is studying ~~erosion~~.

Exercises ——— 1. Assume that the italicized words are not made clear by context. Substitute more specific diction to give a precise meaning.
   a. She is a scientist, but I don't know what her *line* is.
   b. Our *group* thought the *samples* were *peculiar.*
   c. One *aspect* of the *project* is its effect on prices.
   d. What a *terrific* surprise to meet so many *important* people at the same *affair.*
   e. The lab fees for this course are *something else.*

2. Circle the more specific expression in each parenthetical set.

The whole surface of the ice was *(a chaos—full)* of movement. It looked like an enormous *(mass—jigsaw puzzle)* stretching away to infinity and being *(pushed—crunched)* together by some invisible but irresistible force. The impression of its *(titanic—great)* power was heightened by the unhurried deliberateness of the motion. Whenever two thick *(pieces—floes)* came together, their edges *(met—butted)* and *(moved—ground)* against one another for a time. Then, when neither of them showed signs of yielding, they rose *(uncertainly—quiveringly)*, driven by the *(implacable—tremendous)* power behind them. Sometimes they would stop *(altogether—abruptly)* as the unseen forces affecting the ice appeared mysteriously to lose interest. More frequently, though, the two floes—often ten feet thick or more—would continue to rise *(rearing up—tenting up)*, until one or both of them toppled over, creating a pressure ridge.

Eliminating Jargon

Jargon originally meant meaningless chatter. Later it meant the specialized language of a group or profession, as in *habeas corpus* (law) and *cursor* (computer technology). There is no reason not to use learned and technical terms for audiences and situations for which they are appropriate, but to use them unnecessarily when addressing a general audience is a violation of the basic rule that your style should fit your purpose and audience. Jargon in informal writing is pretentious and frustrating to your audience. The following contrast shows inappropriate jargon that results in vague, indirect writing. The version on the left comes from the King James translation of the Bible; the version on the right is George Orwell's "translation" of the same material into modern jargon.

I returned and saw under the sun, that the race is not to the swift, nor the battle to the strong, neither yet bread to the wise, nor yet riches to men of understanding, nor yet favor to men of skill; but time and chance happeneth to them all.

Objective considerations of contemporary phenomena compel the conclusion that success or failure in competitive activities exhibits no tendency to be commensurate with innate capacity, but that a considerable element of the unpredictable must invariably be taken into account.

Although the Biblical version first appeared in 1611, it makes more sense and is easier to read than the "translation," which smothers simplicity and clarity under a blanket of vague, polysyllabic words. As Orwell points out:

> The first contains forty-nine words but only sixty syllables, and all of its words are those of everyday life. The second contains thirty-eight words of ninety syllables; eighteen of its words are from Latin roots, and one from Greek. The first sentence contains six vivid images, and only one phrase ("time and chance") that could be called vague. The second contains not a single fresh, arresting phrase, and in spite of its ninety syllables it gives only a shortened version of the meaning contained in the first. ("Politics and the English Language," *Shooting an Elephant and Other Essays*)

Jargon has three chief characteristics:

▼ Highly abstract, often technical, diction that shows a fondness for learned rather than popular words: *have the capability to* for *can, maximize productivity* for *increase production,* and *utilization of mechanical equipment* for *use of machinery.*

▼ Excessive use of the passive voice. If machines break down, they "are found to be functionally impaired." If a plan does not work, "its objectives were not realized." If management failed to consider the effects of certain changes on the workers, the error is reported like this: "With respect to employee reactions, management seems to have been inadequately advised."

▼ Conspicuous wordiness, as illustrated in the previous examples.

Jargon combines inappropriateness, vagueness, and wordiness into one consistently unintelligible style. Writers who lapse into jargon do so because they believe that ordinary language is not good enough. Like Liza Doolittle, they are trying to make a good impression. But the best way to make a good impression with your writing is to have something to say and to say it clearly.

The only way to revise jargon is to get rid of it. Leaving it in your writing forces your readers to do mentally the rewriting that you should have done, with the difficulty that they may not be sure what you meant.

Notice how the following passage creates ambiguity for the reader.

> (1) Rigorous comprehension and innermost instincts are the features of collaborative inquiry that spelunkers must engage when they delve into the unexplored terrain of a new cave. (2) They must scrutinize the formation of the rocks and the current of the river, establish their directional movement with the assistance of a compass, and maintain a precise topographical record so that they can renegotiate their expedition to its inception. (3) But since they have no established record, they must still commit their full confidence to their instincts when they reach an intersection. (4) At that juncture they must contemplate whether traversing one passageway will bring them into contact with a chamber enlarged by a high ceiling or with a corridor that narrows into a cul-de-sac.

The writer probably consulted a thesaurus to dress up the language of that needlessly "learned" paragraph. If you rewrite the paragraph, reducing each sentence to a summary of what the writer was trying to say, you get this:

1. Spelunkers use knowledge and instincts to explore a new cave.
2. They study rock formations and river currents; they use a compass; and they need to find their way out.
3. Since they have no maps, at intersections they must rely on their instincts.
4. They may turn into big chambers or dead ends.

If you join the revised sentences, you get a paragraph that says all the original was trying to say, but says it more clearly and in fewer words—51 words instead of 119. You might get a still better revision by tinkering with the sentence structure, adding or subtracting words where appropriate:

> When they explore a new cave, spelunkers rely on educated guesswork. They study the rock formation and river current, chart their movement with a compass, and mark their trail so that they can find their way out. But since they have no map, they must trust their instincts at each intersection. They may select a passage that turns into a vaulted chamber or a dead end.

The revised paragraph says nothing that was not said in the revised sentences. But it sharpens the focus by beginning with a clear topic sentence and then explaining that sentence. The pomposities of the original version have been eliminated, and the meaning is conveyed in half the space.

Exercise ——— Using the procedure just shown, revise this paragraph.

> Last month as I was perambulating through the stacks, I happened to encounter a book filled with photographs of volcanoes. Not yet having realized my latent interest in such geological formations, I was surprised at the manner in which this book enthralled my attention. The color displays of the spectacular discharge of Washington's St. Helens and the florid lava flows of Hawaii's Kilauea I found to be particularly disquieting. It was these photographs which led me to the decision to espouse volcanoes as the subject of my research paper.

Eliminating Triteness

The terms *trite, hackneyed,* and *clichéd* are used to describe expressions, once colorful and apt, that have been used so often that they have lost their freshness and force. Like outdated slang, trite expressions once evoked images and conveyed a sense of discovery through language. Striking when new, such phrases become meaningless when they are overused. Note these examples:

apple of her eye	hook, line, and sinker
birds of a feather	lock, stock, and barrel
black sheep	mountains out of molehills
blind as a bat	sober as a judge
budding genius	teeth like pearls
diamond in the rough	thick as thieves
fly in the ointment	water over the dam

Trite diction blocks thought. Writers who use ready-made phrases instead of creating their own soon find it difficult to think beyond stereotyped expressions: any change in personnel becomes a "shakeup"; all hopes become "fond," "foolish," or "forlorn"; defeats are "crushing"; changes in the existing system are "noble experiments" or "dangerous departures"; unexpected occurrences are "bolts from the blue"; and people who "sow wild oats" always have to "pay the piper" even though they are "as poor as church mice."

When you spot triteness in your writing, you should remove it. The way to learn to detect and avoid triteness in your writing is to learn to recognize triteness in the speech and writing of others. Notice the italicized clichés in this paragraph.

> *Money doesn't grow on trees,* and how well I've learned that. What a *rude awakening* when I realized that the odd change I used to ask for at home was not available at school. I had thought my allowance was enormous but, before I knew it, it had *trickled through my fingers.* College has taught me that *"A penny saved is a penny earned."* I have learned to live within my allowance and even to *save something for a rainy day.* What I have learned in college is *not all in the books.* I have learned to *shoulder my responsibilities.*

How many of those phrases do you recognize as prefabricated units that can be inserted into any sentence? If you can identify triteness in another writer's work, you can identify it in your own.

Exercises ———
1. Politics, television, popular music, and sports seem to encourage the use of trite expressions. Although some writers interpret these subjects with originality and insight, most seem to type their texts on a cliché machine. Examine the following paragraph to determine whether it provides any insights into football or simply repeats clichés.

   Whenever the gridiron game is played in the United States—on a sandlot, a high school field, or in a college or professional stadium—the players learn through the school of hard knocks the invaluable lesson that only by the men's blending together like birds of a feather can the team win. It is a lesson they do not forget on the gridiron. Off the field, they duly remember it. In society, the former player does not look upon himself as a lone wolf on the prowl who has the right to do his own thing—that is, to observe only his individual social laws. He knows he is a part of the big picture and must conduct himself as such. He realizes that only by playing as a team man can he do his share in making society what it should be—the protector and benefactor of all. The man who has been willing to make the sacrifice to play football knows that teamwork is essential in this modern day and age and that every citizen must pull his weight in the boat if the nation is to prosper. So he has little difficulty in adjusting to his roles in family life and in the world of business and to his duties as a citizen in the total scheme of things. In short, his football training helps make him a better citizen and person, better able to play the big game of life.

2. Rewrite that paragraph to eliminate the major objections made about it during class discussion.

3. Choose as a general subject a current issue in the world of politics, television, or popular music. Restrict that general subject to a topic that you think is important to students, and write a letter to the campus newspaper expressing your opinion. Then reread your letter to catch any trite language you may have used.

Eliminating Ineffective Imagery

An effective figure of speech can make your writing concrete; a figure that is trite, far-fetched, obscure, or confused mars your writing and distracts your readers. *Mixed metaphors*—metaphors that combine two or more incompatible images in a single figure—are especially ineffective. Consider the following:

> The scientist decided to gauge the political water by throwing his hat into the ring as a trial balloon.

This sentence mixes three overused, equally unimaginative images. "Testing the water" has a literal meaning in cooking and bathing. "Throwing one's hat into the ring" was a conventional way of issuing a challenge in the days of bare-knuckle prize fights. Trial balloons were once used to determine wind direction and velocity. Each of these images can be used in a political context, but fitting all three into one consistent figure of speech is impossible. And because the subject of the sentence is "the scientist," these figures distract the reader by suggesting that the sentence is about science rather than politics. The writer of the sentence should abandon metaphor and simply say, "The scientist tried to evaluate his chances of being nominated by announcing his intention to seek the position."

A poor figure of speech is worse that none at all. Imagery is ruined if the picture it conveys is preposterous or dull. If the figure with which you intended to strengthen your writing weakens it, delete or revise it. Test every figure of speech by *seeing* the picture it represents. If you visualize what your words are saying, then you will see and be able to eliminate ineffective or mixed images during revision.

Exercises ——— These sentences try unsuccessfully to combine discordant elements in the same figure of speech. Visualize the images they suggest, and then revise each sentence by creating an acceptable figure or restating the idea without a figure.

1. A host of music fans flocked into the arena like an avalanche.

2. The president's ill-advised action has thrown the ship of state into low gear, and unless the members of Congress wipe out the party lines and carry the ball as a team, it may take months to get the country back on the track.

3. When I try to focus my microscope, I do something that throws a monkey wrench into the ointment.

4. NASA expressed confidence that the hearing would allow the real facts of the case to come out in the wash.

5. Although the members of our writing group have difficulty forgetting where the hatchet is buried, we decided that was water behind the dam.

Correcting Diction on Your Computer

As you compose, you may often be unable to think of the *right* word. Use the Thesaurus function of your word-processing program to identify a word that is similar to the one you want. Call up that word and see if any of the synonyms listed suggest the word you are looking for.

Although the Thesaurus in some word-processing programs provides a brief definition of every word, don't depend on such definitions when you are making your final choice. Look up words in a standard dictionary to determine their various meanings and connotations. Words that have similar meanings are not interchangeable. For example, only a dictionary will tell you why the underlined word in the second sentence makes the sentence ludicrous: (1) The studio was <u>cluttered</u> with easels; (2) The studio was <u>choked up</u> with easels.

Perhaps the most valuable feature in most word-processing programs is the Spellchecker. But you must know what it will and will not do. It *will* flag every word that does not appear in its dictionary. It will suggest alternatives and enable you to correct your mistakes quickly. But many of the words you may use in your text—proper nouns, for example—will not be in the Spellchecker and so will be flagged as misspelled. You can fix this problem by adding such words to your computer's dictionary. The Spellchecker will *not* catch words that are correctly spelled but misused in the text. For example, it will not catch a common error such as the use of *their* for *there*.

The Spellchecker can function as a kind of Thesaurus. If it flags a word as misspelled, it will suggest a list of other words—one of which you may actually prefer to the one you have misspelled. Again, check your dictionary first. If the new word works, use it instead of your original choice.

The Microscope | James Thurber

In this episode from his classic essay "University Days," humorist James Thurber explains his frustration in trying to see through a microscope. How would you characterize the *appropriateness* of Thurber's diction? On the scale of most formal to least formal, where would you place Thurber's choice of words? Select specific examples to support your choice.

I passed all the other courses that I took at my university, but I could never pass   1
botany. This was because all botany students had to spend several hours a
week in a laboratory looking through a microscope at plant cells, and I could
never see through a microscope. I never once saw a cell through a microscope.
This used to enrage my instructor. He would wander around the laboratory
pleased with the progress all the students were making in drawing the involved,
and so I am told, interesting structure of flower cells, until he came to me. I
would just be standing there. "I can't see anything," I would say. He would begin
patently enough, explaining how anybody can see through a microscope, but he
would always end up in a fury, claiming that I could *too* see through the microscope but just pretended that I couldn't. "It takes away from the beauty of flowers anyway," I used to tell him. "We are not concerned with beauty in this
course," he would say. "We are concerned solely with what I may call the
mechanics of flars." "Well," I'd say, "I can't see anything." "Try it just once
again," he'd say, and I would put my eye to the microscope and see nothing
at all, except now and again a nebulous milky substance—a phenomenon of
maladjustment. You were supposed to see a vivid, restless clockwork of sharply
defined plant cells. "I see what looks like a lot of milk," I would tell him. This,
he claimed, was the result of my not having adjusted the microscope properly,
so he would readjust it for me, or rather for himself. And I would look again
and see milk.

I finally took a deferred pass, as they called it, and waited a year and tried   2
again. (You had to pass one of the biological sciences or you couldn't graduate.)
The professor had come back from vacation brown as a berry, bright-eyed, and
eager to explain cell-structure again to his classes. "Well," he said to me, cheer-
ily, when we met in the first laboratory hour of the semester, "we're going to
see cells this time, aren't we?" "Yes, sir," I said. Students to right of me and to
left of me and in front of me were seeing cells; what's more, they were quietly
drawing pictures of them in their notebooks. Of course, I didn't see anything.

"We'll try it," the professor said to me, grimly, "with every adjustment of   3
the microscope known to man. As God is my witness, I'll arrange this glass so
that you see cells through it or I'll give up teaching. In twenty-two years of
botany, I—" He cut off abruptly for he was beginning to quiver all over, like
Lionel Barrymore, and he genuinely wished to hold onto his temper; his scenes
with me had taken a great deal out of him.

Thurber, James. "University Days." *My Life and Hard Times*. New York: Harper, 1961. 88–90.

So we tried it with every adjustment of the microscope known to man.   4
With only one of them did I see anything but blackness or the familiar lacteal
opacity, and that time I saw, to my pleasure and amazement, a variegated constellation of flecks, specks, and dots. These I hastily drew. The instructor, noting
my activity, came back from an adjoining desk, a smile on his lips and his eyebrows high in hope. He looked at my cell drawing. "What's that?" he
demanded, with a hint of a squeal in his voice. "That's what I saw," I said. "You
didn't, you didn't, you *didn't*!" he screamed, losing control of his temper
instantly, and he bent over and squinted into the microscope. His head
snapped up. "That's your eye!" he shouted. "You've fixed the lens so that it
reflects! You've drawn your eye!"

Knothole Cavern | Edwin Way Teale

In this selection naturalist Edwin Way Teale describes a nighttime discovery
in his garden. In what ways does Teale use *imagery* to describe the events he
observes in the "knothole cavern"? What specific figures of speech does he
use to describe the "larvae of a Syrphid fly, *Eristalis tenax*"?

The drooping branches of the tree, with their thick thatching of green leaves,   1
descend almost to the ground. Supported by the central column of the tree
trunk, they form an arboreal hut that protects me from the rain. Here the drumming of the downpour seems more remote.

For a moment I listen in the darkness before I switch on my light. The   2
beam glides upward along the gray tree trunk. Five feet from the ground, it
encounters the black, unblinking eye of a knothole. A dozen times a day, in full
sunlight, I have passed this opening without a second glance. But now, surrounded by the vast blackness of the night, the three-inch opening assumes a
new interest.

Rain from previous showers has collected in the hollow within. In the   3
beam of my flashlight the scene resembles some unexplored cave or subter-
ranean lake in miniature. The weathered wood, sloping downward along the
roof of this teacup-sized cavern, has the appearance of shelving rock. Half a
dozen sow bugs, like trilobites from a remote geological past, glide away on the
flowing action of a succession of slender legs, to crowd into the darker corners
of the cave. Two black ants are bending down at the edge of the water as
though drinking on the shore of a lake.

On the surface of this knothole pool floats the body of a dead cranefly.   4
While looking at it, I catch a glimpse of one of the sow bugs hurrying from one
dark corner to another with a baby sow bug clinging firmly to its back.

Under the lip of the opening, where I had missed them before, I see a   5
dozen grayish water midgets, hardly more than an eighth of an inch long.
Hanging by the tips of their tails from the surface film of the water, they swing
back and forth in steady, leisurely arcs. They suggest acrobats on gymnasium
rings. Two, side by side, are swinging in unison, first this way, then that. What

Teale, Edwin Way. *Adventures in Nature*. New York: Dodd, 1959. 37–40.

are they? What are they doing? The best guess I can make is that they are some sort of immature gnats living out the underwater stage of their existence.

All around them, and all through this knothole lake, move the lighter, more active forms of the mosquito wigglers. Like slender, whitish tadpoles, these larvae swim about with lashing tails. They start, stop, dart forward again, whip-tails in action. They are the most numerous of the midget swimmers that dwell in this Lilliputian lake. **6**

From the debris at the bottom of the flooded cavern rise a score or more slender white stalks, apparently sprouts from seeds scattered singly and in little clusters. Among these pale vertical columns ascending through the brown water, the tiny wigglers keep up their incessant and seemingly aimless darting and pausing. **7**

As the beam of my flashlight shoots low over the water, I observe a curious thing. The surface is not smooth but has a dozen dimples that suggest the "knots" in an imperfect pane of glass. Under each dimple there are from one to seven of the sprouts. Where there are more than one, the thin stalks come together like the poles of a tepee. Some attraction seems to pull them to a common center. Using a straw, I push one of these clusters apart. With a slow, stately motion, the component stalks swing back and assume their former position. **8**

The dimples above such clusters are larger than where a single sprout reaches the surface. And here is another surprising thing: Not one sprout has pushed above the water. All reach exactly to the surface and no farther. I am puzzling over this when an amazing thing takes place before my eyes. **9**

One of the sprouts, as I watch it, telescopes slowly downward like a moving picture running in reverse. It steadily becomes shorter until it reaches the debris below. The other stalks remain as before. The whitish wigglers keep up their endless darting and halting. And the little acrobats of the surface film continue swinging back and forth in rhythmic oscillations. **10**

But something has happened at the spot where the descending sprout has reached the debris. Half an inch of white is moving along the black decayed wood of the pond-bottom. In a flash, I know. These are no sprouts. These slender stalklike columns are the air-hoses of the world's first diving suits. At the bottom of my knothole cavern are not seeds but some of the strangest, most incredible creatures of the insect world. **11**

These larvae of a Syrphid fly, *Eristalis tenax*, feed upon decaying matter underwater. Their tubelike, telescoping tails reach to the surface and carry air to the creatures below. Aeons before man first appeared on earth, Nature thus invented the prototype of the diving gear. Réaumur, the great natural scientist of eighteenth century France, studied and named this larva. He called it "the rat-tailed maggot" and the name has stuck. **12**

The larvae themselves are at most only two-thirds of an inch long. But their remarkable tails, formed of two tubes, one sliding within the other and both capable of tremendous elongation and contraction, can be extended as much as eight times the length of the larva's body. In his pioneer researches Réaumur added water, little by little, to a vessel in which several of these creatures were feeding. He saw the breathing tubes extend to each new level until the water reached a height of almost six inches. The tails, now no thicker than horsehairs, had stretched to their limit. When more water was added, the larvae either crept up the side of the vessel or floated up to a height from which their breathing tubes could reach the air supply. **13**

Total Eclipse | Annie Dillard

Compare Annie Dillard's comments (page 225) on choosing and using words with her diction in this excerpt from "Total Eclipse." Select specific examples where her word choice exhibits the three qualities of effective diction—appropriateness, specificity, and imagery. How does each example advance her purpose?

T he hill was five hundred feet high. Long winter-killed grass covered it, as high as our knees. We climbed and rested, sweating in the cold; we passed clumps of bundled people on the hillside who were setting up telescopes and fiddling with cameras. The top of the hill stuck up in the middle of the sky. We tightened our scarves and looked around. **1**

East of us rose another hill like ours. Between the hills, far below, was the highway which threaded south into the valley. This was the Yakima valley; I have never seen it before. It is justly famous for its beauty, like every planted valley. It extended south into the horizon, a distant dream of a valley, a Shangri-la. All its hundreds of low, golden slopes bore orchards. Among the orchards were towns, and roads, and plowed and fallow fields. Through the valley wandered a thin, shining river; from the river extended fine, frozen irrigation ditches. Distance blurred and blued the sight, so that the whole valley looked like a thickness or sediment at the bottom of the sky. Directly behind us was more sky, and empty lowlands blued by distance, and Mount Adams. Mount Adams was an enormous, snow-covered volcanic cone rising flat, like so much scenery. **2**

Now the sun was up. We could not see it; but the sky behind the band of clouds was yellow, and far down the valley, some hillside orchards had lighted up. More people were parking near the highway and climbing the hills. It was the West. All of us rugged individualists were wearing knit caps and blue nylon parkas. People were climbing the nearby hills and setting up shop in clumps among the dead grasses. It looked as though we had all gathered on hilltops to pray for the world on its last day. It looked as though we had all crawled out of spaceships and were preparing to assault the valley below. It looked as though we were scattered on hilltops at dawn to sacrifice virgins, make rain, set stone stelae in a ring. There was no place out of the wind. The straw grasses banged our legs. **3**

Up in the sky where we stood the air was lusterless yellow. To the west the sky was blue. Now the sun cleared the clouds. We cast rough shadows on the blowing grass; freezing, we waved our arms. Near the sun, the sky was bright and colorless. There was nothing to see. **4**

It began with no ado. It was odd that such a well-advertised public event should have no starting gun, no overture, no introductory speaker. I should have known right then that I was out of my depth. Without pause or preamble, silent as orbits, a piece of the sun went away. We looked at it through welders' goggles. A piece of the sun was missing; in its place we saw empty sky. **5**

I had seen a partial eclipse in 1970. A partial eclipse is very interesting. It bears almost no relation to a total eclipse. Seeing a partial eclipse bears the **6**

Dillard, Annie. *Teaching a Stone to Talk*. New York: Harper, 1982. 88–93.

same relation to seeing a total eclipse as kissing a man does to marrying him, or as flying in an airplane does to falling out of an airplane. Although the one experience precedes the other, it in no way prepares you for it. During a partial eclipse the sky does not darken—not even when 94 percent of the sun is hidden. Nor does the sun, seen colorless through protective devices, seem terribly strange. We have all seen a sliver of light in the sky; we have all seen the crescent moon by day. However, during a partial eclipse the air does indeed get cold, precisely as if someone were standing between you and the fire. And blackbirds do fly back to their roosts. I had seen a partial eclipse before, and here was another.

What you see in an eclipse is entirely different from what you know. It is 7
especially different for those of us whose grasp of astronomy is so frail that, given a flashlight, a grapefruit, two oranges, and fifteen years, we still could not figure out which way to set the clocks for Daylight Saving Time. Usually it is a bit of a trick to keep your knowledge from blinding you. But during an eclipse it is easy. What you see is much more convincing than any wild-eyed theory you may know.

You may read that the moon has something to do with eclipses. I have 8
never seen the moon yet. You do not see the moon. So near the sun, it is as completely invisible as the stars are by day. What you see before your eyes is the sun going through phases. It gets narrower and narrower, as the waning moon does, and like the ordinary moon, it travels alone in the simple sky. The sky is of course background. It does not appear to eat the sun; it is far behind the sun. The sun simply shaves away; gradually, you see less sun and more sky.

The sky's blue was deepening, but there was no darkness. The sun was a wide 9
crescent, like a segment of tangerine. The wind freshened and blew steadily over the hill. The eastern hill across the highway grew dusky and sharp. The towns and orchards in the valley to the south were dissolving into the blue light. Only the thin river held a trickle of sun.

Now the sky to the west deepened to indigo, a color never seen. A dark 10
sky usually loses color. This was a saturated, deep indigo, up in the air. Stuck up into that unworldly sky was the cone of Mount Adams, and the alpenglow was upon it. The alpenglow is that red light of sunset which holds out on snowy mountaintops long after the valleys and tablelands are dimmed. "Look at Mount Adams," I said, and that was the last sane moment I remember.

I turned back to the sun. It was going. The sun was going, and the world was 11
wrong. The grasses were wrong; they were platinum. Their every detail of stem, head, and blade shone lightness and artificially distinct as an art photographer's platinum print. This color has never been seen on earth. The hues were metallic; their finish was matte. The hillside was a nineteenth-century tinted photograph from which the tints had faded. All the people you see in the photograph, distinct and detailed as their faces look, are now dead. The sky was navy blue. My hands were silver. All the distant hills' grasses were fine-spun metal which the wind laid down. I was watching a faded color print of a movie filmed in the Middle Ages; I was standing in it, by some mistake. I was standing in a movie of hillside grasses filmed in the Middle Ages. I missed my own century, the people I knew, and the real light of day.

I looked at Gary. He was in the film. Everything was lost. He was a plati- 12
num print, a dead artist's version of life. I saw on his skull the darkness of

night mixed with the colors of day. My mind was going out; my eyes were receding the way galaxies recede to the rim of space. Gary was light-years away, gesturing inside a circle of darkness, down the wrong end of a telescope. He smiled as if he saw me; the stringy crinkles around his eyes moved. The sight of him, familiar and wrong, was something I was remembering from centuries hence, from the other side of death: yes, *that* is the way he used to look, when we were living. When it was our generation's turn to be alive. I could not hear him; the wind was too loud. Behind him the sun was going. We had all started down a chute of time. At first it was pleasant; now there was no stopping it. Gary was chuting away across space, moving and talking and catching my eye, chuting down the long corridor of separation. The skin on his face moved like thin bronze plating that would peel.

The grass at our feet was wild barley. It was the wild einkorn wheat which   13
grew on the hilly flanks of the Zagros Mountains, above the Euphrates valley, above the valley of the river we called *River*. We harvested the grass with stone sickles, I remember. We found the grasses on the hillsides; we built our shelter beside them and cut them down. That is how he used to look then, that one, moving and living and catching my eye, with the sky so dark behind him and the wind blowing. God save our life.

From all the hills came screams. A piece of sky beside the crescent sun was   14
detaching. It was a loosened circle of evening sky, suddenly lighted from the back. It was an abrupt black body out of nowhere; it was a flat disk; it was almost over the sun. That is when there were screams. At once this disk of sky slid over the sun like a lid. The sky snapped over the sun like a lens cover. The hatch in the brain slammed. Abruptly it was dark night, on the land and in the sky. In the night sky was a tiny ring of light. The hole where the sun belongs is very small. A thin ring of light marked its place. There was no sound. The eyes dried, the arteries drained, the lungs hushed. There was no world. We were the world's dead people rotating and orbiting around and around, embedded in the planet's crust, while the earth rolled down. Our minds were light-years distant, forgetful of almost everything. Only an extraordinary act of will could recall to us our former, living selves and our contexts in matter and time. We had, it seems, loved the planet and loved our lives, but could no longer remember the way of them. We got the light wrong. In the sky was something that should not be there. In the black sky was a ring of light. It was a thin ring, an old, thin silver wedding band, an old, worn ring. It was an old wedding band in the sky, or a morsel of bone. There were stars. It was all over.

Writing Assignments

Narrate **1.** Mark Twain once said, "The difference between the right word and the nearly right word is the difference between lightning and a lightning bug." Compose a narrative essay about the consequences of your inability to select the right word(s) to explain your behavior on an important occasion.

Observe **2.** Select several students and observe their use of certain words in conversation. Make a list of the words they use most often to describe certain social events on campus. Pay particular attention to their use of slang. Then compile a dictionary of slang for next year's freshman class. Ask your friends to help compose definitions.

Investigate **3.** Interview an expert on your campus (botany professor) or in your community (car mechanic) about some aspect of his or her job. As you conduct the interview, make a list of all the words you don't understand. Ask your expert to help you with your list. Which words would he or she classify as popular, learned, or jargon? Ask your expert to define the words on the jargon list. Then write an essay for uninformed readers explaining some of the jargon they need to know to understand this area of expertise.

Collaborate **4.** Each month *The Atlantic* concludes with a page called "Word Watch." The four or five words presented each month are being tracked by the editors of the *American Heritage Dictionary* to see if they exhibit sustained use over time and therefore merit inclusion in a future edition of the dictionary. In the August 1987 issue, for example, one of the words presented is *dink,* an acronym for "double income, no kids" couples. Your writing group has been asked to conduct a "Word Watch" using a word in *The Atlantic* or a word you have heard on campus. Consider its origin, definition, synonyms. Compile your evidence. Then collaborate on a letter to the editors of the *American Heritage Dictionary* arguing for the inclusion of your word in the next edition of the dictionary.

Read **5.** Select a troublesome word you have encountered in your reading about science—such as *entropy, refraction,* or *void.* Examine the history of the word in the *Oxford English Dictionary.* See if the word is given an expanded definition in a general or specialized encyclopedia such as *Encyclopedia Britannica* or the *McGraw-Hill Encyclopedia of Science and Technology.* Look up some of its synonyms in *Roget's Thesaurus.* Then compose an extended definition of the word, pointing out its denotative and connotative meanings.

Respond **6.** Respond to James Thurber's essay by describing your own experiences seeing what you are supposed to see. You may want to describe your difficulties seeing a microscopic world (a cell) or a cosmic world (a constellation). You may want to expand this assignment to include the "lab report"—that is, to describe the difficulty you had describing *in writing* what you saw to a professor who knew exactly what you were supposed to see.

Analyze **7.** Analyze Edwin Way Teale's use of imagery in "Knothole Cavern." Identify those places in the text where Teale uses similes, metaphors, analogy, personification, and allusion. Pay particular attention to the way Teale uses verbs to create mental pictures. Then write an essay explaining how Teale's use of imagery contributes to his purpose.

Evaluate   **8.**   Evaluate Annie Dillard's diction in the selection from "Total Eclipse." Begin by finding words that document the range of her word choice (from *popular* to *learned*). Next, assess her use of imagery (see in particular her comparison of a partial eclipse with a total eclipse). Then evaluate how Dillard's diction deepens and extends her description of the event.

Argue   **9.**   In an essay designed for a popular nature magazine (or the Life Style section of your Sunday newspaper), argue that physical events create certain psychological reactions. You may want to select an extraordinary event, such as a solar eclipse, tornado, or flood, and speculate on why it produces extreme reactions. Or you may want to select a more common event, such as sunshine, rain, or humidity, and set up correlations between external and internal weather.

Argue   **10.**   When the emperor asked Confucius what could be done to restore harmony to his troubled land, the wise man replied, "Purify the language." Select an example of language that needs purifying from, for example, a political speech or a product warranty. Identify those places in the text that need revision. Then write a letter to the appropriate authority using your revisions to illustrate how effective diction can create social harmony.

10 | Tone and Style

I
n Chapters 8 and 9, you examined sentence structure and diction separately, but you must also consider their joint impact on the tone and style
of a piece of writing. You are generally familiar with the words *tone* and
style, of course. When someone says, "Don't speak to me in that tone," or "The
style of that book is difficult," you know what is meant. In this chapter, however, you will learn that *tone* and *style* are technical concepts that you need to
understand and control to improve your writing.

As you work your way through the stages of the writing process, you try
to sort out what you think about your material and how you want your readers to think about it. For example, Ellen Haack's initial planning draft (in
Chapter 3) captured much of Barry's quirkiness, but her scratch outline
reduced his behavior to abstractions (*food, exercise,* and *culture*). This led her to
eliminate Barry as a subject and adopt an academic tone for her working
hypothesis and discovery draft. She discovered this problem through her
descriptive outline and concluded that her draft sounded scholarly but wasn't
very interesting. By returning to Barry in her new outline and subsequent
draft, she achieved a more entertaining tone and engaging style and revealed
Barry's quirkiness to her readers.

TONE

Essayist Patricia Hampl, like Ellen, finds that the right tone is essential for an
effective writing style.

> The issue of tone is central to me because I want my readers to know that
> another human being is speaking to them. I've never had much interest in
> the objective tone of the godlike narrator. It's supposed to give your writing
> a kind of neutral authority, but I don't think it exists. Even God has a per-
> sonality. There's the God of light. The God of mercy. The philosophical issue
> at stake here is how to maintain the middle position, the position of a human
> being who possesses both authority and reliability. I try to create that balance
> by mixing a formal tone with a more conversational tone. You can deal with
> only so much operatic truth. Then you have to acknowledge the popcorn
> stand and the peanut gallery. (Personal interview)

"When I say 'Please pass the butter,' why do
you say 'Hey, no problem'?"

Drawing by Saxon; © 1987 The New Yorker Magazine, Inc.

Range of Tone: Informative to Affective

As Patricia Hampl suggests, writers can adopt an objective or a subjective tone. You adopt the first when your purpose is to give your readers authoritative information. You adopt the second when your purpose is to affect or influence your readers in some way. The following excerpt exemplifies one of these two extremes of tone.

> The United States was the first nation in history so many of whose citizens could go so far simply in quest of fun and culture. The size of this phenomenon made international travel, for the first time, a major element in world trade, a new problem for the American economy and for American balance of payments, and a new opportunity for the destination countries. In 1970 the Department of Commerce estimated that the expenditures of American trav-

elers overseas had reached $2 billion each year. In the United States, economists began to count foreign travel as a major import, and other countries began to plan for tourism by Americans as a principal export. (Daniel Boorstin, *The Americans: The Democratic Experience*)

Notice the following characterisitics of this passage:

▼ Boorstin is principally concerned with giving readers information about his subject. He assumes that they will be interested in the historic and economic significance of travel.

▼ Boorstin's writing is informative and objective—he does not show his personal feelings. He supports his judgment about America's preoccupation with travel by citing experts: the Department of Commerce and economists.

▼ As a result of Boorstin's purpose and strategies, his tone is informative, factual, and impersonal.

Contrast Boorstin's passage with this one:

I don't know where we got the idea we have to go away for a vacation. I suppose the travel industry sold it to us. The travel business is the second largest industry in the United States. It's always trying to get us to go someplace *else* to spend our money when most of us don't have any trouble spending it right here where we are. The industry tries to make us feel cheap if we don't go on an expensive trip.

Well, I've got my plans all made for my vacation. I'm not going *anywhere*. How do you like that, travel industry? Show me all the luxurious accommodations you want, tempt me with pictures of bikini-clad girls with windswept hair on pearl-white beaches—I'm not going. I'm staying put is what I'm doing. We've been tourists, and none of us likes being a tourist, so this summer I'll be somewhere I've never been on vacation—right where I live. (Andy Rooney, *A Few Minutes with Andy Rooney*)

The sample is quite different from Boorstin's.

▼ Rooney's purpose is to offer his opinion, not to give information. He does tell his readers that the travel industry is the second largest in the United States, but he tells them little more about it—except how it makes him feel.

▼ Rooney's writing is affective and *subjective*. Rooney writes almost exclusively about how *he* feels about the subject of vacations: "I've got my plans," "I'm not going *anywhere*," "I'm staying put." His language reveals his defiant attitude: "How do you like that, travel industry?"

▼ As a result of Rooney's purpose and strategies, his tone is affective, opinionated, and personal.

These two passages represent the extremes of tone on a scale ranging from informative to affective.

Boorstin passage   Rooney passage

◄───►

Informative   *Affective*

Between the extremes, you could place other samples that show varying degrees of objectivity and subjectivity; those in the middle would be equally balanced between the two.

Each time you write, you will have to decide how informative or affective your writing should be. Certain assignments—laboratory reports, summaries of books or events, essay examinations—usually require an informative tone. Persuasive essays, intended to convince a reader to believe or do something, are usually affective. But, as Hampl indicates, a balance of informative and affective elements produces the most flexible and natural tone. The balance in your essays will depend on your subject and purpose.

Inexperienced writers sometimes believe that the way to be objective is to avoid writing in the first person. When you are writing about your own experience, ideas, and feelings, however, you need to use the pronoun *I*. Moreover, a third-person account is not necessarily an objective treatment of the subject. The statement "I saw the car run through a red light" is more objective than "The crazy fool drove through a red light," even though the first sentence contains *I* and the second does not.

Exercises ———— Where on the informative/affective scale would you place the following passages? Examine each passage closely so that you can support your judgment by reference to specific details.

Passage 1

Why is it almost impossible to gaze directly at the Grand Canyon under these circumstances and see it for what it is—as one picks up a strange object from one's back yard and gazes directly at it? It is almost impossible because the Grand Canyon, the thing as it is, has been appropriated by the symbolic complex which has already been formed in the sightseer's mind. Seeing the canyon under approved circumstances is seeing the symbolic complex head on. The thing is no longer the thing as it confronted the Spaniard; it is rather that which has already been formulated—by picture postcard, geography book, tourist folders, and the words *Grand Canyon*. As a result of this preformulation, the source of the sightseer's pleasure undergoes a shift. Where the wonder and delight of the Spaniard arose from his penetration of the thing itself, from a progressive discovery of depths, patterns, colors, shadows, etc., now the sightseer measures his satisfaction *by the degree to which the canyon conforms to the preformed complex*. If it does so, if it looks just like the postcard, he is pleased; he might even say, "Why it is every bit as beautiful as a picture postcard!" He feels he has not been cheated. But if it does not conform, if the colors are somber, he will not be able to see it directly; he will only be conscious of the disparity between what it is and what it is supposed to be. He will say later that he was unlucky in not being there at the right time. The highest point, the term of the sightseer's satisfaction, is not the sovereign discovery of the thing before him; it is rather the measuring up of the thing to the criterion of the preformed symbolic complex. (Walker Percy, "The Loss of the Creature," *The Message in the Bottle*)

Passage 2

Everything comes onto the island: nothing much goes off, even by evaporation. Once it was a gateway to a New World, now it is a portal chiefly to itself. Manhattan long ago abandoned its melting-pot function. Nobody even tries to Americanize the Lebanese or the Lithuanians now, and indeed the ethnic enclaves of the island seem to me to become more potently ethnic each time I visit the place. Nothing could be much more Italian than the Festival of St. Anthony of Padua down on Mulberry Street, when the families of Little Italy stroll here and there through their estate, pausing often to greet volatile contemporaries and sometimes munching the soft-shelled crabs which, spread-eagled on slices of bread like zoological specimens, are offered loudly for sale by street vendors. Harlem has become almost a private city in itself, no longer to be slummed through by whities after dinner, while Manhattan's Chinatown is as good a place as anywhere in the world to test your skill at that universal challenge, trying to make a Chinese waiter smile. (Jan Morris, "Manhattan: The Islanders," *Destinations: Essays from Rolling Stone*)

Passage 3

The next day when I was already in full flight—aboard a northward bound train—I could not have accounted, if it had been demanded of me, for all the varied forces that were making me reject the culture that had molded and shaped me. I was leaving without a qualm, without a single backward glance. The face of the South that I had known was hostile and forbidding, and yet out of all the conflicts and the curses, the blows and the anger, the tension and the terror, I had somehow gotten the idea that life could be different, could be lived in a fuller and richer manner. As had happened, when I had fled the orphan home, I was now running more away from something than toward something. But that did not matter to me. My mood was: I've got to get away; I can't stay here. (Richard Wright, *Black Boy*)

Distance

Another element of tone is the impression of distance between writer and reader.

Consider a professor lecturing to a large class. She is separated from her listeners by her position on a platform; she cannot speak to each student in the audience individually. The situation requires her to speak more slowly, more loudly, and more formally than if she were conferring with a student in her office. The lecture room produces both physical and stylistic distance. Consider the distance in a statement in a printed syllabus that says, "Students are expected to hand in assignments on the date stipulated," and an instructor's after-class remark, "Joe, you've got to get your papers in on time." In the first statement the writer is impersonal and remote; in the second the speaker is personal and close.

The following selections illustrate the difference between writing that tries to get close to the reader and writing that addresses the reader from a distance.

Example 1

Did you ever wonder, looking at a map or whirling a globe, how the intricate shape of continents, shorelines, rivers and mountains came to be mapped, and who designed the system of parallels and meridians? Or how people found out, in the first place, that the earth is shaped like a globe? If we had not been told so I am not ever sure that you or I would have found it out for ourselves. (Erwin Raisz, *Mapping the World*)

Here the distance between writer and reader is very slight. By using the second person, Raisz gives the impression of speaking personally to each reader. His conversational and questioning tone and his diction suggest that he identifies with his readers.

Example 2

The map predates the book (even a fairly ordinary map may contain several books' worth of information). It is the oldest means of information storage, and can present the most subtle facts with great clarity. It is a masterly form of compression, a way of miniaturizing a country or society. Most hill-climbers and perhaps all mountaineers know the thrill at a certain altitude of looking down and recognizing the landscape that is indistinguishable from a map. The only pleasure I take in flying in a jet plane is the experience of matching a coastline or the contour of a river to the corresponding map in my memory. A map can do many things, but I think its chief use is in lessen-ing our fear of foreign parts and helping us anticipate the problems of dislo-cation. Maps give the world coherence. It seems to me one of man's supreme achievements that he knew the precise shape of every continent and practi-cally every river-vein on earth long before he was able to gaze at them whole from the window of a rocketship. (Paul Theroux, "Mapping the World," *Sunrise with Seamonsters*)

This paragraph is addressed not to any particular reader but to all readers. Theroux does not address his readers as "you" or try to appeal to their special interests. He is more interested in what he has to say than in his audience. His tone establishes greater distance between writer and reader than existed in the passage by Raisz.

The impression of distance comes chiefly from sentence structure and dic-tion, the linguistic bases of tone, discussed below under "Style." Remember that the tone of your writing depends in part on decisions you make about the distance, or degree of separation, you want to maintain between yourself and your readers. The decision is not arbitrary; it is related to decisions about your attitude toward your subject, and it should be consistent with your purpose.

STYLE

The *American Heritage Dictionary* defines style as "the way in which something is said or done, as distinguished from its substance." In writing, *style* refers to *how* something is said—the way a writer arranges sentences and words; *sub-stance* means *what* is said—the ideas or message that the writer wishes to con-vey. The difficulty with the dictionary definition is that it assumes that what is said can somehow be examined apart from how it is said. In writing, however, the *what* and the *how* are virtually indistinguishable. The most subtle changes in sentences or diction can change the ideas or message. A simple, though more accurate definition, then, would be, "Style is the way something is written."

How do you describe the way something is written? Consider the following passage from *The Adventures of Huckleberry Finn* by Mark Twain. Huck, staying with the Grangerfords after his raft has been wrecked, has been reading a poem written by the youngest daughter, now dead. The poem, intended to be a sad story about a young man who fell into a well and drowned, is so maudlin and so badly written that it is funny. Huck thinks it is very good. After reading it, he says:

> If Emmeline Grangerford could make poetry like that before she was fourteen, there ain't no telling what she could a done by-and-by. Buck [her younger brother] said she could rattle off poetry like nothing. She didn't ever have to stop and think. He said she would slap down a line, and if she couldn't find anything to rhyme with it she would just scratch it out and slap down another one, and go ahead. She warn't particular; she could write about anything you choose to give her to write about just so it was sadful. Every time a man died, or a woman died, or a child died, she would be on hand with her "tribute" before he was cold. She called them tributes. The neighbors said it was the doctor first, then Emmeline, then the undertaker— the undertaker never got in ahead of Emmeline but once, and then she hung fire on a rhyme for the dead person's name, which was Whistler. She warn't ever the same, after that; she never complained, but she kinder pined away and did not live long.

Notice the following things about this passage:

▼ Mark Twain is having fun with the subject. He knows the poem is sentimental to the point of being ridiculous, and he expects the reader to see that too.

▼ Huck himself is serious. Huck, the narrator, says what a boy like him, but not a man like Twain, would say. Even though Twain is the writer, the *voice* you hear is that of Huck Finn. Twain creates an ironical situation in which everything Huck says about Emmeline's poetry confirms a different judgment in his readers.

▼ The diction is appropriate to the speaker. The humorous effect would be lost if Huck were made to speak like a sophisticated adult. He must speak in his own voice.

▼ All these elements are so interrelated that a change in any one of them would spoil the total effect.

Even this brief sample suggests that when you write something you must consider your attitude toward your subject, your relationship with your readers, and the language you use to express your ideas. The tone of your writing reveals the decisions you have made about the first two. The third is expressed in the choices you make as you develop your purpose. As you have seen throughout this text, a clear sense of purpose guides you through all the choices you make from planning though revision. If these choices are consistent, your writing will exhibit a distinctive *style* that will express your attitude toward and embody your understanding of your purpose.

Range of Style: Sentence Structure, Diction, and Tone

Style, of course, rests finally on language. Look closely at the sentence structure, diction, and tone of the following passages to see what generalizations you can make about them.

Example 1

Airplanes are invariably scheduled to depart at such times as 7:54, 9:21 or 11:37. This extreme specificity has the effect on the novice of instilling in him the twin beliefs that he will be *arriving* at 10:08, 1:43 or 4:22, and that he should get to the airport on time. These beliefs are not only erroneous but actually unhealthy, and could easily be dispelled by an attempt on the part of the airlines toward greater realism. Understandably, they may be reluctant to make such a radical change all at once. In an effort to make the transition easier I offer the following graduated alternatives to "Flight 477 to Minneapolis will depart at 8:03 P.M.":

a. Flight 477 to Minneapolis will depart oh, let's say, eightish.
b. Flight 477 to Minneapolis will depart around eight, eight-thirty.
c. Flight 477 to Minneapolis will depart while it's still dark.
d. Flight 477 to Minneapolis will depart before the paperback is out.
(Fran Leibowitz, "Fran Leibowitz's Travel Hints," *Social Studies*)

Analysis of Example 1:
Sentence Structure

The nine sentences in this passage average only 17 words in length, and almost half of them are set apart in a list of brief announcements. Most of the sentences consist of one or two independent clauses. Only the second sentence has a slightly inverted construction. The rest of the sentences follow a subject-verb-object order.

Diction

In the whole passage there are proportionately few words more than two syllables long. *Invariably, specificity,* and *graduated* are the most notable. Except for *novice* and *erroneous* there are no learned words. There are a few contractions *(let's, it's)* and one example of slang *(eightish).*

Tone

Leibowitz's attitude toward her subject is humorous and ironic. Supposedly informative—after all, she is offering advice—her attitude is really affective because she wants to exploit her readers' exasperation over airline schedules. The distance between writer and reader is slight. Leibowitz writes as a fellow sufferer commenting on a common frustration. You hear the voice of a world-weary crank, slightly angry about a situation over which she has no control.

Summary

With simple sentences and diction, Leibowitz establishes her tone and creates a style that achieves ease and clarity. The diction and the pace of her sentences are those of informal conversation, creating an impression of talking in print. In Chapter 9 the word *colloquial* was used to describe diction of this sort. That term can apply to a style as well. A colloquial style is not common in college writing, but it is by no means inappropriate when it is used—as it is here—to fulfill the writer's purpose.

Now contrast the next example with Leibowitz's writing. Read the following passage aloud, slowly, to hear how it sounds.

Example 2

What a fierce weird pleasure to lie in my berth at night in the luxurious palace-car, drawn by the mighty Baldwin—embodying, and filling me, too, full of the swiftest motion, and most resistless strength! It is late, perhaps midnight or after—distances join'd like magic—as we speed through Harrisburg, Columbus, Indianapolis. The element of danger adds zest to it all. On we go, rumbling and flashing, with our loud whinnies thrown out from time to time, or trumpet-blasts, into the darkness. Passing the homes of men, the farms, barns, cattle—the silent villages. And the car itself, the sleeper, with curtains drawn and lights turn'd down—in the berths the slumberers, many of them women and children—as on, on, on, we fly like lightning through the night—how strangely sound and sweet they sleep! (They say the French Voltaire in his time designated the grand opera and a ship of war the most signal illustrations of the growth of humanity's and art's advance beyond primitive barbarism. Perhaps if the witty philosopher were here these days, and went in the same car with perfect bedding and feed from New York to San Francisco, he would shift his type and sample to one of our American sleepers.) (Walt Whitman, *Specimen Days*)

Analysis of Example 2: Sentence Structure

The paragraph has only eight sentences. Although there are two short sentences (one a fragment), most of the sentences are long. The average sentence length is 26 words, against 17 in the Leibowitz passage; the last three sentences are 42, 32, and 39 words long. The sentences are not simple. Subjects and verbs are often separated—sometimes widely—by modifiers. Several of the sentences exhibit extremely complicated punctuation. Throughout the paragraph, parallel and periodic structures are used for rhythmic and other effects.

Diction

About 27 percent of the words in the passage are more than two syllables long, and it contains a smaller proportion of monosyllables than the Leibowitz example. Whitman's diction is sprinkled with learned words—*resistless, slumberers, barbarism.* Several phrases have a lofty, poetic ring—"embodying, and filling me, too, full of the swiftest motion, and most resistless strength!"

Tone

Whitman is celebrating the mythic adventure of train travel, and his attitude toward his subject is clearly subjective. The distance between writer and reader is great; the emphasis is on the subject, not on the reader. The affective tone is impersonal, dignified, eloquent.

Summary

As in the Leibowitz example, all the components blend into a consistent style. But what a different style! Whitman aims at eloquence, not ease or familiarity. You would not use this style to give directions, explain a process, answer an examination question, or report a story in a newspaper. Whitman's style shares many of the characteristics of nineteenth-century prose, characteristics still found in prose seeking similar effects. It could be called a *grand* style, but the usual name for it is *formal.*

Example 3

In those days differences in vegetation between a main highway and a side road were even greater than now. There weren't many state highways but the best of them stretched straight ahead with mathematical perfection, even though just of gravel. These rights-of-way were usually wide and from the road edge to the boundary fences were mowed pretty much as now, though road building had not been preceded by earth moving. As a result, there were more native plants in among the grass and fewer of those cosmopolitan tramps which take so readily to disturbed habitats. But the side roads, those fascinating side roads, they are mostly gone and there is nothing in the modern road system to compare with them. The wheel track wound here and there, depending upon the slope and the vegetation and the character of the land. Sometimes it was straight for a little way; frequently it wobbled. There was often grass in the roadway outside the actual wheel tracks; shrubs like sumac and elderberry pressed so close to the road that you could smell them as you drove by and children snatched at the flowers. Accommodating drivers of the local stage-line learned to snip off small twigs with a snap of the buggy whip and present them to lady passengers. (Edgar Anderson, "Horse-and-Buggy Countryside," *Landscape*)

Analysis of Example 3: Sentence Structure   This paragraph has nine sentences, all following the standard pattern: subject-verb-object with modifiers and subordinate clauses appearing in predictable places. There are no conspicuous periodic sentences. Sentences do vary in length, from 11 to 38 words, but most fall between 19 and 26, averaging 21 (between the 17-word Leibowitz average and the 26-word Whitman average).

Diction   In this 214-word passage, only 15 words (or about 7 percent) are more than two syllables long. There are a few learned words such as *cosmopolitan* and *habitat*, but they are counterbalanced by popular words such as *snip* and *snap*.

Tone   Anderson's attitude toward his subject is both informative and affective. He wants to inform his readers about country roads, and he wants to describe how it must have looked and felt to ride down one of these roads in a horse-and-buggy. His choice of details—children snatching flowers, stage drivers snipping off flowers with their buggy whips—helps establish his informal, familiar tone. The distance between writer and reader is greater than in the first example but less than in the second example.

Summary   Anderson's style is neither as simple as Leibowitz's nor as involved as Whitman's. It has none of Leibowitz's chattiness and none of the poetry or exaltation that pervades Whitman's writing. Its balance of sentence length, diction, and tone produces a *moderate* style.

Whitman passage	Anderson passage	Leibowitz passage
Formal	*Moderate*	*Colloquial*

The diagram suggests three things.

▼ *The scale indicates degree of formality, from most to least.* It does not measure degree of excellence; no one style is better than another. All three are standard styles, and each is appropriate in some situations—although the moderate style is appropriate for most writing situations.

▼ *Each classification embodies a range.* A particular sample may be more or less formal than others. For example, a legal contract is more formal than Whitman's paragraph.

▼ *There is no clear division between styles.* The overlapping in the diagram is intended to suggest that the moderate style has such a broad range that it may include some formal and colloquial elements. Such inclusions, however, must be consistent with the writer's purpose. Edgar Anderson's use of *habitat,* for example, was justified because his purpose was to identify the characteristics of a particular landscape.

Summary of the Formal, Moderate, and Colloquial Styles

	Formal	*Moderate*	*Colloquial*
Sentences	Relatively long and involved; likely to make considerable use of parallel, balanced, and periodic structures; fragments rare.	Of medium length, averaging between 15 and 25 words; mostly standard structure but with some use of parallel, balanced, and periodic sentences; fragments occasional.	Short, simple structures; mainly subject-verb-object order; almost no use of balanced or periodic sentences; fragments common.
Diction	Extensive vocabulary, some use of learned and abstract words; no slang; almost no contractions or clipped words.	Ranges from learned to colloquial but mostly popular words; both abstract and concrete diction; occasional contractions and clipped words; may contain some inconspicuous slang.	Diction limited to popular and colloquial words, frequent contractions, and clipped words; frequent use of utility words; more slang than in moderate style.
Tone	Always a serious attitude toward an important subject; may be either subjective or objective and informative or affective; no attempt to establish closeness with reader, who is almost never addressed as "you"; personality of the writer often inconspicuous; whole tone usually dignified and impersonal.	Attitude toward subject may be serious or light, objective or subjective, informative or affective; relationship with reader close but seldom intimate; writer often refers to himself or herself as "I" and to reader as "you"; the range of moderate style is so broad that tone can vary from semiformal to semicolloquial.	Attitude toward subject may be serious or light but is usually subjective; close, usually intimate, relation with reader, who is nearly always addressed as "you"; whole tone is that of informal conversation.
Uses	A restricted style used chiefly for scholarly or technical writing for experts, or for essays and speeches that aim at eloquence or inspiration; a distinguished style, but not one for everyday use or practical affairs.	The broadest and most usable style for expository and argumentative writing and for all but the most formal of public speeches; the prevailing style in nontechnical books and magazines, in newspaper reports and editorials, in college lectures and discussions, in all student writing except some fiction.	Light, chatty writing as in letters to close friends; a restricted style that is inappropriate to most college writing except fiction.

Exercises ———— Analyze the sentence structure, diction, and tone of each of the following passages, using supporting details. Then rate each passage on the scale provided.

Most Formal   *Most Colloquial*

Competitors in conquest have overlooked the vital soul of Africa herself, from which emanates the true resistance to conquest. The soul is not dead, but silent, the wisdom not lacking, but of such simplicity as to be counted non-existent in the tinker's mind of modern civilization. Africa is of an ancient age and the blood of many of her peoples is as venerable and as chaste as truth. What upstart race, sprung from some recent, callow century to arm itself with steel and boastfulness, can match in purity the blood of a single Masai Murani whose heritage may have stemmed not far from Eden? It is not the weed that is corrupt; roots of the weed sucked first life from the genesis of earth and hold the essence of it still. Always the weed returns; the cultured plant retreats before it. Racial purity, true aristocracy, devolve not from edict, nor from rote, but from the preservation of kinship with the elemental forces and purposes of life whose understanding is not farther beyond the mind of a Native shepherd than beyond the cultured fumblings of a mortar-board intelligence. (Beryl Markham, *West with the Night*)

We were sitting in a restaurant called Orchid Garden, in the Wanchai district, beginning our first meal in Hong Kong, and I had just sampled something called fish-brain soup. I was about to comment. Alice was looking a bit anxious. She was concerned, I think, that over the years I might have created a vision of Hong Kong in my mind that could not be matched by the reality—like some harried businessman who finally arrives in what he has pictured as the remote, other-worldly peace of a Tahiti beach only to be hustled by a couple of hip beach-umbrella salesmen wearing "Souvenir of Fort Lauderdale" T-shirts. Even before we had a meal, she must have noticed my surprise at discovering that most of the other visitors in Hong Kong seemed to be there for purposes other than eating. That's the sort of thing that can put a visionary off his stride. How would the obsessed mountain climber feel if he arrived in Nepal after years of fantasizing about a clamber up the Himalayas, and found that most of the other tourists had come to observe the jute harvest? It appeared that just about everyone else had come to Hong Kong to shop. Hong Kong has dozens of vast shopping malls—floor after floor of shops run by cheerfully competitive merchants who knock off 10 percent at the hint of a frown and have never heard of sales tax. There are restaurants in some of the shopping malls, but most of the visitors seemed too busy shopping to eat. It was obvious that they would have come to Hong Kong even if it had been one of those British colonies where the natives have been taught to observe the queen's birthday by boiling brussels sprouts for an extra month. That very morning, in the lobby of a hotel, we had noticed a couple in late middle age suddenly drawing close to share some whispered intimacy in what Alice, the romantic, took to be a scene of enduring affection until one of the softly spoken phrases reached her ears—"customs declaration." (Calvin Trillin, "Hong Kong Dream," *Third Helpings*)

If you want to get something done, here is a professional secret: don't try to rush it by laying down the law that it *must be done* within a given time, but come back, each day if need be, and ask again, and do it with a smile. While evidences of irritation are fatal, persistence is never resented if it is clothed in good manners and good temper. When you can't wait any longer, the thing to do is to take an unfair advantage of your Brazilian friend—appeal to him to arrange matters for you because, first, you are in trouble with your principals; second, you are embarrassed by your own failure; third, you are obliged to leave by a given boat and will be humiliated if matters have not been arranged—anything to put it on a personal basis. When you do this your Brazilian is lost. He feels that you have been reasonable and patient and that he cannot throw you to the wolves. And in arranging matters for you he probably has to make a series of appeals more or less similar to yours. (Hugh Gibson, *Rio*)

Some Practical Advice About Style

You have examined the elements of style in passages by other writers. Now you are ready to apply what you have learned to your own writing. As you revise your writing, keep these stylistic considerations in mind.

1. *Let your purpose be your guide.* A clear sense of purpose controls all the choices you make at every stage in writing. Style results from that control.

2. *Generally, choose a moderate style.* There is nothing wrong with a formal or a colloquial style when it is appropriate. Unnecessary formality, however, often leads to pretentiousness and wordiness. The writer tries too hard to be impressive or literary when it would be enough to clearly express his purpose. The colloquial style, if used for serious treatment of a serious subject, can undermine the writer's purpose. The best policy, as Patricia Hampl suggests, is to maintain the middle position, "The position of a human being who possesses both authority and reliability." You can then mix objective and subjective—informative and affective—as your purpose demands.

3. *Keep your style consistent.* Probably the worst stylistic defect is inconsistency. An inconsistent style is not the same as a moderate style in which formal and colloquial elements are balanced for a purpose. Writing that is totally inconsistent has no discoverable purpose and therefore no discoverable style. The inconsistencies in tone and diction that often occur in individual paragraphs, sentences, or words can be removed in revision.

   a. *Inconsistency in tone.* Conspicuous inconsistency in tone is likely to jar a reader. It is most obvious when colloquial elements appear in a formal style or formal elements in a colloquial style. Because a moderate style can range from semiformal to semicolloquial, it can tolerate usages that would be conspicuous in the extreme styles.

   b. *Inconsistency in diction.* As you begin planning and drafting your essay, you gradually commit yourself to a recognizable approach to both your subject and your reader. Your choice of words will either contribute to stylistic consistency or obscure the pattern in your writing.

You are most likely to confuse readers by choosing words that are close but not close enough to your meaning. Do you want to say that your traveling companions are *insensitive, naive,* or *undiscriminating*? Your purpose determines the "best" choice of words.

4. *Try to see your writing as your readers will see it.* This advice may be the hardest to follow. People assume that what is clear to them will be clear to others, but common experience demonstrates that this assumption is not always true. In everyday conversation, a frequently asked question is "What do you mean by that?" Because your readers will not have the opportunity to ask you that question, try to anticipate their need for clarity and completeness.

5. *Be as specific as you can.* Writing is a difficult medium because it is abstract. The word *apple* is more abstract than any apple you ever ate, because it leaves out your actual experience with apples—their shape, size, color, texture, and taste. The problem all writers face is how to make abstractions concrete. The two common solutions are to (a) illustrate the meaning of general statements with examples, and (b) choose words that are specific.

6. *Revise for style.* You revise for style when you undertake global revision. Your style is dependent on your purpose, so if you revise your purpose, you must revise your style. Likewise, if you change your subject or audience, you must make new decisions about sentence structure, diction and tone.

Local revision—arranging your sentences, selecting your words, and adjusting your tone—involves the nuts and bolts of style. In fact, the changes you make in local revision will probably make the most improvement in your style. Follow your local revision with one last reading—just for style. Read the text aloud, or, better yet, listen to it read aloud, and concentrate on its overall effect. Imagine yourself listening to a band or a singer performing a piece of music. As you listen to your own writing, concentrate on the style of the piece and keep alert for any false notes.

The following guidelines provide some basic questions to ask yourself when you revise for style.

Guidelines for Revising Your Style

1. **What is my general impression of my writing?**
   Do I find my writing clear, unambiguous, and likely to engage my readers? Have I carried out my purpose at every level; that is, am I satisfied that the *how* of my writing—its attitude, organization, and language—conveys the *what* of my ideas?

2. **What tone have I established in my writing?**
   Is my tone informative, affective, or a blend of both? How much distance have I maintained between myself and my readers? Is my tone appropriate for my subject and audience? Is it maintained consistently?

3. *How can I characterize the overall style of my writing?*
    Have I written this essay in a moderate style, opting for more or less
    colloquialism or formality as my purpose requires? Does my purpose
    in fact require me to be overtly colloquial or formal?

4. *Are my sentences well constructed and easy on the ear?*
    Have I written sentences varying in length and style so that they hold
    my readers' interest? Have I avoided the choppiness that comes from
    too many basic or loosely coordinated sentences? Have I avoided the
    density that comes from too many complicated sentences with mul-
    tiple subordinate clauses?

5. *Have I used words as effectively as possible?*
    Do the connotations and denotations of my words support my pur-
    pose? Have I avoided unnecessary formalities and slang? Is my lan-
    guage specific and, when appropriate, vivid? Have I inadvertently
    mixed metaphors? Have I used imagery successfully to *heighten* effects,
    not merely to strive after them?

Once you have completed all your revisions and have typed your final
draft, you should proofread your writing very carefully. Proofreading is a close
reading of the final version to catch errors in grammar, spelling, and punctuation, as well as typographical errors, that survived your revisions or crept
into the final copy. Proofreading should be done slowly, preferably aloud. If
possible, you should allow some time to elapse between your final typing and
your proofreading. In that way you are more likely to read with a fresh eye.

Checking Your Tone and Style on Your Computer

Most word-processing programs have a feature that
will check your style: keep track of the length and
variety of your sentences, put an asterisk next to phrases
that seem wordy, and mark constructions—such as "There
are . . ." or "to be . . ."—that it identifies as ineffective.

You may want to consider these points as you edit and
revise. But a computer can make choices between only
two existing options. It cannot analyze subtle nuances or
be creative about solving the problem that appears on the
screen. *Style* is a matter of personal choice. Your imagination and judgment remain the best tools for evaluating
your tone and style.

Third World Driving Hints and Tips | P. J. O'Rourke

In this selection from *Holidays in Hell,* P. J. O'Rourke demonstrates the particular style that he has exhibited as an editor for *The National Lampoon* and as International Affairs Desk Chief at *Rolling Stone.* The title of the essay suggests that its purpose is to inform. At what point in the essay do you realize that O'Rourke's purpose is to entertain? How does his purpose affect his tone?

During the past couple of years I've had to do my share of driving in the Third World—in Mexico, Lebanon, the Philippines, Cyprus, El Salvador, Africa and Italy. (Italy is not technically part of the Third World, but no one has told the Italians.) I don't pretend to be an expert, but I have been making notes. Maybe these notes will be useful to readers who are planning to do something with their Hertz #1 Club cards.   1

Road Hazards

What would be a road hazard anywhere else, in the Third World is probably   2
the road. There are two techniques for coping with this. One is to drive very fast so your wheels "get on top" of the ruts and your car sails over the ditches and gullies. Predictably, this will result in disaster. The other technique is to drive very slowly. This will also result in disaster. No matter how slowly you drive into a ten-foot hole, you're still going to get hurt. You'll find the locals themselves can't make up their minds. Either they drive at 2 m.p.h.—which they do every time there's absolutely no way to get around them. Or else they drive at 100 m.p.h.—which they do coming right at you when you finally get a chance to pass the guy going 2 m.p.h.

Basic Information

It's important to have your facts straight before you begin piloting a car   3
around an underdeveloped country. For instance, which side of the road do they drive on? This is easy. They drive on your side. That is, you can depend on it, any oncoming traffic will be on your side of the road. Also, how do you translate kilometres into miles? Most people don't know this, but one kilometre = ten miles, exactly. True, a kilometre is only 62 per cent of a mile, but if something is one hundred kilometres away, read that as one thousand miles because the roads are 620 per cent worse than anything you've ever seen. And when you see a 50-k.p.h. speed limit, you might as well figure that means 500 *m.p.h.* because nobody cares. The Third World does not have Broderick Crawford and the Highway Patrol. Outside the cities, it doesn't have many police at all. Law enforcement is in the hands of the army. And soldiers, if they feel like it, will shoot you no matter what speed you're going.

Traffic Signs and Signals

Most developing nations use international traffic symbols. Americans may   4
find themselves perplexed by road signs that look like Boy Scout merit badges

O'Rourke, P. J. *Holidays in Hell.* New York: Atlantic Monthly Press, 1988. 78–82.

and by such things as an iguana silhouette with a red diagonal bar across it. Don't worry, the natives don't know what they mean, either. The natives do, however, have an elaborate set of signals used to convey information to the traffic around them. For example, if you're trying to pass someone and he blinks his left turn signal, it means go ahead. Either that or it means a large truck is coming around the bend, and you'll get killed if you try. You'll find out in a moment.

Signalling is further complicated by festive decorations found on many 5 vehicles. It can be hard to tell a hazard flasher from a string of Christmas-tree lights wrapped around the bumper, and brake lights can easily be confused with the dozen red Jesus statuettes and the ten stuffed animals with blinking eyes on the package shelf.

Dangerous Curves

Dangerous curves are marked, at least in Christian lands, by white wooden 6 crosses positioned to make the curves even more dangerous. These crosses are memorials to people who've died in traffic accidents, and they give a rough statistical indication of how much trouble you're likely to have at that spot in the road. Thus, when you come through a curve in a full-power slide and are suddenly confronted with a veritable forest of crucifixes, you know you're dead.

Learning to Drive Like a Native

It's important to understand that in the Third World most driving is done 7 with the horn, or "Egyptian Brake Pedal," as it is known. There is a precise and complicated etiquette of horn use. Honk your horn only under the following circumstances:

1. When anything blocks the road.
2. When anything doesn't.
3. When anything might.
4. At red lights.
5. At green lights.
6. At all other times.

Road-Blocks

One thing you can count on in Third World countries is trouble. There's 8 always some uprising, coup or Marxist insurrection going on, and this means military road-blocks. There are two kinds of military road-block, the kind where you slow down so they can look you over, and the kind where you come to a full stop so they can steal your luggage. The important thing is that you must *never* stop at the slow-down kind of road-block. If you stop, they'll think you're a terrorist about to attack them, and they'll shoot you. And you must *always* stop at the full-stop kind of road-block. If you just slow down, they'll think you're a terrorist about to attack them, and they'll shoot you. How do you tell the difference between the two kinds of road-block? Here's the fun part: you can't!

(The terrorists, of course, have road-blocks of their own. They always 9 make you stop. Sometimes with land mines.)

Animals in the Right of Way

As a rule of thumb, you should slow down for donkeys, speed up for 10 goats and stop for cows. Donkeys will get out of you way eventually, and so will pedestrians. But never actually stop for either of them or they'll take advantage, especially the pedestrians. If you stop in the middle of a crowd of Third World pedestrians, you'll be there buying Chiclets and bogus antiquities for days.

Drive like hell through the goats. It's almost impossible to hit a goat. On the other hand, it's almost impossible *not* to hit a cow. Cows are immune to horn-honking, shouting, swats with sticks and taps on the hind quarters with the bumper. The only thing you can do to make a cow move is to swerve to avoid it, which will make the cow move in front of you with lightning speed. 11

Actually, the most dangerous animals are the chickens. In the United States, when you see a ball roll into the street, you hit your brakes because you know the next thing you'll see is a kid chasing it. In the Third World, it's not balls the kids are chasing, but chickens. Are they practising punt returns with a leghorn? Dribbling it? Playing stick-hen? I don't know. But Third Worlders are remarkably fond of their chickens and, also, their children (population problems notwithstanding). If you hit one or both, they may survive. But you will not. 12

Accidents

Never look where you're going—you'll only scare yourself. Nonetheless, try to avoid collisions. There are bound to be more people in that bus, truck or even on that moped than there are in your car. At best you'll be screamed deaf. And if the police do happen to be around, standard procedure is to throw everyone in jail regardless of fault. This is done to forestall blood feuds, which are a popular hobby in many of these places. Remember the American consul is very busy fretting about that Marxist insurrection, and it may be many months before he comes to visit. 13

If you do have an accident, the only thing to do is go on the offensive. Throw big wads of American money at everyone, and hope for the best. 14

Safety Tips

One nice thing about the Third World, you don't have to fasten your safety belt. (Or stop smoking. Or cut down on saturated fats.) It takes a lot off your mind when average life expectancy is forty-five minutes. 15

The Ugly Tourist | Jamaica Kincaid

Although she now lives in New York and is a staff writer for *The New Yorker*, Jamaica Kincaid has a special perspective on the issues of travel and tourism. Born in St. John's, Antigua, in the West Indies, she has seen and (as she suggests in this excerpt from *A Small Place*) been an "ugly tourist." How would you characterize Kincaid's style—formal, moderate, colloquial? What distinctive features of her style—sentence structure, diction, tone—influence your assessment?

The thing you have always suspected about yourself the minute you become a tourist is true: a tourist is an ugly human being. You are not an ugly person all the time; you are not an ugly person ordinarily; you are not an ugly per- 1

Kincaid, Jamaica. *A Small Place*. New York: Farrar, 1988. 14–9.

son day to day. From day to day, you are a nice person. From day to day, all the people who are supposed to love you on the whole do. From day to day as you walk down a busy street in the large and modern and prosperous city in which you work and live, dismayed, puzzled (a cliché, but only a cliché can explain you) at how alone you feel in this crowd, how awful it is to go unnoticed, how awful it is to go unloved, even as you are surrounded by more people than you could possibly get to know in a lifetime that lasted for millennia, and then out of the corner of your eye you see someone looking at you and absolute pleasure is written all over that person's face, and then you realize that you are not as revolting a presence as you think you are (for that look just told you so). And so, ordinarily, you are a nice person, an attractive person, a person capable of drawing to yourself the affection of other people (people just like you), a person at home in your own skin (sort of; I mean in a way; I mean, your dismay and puzzlement are natural to you, because people like you just seem to be like that, and so many of the things people like you find admirable about yourselves—the things you think about, the things you think really define you—seem rooted in these feelings): a person at home in your own house (and all its nice house things), with its nice back yard (and its nice back-yard things), at home on your street, your church, in community activities, your job, at home with your family, your relatives, your friends—you are a whole person. But one day, when you are sitting somewhere, alone in that crowd, and that awful feeling of displacedness comes over you, and really, as an ordinary person you are not well equipped to look too far inward and set yourself aright, because being ordinary is already so taxing, and being ordinary takes all you have out of you, and though the words "I must get away" do not actually pass across your lips, you make a leap from being that nice blob just sitting like a boob in you amniotic sac of the modern experience to being a person visiting heaps of death and ruin and feeling alive and inspired at the sight of it; to being a person lying on some faraway beach, your stilled body stinking and glistening in the sand, looking like something first forgotten, then remembered, then not important enough to go back for; to being a person marvelling at the harmony (ordinarily, what you would say is the backwardness) and the union these other people (and they are other people) have with nature. And you look at the things they can do with a piece of ordinary cloth, the things they fashion out of cheap, vulgarly coloured (to you) twine, the way they squat down over a hole they have made in the ground, the hole itself is something to marvel at, and since you are being an ugly person this ugly but joyful thought will swell inside you: their ancestors were not clever in the way yours were and not ruthless in the way yours were, for then would it not be you who would be in harmony with nature and backwards in that charming way? An ugly thing, that is what you are when you become a tourist, an ugly, empty thing, a stupid thing, a piece of rubbish pausing here and there to gaze at this and taste that, and it will never occur to you that the people who inhabit the place in which you have just paused cannot stand you, that behind their closed doors they laugh at your strangeness (you do not look the way they look); the physical sight of you does not please them; you have bad manners (it is their custom to eat their food with their hands; you try eating their way, you look silly; you try eating the way you always eat, you look silly); but they do not like the way you speak (you have an accent); they collapse helpless from laughter, mimicking the way they imagine you must look as you carry out some everyday bodily function. They do not like you. *They do not like me!* That thought never actually occurs to you. Still, you feel a little uneasy. Still, you feel a little foolish. Still, you feel a little out of place. But the banality of your own life is very real to you; it drove you to this extreme, spending your days and your nights in the company of people who despise you, people you do not like really, people you would not want to have as your actual neighbour. And so you must devote yourself to puzzling out how much of what you are told is really, really true (Is ground-up bottle glass in peanut sauce really a delicacy around here, or will it do just what you think ground-up bottle glass will do? Is this rare, multicoloured, snout-mouthed fish really an aphrodisiac, or will it cause you to fall asleep permanently?). Oh, the hard work all of this is, and is it any wonder, then, that on your return home you feel the need of a long rest, so that you can recover from your life as a tourist?

That the native does not like the tourist is not hard to explain. For every native of every place is a potential tourist, and every tourist is a native of somewhere. Every native everywhere lives a life of overwhelming and crushing banality and boredom and desperation and depression, and every deed, good and bad, is an attempt to forget this. Every native would like to find a way out, every native would like a rest, every native would like a tour. But some natives—most natives in the world—cannot go anywhere. They are too poor. They are too poor to escape the reality of their lives; and they are too poor to live properly in the place where they live, which is the very place you, the tourist, want to go—so when the natives see you, the tourist, they envy you, they envy your ability to leave your own banality and boredom, they envy your ability to turn their own banality and boredom into a source of pleasure for yourself.

Prague | Patricia Hampl

In this excerpt from her memoirs *A Romantic Education*, Patricia Hampl tries to explain why she revised her intention to visit her grandparents' birthplace. Reread Hampl's comments on tone and style at the beginning of this chapter. Identify the specific passages in Hampl's essay where you sense that "another human being is speaking to" you. Where does Hampl use a formal tone? Where does she use a more conversational tone? How does this mixture help her readers understand the conclusions she forms in the last paragraph?

In May 1975, during the spring music festival that opens every year with a performance of Smetana's "Ma Vlast" ("My Homeland"), I went to Prague for the first time. The lilacs were in bloom everywhere: the various lavenders of the French and Persian lilac, and the more unusual—except in Prague—double white lilac. Huge flat red banners with yellow lettering were hoisted everywhere too, draped across homely suburban factories and from the subtle rose and mustard baroque buildings of Staré Město (the Old City).

The banners were in honor of the thirtieth anniversary of the liberation of Prague by the Soviet Army in May 1945. 30 *Let*, "30 years, " it said everywhere, even on the visa stamp in my passport. Many offices and stores had photo-

Hampl, Patricia. *A Romantic Education*. Boston: Houghton, 1981. 145–48; 149–52.

graphs in their windows, blowups from 1945 showing Russian soldiers accepting spring bouquets from shy little girls, Russian soldiers waving from tanks to happy crowds. For the first time, I was in a city where the end of the Second World War was really celebrated, where history was close at hand. Prague was the first Continental European city I had seen (I had come from London) and it was almost weirdly intact, not modern. On the plane from America to London I had reminded myself that London would be modern; *my* England was so much a product of the nineteenth-century novels and poetry I'd been reading all my life that I knew I would be shocked to see automobiles. And in fact, nothing could prepare me for the slump I felt in London: I wanted the city of Becky Sharpe, of Daniel Deronda, even of Clarissa Dalloway, not the London of Frommer's guidebooks and the thrill of finding lunch for 5 pence.

Prague stopped my tourism flat. The weight of its history and the beauty of its architecture came to me first as an awareness of dirt, a sort of ancient grime I had never seen before. It bewitched me, that dirt, caught in the corners of baroque moldings and decorative cornices, and especially I loved the dusty filth of the long, grave windows at sunset when the light flared against the tall oblongs and caused them to look gilded.   3

I had arrived in a river city, just as I had left one in St. Paul. But the difference . . . On the right bank of the Vltava (in German, the Moldau) the buildings were old—to me. Some of them were truly old, churches and wine cellars and squares dating from the Middle Ages. But the real look, especially of the residential and shopping areas of Nové Město (New City—new since the fourteenth century when Charles IV founded it), was art nouveau, highly decorative, the Bohemian version of the Victorian. Across the river, in Malá Strana (Small Side—Prague's Left Bank), the city became most intensely itself, however; it rose baroquely up, villa by villa, palace crushed to palace, gardens crumbling and climbing, to the castle that ran like a great crown above it on a bluff.   4

The city silenced me. It was just as well I didn't know the language and was traveling alone. There was nothing for me to say. I was here to look.   5

My original intention in going to Prague was simple: to see the place my grandparents had come from, to hear the language they had spoken. I knew Prague was Kafka's city, I knew Rilke had been born here, and I had read his *Letters to a Young Poet* many times. I was a young poet myself. But my visit wasn't for them. Mine was the return of a third generation American, the sort of journey that is so inexplicable to the second generation: "What are you going to *do* there?" my father asked me before I left Minnesota.   6

That spring, the lines at the Prague Čedok office (the government agency that runs tourism in Czechoslovakia) were dotted here and there with young Americans looking for family villages. The young couple in front of me in the line had come from Cleveland. The man was asking a young travel agent, who was dressed in a jeans skirt and wore nail polish the color of an eggplant, how he and his wife could get to a village whose name he couldn't manage to pronounce.   7

"There does not seem to be such a place," she told him. She couldn't find a name on the map with a spelling that corresponded to the one the young man had brought from Cleveland on the piece of paper he was holding out to his wife. ("It's *his* family," she said to me. "I'm Irish.")   8

They decided to set out, anyway, for a village in Moravia that had a similar spelling. "I guess that's the place," the young man said, without much conviction.   9

I asked my father's question: "What are you going to *do* there?"   **10**

"Look around," he said. "Maybe somebody"—he meant a relative—"will   **11**
be there."

My own slip of paper, which I'd brought from St. Paul, had the name of   **12**
my grandmother's village ("spelling approximate," my cousin had written
next to the name when he gave it to me) which was supposed to be near
Třeboň, a small town in southern Bohemia. On the map, Třeboň was set among
lakes (like Minneapolis, I had thought); here, the guidebook said, "the famous
carp" were caught.

Suddenly, just then, as my turn came up, I had no heart for the approxi-   **13**
mate name of the village, for the famous carp, the kind of journey the Cleveland couple had set for themselves. ("We're going to do the same thing in
Ireland," the wife said.) I stepped out of the line, crumpled up my piece of
paper, and left it in an ashtray. The absurdity of trying to get to Třeboň, and
from there to wherever this village with the approximate spelling was supposed to be, lay on me like a plank. I felt like a student who drops out of medical school a semester before graduation; I was almost there and, suddenly, it
didn't matter, I didn't want what I'd been seeking. Apparently I wanted something else.

"Do you want to get something to eat?" I asked the couple from Cleveland.   **14**

But they didn't have time. "We have to split," she said.   **15**

"Yeah," said her husband. "It's a long way. . . ."   **16**

I put Třeboň out of my mind and spent the rest of the week walking aim-   **17**
lessly around Prague. If I had answered my father's question—what was I
doing—I would have said I was sitting in coffeehouses, in between long, aimless walks. A long trip for a cup of coffee, but I was listless, suddenly lacking
curiosity and I felt, as I sat in the Slavia next to the big windows that provide
one of the best views of the Hradčany in the city, that simply by staring out the
window I was doing my bit: there it was, the castle, and I was looking at it. I
had fallen on the breast of the Middle European coffeehouse and I was content
among the putty- and dove-colored clothes, the pensioners stirring away the
hours, the tables of university students studying and writing their papers, the
luscious waste of time, the gossip whose ardor I sensed in the bent heads, lifted
eyebrows—because of course I couldn't understand a word.

In Vienna the coffeehouses—not all of them, thank God—lose their leases   **18**
to McDonald's and fast-food chains. But in Prague the colors just fade and
become more, rather than less, what they were. The coffeehouse is deeply
attached to the idea of conversation, the exchange of ideas, and therefore, to a
political society. In *The Agony of Czechoslovakia '38/'68*, Kurt Weisskopf remembers the Prague coffeehouses before the Second World War.

> You were expected to patronize the coffeehouse of your group, your pro-   **19**
> fession, your political party. Crooks frequented the Golden Goose, or the
> Black Rose in the centre of Prague. Snobs went to the Savarin, whores and
> their prospective clients to the Lind or Julis; commercial travelers occupied
> the front part of Cafe Boulevard, while the rear was the traditional meeting
> place of Stalinists and Trotskyites, glaring at each other as they sat around
> separate marble tables. The rich went to the Urban, "progressive" intellec-
> tuals to the Metro. Abstract painters met at the Union, and surrealists at the

Manes where they argued with impressionists. You were still served by the black-coated waiters if you did not belong, but so contemptuously that you realized how unwelcome your presence was. The papers in their bamboo frames and the magazines in their folders, an essential part of the Central European coffeehouse service, were regrettably not available to intruders. If you went to the wrong coffeehouse you were just frozen out.

But if you fitted in, socially, politically, philosophically, artistically or   20
professionally, well, then the headwaiter and the manager treated you almost as a relative and you were even deemed worthy of credit.

"Rudolf, switch on the light over the Communists, they can't read their   21
papers properly," old Loebl, manager of the Edison, used to instruct the headwaiter. "And see that the Anarchists get more iced water." Once you had ordered your coffee you were entitled to free glasses of iced water brought regularly by the trayload; this was called a "swimming pool."

The water was still brought, as I sat at the marble table of the Slavia   22
though not by the trayload. Perhaps there were political conversations, even arguments: I couldn't tell. But the newspapers were the official ones of the Communist Party, including, in English, the *Daily Worker*. When I asked someone I'd struck up a conversation with, who was quoted as a source on American news, I was told, "Gus Hall," the president of the American Communist Party. "As a typical American?" I asked incredulously. "As the voice of the people," I was told. It struck me as funny, not sinister, although later I realized I was annoyed.

I walked around Prague, hardly caring if I hit the right tourist spots,   23
missing baroque gems, I suppose, getting lost, leaving the hotel without a map as if I had no destination. I just walked, stopping at coffeehouses, smoking unfiltered cigarettes and looking out from the blue wreath around me to other deep-drawing smokers. Everyone seemed to have time to sit, to smoke as if smoking were breathing, to stare into the vacancy of private thought, if their thoughts were private. I was in the thirties, I'd finally arrived in my parents' decade, the men's soft caps, the dove colors of Depression pictures, the acquiescence to circumstance, the ruined quality. For the first time I recognized the truth of beauty: that it is brokenness, it is on its knees. I sat and watched it and smoked (I don't smoke but I found myself buying cigarettes), smoked a blue relation between those coffeehouses and me. For this sadness turned out to be, to me, beautiful. Or rather, the missing quality of beauty, whatever makes it approachable, became apparent in Prague. I could sit, merely breathing, and be part of it. I was beautiful—at last. And I didn't care—at last. I stumbled through the ancient streets, stopped in the smoke-grimed coffeehouses and added my signature of ash, anonymous and yet entirely satisfied. I had ceased even to be a reverse immigrant—I sought no one, no sign of my family or any ethnic heritage that might be mine. I was, simply, in the most beautiful place I had ever seen, and it was grimy and sad and broken. I was relieved of some weight, the odd burden of happiness and unblemished joy of the adored child—or perhaps I was free of beauty itself as an abstract concept. I didn't think about it and didn't bother to wonder. I sat and smoked; I walked and got lost and didn't care because I couldn't get lost. I hardly understood that I was happy: my happiness consisted of encountering sadness. I simply felt *accurate*.

Writing Assignments

Narrate **1.** Write a brief guidebook to a place you remember well and with great affection. Provide a map, a brief (informative) history, and the kind of information your readers will want—how to get there, where to stay, what to see, how much things cost. Reserve a section to explain why this place has special, personal significance for you.

Observe **2.** Select a place you have visited on several occasions and compare how two means of travel—driving a car, or flying in a plane—affected what you saw on your way and altered your attitude toward your destination. Consider why you prefer one style of travel to the other. Then draft an essay, "The Best Way to Get There," describing your observations and the reasons for your choice.

Investigate **3.** In "Girl Talk—Boy Talk," *Science* 85 (January/February 1985), John Pfeiffer reports that researcher "Sally McConnell-Ginet of Cornell finds that women's voices are more colorful—they vary their pitch and change pitch more frequently than do men's voices. In one experiment, women immediately assumed a monotone style when asked to imitate men's speech. McConnell-Ginet regards speaking tunefully as an effective strategy for getting and holding attention, a strategy used more often by women than men." Use McConnell-Ginet's research as a starting point for developing your own investigation of the way gender, class, profession, or place may affect the tone of speech of the people you talk with during your daily travels.

Collaborate **4.** Your writing group has been asked to write and produce a series of language/culture tapes for a group of exchange students visiting your campus for a semester. Make a list of the kind of information you think they should have about America, your region, and campus. Interview other exchange students from that country already on your campus to see what specific difficulties they have encountered. Ask these students to evaluate the sentence structure, diction, and tone in your scripts. Then audition members of your group and select those people with the most engaging *voices* to read the scripts on tape.

Read **5.** Select a place people commonly visit for vacations—the Caribbean, Europe, California, Florida. Collect a range of guidebooks that provide information on the same place—comprehensive *(Baedeker's Great Britain)*, discount *(Great Britain on $50 a Day)*, and quaint *(England's Wonderful Little Hotels and Inns)*. Compare and contrast the tone and style of these books in a review for the "Travel and Leisure" section of your newspaper. Focus on one specific spot— such as Stratford-on-Avon—so that you restrict the terms of your comparison.

Respond **6.** Write a response to P. J. O'Rourke's "Third World Driving Hints and Tips." Your experience driving in other countries or particular sections of our country, for example, may encourage you to imitate O'Rourke's essay, detailing the many comic aspects of driving in a strange place. On the other hand, you may wish to take issue with O'Rourke's attitude toward the people of the *Third World.* In that case, you may want to use specific driving experiences to demonstrate why good guests should learn and respect the customs of their hosts.

Analyze **7.** Study the *you* Jamacia Kincaid addresses in "The Ugly Tourist"—the various contexts *you* inhabits, the reactions *you* elicits, the adjectives *you* ordinarily uses to describe *yourself*, and the changes *you* experiences when encountering people from another country. Then write an explanation of how Kincaid uses this strategy to personalize the conflict between tourists and natives.

Evaluate **8.** Evaluate Patricia Hampl's style (sentence structure, diction, tone) in those sections where she is talking about the history of Prague and those sections where she is talking about herself. Use the information to explain how Prague "silenced" Hampl, "stopped my tourism flat." Then write an essay illustrating how her decision to stop touring and get lost helped her understand this alien culture, helped her feel "accurate."

Argue **9.** Reread Walker Percy's description of the Grand Canyon in this chapter (page 256). Then, using a specific experience to illustrate your case, write an opinion column arguing that tourists adopt a particular style of touring. For example, some tourists see what they expect to see, some see something less than what they were led to believe they would see, and some see something no one else has ever seen.

Argue **10.** Using your own experience, your knowledge of American history, and the readings in this chapter, write a speech for the travel lecture series at your local public library about America's fascination with travel. You could argue, for example, that such fascination is a deficiency: Americans are continually traveling because we are unable to find happiness in any place. Or you could argue that such fascination is a virtue: Americans are flexible, capable of change, and tolerant of other lifestyles.

Readings with a Purpose

11	Readings with a Purpose

11 | Readings with a Purpose

In Part Three you will study seven common strategies writers use to select their subject, analyze their audience, and determine their purpose. Most of this material should seem familiar. You have already examined how these strategies evolve through the writing process (Part One) and give structure to the expression of ideas (Part Two). You have also examined how these strategies emerge in the work of the student and professional writers featured in and at the end of previous chapters. Indeed, you may have experimented with one or more of these strategies as you planned, drafted, and revised your writing assignments. But the collection of essays in this part places these strategies in a new context, giving you the opportunity to learn more about how their special features enable you to write with a purpose.

You will notice that the order of the seven strategies in this part is the same as it was in Chapters 5 and 6, and corresponds roughly to the order of the writing assignments at the end of each chapter:

1. Narration and Description
2. Process Analysis
3. Comparison and Contrast
4. Division and Classification
5. Definition
6. Causal Analysis
7. Argument

In the earlier sections of this book, you were given examples to encourage you to see these strategies as ways to *develop* your writing. For example, you saw that Jane Graham used the first six strategies to discover what she observed on her whale watch and that Matt Fisher used the seventh strategy to generate information for his argument on drug testing. In this section, however, you will be asked to analyze these strategies as ways to *organize* your writing.

To assist you in this project, I have presented each strategy in the same format. The introduction begins with general observations about choosing your subject, audience, and purpose and ends with specific advice about using various features of the strategy effectively. The student essay (complete with annotations) and the professional essay (followed by questions) illustrate the use of those features. "A Sampler of Other Essays" refers you to additional readings in this book that illustrate the same strategy. Part Three concludes with writing assignments, each of which invites you to organize your writing using one of the strategies.

STRATEGY ONE: *Narration and Description*

Selecting Your Subject

Any experience can be narrated and described. In *narration,* you tell a story to make a point; in *description,* you create a picture to evoke the senses. You can select either strategy for a subject, but you will discover that most subjects require you to use them in combination. The best place to look for a subject is your own experience: you can always invent a subject or the details with which you describe it, but you will have more success writing about events and people you know. You will also have more success if you restrict your subject to manageable size—your first trip alone, your last argument with friends—and sort out what makes your story interesting and significant. What is the story in your story?

Analyzing Your Audience

As you think about your essay, consider how much you need to tell your readers and how much you will need to show them. If you are writing from personal experience, few readers will know the story before you tell it. They may know similar stories or have had similar experiences, but they do not know your story. Because you can tell your story in so many different ways—adding or deleting material to fit your purpose—you need to decide how much information your readers need. Do they need to know every detail, only brief summaries of certain parts, or some mixture of detail and summary? You must also decide how much your readers already know and what they expect to learn. If your subject is familiar to most people (for example, working at a fast-food restaurant), your readers will need few technical details to understand your subject. But they will expect you to give them images and insights that create a fresh vision of your subject—for example, portraying the restaurant as a community center.

Determining Your Purpose

You can use narration and description for two purposes. One, you can use them to introduce or illustrate a complicated subject: you might begin an analysis of the energy crisis by telling a story about wastefulness, or you might conclude an argument for gun control by providing a graphic description of a shooting incident. Two, you can use these strategies as the primary method for presenting or analyzing a topic. For example, you might devote an entire essay to recounting your experiences in a foreign country. Although your personal experience forms the core of your essay, your narrative purpose (what happened) and your descriptive purpose (what it looked or felt like) might be linked to larger purposes—for example, explaining how the experience altered your sense of cultural superiority.

Using the Strategy

The key to writing effective narration and description is recognizing that an experience and an essay about that experience are not the same thing. To transform an experience into an essay, you must locate the central *conflict*. It may be a conflict between you and other people, you and the social or natural environment, or aspects of your personality.

Once you have identified the conflict, you must arrange the action so that your readers know how the conflict started, how it developed, and how it was resolved. This coherent sequence of events is called a *plot*. Sometimes you may want to arrange your plot so that it follows a simple chronological pattern, starting at the beginning and describing events as they occur. At other times, you may want to start your essay in the middle or near the end of the event you are describing. After you choose the beginning, middle, and end, you need to establish the *pace* of each section. Sometimes you can narrate events quickly by omitting details, compressing time, and summarizing experience. At other times you must pace events more slowly, adding small details, describing every movement, and using dialogue to render the experience as a fully realized scene.

You can make your scenes and summaries effective by the careful *selection of details.* Simply adding detail is not enough. You must choose those details that satisfy the needs of your reader and advance your purpose. Sometimes you will need to select *objective* or technical details to help your readers understand your subject. At other times you will want to select *subjective* or impressionistic details to appeal to your readers' senses. Occasionally, you may want to select details so that they form a *figurative image* or evoke a *dominant impression.*

Finally, you need to determine your *point of view.* Simply stated, point of view refers to the person and the position of the narrator (point) and the attitude expressed toward the narrative (view). You choose your *person* by deciding whether you want to tell your story in the first person ("I") or third person ("she" or "he"). Your *position* refers to how close you are to the action in time and space. You may be involved in the action or be viewing it as an observer. You may be telling about events as they are happening or many years after they have taken place. You create your attitude once you decide how you want to interpret the events you intend to present.

Inside and Out | Lisa Widenhofer

Introduction: Establish scene and point of view

It was another gloomy day on my Christmas break. This particular afternoon of my Christmas break Mom and I settled down in the sewing room to search through a box of old photographs taken from Grandma's house. So many things had been taken from the house since she had moved into the nursing home that it was hard to get excited about going through yet another box. In previous boxes we had found junk jewelry, outgrown clothes, and little bobbles purchased on sale for some future Christmas. 1

Plot: Introduce conflict

This box, however, was different. Instead of sorting the pitchable objects from the valuables, we were on a mission, of sorts. There was something specific that we hoped to find amidst the curling pictures of Christmases past and New Year's Eve parties of long ago. We were looking for any photos from Grandma and Grandpa's wedding. No one had ever seen any, not even my father. 2

Grandma's house always had a special wall dedicated to everyone's wedding picture, everyone's except for Grandma and Grandpa's own. In all of her trips down memory lane, Grandma never talked about her own wedding. When my brother was married, my future sister-in-law's wedding gown was the talk of the family. Yet no one ever talked about Grandma's gown. And no *Detail: Select details to advance plot* one had really much thought about it. Until now. When we had discovered the box full of old pictures, we hoped to find a wedding picture. Mom now had a special wall of her own dedicated to wedding pictures. It displayed a photo of herself and Dad, my brother Gary and his wife Marianne, Mom's parents, even her grandparents. But Dad's parents' picture was conspicuously missing. 3

Pace: Mix summary and scene

The hours of the afternoon flew by. I shuffled through old black and whites and stopped on occasion to laugh at pictures of my father as a lady-killing six-year-old. Meanwhile, Mom stood up to get something out of the closet, a surprise of some sort. She pulled out a black, plastic covered hanging thing, a dress by the shape of it, and asked me to help her unwrap it. "It's Grandma's," Mom told me. "It almost was thrown away. It was literally wadded up into a ball and jammed in some old newspapers. Your father and I were cleaning out some junk from the attic at Grandma's house and almost missed it hiding in the trash. We didn't even know Grandma still had it." I stood, knees cracking from the hour of kneeling, and lifted the plastic as Mom held the hanger. Sliding from beneath the bag was cream-colored silk, wrinkled like an old woman's face. 4

Detail: Describe dress

It was my grandmother's wedding gown. A page torn from history, a little dirty in places from newsprint and rusting snaps. But the cloth was still intact, not frayed or worn through. The dress was the most simple gown I had seen, but pretty in its own uncomplicated way. Even the cream color of the silk was soothing in its simplicity and held its color true. As Mom held the dress up to the light, I could see that there were tiny gathers along the neckline; long, slim sleeves; and a beautiful, wide train that hung almost four feet below the dress's hemline. 5

Plot: Establish context for dress

As I admired the gown, I remembered Mom telling me about her own   6
wedding dress. The dress Mom picked out for her wedding was not the one
she wore. The dress she had chosen had been replaced by a different one, hand
picked by an imitation of Cinderella's wicked stepmother, Mom's own stepmother. She didn't know or care what happened to that gown. My Mom's
mom, gone from this world for far too many years, had no wedding gown of
her own, either. Her wedding had been rushed in order to have it before World
War II called my Grandpa to battle. This dress of my Dad's mother was the
only wedding gown in our family.

"It still seems pretty well intact, probably even wearable if it was cleaned   7
and pressed carefully," Mom thought aloud. Her fingers glided over the silk,
and she inspected the rusting snaps and hand-sewn seams with an expert eye.

Scene: Use dialogue to introduce photographs

I returned to the box to look for a photograph even more diligently than before.
I breezed by old family photos and pictures of Uncle Steve in his "difficult
stage." And then, there at the bottom of the box sat two large photo savers.

"Check it out, Ma!" I called to Mom, and together we opened the binders   8
to find my grandparents on their wedding day. Grandma looked stunning. The
gown hanging beside me seemed to have jumped from the picture itself.
Grandma wore a long, gorgeous, lace train hanging from the headpiece. It
extended almost three feet past the silk train of the dress. She was so petite and
young. Her arms held a full bouquet of flowers, and her big eyes were warm
and deep.

Detail: Use subjective detail to evoke senses

And then there was Grandpa, looking dashing in his dark suit. I loved him   9
so very much, as I do still. It made my heart both happy and sad to see him so
handsome, so alive. His long, thin face wore a warm smile, and his lean frame
stood tall and proud. I felt that if I stared at the picture hard enough it would
somehow give him back those fifty years to live again, to be with me. Gone for
almost six years, however, Grandpa had passed on, and Grandma was very
sick. They were both so very different from their picture now.

Grandma had moved from her house to Lutheran Home when her heart   10
muscle just couldn't take the strain of living alone anymore. Congestive heart

Pace: Summarize action elsewhere

failure had been tightening its grip on her. It seemed so odd to see the bustling,
cooking, cleaning Grandma that I had always known sitting in the wheelchair
waiting to go down to dinner. But somehow the discovery of the dress and the
photos brought renewed life and energy where it had been once forgotten. I
thought of Grandma sitting, slouched in her favorite chair brought over from
the house. My memory saw her as she so often looked, framed in the open
doorway of the home. I looked again at the wedding picture, her eyes full of
youth and vitality, her face framed in the dark, cardboard picture trim. Different but somehow the same.

Plot: introduce new complication

I sat lost in memories, clutching the dog-eared pictures tight while Mom   11
stood once again to examine the wedding gown. "It has held up pretty well,"
Mom said, as she held the dress at arm's length. Then she looked at me, kneeling there among the photos. "You know," she mused, "it might even fit you.
Wanna try it on?"

Point of View: Present narrator's attitude

The thought seemed eerie. Even thinking that Grandma and I were ever   12
the same size or shape was a new idea. She sat in the home now, shoulders
rounding from worry. She was also heavier now from the fluid that her heart
just couldn't get rid of anymore. I looked again at the young woman in the
photograph. She was so young, so alive, so real. It was a new experience to

think of Grandma not only looking like I do now, but going through the same changes of growing up, through the same frustrations of being not quite a kid, but not quite a grownup either.

I set down the picture, kicked off my tennis shoes and socks to reveal my painted toenails, and carefully stepped into the silky folds of the dress. With deft fingers Mom buttoned up the small buttons, lined up the seams, and straightened the train behind me. And there I stood. I was not the only thing within the dress. It held Grandma, it held memories of a young couple's love, it held new discoveries and old truths. I stared at the sleeves that reached beyond where they should. My fingers glided over the silk, toying for a moment with the small newsprint stain that slightly dulled the otherwise shiny material.

13

I stared at my fingers peeking out of the material, imagining myself as Grandma on her wedding day. Although the dress fit, the extra long sleeves reminded me that the dress was not mine, that I was still the granddaughter dressing up in her grandma's gown. "I can't get over how well it fits you. A little long in the sleeves and a tad big in length, but with heels even that isn't far off. And sleeves can be shortened." Mom was right. The gown fit me, and it was exciting but frightening as well. It was like stepping into the past and the future all at once, becoming aware of my family heritage, feeling it, breathing it as well. I discovered something new in me. Or maybe it was something very old, older than my years, finally surfacing in me.

14

Mom looked at me in silence for a moment. "We have to show Dad and Gary. They're downstairs rummaging through the refrigerator." She snatched up the two photographs of Grandma and Grandpa and then helped me maneuver the train to the stairs and we began to descend, Mom leading the way. The stairs seemed longer than I had remembered. Each step was filled with anticipation. I concentrated on breathing and not stepping on the dress or tripping. I could feel my pulse all the way down to my toes, and my fingers aimlessly clutched that extra material on the long sleeves as a child might hold a security blanket. Mom said, "Hey, Lisa's got something to show you." I heard their footsteps come closer to the stairs. As they spotted me, the men stopped silent. At first glance they probably thought I was reverting to the old days, playing dress-up in Mommy's clothes. Nobody spoke. Suddenly Dad's eyes misted over.

15

"Beautiful," he whispered. I couldn't decide what he meant. Was the word for me, the gown, his mother, or the captivating and swirling dance between memory and imagination?

16

Mom smiled an old smile and handed each man a picture of Grandma and Grandpa's wedding. "Just look." I imagine that Mom was busy with mixed memories of her wedding, imagining Grandma and Grandpa's wedding, and dreaming of mine. The guys looked at the pictures and then back at me. Gary smiled, suggesting he understood completely, that he had the full picture. With half a smile he said, "It looks as if it was made for you, Lis. It's almost creepy. Grandma must have been a lot like you when she was your age." Gary handed the picture back to Mom. I watched him do it through a fuzzy glaze as my eyes began to swell with tears.

17

At that, Dad stepped towards me, put his big hands on my shoulders, and gave me a light kiss on the forehead. "Just beautiful," he muttered. I smiled a half smile, clutched the sleeves with my fingertips, gathered up the gown, revealing my painted toes again, and scooted up the stairs as fast as I could, not

18

even waiting for Mom's aid. The descent down the stairs had been prolonged by anticipation. The return was a blur. I wanted only to hide away, to get into my own clothes, and to quietly sort out my emotions.

Plot: Resolve plot

Once again in the sewing room, I paused for a moment in front of the long   19 mirror. The mirror, like the picture, framed the image of a vital young woman with her Grandma's big, warm eyes, in a simple but beautiful gown. Different but somehow the same. I unbuttoned the silken wedding dress worn so many years ago by my grandmother. Pulling it over my head I felt almost as if I were peeling myself out of a memory. I returned the dress to its hanger and stepped back into my own jeans and sweatshirt, shoes, and socks. Back in my own clothes I looked at the gown hanging once again on the back of the closet door. It hung there still wrinkled and still bursting with memories. I hugged myself and smiled, inside and out. And I shivered, inside and out. And I cried. I had put on my grandmother's wedding gown. I had worn the dress and wear still all that it encompassed. Inside and out.

Point of View: Suggest importance of experience

The Inheritance of Tools | **Scott Russell Sanders**

At just about the hour when my father died, soon after dawn one February morning when ice coated the windows like cataracts, I banged my thumb with a hammer. Naturally I swore at the hammer, the reckless thing, and in the moment of swearing I thought of what my father would say: "If you'd try hitting the nail it would go in a whole lot faster. Don't you know your thumb's not as hard as that hammer?" We both were doing carpentry that day, but far apart. He was building cupboards at my brother's place in Oklahoma; I was at home in Indiana putting up a wall in the basement to make a bedroom for my daughter. By the time my mother called with news of his death—the long distance wires whittling her voice until it seemed too thin to bear the weight of what she had to say—my thumb was swollen. A week or so later a white scar in the shape of a crescent moon began to show above the cuticle, and month by month it rose across the pink sky of my thumbnail. It took the better part of a year for the scar to disappear, and every time I noticed it I thought of my father.

The hammer had belonged to him, and to his father before him. The three of us have used it to build houses and barns and chicken coops, to upholster chairs and crack walnuts, to make doll furniture and bookshelves and jewelry boxes. The head is scratched and pockmarked, like an old plowshare that has been working rocky fields, and it gives off the sort of dull sheen you see on fast creek water in the shade. It is a finishing hammer, about the weight of a bread loaf, too light really for framing walls, too heavy for cabinetwork, with a curved claw for pulling nails, a rounded head for pounding, a fluted neck for looks, and a hickory handle for strength.

The present handle is my third one, bought from a lumberyard in Tennessee down the road from where my brother and I were helping my father build his retirement house. I broke the previous one by trying to pull sixteen-penny nails out of floor joists—a foolish thing to do with a finishing hammer, as my father pointed out. "You ever hear of a crowbar?" he said. No telling how many handles he and my grandfather had gone through before me. My grandfather used to cut down hickory trees on his farm, saw them into slabs, cure the planks in his hayloft, and carve handles with a drawknife. The grain in hickory is crooked and knotty, and therefore tough, hard to split, like the grain in the two men who owned this hammer before me.

After proposing marriage to a neighbor girl, my grandfather used this hammer to build a house for his bride on a stretch of river bottom in northern Mississippi. The lumber for the place, like the hickory for the handle, was cut on his own land. By the day of the wedding he had not quite finished the house, and so right after the ceremony he took his wife home and put her to work. My grandmother had worn her Sunday dress for the wedding, with a fringe of lace tacked on around the hem in honor of the occasion. She removed

1

2

3

4

Sanders, Scott Russell. "The Inheritance of Tools." *The Paradise of Bombs*. Athens: U of Georgia P, 1987. 102–10.

this lace and folded it away before going out to help my grandfather nail siding on the house. "There she was in her good dress," he told me some fifty-odd years after that wedding day, "holding up them long pieces of clapboard while I hammered, and together we got the place covered up before dark." As the family grew to four, six, eight, and eventually thirteen, my grandfather used this hammer to enlarge his house room by room, like a chambered nautilus expanding his shell.

By and by the hammer was passed along to my father. One day he was up   5 on the roof of our pony barn nailing shingles with it, when I stepped out the kitchen door to call him for supper. Before I could yell, something about the sight of him straddling the spine of that roof and swinging the hammer caught my eye and made me hold my tongue. I was five or six years old, and the world's commonplaces were still news to me. He would pull a nail from the pouch at his waist, bring the hammer down, and a moment later the *thunk* of the blow would reach my ears. And that is what had stopped me in my tracks and stilled my tongue, that momentary gap between seeing and hearing the blow. Instead of yelling from the kitchen door, I ran to the barn and climbed two rungs up the ladder—as far as I was allowed to go—and spoke quietly to my father. On our walk to the house he explained that sound takes time to make its way through air. Suddenly the world seemed larger, the air more dense, if sound could be held back like any ordinary traveler.

By the time I started using this hammer, at about the age when I dis-   6 covered the speed of sound, it already contained houses and mysteries for me. The smooth handle was one my grandfather had made. In those days I needed both hands to swing it. My father would start a nail in a scrap of wood, and I would pound away until I bent it over.

"Looks like you got ahold of some of those rubber nails," he would tell   7 me. "Here, let me see if I can find you some stiff ones." And he would rummage in a drawer until he came up with a fistful of more cooperative nails. "Look at the head," he would tell me. "Don't look at your hands, don't look at the hammer. Just look at the head of that nail and pretty soon you'll learn to hit it square."

Pretty soon I did learn. While he worked in the garage cutting dovetail   8 joints for a drawer or skinning a deer or tuning an engine, I would hammer nails. I made innocent blocks of wood look like porcupines. He did not talk much in the midst of his tools, but he kept up a nearly ceaseless humming, slipping in and out of a dozen tunes in an afternoon, often running back over the same stretch of melody again and again, as if searching for a way out. When the humming did cease, I knew he was faced with a task requiring great delicacy or concentration, and I took care not to distract him.

He kept scraps of wood in a cardboard box—the ends of two-by-fours,   9 slabs of shelving and plywood, odd pieces of molding—and everything in it was fair game. I nailed scraps together to fashion what I called boats or houses, but the results usually bore only faint resemblance to the visions I carried in my head. I would hold up these constructions to show my father, and he would turn them over in his hands admiringly, speculating about what they might be. My cobbled-together guitars might have been alien spaceships, my barns might have been models of Aztec temples, each wooden contraption might have been anything but what I had set out to make.

Now and again I would feel the need to have a chunk of wood shaped or   10 shortened before I riddled it with nails, and I would clamp it in a vice and scrape at it with a handsaw. My father would let me lacerate the board until my arm gave out, and then he would wrap his hand around mine and help me finish the cut, showing me how to use my thumb to guide the blade, how to pull back on the saw to keep it from binding, how to let my shoulder do the work.

"Don't force it," he would say, "just drag it easy and give the teeth a chance to bite."   11

As the saw teeth bit down the wood released its smell, each kind with its own fragrance, oak or walnut or cherry or pine—usually pine, because it was the softest and the easiest for a child to work. No matter how weathered and gray the board, no matter how warped and cracked, inside there was this smell waiting, as of something freshly baked. I gathered every smidgen of sawdust and stored it away in coffee cans, which I kept in a drawer of the workbench. When I did not feel like hammering nails I would dump my sawdust on the concrete floor of the garage and landscape it into highways and farms and towns, running miniature cars and trucks along miniature roads. Looming as huge as a colossus, my father worked over and around me, now and again bending down to inspect my work, careful not to trample my creations. It was a landscape that smelled dizzyingly of wood. Even after a bath my skin would carry the smell, and so would my father's hair, when he lifted me for a bedtime hug.   12

I tell these things not only from memory but also from recent observation, because my own son now turns blocks of wood into nailed porcupines, dumps cans full of sawdust at my feet and sculpts highways on the floor. He learns how to swing a hammer from the elbow instead of the wrist, how to lay his thumb beside the blade to guide a saw, how to tap a chisel with a wooden mallet, how to mark a hole with an awl before starting a drill bit. My daughter did the same before him, and even now, on the brink of teenage aloofness, she will occasionally drag out my box of wood scraps and carpenter something. So I have seen my apprenticeship to wood and tools reenacted in each of my children, as my father saw his own apprenticeship renewed in me.   13

The saw I use belonged to him, as did my level and both of my squares, and all four tools had belonged to his father. The blade of the saw is the bluish color of gun barrels, and the maple handle, dark from the sweat of hands, is inscribed with curving leaf designs. The level is a shaft of walnut two feet long, edged with brass and pierced by three round windows in which air bubbles float in oil-filled tubes of glass. The middle window serves for testing whether a surface is horizontal, the others for testing whether it is plumb or vertical. My grandfather used to carry this level on the gun rack behind the seat in his pickup, and when I rode with him I would turn around to watch the bubbles dance. The larger of the two squares is called a framing square, a flat steel elbow so beat up and tarnished you can barely make out the rows of numbers that show how to figure the cuts on rafters. The smaller one is called a try square, for marking right angles, with a blued steel blade for the shank and a brass-faced block of cherry for the head.   14

I was taught early on that a saw is not to be used apart from a square: "If you're going to cut a piece of wood," my father insisted, "you owe it to the tree to cut it straight."   15

Long before studying geometry, I learned there is a mystical virtue in right angles. There is an unspoken morality in seeking the level and the plumb. A house will stand, a table will bear weight, the sides of a box will hold together only if the joints are square and the members upright. When the bubble is lined up between two marks etched in the glass tube of a level, you have aligned   16 yourself with the forces that hold the universe together. When you miter the corners of a picture frame, each angle must be exactly forty-five degrees, as they are in the perfect triangles of Pythagoras, not a degree more or less. Otherwise the frame will hang crookedly, as if ashamed of itself and of its maker. No matter if the joints you are cutting do not show. Even if you are butting two pieces of wood together inside a cabinet, where no one except a wrecking crew will ever see them, you must take pains to insure that the ends are square and the studs are plumb.

I took pains over the wall I was building on the day my father died. Not   17
long after that wall was finished—paneled with tongue-and-groove boards of yellow pine, the nail holes filled with putty and the wood all stained and sealed—I came close to wrecking it one afternoon when my daughter ran howling up the stairs to announce that her gerbils had escaped from their cage and were hiding in my brand-new wall. She could hear them scratching and squeaking behind her bed. Impossible! I said. How on earth could they get inside my drum-tight wall? Through the heating vent, she answered. I went downstairs, pressed my ear to the honey-colored wood, and heard the scritch scritch of tiny feet.

"What can we do?" my daughter wailed. "They'll starve to death, they'll   18
die of thirst, they'll suffocate."

"Hold on," I soothed. "I'll think of something."   19

While I thought and she fretted, the radio on her bedside table delivered   20
us the headlines. Several thousand people had died in a city in India from a poisonous cloud that had leaked overnight from a chemical plant. A nuclear-powered submarine had been launched. Rioting continued in South Africa. An airplane had been hijacked in the Mediterranean. Authorities calculated that several thousand homeless people slept on the streets within sight of the Washington Monument. I felt my usual helplessness in face of all these calamities. But here was my daughter weeping because her gerbils were holed up in a wall. This calamity I could handle.

"Don't worry," I told her. "We'll set food and water by the heating vent   21
and lure them out. And if that doesn't do the trick, I'll tear the wall apart until we find them."

She stopped crying and gazed at me. "You'd really tear it apart? Just for   22
my gerbils? The *wall*?" Astonishment slowed her down only for a second, however, before she ran to the workbench and began tugging at drawers, saying, "Let's see, what'll we need? Crowbar. Hammer. Chisels. I hope we don't have to use them—but just in case."

We didn't need the wrecking tools. I never had to assault my handsome   23
wall, because the gerbils eventually came out to nibble at a dish of popcorn. But for several hours I studied the tongue-and-groove skin I had nailed up on the day of my father's death, considering where to begin prying. There were no gaps in that wall, no crooked joints.

I had botched a great many pieces of wood before I mastered the right   24
angle with a saw, botched even more before I learned to miter a joint. The knowledge of these things resides in my hands and eyes and the webwork of muscles, not in the tools. There are machines for sale—powered miter boxes and radial arm saws, for instance—that will enable any casual soul to cut proper angles in boards. The skill is invested in the gadget instead of the person who uses it, and this is what distinguishes a machine from a tool. If I had to

earn my keep by making furniture or building houses, I suppose I would buy powered saws and pneumatic nailers; the need for speed would drive me to it. But since I carpenter only for my own pleasure or to help neighbors or to remake the house around the ears of my family, I stick with hand tools. Most of the ones I own were given to me by my father, who also taught me how to wield them. The tools in my workbench are a double inheritance, for each hammer and level and saw is wrapped in a cloud of knowing.

All of these tools are a pleasure to look at and to hold. Merchants would never paste NEW NEW NEW! signs on them in stores. Their designs are old because they work, because they serve their purpose well. Like folksongs and aphorisms and the grainy bits of language, these tools have been pared down to essentials. I look at my claw hammer, the distillation of a hundred generations of carpenters, and consider that it holds up well beside those other classics—Greek vases, Gregorian chants, *Don Quixote,* barbed fishhooks, candles, spoons. Knowledge of hammering stretches back to the earliest humans who squatted beside fires chipping flints. Anthropologists have a lovely name for those unworked rocks that served as the earliest hammers. "Dawn stones" they are called. Their only qualification for the work, aside from hardness, is that they fit the hand. Our ancestors used them for grinding corn, tapping awls, smashing bones. From dawn stones to this claw hammer is a great leap in time, but no great distance in design or imagination.

On that iced-over February morning when I smashed my thumb with the hammer, I was down in the basement framing the wall that my daughter's gerbils would later hide in. I was thinking of my father, as I always did whenever I built anything, thinking how he would have gone about the work, hearing in memory what he would have said about the wisdom of hitting the nail instead of my thumb. I had the studs and plates nailed together all square and trim, and was lifting the wall into place when the phone rang upstairs. My wife answered, and in a moment she came to the basement door and called down softly to me. The stillness in her voice made me drop the framed wall and hurry upstairs. She told me my father was dead. Then I heard the details over the phone from my mother. Building a set of cupboards for my brother in Oklahoma, he had knocked off work early the previous afternoon because of cramps in his stomach. Early this morning, on his way into the kitchen of my brother's trailer, maybe going for a glass of water, so early that no one else was awake, he slumped down on the linoleum and his heart quit.

For several hours I paced around inside my house, upstairs and down, in and out of every room, looking for the right door to open and knowing there was no such door. My wife and children followed me and wrapped me in arms and backed away again, circling and staring as if I were on fire. Where was the door, the door, the door? I kept wondering. My smashed thumb turned purple and throbbed, making me furious. I wanted to cut it off and rush outside and scrape away the snow and hack a hole in the frozen earth and bury the shameful thing.

I went down into the basement, opened a drawer in my workbench, and stared at the ranks of chisels and knives. Oiled and sharp, as my father would have kept them, they gleamed at me like teeth. I took up a clasp knife, pried out the longest blade, and tested the edge on the hair of my forearm. A tuft came away cleanly, and I saw my father testing the sharpness of tools on his own skin, the blades of axes and knives and gouges and hoes, saw the red hair shaved off in patches from his arms and the backs of his hands. "That will cut bear," he would say. He never cut a bear with his blades, now my blades, but he cut deer, dirt, wood. I closed the knife and put it away. Then I took up the hammer and went back to work on my daughter's wall, snugging the bottom plate against a chalkline on the floor, shimming the top plate against the joists overhead, plumbing the studs with my level, making sure before I drove the first nail that every line was square and true.

Questions About Strategy

1. How does Scott Russell Sanders use the opening and closing scenes to establish and resolve the conflicts in his plot?
2. How does Sanders mix summary and scene to interpret the significance of the tools?
3. How does Sanders's selection of details—his smashed thumb, his daughter's gerbils, his father's tools—enrich and advance the purpose of his essay?

A Sampler of Other Essays

1. Jane Graham, "Watching Whales" (student essay), p. 121
2. John McPhee, "Grizzly," p. 123
3. Edwin Way Teale, "Knothole Cavern," p. 246
4. Patricia Hampl, "Prague," p. 272

STRATEGY TWO: *Process Analysis*

Selecting Your Subject

Because a *process* is an operation that moves through a series of steps to bring about a desired result, you could consider almost any procedure—from brushing your teeth to investing in the stock market—a possible subject. But selecting the appropriate subject for a process analysis essay requires some planning. You should know your subject thoroughly so that you can divide it into steps and analyze its movement from beginning to end. You should also select a process that you can analyze effectively in an essay—brushing your teeth is too simple; investing in the stock market is too complex. And finally you should select a subject whose individual steps and final results require thoughtful analysis and evaluation.

Analyzing Your Audience

When you write a process analysis essay, you must think carefully about your audience. First, you need to decide whether you are writing *to* an audience or *for* an audience. If you are writing to an audience, you can address your readers directly: "If you want to send a message by E-mail, follow these four steps." If you are writing *for* an audience, you may want to assume a more formal point of view: "Although many Americans say they are interested in computers, few know how computers work." Second, you need to determine how much your readers know about the process you intend to analyze. Your decision to write about the process suggests that you are an expert. If you suspect your readers are also knowledgeable, you can write your analysis with certain assumptions. For example, if you are writing about E-mail, you can assume that you don't need to define it or explain why someone would want to use it. On the other hand, if you think that your intended audience knows almost nothing about a process, you can take nothing for granted: You will need to define E-mail, explain its purpose, and inch your way through an analysis of how it works.

Determining Your Purpose

Usually you write a process analysis to accomplish one of two purposes: *to give directions* or *to provide information.* In the first case you want to help your readers do something they want to do (record a television program on a VCR). In the second case you want to satisfy your readers' curiosity about some process they'd like to know about but are unlikely to perform (repair a television satellite). You might also write a process analysis to demonstrate that a task that looks difficult is really easy (operating a cellular phone) or that a task that looks easy is really complex (installing an answering machine).

Using the Strategy

The best way to organize a process analysis essay is to follow these five steps.

1. Overview
2. Special Terms
3. Sequence of Steps
4. Examples
5. Results

The first two steps help your readers understand the process, the next two show the process in action, and the last helps them evaluate its final results.

Begin your analysis with an *overview* of the whole process. Such an overview includes (1) defining the objective of the process, (2) identifying (and numbering) the steps in the sequence, (3) grouping small steps into larger organizational units, and (4) calling attention to those steps or units that are crucial to the success of the procedure and therefore require the most detailed analysis.

Each process has its own *special terms* for tools, tasks, and methods. You can define these at the beginning, so your readers will recognize them when you use them later. Or you can define when you introduce them. Your readers may have difficulty remembering new terminology out of context, so it's often easier to define your terms throughout the course of the essay, pausing to explain their special meaning when you use them in your analysis.

You must present your process analysis in a clear *sequence of steps*. Such a presentation interprets the reason for each step and, where appropriate, provides the following advice:

1. *Do not omit any step.* A sequence is a sequence because all steps depend on one another. Omitting a step can have disastrous consequences.

2. *Do not reverse steps.* A sequence is a sequence because each step must be performed in a necessary and logical order. Reversing steps is not an option if you want to obtain the desired result.

3. *Suspend certain steps.* Occasionally, a series of steps must be suspended, and another completed, before the sequence can resume.

4. *Do not overlook steps within steps.* Every sequence has a series of smaller steps buried within each step. Make sure your readers understand how these little, unstated steps contribute to the process.

5. *Avoid certain steps.* It is often tempting to try out steps that appear logical but are in fact harmful. As an expert, you have the task of alerting your readers to the consequences of modifying the process with such innovations.

You may want to use several kinds of *examples* to illustrate the steps in the process. You can use graphs, charts, and blueprints to outline the operation. You can clarify the process by using examples from your own experience or the experience of experts. Such testimony offers you the opportunity to suggest shortcuts or *variations* in the process you are analyzing. You can help your readers understand a complex process by *comparing* it to a similar and simpler process they already know.

Although your analysis will tend to focus on the movement of the process through its various steps, you should also try to establish criteria for evaluating the final *results*. You can move to this last step by asking two questions:

1. How do you know it's done? and

2. How do you know it's good?

Anatomy of a Garage Band | Rob Sturma

Introduction: Establish reader's interest in process

S omebody famous once said something about music having charms to soothe somebody, or something like that. This makes sense. If you take a look at any community, whether it be a sprawling metropolis, a college town, or your little neck of the woods, somebody out there is making music. The reasons are varied: some people enjoy the sense of community it brings, some find that it helps them to express their feelings, and, well, some just think it's cool. Admit it, somewhere in your deepest, primordial urges exists the need to hammer away on a cheap guitar and bring a basement full of enthralled party-goers to some form of screaming frenzy. The need to satisfy this urge is why you, my friend, must join a garage band. So let's get to it.

Overview: Define the garage band

Examples: Illustrate with Lovejunkies

For those uninitiated into the ragtag world of rock 'n' roll, some definitions must be set. A garage band is a loose amalgamation of people you know or meet who fancy themselves musicians, and with or without the incentive of fame or fortune, choose to form a collective in which they can produce the liberating sounds that we know homogeneously as rock 'n' roll. In layman's terms, it's a bunch of dudes who want to jam. We'll take a look at one particular band of this ilk, the Lovejunkies, and follow them through the steps of achieving garage-band status. The Lovejunkies play what they call "college-pop," which ranges from alternative rock to universally embraced cover tunes to sophomoric '70's heavy metal (this is known within the garage world as "manly rock" for obvious lyrical reasons; see "Cooper, Alice").

Overview: Identify and number first step

According to these local veterans, your first step to amplified bliss is getting your band together. Best friends and roommates are always a good jump-off point, and from there it's a matter of filling in the musical blanks, as it were. Enlisting the talents of a specialist is not always an easy task; when the Lovejunkies needed a new drummer, their ideal choice was an accomplished musician, but they advertised realistically for someone "who will show up for rehearsal." This can turn out okay, though. You may be pleasantly surprised by the sounds emanating from your first jam session. If not, well, that's what rehearsal is for.

Sequence of Steps: Suspend one step to complete another

Before you delve into the rehearsal process and all that goes with it, you must make sure that your band's name will leave its imprint on the world. Creativity counts; no points are awarded for using another band's name. Let's face it, a band called The New Beatles leave themselves little room for creative expansion. Citing your influences is okay, though; the Lovejunkies' lead singer Joe dug the bands Love Cowboys and the Cowboy Junkies. See how simple it can be? He took out the "cowboy," and voila! Like the phoenix, a new band emerges. Feel free, though, to use any appropriate method to dub your ensemble. Names like Freaks of Nature, Neurotic Box, Wishful Thinking, and The Uninvited are all monickers that help to bring a clearer picture of their namesakes' stylistic contributions. Remember, if the New Fast Automatic Daffodils can nominally exist, nothing is too far-fetched.

At this point, let's assume that your posse of players has been assembled. You've got some drums, a bass, a few guitars, and somebody who likes to refer

1

2

3

4

5

*Special Terms: Intro-
duce and define special
terminology*

to him or herself as a "vocal stylist" (this is the proper term as the word "singer" often has little to do with a garage band. See "Pistols, Sex"). A prudent direction to take would be to decide what type of music you'll be indulging in. The Lovejunkies, as already mentioned, play "college-pop," which is an appropriate choice for their target college audience. Go figure. Some of their tunes can range in musical style, but be warned. As exciting as stylistic fusion can be, an AC/DC drum line does not always fare well coupled with a Police guitar riff and an R.E.M. vocal (if that last sentence seems far too buried in subreference, then perhaps you should think about forming a polka band instead). As everyone's tastes will forever vary, you will learn that the term "creative differences" significantly figures into the rehearsal process. If all else fails, a rousing rendition of "Louie, Louie" is always a crowd pleaser.

*Sequence of Steps: Do
not omit certain steps*

Let's assume, then, that your band has established their style. You might   6
do well to assemble a set list, or a list of songs that you plan to practice and practice and practice and eventually perform and then practice some more. You must, I repeat, must, love these songs, for just as your audiences begin to share your aesthetic enthusiasm, you will begin to hate them. Get used to this, as part of paying your musical dues consists of driving the same ten to twenty songs into the ground. Your audience may not know art, but they know what they like. Suffer.

Intertwined within the set list dilemma lies the age-old question: Are we a   7
cover band, or do we do originals? Well, wake up, silly. Cover bands make money. Never presume that anyone wants to hear your silly little songs when they could listen to "My Sharona" for the two-thousandth time. Nothing against "My Sharona," mind you. Songs become popular for a reason. I digress, however.

*Sequence of Steps: Do
not overlook certain
steps*

The path to garagedom, as chosen by the Lovejunkies, has been to become   8
a cover band (i.e., "gig-getters") who occasionally play an original song or two (i.e., "Hey, this ain't Free Bird"). Then, as their popularity grew, they managed to sneak more and more originals into their set. Subversive? Yes, but someone needs to enlighten the masses.

Your other option, of course, is to scrap all of that advice and just kick out   9
your own jams. It's your creative life, friend.

*Sequence of Steps:
Summarize first
process (forming the
band); introduce
related process
(employing the band)*

Okay, now let's take a little inventory. You have a band (well, most of the   10
time, y'see, because your lead guitarist can only rehearse on Wednesday and that's a bad night for your bass player), you've got a slammin' name (so maybe it's been changed a few times, but "The Pat Sajak Experience" wasn't the image you needed anyway), and you have a vast array of songs (except I guess you'll have to drop "Layla" because your drummer insists on playing it reggae style). Let's get some gigs—er, excuse me, procure some performance dates. The secret to your success? Beats the heck out of me. I've heard bands who can't play a lick get booked into every venue in town, while others with genuine talent are shoved into playing nonstop basement parties and charity shows. If it's about anything, I guess, it's about promotion.

*Sequence of Steps:
Explain hidden steps*

1. Contact clubs

This is the point where you or someone who fancies themself your man-   11
ager begins to visit every bar, restaurant, or club in town that supports and books live bands. Make sure, or course, that it's not a theme bar, as restless country music fans will not appreciate your killer interpretation of David Bowie material. So, appropriate venue established, do your best to bother the folks in charge of booking bands. Bug 'em, bug 'em, and bug 'em some more.

Your only weapons are some kind of publicity package (usually a band photo and maybe a little something about yourselves) and some form of demo tape (about 4 or 5 songs, recorded any way possible. The Lovejunkies did one on a four-track mixer in Joe's living room). Ninety percent of the time, persistence pays off. If not, hey, keep trying. The only thing more important than persistence is the unrivaled ability to wear down your opponent. And who says rock 'n' roll isn't a contact sport?

Let's say, for the sake of the narrative, that you now have a place to play. 12 You've almost reached your larger goal and I have but one word for you: flyers.

2. Produce publicity

Familiarize yourself with the local copy shop, as they will be the people 13 giving you more for your advertising dollar. After you have designed your provocatively eye-catching yet chock full of all pertinent information-type 8 1/2" × 11" flyer, you will be spending all kinds of money you don't have copying said flyer onto hundreds of once again eye-catching yet not too brightly colored so as to be distracting pieces of paper. Yes, I said hundreds. You will then proceed to tape, staple, hand out, and otherwise rid yourself of these relatively cheap advertisements. Saturation of your market is essential, as half of your flyers will be torn down and/or thrown away. Don't be offended by this; after all, you are being noticed.

Results: How do you know it's done?

Whew. You've made it through the toughest parts of your ascendance to 14 local stardom; now you need only to perform, bask in your 15 minutes of fame, and start the process all over again. At best, you will over time establish your band as a crowd-pleaser and a fresh, new talent. At worst, you'll never even hit the stage because yet another member has quit to pursue a solo career playing his unique brand of acoustic funk. Problems will inevitably occur. You may not always get paid. You may have to borrow an amplifier from that metal band that you hate. You may have a serious debate, as did Tim, the Lovejunkies' guitarist, whether or not to use your grocery money for guitar strings. Will you let these petty things drag you down? Will you be defeated? Heck, no, you shout. And well you should.

Sequence of Steps: Avoid certain steps

Results: How do you know it's good?

You have become part of a larger family, and the music binds you together. 15 It doesn't matter whether you've been trying to hold one band together for five years (see "Lovejunkies, The"), or whether you've been in seven different bands in the past three months (see "Former Members of the Lovejunkies, Many"). The need to play is bigger than you, than your garage band; it's bigger than you ever dreamed. I think that the rock legends KISS put it best when they made the proclamation, "God gave rock 'n' roll to you." See? It's unavoidable. You're trapped.

So, to paraphrase somebody famous who once said something some time 16 ago; it's time to plug in, turn up, and rock out. If you're really good, fantastically original, or just plain lucky, somebody who's not famous may someday recognize you as somebody who is . . . or something like that.

How to Get a Job as a "Swing Dancer" in a Hit Broadway Show | Bob Evans

After a musical has opened in New York and has had the rare privilege of getting unanimous raves from the critics, everyone from the producers, writers, and directors right on down to the chorus relaxes to bask in the sunlight of critical acceptance, public support, and financial gain.   1

The dancers, especially, enjoy the hit in a strange sort of way. They immediately go back to the strenuous activity of daily jazz and ballet classes, masochistically stretching and twisting in order to stay in shape for auditions when this show eventually closes. After the strenuous activity of daytime classes, the theatre often becomes a place to rest up and recuperate for tomorrow's classes. Out come the magazines, books, knitting, and small change for poker games, and even possibly TV with the sound turned way down; the whole thing takes on the atmosphere of a USO.   2

At this point the management, in the flush of success, decides that it can afford an extra dancer to cover the possibility that dancers will be out sick from time to time. Now, as a rule, dancers are never sick during the rehearsal and out-of-town tryout periods unless they have fallen out of a window or been run over, but once the show is back in New York for a long run, illness becomes really fashionable. This extra dancer is known in the trade as a "swing dancer." It takes a good dancer to fill the job because it requires the ability to dance every position in every number and adjust to a variety of partners. Also, it means no cocktails before coming to work nights.   3

The management informs Equity, the theatrical union, to notify its members of an audition, but they are not told the nature of the job so that the turnout will be full strength. The inference is that the audition will be for the much-treasured straight replacement in the show, but word usually leaks out anyway that it's for the swing job. Regardless of that, everyone goes for the simple reason that everyone needs a job.   4

There are usually seventy-five to a hundred eager perspirants for this one position, stretching, kicking, and limbering up all over the stage. (Actually, both a boy and a girl are hired to cover all the dancers' steps and positions.) The step chosen for the audition is always the hardest one in the show. This movement is probably done only once in a number for, say, two measures, but at the audition the dancers get the dubious privilege of doing it over and over again all afternoon in a cold and dim theatre. After anywhere from three to five grueling hours of elimination, interspersed with occasional line-ups to see who is still standing (similar in method to the longshoremen's shape-up), a dancer is picked and told the job is his. He accepts, of course, because all that torture has convinced him how lucky he was to be picked out of all those other good dancers who were also tearing themselves limb from limb to get the job.   5

Evans, Bob. "How to Get a Job as a 'Swing Dancer' in a Hit Broadway Show." *Harper's Magazine* January 1965: 28–31.

The dancers with whom the swing boy will be working can be divided into roughly two groups. Group one becomes entrenched like wood ticks on a hunting dog for a long run in the show. To qualify for this group you must eventually bring some or all of the following items to the theatre: coffee, tea, sugar, powdered milk, spoons, knives and forks, glasses and cups, hot plates, coffee pots, extra umbrellas and rubbers, aspirin, toothpaste and brush, mouthwash, all shaving things, books, magazines, foam-rubber cushions, plus any other creature comforts that the theatre lacks. Often these dressing rooms wind up being more comfortable and convenient than apartments. When the show closes it usually takes two or three trips with a couple of suitcases to clean the dressing table off. **6**

Group two is made up of the "I can't wait to get the hell out of this show" type who has been bored with the show practically from the first day of rehearsal. Since these individuals consider their talents wasted and/or ignored, they don't "dig in" so they won't have too much to cart away when they make a hasty exit out of the present hit into a brand-new flop. They shave at home and bring coffee in containers. Their dressing room table is bare save for makeup and possibly a few essentials such as framed photos of themselves and perhaps the *New York Times* crossword puzzle so that they don't have to talk to anybody in the dressing room. Downstairs in the "recreation area," which is really the basement of the theatre, Group one has taken all the chairs and the well-lit areas. At the same time Group two is going around driving everyone to distraction with anarchy and insurrection. This is the grim, battle scarred atmosphere that the swing boy walks into. **7**

Your first evening you report to the theatre in your best suit, which you hope is still in style, as you will no doubt go out front to watch the show. While you wait backstage, the girl dancers smile at you sweetly and say good evening, for no one except the stage manager stands around backstage with a suit on and so they think you must be someone important from the front office. When they find out you're just the extra dancer they all relax again and lose themselves in reveries of self-appreciation. **8**

Under normal conditions it would be a lot of fun to go out front and watch a Broadway show free, but right now the only thing on your mind is to find out how hard the dancing is and hope that there aren't any acrobatic tricks or lifts you can't do. Everything else in the show, including the principals and the plot, is unimportant. All that counts is eight dancing boys and their partners, to watch all at once. If the first act is loaded with hard dances, you think maybe you can just quietly disappear during the intermission and never be heard from again. If the dancing hasn't scared you away, you go up to the dressing room after the curtain where everyone will ask you how you liked the show. What is really meant by this is "How was I?" and you should have some compliments ready because each dancer is sure that he is as exciting on stage as Jack the Ripper would be at the Annual Streetwalkers' Picnic. It's always a good idea to get as many people as you can on your side in the beginning, because you'll need them later on when your popularity wanes. **9**

The next night you are introduced to the wardrobe mistress, the threat of the threads. She didn't especially like you even before she met you. Nothing personal, of course, but the swing boy creates a new problem for her. He must have costumes to cover every dance possibility, and the management has suggested that she whip up a complete wardrobe out of the stuff discarded from numbers and finales out of town. Since the management doesn't expect to see a **10** bill for new costumes up at the office it doesn't get one, because the wardrobe mistress wants to be sure the firm considers her for their new show next year. All in all, this puts quite a strain on her as she usually hasn't any dancers' costumes left over, but there always seem to be plenty of overly large singers' costumes which are destined to make the new boy look like the comedy relief in the show. Everything is basted; they're afraid to cut material since the swing boy may not work out and the next one may be taller or something.

From rehearsal days to the time the show opens in New York there have   11
been so many changes in the numbers that the dance captain is often as confused as the swing boy because he hasn't had a chance to see what the other dancers have been doing behind his back for three months. Naturally, you learn the dance captain's part first until he can find out what the rest of the dancers have been up to. The best way for him to find out is to call a rehearsal, the purpose of which is supposed to be for you to learn all the parts, but actually the dance captain is so busy asking everybody one by one, "Now exactly what movement are you doing on this count?" that you never get to do any of the parts. But you've got an ace in the hole. You have gone to the five-and-ten and bought yourself a jumbo-size notebook and you are diligently writing down every movement and/or count, or a least you had better be doing it because these notes may be your only contact with reality and may save your life when the time comes . . . providing you can dope out what you have written down.

After a few weeks of watching and a whole notebook full of counts, half of   12
which are all wrong, the inevitable happens. When you arrive at the theatre one evening, a half-hour early to be on the safe side, before you even sign in, you're hit with the news that you're on tonight. Naturally the boy who is out is the one you haven't been watching and you haven't the vaguest idea what he does or where he goes in the numbers. Eighty pages of counts and positions, and not one page for the sick dancer, who is out because he wants to catch a television show he danced on that was taped during the past summer. Incidentally, when some of the more considerate dancers feel they are going to be out, say for a matinee, they give you a hint by coughing and trying to look ill the night before so that you can watch them on stage and not be caught the next evening with your notes down.

It's very exciting for the whole cast when the swing boy is going on for the   13
first time. It gives them something to look forward to that evening. The rest of the dancers arrive and tell you that everything is going to be fine and that you will be just great, which is about as honest as an income-tax return. After putting on a very bad makeup, with one eyebrow penciled in thicker than the other, you rush down to the basement to get into your basted singer's costume because you're going to rehearse three lifts with one girl or one lift with three girls—it really doesn't matter anymore since it's already too late to learn anything. The first girl says something like this, which is supposed to be reassuring but which really makes you feel helpless:

"Don't worry about a thing, honey; all you have to do is just grab me and   14
I'll do all the rest."

You're dispensable, right off the bat! After three minutes of practicing five   15
lifts, or five minutes of practicing three lifts, you stand there with a possible double hernia while the girls leave with such reassuring phrases as, "It'll be great." "Don't be afraid, you won't drop me, only please be careful of that right thumb you sprained in rehearsal . . . it's still very sore." "Good luck, honey"

(with a kiss thrown back). As soon as they reach the dressing room, the first one rolls her eyes and says, "Boy, what a night this is going to be!" The other one says, "Yeah, well, I'm glad my folks saw the show last week." The third one says, "Oh, boy, are my ribs going to be sore tomorrow."

I guess we don't have to go into the details of the performance because it happens just the way everyone expected, only worse. It doesn't seem to work out like that classic Ruby Keeler movie where you're brilliant going on for the first time and everyone just loves you for saving the show. What happens is this: When you aren't counting out loud, you're looking for the girl you're supposed to be lifting right this second, who looks entirely different with her stage makeup on. You can't find anybody because all the girls are dressed alike except for different lace work at the hem of their costumes which you probably couldn't see even if you weren't nervous, so you run to a girl singer instead of your partner and try to lift her. The leading man, who is singing stage center right in the way of all the dancers, hasn't seen you at all up until this minute, and he muffs a lyric trying to figure out who the new singer is and why he's dancing in the number in the first place. If you don't kick the leading lady, who is in the way also, you will at least muss up her intricate hour-and-a-half hairdo as you go flying past. All during this your basted singer's costume is coming apart at the seams. At the blackout at the end of the number, someone luckily pulls you back out of the way of the fast-falling, one-and-a-half-ton curtain, but you get smashed anyway by an avalanche of stagehands rushing onstage to clear the set in the dark. **16**

Back in the dressing room, the hollow consolation of the other dancers ring all around you: "That was great for the first time. Nobody could have done better." "The audience doesn't know what's going on in the dance numbers anyway. They'd never catch all those little goofs you were making. Maybe the only one they really did see was when your shoe flew off into the orchestra pit after you cartwheeled the wrong way into the desk." "I guess I shouldn't have told you the choreographer was out front watching. It didn't make you nervous, did it? He probably wasn't even watching you." **17**

After the show, the swing boy either goes home to sulk in front of the television set with a beer, or else he goes all out and gets potted at some bar. So the next time you see a dancer at a bar loaded and babbling incoherently, please be tolerant. It is just possible that he is a swing boy and he really isn't celebrating anything. **18**

Questions About Strategy

1. What kinds of information does Bob Evans provide in his overview section?
2. How does Evans illustrate the sequence of steps that the swing dancer must follow to prepare himself for the performance?
3. How does Evans evaluate the difference between successful practice and performance?

A Sampler of Other Essays

1. Wallace Armstrong, "Brandon's Clown" (student essay), p. 20
2. P. J. O'Rourke, "Third World Driving Hints and Tips," p. 268

3. Annie Dillard, "Total Eclipse," p. 248

4. Richard Selzer, "The Knife," p. 220

STRATEGY THREE: *Comparison and Contrast*

Selecting Your Subject

As you shop around for subjects, you will find that you can compare anything from the trivial (regular gum with sugarless gum) to the really serious (a career as a doctor with a job in a pharmaceutical company). Technically speaking, when you *compare* you are looking for similarities; when you *contrast* you are looking for differences. In practice, the operations are part of the same process. When you look for what's similar, you will also notice what's different. The challenge in selecting a subject for such analysis is to avoid what is commonly called the "so-what" problem. You can always make a list of differences and similarities. This is blue; that's red. This is round, that's square. So what! To convert a list of comparisons into a comparison and contrast essay, you need to see your subject as part of a larger project—to demonstrate that one object is better than another or to reveal a particular relationship between two objects.

Analyzing Your Audience

As you plan a comparison and contrast essay, think about what your readers already know and what they expect to learn. If you're confident that your readers know a lot about the items you are comparing (two television shows), you can spend less time on pointing out similarities and more time on your reasons for making the comparison. When your readers know little about the items (two Chinese folktales), you'll have to describe each, using examples they are familiar with before you can point out important contrasts. If your readers know about only one item in the pair (the American film, but not the French film on which it was based), then use the familiar item to describe the unfamiliar. As you think about what your readers expect, remember they want your essay to be fairly balanced, not 90 percent on the American film and 10 percent on the French film. When your essay is so unbalanced, you will disappoint your readers who expect to learn about both items being compared.

Determining Your Purpose

You can take two approaches to writing comparison and contrast essays; each has a different purpose. When you write a *strict* comparison, you compare only those things in the same category—actors with actors, musicians with musicians, but not actors with musicians. Although subjects often inhabit several categories at the same time, your purpose is to find what your subjects have in common. For example, how are jazz musicians and classical musicians alike, even if their music is quite different? Often, in a strict comparison, your purpose is to make a judgment and a choice. When you write a *fanciful* comparison, you try to compare in an imaginative, illuminating way, two things that don't seem at all alike. You can use such comparisons to help your readers understand a complex idea (how a highway system and the new computer networks are alike) or to expand their concept of your subject (how the increased use of drugs is an epidemic). You may find it difficult to sustain a fanciful comparison for a whole essay. But you can construct such a comparison to help your readers see new connections between unlike things.

Using the Strategy

You can use two basic strategies for organizing a comparison and contrast essay. With the *divided* or *subject-by-subject* pattern, you present all your information on one topic before introducing information on the other topic. With the *alternating* or *point-by-point* pattern, you work your way through the comparison point by point, giving information on one aspect of the first topic, then on the same aspect of the other topic.

Although both methods are useful, you'll discover that each has weaknesses. The divided pattern works especially well in short essays, where your reader can easily keep track of your points. Its weakness, however, is that you can slip into writing two separate essays. The alternating pattern works well when you want to show the two subjects side by side according to their points of comparison. You'll find it particularly useful in longer essays when you want to discuss many complex points of comparison. Its weakness is that it may reduce your analysis to exercise, encouraging you to compose a simple list.

Often you can make the best of both worlds by *combining strategies*. For example, you could start with a divided pattern to give a unified, overall view of each subject, then shift to an alternating pattern to illustrate the larger purpose of your comparison. Or you could establish the points you want to make using the alternating pattern and then move on to a longer, detailed analysis of each topic.

To write a successful comparison and contrast essay, keep three guidelines in mind:

1. *balance* the various selections of your comparison;

2. *include reminders,* such as transitional phrases and sentences, to help your readers connect the points of your comparison; and

3. *supply reasons* to support your purpose and to explain why you are making the comparison.

Same Goal/Different Plan | Kris Modlin

*"*B*id 'em if you got 'em!"*   1

Pattern: Establish points of comparison

My brother's exasperated encouragement rings in my ears each time we   2
play euchre. He believes in decisive action. I believe in deliberate choices.

"Don't rush me. I'm thinking."   3

My reply is as predictable as his command. I like to mull over my options.   4

Purpose: Contrast differences in politics and religion with similarity of objective

Whenever my family gets together for birthdays, Mother's Day, Labor   5
Day, or Christmas, we play cards, most often doubledeck bid euchre. Once, I
don't remember exactly when, we drew for partners. Somehow my brother and
I, so different in our political and religious beliefs despite our similar upbringing, became a team challenging my mother and sister-in-law. To our great surprise the pairing clicked, making us an almost unbeatable twosome. When we
can concentrate on winning rather than tiptoeing around our opposing opinions, my brother and I bridge our differences and recreate the closeness of our
childhood.

Pattern:
A. Politics
1. Brother

Sixteen years older than I and the hero of my childhood, my brother reigns   6
as our family's political black sheep. His conservative accountant mind
embraces enthusiastically every plank of the Republican platform. He believes
individual states run best with little or no interference from the federal government, an odd stand for the great-great-grandson of a Quaker abolitionist active
in the Underground Railroad and the grandson of a depression farmer whose
lands were saved by FDR's moratorium on loan interest. Still, my brother
praises corporate tax breaks because they stimulate the economy and de-
nounces military cutbacks because they endanger our country.

2. Writer

So, to maintain peaceful coexistence, I rarely discuss politics with him,   7
partially because some vestige of hero worship remains, but mostly because I
envision a world more closely aligned with the liberal ideals of the Democratic
party—a vision shared by most of my other relatives. I believe the federal government should legislate equality in all states and place people before economics. Thus, I condemn our present tax structure that forces the middle class to
pay a higher percentage of their income than the rich do, and I support balanc-
ing the federal budget by halting military buildups rather than cutting free
lunch programs for needy school children.

B. Religion
1. Brother

My brother's conservatism also permeates his religion. The fundamental-   8
ist faith he adopted provides clear, if not easy, standards to uphold such as forbidding divorce and perpetuating male dominance in the church. His literal
interpretation of the Bible, including baptism by immersion and weekly com-
munion, establishes an absolute line between black and white, between the
damned and the saved, leaving little room for gray spaces. He is not fanatical
about any of this.

He simply lives his faith, preferring to convert others by example rather   9
than by pushy sermons.

2. Writer

Although I once attended the same church as my brother, my religion has   10
grown away from his simple faith. I have no argument with the teachings of

Jesus, but I cannot accept the narrow, sexist vision of Paul nor the immense burden of guilt embedded in most Christian doctrine. I believe each person should look within her own mind and imagination, searching for a connection between herself and her world—a connection that will create a sense of responsibility, not guilt. Perhaps that search will lead to Christianity. Perhaps not.

Transition: Connect comparison to card game

Obviously, the old adage, "Don't discuss politics or religion," applies to my brother and me. But when the euchre game begins, our political and religious differences cease to matter. Our sole goal is winning, and after years of being partners, we both know how the other will play. 11

C. Card-playing style

1. Brother

He always sorts his hand without expression and then bids precisely what his cards dictate, adhering to his "bid 'em if you got 'em" philosophy. Next he analytically plays his hand, keeping track of what cards have been played and appearing to know what cards each player holds in her hand. His manner is calm. He prefers to surprise his mother and his wife by silently sneaking a trick to make his bid or to set them, which usually results in at least one of them yelling or throwing her cards at him while he laughs. 12

2. Writer

I, too, sort my cards without expression, but when bidding I often give away a good hand by sitting up straight and scooting to the edge of my chair. My risky "bid 'em if you got 'em" practice causes me to overbid my hand sometimes. I believe my partner's always good for one trick, and I'm usually right. As the hand progresses, I pull in the cards, talking faster and faster, sometimes louder and louder, drawing attention away from my brother as he sneaks in the crucial winning trick. 13

Conclusion: Supply reasons for making comparison

After each hand is played, we rehash it as the next one is dealt. What *could* we have done? What *should* we have done? Why does it matter? It does. The discussion is cards, a common interest, a sharing not often possible in the different paths our two lives have taken. Over the years, the card game has helped me respect the differences between us while still valuing our brother and sister relationship. When we do discuss politics and religion, my brother and I discover that, as in euchre, our goals are similar but our game plan differs. He's conservative. I hesitate and then take a chance. Our euchre ritual strengthens our bond, a bond we obviously didn't choose to create, but one we choose to continue. 14

Two Traditions of Storytelling | Shirley Brice Heath

In Roadville
A Piece of Truth

R oadville residents worry about many things. Yet no Roadville home is a   1
somber place where folks spend all their time worrying about money, their
children's futures, and their fate at the hands of the mill. They create numerous
occasions for celebration, most often with family members and church friends.
On these occasions, they regale each other with "stories." To an outsider, these
stories seem as though they should be embarrassing, even insulting to people
present. It is difficult for the outsider to learn when to laugh, for Roadville people seem to laugh at the story's central character, usually the story-teller or
someone else who is present.

A "story" in Roadville is "something you tell on yourself, or on your   2
buddy, you know, it's all in good fun, and a li'l something to laugh about."
Though this definition was given by a male, women define their stories in similar ways, stressing they are "good fun," and "don't mean no harm." Stories
recount an actual event either witnessed by others or previously told in the
presence of others and declared by them "a good story." Roadville residents
recognize the purpose of the stories is to make people laugh by making fun of
either the story-teller or a close friend in sharing an event and the particular
actions of individuals within that event. However, stories "told on" someone
other than the story-teller are never told unless the central character or someone who is clearly designated his representative is present. The Dee children
sometimes tell stories on their father who died shortly after the family moved
to Roadville, but they do so only in Mrs. Dee's presence with numerous positive adjectives describing their father's gruff nature. Rob Macken, on occasion,
is the dominant character in stories which make fun of his ever-present willingness to point out where other folks are wrong. But Rob is always present on
these occasions, and he is clearly included in the telling ("Ain't that right,
Rob?" "Now you know that's the truth, hain't it?"), as story-tellers cautiously
move through their tale about him, gauging how far to go by his response to
the story.

Outside close family groups, stories are told only in sex-segregated   3
groups. Women invite stories of other women, men regale each other with tales
of their escapades on hunting and fishing trips, or their run-ins (quarrels) with
their wives and children. Topics for women's stories are exploits in cooking,
shopping, adventures at the beauty shop, bingo games, the local amusement
park, their gardens, and sometimes events in their children's lives. Topics for
men are big-fishing expeditions, escapades of their hunting dogs, times they
have made fools of themselves, and exploits in particular areas of their expertise (gardening and raising a 90-lb pumpkin, a 30-lb cabbage, etc.). If a story
is told to an initial audience and declared a good story on that occasion, this

Heath, Shirley Brice. "Two Traditions of Storytelling." *Ways with Words*. New York: Cambridge
UP, 1983. 149–53; 166–69; 187–89.

audience (or others who hear about the story) can then invite the story-teller to retell the story to yet other audiences. Thus, an invitation to tell a story is usually necessary. Stories are often requested with a question: "Has Betty burned any biscuits lately?" "Brought any possums home lately?" Marked behavior—transgressions from the behavioral norm generally expected of a "good hunter," "good cook," "good handyman," or a "good Christian"—is the usual focus of the story. The foolishness in the tale is a piece of truth about everyone present, and all join in a mutual laugh at not only the story's central character, but at themselves as well. One story triggers another, as person after person reaffirms a familiarity with the kind of experience just recounted. Such stories test publicly the strength of relationships and openly declare bonds of kinship and friendship. When the social bond is currently strong, such stories can be told with no "hard feelings." Only rarely, and then generally under the influence of alcohol or the strain of a test in the relationship from another source (job competition, an unpaid loan), does a story-telling become the occasion for an open expression of hostility.

Common experience in events similar to those of the story becomes an   4
expression of social unity, a commitment to maintenance of the norms of the church and of the roles within the mill community's life. In telling a story, an individual shows that he belongs to the group: he knows about either himself or the subject of the story, and he understands the norms which were broken by the story's central character. Oldtimers, especially those who came to Roadville in the 1930s, frequently assert their long familiarity with certain norms as they tell stories on the young folks and on those members of their own family who moved away. There is always an unspoken understanding that some experiences common to the oldtimers can never be known by the young folks, yet they have benefited from the lessons and values these experiences enabled their parents to pass on to them.

In any social gathering, either the story-teller who himself announces he   5
has a story or the individual who invites another to tell a story is, for the moment, in control of the entire group. He manages the flow of talk, the staging of the story, and dictates the topic to which all will adhere in at least those portions of their discourse which immediately follow the story-telling. At a church circle meeting, many of the neighborhood women had gathered, and Mrs. Macken was responsible for refreshments on this occasion. The business and lesson of the circle had ended, and she was preparing the refreshments, while the women milled about waiting for her to signal she was ready for them. Mrs. Macken looked up from arranging cookies on a plate and announced Sue had a story to tell. This was something she could not normally have done, since as a relative newcomer, a schoolteacher, and a known malcontent in Roadville, her status was not high enough to allow her to announce a story for someone who was as much of an oldtimer as Sue. However, as the hostess of the circle, she had some temporary rank.

Roadville Text IV

Mrs. Macken:	Sue, you oughta tell about those rolls you made the other 6
	day, make folks glad you didn't try to serve fancy rolls
	today.
Mrs. Dee:	Sue, what'd you do, do you have a new recipe? 7
Mrs. Macken:	You might call it that 8
	[
Sue:	I, hh wanna =

Martha:	= Now Millie [Mrs. Macken], you hush and let Sue give us *her* story. **9**
Sue:	Well, as a matter of fact, I did have this new recipe, one I **10** got out of *Better Homes and Gardens,* and I thought I'd try it, uh, you see, it called for scalded milk, and I had just started the milk when the telephone rang, and I went to get it. It was Leona/*casting her eyes at Mrs. Macken/.* I thought I turned the stove off, and when I came back, the burner was off, uh, so I didn't think anything about it, poured the milk in on the yeast, and went to kneading. Felt a little hot. Well, anyway, put the stuff out to rise, and came back, and it looked almost like Stone Mountain, thought that's a strange recipe, so I kneaded it again, and set it out in rolls. This time I had rocks, uh, sorta like 'em, the kind that roll up all smooth at the beach. Well, I wasn't gonna throw that stuff all out, so I cooked it. Turned out even harder than those rocks, if that's possible, and nobody would eat 'em, couldn't even soften 'em in butter-milk. I was trying to explain how the recipe was so funny, you know, see, how I didn't know what I did wrong, and Sally piped up and said 'Like yeah, when you was on the phone, I came in, saw this white stuff a-boiling, and I turned it off.' (pause) Then I knew, you know, that milk was too hot, killed the yeast/*looking around at the women/.* Guess I'll learn to keep my mind on my own business and off other folks'.

The story was punctuated by gestures of kneading, turns of the head in puzzle- **11** ment, and looks at the audience to see if they acknowledged understanding of the metaphors and similes. Stone Mountain is a campground in the region which everyone at the circle meeting had visited; it rises out of the ground like a giant smooth-backed whale. The beach is a favorite summer vacation spot for Roadville families, and the women often collect the smooth rocks from the beach to put on top of the dirt in their flower pots.

Several conventions of stories and story-telling in Roadville stand out in **12** this incident. The highest status members present, Mrs. Dee and her grand-daughter Martha, reannounce Sue's story and subtly convey that Mrs. Macken stepped out of line by asking Sue to tell a story on this occasion. Within her narrative, Sue follows a major requirement of a "good story": it must be factual, and any exaggeration or hyperbole must be so qualified as to let the audience know the story-teller does not accept such descriptions as literally true. Sue qualifies her Stone Mountain description with "almost," her equation of the rolls with rocks by "sorta like 'em," and her final comparison of the rolls to rocks with "if that's possible." She attempts to stick strictly to the truth and exaggerates only with hedges and qualifications.

Perhaps the most obligatory convention Sue follows is that which requires **13** a Roadville story to have a moral or summary message which highlights the weakness admitted in the tale. "Stories" in these settings are similar to testimo-nials given at revival meetings and prayer sessions. On these occasions, indi-viduals are invited to give a testimonial or to "tell your story." These narratives are characterized by a factual detailing of temporal and spatial descriptions and recounting of conversations by direct quotation ("Then the Lord said to me:"). Such testimonials frequently have to do with "bringing a young man to his senses" and having received answers to specific prayers. The detailing of the actual event is often finished off with Scriptural quotation, making it clear that the story bears out the promise of "the Word." Sue's story is confession-like, and its summing up carries a double meaning, both a literal one ("on my own business" = cooking) and a figurative one ("on my own business" = general affairs). Any woman in the group can quote Scripture describing the sins of which the tongue is capable (for example, James 3:6 which likens the tongue to a fire which spreads evil). . . .

In Trackton
Talkin' Junk

Trackton folks see the truth and the facts in stories in ways which differ   14
greatly from those of Roadville. Good story-tellers in Trackton may base their stories on an actual event, but they creatively fictionalize the details surrounding the real event, and the outcome of the story may not even resemble what indeed happened. The best stories are "junk," and anyone who can "talk junk" is a good story-teller. Talkin' junk includes laying on highly exaggerated compliments and making wildly exaggerated comparisons as well as telling narratives. Straightforward factual accounts are relatively rare in Trackton and are usually told only on serious occasions: to give a specific piece of information to someone who has requested it, to provide an account of the troubles of a highly respected individual, or to exchange information about daily rounds of activities when neither party wishes to intensify the interaction or draw it out. Trackton's "stories," on the other hand, are intended to intensify social interactions and to give all parties an opportunity to share in not only the unity of the common experience on which the story may be based, but also in the humor of the wide-ranging language play and imagination which embellish the narrative.

From a very early age, Trackton children learn to appreciate the value of a   15
good story for capturing an audience's attention or winning favors. Boys, especially on those occasions when they are teased or challenged in the plaza, hear their antics become the basis of exaggerated tales told by adults and older children to those not present at the time of the challenge. Children hear themselves made into characters in stories told again and again. They hear adults use stories from the Bible or from their youth to scold or warn against misbehavior. The mayor captures the boys' conflict in the story of King Solomon which features a chain of events and resolution of a conflict similar to that in which they are currently engaged. Children's misdeeds provoke the punchline or summing up of a story which they are not told, but are left to imagine: "Dat policeman'll come 'n git you, like he did Frog." The story behind this summary is never told, but is held out as something to be recreated anew in the imagination of every child who hears this threat.

Trackton children can create and tell stories about themselves, but they   16
must be clever if they are to hold the audience's attention and to maintain any extended conversational space in an on-going discourse. Young children repeatedly try to break into adult discourse with a story, but if they do not succeed in relating the first few lines of their story to the on-going topic or otherwise exciting the listeners' interests, they are ignored. An adult's accusation, on the other hand, gives children an open stage for creating a story, but this one must also be "good," i.e., highly exaggerated, skillful in language play, and full

of satisfactory comparisons to redirect the adult's attention from the infraction provoking the accusation.

Adults and older siblings do not make up sustained chronological narratives specially for young children, and adults do not read to young children. The flow of time in Trackton, which admits few scheduled blocks of time for routinized activities, does not lend itself to a bedtime schedule of reading a story. The homes provide barely enough space for the necessary activities of family living, and there is no separate room, book corner, or even outdoor seat where a child and parent can read together out of the constant flow of human interactions. The stage of the plaza almost always offers live action and is tough competition for book-reading. Stories exchanged among adults do not carry moral summaries or admonitions about behavior; instead they focus on detailing of events and personalities, and they stress conflict and resolution or attempts at resolution. Thus adults see no reason to direct these stories to children for teaching purposes. When stories are told among adults, young children are not excluded from the audience, even if the content refers to adult affairs, sexual exploits, crooked politicians, drunk ministers, or wayward choirleaders. If children respond to such stories with laughter or verbal comments, they are simply warned to "keep it to yo'self." Some adult stories are told only in sex-segregated situations. Men recount to their buddies stories they would not want their wives or the womenfolk to know about; women share with each other stories of quarrels with their menfolk or other women. Many men know about formulaic toasts (long epic-like accounts of either individual exploits or struggles of black people) from visitors from up-North or men returned from the armed services, but these are clearly external to the Trackton man's repertoire, and they do not come up in their social gatherings. Instead, Trackton men and their friends focus on stories which tell of their own current adventures or recount fairly recent adventures of particular personalities known to all present. All of these are highly self-assertive or extol the strength and cleverness of specific individuals. **17**

Women choose similar topics for their stories: events which have happened to them, things they have seen, or events they have heard about. Considerable license is taken with these stories, however, and each individual is expected to tell the story, not as she has heard it, but with her own particular style. Women tell stories of their exploits at the employment office, adventures at work in the mill, or episodes in the lives of friends, husbands, or mutual acquaintances. Laced through with evaluative comments ("Didja ever hear of such a thing?" "You know how he ak [act] when he drunk." "You been like dat."), the stories invite participation from listeners. In fact, such participation is necessary reinforcement for the story-teller. Perhaps the most characteristic feature of story-telling by adults is the dramatic use of dialogue. Dovie Lou told the following story one afternoon to a group of six women sitting on the porch of Lillie Mae's house. The Henning family was transient and had been in Trackton only a few weeks. **18**

Trackton Text V

Now you know me—I'm Dovie Lou, and you may think I'ma put up wid that stuff off Hennin's ol' lady, right? Who, who, after all, gives a hoot about her—or him, for dat matter? I been here quite a while—gonna be here a time yet too. She holler off her porch "Yo man, he over in Darby Sat'day nite." I say "Shit, what you know 'bout my man? My man." It was a rainy night, you know ain't no use gettin' fussied up to go out on a night like dat. Tessie 'n I go play **19** bingo. But dat ol' woman, she ak like she some Channel Two reporter or sump'n:

> "P. B. Evans was seen today on the corner of Center and Main Street. He hadda bottle in each hip pocket, and one under his Lóndon Fóg hat. Sadie Lou [a well-known stripper in a local topless bar] was helpin' him across the street, holin' her white mink in front of him to keep his shíny shoes from gettin' wet. The weather tomorrow promises to be cloudy for some."

What she think she doin', tellin' *me/looks around to audience/*'bout my ol' man? Sayin' "He lookin' mighty fine, yes sireeeeee." (long pause) She betta keep/*casting a sharp look in the direction of the Hennings' house/*her big mouf 'n stay shut up in dat house. [20]

Throughout the story, the audience laughed, nodded, and provided "yeah," "you right," "you know it." Dovie Lou's shift to the exaggerated Standard English of the Channel Two reporter brought gales of laughter from the audience. [21]

Numerous cultural assertions are made in the story. The evaluative introduction establishes Dovie Lou as an oldtimer, a fixture in the neighborhood, and Henning and his old lady as relative newcomers. Dovie Lou announces herself a victor before the story begins. Later, she makes it clear that she knew her man, P. B. Evans, was out that night, and that she had had a chance to go out with him, but had decided it was not worth getting "fussied up" to go out in the rain. Instead, she and a girlfriend had gone to play bingo. She uses the TV report to show exaggeration, to report her man out with a famous stripper, and also to brag about the fancy dress of her man who wears name-brand clothes and has a reputation for keeping himself "fine." The final point of the story asserts that her animosity to the Henning woman is not over. Dovie Lou warns that the newcomer should stay inside and not join the neighborhood women on their porches. Once Dovie Lou's anger wears off or she is reunited with her man publicly, she can fend off Henning's wife's stories. Dovie Lou's story is based on fact: Henning's wife had said something to Dovie Lou about her man being out with another woman. But beyond this basis in fact, Dovie Lou's story is highly creative, and she ranges far from the true facts to tell a story which extols her strengths and announces her faith in her ultimate victory over both her wayward man and her "big-mouth" neighbor. . . . [22]

The Traditions of Story-Telling

People in both Trackton and Roadville spend a lot of time telling stories. Yet the form, occasions, content, and functions of their stories differ greatly. They structure their stories differently; they hold different scales of features on which stories are recognized as *stories* and judged as good or bad. The patterns of interaction surrounding the actual telling of a story vary considerably from Roadville to Trackton. One community allows only stories which are factual and have little exaggeration; the other uses reality only as the germ of a highly creative fictionalized account. One uses stories to reaffirm group membership and behavioral norms, the other to assert individual strengths and powers. Children in the two communities hear different kinds of stories, they develop competence in telling stories in highly contrasting ways. [23]

Roadville story-tellers use formulaic openings: a statement of a comparison or a question asked either by the story-teller or by the individual who has invited the telling of the story. Their stories maintain a strict chronicity, [24] with direct discourse reported, and no explicit exposition of meaning or direct expression of evaluation of the behavior of the main character allowed. Stories end with a summary statement of a moral or a proverb, or a Biblical quotation. Trackton story-tellers use few formulaic openings, except the story-teller's own introduction of himself. Frequently, an abstract begins the story, asserting that the point of the story is to parade the strengths and victories of the story-teller. Stories maintain little chronicity; they move from event to event with numerous interspersions of evaluation of the behaviors of story characters and reiterations of the point of the story. Stories have no formulaic closing, but may have a reassertion of the strengths of the main character, which may be only the opening to yet another tale of adventure.

In Roadville, a story must be invited or announced by someone other than   25
the story-teller. Only certain community members are designated good story-tellers. A story is recognized by the group as an assertion of community membership and agreement on behavioral norms. The marked behavior of the story-teller and audience alike is seen as exemplifying the weaknesses of all and the need for persistence in overcoming such weaknesses. Trackton story-tellers, from a young age, must be aggressive in inserting their stories into an on-going stream of discourse. Story-telling is highly competitive. Everyone in a conversation may want to tell a story, so only the most aggressive wins out. The stress is on the strengths of the individual who is the story's main character, and the story is not likely to unify listeners in any sort of agreement, but to provoke challenges and counterchallenges to the character's ways of overcoming an adversary. The "best stories" often call forth highly diverse additional stories, all designed not to unify the group, but to set out the individual merits of each member of the group.

Roadville members reaffirm their commitment to community and church   26
values by giving factual accounts of their own weaknesses and the lessons learned in overcoming these. Trackton members announce boldly their individual strength in having been creative, persistent, and undaunted in the face of conflict. In Roadville, the sources of stories are personal experience and a familiarity with Biblical parables, church-related stories of Christian life, and testimonials given in church and home lesson-circles. Their stories are tales of transgressions which make the point of reiterating the expected norms of behavior of man, woman, hunter, fisherman, worker, and Christian. The stories of Roadville are true to the facts of an event; they qualify exaggeration and hedge if they might seem to be veering from an accurate reporting of events.

The content of Trackton's stories, on the other hand, ranges widely, and there is "truth" only in the universals of human strength and persistence   27
praised and illustrated in the tale. Fact is often hard to find, though it is usually the seed of the story. Playsongs, ritual insults, cheers, and stories are assertions of the strong over the weak, of the power of the person featured in the story. Anyone other than the story-teller/main character may be subjected to mockery, ridicule, and challenges to show he is not weak, poor, or ugly.

In both communities, stories entertain; they provide fun, laughter, and frames for other speech events which provide a lesson or a witty display of ver-   28
bal skill. In Roadville, a proverb, witty saying, or Scriptural quotation inserted into a story adds to both the entertainment value of the story and to its unifying role. Group knowledge of a proverb or saying, or approval of Scriptural quotation reinforces the communal experience which forms the basis of Road-

ville's stories. In Trackton, various types of language play, imitations of other community members or TV personalities, dramatic gestures and shifts of voice quality, and rhetorical questions and expressions of emotional evaluations add humor and draw out the interaction of story-teller and audience. Though both communities use their stories to entertain, Roadville adults see their stories as didactic: the purpose of a story is to make a point—a point about the conventions of behavior. Audience and story-teller are drawn together in a common bond through acceptance of the merits of the story's point for all. In Trackton, stories often have no point; they may go on as long as the audience enjoys the story-teller's entertainment. Thus a story-teller may intend on his first entry into a stream of discourse to tell only one story, but he may find the audience reception such that he can move from the first story into another, and yet another. Trackton audiences are unified by the story only in that they recognize the entertainment value of the story, and they approve stories which extol the virtues of an individual. Stories do not teach lessons about proper behavior; they tell of individuals who excel by outwitting the rules of conventional behavior.

Questions About Strategy

1. How does Shirley Brice Heath use the phrases "A Piece of Truth" and "Talkin' Junk" to divide the two types of storytelling she compares?

2. What observations does she make about the context and the Roadville and Trackton texts?

3. How does Heath use the alternating pattern to establish the larger purpose of her comparison in the section titled "The Traditions of Story-Telling"?

A Sampler of Other Essays

1. Jill Taraskiewicz, "The Recycling Controversy" (student essay), p. 465
2. Marie Winn, "Television and Reading," p. 46
3. Suzanne Britt Jordan, "The Lean and Hungry Look," p. 73
4. Mary Field Belenky *et al.*, "What Does a Woman Need to Know?", p. 373

STRATEGY FOUR:
Division and Classification

Selecting Your Subject

To find a suitable subject for a division and classification essay, you need to think about the world in terms of categories. Like the producers of the television game show "Jeopardy," you will never run out of categories, but you need to know how to divide and classify them. When you *divide*, you move downward from some concept (television news) to some system of subcategories within that concept (news, sports, and weather). When you *classify*, you move upward from specific examples (individual news commentators) to some feature they have in common (trustworthiness). Although you can select either strategy for a subject, you will find that the subjects you know best encourage you to use the strategies together. For example, you might divide a college sports program into its units (football, basketball, hockey, volleyball, etc.) and then classify these units according to their budgets (most money for football, least money for volleyball).

Analyzing Your Audience

As with any writing assignment, when you write a classification essay you need to think about what your readers already know and what they expect (or need). If you're writing on a new subject (social ceremonies in primitive societies) or explaining a specialized system (the botanist's procedure for identifying plants), your readers need precise definitions and many illustrations for each subcategory. If your readers already know how your subject is classified (G, PG, PG-13, R, NC-17, and X ratings for films), then you don't need to provide elaborate definitions, but you may want to use your illustrations to analyze whether the system works. If you're classifying rock musicians, your readers are likely to regard your system as self-enclosed—something to quibble with, but not something they're likely to use in their everyday lives. On the other hand, if you are classifying stereo equipment, your readers may want to use your system when they shop. In that case, you will need to divide your subject into all its possible categories and illustrate each category with concrete examples.

Determining Your Purpose

Your chief purpose in writing a classification essay is to *explain* how a system is organized. You might want to explain an established system, such as the Library of Congress system for classifying books. At a deeper level, however, your purpose might be to define, analyze, and justify the principle that underlies the system. You can also write classification essays to *entertain* or to *persuade*. If you classify to entertain (classifying fools, for example), you have an opportunity to be clever and witty, pointing out the dramatic features of each category and providing striking examples of each type. If you classify to persuade, however, you need to be thoughtful and reasonable, as, for example, when you try to convince your readers that a new or controversial rezoning plan for land use is superior to the one already in place.

Using the Strategy

When you write a classification essay, *divide your subject* into major categories that exhibit a common trait, then subdivide those categories into smaller units. Next, arrange *your categories* into a sequence that shows a logical or dramatic progression. Finally, *divide each of your categories*. First, show how a category is different from others, and second, discuss its most vivid examples. To make this strategy succeed, however, you must be sure that your classification system is *consistent, complete, emphatic,* and *significant.*

When you divide your subject into categories, *apply the same principle of selection to each class.* You may find this difficult if you are trying to explain an established but inconsistent system. You have only to visit a record store to realize that music is often sorted into categories that overlap and cross over. For example, a Linda Ronstadt album could be classified as *country, pop, rock, standard,* or *female vocal.* To avoid such tangles, you may decide to create your own system, as Sarah did in Chapter 4 when she classified consumers according to how much they use coupons (p. 85).

After you have divided your subject into separate and consistent categories, *make sure your division is complete.* The simplest division separates a subject into A and Not-A. Although you can use this system to tell your readers something about one category (musicians), you won't be able to tell them much about the other (nonmusicians). For this reason, you should try to exhaust your subject by finding *at least three* categories and by acknowledging those examples that won't fit into your system.

Once you have divided your subject, *arrange your categories and examples in an emphatic order.* This strategy encourages you and your readers to think of your categories in some sort of ascending order—from first to last, from simple to complex, from least expensive to most expensive. This technique helps you to show how a category changes, to demonstrate variety in similarity, to distinguish good from bad.

Finally, you need to show *the significance of your system of classification.* The strength of the classifying process is that you can use it to analyze a subject by any number of systems. Its weakness is that you are tempted to classify a subject using all kinds of trivial or pointless categories. You can classify people by their educational backgrounds, their work experience, or their significant achievements; you can also classify them by their shoe size, favorite color, or tastes in ice cream. At the least, you need to demonstrate that your system counts because it analyzes a subject according to a significant subdivision.

Listmakers | Larry Bush

Introduction: Divide subject into three categories

W hat's the big deal with lists? They are everywhere—on your refrigerator, on your computer screen, and in virtually every section of the newspaper. Somebody's always coming out with a new list of best sellers, worst picks, or top tens. Irving Wallace even wrote a book entitled *The Book of Lists.* Apparently people can't think about any subject without a list. Well, that's not entirely true. Not everybody thinks about lists in the same way. I have a list. The way I figure it, listmakers can be divided into one of three categories depending on their attitude toward lists.   1

Thesis: Establish single principle of division

Arrangement: Use numbers to establish order of classification

Category one: Casual listmakers make lists only on rare occasions. They don't make shopping lists unless they have to purchase more than twelve items. They never make Christmas lists for themselves or for others. Even when they make lists, they don't know how to use them. They forget to look at their list as they stroll through the grocery store. They never check things off their lists when they do their Christmas shopping. They often lose their lists without realizing it. And they have great difficulty reading (much less understanding) other people's lists.   3

Casual listmakers are actually proud of their "list-less-ness." They proclaim that they don't need lists to run their lives. They can make choices and solve problems without constantly consulting some piece of paper. They view those who are obsessed with lists as slaves to a silly system. When asked, they reply that they have never heard of Irving Wallace's *The Book of Lists.*   4

Completeness: List information for each category

Category two: Careful listmakers make lists for most occasions. They always make detailed shopping and Christmas lists, and they usually make daily, or at least weekly, lists of things to do. They are fairly conscientious about using lists to organize their future plans, and checking these lists to see if they have forgotten something they have planned to do. They often make a new list of things they failed to do on their old list. They like to read other people's lists because they see such systems, however trivial, as interesting and entertaining.

Careful listmakers actually need their lists. They explain that if they can   5 control their lists they can control their lives. They think (or hope) they live organized lives because they make lists. They view those who live without lists as disorganized, deficient—even irresponsible. When asked, careful listmakers admit that they have skimmed Wallace's *The Book of Lists,* but did not buy it because it wasn't on their shopping list.

Consistency: Cite Wallace's **The Book of Lists** *for each category*

Emphasis: Clarify emphatic order by arranging system by terms **casual, careful, compulsive**

Category three: Compulsive listmakers make lists for absolutely every   6 occasion. They make lists by the day, by the hour, and by the portion of the hour. They make shopping lists for their family and Christmas lists for their friends. Compulsive listmakers are always inventing new ways to use their lists. They love to write things down so they can check them off. They are at their creative best devising elaborate cross-referencing systems to keep lists of their lists. They have to read, analyze, and debate the details on other people's lists.

Compulsive listmakers cannot live without their lists. They believe that [7] lists (and those who make them) rule the world. These "listamaniacs" cannot think or learn about anything without making a list. They view the "list-less" as hopelessly and extremely lost. When asked, they confess that they had a religious experience when they found *The Book of Lists* listed in the data base of their public library. They immediately placed it on their shopping list, checked it off when they purchased it, and now hide this from their family and friends as though it were some sacred relic. They occasionally post tantalizing lists from the book on the refrigerator or the office bulletin board. They also compiled a list of all the people to whom they have given copies of the book and a list of their reactions to it—subdivided into two smaller lists of those people who 1. liked it and 2. loved it.

Significance: Point to significance of system by illustrating how exceptions can be included

Not everyone falls into one of these three categories. Although most [8] people like lists because they represent the orderly way they think they think—top to bottom, first to last—there are people who seem to think in other patterns. According to Wallace, these "holistic" thinkers can be listed in the following categories . . .

The Plot Against People | Russell Baker

I nanimate objects are classified into three major categories—those that don't   1
work, those that break down and those that get lost.

The goal of all inanimate objects is to resist man and ultimately to defeat   2
him, and the three major classifications are based on the method each object
uses to achieve its purpose. As a general rule, any object capable of breaking
down at the moment when it is most needed will do so. The automobile is typical of the category.

With the cunning typical of its breed, the automobile never breaks down   3
while entering a filling station with a large staff of idle mechanics. It waits until
it reaches a downtown intersection in the middle of the rush hour, or until it is
fully loaded with family and luggage on the Ohio Turnpike.

Thus it creates maximum misery, inconvenience, frustration and irritabil-   4
ity among its human cargo, thereby reducing its owner's life span.

Washing machines, garbage disposals, lawn mowers, light bulbs, auto-   5
matic laundry dryers, water pipes, furnaces, electrical fuses, television tubes,
hose nozzles, tape recorders, slide projectors—all are in league with the automobile to take their turn at breaking down whenever life threatens to flow
smoothly for their human enemies.

Many inanimate objects, of course, find it extremely difficult to break   6
down. Pliers, for example, and gloves and keys are almost totally incapable of
breaking down. Therefore, they have had to evolve a different technique for
resisting man.

They get lost. Science has still not solved the mystery of how they do it,   7
and no man has ever caught one of them in the act of getting lost. The most
plausible theory is that they have developed a secret method of locomotion
which they are able to conceal the instant a human eye falls upon them.

It is not uncommon for a pair of pliers to climb all the way from the cellar   8
to the attic in its single-minded determination to raise its owner's blood pressure. Keys have been known to burrow three feet under mattresses. Women's
purses, despite their great weight, frequently travel through six or seven rooms
to find hiding space under a couch.

Scientists have been struck by the fact that things that break down virtu-   9
ally never get lost, while things that get lost hardly ever break down.

A furnace, for example, will invariably break down at the depth of the first   10
winter cold wave, but it will never get lost. A woman's purse, which after all
does have some inherent capacity for breaking down, hardly ever does; it
almost invariably chooses to get lost.

Some persons believe this constitutes evidence that inanimate objects are   11
not entirely hostile to man, and that a negotiated peace is possible. After all,
they point out, a furnace could infuriate a man even more thoroughly by get-

Baker, Russell. "The Plot Against People." *New York Times* 18 June 1968: 46.

ting lost than by breaking down, just as a glove could upset him far more by breaking down than by getting lost.

Not everyone agrees, however, that this indicates a conciliatory attitude among inanimate objects. Many say it merely proves that furnaces, gloves and pliers are incredibly stupid. 12

The third class of objects—those that don't work—is the most curious of all. These include such objects as barometers, car clocks, cigarette lighters, flashlights and toy-train locomotives. It is inaccurate, of course, to say that they never work. They work once, usually for the first few hours after being brought home, and then quit. Thereafter, they never work again. 13

In fact, it is widely assumed that they are built for the purpose of not working. Some people have reached advanced ages without ever seeing some of these objects—barometers, for example—in working order. 14

Science is utterly baffled by the entire category. There are many theories about it. The most interesting holds that the things that don't work have attained the highest state possible for an inanimate object, the estate to which things that break down and things that get lost can still only aspire. 15

They have truly defeated man by conditioning him never to expect anything of them, and in return they have given man the only peace he receives from inanimate society. He does not expect his barometer to work, his electric locomotive to run, his cigarette lighter to light or his flashlight to illuminate, and when they don't, it does not raise his blood pressure. 16

He cannot attain that peace with furnaces and keys and cars and women's purses as long as he demands that they work for their keep. 17

Questions About Strategy

1. What principle does Russell Baker use to divide objects into three categories?

2. What does Baker accomplish by scrambling in the body of his essay the sequence of categories he presents in his opening sentence?

3. What significance does Baker attribute to his last category?

A Sampler of Other Essays

1. Ellen Haack, "A Man with All Reasons" (student essay), p. 71
2. Richard Saul Wurman, "The Five Rings," p. 44
3. Desmond Morris, "Territorial Behavior," p. 113

STRATEGY FIVE: *Definition*

Selecting Your Subject

All writing is defining. When you write about any subject, you select and connect words that have established meanings. Often, as you compose, you pause to define a special term or define the special way you intend to use a term.

When you use definition as a strategy for several paragraphs or a whole essay, however, you have usually stumbled on to a word that needs extended definition. Such words may intrigue you because they seem different (chutzpah), difficult (entropy), or vague (stress). The word *definition* comes from *de* (with regard to) and *finite* (limits). When you are selecting a subject for an extended definition, you are looking for a word whose use or misuse has raised questions or created problems for you and your readers. You hope to clarify the situation by establishing limits for what this word can and cannot mean.

Analyzing Your Audience

Before you use definition as a writing strategy, think about what your readers already know *or* think they know about the word you have selected to define. Most of your readers may already have a working definition for a word such as *class*. You need to consider these common definitions—how they have been used and misused—as you organize your essay. If you assure your readers that you are familiar with the meanings they know, you may entice them to consider your explanation of the problems these definitions have caused. Similarly, you need to be alert to the problems or questions your readers may have with your attempt to define your term. They may expect you to define other terms before they consider your definition of your term. For example, in order for your readers to follow your definition of *white-collar crime*, they may need definitions for a cluster of related words, such as *insider trading, junk bonds,* and *privilege.*

Determining Your Purpose

Your primary purpose in writing a definition is to identify the *special nature* of something. On some occasions, you will need to explain the *exact use* of a particular word or concept. If you are trying to write about a new computer software system, your purpose may be to restrict the meanings of a word such as *file* to a specific one. On other occasions, you will want to argue for the *expanded use* of a word. If you are trying to discuss a historical movement, your purpose may be to open up the use of a word such as *culture* to a variety of interpretations. On still other occasions, you will need to interpret the *conflicting uses* of a controversial word. If you are trying to analyze a social problem, your purpose may be to balance the various uses of a word such as *euthanasia* so that you don't alienate the opposing sides before you have an opportunity to present your definition.

Using the Strategy

You can select one strategy for defining or use several in combination. Perhaps the most straightforward method for defining anything is *giving examples.* This technique is as natural as a child reading *horse* or *giraffe* in its book and then pointing to the picture on the opposite page. The examples you "point" to should be concrete and cogent. If you introduce vague or unusual examples, you are likely to confuse rather than clarify your discussion.

You can also define by *analyzing qualities* or *attributing characteristics*. These methods build on the procedures followed in dictionaries and thesauruses, which define a word with similar words, or synonyms. Such methods suggest the nuances of a word and avoid the problem of circular definition. For example, to avoid definitions such as "a *charming* person is someone who has *charm*," consider how the following list of synonyms for *charming* might help you identify qualities or characteristics: *pleasant, agreeable, sensual, glamorous, poised, eloquent, tasteful.*

Two other methods that can help you define a term are *defining negatively* and *giving functions.* Most dictionaries provide *antonyms* as well as synonyms to clarify the meaning of a word. For example, you could define *charming* by discussing the meanings of *vulgar.* A more complex procedure might involve using synonyms to define negatively. That is, you could say that a *charming* person may be *sensual* but not *sexual.* Sometimes the most significant (defining) fact about a person, object, or institution is what he, she, or it does. When you define a person as *charming,* you might consider what he or she does: for example, "a charming person *anticipates, empathizes with,* and *responds to* the concerns of others."

Finally, because definition is essential to the writing process, you may find yourself combining it with other strategies. In process analysis you need to define special terms. In comparison and contrast, you need to define the differences and similarities between the subjects of your comparison. In division and classification, you need to define the subcategories you explain. And in any causal analysis or argument you must define your terms.

Depression | Sue Kirby

Introduction: Establish misunderstanding of word

Depression is a disabling illness we are reluctant to see. People of all ages and socioeconomic groups suffer from depression. Many do not seek treatment because they don't recognize the symptoms. Depression is frequently misidentified as "the blues." "You'll get over it" and "Cheer up" is what people often say to a depressed person. "Look on the bright side." The well-wisher's intent is to snap the person out of the symptoms. Attempts are often made to identify the event that caused the depression. This minimizes the depressed person's experience and implies that if he were stronger willed, he would be well. I have been clinically depressed, and I know that if all it took was wanting to get better, no one would ever be truly depressed. Although traumatic or stressful events may make an individual more vulnerable to depression, it is not the events that must be overcome.

Analyze qualities

Depression is not merely feeling unhappy or sad but a pervasive feeling of hopelessness and sadness that is unrelenting. Day in and day out most of every day the person with depression is bombarded with negative thoughts, self-doubts, and guilt. Sleep and appetite disturbances almost always accompany depression and affect the overall health of the individual with depression. The person usually has difficulty concentrating. Motivation and interest in work or activities a person once found pleasurable disappear.

Attribute characteristics

Thoughts of suicide are common and make depression a life-threatening illness. Frequently the depressed person obsesses about suicide. Because depression affects the person's ability to think clearly, logical approaches to talk the person out of suicide rarely are helpful.

Give examples

The best intervention begins with an honest assessment of the depressed person's thoughts and intents about self-harm. Simply asking the person if he has any thoughts of suicide or self-harm creates an open, honest dialogue. It is important to offer acceptance of the person's thoughts and feelings without condoning suicide as an option. Empathy can be affirming and comforting to the person. Assuring that you will assist the person to get help and work to keep your friend safe from acting upon suicidal thoughts are powerful interventions in suicide prevention.

Clarify purpose for definition

Depression can be treated. Many people suffer needlessly not only due to lack of recognition of the illness but due to stigma associated with mental illness. Although it is a common illness, people are reluctant to acknowledge they have been treated for depression; that is why I am writing this paper today. Until the Americans with Disabilities Act was enacted this year, employers readily discriminated against persons treated for a mental illness such as depression. Insurance companies rarely provide the same levels of coverage for treatment of a psychiatric illness as are allowed for other illnesses. Many physicians are reluctant to diagnose their patients with depression because of society's stigma or their own prejudices.

Conclusion: Explain that misunderstanding can be resolved

Depression can be identified and treated. By acknowledging the symptoms, we enable persons suffering with depression to get the treatment needed and make depression a visible illness.

Codependency | Carol Tavris

"Codependency" was originally a term that referred to the spouses of alcoholics, who faced specific common problems. The term quickly absorbed the disease language that was being applied to drug addicts, and from there it was only a short leap to cover "love addicts" as well. Today it seems that the codependency bug has bitten virtually everybody: relatives of alcoholics; anyone in a relationship with any sort of "holic" (foodaholic, workaholic, or sexaholic); people living with partners who are mentally disturbed, chronically ill, or, adds [Melody] Beattie, generally "irresponsible"; parents of rebellious teenagers or children with behavior problems; professionals in helping occupations, and so on.

Oddly enough for a disease that has afflicted so many victims, no one really agrees on what codependency is or defines its symptoms the same way. "There are almost as many definitions of codependency as there are experiences that represent it," says Beattie. Her own definition of a codependent person is "one who has let another person's behavior affect him or her, and who is obsessed with controlling that person's behavior." (This definition excludes only a few saints and hermits.) Codependency is "an addiction to dysfunctional love relationships," says Lynne Namka, "a preoccupation of meeting the needs of other persons to the point of feeling responsible for them at the expense of yourself."

And in a veritable flourish of psychobabble, Anne Wilson Schaef defines codependency as "a disease process whose assumptions, beliefs and lack of spiritual awareness lead to a process of nonliving which is progressive." (A disease that holds assumptions? A process of nonliving, which one apparently is mistaken in thinking means "dead," that can progress?) To Schaef, codependency is a "progressive, fatal disease" that covers up other "addictions" to sex and love.

"Some therapists," Beattie acknowledges, "have proclaimed: 'Codependency is *anything*, and *everyone* is codependent.'" This is a curious kind of disease; what physician would write a book on diabetes, saying "Diabetes is *anything*, and *everyone* is diabetic"? But codependency writers are not fazed by such matters, which they regard as defensive quibbling. If a woman is skeptical, that's more evidence that she is codependent. "Your judgmentalism," writes Schaef, "is a characteristic of the disease." If this is a disease, it's a very social one: social in manufacture and in treatment.

The vagueness of these definitions makes it easier, of course, for everyone to have at least one of the symptoms of the problem. It is the formula for wildfire fads and best-sellerdom—if everybody has the problem, everybody needs to read about the cure or join the right group. Just as they share the disease view of addiction, codependency books propose a common cure: the Alcoholics Anonymous twelve-step method, based on a "spiritual awakening" in which the sufferer hands over his or her addiction to a "Higher Power" for

Tavris, Carol. "Codependency." *The Mismeasure of Women.* New York: Simon, 1992. 193–7.

salvation. Codependency books are full of warm admonitions to forgive your-self, "celebrate your perfection," and give yourself "permission to be precious." Reading these books therefore feels somewhat like listening to friendly ser-mons that emphasize the healing power of love. They make perfect sense at the time, and the advice is undeniably good; but an hour later the reader is hungry for substance, and she may be forgiven for wondering the next day how to *implement* these wise ideas. Following the Ten Commandments is a good idea too, but history shows the regrettably human gap between knowing what you should do and being able to do it.

I do not wish to disparage any program or belief that helps people take   6
control of their lives, change bad habits, or break a cycle of abuse. And, cer-tainly, codependency programs do alert people to one key cause of their trou-bles: the network of family relationships that enmeshes them. Individuals in families are part of a pattern of reciprocal influences. When one family member takes on the role of "person with problem" (for example becoming depressed, drinking too much, not working), the spouse—wife *or* husband—will often fall into the corresponding role of rescuer and problem solver. It is helpful for peo-ple to realize that the rescuer role, born out of a natural desire to help the loved relative, can backfire, making the spouse with the problem feel less competent, more hopeless, more determined to resist help. Moreover, it is essential for people to learn to set limits on the destructive behavior of others.

But family-systems therapy, from which much of codependency language   7
derives, does not regard family conflicts and even destructive patterns of behavior as a result of individual sickness or pathology. It is normal to want to help a family member or friend in trouble; the problem arises only when a spouse becomes *excessively* involved with solving the other person's problems and stops attending to his or her own needs entirely.

The symptoms of codependency, however, do not discriminate between   8
such excessive, self-obliterating behaviors and normal caretaking or healthy selflessness. Take a close look again at the symptoms that the codependency movement wants to "cure:"

1. You "cover" for another person's bad behavior.
2. You frequently talk and worry about other people's problems instead of your own.
3. You take on more responsibility than you should in relationships.
4. You ignore your own needs to meet someone else's.
5. You worry that if you leave a relationship, the other person will fall apart.
6. Your self-esteem depends on what others say and think about you, or on your possessions or job.
7. You want to be a good person.
8. You need other people.
9. You are dependent on your relationships.
10. You are too unselfish.

The person who has these problems is familiar, all right; she is . . . the   9
stereotypic woman. The qualities of the codependent person are most of the hallmarks of the female role, writ large. They represent a blueprint of the obli-

gations a "good woman" is taught to value and enjoy, the most basic of which is caring for others. They consist of expectations for proper female behavior that form the basis of most women's self-esteem. The many men who "suffer" from needing and caring for their partners have the additional burden of worrying about their "unmanliness."

These symptoms of codependency describe traditional role relations in America. For example, Robin Norwood, in *Women Who Love Too Much*, argues that women who choose abusive or unavailable men, another apparent symptom of codependence, come from "dysfunctional" families in which the father is unavailable and the mother is inadequate. The daughter spends considerable energy trying to win her father's love by being good, helpful, ladylike, and otherwise perfect. As an adult, she pursues men who are unavailable or who treat her abusively, trying to get from them what she didn't get from her father. But if the man does love her, she loses interest. She's self-defeating to boot. 10

Certainly this description fits the experiences of many women. But is it really for the intrapsychic reason Norwood offers? The pattern of the "absent" father and the "inadequate" (i.e., submissive) mother reflects traditional sex-role patterns characteristic of most middle-class families a generation ago. Countless numbers of parents are now being blamed for "toxic" forms of child-rearing that were simply the expected way of doing things at the time. And as for girls learning to be ladylike, good, and helpful to win the "absent" father's love—well, that's what they learned to win the "present" father's love, and the mother's love, and the love of anyone else who happened to be around. It was the message of the times. Little girls were supposed to be good, period. That was their job. 11

And what does a codependent have to do to be cured? A Codependents Anonymous leaflet entitled "Ways to Become Less Dependent" reminds group members that "Independence, not dependence, promotes effective living, healthy parenting, and rewarding interpersonal relationships. Similarly, the hallmark of effective marriage is minimal fusion and optimal autonomy." A recovering codependent has learned to: 12

▼ Become independent.
▼ Be selfish without feeling guilty.
▼ Become self-reliant.
▼ Live serenely, without being hooked by the unhappiness and problems of others.
▼ Develop more of a "self."
▼ Just say no to the demands of others.
▼ Want to be loved without being needed.

Are these qualities familiar? The codependent-no-more person is . . . the stereotypic male! "For a codependent to be recovered," writer Alison Humes observes, "her heart would not leap at the sound of another's voice or at the prospect of its departure. She would not want or need to be needed. Once she had a sense of herself and others as self-sufficient human beings, and once she was in touch with all of her feelings, she would be able to find and enjoy non-addictive mature love. That this definition of 'perfection' is so resoundingly male is, of course, suitably ironic." 13

There, in a nutshell, is the fatal flaw in the codependency movement: It is   **14**
based on a model of the normalcy of men. "By labeling the traits of caretaking a
disease," Humes argues, codependency "leaves no room for a positive view of
women's abilities to take care of others." By and large, "caring too much" is
regarded as the problem, not the corresponding "illness," caring too little.
Some of the men in the codependency movement, such as Earnie Larson, do
emphasize the problems for men who are unable to express their feelings,
admit their needs, or reveal their affections. In general, however, the movement
scolds women for having the very qualities they were raised to cultivate.

Questions About Strategy

1. How does Carol Tavris give examples of other definitions to demonstrate
   the common misunderstanding of *codependency*?
2. How does Tavris use lists to analyze characteristics of the codependent
   person and the independent one?
3. How does Tavris combine her definition of codependency with her larger
   argument about gender?

A Sampler of Other Essays

1. Richard Gant, "The Meaning of Heritage in 'Everyday Use'" (student
   essay), p. 397
2. Yi-Fu Tuan, "Fear," p. 116
3. Bill Barich, "La Frontera," p. 186
4. Andy Rooney, "New Products," p. 94

STRATEGY SIX: *Causal Analysis*

Selecting Your Subject

When you look for a subject for causal analysis, you are simply being curious.
You want to find out why something happened (cause) and what results it produced (effects). Any subject you choose—from why your car won't start to
what you can see through a satellite telescope—will have multiple causes and
effects. The interrelationship between causes and effects is what makes a particular subject interesting. But to manage your subject effectively, you will
need to sort out minor or remote causes so that you can focus on the major
causes and effects you want to analyze. You will also need to decide which
part of the process seems most significant—the causes or the effects. Do you
want to explain why your car wouldn't start, or analyze what happened when
you couldn't use your car?

Analyzing Your Audience

You can assume that your readers, like you, are always curious about why something happens and what results it produces. But you cannot assume that your readers will remain curious for very long if you simply list causes or point to effects. They expect you to show them the connection—they want to know how the causal relationship works. For that reason you must consider some of the following questions: How ready are your readers to follow your analysis? What sort of context do you need to give them to help them see the significance of your subject? How much and what kind of evidence will they need to accept your assertion about the connection between the causes and effects you describe?

Determining Your Purpose

When you write a causal analysis, you're likely to have one of three purposes. Frequently, you are writing to *explain* how and why things happen. If you are trying to explain how to establish the price of a product or why you exceeded your budget, your purpose is to *isolate* specific causes and effects. At other times, you are writing to *speculate* about the possible causes or potential effects of a certain chain of events. If you are trying to speculate about a new style in fashion, your purpose is to theorize, to *expand* the range of possible causes and consequences. And of course, you can use causal analysis to *argue* that a certain relationship exists between one set of events and another. If you are trying to argue that the consumption of alcohol causes heart disease, your purpose is to acknowledge the possibility of other causal relationships before presenting your best evidence for the relationship you consider the most probable.

Using the Strategy

You can organize your causal analysis in two ways: (1) you can start with some event or idea and work backward, identifying, analyzing, and speculating about its causes; or (2) you can begin with some event or idea and move forward, theorizing, considering, or forecasting effects. Whether you decide to emphasize causes or effects, you will discover that the motion of life makes your starting point somewhat arbitrary. All causes have effects, which in turn become causes. The more efficient way to bring this process under control in your writing is to (1) state your claim early, (2) explain the connection you are attempting to demonstrate, and (3) present the evidence for connections you intend to analyze.

To write an effective causal analysis, you should also avoid the following problems.

1. *Exaggerated claim.* Don't overstate your case, particularly when you are writing about complex situations that involve people. Many plausible cause-and-effect relationships are difficult to prove conclusively, so present

your analysis as a possible explanation rather than the only explanation.

2. *Hasty generalization.* Don't oversimplify the cause-and-effect relationship. Important events are seldom the result of one simple cause, and rarely produce one simple effect. For that reason, qualify your assertions with phrases such as "a major cause," "one result," or "an immediate effect."

3. *Circular cause.* Don't chase your own tail by analyzing effects that are already imbedded in the cause. Circular readings can produce sentences such as "There weren't enough tickets for the concert because there were too many people in line."

As these problems suggest, causal analysis can be tricky. But that doesn't mean you should avoid using this strategy until you are absolutely sure of your information. You can't always wait to make an analysis or forecast. The best you can do is observe carefully, speculate intelligently, and, when appropriate, qualify your analysis.

Only Child Policy | Yili Shi

Introduction: Establish context and cause of the policy

The biggest problem facing the People's Republic of China in its attempt to build a modern socialist state is its own population. One out of every four people in the world lives in China. This enormous population of over one billion people causes incredibly complex difficulties in virtually every aspect of daily life. In 1979, the Chinese government made a dramatic step to control the growth of this population by declaring that each family could produce only one child. Given the size of the population, the speed at which it was growing, and the strains it was placing on any attempt to chart China's future, the "only child policy" seemed logical and necessary. But implementing it has caused a wide range of social and psychological problems for China's families and their children.

Thesis: Assert that policy has social and psychological effects

Analysis: Consider the immediate effect of policy on traditional family

The immediate problem was that the policy contradicted the long established values of the Chinese family. According to tradition, a family's prosperity is judged by the number of children it produces. In particular, sons are valued because they carry on the family name, cultivate and harvest the family farm, and create additional workers for the family when they marry. By contrast, daughters give up their family name when they marry, move to another place, and work for the prosperity of another family. Given such values, traditional families, especially those in rural areas, resisted the only child policy or sabotaged it by killing baby girls in the hopes that the next "only" child would be a boy.

Analysis: Consider how policy affects aging in city families

The only child policy created another set of problems for families in the city. They looked at the inevitable imbalance between old and young (4:2:1—four grandparents, two parents, and one child) and began to wonder who would take care of them in their old age. On the farm, the eldest son inherits the land and the responsibility for taking care of his parents and aging relatives. In the city, the eldest son has no land and sees his parents and grandparents as an expensive obligation. He prefers to live in his own place, or live off his parents if he can't find a place. In either case, he searches for some form of independence and submits to the wishes of his wife rather than his parents. By contrast, city girls, even after they marry, stay in close contact with their family. They ask their husbands to work for the family, donate money for clothes and food, and look after aging parents and grandparents.

Analysis: Discuss unplanned social effects of policy

Once families accepted the only child policy, they faced the problem of exceptions. What would a family do if it did not plan effectively? Rich families could pay the fine for violating the policy, but poor families would have to find some other, no doubt unpleasant, solution. And what about divorce? If a couple has one child and then decides to separate, who gets the child, who gets to produce another child, and who decides who gets what?

Analysis: Speculate about psychological effects of policy

The biggest problem caused by the implementation of the only child policy was the fear that only children will develop undesirable personalities. If a newly married couple realizes even before their child is born that this child is going to be their only child, how will this knowledge affect the way they raise the child? Will they be over-protective, over-indulgent, catering to their child's every wish and whim? If an only child grows up without siblings, without having to compete for attention and affection, how will he relate to the world outside the family?

The only child policy will be a disaster if it creates a country of self-centered, spoiled brats who do not care about their families, and who do not know how to work and play with others, much less lead their nation into the next century.

6

Conclusion: Suggest possible long-term effects caused by policy

Apparently, the result of China's only child policy will be the creation of other policies—a policy to establish classes to teach Chinese families how to interpret their new tradition; a policy to establish nursing homes to care for elderly citizens in case their children abandon them; and a policy to establish counseling centers to help parents and only children work out their psychological problems.

7

Carrie Buck's Daughter | Stephen Jay Gould

The Lord really put it on the line in his preface to that prototype of all pre- 1
scription, the Ten Commandments:

> . . . for I, the Lord thy God, am a jealous God, visiting the iniquity of the
> fathers upon the children unto the third and fourth generation of them
> that hate me (Exod. 20:5).

The terror of this statement lies in its patent unfairness—its promise to 2
punish guiltless offspring for the misdeeds of their distant forebears.

A different form of guilt by genealogical association attempts to remove 3
this stigma of injustice by denying a cherished premise of Western thought—
human free will. If offspring are tainted not simply by the deeds of their parents but by a material form of evil transferred directly by biological inheritance,
then "the iniquity of the fathers" becomes a signal or warning for probable misbehavior of their sons. Thus Plato, while denying that children should suffer
directly for the crimes of their parents, nonetheless defended the banishment of
a personally guiltless man whose father, grandfather, and great-grandfather
had all been condemned to death.

It is, perhaps, merely coincidental that both Jehovah and Plato chose three 4
generations as their criterion for establishing different forms of guilt by association. Yet we maintain a strong folk, or vernacular, tradition for viewing triple
occurrences as minimal evidence of regularity. Bad things, we are told, come in
threes. Two may represent an accidental association; three is a pattern. Perhaps,
then, we should not wonder that our own century's most famous pronounce-
ment of guilt employed the same criterion—Oliver Wendell Holmes's defense
of compulsory sterilization in Virginia (Supreme Court decision of 1927 in *Buck
v. Bell*): "three generations of imbeciles are enough."

Restrictions upon immigration, with national quotas set to discriminate 5
against those deemed mentally unfit by early versions of IQ testing, marked
the greatest triumph of the American eugenics movement—the flawed heredi-
tarian doctrine, so popular earlier in our century and by no means extinct
today, that attempted to "improve" our human stock by preventing the propagation of those deemed biologically unfit and encouraging procreation among
the supposedly worthy. But the movement to enact and enforce laws for compulsory "eugenic" sterilization had an impact and success scarcely less pronounced. If we could debar the shiftless and the stupid from our shores, we
might also prevent the propagation of those similarly afflicted but already here.

The movement for compulsory sterilization began in earnest during the 6
1890s, abetted by two major factors—the rise of eugenics as an influential political movement and the perfection of safe and simple operations (vasectomy for
men and salpingectomy, the cutting and tying of Fallopian tubes, for women)
to replace castration and other socially unacceptable forms of mutilation.

Gould, Stephen Jay. *The Flamingo's Smile*. New York: Norton, 1985. 306–318.

Indiana passed the first sterilization act based on eugenic principles in 1907 (a few states had previously mandated castration as a punitive measure for certain sexual crimes, although such laws were rarely enforced and usually overturned by judicial review). Like so many others to follow, it provided for sterilization of afflicted people residing in the state's "care," either as inmates of mental hospitals and homes for the feeble-minded or as inhabitants of prisons. Sterilization could be imposed upon those judged insane, idiotic, imbecilic, or moronic, and upon convicted rapists or criminals when recommended by a board of experts.

By the 1930s, more than thirty states had passed similar laws, often with   7
an expanded list of so-called hereditary defects, including alcoholism and drug addiction in some states, and even blindness and deafness in others. These laws were continually challenged and rarely enforced in most states; only California and Virginia applied them zealously. By January 1935, some 20,000 forced "eugenic" sterilizations had been performed in the United States, nearly half in California.

No organization crusaded more vociferously and successfully for these   8
laws than the Eugenics Record Office, the semiofficial arm and repository of data for the eugenics movement in America. Harry Laughlin, superintendent of the Eugenics Record Office, dedicated most of his career to a tireless campaign of writing and lobbying for eugenic sterilization. He hoped, thereby, to eliminate in two generations the genes of what he called the "submerged tenth"—"the most worthless one-tenth of our present population." He proposed a "model sterilization law" in 1922, designed

> to prevent the procreation of persons socially inadequate from defective inheritance, by authorizing and providing for eugenical sterilization of certain potential parents carrying degenerate hereditary qualities.

This model bill became the prototype for most laws passed in America,   9
although few states cast their net as widely as Laughlin advised. (Laughlin's categories encompassed "blind, including those with seriously impaired vision; deaf, including those with seriously impaired hearing; and dependent, including orphans, ne'er-do-wells, the homeless, tramps, and paupers.") Laughlin's suggestions were better heeded in Nazi Germany, where his model act inspired the infamous and stringently enforced *Erbgesundheitsrecht*, leading by the eve of World War II to the sterilization of some 375,000 people, most for "congenital feeble-mindedness," but including nearly 4,000 for blindness and deafness.

The campaign for forced eugenic sterilization in America reached its cli-   10
max and height of respectability in 1927, when the Supreme Court, by an 8–1 vote, upheld the Virginia sterilization bill in *Buck v. Bell*. Oliver Wendell Holmes, then in his mid-eighties and the most celebrated jurist in America, wrote the majority opinion with his customary verve and power of style. It included the notorious paragraph, with its chilling tag line, cited ever since as the quintessential statement of eugenic principles. Remembering with pride his own distant experiences as an infantryman in the Civil War, Holmes wrote:

> We have seen more than once that the public welfare may call upon the best citizens for their lives. It would be strange if it could not call upon those who already sap the strength of the state for these lesser sacrifices. . . . It is better for all the world, if instead of waiting to execute degenerate offspring for crime, or to let them starve for their imbecility, society can pre-

vent those who are manifestly unfit from continuing their kind. The principle that sustains compulsory vaccination is broad enough to cover cutting the Fallopian tubes. Three generations of imbeciles are enough.

Who, then, were the famous "three generations of imbeciles," and why should they still compel our interest? 11

When the state of Virginia passed its compulsory sterilization law in 1924, Carrie Buck, an eighteen-year-old white woman, lived as an involuntary resident at the State Colony for Epileptics and Feeble-Minded. As the first person selected for sterilization under the new act, Carrie Buck became the focus for a constitutional challenge launched, in part, by conservative Virginia Christians who held, according to eugenical "modernists," antiquated views about individual preferences and "benevolent" state power. (Simplistic political labels do not apply in this case, and rarely in general for that matter. We usually regard eugenics as a conservative movement and its most vocal critics as members of the left. This alignment has generally held in our own decade. But eugenics, touted in its day as the latest in scientific modernism, attracted many liberals and numbered among its most vociferous critics groups often labeled as reactionary and antiscientific. If any political lesson emerges from these shifting allegiances, we might consider the true inalienability of certain human rights.) 12

But why was Carrie Buck in the State Colony and why was she selected? Oliver Wendell Holmes upheld her choice as judicious in the opening lines of 1927 opinion: 13

> Carrie Buck is a feeble-minded white woman who was committed to the State Colony. . . . She is the daughter of a feeble-minded mother in the same institution, and the mother of an illegitimate feeble-minded child.

In short, inheritance stood as the crucial issue (indeed as the driving force behind all eugenics). For if measured mental deficiency arose from malnourishment, either of body or mind, and not from tainted genes, then how could sterilization be justified? If decent food, upbringing, medical care, and education might make a worthy citizen of Carrie Buck's daughter, how could the State of Virginia justify the severing of Carrie's Fallopian tubes against her will? (Some forms of mental deficiency are passed in inheritance in family lines, but most are not—a scarcely surprising conclusion when we consider the thousand shocks that beset us all during our lives, from abnormalities in embryonic growth to traumas of birth, malnourishment, rejection, and poverty. In any case, no fair-minded person today would credit Laughlin's social criteria for the identification of hereditary deficiency—ne'er-do-wells, the homeless, tramps, and paupers—although we shall soon see that Carrie Buck was committed on these grounds.) 14

When Carrie Buck's case emerged as the crucial test of Virginia's law, the chief honchos of eugenics understood that the time had come to put up or shut up on the crucial issue of inheritance. Thus, the Eugenics Record Office sent Arthur H. Estabrook, their crack fieldworker, to Virginia for a "scientific" study of the case. Harry Laughlin himself provided a deposition, and his brief for inheritance was presented at the local trial that affirmed Virginia's law and later worked its way to the Supreme Court as *Buck v. Bell*. 15

Laughlin made two major points to the court. First, that Carrie Buck and her mother, Emma Buck, were feeble-minded by the Stanford-Binet test of IQ then in its own infancy. Carrie scored a mental age of nine years, Emma of 16 seven years and eleven months. (These figures ranked them technically as "imbeciles" by definitions of the day, hence Holmes's later choice of words—though his infamous line is often misquoted as "three generations of idiots." Imbeciles displayed a mental age of six to nine years; idiots performed worse, morons better, to round out the old nomenclature of mental deficiency.) Second, that most feeble-mindedness resides ineluctably in the genes, and that Carrie Buck surely belonged with this majority. Laughlin reported:

> Generally, feeble-mindedness is caused by the inheritance of degenerate qualities; but sometimes it might be caused by environmental factors which are not heredity. In the case given, the evidence points strongly toward the feeble-mindedness and moral delinquency of Carrie Buck being due, primarily, to inheritance and not to environment.

Carrie Buck's daughter was then, and has always been, the pivotal figure   17
of this painful case. I noted in beginning this essay that we tend (often at our peril) to regard two as potential accident and three as an established pattern. The supposed imbecility of Emma and Carrie might have been an unfortunate coincidence, but the diagnosis of similar deficiency for Vivian Buck (made by a social worker, as we shall see, when Vivian was but six months old) tipped the balance in Laughlin's favor and led Holmes to declare the Buck lineage inherently corrupt by deficient heredity. Vivian sealed the pattern—*three* generations of imbeciles are enough. Besides, had Carrie not given illegitimate birth to Vivian, the issue (in both senses) would never have emerged.

Oliver Wendell Holmes viewed his work with pride. The man so   18
renowned for his principle of judicial restraint, who had proclaimed that freedom must not be curtailed without "clear and present danger"—without the equivalent of falsely yelling "fire" in a crowded theater—wrote of his judgment in *Buck v. Bell*: "I felt that I was getting near the first principle of real reform."

And so *Buck v. Bell* remained for fifty years, a footnote to a moment of   19
American history perhaps best forgotten. Then, in 1980, it reemerged to prick our collective conscience, when Dr. K. Ray Nelson, then director of the Lynchburg Hospital where Carrie Buck had been sterilized, researched the records of his institution and discovered that more than 4,000 sterilizations had been performed, the last as late as 1972. He also found Carrie Buck, alive and well near Charlottesville, and her sister Doris, covertly sterilized under the same law (she was told that her operation was for appendicitis), and now, with fierce dignity, dejected and bitter because she had wanted a child more than anything else in her life and had finally, in her old age, learned why she had never conceived.

As scholars and reporters visited Carrie Buck and her sister, what a few   20
experts had known all along became abundantly clear to everyone. Carrie Buck was a woman of obviously normal intelligence. For example, Paul A. Lombardo of the School of Law at the University of Virginia, and a leading scholar of *Buck v. Bell*, wrote in a letter to me:

> As for Carrie, when I met her she was reading newspapers daily and joining a more literate friend to assist at regular bouts with the crossword puzzles. She was not a sophisticated woman, and lacked social graces, but mental health professionals who examined her in later life confirmed my impressions that she was neither mentally ill nor retarded.

21

On what evidence, then, was Carrie Buck consigned to the State Colony for Epileptics and Feeble-Minded on January 23, 1924? I have seen the text of her commitment hearing; it is, to say the least, cursory and contradictory. Beyond the bald and undocumented say-so of her foster parents, and her own brief appearance before a commission of two doctors and a justice of the peace, no evidence was presented. Even the crude and early Stanford-Binet test, so fatally flawed as a measure of innate worth (see my book *The Mismeasure of Man*, although the evidence of Carrie's own case suffices) but at least clothed with the aura of quantitative respectability, had not yet been applied.

When we understand why Carrie Buck was committed in January 1924, 22 we can finally comprehend the hidden meaning of her case and its message for us today. The silent key, again as from the first, is her daughter Vivian, born on March 28, 1924, and then but an evident bump on her belly. Carrie Buck was one of several illegitimate children borne by her mother, Emma. She grew up with foster parents, J. T. and Alice Dobbs, and continued to live with them as an adult, helping out with chores around the house. She was raped by a relative of her foster parents, then blamed for the resulting pregnancy. Almost surely, she was (as they used to say) committed to hide her shame (and her rapist's identity), not because enlightened science had just discovered her true mental status. In short, she was sent away to have her baby. Her case never was about mental deficiency; Carrie Buck was persecuted for supposed sexual immorality and social deviance. The annals of her trial and hearing reek with the contempt of the well-off and well-bred for poor people of "loose morals." Who really cared whether Vivian was a baby of normal intelligence; she was the illegitimate child of an illegitimate woman. Two generations of bastards are enough. Harry Laughlin began his "family history" of the Bucks by writing: "These people belong to the shiftless, ignorant and worthless class of anti-social whites of the South."

We know little of Emma Buck and her life, but we have no more reason to 23 suspect her than her daughter Carrie of true mental deficiency. Their supposed deviance was social and sexual; the charge of imbecility was a cover-up, Mr. Justice Holmes notwithstanding.

We come then to the crux of the case, Carrie's daughter, Vivian. What evi- 24 dence was ever adduced for her mental deficiency? This and only this: At the original trial in late 1924, when Vivian Buck was seven months old, a Miss Wilhelm, social worker for the Red Cross, appeared before the court. She began by stating honestly the true reason for Carrie Buck's commitment:

> Mr. Dobbs, who had charge of the girl, had taken her when a small child, had reported to Miss Duke [the temporary secretary of Public Welfare for Albemarle County] that the girl was pregnant and that he wanted to have her committed somewhere—to have her sent to some institution.

Miss Wilhelm then rendered her judgment of Vivian Buck by comparing 25 her with the normal granddaughter of Mrs. Dobbs, born just three days earlier:

> It is difficult to judge probabilities of a child as young as that, but it seems to me not quite a normal baby. In its appearance—I should say that perhaps my knowledge of the mother may prejudice me in that regard, but I saw the child at the same time as Mrs. Dobbs' daughter's baby, which is only three days older than this one, and there is a very decided difference in the development of the babies. That was about two weeks ago. There is a look about it that is not quite normal, but just what it is, I can't tell.

This short testimony, and nothing else, formed all the evidence for the   26
crucial third generation of imbeciles. Cross-examination revealed that neither
Vivian nor the Dobbs grandchild could walk or talk, and that "Mrs. Dobbs'
daughter's baby is a very responsive baby. When you play with it or try to
attract its attention—it is a baby that you can play with. The other baby is not.
It seems very apathetic and not responsive." Miss Wilhelm then urged Carrie
Buck's sterilization: "I think," she said, "it would at least prevent the propagation of her kind." Several years later, Miss Wilhelm denied that she had ever
examined Vivian or deemed the child feeble-minded.

Unfortunately, Vivian died at age eight of "enteric colitis" (as recorded on   27
her death certificate), an ambiguous diagnosis that could mean many things
but may well indicate that she fell victim to one of the preventable childhood
diseases of poverty (a grim reminder of the real subject in *Buck v. Bell*). She is
therefore mute as a witness in our reassessment of her famous case.

When *Buck v. Bell* resurfaced in 1980, it immediately struck me that   28
Vivian's case was crucial and that evidence for the mental status of a child who
died at age eight might best be found in report cards. I have therefore been trying to track down Vivian Buck's school records for the past four years and have
finally succeeded. (They were supplied to me by Dr. Paul A. Lombardo, who
also sent other documents, including Miss Wilhelm's testimony, and spent several hours answering my questions by mail and Lord knows how much time
playing successful detective in re Vivian's school records. I have never met Dr.
Lombardo; he did all this work for kindness, collegiality, and love of the game
of knowledge, not for expected reward or even requested acknowledgment. In
a profession—academics—so often marred by pettiness and silly squabbling
over meaningless priorities, this generosity must be recorded and celebrated as
a sign of how things can and should be.)

Vivian Buck was adopted by the Dobbs family, who had raised (but later   29
sent away) her mother, Carrie. As Vivian Alice Elaine Dobbs, she attended the
Venable Public Elementary School of Charlottesville for four terms, from September 1930 until May 1932, a month before her death. She was a perfectly normal, quite average student, neither particularly outstanding nor much
troubled. In those days before grade inflation, when C meant "good, 81–87" (as
defined on her report card) rather than barely scraping by, Vivian Dobbs
received A's and B's for deportment and C's for all academic subjects but mathematics (which was always difficult for her, and where she scored D) during
her first term in Grade 1A, from September 1930 to January 1931. She improved
during her second term in 1B, meriting an A in deportment, C in mathematics,
and B in all other academic subjects; she was placed on the honor roll in April
1931. Promoted to 2A, she had trouble during the fall term of 1931, failing
mathematics and spelling but receiving A in deportment, B in reading, and C
in writing and English. She was "retained to 2A" for the next term—or "left
back" as we used to say, and scarcely a sign of imbecility as I remember all my
buddies who suffered a similar fate. In any case, she again did well in her final
term, with B in deportment, reading, and spelling, and C in writing, English,
and mathematics during her last month in school. This daughter of "lewd and
immoral" women excelled in deportment and performed adequately, although
not brilliantly, in her academic subjects.

In short, we can only agree with the conclusion that Dr. Lombardo has   30
reached in his research on *Buck v. Bell*—there were no imbeciles, not a one,

among the three generations of Bucks. I don't know that such correction of cruel but forgotten errors of history counts for much, but I find it both symbolic and satisfying to learn that forced eugenic sterilization, a procedure of such dubious morality, earned its official justification (and won its most quoted line of rhetoric) on a patent falsehood.

Carrie Buck died last year. By a quirk of fate, and not by memory or design, she was buried just a few steps from her only daughter's grave. In the umpteenth and ultimate verse of a favorite old ballad, a rose and a brier—the sweet and the bitter—emerge from the tombs of Barbara Allen and her lover, twining about each other in the union of death. May Carrie and Vivian, victims in different ways and in the flower of youth, rest together in peace.   31

Questions About Strategy

1. How does Stephen Jay Gould establish a context for his analysis of the causal analysis that guided the reasoning in *Buck v. Bell*?

2. What evidence does Gould use to support his argument that Carrie Buck's treatment was motivated by prejudice and shame rather than concern over her mental abilities?

3. How does Gould connect his analysis of Carrie Buck to his readers' knowledge of contemporary social problems?

A Sampler of Other Essays

1. Sarah Penning, "The Coupon Conspiracy" (student essay), p. 89
2. Howard Gardner, "The Compositions of Mozart's Mind," p. 19
3. Brent Staples, "Black Men and Public Space," p. 184
4. Diane Ackerman, "The Painter's Eye," p. 217

STRATEGY SEVEN: *Argument*

Selecting Your Subject

As you think about possible subjects for an argument, think of yourself as an attorney in a courtroom. You have collected your evidence and formed an opinion about your subject, but the other attorney has also collected evidence and formed an opinion that challenges yours. In other words, when you look for a subject, look for the opposition. When you do, you will discover that some subjects are not worth an argument. You can argue about *facts*—who scored the most touchdowns. You can argue about *opinions*—what's the best movie. The first argument can be settled quickly by checking a reference book; the second argument can never be settled because such opinions are based on preference or prejudice. The best subject for an argument is one that can be debated by sensible people presenting evidence, appealing to authorities, and rendering judgments that follow from careful reasoning. See, for example, the various arguments for and against drug testing that Matt Fisher considers in Chapter 6.

Analyzing Your Audience

You can never write an argument in a vacuum. If you are an attorney, for example, you are making your argument to a small audience (the jury) and several larger audiences (the people standing outside the courtroom or reading about the trial in a newspaper). The first group is impartial and willing to listen to both sides. The second group contains people who have already made up their minds or who are only vaguely aware of the issues in the trial. Good writers, like good attorneys, must identify readers (friendly and hostile), speculate about potential readers (detached and disinterested), and present all groups with evidence that they will see as appropriate, significant, and reliable. See "Analyzing the Audience" in Chapter 6 (pages 136–137).

Determining Your Purpose

The most obvious purpose for conducting an argument is to settle a dispute about some controversy or conflict. You make your best case and let the jury, your readers, decide. But you may write arguments for other purposes. Sometimes you may argue to *support a cause,* composing an editorial in favor of subsidized child care on your campus. You may also argue to *promote change,* drafting a petition to reduce student fees. Sometimes you may argue to *refute a theory,* composing a history paper on why you think the antislavery movement was not the chief cause of the Civil War. You can also write arguments to *arouse sympathy,* circulating an essay to support better laws against child abuse. Or sometimes you may argue to *find agreement,* helping apartment residents reach a consensus about a policy on pets. Each of these purposes suggests a slightly different strategy for organizing and presenting your argument.

Using the Strategy

Two related strategies for conducting an argument are *induction* and *deduction.* In induction, you present a series of individual examples until a particular pattern emerges. Then you make an inductive leap and claim that these examples provide sufficient evidence for your general conclusion. In deduction, you present a general assertion and then attempt to prove its validity by examining individual examples. The two processes are interrelated because to organize your evidence by *induction* you have to begin with *deduction.* That is, your introduction presents your thesis statement, the generalization you hope to prove by analyzing your individual examples.

Another strategy for organizing an argument borrows from comparison and contrast. In this strategy, you (1) present your opponent's side and then your side (divided pattern), or (2) present one point of your opponent's argument, then refute it, assert your point, and move on to the next point (alternating pattern). Another version of this strategy compares each set of points to demonstrate areas of agreement rather than disagreement. In all three methods, you should present the other side first—in a fair and balanced way—and then present your side as the conclusion or accommodation that makes more sense.

As you arrange your argument, avoid oversimplifying or distorting your evidence. An error due to faulty reasoning is called a *fallacy* (see Chapter 6, pages 145–146). When you purposely make such errors to deceive people, you are guilty of *fraud*.

Finally, you need to use the *three appeals* of any argument: *logical, emotional,* and *ethical*. In the logical appeal, use rational methods, such as making claims and citing evidence to support your case. Because such methods appeal to your readers' intelligence, they are probably the best strategies for making your argument convincing. But emotional and ethical appeals have their value too. *Connotative language* and *dramatic examples* appeal to your readers' emotions and persuade them to accept your argument. *Expert testimony* and a *reasonable tone* appeal to your readers' desire for trustworthiness and convince them that they should believe in your competence. Although emotional and ethical appeals must be used with caution (see Chapter 6, pages 141–142), they can enrich and enlighten an otherwise dry and uninspiring argument.

The Humanities Controversy | Robin Jensen

Introduction: Identify contending sides

For the last ten years, American education has been engaged in a complex and contentious debate about what books ought to be taught in the university's basic humanities course. On the one side, the traditionalists argue that students should be taught the great books of Western civilization. On the other side, the multiculturalists argue that students should be taught the great books of other civilizations, including the neglected works of minority writers within our culture. Like all controversies, each side presents compelling evidence to support its position. But their categorical assertions often prevent them from seeing what is really at stake in the controversy. In this case, the battle over what students should be taught has overlooked the question of how they learn.

Thesis: Assert new position

Arrangement: Present traditional view of humanities

According to the traditionalists, the problem began in the sixties when American educators exhibited what William J. Bennett has characterized as a "loss of nerve" (*To Reclaim* 1). Confronted by the emergence of ethnic studies and the challenges of the civil rights movement, American educators ceased to argue for a unified humanities curriculum that celebrated the achievements of Western civilization. Instead, they opened up the university curriculum to a bewildering array of specialized courses, producing what Allan Bloom has called "educational anarchy" (337).

Evidence: Cite expert testimony

The result, according to Bloom, is that "the university now offers no distinctive visage . . . no vision . . . of what an educated human being is" (337). Graduates now are distinguished by what they do not know. In his *To Reclaim a Legacy: A Report on the Humanities in Higher Education*, Bennett cites the following figures: "A student can obtain a bachelor's degree from 75 percent of all American colleges and universities without having studied European history, from 72 percent without having studied American literature or history, and from 86 percent without having studied the civilizations of classical Greece and Rome" (1–2). Several years later, in her *Humanities in America: A Report to the President, the Congress and the American People*, Lynn V. Cheney continues to tabulate the crisis: "It is possible to graduate now, as it was five years ago, from almost 80 percent of the nation's four-year colleges and universities without taking a course in the history of Western civilization" (5).

Evidence: Cite examples of negative results

Such statistics explain E. D. Hirsch, Jr.'s call for "cultural literacy." He argues that "at the heart of modern nationhood is the teaching of literacy and a common culture through a national system of education" (73). When nations do not preserve and perpetuate a common culture, Hirsch argues, they become like China, "a polyglot nation of mutually unintelligible dialects. . . . [un]able to function successfully as a modern industrial and economic unit" (76). To avoid such disasters, Hirsch offers a list of terms, "What Literate Americans Know," and encourages teachers to begin teaching it (146–215).

Arrangement: Refute traditionalist position

Hirsch's argument assumes that the great tradition of Western civilization can be represented by a basic list and that although there is *other* information citizens could learn, learning *this* information is crucial to "our national survival, as well as our national identity" (Stimpson 29). We should study Western

1

2

3

4

5

civilization because it is ours (Bennett "Why the West?" 39), and because it "forms the basis of our society's laws and instructions" (Cheney 12).

Arrangement: Present multiculturalist position

Although traditionalists such as Hirsch make a persuasive argument, Rick Simonson and Scott Walker, the editors of *Multi-Cultural Literacy: Opening the American Mind*, remain unconvinced, finding their opponents' position "over-ridingly static" and "shallow" (x). The traditionalists, they argue, "seem to think that most of what constitutes contemporary American and world culture was immaculately conceived by a few men in Greece around 900 B.C., came to its full expression in Europe a few centuries later, and began to decline around the middle of the nineteenth century" (x). **6**

Evidence: Suggest that traditionalist position is outdated

The multiculturalist side in the humanities controversy focuses on the "out-dated" notion of the traditionalists' definition of culture (Simonson and Walker x). What the traditionalists see as the fragmentation of Western civiliza-tion, the multiculturalists see as the fulfillment of "a more democratic society in which there will be greater equality in all spheres of life" (Appleton 6). Instead of celebrating the superiority of *our* culture, the multiculturalists argue that "Americans need to broaden their awareness and understanding of the cultures of the rest of the world" (Simonson and Walker xiii). **7**

Emotional Appeal: Use effective analogy

The obvious reason for studying other cultures is, as Mary Louise Pratt points out, that our cultural identity is being reformed by the economic, political, and social changes throughout the world (8). The goods Americans buy, the treaties they sign, and many of the students who enroll in their universities are no longer the products of a uniform Western culture. "To see . . . an entire cul-tural tradition as if it were a self-contained whole is," as one of Pratt's colleagues comments, "like listening to only one side of a phone conversation" (13). **8**

Evidence: Cite expert testimony

Another reason for studying other cultures is to see how they challenge the basic assumptions of our culture (Graff 62). Sometimes those challenges come from cultures across the globe; sometimes they come from cultures that have been suppressed in our own back yard. As Gerald Graff points out, it is easy to celebrate the glories of Western civilization if we exclude those who are likely to "make trouble" (62). Afro-American scholar Henry Louis Gates, Jr. explains why those who "make trouble" want to challenge the traditionalists' view of the humanities: **9**

> the teaching of an aesthetic and political order in which no women or peo-ple of color were even able to discover the reflection or representation of their images, or hear the resonances of their cultural voices. . . . represents the return of an order in which my people were the subjugated: the voice-less, the invisible, the unrepresented and the unrepresentable. (105)

Or as Diane Ravitch points out, human history is the story of "the clash of dif-ferent cultures, races, ethnic groups and religions" (340). If we want to live together, then we must learn to understand the differences that divide us.

Arrangement: Balance both sides and then introduce new position

As in all controversies, both sides in the traditionalist-multiculturalist debate make valid arguments. Students should be taught the culture that formed their heritage; they should also be taught that culture is not a static product, like a statue in a museum, but a dynamic process in which different voices challenge and complement each other (Stimpson 30). Students should be taught cultures other than their own; they should also be taught that these other cultures suffer from the same superiority complex that has made Western civilization ethnocentric (Bloom 36). **10**

Evidence: Cite one way to resolve controversy

The simplest way to resolve this controversy is to acknowledge the claims 11 of both sides: Teach students courses in Western civilization *and* courses in non-Western civilization. But this solution only perpetuates what Graff calls the "add-on" principle of curricular change:

> by this principle, whenever a new and challenging idea or method arises, it is assimilated into the university by the device of *adding* another unit to the existing aggregate. The result is that established departments and factions do not have to confront the challenge of the new idea or even notice its existence (57).

Thus, universities could teach both versions of the humanities in separate courses, creating a curriculum that everybody needs and nobody wants.

Evidence: Suggest second way to resolve controversy

Another way to resolve the controversy would be to combine the two 12 courses. But even if teachers would be willing to entertain such a compromise, they could not produce it. As Catharine Stimpson points out, "no curriculum . . . can do all of earthly time, all of earthly space" (31). And combining curriculums often forces teachers to look for common ground and to erase the differences that created the opposing cultures in the first place (Graff 56).

Appeal: Cite students to make emotional appeal

In their constant fussing about books, both sides seem preoccupied by 13 what students need to be taught rather than how students can learn (Emig 88). To learn effectively, students need to participate in their own education (Emig 93). But both sides see students as passive and powerless—children who need to be given lots of information (Trimbur 118). The official curriculum may focus on the classic debates in ancient Greece or the contemporary debates between "Third World" and "First World" cultures, but the "unofficial" curriculum tells students to keep quiet and take notes.

Arrangement: Present solution

Studying the humanities should engage students in a conversation, a "cul- 14 tural conversation they have a stake in" (Graff 65). To create this conversation, teachers will need to give students time to talk. Instead of telling them what to think about "the *Norton Anthology of World Masterpieces*, we might ask them to think about what is implied by the word 'World' in the title of a volume that collects works exclusively from the Western tradition" (Trimbur 117–18). Instead of trying to cover centuries of cultural achievement, in all parts of the world, teachers might invite students to examine one historical period to see "what was happening simultaneously in many places, and how each place thought of the others, if indeed they did" (Stimpson 31).

Conclusion: Cite students to make ethical appeal

Such invitations will help students see that culture is not something that 15 has "washed up on the beach of history" (Gates 104). Culture is created by constant arguments about what voices to include and what voices to exclude. Indeed, the argument about what books should be taught in the humanities course is part of that process. Rather than waiting for one side to win or for both sides to resolve their disagreements (Graff 52), students should be encouraged to examine the causes and effects of the conflict. The real crisis in the humanities controversy is that for the most part students have not been consulted. To "claim" their legacy they need to participate in the complex and contentious controversy. They need to do more than take humanities; they need to take part in creating humanities.

Works Cited

Appleton, Nicholas. *Cultural Pluralism in Education: Theoretical Foundations*. New York: Longman, 1983.

Bennett, William J. *To Reclaim a Legacy: A Report on the Humanities in Higher Edu-cation*. Washington, D.C.: National Endowment for the Humanities, 1984.

—. "Why the West?" *National Review* 27 May 1988: 37–39.

Bloom, Allan. *The Closing of the American Mind: How Higher Education Has Failed Democracy and Impoverished the Souls of Today's Students*. New York: Simon, 1987.

Cheney, Lynn V. *Humanities in America: A Report to the President, the Congress and the American People*. Washington, D.C.: National Endowment for the Humanities, 1988.

Emig, Janet. "Our Missing Theory." *Conversations: Contemporary Critical Theory and the Teaching of Literature*. Eds. Charles Moran and Elizabeth Penfield. Urbana: NCTE, 1990: 87–96.

Gates, Henry Louis, Jr. "The Master's Pieces: On Canon Formation and the African-American Tradition." *South Atlantic Quarterly* 89 (Winter 1990): 89–112.

Graff, Gerald. "Teach the Conflicts." *South Atlantic Quarterly* 89 (Winter 1990): 51–67.

Hirsch, E. D. *Cultural Literacy: What Every American Needs to Know*. Boston: Houghton, 1987.

—. *The Dictionary of Cultural Literacy*. Boston: Houghton, 1988.

Pratt, Mary Louise. "Humanities for the Future: Reflections on the Western Cul-ture Debate at Stanford." *South Atlantic Quarterly* 89 (Winter 1990): 7–25.

Ravitch, Diane. "Multiculturalism: *E Pluribus Plures.*" *American Scholar* 59 (Sum-mer 1990): 337–54.

Simonson, Rick and Scott Walker, eds. *Multi-Cultural Literacy: Opening the Amer-ican Mind*. St. Paul, MN: Graywolf, 1988.

Stimpson, Catharine R. "Is There a Core in the Curriculum? And Is It Really Necessary?" *Change* 20 (Mar.–Apr. 1988): 26–31.

Trimbur, John. "*To Reclaim a Legacy*, Cultural Literacy and the Discourse of Crisis." *Liberal Education* 72 (Summer 1986): 109–19.

Affirmative Action: The Price of Preference | Shelby Steele

I n a few short years, when my two children will be applying to college, the affirmative action policies by which most universities offer black students some form of preferential treatment will present me with a dilemma. I am a middle-class black, a college professor, far from wealthy, but also well removed from the kind of deprivation that would qualify my children for the label "disadvantaged." Both of them have endured racial insensitivity from whites. They have been called names, have suffered slights, and have experienced firsthand the peculiar malevolence that racism brings out in people. Yet, they have never experienced racial discrimination, have never been stopped by their race on any path they have chosen to follow. Still, their society now tells them that if they will only designate themselves as black on their college applications, they will likely do better in the college lottery than if they conceal this fact. I think there is something of a Faustian bargain in this. 1

Of course, many blacks and a considerable number of whites would say that I was sanctimoniously making affirmative action into a test of character. They would say that this small preference is the meagerest recompense for centuries of unrelieved oppression. And to these arguments other very obvious facts must be added. In America, many marginally competent or flatly incompetent whites are hired everyday—some because their white skin suits the conscious or unconscious racial preference of their employer. The white children of alumni are often grandfathered into elite universities in what can only be seen as a residual benefit of historic white privilege. Worse, white incompetence is always an individual matter, while for blacks it is often confirmation of ugly stereotypes. The Peter Principle was not conceived with only blacks in mind. Given that unfairness cuts both ways, doesn't it only balance the scales of history that my children now receive a slight preference over whites? Doesn't this repay, in a small way, the systematic denial under which their grandfather lived out his days? 2

So, in theory, affirmative action certainly has all the moral symmetry that fairness requires—the injustice of historical and even contemporary white advantage is offset with black advantage; preference replaces prejudice, inclusion answers exclusion. It is reformist and corrective, even repentent and redemptive. And I would never sneer at these good intentions. Born in the late forties in Chicago, I started my education (a charitable term in this case) in a segregated school and suffered all the indignities that come to blacks in a segregated society. My father, born in the South, only made it to the third grade before the white man's fields took permanent priority over his formal education. And though he educated himself into an advanced reader with an almost professorial authority, he could only drive a truck for a living and never earned more than ninety dollars a week in his entire life. So yes, it is crucial to my sense of citizenship, to my ability to identify with the spirit and the interests of 3

Steele, Shelby. "Affirmative Action: The Price of Preference." *The Content of Our Character.* New York: Harper, 1990. 111–25.

America, to know that this country, however imperfectly, recognizes its past sins and wishes to correct them.

Yet good intentions, because of the opportunity for innocence they offer us, are very seductive and can blind us to the effects they generate when implemented. In our society, affirmative action is, among other things, a testament to white goodwill and to black power, and in the midst of these heavy investments, its effects can be hard to see. But after twenty years of implementation, I think affirmative action has shown itself to be more bad than good and that blacks—whom I will focus on in this essay—now stand to lose more from it than they gain. 4

In talking with affirmative action administrators and with blacks and whites in general, it is clear that supporters of affirmative action focus on its good intentions while detractors emphasize its negative effects. Proponents talk about "diversity" and "pluralism"; opponents speak of "reverse discrimination," the unfairness of quotas and set-asides. It was virtually impossible to find people outside either camp. The closest I came was a white male manager at a large computer company who said, "I think it amounts to reverse discrimination, but I'll put up with a little of that for a little more diversity." I'll live with a little of the effect to gain a little of the intention, he seemed to be saying. But this only makes him a halfhearted supporter of affirmative action. I think many people who don't really like affirmative action support it to one degree or another anyway. 5

I believe they do this because of what happened to white and black Americans in the crucible of the sixties when whites were confronted with their racial guilt and blacks tasted their first real power. In this stormy time white absolution and black power coalesced into virtual mandates for society. Affirmative action became a meeting ground for these mandates in the law, and in the late sixties and early seventies it underwent a remarkable escalation of its mission from simple anti-discrimination enforcement to social engineering by means of quotas, goals, timetables, set-asides and other forms of preferential treatment. 6

Legally, this was achieved through a series of executive orders and EEOC guidelines that allowed racial imbalances in the workplace to stand as proof of racial discrimination. Once it could be assumed that discrimination explained racial imbalances, it became easy to justify group remedies to presumed discrimination, rather than the normal case-by-case redress for proven discrimination. Preferential treatment through quotas, goals, and so on is designed to correct imbalances based on the assumption that they always indicate discrimination. This expansion of what constitutes discrimination allowed affirmative action to escalate into the business of social engineering in the name of anti-discrimination, to push society toward statistically proportionate racial representation, without any obligation of proving actual discrimination. 7

What accounted for this shift, I believe, was the white mandate to achieve a new racial innocence and the black mandate to gain power. Even though blacks had made great advances during the sixties without quotas, these mandates, which came to a head in the very late sixties, could no longer be satisfied by anything less than racial preferences. I don't think these mandates in themselves were wrong, since whites clearly needed to do better by blacks and blacks needed more real power in society. But, as they came together in affirmative action, their effect was to distort our understanding of racial discrimination in a way that allowed us to offer the remediation of preference on the basis 8 of mere color rather than actual injury. By making black the color of preference, these mandates have reburdened society with the very marriage of color and preference (in reverse) that we set out to eradicate. The old sin is reaffirmed in a new guise.

But the essential problem with this form of affirmative action is the way it leaps over the hard business of developing a formerly oppressed people to the point where they can achieve proportionate representation on their own (given equal opportunity) and goes straight for the proportionate representation. This may satisfy some whites of their innocence and some blacks of their power, but it does very little to truly uplift blacks.   9

A white female affirmative action officer at an Ivy League university told me what many supporters of affirmative action now say: "We're after diversity. We ideally want a student body where racial and ethnic groups are represented according to their proportion in society." When affirmative action escalated into social engineering, diversity became a golden word. It grants whites an egalitarian fairness (innocence) and blacks an entitlement to proportionate representation (power). *Diversity* is a term that applies democratic principles to races and cultures rather than to citizens, despite the fact that there is nothing to indicate that real diversity is the same thing as proportionate representation. Too often the result of this on campuses (for example) has been a democracy of colors rather than of people, an artificial diversity that gives the appearance of an educational parity between black and white students that has not yet been achieved in reality. Here again, racial preferences allow society to leapfrog over the difficult problem of developing blacks to parity with whites and into a cosmetic diversity that covers the blemish of disparity—a full six years after admission, only about 26 percent of black students graduate from college.   10

Racial representation is not the same thing as racial development, yet affirmative action fosters a confusion of these very different needs. Representation can be manufactured; development is always hard-earned. However, it is the music of innocence and power that we hear in affirmative action that causes us to cling to it and to its distracting emphasis on representation. The fact is that after twenty years of racial preferences, the gap between white and black median income is greater than it was in the seventies. None of this is to say that blacks don't need policies that ensure our right to equal opportunity, but what we need more is the development that will let us take advantage of society's effort to include us.   11

I think that one of the most troubling effects of racial preferences for blacks is a kind of demoralization, or put another way, an enlargement of self-doubt. Under affirmative action the quality that earns us preferential treatment is an implied inferiority. However this inferiority is explained—and it is easily enough explained by the myriad deprivations that grew out of our oppression—it is still inferiority. There are explanations, and then there is the fact. And the fact must be borne by the individual as a condition apart from the explanation, apart even from the fact that others like himself also bear this condition. In integrated situations where blacks must compete with whites who may be better prepared, these explanations may quickly wear thin and expose the individual to racial as well as personal self-doubt.   12

All of this is compounded by the cultural myth of black inferiority that blacks have always lived with. What this means in practical terms is that when blacks deliver themselves into integrated situations, they encounter a nasty   13 little reflex in whites, a mindless, atavistic reflex that responds to the color black with alarm. Attributions may follow this alarm if the white cares to indulge them, and if they do, they will most likely be negative—one such attribution is intellectual ineptness. I think this reflex and the attributions that may follow it embarrass most whites today, therefore, it is usually quickly repressed. Nevertheless, on an equally atavistic level, the black will be aware of the reflex his color triggers and will feel a stab of horror at seeing himself reflected in this way. He, too, will do a quick repression, but a lifetime of such stabbings is what constitutes his inner realm of racial doubt.

The effects of this may be a subject for another essay. The point here is that 14 the implication of inferiority that racial preferences engender in both the white and black mind expands rather than contracts this doubt. Even when the black sees no implication of inferiority in racial preferences, he knows that whites do, so that—consciously or unconsciously—the result is virtually the same. The effect of preferential treatment—the lowering of normal standards to increase black representation—puts blacks at war with an expanded realm of debilitating doubt, so that the doubt itself becomes an unrecognized preoccupation that undermines their ability to perform, especially in integrated situations. On largely white campuses, blacks are five times more likely to drop out than whites. Preferential treatment, no matter how it is justified in the light of day, subjects blacks to a midnight of self-doubt, and so often transforms their advantage into a revolving door.

Another liability of affirmative action comes from the fact that it indirectly 15 encourages blacks to exploit their own past victimization as a source of power and privilege. Victimization, like implied inferiority, is what justifies preference, so that to receive the benefits of preferential treatment one must, to some extent, become invested in the view of one's self as a victim. In this way, affirmative action nurtures a victim-focused identity in blacks. The obvious irony here is that we become inadvertently invested in the very condition we are trying to overcome. Racial preferences send us the message that there is more power in our past suffering than our present achievements—none of which could bring us a *preference* over others.

When power itself grows out of suffering, then blacks are encouraged to 16 expand the boundaries of what qualifies as racial oppression, a situation that can lead us to paint our victimization in vivid colors, even as we receive the benefits of preference. The same corporations and institutions that give us preference are also seen as our oppressors. At Stanford University minority students—some of whom enjoy as much as $15,000 a year in financial aid—recently took over the president's office demanding, among other things, more financial aid. The power to be found in victimization, like any power, is intoxicating and can lend itself to the creation of a new class of super-victims who can feel the pea of victimization under twenty mattresses. Preferential treatment rewards us for being underdogs rather than for moving beyond that status—a misplacement of incentives that, along with its deepening of our doubt, is more a yoke than a spur.

But, I think, one of the worst prices that blacks pay for preference has to 17 do with an illusion. I saw this illusion at work recently in the mother of a middle-class black student who was going off to his first semester of college. "They owe us this, so don't think for a minute that you don't belong there." This is the logic by which many blacks, and some whites, justify affirmative action—it is something "owed," a form of reparation. But this logic overlooks a much harder and less digestible reality, that it is impossible to repay blacks living today for the historic suffering of the race. If all blacks were given a million dollars tomorrow morning it would not amount to a dime on the dollar of three centuries of oppression, nor would it obviate the residues of that oppression that we still carry today. The concept of historic reparation grows out of man's need to impose a degree of justice on the world that simply does not exist. Suffering can be endured and overcome, it cannot be repaid. Blacks cannot be repaid for the injustice done to the race, but we can be corrupted by society's guilty gestures of repayment.

Affirmative action is such a gesture. It tells us that racial preferences can do for us what we cannot do for ourselves. The corruption here is in the hidden incentive *not* to do what we believe preferences will do. This is an incentive to be reliant on others just as we are struggling for self-reliance. And it keeps alive the illusion that we can find some deliverance in repayment. The hardest thing for any sufferer to accept is that his suffering excuses him from very little and never has enough currency to restore him. To think otherwise is to prolong the suffering.   18

Several blacks I spoke with said they were still in favor of affirmative action because of the "subtle" discrimination blacks were subject to once on the job. One photojournalist said, "They have ways of ignoring you." A black female television producer said, "You can't file a lawsuit when your boss doesn't invite you to the insider meetings without ruining your career. So we still need affirmative action." Others mentioned the infamous "glass ceiling" through which blacks can see the top positions of authority but never reach them. But I don't think racial preferences are a protection against this subtle discrimination; I think they contribute to it.   19

In any workplace, racial preferences will always create two-tiered populations composed of preferreds and unpreferreds. This division makes automatic a perception of enhanced competence for the unpreferreds and of questionable competence for the preferreds—the former earned his way, even though others were given preference, while the latter made it by color as much as by competence. Racial preferences implicitly mark whites with an exaggerated superiority just as they mark blacks with an exaggerated inferiority. They not only reinforce America's oldest racial myth but, for blacks, they have the effect of stigmatizing the already stigmatized.   20

I think that much of the "subtle" discrimination that blacks talk about is often (not always) discrimination against the stigma of questionable competence that affirmative action delivers to blacks. In this sense, preferences scapegoat the very people they seek to help. And it may be that at a certain level employers impose a glass ceiling, but this may not be against the race so much as against the race's reputation for having advanced by color as much as by competence. Affirmative action makes a glass ceiling virtually necessary as a protection against the corruptions of preferential treatment. This ceiling is the point at which corporations shift the emphasis from color to competency and stop playing the affirmative action game. Here preference backfires for blacks and becomes a taint that holds them back. Of course, one could argue that this taint, which is, after all, in the minds of whites, becomes nothing more than an excuse to discriminate against blacks. And certainly the result is the same in either case—blacks don't get past the glass ceiling. But this argument does not   21 get around the fact that racial preferences now taint this color with a new theme of suspicion that makes it even more vulnerable to the impulse in others to discriminate. In this crucial yet gray area of perceived competence, preferences make whites look better than they are and blacks worse, while doing nothing whatever to stop the very real discrimination that blacks may encounter. I don't wish to justify the glass ceiling here, but only to suggest the very subtle ways that affirmative action revives rather than extinguishes the old rationalizations for racial discrimination.

22 In education, a revolving door; in employment, a glass ceiling.

23 I believe affirmative action is problematic in our society because it tries to function like a social program. Rather than ask it to ensure equal opportunity we have demanded that it create parity between the races. But preferential treatment does not teach skills, or educate, or instill motivation. It only passes out entitlement by color, a situation that in my profession has created an unrealistically high demand for black professors. The social engineer's assumption is that this high demand will inspire more blacks to earn Ph.D.'s and join the profession. In fact, the number of blacks earning Ph.D.'s has declined in recent years. A Ph.D. must be developed from preschool on. He requires family and community support. He must acquire an entire system of values that enables him to work hard while delaying gratification. There are social programs, I believe, that can (and should) help blacks *develop* in all these areas, but entitlement by color is not a social program; it is a dubious reward for being black.

24 It now seems clear that the Supreme Court, in a series of recent decisions, is moving away from racial preferences. It has disallowed preferences except in instances of "identified discrimination," eroded the precedent that statistical racial imbalances are *prima facie* evidence of discrimination, and in effect granted white males the right to challenge consent degrees that use preference to achieve racial balances in the workplace. One civil rights leader said, "Night has fallen on civil rights." But I am not so sure. The effect of these decisions is to protect the constitutional rights of everyone rather than take rights away from blacks. What they do take away from blacks is the special entitlement to more rights than others that preferences always grant. Night has fallen on racial preferences, not on the fundamental rights of black Americans. The reason for this shift, I believe, is that the white mandate for absolution from past racial sins has weakened considerably during the eighties. Whites are now less willing to endure unfairness to themselves in order to grant special entitlements to blacks, even when these entitlements are justified in the name of past suffering. Yet the black mandate for more power in society has remained unchanged. And I think part of the anxiety that many blacks feel over these decisions has to do with the loss of black power they may signal. We had won a certain specialness and now we are losing it.

25 But the power we've lost by these decisions is really only the power that grows out of our victimization—the power to claim special entitlements under the law because of past oppression. This is not a very substantial or reliable power, and it is important that we know this so we can focus more exclusively on the kind of development that will bring enduring power. There is talk now that Congress will pass new legislation to compensate for these new limits on affirmative action. If this happens, I hope that their focus will be on development and anti-discrimination rather than entitlement, on achieving racial parity rather than jerry-building racial diversity.

I would also like to see affirmative action go back to its original purpose of 26 enforcing equal opportunity—a purpose that in itself disallows racial preferences. We cannot be sure that the discriminatory impulse in America has yet been shamed into extinction, and I believe affirmative action can make its greatest contribution by providing a rigorous vigilance in this area. It can guard constitutional rather than racial rights, and help institutions evolve standards of merit and selection that are appropriate to the institution's needs yet as free of racial bias as possible (again, with the understanding that racial imbalances are not always an indication of racial bias). One of the most important things affirmative action can do is to define exactly what racial discrimination is and how it might manifest itself within a specific institution. The impulse to discriminate *is* subtle and cannot be ferreted out unless its many guises are made clear to people. Along with this there should be monitoring of institutions and heavy sanctions brought to bear when actual discrimination is found. This is the sort of affirmative action that America owes to blacks and to itself. It goes after the evil of discrimination itself, while preferences only sidestep the evil and grant entitlement to its *presumed* victims.

But if not preferences, then what? I think we need social policies that are 27 committed to two goals: the educational and economic development of disadvantaged people, regardless of race, and the eradication from our society—through close monitoring and severe sanctions—of racial, ethnic, or gender discrimination. Preferences will not deliver us to either of these goals, since they tend to benefit those who are not disadvantaged—middle-class white women and middle-class blacks—and attack one form of discrimination with another. Preferences are inexpensive and carry the glamour of good intentions—change the numbers and the good deed is done. To be against them is to be unkind. But I think the unkindest cut is to bestow on children like my own an undeserved advantage while neglecting the development of those disadvantaged children on the East Side of my city who will likely never be in a position to benefit from a preference. Give my children fairness; give disadvantaged children a better shot at development—better elementary and secondary schools, job training, safer neighborhoods, better financial assistance for college, and so on. Fewer blacks go to college today than ten years ago; more black males of college age are in prison or under the control of the criminal justice system than in college. This despite racial preferences.

The mandates of black power and white absolution out of which prefer- 28 ences emerged were not wrong in themselves. What was wrong was that both races focused more on the goals of these mandates than on the means to the goals. Blacks can have no real power without taking responsibility for their own educational and economic development. Whites can have no racial innocence without earning it by eradicating discrimination and helping the disadvantaged to develop. Because we ignored the means, the goals have not been reached, and the real work remains to be done.

Questions About Strategy

1. At the beginning of the essay, how does Shelby Steele use his own experience to establish the ethical appeal of his argument?

2. How does Steele compare the positions of blacks and whites arguing for affirmative action?

3. What kind of evidence does Steele use to support his reinterpretation of the purpose of affirmative action?

A Sampler of Other Essays

1. Matt Fisher, "Drug Abuse in the Work Place" (student essay), p. 154
2. Marya Mannes, "Packaged Deception," p. 97
3. H. L. Mencken, "The Penalty of Death," p. 150
4. Anna Quindlen, "Execution," p. 152

Writing Assignments

Narrate **1.** Make a list of the special objects you have inherited from members of your family—photographs, tools, clothing. Select one that has become legendary in your family. Then narrate the story of that object, using descriptive details, to make some point about a lesson you inherited with the object.

Observe **2.** Select someone who does an unusual job—a mechanic, a stockbroker, an actor, a psychic—and ask him or her to analyze a process he or she follows to complete one aspect of his or her job successfully. Use this explanation to prove that a complex job can be made simple or that a job that appears simple can be more difficult than it seems.

Investigate **3.** Interview members of two groups of students (for example, male and female, black and white, young and old) about what kinds of jokes make them laugh. Then report your findings in an essay that compares the two groups according to their sense of humor.

Collaborate **4.** Collect information from the members of your writing group on the types of writing teachers they have encountered in their years of schooling. Establish at least three categories of teachers. Then classify them, explaining the strengths and weaknesses of the members of each category.

Read **5.** Select a word that has always bothered you and that has had significant meaning in your life. Search your library's data base for books that might define this word. Then use this information, together with your own experience, to compose an extended definition of the word.

Report **6.** Respond to one of the essays in this section by writing a letter to its author about the features in his or her essay you found particularly enjoyable. You may also want to identify those sections of his or her essay you found difficult to understand. In the latter case, you may want to list the kind of information you need to clarify your misunderstanding.

Analyze **7.** Identify and analyze the unforeseen consequences of some policy enacted in your school or community. Consider what prompted the creation of the policy. Finally, speculate about the policy's future.

Evaluate **8.** Read the two essays (student and professional) that illustrate one of the strategies in this section and the four essays listed in "A Sampler of Other Essays." Then evaluate which of the six essays makes the most effective use of the strategy. Explain the reasons for your choice.

Argue **9.** Draft a letter to the Minority or Ethnic Studies departments on your campus arguing that all minority students should be required to take a traditional version of the course in Western civilization. Find and use sources to support one of the following arguments: (1) all students—regardless of gender, race, and class—are entitled to know the version of the humanities that has been taught by the dominant culture; or (2) minority students should learn how to challenge the assumptions and assertions contained in the language of the traditional humanities course.

Argue **10.** Conduct some research on the cultural backgrounds of the students and faculty on your campus. How many students and faculty come from minority or other cultures? How many citizens in your state or region come from the same culture? How many opportunities does your university offer to faculty and students to study the cultural history of these groups? Once you have completed your research, write a letter to your state legislature's Education Committee presenting your research and suggesting reasons why they should fund more students and faculty from culturally diverse backgrounds.

Special Assignments

12 | The Essay Examination

The essay examination is one of the most practical of all academic writing assignments. By asking you to compose an answer to a specific question, with a limited amount of time for organizing your thoughts, it calls on most of the skills you have developed as a writer. As historian T. H. White points out in his book *In Search of History*, "One must grasp the question quickly; answer hard, with minimum verbiage; and do it all against a speeding clock."

Instructors frequently complain that students produce their worst writing on essay examinations. Of course, the "speeding clock" makes it impossible for you to work slowly and carefully through the stages of planning, drafting, and revising your responses. And certainly, the pressure of taking an examination does not encourage stylistic polish. But in spite of these limitations, you can still plan what you want to say, develop your purpose into an adequate essay, and reserve some time to review and proofread your answer. If you simply begin writing without using those strategies, you are likely to produce an essay that is irrelevant, inadequate, unclear, and even self-contradictory.

If you practice the major principles of purposeful writing discussed in this book, you will be able to improve the quality of your essay answers. Of course, you will not learn the subject matter of your examinations in this chapter. But many weak responses to essay examination questions are caused not by ignorance of the subject matter but by carelessness, haste, or panic. The recommendations in this chapter will help you avoid such pitfalls.

READ THE QUESTION CAREFULLY

Before you begin to answer any part of an examination, read the question carefully to see what it asks you to write about and how it asks you to write about it. If you misinterpret the question, your answer may be inadequate, even if it shows detailed knowledge of the subject and is otherwise well written. Essay questions are generally carefully written to identify a specific subject and indicate a specific approach. So before you begin to write, ask yourself, "What subject does this question require me to write about and how does it require me to write about it?" Look for key words—such as *evaluate*, *trace*, or *contrast*—that indicate the appropriate organization for your information. If you are asked to *analyze* a passage, a summary or a paraphrase will not satisfy the requirement.

UPI/Bettmann Newsphotos

If you are asked to *compare* two characters in a play, a description of each character may not develop the comparison. *Never begin to write until you have a clear idea of the form and content of the answer required.*

Study the following question and the two answers to it to see the difference in answers derived from a careful and from a careless reading of the question.

Examination Question

FDR and JFK had different conceptions of the presidential press conference. Using these two photographs as evidence, describe and contrast their conceptions.

Answer 1

FDR and JFK had different conceptions of the presidential press conference. FDR saw it as a private discussion with a small group of friendly reporters; JFK saw it as a public performance in front of a large audience that included reporters and the American people. In the two photographs, these contrasting views can be seen in each president's choice of setting, characters, and activity.

FDR chose the Oval Office for his intimate press conferences. The informality of this setting is illustrated by the small group of reporters

Photo courtesy The John F. Kennedy Library, Boston, Photo No. AR 6703B.

standing close to the president, the bouquet of flowers on his desk, and
the good will evident in the president's smile. By contrast, JFK chose
the auditorium at the State Department for his more imposing press
conferences. The formality of this setting is illustrated by the way
reporters are separated from the president by theater seating, by the
elevated stage and rostrum, and by the microphones on the lectern.
Instead of the casual bouquet of flowers, the flags and official seals of
the president suggest that this press conference is a ceremonial
occasion.

FDR invited thirty or so reporters to his weekly press conferences.
He thought of them as "family" and was eager to talk with them about
various issues of public policy. Because all of them were print
journalists, he provided them with information that they could use to
write their stories. JFK held open news conferences, and usually the
four-hundred-seat auditorium was filled to overflowing. He thought of
reporters as "friendly adversaries" and enjoyed making news by
sparring with them on live television. In the first photo, FDR seems

prepared to answer questions by himself. In the second, JFK is flanked by a group of advisors who can help him if he is asked a complicated question.

The drama captured in the FDR photo suggests the activity of a family council. FDR allowed each reporter to ask questions, but he conducted his conferences like after-dinner discussions, lecturing leisurely to reporters about the state of the economy or foreign policy and dictating when they could or could not quote him directly. JFK called on reporters, but since he staged his press conferences as thirty-minute television shows, he had to be selective about which questions he acknowledged and which answers he developed in detail. In the first photo, FDR seems like a beneficent father who has stopped discussion to pose for a family photograph. In the second, JFK seems like a matinee idol performing not just for the reporters in the room but for the millions of people watching on television.

This is an excellent response to the examiner's question. The first paragraph asserts a basic contrast in the two presidents' conception of the press conference that is based on supporting evidence from the photographs. The three paragraphs that follow use the alternating pattern to contrast FDR's and JFK's choice of, respectively, setting, characters, and dramatic activity. Each detail develops the contrast announced in the opening paragraph. There are no digressions. And each paragraph concludes with a brief summary that re-affirms the basic contrast. The writer knows what the question requires. That determines her purpose and controls what she has to say.

Answer 2

The photograph of FDR's press conference is very crowded. About twenty people, not all of them smiling, are trying to squeeze themselves into the shot. It is not clear from the photograph that all these people are reporters—only one seems to be writing. All seem aware of the photographer, who has apparently asked them to stop their discussion and pose. The president's desk is covered, but not cluttered, with paper. Other objects on his desk are an inkstand, a telephone, and a large bouquet of flowers. The president is seated in a large, comfortable chair. Because FDR was crippled by polio, photographers agreed to maintain the illusion of his good health by taking his picture only when he was seated. His smile suggests that the press conference has been productive.

The photograph of JFK's press conference is also crowded, but most of the reporters are seated in (or standing around the rim of) an auditorium, while the president stands on a platform behind a large lectern. Some of his advisors appear to be seated on his left. Near the double doors to his right are two television cameras. Behind the windows on the second floor is the control center. Barely visible behind the glass are the technicians who control the light and sound for the president's performance and broadcast it to the American public. The president seems to be making a thoughtful reply to an important question. Most of the reporters in the room are either listening to his response or writing significant quotes in their notebooks.

Even though it shows good observation of details, answer 2 is unsatisfactory, chiefly because it does not respond directly to the question. The purpose imposed by the directions was to use the two photographs to *describe and contrast* the different conceptions FDR and JFK had of the presidential press conference. Answer 2 describes each photograph separately but pays almost no attention to the contrast the descriptions were to demonstrate. The writer digresses by mentioning FDR's polio, which is irrelevant to the description of the press conference. This answer lacks a thesis; it tells readers what each press conference looks like but says nothing about the two presidents' differing conceptions of them.

THINK OUT YOUR ANSWER
BEFORE WRITING

Plan your answer before you begin to write it. Because in an essay examination you will have almost no chance for composing a discovery draft or for extensive revising, your answer must be drafted correctly the first time. Most examination questions attempt to restrict your subject, specify a method of development and organization, and suggest a thesis. Thinking about the implications of the information given in the question itself will bring to mind explanatory or illustrative details that you can use in your answer. For many questions, it is wise to start, as you learned in Chapter 3, by making a scratch outline to organize the information you want to use and then formulating a thesis statement or, in the case of brief answers, a topic sentence.

Answer 1 below shows a carefully planned response to this question:

Explain how the Arctic region supports various forms of plant and animal life.

The student thinks over the question and frames a topic sentence:

The seasonal changes in the permafrost enable the Arctic region to support various forms of plant and animal life.

The topic sentence (or thesis) shows that the writer understands that the question is asking him to discuss *how* a specific characteristic of the Arctic region—the seasonal changes in the permafrost—supports various forms of plant and animal life. His topic sentence will require him to define *permafrost,* to explain how seasonal changes affect it, and to demonstrate how these changes support plant and animal life. Notice how his answer satisfies the requirements of both the question and his own topic sentence.

Answer 1

The seasonal changes in the permafrost enable the Arctic region to support various forms of plant and animal life. During most of the year the ground is covered with snow, and permafrost freezes the sublayers of the soil to depths ranging from 50 to 4,800 feet. But during the spring months the snow melts and the top layer of the permafrost thaws into a swampy marsh. This layer is not deep enough to support trees, whose roots need from 4 to 8 feet of unfrozen soil to grow, but it does support a wide variety of stunted vegetation, composed mostly of mosses, lichens, and grasses. These plant communities, some featuring brightly colored flowers, support the life of insects, migrating birds, and grazing mammals such as reindeer.

This answer is an excellent example of purposeful writing in a paragraph: topic sentence, followed by supporting detail, followed by a concluding sentence that expands the reference to "plant and animal life." Because the writer planned his whole answer from beginning to end, he controls his paragraph and demonstrates his understanding of the content behind the question.

Answer 2 does not show the same careful thought about the requirements of the question or the use of an appropriate topic sentence to control the answer. Instead the student plunges into a summary of the facts without considering how they relate to the question she is supposed to be answering.

Answer 2

The Arctic region is able to support a wide range of plant and animal life. Although most of the area is virtually treeless, it does support specialized vegetation such as grasses and sedges. These plants have brightly colored flowers but thrive in swampy soil that makes walking extremely difficult. They provide habitation for many insects, including flies and mosquitoes that make what appears to be a beautiful meadow unbearable for most travelers. The most common mammals in this region are lemming, reindeer, Arctic fox, and wolf. Birds, mainly hawks, also migrate to the Arctic region during the summer months.

This paragraph does not answer the question. It catalogues the variety of plant and animal life in the Arctic region but fails to analyze the factor (the spring thaw of the top layer of the permafrost) that enables this life to thrive. The answer also digresses by its allusion to the difficulties encountered by travelers.

Failure to read the question carefully enough to see what it asks and failure to plan your answer are related faults. If you know the subject, careful reading of the question will suggest an answer, and planning the answer will give you a check against the wording in the question. If you miss the first step, you will probably miss the second also.

WRITE A COMPLETE ANSWER

Unless the directions specify a short answer, do not write a one- or two-sentence response in an essay examination. Be sure to distinguish between a short-answer test and an essay examination. A short-answer test tests your ability to recall facts, and each question can usually be answered in one or two minutes. Usually there are from twenty to thirty such questions in a fifty-minute quiz. An essay examination, by contrast, tests your ability to interpret facts—to select and organize information that supports a thesis. Because such an answer requires more extended writing, the examiner assumes that you may need as much as fifty minutes to compose each answer. Sometimes the directions specify how much time to allow for each answer, but if they do not, the number of questions in the test indicates approximately how much time you should devote to each answer.

A complete answer is one that deals with the subject as fully as possible within the time limits. An answer that is complete for a short-answer test will be inadequate for an essay examination. For example, with a few additions, the second sentence of answer 1 contrasting FDR's and JFK's conceptions of press conferences would be a complete answer for a short-answer test.

FDR saw [the presidential press conference] as a private discussion with a small group of friendly reporters; JFK saw it as a public performance in front of a large audience that included reporters and the American people.

But this would be an inadequate answer for an essay examination because it lacks the detailed analysis of the two photographs required by the question.

The answers to the following essay examination question further illustrate the difference between a complete and an incomplete answer.

What lessons did American military strategists learn from the French experience in Vietnam?

Answer 1

American military strategists learned little from the French experience in Vietnam because, like the French, they failed to understand the culture of the country and the dedication of the enemy. For example, the Americans ignored the lesson of the French "agroville" experiment when they adopted the Strategic Hamlet program. Both programs violated ancient Vietnamese traditions by removing peasants from their sacred villages and herding them into secure but alien fortresses. In each case, many peasants sneaked back to their homes, and those who remained nursed a growing hostility toward those who were trying to save them.

Similarly, the U.S. did not understand the lesson of Dien Bien Phu. The French assumed that a massive increase in highly trained forces could overpower a poorly armed enemy. At Dien Bien Phu, however, the Vietminh used superhuman effort to haul their small supply of large guns through dense jungles to trap and capture the superior French forces. Like the French, American military and political leaders failed to learn that increases in personnel and weapons were insufficient to dispose of a dedicated army fighting for its homeland.

Answer 2

The United States never made the error of Dien Bien Phu, where the French troops were in a valley by enemy artillery. But, by and large, the United States repeated the central French mistake of failing to understand the country it was trying to save from communism.

Answer 2 is incomplete for two reasons: first, it does not mention the real lesson of Dien Bien Phu (that a small, dedicated army can outmaneuver large forces), and second, it fails to illustrate how the Americans repeated the central French mistake of ignoring the culture of the country it was trying to help. Although the second answer may be adequate for a short-answer examination, it is not developed in enough detail for an essay examination.

Completeness in an essay examination resembles completeness in paragraphs (discussed in Chapter 7). The topic sentence of a paragraph or the thesis of an essay is necessarily a general statement. To make that statement clear and convincing, you must develop it with specific details. This is especially true when an examination question, such as the one on Vietnam, calls for a judgment. Your judgment is only an assertion until you support it with evidence. If the writer of answer 1 on Vietnam had stopped with the assertion in his first sentence, he would have written an incomplete answer. His explanatory details provide the evidence that makes his answer complete.

DO NOT PAD YOUR ANSWER

Padding an answer with needless repetition or irrelevant detail is more likely to hurt than to help. A padded answer suggests that you are trying to conceal a lack of knowledge. Graders are not easily persuaded that an answer is good just because it is long. They are more likely to be annoyed at having to sort through all the padding to find the information that might be relevant to the question. It is your responsibility to select, present, and develop the essential information called for in the question.

The answer below is a padded response to the question of what lessons American strategists learned from the French experience in Vietnam. The grader's comments identify the two major weaknesses of the answer—failure to explain the lesson learned and the useless repetition of the content of the first paragraph in the second. The thesis statement reveals that the writer was not prepared to answer the question. She said all she had to say in the first paragraph, but she seemed to feel that saying it over again, from a slightly different perspective, would somehow make her answer acceptable. Through the use of marginal comments and editorial suggestions, the grader calls attention to these deficiencies.

What specific lesson did the United States learn from the French defeat at Dien Bien Phu?

vague

The Americans learned a <u>great deal</u> from the French war with the revolutionary army called the Vietminh, headed by the communist leader Ho Chi Minh. Throughout their war with these guerrillas, the French continuously increased their troop commitments ~~to higher and higher numbers~~ because they believed that more soldiers and more guns could bring about a speedy victory against a small and poorly armed enemy. At Dien Bien Phu, the French parachuted over 6,000 crack troops into a valley to begin an all-out assault on the Vietminh. But they did not realize that the enemy had worked its way through the jungles to occupy the high ridges above the valley where it had a superior military position.

This paragraph merely restates the ideas in paragraph 1 and further delays your response to the question about what Americans may have learned from this battle.

~~The capture of the French troops at Dien Bien Phu is an example of how important military mistakes are often made by miscalculation of the enemy's strategy. The French assumed that they could confront the enemy in a traditional ground war. But because the Vietminh was a guerrilla army, it never allowed the French the opportunity to engage in this kind of military action. Instead, it hauled its guns to the top of a high ridge and surprised the French.~~

Your problem seems to begin with your vague thesis sentence. You seen uncertain about what the United States learned from the French, so you simply present (rather than interpret) the facts of Dien Bien Phu.

PROOFREAD YOUR ANSWER

Reserve some time at the end of the examination to reread and correct your answer. You will not have time to write a second draft, but you may have enough time for a quick review and revision. First, reread the question. Then, as you read your answer, determine whether you supplied all the required information. Sometimes a subtle change in diction or sentence structure will clarify your answer. At other times you may need to add a sentence or paragraph to develop or redirect your answer. Use a caret (∧) to indicate where such insertions belong, then place the additional information in a numbered box in the margin or at the end of your paper. Help your instructor follow these revisions by writing a brief note near the insertion. If the writer of the essay answer above has reserved time for such revisions, she might have sharpened her thesis, added a few sentences about what the United States learned from Dien Bien Phu, and deleted the repetitious second paragraph.

Review
Exercises ——— Examine each of the following paired answers to questions on literature, psychology, and cultural geography. Decide which is the better answer, and be prepared to explain the reasons for your choice. Even if you are unfamiliar with the subjects, you should be able to decide which answer satisfies the requirements of the question.

Question 1   Just before he dies, Laertes says to Hamlet, "Mine and my father's death come not on thee, nor thine on me." In view of the facts of the play, how do you interpret this statement?

Answer 1   Laertes' statement fits some of the facts but not all of them and is best understood as a request to let bygones be bygones. True, Hamlet is not responsible for Laertes' death, because Hamlet thought he was engaging in a friendly bout with blunted swords. When he picked up Laertes' sword in the mix-up, he did not know it was poisoned. Since Laertes deliberately put the poison there, he was responsible for both Hamlet's death and his own. Hamlet killed Polonius by mistake, thinking that the person behind the curtain was the king. To that extent it was an accidental killing, but a killing nevertheless. I think Laertes' statement is intended not as a literal description of the facts but as a reconciliation speech. I interpret the statement to mean: "We have both been the victims of the king's treachery. Forgive me for your death, as I forgive you for mine and my father's."

Answer 2   Laertes returns from France and learns that his father has been killed by Hamlet. He is almost mad with grief and rage, and in a stormy scene with the king he demands revenge. He and the king conspire to arrange a duel between Laertes and Hamlet in which Laertes will use a poisoned sword. The duel takes place after Ophelia's funeral, and Laertes cuts Hamlet with the poisoned sword. Then, in a scuffle, their swords are knocked from their hands, and Hamlet picks up Laertes' poisoned sword and wounds him. Meanwhile the king has put poison in a goblet of wine he intends for Hamlet, but the queen drinks the wine by mistake. When Hamlet sees that she is dying, he kills the king; then both Hamlet and Laertes die.

Question 2   Explain the chief differences between neurosis and psychosis.

Answer 1

The chief differences between neurosis and psychosis are the extent to which a person is alienated from reality and his or her chances of making a workable adjustment to normal living. The boundary between the two cannot be precisely drawn; therefore the differences are best illustrated at their extremes.

A person suffering from neurosis may feel serious anxieties but still be able to handle the ordinary activities of daily living. For example, a woman may have a phobia about being left alone with a red-headed man because a male with red hair once assaulted her. But as long as she avoids that particular situation, she is able to fulfill her domestic and business responsibilities. Through psychiatric counseling she may learn to understand the cause of her phobia and either get rid of it or control it. Fears of heights and of crowds are examples of other neuroses. They are not central to the way one organizes one's life and can be alleviated either by counseling or by avoidance of situations in which the neurotic response is likely to occur.

A psychotic person is so divorced from reality that in severe cases, like paranoid schizophrenia, he or she lives in a private world that has little relation to the real one. A man who thinks he is Moses and feels a divinely granted right to punish those who break any of the Ten Commandments has reorganized experience around a delusion that makes life bearable for him. His delusion is necessary to his continued existence. In a sense he has found a therapy that works for him. He will resist psychiatric help because he thinks he no longer has any problem: it is the sinners who have problems. Such a person may be helped to some degree by specialized, institutional care, but the chances of a complete recovery are slim.

Between these extremes are conditions classifiable as either neurosis or psychosis. In such cases psychiatrists may disagree in their diagnoses.

Answer 2

Because there is some neurosis in all of us, we all utilize defense mechanisms against our frustrations. For that matter, a psychotic person may also use such defenses, but is less likely to be aware of what he or she is doing. We may repress our frustrations—simply refuse to think about them. Or we may defend by consciously developing characteristics that are the opposite of those we disapprove of. For example, a person who is troubled by a tendency toward greediness may force himself or herself to generously give away prized possessions. We can also escape frustration and low self-esteem by projection of our faults, blaming them on other people. Or we can use rationalization by devising excuses to justify our behavior. Finally, we may save our pride by fantasizing. That is, a young man may imagine that the girl who has declined to date him is cheering wildly in a basketball gymnasium when he sets a new scoring record and that she will be waiting for him with bated breath at the locker-room door.

Neurotic people may need the help that defense mechanisms can give them, but excessive use of such devices can make a problem worse. And if a neurotic condition becomes so serious that the person is out of touch with the real world and locked into his or her private world, that person is psychotic. As I think back over my answer, it seems to me that a psychotic person would be more likely to use some of these mechanisms than others.

Question 3

Contrast the different concepts of *border* that are illustrated by these two maps of North America.

Answer 1

These two maps provide a dramatic contrast between the geopolitical and theoretical concepts of <u>border</u>. The first map designates the official borders of the United States, which have been formed by three methods. First, there are <u>natural</u> borders. Rivers such as the Ohio and Mississippi, lakes such as Michigan and Erie, and mountains such as the Smokies and Sierra Nevada provide natural ways to separate various regions of the country from one another. Second, the map documents <u>historical</u> borders that were negotiated as the result of specific military conflicts—for example, the border separating Canada and Maine was negotiated to end the Aroostook War (1842), and the border separating Mexico and Texas was negotiated to end the Mexican War (1848). And third, this map illustrates <u>political</u>

Map by Graf-Tech, Inc.

borders that were formed by the process of achieving statehood. After the formation of the thirteen original colonies, large blocks of land, particularly west of the Mississippi, were shaped by local politicians and federal agencies into territories that eventually became states. The borders of these structures—for example, Colorado and Oklahoma— were often drawn without reference to the contours of the land or the interests of the inhabitants.

By contrast, the second map illustrates Joel Garreau's theory that the United States can be understood only by reshaping its borders into "the nine nations of North America." By ignoring the principles used to establish the borders of the first map, Garreau is able to speculate about how people's attitudes toward issues such as economics and ecology give rise to more natural alliances—and hence more meaningful borders—than those on the geopolitical map. For example, Garreau says that the neatly boxed borders of Colorado make no sense. The wheat farmers in the eastern part of the state feel a more natural alliance with farmers in "The Breadbasket" than with the

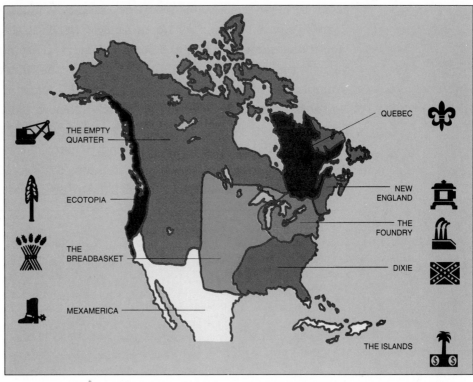

THE EMPTY QUARTER

ECOTOPIA

THE BREADBASKET

MEXAMERICA

QUEBEC

NEW ENGLAND

THE FOUNDRY

DIXIE

THE ISLANDS

© Robert Anthony, Inc. 1987. From *Nine Nations of North America,* by Joel Garreau, © Houghton Mifflin Co.

industrialists in Denver who want to mine the resources of "The Empty Quarter." Similarly, the thin strip along the Pacific coast contains not three states, but two nations. What separates them, Garreau argues, is their attitude toward water. "Ecotopia" is the only place in the West with enough water, whereas "MexAmerica" must suck water from other places to support its dry, sunny climate.

Answer 2

 The first map illustrates the international borders separating the United States from Canada and Mexico, and the national borders separating the states. Some of these borders are irregular because they are formed by the shoreline of the ocean or the banks of a river. Other borders are extremely regular because they were drawn by surveyors who were marking out plots of land for the United States government. For example, the borders of the western states look like rectangular blocks, whereas the borders of the eastern states look like oddly shaped pieces of a puzzle.

 The second map does not acknowledge the borders that separate the United States from Canada and Mexico, or the borders that separate the various states from one another. It illustrates Joel Garreau's nine "nations" of North America. Each nation has an identifying name, symbol, and border. Some of these nations are vaguely recognizable as traditional regions in the United States. For example, the borders of "The Foundry" enclose most of the industrial Northeast, whereas the borders of "Dixie" enclose most of the Old South. But most of the map rearranges the traditional borders of North America. For example, "The Empty Quarter" includes most of the underdeveloped land of the United States and Canada, and "MexAmerica" joins southern California, the Southwest, and Mexico.

The Value of C | Jean Shepherd

In this excerpt, humorist Jean Shepherd remembers the one time he could not avoid a question in algebra and the extraordinary luck he had in formulating an answer. In what ways does Shepherd avoid *reading the question carefully* and *thinking out his answer*? What kind of guerrilla tactics does he employ as alternative strategies?

1 Wednesday, two days before the end, arrived like any other spring day. A faint breeze drifted from the south, bringing with it hints of long summer afternoons to come, of swung bats, of nights in the lilac bushes. But not for such as me. I stumped into algebra class feeling distinctly like the last soul aboard the *Titanic* as she was about to plunge to the bottom. The smart-asses were already in their seats, laughing merrily, the goddamn A's and B's and C's and even the M's. I took my seat in the back, among the rest of the condemned. Schwartz sat down sullenly and began his usual moan. Helen Weathers squatted toadlike, drenched in sweat. The class began, Pittinger's chalk squeaked, hands waved. The sun filtered in through the venetian blinds. A tennis ball pocked back and forth over a net somewhere. Faintly, the high clear voices of the girls' glee club sang, "Can you bake a cherry pie, charming Billy?" Birds twittered.

2 My knot of fear, by now an old friend, sputtered in my gut. In the past week, it had grown to roughly the size of a two-dollar watermelon. True I had avoided being called on even once the entire year, but it was a hollow victory and I knew it. Minute after minute inched slowly by as I ducked and dodged, Pittinger firing question after question at the class. Glancing at my Pluto watch, which I had been given for Christmas, I noted with deep relief that less than two minutes remained before the bell.

3 It was then that I made my fatal mistake, the mistake that all guerrilla fighters eventually make—I lost my concentration. For years, every fiber of my being, every instant in every class, had been directed solely at survival. On this fateful Wednesday, lulled by the sun, by the gentle sound of the tennis ball, by the steady drone of Pittinger's voice, by the fact that there were just two minutes to go, my mind slowly drifted off into a golden haze. A tiny mote of dust floated down through a slanting ray of sunshine. I watched it in its slow, undulating flight, like some microscopic silver bird.

4 "You're the apple of my eye, darling Billy . . . I can bake a cherry pie . . ."

5 A rich maple syrup warmth filled my being. Out of the faint distance, I heard a deadly rasp, the faint honking of disaster.

6 For a stunned split second, I thought I'd been jabbed with an electric cattle prod. Pittinger's voice, loud and commanding, was pronouncing my name. He was calling on ME! Oh, my God! With a goddamn minute to go, he had nailed me. I heard Schwartz bleat a high, quavering cry, a primal scream. I knew what it meant: If they got him, the greatest master of them all, there's no hope for ANY of us!

Shepherd, Jean. *A Fistful of Fig Newtons*. New York: Doubleday, 1981. 192–95.

As I stood slowly at my seat, frantically bidding for time, I saw a great 7
puddle forming around Helen Weathers. It wasn't all sweat. Chester had sunk
to the floor beneath his desk, and behind me Zynzmeister's beads were clatter-
ing so loudly I could hardly hear his Hail Marys.

"Come to the board, please. Give us the value of C in this equation." 8

In a stupor of wrenching fear, I felt my legs clumping up the aisle. On all 9
sides the blank faces stared. At the board—totally unfamiliar territory to me—I
stared at the first equation I had ever seen up close. It was well over a yard and
a half long, lacerated by mysterious crooked lines and fractions in parentheses,
with miniature twos and threes hovering above the whole thing like tiny bar-
nacles. Xs and Ys were jumbled in crazy abandon. At the very end of this
unholy mess was a tiny equal sign. And on the other side of the equal sign was
a zero. Zero! All this crap adds up to nothing! Jesus Christ! My mind reeled at
the very sight of this barbed-wire entanglement of mysterious symbols.

Pittinger stood to one side, arms folded, wearing an expression that said, 10
At last I've nailed the little bastard! He had been playing with me all the time.
He knew!

I glanced back at the class. It was one of the truly educational moments of 11
my life. The entire mob, including Schwartz, Chester, and even Zynzmeister,
were grinning happily, licking their chops with joyous expectation of my imminent crucifixion. I learned then that when true disaster strikes, we have no
friends. And there's nothing a phony loves more in this world than to see
another phony get what's coming to him.

"The value of C, please," rapped Pittinger. 12

The equation blurred before my eyes. The value of C. Where the hell was 13
it? What did a C look like, anyway? Or an A or a B, for that matter. I had forgotten the alphabet.

"C, please." 14

I spotted a single letter C buried deep in the writhing melange of Ys and 15
Xs and umlauts and plus signs, brackets, and God knows what all. One tiny C.
A torrent of sweat raged down my spinal column. My jockey shorts were
soaked and sodden with the sweat and stink of execution. Being a true guerrilla from years of the alphabetical ghetto, I showed no outward sign of panic,
my face stony; unyielding. You live by the gun, you die by the gun.

"C, please." Pittinger moodily scratched at his granite chin with thumb 16
and forefinger, his blue beard rasping nastily.

"Oh my darling Billy boy, you're the apple of my eye . . ." 17

Somewhere birds twittered on, tennis racquet met tennis ball. My moment 18
had finally arrived.

Now, I have to explain that for years I had been the leader of the atheistic 19
free-thinkers of Warren G. Harding School, scoffers all at the Sunday School
miracles taught at the Presbyterian church; unbelievers.

That miracle stuff is for old ladies, all that walking on water and birds fly- 20
ing around with loaves of bread in their beaks. Who can believe that crap?

Now, I am not so sure. Ever since that day in Pittinger's algebra class I 21
have had an uneasy suspicion that maybe something mysterious is going on
somewhere.

As I stood and stonily gazed at the enigmatic Egyptian hieroglyphics of 22
that fateful equation, from somewhere, someplace beyond the blue horizon, it
came to me, out of the mist. I heard my voice say clearly, firmly, with decision:

"C . . . is equal to three." 23

Pittinger staggered back; his glasses jolted down to the tip of his nose. 24

"How the hell did you know?!" he bellowed hoarsely, his snap-on bow tie 25 popping loose in the excitement.

The class was in an uproar. I caught a glimpse of Schwartz, his face pale 26 with shock. I had caught one on the fat part of the bat. It was a true miracle. I had walked on water.

Instantly, the old instincts took over. In a cool, level voice I answered 27 Pittinger's rhetorical question.

"Sir, I used empirical means." 28

He paled visibly and clung to the chalk trough for support. On cue, the 29 bell rang out. The class was over. With a swiftness born of long experience, I was out of the room even before the echo of the bell had ceased. The guerrilla's code is always hit and run. A legend had been born.

What Does a Woman Need to Know? | **Mary Field Belenky**
Bythe McVicker Clinchy
Nancy Ruth Goldberger
Jill Mattack Torule

This selection from *Women's Ways of Knowing* compares two stories about the "limitations of firsthand experience as a source of knowledge." What important differences between the teachers and students in the two stories can you identify? How do the authors use this information to support the main point in their concluding paragraph?

We begin with the reminiscences of two ordinary women, each recalling an 1 hour during her first year at college. One of them, now middle aged, remembered the first meeting of an introductory science course. The professor marched into the lecture hall, placed upon his desk a large jar filled with dried beans, and invited the students to guess how many beans the jar contained. After listening to an enthusiastic chorus of wildly inaccurate estimates the professor smiled a thin, dry smile, revealed the correct answer, and announced, "You have just learned an important lesson about science. Never trust the evidence of your own senses."

Thirty years later, the woman could guess what the professor had in mind. 2 He saw himself, perhaps, as inviting his students to embark upon an exciting voyage into a mysterious underworld invisible to the naked eye, accessible only thorough scientific method and scientific instruments. But the seventeen-year-old girl could not accept or even hear the invitation. Her sense of herself as a knower was shaky, and it was based on the belief that she could use her own firsthand experience as a source of truth. This man was saying that this belief was fallacious. He was taking away her only tool for knowing and

---

Belenky, Mary Field, et al. *Women's Ways of Knowing: The Development of Self, Voice and Mind.* New York: Basic, 1986. 191–93.

providing her with no substitute. "I remember feeling small and scared," the woman says, "and I did the only thing I could do. I dropped the course that afternoon, and I haven't gone near science since."

The second woman, in her first year at college, told a superficially similar but profoundly different story about a philosophy class she had attended just a month or two before the interview. The teacher came into class carrying a large cardboard cube. She placed it on the desk in front of her and asked the class what it was. They said it was a cube. She asked what a cube was, and they said a cube contained six equal square sides. She asked how they knew that this object contained six equal square sides. By looking at it, they said. "But how do you know?" the teacher asked again. She pointed to the side facing her, and, therefore, invisible to the students; then she lifted the cube and pointed to the side that had been face down on the desk, and, therefore, also invisible. "We can't look at all six sides of a cube at once, can we? So we can't exactly *see* a cube. And yet, you're right. You know it's a cube. But you know it not just because you have eyes but because you have intelligence. You invent the sides you cannot see. You use your intelligence to create the 'truth' about cubes."

The student said to the interviewer,

It blew my mind. You'll think I'm nuts, but I ran back to the dorm and I called my boyfriend and I said, "Listen, this is just incredible," and I told him all about it. I'm not sure he could see why I was so excited. I'm not sure I understand it myself. But I really felt, for the first time, like I was really in college, like I was—I don't know—sort of *grown up.*

Both stories are about the limitations of firsthand experience as a source of knowledge—we cannot simply see the truth about either the jar of beans or the cube—but there is a difference. We can know the truth about cubes. Indeed, the students did know it. As the science professor pointed out, the students were wrong about the beans; their senses had deceived them. But, as the philosophy teacher pointed out, the students were right about the cube; their minds had served them well.

The science professor was the only person in the room who knew how many beans were in that jar. Theoretically, the knowledge was available to the students; they could have counted the beans. But faced with that tedious prospect, most would doubtless take the professor's word for it. He is authority. They had to rely upon his knowledge rather than their own. On the other hand, every member of the philosophy class knew that the cube had six sides. They were all colleagues.

The science professor exercised his authority in a benign fashion, promising the students that he would provide them with the tools they needed to excavate invisible truths. Similarly, the philosophy teacher planned to teach her students the skills of philosophical analysis, but she was at pains to assure them that they already possessed the tools to construct some powerful truths. They had built cubes on their own, using only their own powers of inference, without the aid of elaborate procedures or fancy apparatus or even a teacher. Although a teacher might have told them once that a cube contained six equal square sides, they did not have to take the teacher's word for it; they could have easily verified it for themselves.

The lesson the science professor wanted to teach is that experience is a source of error. Taught in isolation, this lesson diminished the student, rendering her dumb and dependent. The philosophy teacher's lesson was that although raw experience is insufficient, by reflecting upon it the student could arrive at truth. It was a lesson that made the student feel more powerful ("sort of grown up").

No doubt it is true that, as the professor in May Sarton's novel *The Small Room* says, the "art" of being a student requires humility. But the woman we interviewed did not find the science lesson humbling; she found it humiliating. Arrogance was not then and is not now her natural habitat. Like most of the women in our sample she lacked confidence in herself as a thinker; and the kind of learning the science teacher demanded was not only painful but crippling. 10

In thinking about the education of women, Adrienne Rich writes, "Suppose we were to ask ourselves, simply: What does a woman need to know?" A woman, like any other human being, does need to know that the mind makes mistakes; but our interviews have convinced us that every woman, regardless of age, social class, ethnicity, and academic achievement, needs to know that she is capable of intelligent thought, and she needs to know it right away. Perhaps men learn this lesson before going to college, or perhaps they can wait until they have proved themselves to hear it; we do not know. We do know that many of the women we interviewed had not yet learned it. 11

In Laboratory with Agassiz | Samuel H. Scudder

In this memoir, scientist Samuel H. Scudder (1837–1911) recalls how his teacher, Louis Agassiz (1807–1873), required him to examine a fish in scrupulous detail, reflect on what he had seen, and speculate on what he had not expected to see. What does Scudder learn by following Agassiz's injunction to "look, look, look"? What would Agassiz consider a *complete* answer to his examination?

It was more than fifteen years ago that I entered the laboratory of Professor Agassiz, and told him I had enrolled my name in the Scientific School as a student of natural history. He asked me a few questions about my object in coming, my antecedents generally, the mode in which I afterwards proposed to use the knowledge I might acquire, and, finally, whether I wished to study any special branch. To the latter I replied that, while I wished to be well grounded in all departments of zoology, I purposed to devote myself specially to insects. 1

"When do you wish to begin?" he asked. 2

"Now," I replied. 3

This seemed to please him, and with an energetic "Very well!" he reached from a shelf a huge jar of specimens in yellow alcohol. "Take this fish, " he said, "and look at it; we call it a haemulon; by and by I will ask what you have seen." 4

With that he left me, but in a moment returned with explicit instructions as to the care of the object entrusted to me. 5

Scudder, Samuel H. *Every Saturday*. 4 April 1874. 369–70.

"No man is fit to be a naturalist," said he, "who does not know how to   6
take care of specimens."

I was to keep the fish before me in a tin tray, and occasionally moisten the   7
surface with alcohol from the jar, always taking care to replace the stopper
tightly. Those were not the days of ground-glass stoppers and elegantly shaped
exhibition jars; all the old students will recall the huge necklace glass bottles
with their leaky, wax-besmeared corks, half eaten by insects, and begrimed
with cellar dust. Entomology was a cleaner science than ichthyology, but the
example of the Professor, who had unhesitatingly plunged to the bottom of the
jar to produce the fish, was infectious; and though this alcohol had a "very
ancient and fishlike smell," I really dared not show any aversion within these
sacred precincts, and treated the alcohol as though it were pure water. Still I
was conscious of a passing feeling of disappointment, for gazing at a fish did
not commend itself to an ardent entomologist. My fiends at home, too, were
annoyed when they discovered that no amount of eau-de-Cologne would
drown the perfume which haunted me like a shadow.

In ten minutes I had seen all that could be seen in that fish, and started in   8
search of the Professor—who had, however, left the Museum; and when I
returned, after lingering over some of the odd animals stored in the upper
apartment, my specimen was dry all over. I dashed the fluid over the fish as if
to resuscitate the beast from a fainting fit, and looked with anxiety for a return
of the normal sloppy appearance. This little excitement over, nothing was to be
done but to return to a steadfast gaze at my mute companion. Half an hour
passed—an hour—another hour; the fish began to look loathsome. I turned it
over and around; looked it in the face—ghastly; from behind, beneath, above,
sideways, at three-quarter's view—just as ghastly. I was in despair; at an early
hour I concluded that lunch was necessary; so, with infinite relief, the fish was
carefully replaced in the jar, and for an hour I was free.

On my return, I learned that Professor Agassiz had been at the Museum,   9
but had gone, and would not return for several hours. My fellow-students were
too busy to be disturbed by continued conversation. Slowly I drew forth that
hideous fish, and with a feeling of desperation again looked at it. I might not
use a magnifying-glass; instruments of all kinds were interdicted. My two
hands, my two eyes, and the fish: it seemed a most limited field. I pushed my
finger down its throat to feel how sharp the teeth were. I began to count the
scales in the different rows, until I was convinced that was nonsense. At last a
happy thought struck me—I would draw the fish; and now with surprise I
began to discover new features in the creature. Just then the Professor returned.

"That is right," said he; "a pencil is one of the best of eyes. I am glad to   10
notice, too, that you keep your specimen wet, and your bottle corked."

With these encouraging words, he added: 11

"Well, what is it like?"   12

He listened attentively to my brief rehearsal of the structure of parts   13
whose names were still unknown to me: the fringed gill-arches and movable
operculum; the pores of the head, fleshy lips and lidless eyes; the lateral line,
the spinous fins and forked tail; the compressed and arched body. When I finished, he waited as if expecting more, and then, with an air of disappointment:

"You have not looked very carefully; why," he continued more earnestly,   14
"you haven't even seen one of the most conspicuous features of the animal,

which is plainly before your eyes as the fish itself; look again, look again!" and
he left me to my misery.

I was piqued. I was mortified. Still more of that wretched fish! But now I   15
set myself to my task with a will, and discovered one new thing after another,
until I saw how just the Professor's criticism had been. The afternoon passed
quickly; and when, towards its close, the Professor inquired:

"Do you see it yet?"   16

"No," I replied, "I am certain I do not, but I see how little I saw before." 17

"That is next best," said he, earnestly, "but I won't hear you now; put   18
away your fish and go home; perhaps you will be ready with a better answer in
the morning. I will examine you before you look at the fish."

This was disconcerting. Not only must I think of my fish all night, study-   19
ing, without the object before me, what this unknown but most visible feature
might be; but also, without reviewing my discoveries, I must give an exact
account of them the next day. I had a bad memory; so I walked home by
Charles River in a distracted state, with my two perplexities.

The cordial greeting from the Professor the next morning was reassuring;   20
here was a man who seemed to be quite as anxious as I that I should see for
myself what he saw.

"Do you perhaps mean," I asked, "that the fish has symmetrical sides with   21
paired organs?"

His thoroughly pleased "Of course! Of course!" repaid the wakeful hours of   22
the previous night. After he had discoursed most happily and enthusiastically—
as he always did—upon the importance of this point, I ventured to ask what I
should do next.

"Oh, look at your fish!" he said, and left me again to my own devices. In a 23
little more than an hour he returned, heard my new catalogue.

"That is good, that is good!" he repeated; "but that is not all; go on"; and 24
so for three long days he placed that fish before my eyes, forbidding me to look
at anything else, or to use any artificial aid. "Look, look, look," was his
repeated injunction.

This was the best entomological lesson I ever had—a lesson whose influ-   25
ence has extended to the details of every subsequent study; a legacy the Professor had left to me, as he has left it to so many others, of inestimable value,
which we could not buy, with which we cannot part.

A year afterward, some of us were amusing ourselves with chalking out-   26
landish beasts on the Museum blackboard. We drew prancing starfishes; frogs
in mortal combat; hydra-headed worms; stately crawfishes, standing on their
tails, bearing aloft umbrellas; and grotesque fishes with gaping mouths and
staring eyes. The Professor came in shortly after, and was as amused as any at
our experiments. He looked at the fishes.

"Haemulons, every one of them," he said; "Mr. _____ drew them."   27

True; and to this day, if I attempt a fish, I can draw nothing but haemulons. 28

The fourth day, a second fish of the same group was placed beside the   29
first, and I was bidden to point out the resemblances and differences between
the two; another and another followed, until the entire family lay before me,
and a whole legion of jars covered the table and surrounding shelves; the odor
had become a pleasant perfume; and even now, the sight of an old, six-inch,
worm-eaten cork brings fragrant memories.

The whole group of haemulons was thus brought in review; and whether   30
engaged upon the dissection of the internal organs, the preparation and examination of the bony framework, or the description of the various parts, Agassiz's training method of observing facts and their orderly arrangement was ever accompanied by the urgent exhortation not be content with them.

"Facts are stupid things," he would say, "until brought into connection   31
with some general law."

At the end of eight months, it was almost with reluctance that I left these   32
friends and turned to insects; but what I had gained by this outside experience has been of greater value than years of later investigation in my favorite groups.

Writing Assignments

Narrate   **1.** List the memorable examinations you have faced in your academic career—those where you studied the wrong thing, misread the question, or earned a high grade. Select one that taught you a lesson you were not expecting to learn about yourself. Then write a narrative of that experience addressed to a specific audience (e.g., a group of high school students).

Observe   **2.** Take your journal to the library (or some other place where students are studying for examinations). Select a group of students. Log the amount of time each one seems to devote to certain activities—reading, writing, staring, talking to others, and so on. Then write a column (perhaps a humorous one) for your student paper in which you classify the behavior of students on "The Night Before the Big One."

Investigate   **3.** Interview one of your favorite teachers about his or her philosophy of examinations. Begin by asking about his or her own experience as a student taking exams. Then ask about the assumptions and expectations that were buried in a recent exam (perhaps one you took). How would the teacher have prepared for the exam? What specific thinking and writing strategies did the exam require? What specific problems did the teacher encounter in evaluating the answers? Finally use the information from your interview to compose an essay entitled "How to Succeed in Professor X's Class."

Collaborate   **4.** Your writing group has been asked to compose a study guide for one of the General Studies courses that requires essay examinations—History 101, Anthropology 151, Philosophy 100, or a comparable course. Determine which members of your group (or students you know) have performed successfully or unsuccessfully in the class. Establish the reasons for their performance. Visit several sections of the class, take notes on the lectures, read the text. Study an old examination question and some exemplary answers. What writing strategies do successful students seem to use? Do students know these strategies in advance or do teachers coach them? What seems to be the main cause of student failure? Collect your data and, with the help of teachers or tutors, write a guide that suggests ways to overcome the problems you have discovered.

Read   **5.** Visit the study skills center on your campus. Talk to teachers and tutors about the research they use to counsel students. Read one research study that has developed a successful method for helping students prepare for written examinations. You may want to test the findings of the study by using its methodology in your next examination. Then write an essay on "What They Never Told Me about Writing Essay Examinations."

Respond   **6.** Respond to Jean Shepherd's "The Value of C" by recalling an experience (or a dream) in which you had to take an examination on a subject about which you knew nothing (or next to nothing). How did you feel—about yourself, your teacher, the subject, education? How did you react to your feelings? Then write an essay that tries to show your readers what it feels like to be unprepared.

Analyze   **7.**   Examine the gender stereotypes illustrated in the two examples in "What Does a Woman need to Know?" How are men (particularly the male professor) characterized in the selection? What gender stereotypes are represented by the women students? Using this hypothesis, and your own observations about the way men and women use and abuse authority in education, analyze the concluding paragraph of this selection.

Evaluate   **8.**   Study the teaching-learning process as it is exemplified in Samuel H. Scudder's "In Laboratory with Agassiz." This essay was written about education in the nineteenth century at Harvard University. How have things changed? For example, how would you and your friends define a good teacher? How would you assess Louis Agassiz's ability as a teacher? How would you assess Scudder's abilities as a student? How would students you know respond to Agassiz's assignment? Use your answers to these questions to draft a speech that evaluates the motivation of contemporary teachers and students for a specific audience (the local PTA, teachers' union, or state legislature.)

Argue   **9.**   In a letter to the chair of your department major or some other administrator, argue that most teachers do not prepare students to take their examinations. Describe the kinds of teachers whose philosophy of testing or inattentiveness to students' need for guidance renders them unable to provide advance coaching on how to do well on a written examination. By contrast, describe the kind of teachers who employ specific strategies to help students prepare for and perform well on written examinations.

Argue   **10.**   In a letter to the Dean of Undergraduate Programs, argue that teachers who understand the writing process—particularly, the need for planning, drafting, and revising—should not give impromptu or timed written examinations. Acknowledge teacher arguments—(1) students need to learn to write under pressure, (2) teachers need to verify that student work is original—but provide examples and alternatives that demonstrate how teachers can design writing assignments to help students learn more effectively.

13 | The Critical Essay

The critical essay helps readers understand a subject. The word *critical* means "to separate, discern, or choose." Thus, the critical essay attempts to enhance the reader's understanding of a subject by analyzing its parts and interpreting its meaning. It may deal with any subject worthy of serious study—a painting, a film, a social movement. In most writing classes, however, the critical essay assignment focuses on literature. Although procedures for composing a critical essay resemble procedures followed in writing other essays, the success of the critical essay depends on another process—the informed reading of imaginative literature.

BASIC ELEMENTS OF LITERATURE

Reading literature is different from reading a newspaper or magazine. In reading those texts, you may be a "speed reader," grasping the main point early, skimming through the middle, and glancing at the end to see how it turns out. Such habits can cause trouble when you read a poem or a play. As novelist William Gass points out, reading a work of literature is a "slow, old-fashioned . . . complicated, profound, silent, still, very private, very solitary yet civilizing activity" ("Of Speed-Readers and Lip-Movers"). To engage in that sort of reading, you need to distinguish among three literary genres—*fiction, poetry,* and *drama,* each with its own history, conventions, and subcategories—and recognize five elements common to nearly every literary work—*plot, characterization, setting, point of view,* and *theme.*

These elements may be combined with such subtlety that you may not see them as separate concepts, or one or two of them may be given special attention. Some works may require you to consider additional elements. In much poetry, for example, you will need to consider rhyme, sound patterns, meter, and form. In considering dramatic productions, you will need to evaluate actors, costumes, lighting, and sets. But in most cases, your ability to recognize the interaction of the five basic elements will enable you to complete the informed reading essential for writing a critical essay.

Plot

The plot is a coherent, unified, and meaningful sequence of events that forms the beginning, middle, and end of a work of literature. The author must begin by revealing where and when the events take place, who the characters are, and what situation has brought them together. This introductory material is termed the *exposition*. In some cases, as in a brief poem, the exposition may be short because the author expects the readers to understand immediately the circumstances and setting. In other cases, such as in a complex drama, the playwright may need to provide a lengthy exposition to help the audience understand the events that are about to occur.

The middle section of the plot begins when a new set of complications develops to disrupt the existing order. These complications are almost always the result of *conflict*—conflicts among characters, conflicts between characters and their environment, conflicts in the thoughts, desires, or choices of a single character. In some works, all three types of conflict occur together. As conflict intensifies, a moment of crisis, called the *climax*, is reached. The climax usually marks the end of the major action of the plot. All that remains is the revelation of the consequences of whatever occurred during the climax. This final clarification or unraveling of the plot is called the *dénouement*, from a French word that means to untangle knots.

All plots have a beginning, middle, and end, but they do not always follow a chronological or predictable sequence. Some begin in the middle of the action or near the end. In such instances, the author may use a *flashback* to take the reader back in time to witness a scene that explains the current action. Early in a work, an author may use *foreshadowing* to suggest how the action might be resolved. Occasionally such hints turn out to be false clues, and the plot resolves itself in an unexpected way. This reversal of expectations is called *situational irony*.

Characterization

The method by which an author creates, reveals, and develops characters is called *characterization*. An author may describe characters directly, telling the reader what people look like, how they behave, and what they think; or an author may reveal characters indirectly, suggesting their appearance, personality, and values through their words and deeds or through the words and deeds of others.

A literary work usually focuses on a single character. In a poem, this character is often the speaker, who reveals thoughts or describes events. In fiction or drama, this character, the *protagonist*, is often opposed by another character or characters, the *antagonist*. The antagonist need not be a person; it might be the environment, society, or some aspect of the protagonist's personality.

Central characters who change in some significant way as a result of the conflicts they must resolve are often called *dynamic*. Characters who remain unchanged by the experiences they encounter are called *static*. Another way to distinguish between characters is to use the terms *round* and *flat*. A round character, usually the central character, is a fully developed, complex, often contradictory personality. A flat character, usually a minor character, possesses no depth or complexity but is so predictable in words and deeds that he or she is often called a stock character, or *stereotype*.

In thinking about literary characters, your main concern is to interpret their behavior. When a character makes choices or fails to make choices, you need to explain his or her *motivation*. In some cases, motivation can be explained by acknowledging that the character is responding to external factors such as social expectations. In other cases, motivation can be explained only by assessing internal factors such as psychological perception. A mixture of social and psychological factors motivates the most complex characters. When characters reveal their inability to understand their own motivation, making choices that the reader knows are uninformed or incorrect, they create a situation known as *dramatic irony.*

Setting

In simple terms, setting is the place, time, and social context established by a work of literature. Sometimes an author's choice of a physical place—a living room in a play, for example—seems relatively insignificant. More often, an author chooses a specific physical location—a farm in the rural South, a ghetto in the urban North—because it embodies the conflict in the plot and the choices available to the characters. Similarly, some authors seem to be indifferent to the constraints of time. A poet may evoke a mood in a kind of timeless present; a novelist may establish a story in a particular historical period. To interpret a literary work effectively, you need to determine the author's purpose in ignoring or exploiting restrictions of place and time.

The combination of place and time creates the *social context* for a literary work. Certain stories, poems, and plays evolve from the assumptions, rituals, and shared beliefs that shape the characters and their world. Understanding this context may help you explain an author's *tone,* or attitude toward the world he or she is describing, or an author's use of *symbols*, the evocation of artifacts, images, and ideas that illuminate the meaning of the work.

Point of View

Literally, point of view is the position one occupies in viewing an object. Applied to literature, the phrase refers to both *position* (the narrator's or speaker's proximity to the action in time and space) and *person* (the narrator's or speaker's personality and attitude). The term *narrator* is usually reserved for novels and short stories; the term *speaker* is used for poems. Neither term suits drama, because in a play the action unfolds as each character speaks.

In determining how to reveal the action and ideas in a literary work, an author may choose from four basic points of view.

▼ *Third-person omniscient* The narrator, usually assumed to be the author, tells the story. He or she can move at will through time, across space, and into the minds of each character to tell the reader anything that is necessary to understand the story.

▼ *Third-person limited omniscient* Although the author is still the narrator, he or she gives up total omniscience and limits the point of view to the experience and perception of one character in the story. Instead of knowing everything, the reader knows only what this one character knows or is able to learn.

▼ *First person*   The author selects one character to tell the story or express an idea. The character may be involved in the action or reflect on it from afar. This character may tell about events as they are happening or recall events many years after they have taken place.

▼ *Dramatic*   The author presents the external action of the story directly, as if it were being acted on stage or filmed by a movie camera. The author does not attempt to comment on or interpret the character's actions, thoughts, or feelings. All the reader knows about the action is inferred from the character's public words and deeds.

Through your ability to identify a point of view, you can understand other literary elements, such as *tone* and *style.* In Chapter 10, you learned how to use tone and style to enhance the purpose of your writing. In a work of imaginative literature, the tone and style of the narrator or speaker also further the author's purpose. The tone may be straightforward or ironic, bitter or enthusiastic. The style may be colloquial or formal, simple or complex. In each case the author makes choices that shape the meaning of the work. Your ability to assess the significance of these choices will help you interpret a work more effectively.

Theme

In addition to showing characters in conflict, a work of literature expresses several ideas about human experience. Different readers, working from different perspectives, may respond to the same work in dramatically different ways. Their disagreement prompts further discussion and analysis, encouraging additional reading of a work to find support for a particular interpretation.

To discover and state the theme that seems to integrate your perceptions and responses to a literary work, look for general statements about human experience. These statements are sometimes presented by the omniscient narrator and sometimes by individual characters. In the case of statements by a character, you need to examine the statement in light of your understanding of events. A character who makes a generalization that seems directly opposite to the author's intended meaning may be using *verbal irony.*

If you cannot find any direct statement of theme, ask yourself what the central characters have learned from their experience, or ask yourself what you have learned, from reading of this experience, that the characters have somehow failed to perceive.

You may also gain insight into theme by looking at how authors express their meaning through literary devices such as symbol and allusion. A *symbol* is a person, act, or thing that has both literal significance and metaphorical meaning. A symbol often pulls together several complex, interrelated ideas. An author may use one symbol or a series of related symbols to suggest a theme. An *allusion* suggests a thematic connection between some aspect of the story and something similar in literature, history, or myth. Such references suggest significant comparisons or ironic contrasts that illuminate the theme.

*Guidelines for Reading Literature*_____

Now that you have some knowledge of the basic elements that interact within any work of literature, you need to approach the reading of a specific work by following some practical reading strategies. Some of these strategies resemble those discussed in Chapter 2 (pages 37–39). Others are especially suited to reading literature.

Preview

It is often possible to learn a few important things about a literary work before you read it.

▼ Begin with a careful consideration of the title, which, as the first clue to the world you are about to enter, may reveal significant information about what you are about to discover. After you have finished reading, you should reconsider the title to see if your first impression was accurate. In most instances, you will discover that the title anticipated what you found and provides a focus for your interpretation.

▼ Next, consider what you know about the author. If you have read other works by the same author, you may be familiar with her or his themes or techniques. Read whatever introduction or headnote is provided; it may contain important biographical information. If such information is not provided, you may want to use a standard reference guide such as *Who's Who* to find out something about the author's life and work.

▼ Finally, consider the genre of the literary work. Recalling the basic differences between genres may give you some initial insight into the text you are about to read.

Read

As you read a literary text, do not be a passive observer, simply absorbing words and turning pages. Be an active reader, analyzing characters and speculating about their behavior.

▼ As you read, annotate the work. Use any convenient method. Underline words or sentences that seem important, mark transitions, or put an asterisk next to statements that may help you once you begin to compose your interpretation.

▼ Ask yourself questions about what you are reading. If you are confused about a character's motives, reactions, or observations, take time to write out your questions in the margin of the work. Even though further reading may answer your questions, the act of writing them down encourages you to analyze what seems to be happening and why.

▼   As you read, and particularly when you reread a work, mark the places in the text where the five basic elements are more apparent—for example, divisions within the plot, clues to character motivation, shifts in point of view.

Review

Once you have finished reading a work, you will want to reread it, both to analyze how it achieves its effect and to contemplate the ways it might be interpreted. A poem with a difficult meter or one that remains opaque after a first reading, or a story whose ending surprised you, may send you back to the text for an immediate rereading, causing you to postpone using the following planning strategies. Often, however, using these strategies immediately after a first reading produces unexpected insights and interesting questions to guide your second reading.

▼   Make a list of the ideas and images that come to mind as you think about the work. You need not organize this information according to any particular pattern. Consult your memory to determine what aspects of the story made the strongest impression.

▼   Using the freewriting techniques you learned in Chapter 2, compose a more extended response to the story, using statements or questions or both. Your purpose is to write out your immediate reaction to the work. Did you like it or not? More important, what confused you about the characters and the way they attempted to resolve their problems?

▼   Compose (or consult) a series of questions about the five basic elements in the work. Some anthologies (or instructors) provide such questions. These questions, like yours, are composed by active readers who are attempting to achieve an informed reading of the work. You may discover that you have already answered some of them in your first reading. Other questions, however, may send you back to the work to look more closely at specific elements of plot, characterization, setting, point of view, or theme.

Now use these guidelines to read and draft your initial responses to the following short story. A headnote introduces the author, and study questions are provided in the exercise on pages 394–395.

Everyday Use | Alice Walker

Alice Walker was born in 1944 in Eatonton, Georgia. After graduating from Sarah Lawrence College, she became active in the civil rights movement, helping to register voters in Georgia, teaching in the Head Start program in Mississippi, and working on the staff of the New York City welfare department. In subsequent years she developed her own writing career while working as

Walker, Alice. *In Love & Trouble.* New York: Harcourt, 1973. 47–59.

writer-in-residence at several universities. She has written a biography for children, *Langston Hughes, American Poet* (1973), edited an important literary anthology, *I Love Myself When I'm Laughing . . . and Then Again When I'm Looking Mean and Impressive: A Zora Neale Hurston Reader* (1979), and compiled two collections of her essays, *In Search of Our Mothers' Gardens* (1983) and *Living by the Word* (1988). These works reveal her interest in the themes of sexism and racism, themes embodied in her four widely acclaimed novels: *The Third Life of Grange Copeland* (1970), *Meridian* (1976), *The Color Purple* (1982), and *The Temple of My Familiar* (1989). Her stories, collected in *Love & Trouble: Stories of Black Women* (1973) and *You Can't Keep a Good Woman Down* (1981), also examine the complex experiences of black women.

for your grandmamma

I will wait for her in the yard that Maggie and I made so clean and wavy yesterday afternoon. A yard like this is more comfortable than most people know. It is not just a yard. It is like an extended living room. When the hard clay is swept clean as a floor and the fine sand around the edges lined with tiny, irregular grooves anyone can come and sit and look up into the elm tree and wait for the breezes that never come inside the house.   1

Maggie will be nervous until after her sister goes: she will stand hopelessly in corners homely and ashamed of the burn scars down her arms and legs, eyeing her sister with a mixture of envy and awe. She thinks her sister has held life always in the palm of one hand, that "no" is a word the world never learned to say to her.   2

You've no doubt seen those TV shows where the child who has "made it" is confronted, as a surprise, by her own mother and father, tottering in weakly from backstage. (A pleasant surprise, of course: What would they do if parent and child came on the show only to curse out and insult each other?) On TV mother and child embrace and smile into each other's faces. Sometimes the mother and father weep, the child wraps them in her arms and leans across the table to tell how she would not have made it without their help. I have seen these programs.   3

Sometimes I dream a dream in which Dee and I are suddenly brought together on a TV program of this sort. Out of a dark and soft-seated limousine I am ushered into a bright room filled with many people. There I meet a smiling, gray, sporty man like Johnny Carson who shakes my hand and tells me what a fine girl I have. Then we are on the stage and Dee is embracing me with tears in her eyes. She pins on my dress a large orchid, even though she has told me once that she thinks orchids are tacky flowers.   4

In real life I am a large, big-boned woman with rough, man-working hands. In the winter I wear flannel nightgowns to bed and overalls during the day. I can kill and clean a hog as mercilessly as a man. My fat keeps me hot in zero weather. I can work all day, breaking ice to get water for washing. I can eat pork liver cooked over the open fire minutes after it comes steaming from the hog. One winter I knocked a bull calf straight in the brain between the eyes with a sledge hammer and had the meat hung up to chill before nightfall. But of course all this does not show on television. I am the way my daughter would want me to be: a hundred pounds lighter, my skin like an uncooked barley   5 pancake. My hair glistens in the hot bright lights. Johnny Carson has much to do to keep up with my quick and witty tongue.

But that is a mistake. I know even before I wake up. Who ever knew a Johnson with a quick tongue? Who can even imagine me looking a strange white man in the eye? It seems to me I have talked to them always with one foot raised in flight, with my head turned in whichever way is farthest from them. Dee, though. She would always look anyone in the eye. Hesitation was no part of her nature.   6

"How do I look, Mama?" Maggie says, showing just enough of her thin body enveloped in pink skirt and red blouse for me to know she's there, almost hidden by the door.   7

"Come out into the yard," I say.   8

Have you ever seen a lame animal, perhaps a dog run over by some careless person rich enough to own a car, sidle up to someone who is ignorant enough to be kind to him? That is the way my Maggie walks. She has been like this, chin on chest, eyes on ground, feet in shuffle, ever since the fire that burned the other house to the ground.   9

Dee is lighter than Maggie, with nicer hair and a fuller figure. She's a woman now, though sometimes I forget. How long ago was it that the other house burned? Ten, twelve years? Sometimes I can still hear the flames and feel Maggie's arm sticking to me, her hair smoking and her dress falling off her in little black papery flakes. Her eyes seemed stretched open, blazed open by the flames reflected in them. And Dee. I see her standing off under the sweet gum tree she used to dig gum out of; a look of concentration on her face as she watched the last dingy gray board of the house fall in toward the red-hot brick chimney. Why don't you do a dance around the ashes? I'd wanted to ask her. She had hated the house that much.   10

I used to think she hated Maggie, too. But that was before we raised the money, the church and me, to send her to Augusta to school. She used to read to us without pity; forcing words, lies, other folks' habits, whole lives upon us two, sitting trapped and ignorant underneath her voice. She washed us in a river of make-believe, burned us with a lot of knowledge we didn't necessarily need to know. Pressed us to her with the serious way she read, to shove us away at just the moment, like dimwits, we seemed about to understand.   11

Dee wanted nice things. A yellow organdy dress to wear to her graduation from high school; black pumps to match a green suit she'd made from an old suit somebody gave me. She was determined to stare down any disaster in her efforts. Her eyelids would not flicker for minutes at a time. Often I fought off the temptation to shake her. At sixteen she had a style of her own; and knew what style was.   12

I never had an education myself. After second grade the school was closed down. Don't ask me why: in 1927 colored asked fewer questions than they do now. Sometimes Maggie reads to me. She stumbles along good-naturedly but can't see well. She knows she is not bright. Like good looks and money, quickness passed her by. She will marry John Thomas (who has mossy teeth in an earnest face) and then I'll be free to sit here and I guess just sing church songs to myself. Although I never was a good singer. Never could carry a tune. I was always better at a man's job. I used to love to milk till I was hoofed in the side   13 in '49. Cows are soothing and slow and don't bother you, unless you try to milk them the wrong way.

I have deliberately turned my back on the house. It is three rooms, just like   **14**
the one that burned, except the roof is tin; they don't make shingle roofs any more. There are no real windows, just some holes cut in the sides, like the portholes in a ship, but not round and not square, with rawhide holding the shutters up on the outside. This house is in a pasture, too, like the other one. No doubt when Dee sees it she will want to tear it down. She wrote me once that no matter where we "choose" to live, she will manage to come see us. But she will never bring her friends. Maggie and I thought about this and Maggie asked me, "Mama, when did Dee ever *have* any friends?"

She had a few. Furtive boys in pink shirts hanging about on washday after   **15**
school. Nervous girls who never laughed. Impressed with her they worshiped the well-turned phrase, the cute shape, the scalding humor that erupted like bubbles in lye. She read to them.

When she was courting Jimmy T she didn't have much time to pay to us, but   **16**
turned all her faultfinding power on him. He *flew* to marry a cheap gal from a family of ignorant flashy people. She hardly had time to recompose herself.

When she comes I will meet—but there they are!   **17**

Maggie attempts to make a dash for the house, in her shuffling way, but I   **18**
stay her with my hand, "Come back here," I say. And she stops and tries to dig a well in the sand with her toe.

It is hard to see them clearly through the strong sun. But even the first   **19**
glimpse of leg out of the car tells me it is Dee. Her feet were always neat-looking, as if God himself had shaped them with a certain style. From the other side of the car comes a short, stocky man. Hair is all over his head a foot long and hanging from his chin like a kinky mule tail. I hear Maggie suck in her breath. "Uhnnnh," is what it sounds like. Like when you see the wriggling end of a snake just in front of your foot on the road. "Uhnnnh."

Dee next. A dress down to the ground, in this hot weather. A dress so loud it   **20**
hurts my eyes. There are yellows and oranges enough to throw back the light of the sun. I feel my whole face warming from the heat waves it throws out. Earrings, too, gold and hanging down to her shoulders. Bracelets dangling and making noises when she moves her arm up to shake the folds of the dress out of her armpits. The dress is loose and flows, and as she walks closer, I like it. I hear Maggie go "Uhnnnh" again. It is her sister's hair. It stands straight up like the wool on a sheep. It is black as night and around the edges are two long pigtails that rope about like small lizards disappearing behind her ears.

"Wa-su-zo-Tean-o!" she says, coming on in that gliding way the dress   **21**
makes her move. The short, stocky fellow with the hair to his navel is all grinning and he follows up with "Asalamalakim, my mother and sister!" He moves to hug Maggie but she falls back, right up against the back of my chair. I feel her trembling there and when I look up I see the perspiration falling off her chin.

"Don't get up," says Dee. Since I am stout it takes something of a push. You   **22**
can see me trying to move a second or two before I make it. She turns, showing white heels through her sandals, and goes back to the car. Out she peeks next with a Polaroid. She stoops down quickly and lines up picture after picture of me sitting there in front of the house with Maggie cowering behind me. She

never takes a shot without making sure the house is included. When a cow comes nibbling around the edge of the yard she snaps it and me and Maggie *and* the house. Then she puts the Polaroid in the back seat of the car, and comes up and kisses me on the forehead.

Meanwhile Asalamalakim is going through the motions with Maggie's   23
hand. Maggie's hand is as limp as a fish, and probably as cold, despite the sweat, and she keeps trying to pull it back. It looks like Asalamalakim wants to shake hands but wants to do it fancy. Or maybe he don't know how people shake hands. Anyhow, he soon gives up on Maggie.

"Well," I say. "Dee."   24

"No, Mama," she says. "Not 'Dee,' Wangero Leewanika Kemanjo!"   25

"What happened to 'Dee'?" I wanted to know.   26

"She's dead," Wangero said. "I couldn't bear it any longer being named after   27
the people who oppress me."

"You know as well as me you was named after your aunt Dicie," I said.   28
Dicie is my sister. She named Dee. We called her "Big Dee" after Dee was born.

"But who was *she* named after?" asked Wangero.   29

"I guess after Grandma Dee," I said.   30

"And who was she named after?" asked Wangero.   31

"Her mother," I said, and saw Wangero was getting tired. "That's about as   32
far back as I can trace it," I said. Though, in fact, I probably could have carried it back beyond the Civil War through the branches.

"Well," said Asalamalakim, "there you are."   33

"Uhnnnh." I heard Maggie say.   34

"There I was not," I said, "before 'Dicie' cropped up in our family, so why   35
should I try to trace it that far back?"

He just stood there grinning, looking down on me like somebody inspecting   36
a Model A car. Every once in a while he and Wangero sent eye signals over my head.

"How do you pronounce this name?" I asked.   37

"You don't have to call me by it if you don't want to," said Wangero.   38

"Why shouldn't I?" I asked. "If that's what you want us to call you, we'll   39
call you."

"I know it might sound awkward at first," said Wangero.   40

"I'll get used to it," I said. "Ream it out again."   41

Well, soon we got the name out of the way. Asalamalakim had a name twice   42
as long and three times as hard. After I tripped over it two or three times he told me to just call him Hakim-a-barber. I wanted to ask him was he a barber, but I didn't really think he was, so I didn't ask.

"You must belong to those beef-cattle peoples down the road," I said. They   43
said "Asalamalakim" when they met you, too, but they didn't shake hands. Always too busy: feeding the cattle, fixing the fences, putting up salt-lick shelters, throwing down hay. When the white folks poisoned some of the herd the men stayed up all night with rifles in their hands. I walked a mile and a half just to see the sight.

Hakim-a-barber said, "I accept some of their doctrines, but farming and rais-   44
ing cattle is not my style." (They didn't tell me, and I didn't ask, whether Wangero [Dee] had really gone and married him.)

We sat down to eat and right away he said he didn't eat collards and pork   45
was unclean. Wangero, though, went on through the chitlins and corn bread, the

greens and everything else. She talked a blue streak over the sweet potatoes. Everything delighted her. Even the fact that we still used the benches her daddy made for the table when we couldn't afford to buy chairs.

"Oh, Mama!" she cried. Then turned to Hakim-a-barber. "I never knew how **46** lovely these benches are. You can feel the rump prints," she said running her hands underneath her and along the bench. Then she gave a sigh and her hand closed over Grandma Dee's butter dish. "That's it!" she said. "I knew there was something I wanted to ask you if I could have." She jumped up from the table and went over in the corner where the churn stood, the milk in its clabber by now. She looked at the churn and looked at it.

"This churn top is what I need," she said. "Didn't Uncle Buddy whittle it out **47** of a tree you all used to have?"

"Yes," I said   **48**

"Uh huh," she said happily. "And I want the dasher, too."   **49**

"Uncle Buddy whittle that, too?" asked the barber.   **50**

Dee (Wangero) looked at me.   **51**

"Aunt Dee's first husband whittled the dash," said Maggie so low you   **52** almost couldn't hear her. "His name was Henry, but they called him Stash."

"Maggie's brain is like an elephant's," Wangero said, laughing. "I can use   **53** the churn top as a centerpiece for the alcove table," she said, sliding a plate over the churn, "and I'll think of something artistic to do with the dasher."

When she finished wrapping the dasher the handle stuck out. I took it for a   **54** moment in my hands. You didn't even have to look close to see where hands pushing the dasher up and down to make butter had left a kind of sink in the wood. In fact, there were a lot of small sinks; you could see where thumbs and fingers had sunk into the wood. It was beautiful light yellow wood, from a tree that grew in the yard where Big Dee and Stash had lived.

After dinner Dee (Wangero) went to the trunk at the foot of my bed and   **55** started rifling through it. Maggie hung back in the kitchen over the dishpan. Out came Wangero with two quilts. They had been pieced by Grandma Dee and then Big Dee and me had hung them on the quilt frames on the front porch and quilted them. One was in the Lone Star pattern. The other was Walk Around the Mountain. In both of them were scraps of dresses Grandma Dee had worn fifty and more years ago. Bits and pieces of Grandpa Jarrell's Paisley shirts. And one teeny faded blue piece, about the size of a penny matchbox, that was from Great Grandpa Ezra's uniform that he wore in the Civil War.

"Mama," Wangero said sweet as a bird. "Can I have these old quilts?"   **56**

I heard something fall in the kitchen, and a minute later the kitchen door   **57** slammed.

"Why don't you take one or two of the others?" I asked. "These old things   **58** was just done by me and Big Dee from some tops your grandma pieced before she died."

"No," said Wangero, "I don't want those. They are stitched around the bor-   **59** ders by machine."

"That'll make them last better," I said.   **60**

"That's not the point," said Wangero. "These are all pieces of dresses   **61** Grandma used to wear. She did all this stitching by hand. Imagine!" She held the quilts securely in her arms, stroking them.

"Some of the pieces, like those lavender ones, come from old clothes her   **62** mother handed down to her," I said, moving up to touch the quilts. Dee

(Wangero) moved back just enough so that I couldn't reach the quilts. They already belonged to her.

"Imagine!" she breathed again, clutching them closely to her bosom.   63

"The truth is," I said, "I promised to give them quilts to Maggie, for when   64
she marries John Thomas."

She gasped like a bee had stung her.   65

"Maggie can't appreciate these quilts!" she said. "She'd probably be back-   66
ward enough to put them to everyday use."

"I reckon she would," I said. "God knows I been saving 'em for long enough   67
with nobody using 'em. I hope she will!" I didn't want to bring up how I had
offered Dee (Wangero) a quilt when she went away to college. Then she had
told me they were old-fashioned, out of style.

"But they're *priceless!* she was saying now, furiously; for she has a temper.   68
"Maggie would put them on the bed and in five years they'd be in rags. Less
than that!"

"She can always make some more," I said. "Maggie knows how to quilt."   69

Dee (Wangero) looked at me with hatred. "You just will not understand. The   70
point is these quilts, *these* quilts!"

"Well," I said, stumped. "What would *you* do with them?"   71

"Hang them," she said. As if that was the only thing you *could* do with quilts.   72

Maggie by now was standing in the door. I could almost hear the sound her   73
feet made as they scraped over each other.

"She can have them, Mama," she said, like somebody used to never winning   74
anything, or having anything reserved for her. "I can 'member Grandma Dee
without the quilts."

I looked at her hard. She had filled her bottom lip with checkerberry snuff   75
and it gave her face a kind of dopey, hangdog look. It was Grandma Dee and
Big Dee who taught her how to quilt herself. She stood there with her scarred
hands hidden in the folds of her skirt. She looked at her sister with something
like fear but she wasn't mad at her. This was Maggie's portion. This was the
way she knew God to work.

When I looked at her like that something hit me in the top of my head and ran   76
down to the soles of my feet. Just like when I'm in church and the spirit of God
touches me and I get happy and shout. I did something I never had done before:
hugged Maggie to me, then dragged her on into the room, snatched the quilts
out of Miss Wangero's hands and dumped them into Maggie's lap. Maggie just
sat there on my bed with her mouth open.

"Take one or two of the others," I said to Dee.   77

But she turned without a word and went out to Hakim-a-barber.   78

"You just don't understand," she said, as Maggie and I came out to the car.   79

"What don't I understand?" I wanted to know.   80

"Your heritage," she said. And then she turned to Maggie, kissed her, and   81
said, "You ought to try to make something of yourself, too, Maggie. It's really a
new day for us. But from the way you and Mama still live you'd never know it."

She put on some sunglasses that hid everything above the tip of her nose   82
and her chin.

Maggie smiled; maybe at the sunglasses. But a real smile, not scared. After   83
we watched the car dust settle I asked Maggie to bring me a dip of snuff. And
then the two of us sat there just enjoying, until it was time to go in the house
and go to bed.

PLANNING THE CRITICAL ESSAY

An informed reading of a literary work is the most important stage in planning the critical essay. But to transform your reading into writing, you need to try out some of the thinking-in-writing strategies suggested as review activities (page 386). For example, after Richard Gant read "Everyday Use," he made a list of the characters, scenes, and images that he remembered most vividly.

> Mama—fat, proud, smart—sledgehammer
> Johnny Carson reunion vs. real reunion
> Maggie—fire, ugly, afraid of Dee, knows how to make a quilt
> Dee—educated, ashamed of family (Wangero), Hakim-a-barber
> Butter dish, churn
> Quilts—bits and pieces, suddenly fashionable
> Hang on the wall
> Mama's choice

After looking over this list, Richard decided to focus his attention on Dee's attempt to take the quilts. In a freewriting exercise, he explored his reaction to this event:

> I was really furious with Dee, or Wangero, or whatever her name is. She didn't want those quilts when she was in college. Out of style. Now that they're "in," she wants to hang one in her apartment. Probably put spotlights on them with a brass plaque explaining how priceless they are. Good thing Mama saw through her. Maggie would have given them to her. She can always make others. But that's not the point. It's the principle. They're Maggie's quilts. Shouldn't have to give them up.

Not everybody reacts to a particular literary work in the same way. For example, Julia Miller's freewriting exercise expresses a slightly different interpretation of Dee's behavior.

> Dee is not completely at fault for the way she acts. She's what her family wanted her to become—educated. Mama and Maggie think she's famous. Johnny Carson. Every family has somebody that outgrows it. Dee lives in a different world. Different values. Car, dress, bracelets, boyfriend. Wangero. Trying to discover roots. Knows what style is. People should respect heritage. Try to make something out of themselves.

By contrast to Richard's emotional reaction to the story, Julia's response seems thoughtful and objective. Her analysis may explain Dee's behavior, but it does not account for Mama's decision to give the quilts to Maggie. Richard, on the other hand, may need to think through the reasons for his anger, but his assessment provides a more complete picture of the story's events. Obviously, Julia and Richard have a great deal to discuss with each other about "Everyday Use." Each response may add some insight to the other, prompting both writers to rethink their views and perhaps return to the story to look for evidence that supports their positions.

To test their reactions to the story, they need to consider the five basic elements contributing to the story's effect. One way is to compose and answer questions about these elements or attempt to answer questions provided by their instructor.

Exercises ——— Answer the following questions about how the five basic elements interact in "Everyday Use." Respond to each question in three or four sentences. For some questions, you may need to reread sections of the story before you compose your answer.

Questions About Plot

1. How does Mama's dream about a family reunion on television introduce the conflicts in the story?
2. How does Mama's decision to give the quilts to Maggie mark the climax of the story?
3. How do Wangero's comments about heritage and self-development bring the story to an ironic conclusion?

Questions About Characterization

1. How does Mama's description of her working ability establish her character?
2. How do Maggie's scars explain her lack of self-esteem?
3. How do Dee's attire, boyfriend, and new name justify Mama's comment that Dee "knew what style was"?

Questions About Setting

1. How do Mama's opening and closing comments about the yard evoke the physical and social setting of the story?
2. Why does Mama suspect that Dee will want to "tear down" the house?
3. Why does Wangero photograph the house and pay so much attention to the benches, churn, and quilts?

Questions About Point of View

1. Why is it appropriate for Mama to tell this story? For example, how might the story change if it were told by Maggie or Dee?
2. What is Mama's attitude toward Maggie's accident and Dee's education?

3. What attitude toward her story does Walker suggest by her dedication, *"for your grandmamma"*?

   Questions About Theme

1. How does the conflict about the quilts symbolize the themes of tradition and progress?

2. How do you interpret Wangero's comment that her sister should "make something" of herself?

3. How do you interpret Mama's observation that "Maggie knows how to quilt"?

DRAFTING THE CRITICAL ESSAY

After you have worked your way through several thinking-in-writing strategies, you should have learned enough about a particular literary work to draft your essay.

Selecting Your Subject

Sort through the subject ideas you uncovered during planning. Even a subject assigned by your instructor and restricted to a specific aspect of a story, poem, or play should enable you to integrate your planning material into a unified essay. If your instructor asks you to select your own subject, be sure to restrict it to a specific aspect of the work. You cannot discuss everything you know about "Everyday Use," for example, but you can focus your attention on an aspect of the story that will enable you to compose a thoughtful and thorough analysis.

Analyzing Your Audience

You must assume that your audience for a critical essay is a group of informed readers. This means that your readers have read the story you are about to interpret and have probably formed their own opinions about its meaning and significance. For that reason, you do not need to summarize the plot. But you do need to analyze relevant aspects of the plot (and even quote certain passages) so that your readers can see how you arrived at your interpretation.

Determining Your Purpose

Restricting your subject will help determine your purpose, but remember that you need to prove something about your subject. In a critical essay on a literary work, this means proving that your particular interpretation is supported by a careful examination of the text. To put your purpose into operation, compose a thesis that embodies the interpretation you are trying to prove.

As Richard began drafting his essay on "Everyday Use," he decided that he wanted to restrict his subject to the conflicting attitudes toward the word *heritage* that he discovered in the story. He began by making a scratch outline, grouping words and details that reveal how Mama and Dee might use the word.

1. <u>Mama</u>
   House-yard-homestead
   Hard work, hog killing
   Family—children, all the Dees (Civil War)
   Church songs
   Skills—whittling, quilts
   Saving for "everyday use"
   Can always make another

2. <u>Dee</u>
   School—discovers other habits (heritages)
   Wanted nice things—style (vs. heritage)
   Rediscovers heritage: Afro, pigtails, jewelry
   New name (oppression vs. tradition)
   Photographs—artifacts, something artistic
   Skills—admired, appreciated, priceless
   New Day

Making this simple division lets Richard see the significance of some aspects of the story that were not on his original list or in his freewriting exercise and lets him draft a preliminary hypothesis about this information.

In "Everyday Use," Alice Walker presents two attitudes toward heritage: Mama's and Maggie's is something used every day, and Wangero's is a matter of what is in style.

As he thinks about this hypothesis, Richard decides to use his knowledge of the basic elements of literature to provide a more critical perspective on his material. He revises his thesis to focus on *how* Alice Walker develops this *theme* through *characterization*.

In "Everyday Use," Alice Walker presents contrasting attitudes toward heritage through her characters' appearance, actions, and appreciation of family possessions.

The advantage of this thesis is that it sets up a structure for Richard's essay. He can contrast the two attitudes toward heritage as he contrasts the characters in three separate sections: (a) *appearance,* (b) *actions,* and (c) *appreciation of family possessions.* His use of the various stages of the reading and writing process enables him to compose the following draft.

THE MEANING OF HERITAGE IN "EVERYDAY USE"
Richard Gant

Alice Walker's short story "Everyday Use" is about the conflict   1
between a mother and a daughter over their <u>heritage</u>. Heritage for
Mama and her daughter Maggie is a matter of everyday living, or
"everyday use" as the title of the story suggests. Mama and Maggie
are not conscious of their heritage because it is so much a part of
their lives. For Mama's daughter Dee, however, heritage is a matter
of style, a fashionable obsession with one's roots. Walker develops
these contrasting attitudes through her characters' appearance,
actions, and appreciation of family possessions.

The description of the characters in the story introduces the con-   2
flicting attitudes toward heritage. Mama admits that she is fat and
manly. Her hands are calloused and rough from a lifetime of hard
work. Maggie is described as homely, wearing a pink skirt and red
blouse, and bearing scars from a fire that burned down the family
home. Dee, however, is beautiful and stylish, wearing a striking,
brightly colored African dress, earrings, bracelets, sunglasses, and
hair in the full-bodied African style that, according to Mama, "stands
straight up like the wool on a sheep." Even Dee's feet are pretty, "as
if God himself had shaped them with a certain style."

The characters' actions further develop the theme of heritage.   3
By telling us that she can butcher hogs "as mercilessly as a man" or
break ice "to get water for washing," Mama suggests that she
possesses necessary survival skills. She is at home in her world,
sweeping the front yard as though it were "an extended living
room." And she prepares and eats chitlins, corn bread, and collards
because they are inexpensive and readily available. Although she is
less assertive, Maggie displays similar domestic skills, particularly
her ability to make quilts. Both women live their heritage. Dee,
however, thinks of herself as outside this world. When she was a
girl, she used to read things to her family that they "didn't
necessarily need to know," washing them "in a river of make-
believe." She wanted to dress nicely and impress others with a "well-
turned phrase." Now that she has become educated and fascinated
by African culture, she changes her name to Wangero Leewanika
Kemanjo. She does not want to bear the name of the "people who

oppress me," even though, ironically, her name has a long history in the family. Unaware of this inconsistency, Wangero returns home with her Muslim boyfriend, Hakim-a-barber, to take pictures of her mother and sister with the house and cow, probably to show her friends the "down-home" aura of the homestead.

The characters' appreciation of certain family possessions intensifies the difference between the two notions of heritage. Dee-Wangero rediscovers Mama's wooden benches: "I never knew how lovely these benches are. You can feel the rump prints." She also views the churn top and the dasher as quaint because they were created by a primitive skill, whittling, and because she can use them to create something else, such as an artistic centerpiece for her alcove table. And finally, she is captivated by the quilts that Grandma Dee and Big Dee stitched together out of bits and pieces of family clothing from as far back as the Civil War. She wants to hang them on a wall as she would priceless paintings. To Mama and Maggie, however, these objects are indispensable to their everyday living. The churn top, dasher, benches, and quilts are for "everyday use," not for stylish decoration.

At the climax of the story, Maggie is tempted to give her quilts to Dee-Wangero. Mama has been saving them for Maggie to use when she starts her own home, but Maggie says that she can remember "Grandma Dee without the quilts." Mama acknowledges that Maggie "can always make some more," and then suddenly she feels "something hit me in the top of my head and run down to the soles of my feet." She hugged Maggie, "snatched the quilts out of Miss Wangero's hands and dumped them into Maggie's lap." This decision leaves Maggie speechless and Dee-Wangero momentarily annoyed. But clearly Mama and Maggie understand their heritage better than Dee-Wangero thinks they do. The final scene of the story reveals the difference between an artificial and a real heritage. Dee-Wangero puts on her sunglasses and rides away in the dust, while Mama and Maggie finish the day by sitting there "just enjoying."

REVISING THE CRITICAL ESSAY

To assess what you have accomplished in your draft, use the strategies for global and local revision that you have already learned to clarify the focus and development of your text. To complete this revision process, however, reread the literary work, using your draft as a guide. If your draft helps you understand the interaction of the basic elements in the work, then you have probably composed a fairly complete essay. But if, as you reread the work, you discover important features of plot, characterization, setting, point of view, or theme that you have overlooked or underestimated, then you may need to revise your essay. Sometimes such discoveries will require you to rethink the wording of your thesis or the transitions between the major divisions of your paper. At other times, they will remind you that by adding a detail, modifying an assertion, or quoting a particular passage, you can make a more compelling case for your interpretation.

Poem/Student Essay

Examine Edwin Arlington Robinson's poem "Mr. Flood's Party" by using the reading strategies described in the Guidelines for Reading Literature (pages 385–386). Then read Julia Miller's essay, "Old Eben and Mr. Flood." In what ways does your response differ from the student's response? What aspects of the poem did you overlook in your reading? What aspects did she overlook in her writing?

Mr. Flood's Party | Edwin Arlington Robinson

Old Eben Flood, climbing alone one night
Over the hill between the town below
And the forsaken upland hermitage
That held as much as he should ever know
On earth again of home, paused warily.   5
The road was his with not a native near;
And Eben, having leisure, said aloud,
For no man else in Tilbury Town to hear:

"Well, Mr. Flood, we have the harvest moon
Again, and we may not have many more;   10
The bird is on the wing, the poet says,
And you and I have said it here before.
Drink to the bird." He raised up to the light
The jug that he had gone so far to fill,
And answered huskily: "Well, Mr. Flood,   15
Since you propose it, I believe I will."

Alone, as if enduring to the end
A valiant armor of scarred hopes outworn,
He stood there in the middle of the road
Like Roland's ghost winding a silent horn.   20
Below him, in the town among the trees,
Where friends of other days had honored him,
A phantom salutation of the dead
Rang thinly till old Eben's eyes were dim.

Then, as a mother lays her sleeping child   25
Down tenderly, fearing it may awake,
He set the jug down slowly at his feet
With trembling care, knowing that most things break;
And only when assured that on firm earth
It stood, as the uncertain lives of men   30
Assuredly did not, he paced away,
And with his hand extended paused again:

Collected Poems of Edwin Arlington Robinson. New York: Macmillan, 1921. 573–5.

"Well, Mr. Flood, we have not met like this
In a long time; and many a change has come
To both of us, I fear, since last it was   35
We had a drop together. Welcome home!"
Convivially returning with himself,
Again he raised the jug up to the light;
And with an acquiescent quaver said:
"Well, Mr. Flood, if you insist, I might.   40

"Only a very little, Mr. Flood—
For auld lang syne. No more sir; that will do."
So, for the time, apparently it did,
And Eben evidently thought so too;
For soon amid the silver loneliness   45
Of night he lifted up his voice and sang,
Secure, with only two moons listening,
Until the whole harmonious landscape rang—

"For auld lang syne." The weary throat gave out,
The last word wavered, and the song was done.   50
He raised again the jug regretfully
And shook his head, and was again alone.
There was not much that was ahead of him,
And there was nothing in the town below—
Where strangers would have shut the many doors   55
That many friends had opened long ago.

Old Eben and Mr. Flood | Julia Miller

"Mr. Flood's Party" embraces two separate worlds. The first world is one   1
of reality, consisting of Eben's consciousness of his present state, in
which he is lonely and desolate; the other world is one of illusion, made up of
Mr. Flood's dreams of his fellowship with friends of bygone days. The distinction
between the poem's two worlds is emphasized by the figure of the "two moons."
One moon is real, but the other moon is just a part of Mr. Flood's illusion.

Robinson begins the poem by placing Eben in the world of reality. In the   2
first words of the first line, "Old Eben Flood, climbing alone," the reader gets a
hint of Eben's age and solitude. In the next line, the phrase "Over the hill" continues to express the concept of age. Eben's position "between the town
below/And the forsaken upland hermitage" strengthens the idea of loneliness.
Here, he is caught in the middle. In the words of the last stanza, "there was
nothing in the town below," and yet "There was not much that was ahead of
him." The world of reality continues for Eben in the second stanza. In addressing himself, Eben recognizes his age in the passage: "we have the harvest
moon/Again, and we may not have many more." He also acknowledges the
movement of time in the statement, "The bird is on the wing." On this note old
Eben takes a drink, and his world of reality begins to fade.

In the third stanza, Eben is still aware of his state of solitude, but this   3
awareness has taken on a heroic quality. He is described as "enduring to the
end/A valiant armor of scarred hopes outworn." This is a very noble image of

Mr. Flood, who has merely outlasted his expectations and outlived his time. "Like Roland's ghost winding a silent horn," so Mr. Flood calls for the help of his comrades by raising the jug to his mouth. In the world of illusion, Flood's friends answer the call. At the end of the third stanza, these "friends of other days" who "had honored him" greet Mr. Flood in a "phantom salutation of the dead." Old Eben's desolation is forgotten in this illusion. He is living in a dream of the past through his imagined reunion with his deceased friends. Feeling secure in the company of his party, Mr. Flood sings "For auld lang syne."

Robinson then informs the reader that "The weary throat gave out,/The   4
last word wavered, and the song was done." Likewise, Mr. Flood's world of illusion fades, and the party is over.

As the party ends, the world of reality returns. Eben, as if he were waking   5
from a dream, "shook his head, and was again alone." In the line that states, "There was not much that was ahead of him," Eben recognizes that there is neither much left of his life, nor much left in his life. The words of the last three lines sum up Eben's situation: "there was nothing in the town below—/Where strangers would have shut the many doors/That many friends had opened long ago." In the realm of reality, Eben knows that the world has changed. He also knows that all of his contemporaries are gone. As the poem ends, Eben returns to being a lonely old man with time passing rapidly by him.

In conclusion, the name Eben Flood is most appropriate for the main char-   6
acter in this poem. The name can be broken down into "ebb and flood." The flood describes the high tide of Eben's life. This is the period in which Eben had friends and hopes. At that time, life held much in store for him. The image of the flood also describes the flood of memories from his past, which pour in the flood from the jug. All of Mr. Flood's dreams of a bygone era comprise the world of illusion. The ebb describes the decline of Eben's life and the low level of his present existence. The ebb also represents the world of reality, in which Mr. Flood must face up to loneliness, desolation, and age. Eben may always want to live in the flood of illusion, but he must always return to the ebb of reality. After all, time and tide wait for no man.

Writing Assignments

Narrate   **1.**   List three or four of your favorite stories, such as the ones that were read to you as a child, the first one you read on your own, and those that gave you particular pleasure or difficulty in school. Select one from the list and, making use of the basic elements of literature (plot, characterization, setting, point of view, and theme), compose a narrative about your experience with that story.

Observe   **2.**   Select a member of your family or a teacher who is a gifted storyteller. Document those techniques of storytelling that make your storyteller effective. Another version of this assignment would be to document the skills of your favorite show-business storyteller (e.g., Bill Cosby, Whoopi Goldberg, Garrison Keillor, Hal Holbrook as Mark Twain). Or you may want to document the flaws of someone you know who *thinks* he or she is a good storyteller but who usually bores an audience to distraction. After you have collected your information, identify the most telling talents of a good storyteller.

Investigate   **3.**   Interview someone on your campus or in your community who writes stories for a living—a creative writer on your faculty, a columnist on your local newspaper, a local master of ceremonies who is famous for his or her stories. Select a specific text (or performance) as evidence and then question its creator about how he or she created it. What came first—the plot, the characters, the point of view? What difficulties did the creator have in fashioning and presenting the text? What point does the creator hope his or her readers will see in the story? Then write a profile for the entertainment section of your newspaper that gives your readers the inside story on how the story was made.

Collaborate   **4.**   Your writing group has been asked to perform a dramatic version of "Everyday Use." Conduct what's called a story conference to map the set, select the props, pick those parts of the story (especially dialogue) that can be dramatized effectively, case the members of your group for different parts, and discuss how your audience might interpret (or misinterpret) your version of the story. Do not depend on improvisation. Write down your adaptation as you would a playscript. Perform it. Then wait for the reviews.

Read   **5.**   Following the Guidelines for Reading Literature (pages 385–386), examine the two poems printed here. Then compose a critical essay on this topic; compare the tension between romantic love and everyday reality in Richard Wilbur's "A Late Aubade" and Adrienne Rich's "Living in Sin."

A Late Aubade | Richard Wilbur

You could be sitting now in a carrel
Turning some liver-spotted page,
Or rising in an elevator-cage
Toward Ladies' Apparel.

You could be planting a raucous bed
Of salvia, in rubber gloves,
Or lunching through a screed of someone's loves
With pitying head,

5

Or making some unhappy setter
Heel, or listening to a bleak   10
Lecture on Schoenberg's serial technique.
Isn't this better?

Think of all the time you are not
Wasting, and would not care to waste,
Such things, thank God, not being to your taste.   15
Think what a lot

Of time, by woman's reckoning,
You've saved, and so may spend on this,
You who had rather lie in bed and kiss
Than anything.   20

It's almost noon, you say? If so,
Time flies, and I need not rehearse
The rosebuds-theme of centuries of verse.
If you *must* go,
                                                                                 25
Wait for a while, then slip downstairs
And bring us up some chilled white wine,
And some blue cheese, and crackers, and some fine
Ruddy skinned pears.

Living in Sin | Adrienne Rich

She had thought the studio would keep itself;
no dust upon the furniture of love.
Half heresy, to wish the taps less vocal,
the panes relieved of grime. A plate of pears,
a piano with a Persian shawl, a cat   5
stalking the picturesque amusing mouse
had risen at his urging.
Not that at five each separate stair would writhe
under the milkman's tramp; that morning light
so coldly would delineate the scraps   10
of last night's cheese and three sepulchral bottles;
that on the kitchen shelf among the saucers
a pair of beetle-eyes would fix her own—
envoy from some village in the moldings . . .
Meanwhile, he, with a yawn,   15
sounded a dozen notes upon the keyboard,
declared it out of tune, shrugged at the mirror,
rubbed at his beard, went out for cigarettes;
while she, jeered by the minor demons,
pulled back the sheets and made the bed and found   20
a towel to dust the table-top,
and let the coffee-pot boil over on the stove.
By evening she was back in love again,
though not so wholly but throughout the night
she woke sometimes to feel the daylight coming   25
like a relentless milkman up the stairs.

Respond 6. Consider the issues in Alice Walker's "Everyday Use" from the point of view of Dee (Wangero). Then write a narrative in the voice of Dee (Wangero) explaining how specific experiences in your education have enabled you to understand and appreciate your heritage.

Analyze 7. Read the title essay in Alice Walker's *In Search of Our Mothers' Gardens* (New York: Harcourt, 1983: 231–43). Analyze Walker's portrait of her mother in the essay. Then compare it to her portrait of Mama in "Everyday Use."

Evaluate 8. Evaluate the effectiveness of Julia Miller's essay on Edwin Arlington Robinson's "Mr. Flood's Party." To supplement your own response, you may wish to read some other critical commentaries on the poem. See, for example, Hoyt Franchere, *Edwin Arlington Robinson* (New York: Twayne, 1968); or Francis Murphy, *Edwin Arlington Robinson: A Collection of Critical Essays* (Englewood Cliffs, N.J.: Prentice, 1970). Then write to Julia about those aspects of the poem that you and other commentators have noticed and that she might want to consider should she decide to revise her essay.

Argue 9. Read biographical accounts of several African-American women writers— Paule Marshall, Toni Morrison, *and* Alice Walker. Then argue that these women discovered the significance of their heritage by reading books in school rather than making quilts at home.

Argue 10. Compile a brief anthology of poems that focus on a theme—childhood, education, nature, war. Select and organize the poems so that they develop engaging perspectives on the theme. Then write an introduction presenting the specific thesis your readers will discover by reading your anthology.

14 | Planning the Research Paper

You will probably write a number of research papers (also called library or term papers) during your formal education, papers that will figure prominently in your course grades but also provide you with an opportunity to discover new ways of thinking and writing. Noted historian Barbara Tuchman remembers researching her undergraduate honors thesis as "the single most formative experience of my career. . . . It was not a tutor or a teacher or a fellow student or a great book or the shining example of some famous lecturer. . . . It was the stacks at Widener [library]. They were *my* Archimedes' bathtub, my burning bush, my dish of mold where I found my personal penicillin" (Barbara Tuchman, "In Search of History," *Practicing History*).

The assignment to write a research paper is similar to other writing assignments in that you must discover information to fulfill a specific purpose. But it differs from other writing assignments in that your major source of information is not memory, observation, or informal reading (as in most personal essays), your textbook or lecture notes (as in the essay examination), or one or more literary texts (as in the critical essay) but—as Tuchman suggests—the books, articles, and documents housed in your university library. Locating the information you need and then using it in your paper requires skills in thinking, reading, and writing that you do not draw on in other assignments.

Chapter 14 introduces the stages you must work through in *planning* a research paper:

▼ Understanding the assignment
▼ Making a schedule
▼ Selecting a subject
▼ Finding sources
▼ Evaluating sources
▼ Taking notes
▼ Filling gaps

Chapter 15 takes up the stages involved in *writing* the paper. In these chapters you will follow Jill Taraskiewicz, a student writer, as she plans, drafts, and revises her paper on the controversy over recycling. Jill's final paper appears fully annotated at the end of Chapter 15 so that you can see how she made important decisions about her sources and used those sources to clarify her own position in the controversy.

UNDERSTANDING THE ASSIGNMENT

Before you begin working, you need to determine the kind of paper you are to write. There are two basic kinds of research papers. In one you are expected to compile a *survey*; in the other you are expected to conduct an *argument*.

The Survey

The survey is a factual review of what other researchers have written about a subject. When you select a subject for a survey, focus on an issue or problem that has provoked extensive commentary or controversy, such as the causes of acid rain, the effects of gun control, the merits of educational reform. Imagine that your readers are curious about your subject but uncommitted to any particular position. They expect you to examine all sides of the subject objectively and to document your sources accurately so that they can read more about the subject. Your purpose is not to present your own argument about the subject but to identify and summarize the major arguments of others.

The Argument

The argument presents your analysis of a subject that has been researched by others; you interpret the information you uncovered in your research. You work from the perspective you have chosen, and you devise your own method of organizing and analyzing sources. Imagine that your readers are curious and uncommitted but ready to be convinced by a compelling argument. They expect you to acknowledge opinions that do not support your own, but they also expect you to present a forceful analysis, citing the proper authorities to support your viewpoint. Your purpose is not to compile a neutral summary of what others have written but to make your own contribution to a growing body of knowledge. (See Chapter 6, "Argument.")

MAKING A SCHEDULE

Your instructor will specify when your paper is due and may require you to submit your work in stages so that both of you can track your progress. If your instructor does not provide a timetable, make one yourself. Start with the deadline and then work backward through the process, assigning a specific amount of time to each stage. Be cautious; allow yourself plenty of time to complete each activity. Be conscientious; work in the library for a certain number of hours each week. And be pragmatic; produce some kind of written material (journal entries, note cards, drafts) at the end of each stage. Post your schedule in a prominent place and consult it often. A schedule for a research paper might look like this:

Time	Activity	Written Product
Week 1	Study assignment. Make out schedule. Use journal to assess subject, audience, and purpose. Pick general subject. Read background material.	Schedule; journal entries; general subject; notes on background reading
Week 2	Select a specific subject. Formulate several hypotheses. Begin compiling bibliography of possible sources.	Specific subject; several hypotheses; source cards
Week 3	Locate and evaluate possible sources. Begin reading and taking notes.	Note cards
Week 4	Restrict subject. Analyze most valuable sources. Identify gaps in research.	Restricted-subject note cards; new source cards
Week 5	Locate and read additional sources. Take notes.	New note cards
Week 6	Select hypothesis. Develop outline.	Hypothesis; outline
Week 7	Write first draft. Prepare revision agenda for next draft. New outline.	First draft; revision agenda; new outline
Week 8	Write final draft. Check quotations. Complete documentation. Compile works cited list. Type and proofread final manuscript.	Completed assignment

Even if you start planning your paper the day you receive your assignment and follow a schedule like this one, inevitably you will have to adjust your timetable as your work proceeds. A good rule of thumb is to add two weeks to your schedule for unexpected difficulties. You may need this time for situations like these:

▼ *Some things take more time than you planned.* Because the article you must read by Friday has to be ordered through interlibrary loan, you have to wait two weeks to complete your background reading.

▼ *Some stages prove more difficult than you expected.* Because your search strategy turns up only a few sources that deal directly with your subject, you have to find new sources or a new angle on your subject.

▼ *Deadlines on your schedule have to be adjusted, making it more difficult to meet subsequent deadlines.* Difficulties composing the final draft cut into time set aside for typing and proofreading.

Writers who start promptly, map out a reasonable timetable, make allowances for setbacks, and work efficiently can produce a research paper on time. Those who leave everything to the last minute will discover too late that they cannot throw together a satisfactory paper overnight. You need to live with your project for several weeks, reading and assimilating sources. A realistic schedule is a written reminder of your goal and encourages you to work at a steady pace, committing your discoveries and ideas to writing as soon as possible.

SELECTING A SUBJECT

Selecting a subject for a research paper is like staking a prospector's claim. You *hope* the claim will produce gold, but you won't *know* until you begin digging. Some instructors, therefore, ask students to select a subject from a pretested list. If your instructor instead asks you to select your own subject, assess potential subjects according to the following criteria of successful research subjects. (Review "Guidelines for Selecting Your Subject" in Chapter 1 on page 9.)

1. *Select a subject you can research.* This may seem an obvious requirement, but many subjects cannot be researched.
   a. *Some subjects are too autobiographical.* A paper that draws primarily on your own experience—"Growing Up in Oklahoma City"—does not require you to search for information in other sources.
   b. *Some subjects are too subjective.* No amount of research will resolve a question of personal taste, such as "Which is the better poet—Yeats or Eliot?"
   c. *Some subjects are too restricted.* A mechanical process—"How to Operate a VCR"—that can be explained by only one source does not require significant research.
   d. *Some subjects are too current.* Events that produce today's headlines—"Scandal at the State House"—have not been studied in sufficient depth for you to find enough information about them.
   e. *Some subjects are too specialized.* A subject such as "Reactions of German-American Pacifists to the Great Sioux Massacre of 1864" cannot be researched if your library does not own or have access to the required special documents.

2. *Select a subject you can restrict.* Before you begin your research, you may worry that you will not be able to find enough information. Once you begin, however, you are likely to find that nearly every source reveals new aspects of your subject. Instead of feeling overwhelmed, take control of your subject and reduce it to a manageable size. Two factors will help you:

a. *The time you scheduled for planning your paper.* Whether you select a subject that you already know something about or one that is new to you, be realistic about how much you can learn in the time available. A subject such as heart disease, for example, will lead to more sources than you will have time to read, analyze, and understand. Restrict your subject to a specific aspect of heart disease, such as one of its suspected causes. Restricting your subject even further, to one method used to control a cause of heart disease, might lead to an even better focus for your paper.

b. *The space available to develop your paper.* If your assignment restricts the length of your paper, be realistic about how much you can cover in the specified number of pages. A subject such as word processors, for example, will have more sources than can be listed in ten pages, let alone usefully developed into an argument. Restricting your subject to changes in American business correspondence or even changes in *one* American business's correspondence with its customers will be more manageable.

3. *Select a subject you can live with.* Writing a research paper requires you to work with one subject for a long time. If this subject does not fascinate you, if you do not care about the questions it poses or the answers you can provide, you will become bored; your planning will be careless and your writing uninspired. Be sure to select a subject that holds your interest.

4. *Select a subject that will appeal to other readers.* Although the immediate audience for your research paper is your instructor, imagine at least two other audiences. One is the authors you have come to know while doing your research. In a sense, you are carrying on an extended conversation with these writers about a new direction in an area familiar to them. The other audience is the intelligent general reader, who is always interested in new information or new approaches. You are asking this reader to consider your thesis. As you select your subject, strike a balance between the expectations of these two audiences. Previous researchers should consider your work substantive, not trendy; the general reader should find it innovative, not shopworn.

5. *Select a subject you can prove something about.* If you are writing an *argument*, not a *survey*, the purpose of your paper is to use sources to support a thesis. You must be sure to select a subject that will yield a thesis, not a summary of other researchers' arguments. Your subject must be focused, so that you can control your evidence to support your argument, and complex, so that you can develop and sustain your argument throughout your paper.

Exercise ———— One way to discover a subject is to explore, in your journal, what you already know about related subjects. Jill tries this approach as she thinks about possible subjects for a research paper on the environment for her English composition class. Read her journal entry and then discuss how she has applied the above criteria for selecting a subject.

9/16 Got research paper assignment. Johnson says write about some issue or controversy. Rain forest—never seen one. Spotted owl—never seen one. Ozone layer—can't see it. What I can see is all the clutter in this study lounge. Bulletin board—announcements for lectures, films; ads for roommates, spring break, magazines. Tables—discarded newspapers, class notes, quizzes, memos, candy wrappers. Where does all this paper come from? Where does it go? Trash can next to the vending machines—RECYCLE. My books have recycling symbol on the spine. Today's trash makes tomorrow's texts. At least that's the promise. Everybody says they are <u>into</u> recycling. But does it work? Johnson says I have to prove something about my subject. Recycling—Fad? Fraud? Final Solution?

FINDING SOURCES

Once you have selected your general subject, begin the formal process of researching it in the library. Most libraries, like most cities, try to help visitors by providing tours, publishing maps and directories, and hiring guides (librarians) to work at specific locations throughout the building. Because no two libraries are organized exactly alike, even the most experienced researchers depend on this kind of assistance to help them work in an unfamiliar library.

One reason you will need this advice is that in the last five years libraries, like most other institutions in our culture, have gone through a technological revolution. They still provide traditional resources, but more and more libraries also are providing computerized versions of nearly every reference tool mentioned in this chapter. The card catalogue is available on On-line Public Access Catalogue (OPAC), and most periodical indexes are available on Compact Disk–Read Only Memory (CD–ROM). In addition, most libraries now provide a battery of terminals and printers at convenient locations throughout the building and computer ports in other buildings (including faculty offices and student dormitory rooms) all over campus.

Clearly such technological devices change the way researchers track and compile their sources. But not every library has the same technological capacity. And every technological wonder has built-in limitations that can often frustrate rather than facilitate your research. You will save yourself much needless confusion at the outset if you realize that your best allies are librarians. No matter how difficult or ridiculous your question seems, the librarians have probably heard it or one like it before. And if they cannot give you an answer, they can show you where and how to look for one. Indeed, they can direct you to many more sources than are mentioned in this chapter. You have already considered how to select a subject. Librarians will help you formulate a *search strategy*—a systematic procedure for finding information on your subject. The Search Strategy diagram below shows you the sequence of steps in a search strategy.

Background Information

Read several overviews of your general subject so that you can learn about its history, major themes, and principal figures. Such background information can be found in general and specialized encyclopedias located in the reference collection of the library.

General Encyclopedias These reference works, written for a general audience, cover a wide variety of subjects. The entries, generally arranged in alphabetical order, are not technical or scholarly, but they often contain a brief list of sources that do treat the subject in depth. You can find the main entry about your general subject by looking in the appropriate volume. To locate every reference to your subject in the encyclopedia, you can consult the index, which is usually the last volume. The latter method enables you to see how your subject is subdivided and cross-referenced, and reading the additional entries may give you a perspective that will help you restrict or revise your subject. Standard encyclopedias include

Collier's Encyclopedia
New Columbia Encyclopedia
Encyclopedia Americana
New Encyclopaedia Britannica
World Book

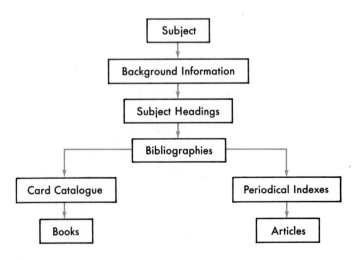

Search strategy

Subject → Background Information → Subject Headings → Bibliographies → Card Catalogue → Books; Bibliographies → Periodical Indexes → Articles

Specialized Encyclopedias   These books are usually devoted to one or two disciplines or to specific subject areas. They provide a narrow, detailed coverage of particular topics. The entries tend to be more technical than those in a general encyclopedia, with longer lists of sources. Because specialized encyclopedias are available on a wide range of academic and general interest subjects, you will need to use OPAC or the card catalogue to locate them. Look up your general subject and then look for the subheading "Dictionaries." The *Encyclopedia of Philosophy*, for example, is listed under the subject heading "Philosophy—Dictionaries." The following brief list of specialized encyclopedias shows the variety of material available.

> *International Encyclopedia of Higher Education*
> *McGraw-Hill Encyclopedia of Science and Technology*
> *Rock On: The Illustrated Encyclopedia of Rock 'n' Roll*

Biographical Sources   These works give brief accounts of notable figures, listing such information as family history, educational background, major accomplishments, and significant publications. A short list of additional sources is often included. If your background reading points to one or two people significant in the development of your general subject, you should research these figures in a biographical source. Some examples are

> *Biography Index*
> *Dictionary of American Biography*
> *International Who's Who*

Exercise ———— Jill uses her journal to take notes on the information she discovered about recycling in encyclopedias. Read her notes and consider how her background reading helps her shape her subject. Note her initial frustrations at being unable to find information on her subject and how she overcomes these difficulties. Also note how the information she does find enriches and expands her original subject, causing her some confusion.

9/18 Great start. <u>None</u> of the encyclopedias had citations on recycling. Am I crazy or what? Are these encyclopedias <u>that</u> dated? HELP! Librarian suggested I check the index volume to see if recycling was listed in some other way like waste management. DAH! Felt like a real dummy. Bingo! Recycling is listed but cross-referenced under different headings. <u>Collier's</u>—renewable resources. <u>World Book</u>—environmental pollution. <u>Britannica</u>—industrial waste. <u>Collier's</u> claims that recycling of inorganic materials (metal, glass) is commonplace. Recycling organic materials (newsprint) is practical but supply is so large that better technologies will be required. <u>World Book</u>—definition:

"The reprocessing of waste products for reuse is called <u>recycling</u>." Lists products that can be recycled (cans, newspapers, glass, tires), but doesn't mention difficulties in the process. <u>Britannica</u> has detailed discussion of the complex process of recycling newspapers—<u>de-inking</u>.

Librarian showed me how reference books were listed in OPAC. (And for future reference how the periodicals that the library owned were also listed in OPAC). Used K=recycling and found <u>Recycling in America: A Reference Handbook</u>. Great source! Chronology of recycling: 400 B.C.—1st municipal dump (Athens); 105 A.D.—Ts'ai Lun invents paper in China using reclaimable materials like rags; 200 A.D.—1st garbage men (Rome); 1868—John Wesley Hyatt invents plastic; 1885—1st incinerator (Govenor's Island); 1948—Fresh Kill Land Fill opens on Staten Island. Now so big that it was one of two man-made structures that the astronauts could see from moon (Great Wall—China). "MURFs" (material recovery centers). 3Rs (reduce, reuse, recycle). Seattle is model recycling city. Biographical sketches of recycling innovators. Laws and agencies (by state) on recycling. Great annotated bibliography—books, articles, newsletters, video/audio tapes, curriculum guides—even children's books. Sources are somewhat dated. Need to check periodical data base. But bibliography should help focus my search.

Subject Headings

When you have done some background reading, you will discover that there are many ways to classify, subdivide, and cross-reference your topic. This cluster of categories should tell you three things:

1. You must restrict your general subject (in Jill's case, waste management) to the specific subject you want to write about (recycling).
2. You may find your specific subject listed under several headings (renewable resources, environmental pollution, industrial waste).
3. You may have to read material that does not deal directly with your subject in order to develop a perspective that will help you organize your information (the invention of plastic, the technology of incinerators, the history of the environmental movement, the philosophy of urban design).

The best way to discover subject headings related to your subject is to consult the reference book entitled *Library of Congress Subject Headings*. This guide, usually located near the card catalogue and main OPAC terminals, shows you how your subject is classified and cross-referenced in the library's various data bases. Sometimes you will have to use some ingenuity to determine how your subject might be listed. For example, Jill found that the broadest term for her subject was "conservation of natural resources." But she also found cross-references to "pollution control industry," "refuse disposal," and "energy conservation" that might direct her to sources on recycling.

Throughout your research you will revise your subject headings. Some will be eliminated because the information on them is not related to your subject. Others will be added because they lead you to sources that give you valuable insights. In fact, one of the most powerful features of the computerized systems is the *keyword,* a feature that encourages you to strike out in a new direction, using a word or combination of words to find a new angle on your subject. If the keyword is listed in a publication's title, subject headings, description or *abstract,* the publication will appear on your computer screen in a list of possible sources.

For example, Jill added to her initial headings, "recycling" and "waste management," the following: "refuse disposal," "waste paper," "de-inking," "plastics," "trash," and "rubbish." She considered but discarded "energy conservation" and "salvage." Although her subject may seem to be getting out of control, Jill is actually developing several hypotheses about the controversy over recycling. The hypothesis she selects will help her shape her draft.

Bibliographies

When you have compiled a preliminary list of subject headings, you are ready to begin building your bibliography. You begin with a *working bibliography,* a list of books and articles you intend to consult as you plan your paper. (When you finish writing your research paper, you will have a *final bibliography,* a typewritten list of *works cited.*) Consult a reference guide to reference books, such as the American Library Association's *Guide to Reference Books* (10th ed., 1986), compiled by Eugune P. Sheehy, or its supplement, which covers the period from 1985 to 1990, compiled by Robert Balay. These guides will tell you if there is a specialized bibliography on your subject. Specialized bibliographies not only save you time but also ensure that you consult the most significant sources. Such bibliographies are often *annotated,* providing a brief description (and sometimes an evaluation) of each book and article listed. However, specialized bibliographies may not cover recent works. A bibliography published in 1950, for example, leaves you to track down the research done in the decades since.

Three other sources of information on specialized bibliographies are the

▼ *Bibliography Index,* a reference work that lists articles, parts of books, and pamphlets devoted in whole or in part to bibliographies.

▼ Card catalogue or OPAC under your subject headings (S=) or keywords (K=) and the subheading "Bibliography": for example, K=recycling and bibliography.

▼ Catalogue card under your subject heading or OPAC entry, which may contain a bibliography, as in the following example:

```
Search Request:    K=RECYCLING AND BIBLIOGRAPHY
BOOK - Record 2 of 67 Entries Found
-------------------------------------------------------------------
Author:         Kimball, Debi.

Title:          Recycling in America : a reference handbook / Debi
                Kimball.

Published:      Santa Barbara, Calif. : ABC-CLIO, c1992.

Subjects:       Recycling (Waste, etc.)--United States.
                Recycling (Waste, etc.)--Law and legislation--United
                States.
                Recycling (Waste, etc.)--Bibliography.
-------------------------------------------------------------------
LOCATION:                      CALL NUMBER:          STATUS:
Reference Collection           TD794.5 .K55 1992     Not checked out
(Non-Circulating)
```

Bibliography note ⟶

Card Catalogue/OPAC

After locating a specialized bibliography or determining that none is available, begin constructing your bibliography with the two major research tools in the library—the *card catalogue/OPAC* and the *periodical indexes/CD–ROMs*. The card catalogue, arranged alphabetically, lists books and other material in the library by subject, author, and title. OPAC lists material in the same format but also enables you to find sources using keywords.

Author Card/A=   If you know the author of a book on your subject or suspect that a certain author might have written about the subject, look in the card catalogue for the *author*, or *main card*. If you are working with OPAC, strike A= and type the author's name (last name first). The screen will display all the books the author has written. Type the number of the book you want and the author card will appear on the screen.

Title Card/T=   If you know the title of the book you want but have forgotten the author, or if you suspect one of your subject headings might be included in the title, look for a *title card* in the catalogue or strike T= and type the title on your OPAC terminal.

Subject Card/S=   If you know only your subject or several related subject areas, look for the *subject card* in the catalogue. If you are working with OPAC, your screen will tell you how many books on that subject the library owns and will list the books according to date of publication (most recent first). Once you have selected the book you want, your screen will display the complete subject card.

Key Word/K=   If you are using OPAC, type a keyword to start your search. You can also use a variety of keyword combinations to restrict the range of your search. However you find your source card, it will give you all sorts of useful information:

Source Card

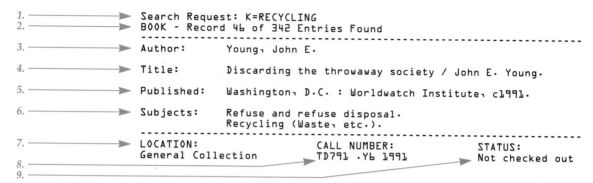

1. ──────▶ Search Request: K=RECYCLING
2. ──────▶ BOOK - Record 46 of 342 Entries Found
    -
3. ──────▶ Author: Young, John E.
4. ──────▶ Title: Discarding the throwaway society / John E. Young.
5. ──────▶ Published: Washington, D.C. : Worldwatch Institute, c1991.
6. ──────▶ Subjects: Refuse and refuse disposal.
                           Recycling (Waste, etc.).
    -
7. ──────▶ LOCATION: CALL NUMBER: STATUS:
            General Collection   ▶ TD791 .Y6 1991   ▶ Not checked out
8.
9.

1. *Search request.* The search request reminds you how you found the source you are looking at on your screen. If you decide to use another search request—for example, REFUSE—the search request will keep track of your search strategy.

2. *Record of entries found.* The record indicates how many sources owned by the library are listed under this search word. It also tells you where this source is on that list.

3. *Author's name.* The last name appears first, followed by first name and middle initial, depending on how the author's name appears on the title page.

4. *Title.* The title is given as it appears on the title page.

5. *Imprint.* The imprint information includes the place of publication, the publisher, and year of publication.

6. *Tracings.* These list the subject headings under which the book is catalogued. Tracings are most useful for identifying other subject areas that might pertain to your subject.

7. *Location.* Some versions of OPAC will tell you whether your source is located in the general collection or in some special collection of the main library or another library on campus.

8. *Call number and location symbol.* These letters and numbers, in the exact order in which they appear on the card, constitute the call number, which indicates the book's location on the library's shelves.

9. *Status.* Some versions of OPAC will tell you whether the book you want is on the shelf or has been checked out. In the latter case, OPAC will also tell you when the book is due to be returned or if it is overdue.

After you have located the book you want in the card catalogue or OPAC, write down the call number or print out your data on the printer connected to your terminal, then locate the book on the shelf. Most libraries are arranged according to the *Library of Congress system,* although some libraries retain portions of the *Dewey decimal system* for older or specialized parts of their collections.

Library of Congress

A	General works	M	Music
B	Philosophy, Psychology, Religion	N	Fine Arts
C–D	History and Topography (except America)	P	Language and Literature
		Q	Science
E–F	America	R	Medicine
G	Geography, Anthropology, Sports and Games	S	Agriculture and Forestry
		T	Engineering and Technology
H	Social Sciences		
J	Political Science	U	Military Science
K	Law	V	Naval Science
L	Education	Z	Bibliography and Library Science

Dewey Decimal System   In the Dewey decimal system, materials are arranged by numbers that represent subject areas.

000–099	General works	600–699	Technology (applied sciences)
100–199	Philosophy and related disciplines	700–799	The arts. Fine and decorative arts
200–299	Religion	800–899	Literature (belles-lettres)
300–399	Social sciences	900–999	General geography and history and their auxiliaries
400–499	Language		
500–599	Pure sciences		

Knowing which classification system your library uses will help you find a specific book. However, because in both systems books are shelved by subject, browsing through the shelves may enable you to find intriguing titles you failed to notice when you were thumbing through the card catalogue or scrolling down the screen of the OPAC terminal. For example, browsing through the shelf where she found John E. Young's *Discarding the Throwaway Society*, Jill discovered other books on recycling. Similarly, by browsing in the general area designated "Environmental Technology (TD)," she found books on a wide range of issues related to her subject.

Periodical Indexes/CD–ROMs

Periodicals (magazines and journals) exist on almost every conceivable subject. Their value in research is their currency and specificity, and back issues can show the ways your subject has been treated in the past. Indexes to periodicals are of two types, general and specific, and are available in two formats—printed volumes and computer disks (CD–ROMs).

General indexes list articles from hundreds of nontechnical and scholarly magazines. Individual articles are classified by author, subject, and keywords. The most useful general indexes are *Readers' Guide to Periodical Literature* and EXAC, *Expanded Academic Index*. The *Readers' Guide* is bound in individual volumes and organized by year. EXAC is usually located in a library's main computer terminals, along with OPAC and several other special computerized indexes. Each has advantages and disadvantages: *Readers' Guide* covers a long historical period (volume 1 was published in 1900), but checking each volume is time-consuming and cumbersome. EXAC is quick and efficient, but it only covers the period 1988 to the present.

Subject indexes list articles on specific subjects. The articles tend to be more detailed and scholarly than those listed in the general indexes. Here is a brief sampling of the subject indexes available both in print and on computerized disk:

Art Index   Humanities Index

Business Periodicals Index   Music Index

General Science Index   Social Science Index

Note: A computer index tells the reader how many articles it has found on a specific subject. In the two examples below, Jill found 1,402 entries in EXAC and 6,412 in the Business Information Index. She scrolled through each list and selected articles she thought might be worth reading. Notice that some periodicals provide an abstract, which helps readers by summarizing the most important information in an article.

EXAC (CD–ROM)

```
Author:          Van Voorst, Bruce
Title:           The recycling bottleneck.
Description:     (photograph)
Journal:         Time  Sept 14 1992, v140, n11, p52 (3)
ISSN:            0040-781X

Subjects:        Recycling (Waste, etc.)--Economic aspects

                 Recycling industry--Economic aspects
```

Business Index (CD–ROM)

```
Title:           Prudential says recycling firm could be big winner.
                 (Pure Tech International Inc.) (Financial News-
                 Front)
Journal:         Chemical Marketing Reporter May 18 1992, v241, n20,
                 p17(1)
ISSN:            0090-0907
Abstract:        Plastics recycling firm Pure Tech International Inc
                 is a growing company whose stock represents a good
                 investment, according to Prudential Securities Inc
                 analyst Len Bogner. Pure Tech stock is trading
                 around $8 1/2 per share in May 1992, and Bogner
                 believes the stock will be trading over $20 per
                 share by the end of 1993. Bogner is particularly
```

```
                                impressed with Pure Tech's 15%-20% cost advantage
                                over other plastic recyclers and predicts Pure
                                Tech will have $35-$40 million in sales by 1995.
                 Subjects:      Recycling industry--Rating
```

Readers' Guide (Print)

RECYCLING (WASTE, ETC.)

See also

Anti-freeze solutions—Recycling

Building materials—Recycling

Cans—Recycling

Computer programming—Recycling

Decoration and ornament, Architectural—Recycling

Electric batteries—Recycling

Farm waste—Recycling

Grain mash—Recycling

Leaves—Recycling

Newspapers—Recycling

Plastics—Recycling

Polystyrene—Recycling

Recycle Signal (Organization)

Refuse as fuel

Scrap metal—Recycling

Southampton Recycling (Organization)

Space stations—Recycling

Tires—Recycling

Toilet paper—Recycling

Waste paper—Recycling

Water reuse

Wood—Recycling

Airlines step up recycling efforts, strive to cut discharge of wastes. J. T. McKenna. il *Aviation Week & Space Technology* 135:92-3 N 25 '91

Bringing the planet home. S. H. Stocking. il *Ladies' Home Journal* 108:94 Mr '91

Cafeteria ecology [school programs] S. Marbert. *The Education Digest* 57:66-8 S '91

Cleanup at the workplace. K. Springen. il *Ladies' Home Journal* 108:98 Ja '91

DejaShoe [footwear manufactured from recycled materials by J. Lewis] il *Buzzworm* 3:94 Mr/Ap '91

Getting down to earth. K. Knight. *Essence* 22:110 My '91

"No one wants to shoot Snow White" [landfills vs. recycling] M. Berss. il *Forbes* 148:40-2 O 14 '91

Peddling the virtues of recycling. E. M. Ros. il *Publishers Weekly* 238:35-7 My 31 '91

Quick-and-easy kitchen recycling center. il *Better Homes and Gardens* 69:50 S '91

The recycler's garden [work of B. Whitman in Beaumont, Tex.] D. M. Sitton. il por *Organic Gardening* 38:62-4 N '91

Recycling & reusing. M. D. Brown. il *Current Health 2* 17:25-7 F '91

Recycling at home. *Southern Living* 26:97 F '91

The recycling game [publishing industry] W. Nixon. il *Publishers Weekly* 238:11-14 Jl 25 '91

General Science Index (Print)

Waste, Utilization of

See also

Refuse as fuel

Sewage sludge as fertilizer

Amino acid hydrolysate from crab processing waste. A. S. Jaswal. bibl il *J Food Sci* 55:379-80+ Mr/Ap '90

Are plastics really the landfill problem? P. R. Lantos. bibl il *Chemtech* 20:473-5 Ag '90

Baking properties of bread and cookies incorporating distillers' or brewer's grain from wheat or barley. B. A. Rasco and others. bibl il *J Food Sci* 55:424-9 Mr/Ap '90

Biorecycling-welcome in backyards? *Environment* 32:22 Jl/Ag '90

Cadmium charges: the environmental costs of batteries are stacking up. D. Erickson. il *Sci Am* 264:122 My '91

Cartons counterattack in battle of the bottle. *New Sci* 128:27 D 8 '90

Characterization of oyster shucking liquid wastes and their utilization as oyster soup. C. Y. Shiau and T. Chai. bibl il *J Food Sci* 55:374-8 Mr/Ap '90

Conserving at the office. il *Int Wildl* 20:25 N/D '90

Corporate America buys in. F. Hoke. *Environment* 32:21-2 Je '90

Demonstrating solutions to the solid-waste crisis. T. Whelan and A. Schwartz. il *Audubon* 92:142-3 Mr '90

Design for disassembly. *Environment* 32:24 O '90

Dieldrin in the food chain: potential health effects of recycled animal manure. A. El-Ahraf and others. bibl il *J Environ Health* 53:17-19 Jl/Ag '90

Dietary fiber ingredients obtained by processing brewer's dried grain. V. K. Chaudhary and F. E.Weber. bibl il *J Food Sci* 55:551+ Mr/Ap '90

Garbage [Environmental magazine, Garbage, printed on recycled paper] *Audubon* 92:14+ Mr '90

Just plug it into that cherry tomato over there. W. B. Travis. il *Sierra* 75:20-1 My/Je '90

Kindly virus. F. Graham, Jr. il *Audubon* 92:10+ N '90

Landfill lodes. R. E. Fahey. il *Nat Hist* p58-60 My '90

The metamorphosis of Keep America Beautiful. T. Williams. il *Audubon* 92:124-6+ Mr '90

Miles to go for scrap tires. F. Hoke. il *Environment* 32:23 Je '90

Modern middens. D. C. Wilson and W. L. Rathje. il *Nat Hist* p54-8 My '90

Most periodical indexes (CD–ROMs and printed volumes) are located in the reference area of your library. When you have selected the best indexes for your subject, look under your subject headings to find major listings and then check any subheadings or cross-references for additional information. When you find your entry, you will see that it contains (1) the title of the article, (2) the name of the author, (3) the title of the periodical (or an abbreviated version of the title), (4) the volume of the periodical, (5) page references, and (6) the date of publication.

In the case of printed indexes, you will need to copy this information onto a source card (see "Taking Notes," pages 425–430). In the case of computerized indexes, you will need to read through the sources available and print the most promising entries (see "Taking Notes," pages 425–430).

Jill checked *Readers' Guide, EXAC, General Science Index*, and *Business Index* for periodical sources. In *Readers' Guide*, she discovered several cross-references that enabled her to restrict her subject (recycling) to the problem of recycling specific kinds of material (newspapers-recycling). Indeed, when she placed "newspapers" before "recycling," she reduced the list of sources in EXAC from 1402 to 48. She scrolled through this shorter list and picked four publications that focused on the effectiveness of the technology used to recycle newspapers. In *General Science Index*, she discovered an article, "Are Plastics Really the Landfill Problem?" that suggested she needed to expand her subject again to consider the claims of other kinds of waste-management systems (e.g., landfills). When she looked in the *Business Index*, she discovered that the articles listed often focused on the cost and effectiveness of recycling, as opposed to landfills and incinerators. Although these discoveries seem to constantly reshape Jill's topic, they actually help her sort her sources into subcategories and begin to refine the subject and purpose of her research.

Newspapers, Documents, Microforms, and Computer Searches

In addition to the card catalogue/OPAC and periodical indexes/CD–ROMs, four other tools will help you find information on your subject.

Newspapers   Many major newspapers, such as the *New York Times, The Times* (London), and the *Washington Post*, publish their own indexes in both printed and computerized form. Newspapers give day-to-day accounts of events and provide details often omitted in later, more general discussions. Consulting them will help you identify important factual information about your subject and enable you to trace its historical development.

Government Documents and Publications   The U.S. government publishes an enormous amount of information on a wide variety of subjects. These publications are housed in a separate area of the library and catalogued according to a separate classification system. There are print and computer disk indexes to this information, such as *American Statistics Index* and the *Monthly Catalogue of United States Government Publications*, but to use the collection effectively you will need help from someone familiar with government documents. A documents librarian or a member of your library's reference staff will be able to provide this guidance.

Microforms   Most libraries do not have space for all the documents they wish to keep. Thus many periodicals and other materials are photographically reduced in size and stored on *microfilm* (reels of film), *microfiche* (transparent sheets of film), or *microcard* (opaque prints). With the aid of mechanical viewers you can enlarge and read these documents easily or make photocopies of the enlarged images. Librarians can tell you which books and periodicals are stored in microform and show you how to operate the microreaders.

"Excuse me, I'm lost. Can you direct me to the information superhighway?"

Drawing by W. Miller; © 1994 The New Yorker Magazine, Inc.

Computer Search   With the increasing use of computers throughout the library, the specialized computer search is no longer an essential tool for most researchers. But not all libraries own every computerized index and some disks do not pick up specialized sources.

If your library offers computer searches, consult with the librarian about your subject and subject headings to determine if a computer search is appropriate. If so, the librarian will use your subject headings to search data bases for books, articles, and other documents. Computer searches may cost as little as $10; some cost a good deal more. Your librarian can advise you whether, given your subject, you should invest in the service.

EVALUATING SOURCES

To compile a working bibliography of books and articles that might pertain to your subject, you must decide which items are likely to prove most useful. The best way to make this decision is through careful reading, but you will *never* have time to read every possible source. The computer can be frustrating to use simply because it produces so many sources. If Jill attempts to read everything she finds on recycling, she will never finish reading, much less begin writing. If she decides to read, in addition, all the books and articles she can find on waste management, she will spend her life trying to keep up with an ever-growing reading list.

All researchers need guidelines and shortcuts to help them make intelligent guesses about the potential value of the sources they uncover. Following such guidelines will help you eliminate some sources immediately, discard others after determining that they do not focus on your subject, and concentrate on the ones that will make the most significant contribution to your research.

Guidelines for Evaluating Sources

1. **The source should be relevant.**
   Whether a particular source is relevant is not always apparent. When you first begin your research, your lack of perspective on your subject may make every source seem potentially relevant. Sometimes the titles of articles and books may be misleading or vague, leading you to examine a work unrelated to your subject or to assume that a work is too general or theoretical when it actually focuses on an essential aspect of your subject. Finally, your reading will occasionally change the status of some sources. What seemed irrelevant to yesterday's perspective on your subject may suddenly seem crucial to today's more informed definition of your purpose. The key to assessing the relevance of a source is to restrict your subject. The sooner you limit your subject, the sooner you can determine the relevance of a particular book or article.

2. **The source should be current.**
   You want to be sure that the information in your sources is reliable and up to date. A paper on the latest cures for cancer should not rely on an article published in 1945. On the other hand, if you are analyzing the public's attitude toward cancer at different times, the 1945 article might be relevant. Not all old works are dated, however. Experts in many subjects acknowledge classic, or standard, books or articles that have advanced major interpretations. You should read those that pertain to your subject.

3. **The source should be comprehensive.**
   Some sources will focus on an extremely narrow aspect of your subject; others will cover its every feature and many related topics as well. Always begin your reading with the most comprehensive source, because it will probably provide the essential information contained in the more specialized sources, and you may not have to read the second source.

4. **The source should direct you to other sources.**
   Catalogue cards will show whether a book contains a bibliography. Skimming will reveal whether an article contains extensive notes. The most helpful notes include annotations about the sources cited. Books

and articles that describe and evaluate other sources help you decide whether you want to read the sources you already found and point you toward sources you have overlooked.

Shortcuts for Evaluating Sources

Locate Annotated Bibliographies   If you are lucky enough to find an annotated bibliography on your subject or if the notes in an article contain extensive annotations, you can determine quickly whether the sources they describe are worth reading.

Read Book Reviews   If you want to determine whether a particular book is reliable, see how it was reviewed when it was first published. Reference guides, such as the *Book Review Digest* and the *New York Times Index*, contain either summaries of or references to book reviews that should help you evaluate the book's content and critical reception.

Obtain the Advice of Experts   Many people on your campus or in your community are experts on certain subjects. A quick phone call or visit to these people can help you identify the "must-reads" or classic treatments of your subject. They can also direct you to annotated bibliographies and special indexes. And, finally, they can refer you to unusual sources that you would not find by using a normal search strategy. Such books and articles, often dealing with related subjects, may introduce you to new ideas or new methods of interpretation.

Review the Table of Contents   To determine the way a book develops its major ideas, study the table of contents. The chapter titles and subheadings work like an outline, giving you a general sense of the author's understanding, treatment, and organization of the subject.

Read the Introduction   To discover the particular focus of a source, read its introduction—the preface and often the first chapter of a book, the first few paragraphs of an article. A few pages is usually enough to detect the author's thesis and decide whether it is relevant and the source valuable.

Browse Through the Index   An index works like a miniature card catalogue, helping you see whether a source has information on your subject, how it classifies and cross-references your subject, how much information it devotes to each of your subject's features, and precisely where that information is located.

Exercise ————   The following titles came from Jill's working bibliography for her paper on the controversy over recycling. (Jill is using the Modern Language Association's citation form, described in Chapter 15 on pages 446–460.) Using the "Guidelines for Evaluating Sources" (pages 423–424), what guesses would you make about the usefulness of these sources to Jill's project?

Brenner, Brian. "Recycling: The Newest Wrinkle in Waste Management's Bag." Business Week 5 March 1990.

Brewer, C. G. "Sources of Household Waste." Outlook 5 Jan. 1904: 29–33.

Gibbons, Gail. Recycle! A Handbook for Kids. Boston: Little, Brown, 1992.

Crown, Judith. "McDonald's Aim to Recycle Trash, Image." Crain's Chicago Business 19 Apr. 1990: 3–4.

Goodwin, Morgan. "Recycling Old Landfills Turns Out to Be Good for Lancaster County." American Metal Market 14 Aug. 1992: 8.

McAllister, Celia. "Save the Trees—And You May Save a Bundle." Business Week 4 Sept. 1989: 118.

Pavoni, Joseph L. Handbook of Solid Waste Disposal. New York: Van Nostrand, 1975.

Glenn, Jim, and David Riggle. "The State of Garbage in America." Bio Cycle 32 (Apr. 1991): 34–38.

Toto, Taryn. "Nasty Things That Live in the Rubbish." New Scientist 20 Apr. 1991: 13.

Gialanella, Mario, and Louis Luedtke. "Air Pollution Control and Waste Management." American City and County 106 (Jan. 1991): SW/RR 17–32.

TAKING NOTES

As you find your sources and select those that you suspect will prove most useful, start making source cards (or printing the sources on your computer screen) and begin taking notes.

Source Cards/Print Screen

The traditional procedure for keeping track of your sources is to fill out a 3" × 5" source card for every item you intend to read. The card will help you keep track of each source from the beginning of your research (when you locate the source in the card catalogue or periodical index) to the point at which you type up the results of your research (when you enter the source in your list of works cited).

The more recently developed procedure is to take advantage of the availability of computer terminals and printers and simply print the source that appears on your computer screen. Each procedure has advantages and disadvantages. The source card takes time to fill out but is easier to code and sort as you work on your paper. The computer printout is more quickly done (and more accurate), but the computer paper is difficult to sort and is easily damaged or misplaced. Here is a sample source card and the computer printout for the same source.

Source Card

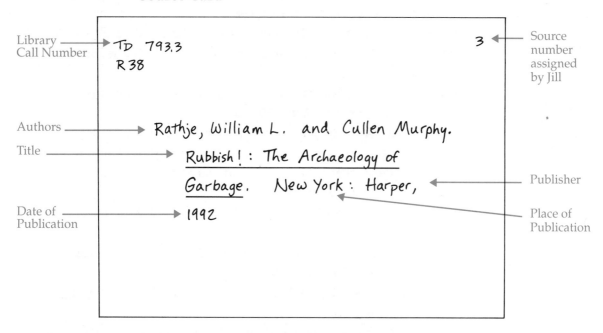

Library Call Number

Authors

Title

Date of Publication

Source number assigned by Jill

Publisher

Place of Publication

On the card (handwritten):

TD 793.3
R 38

3

Rathje, William L. and Cullen Murphy.
Rubbish! : The Archaeology of
Garbage. New York : Harper,
1992

Print Screen (Computer Printout)

Source number assigned by Jill

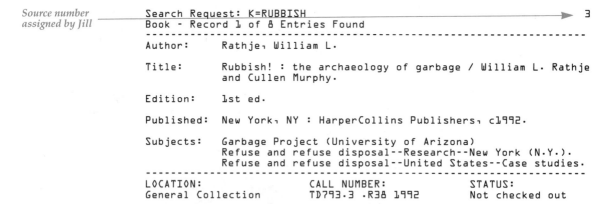

```
Search Request: K=RUBBISH                                          3
Book - Record 1 of 8 Entries Found
-----------------------------------------------------------------
Author:     Rathje, William L.

Title:      Rubbish! : the archaeology of garbage / William L. Rathje
            and Cullen Murphy.

Edition:    1st ed.

Published:  New York, NY : HarperCollins Publishers, c1992.

Subjects:   Garbage Project (University of Arizona)
            Refuse and refuse disposal--Research--New York (N.Y.).
            Refuse and refuse disposal--United States--Case studies.
-----------------------------------------------------------------
LOCATION:                 CALL NUMBER:          STATUS:
General Collection        TD793.3 .R38 1992     Not checked out
```

Two pieces of information on the source card/print screen will help you during your research. The *call number* (at the left on the source card and at the bottom of the computer printout) enables you to locate the book in the library. The *source number* (in upper right) enables you to code your sources so that you can identify the source without recopying the bibliographic information. Note that Jill has copied the bibliographic information on Rathje and Murphy's book onto her source card in the format she will use when she types her list of works cited (see "Listing Sources," pages 452–459). In contrast, she will have to rearrange the information on the computer printout so that it will conform to the appropriate format. If you use source cards, remember to copy the information accurately, even though you are not yet sure which sources will surface in your paper. If you rely on computer printouts, remember to arrange the bibliographic information in the correct format if you decide to cite it in your paper.

After you make your source cards or print the sources you find on your screen, use the "Guidelines for Evaluating Sources" on pages 423 to 424 to establish some priorities for your reading. What sources seem most crucial? What sources will take the most time to read? What sources are likely to help you find other sources? Sort through your information and plan your reading to make the best use of your time.

Note Cards

Note taking is the most critical stage in the research process because it demands that you read, select, interpret, and evaluate the information that will form the substance of your paper. When you return the books and articles to the library, your notes will be your only record of your research. If you have taken notes carelessly, you will be in trouble when you begin writing. Many students inadvertently plagiarize because they work from inaccurate notes. The wise procedure is to take notes very carefully from the beginning.

There are two basic methods for taking notes. In the traditional method, researchers use large cards (4"× 6" or 5"× 7") for notes and small cards (3"× 5") for sources. These two sizes make it easy to distinguish between types of cards, and the large cards provide more room for information. Just as your source card may become part of your list of works cited, each of your note cards may produce one of the ideas you will present in the body of your text. Make a separate card for every important piece of information you discover in each source. Identify the note card with the source-card number, the author(s), and the pages where you found the information. By using a separate card for each note you can shuffle your cards as you begin to look for ways to organize your material. As you become familiar with your subject, write a subheading at the top of each card.

In the newer method of taking notes, researchers type notes from each of their sources into a computer file. (See "Planning Your Research Paper on Your Computer," page 43.) They begin by entering the information on the printout from the library data base according to the documentation style they will use in their works cited list. Then they read and compose their notes on the screen. The citation serves to identify the source of all the notes composed beneath it, but researchers still need to enter the page number for each note and compose subheadings to help them organize their material.

The advantage of this method is that you can create your own data base on a subject, using the keyword function to re-search your notes for information on particular subheadings. You can also use the cut-and-paste feature to collect information on each subheading from different sources and place it in a new file, thus performing the traditional step of shuffling note cards with various subheadings. The disadvantage of this method is that you must read and take notes at your computer terminal. Sometimes it is easier (or even necessary) to take notes the traditional way—as you read a book in the study lounge or examine a document in a special collection of the library.

No matter which method you use, begin by reading quickly through your source to determine if it contains any worthwhile information. If it does, then during a second, more careful reading, use one of these three methods to take notes: *quoting, summarizing, paraphrasing*. At the end of each note leave some room for a personal comment—for example, ideas on how you might make use of this information in your paper.

To understand how to read, react, and write during the note-taking process, consider Jill's response to the following passage from William L. Rathje and Cullen Murphy's *Rubbish! The Archaeology of Garbage*. Her responses are recorded on her note card and in her computer file.

> For consumers, buying recycled products would represent a minimal investment of time and energy. But consumers will have to become garbage literate, because labels can be deceptive. For example, the word "recycled" on a package generally means not that a product has been made, at least in part, out of something that a consumer once bought and then turned in for recycling, but rather that it has been made in part with scrap left over from the normal manufacturing process—business as usual in any well-run factory. The label one needs to look for is "post-consumer recycled," and ideally the label will include a percentage, as in "30 percent post-consumer recycled." Anything over 10 percent is worthwhile. Consumers also need to know the pertinent legends and markings on labels, which indicate that various paper and plastic items are major players in the recycling loop. (New organizations such as Green Seal may increasingly be able to provide guidance on this and related matters.) Individuals, by the way, aren't the only consumers who can help sustain recycling by buying recycled products; so can governments, and so can businesses.

Note Card

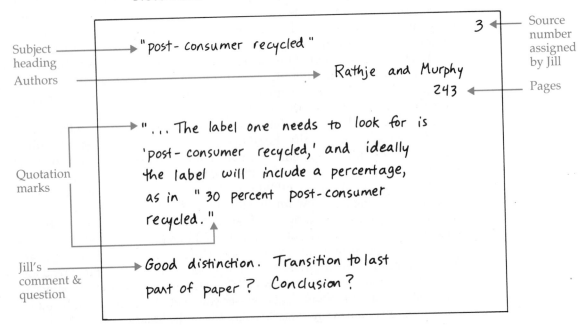

Computer Notes

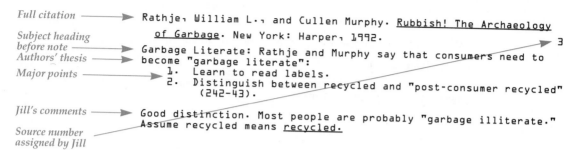

Full citation

Subject heading before note

Authors' thesis

Major points

Jill's comments

Source number assigned by Jill

Rathje, William L., and Cullen Murphy. <u>Rubbish! The Archaeology of Garbage</u>. New York: Harper, 1992.

Garbage Literate: Rathje and Murphy say that consumers need to become "garbage literate":
1. Learn to read labels.
2. Distinguish between recycled and "post-consumer recycled" (242-43).

Good distinction. Most people are probably "garbage illiterate." Assume recycled means <u>recycled</u>.

3

Quoting Sources

Quoting an author's text word for word is the easiest way to record information, but you should use this method selectively. Quote only the passages that deal directly with your subject in particularly memorable language. When you write a quotation on your note card, place quotation marks at the beginning and end of the passage to indicate you are quoting. If you decide to leave out part of the text, use *three* ellipsis points (. . .) to indicate that you have omitted words from the beginning or middle of the sentence and *four* ellipsis points (. . . .) to indicate that you have omitted the end of a sentence or one or more sentences. (See discussion of ellipsis points in Section 28 of the "Handbook of Grammar and Usage.") Finally, proofread your quotation against the original to confirm that every word and mark of punctuation is in its proper place.

Summarizing Sources

Summarizing an author's views is an effective way to record the essence of a text. Use this method when the author states a thesis or analyzes evidence in a way that either anticipates or contradicts your emerging perception of your argument. Use key words or two or three phrases to briefly restate the author's principal points.

Paraphrasing Sources

Paraphrasing an author's views is both the most useful and the most misused method of note taking. It is *not* simply a casual way for you to reproduce the author's views nearly word for word without using quotation marks. Rather, paraphrasing requires you to think through what the author has said and then restate the information *in your own words*. To accomplish this objective you must understand what the author has said and then reformulate her or his opinion without adding or deleting significant information and without distorting the intent of the original passage. The paraphrase combines the advantages of quoting and summarizing because it allows you to reproduce the essence of the author's argument and adapt it to the flow of your own argument.

Computer Notes

Brief citation using → `Rathje and Murphy (cont'd)`   3
authors' names

`According to Rathje and Murphy, people need to become "garbage lit-`
Paraphrase subject → `erate" because most recycling labels are deceptive (242).`
heading after note   `Recycling Labels.`

Jill's comment and → `Good term--"garbage literate." Should I have a whole section of the`
question   `paper on how to read labels?`
Source number
assigned by Jill
Page

Exercise ──────   Read the following passage by Bruce Van Voorst and then, following the procedures discussed above, compose three types of notes: first, quote a few
important sentences; second, summarize the major point of the passage; and
third, paraphrase a major section of Van Voorst's argument. At the bottom of
each note, indicate why it is significant and how you might use it in a paper.

> To be sure, recycling is in vogue. Citizen participation is at an all-time high;
> curbside collection programs have exploded from 600 in 1989 to 4,000 today.
> But the dirty secret, and it's not a little one, is that major quantities of the
> material being collected never actually get recycled. More than 10,000 tons of
> old newspapers have piled up in waterfront warehouses in New Jersey, and a
> congressional committee has heard testimony that the nationwide figure tops
> 100 million tons. At the Pentagon, employees looking out over the parking lot
> can watch paper they've carefully segregated in the office being tossed into a
> single Dumpster, destined for an incinerator. The used-glass market has been
> so soft that Waste Management of Seattle, Inc. is stuck with a mini-mountain
> of 6,000 tons of bottles from neighborhood collections. In the Minneapolis–
> St. Paul area, haulers have run out of storage space and are incinerating some
> recyclable goods. "It's like having your suitcase all packed with no place to
> go," laments Amy Perry, solid-waste program director for the nonprofit
> Massachusetts Public Interest Research Group.
>   The problem is that the economics of recycling are out of whack. Enthusi-
> asm for collecting recyclables has raced ahead of the capacity in many areas
> to process and market them. Right now, says Victor Bell, a veteran Rhode
> Island recycling expert, "the market can't keep up with the recycling binge."
> In recent years many states and municipalities have passed laws mandating
> the collection of newspapers, plastics, glass and paper. But arranging for pro-
> cessing—and finding a profit in it—has proved tricky. As trucks loaded with
> recyclable materials arrive at processors, backlogs develop. Worse, the glut
> has depressed already soft prices for used paper and plastics.

Photocopying

Photocopying has had as great an impact on research as have microtexts and
computer databases. When you discover a particularly valuable source, copying all of it (if it is an article) or major portions of it (if it is a book) may seem to

───────

Van Voorst, Bruce. "The Recycling Bottleneck." *Time* 14 Sept. 1992: 52.

be the most efficient thing to do. You can cut out appropriate passages and paste them onto individual note cards, thus ensuring that you have precise quotations. You can even review the pertinent information in the original when you begin to write.

But if you decide to photocopy every source you uncover, you will waste a lot of time, paper, and money. The purpose of reading and note taking is to extract the essence of an article or book, to identify the information most pertinent to your argument. Photocopying is not an alternative to evaluating your sources. Compiling a large stack of paper only postpones your examination, reading, and assessment of the material.

Planning Your Research Paper on Your Computer

As you read this sentence, the advances in computer technology have changed much of the information in this chapter on how to find sources in your library. Despite these changes, however, the job of *planning* your research paper remains the same. Computer data bases may help you locate 10,000 sources on your subject, but you will never have time to read them all, much less cite them. You need a few basic strategies to find, organize, and assess those sources that will support the arguments you are making in your research paper.

Begin by creating a single file on the subject of your paper (recycling). Rather than open a file for each source you consult, create a single data base of sources, notes, and comments. As you discover additional descriptors that restrict your subject or lead to promising sources (newspapers and recycling), add them to your notes. Similarly, as you see your notes begin to cluster around certain topics (landfills), insert these keywords into your data.

Once you have created your data base, use the search feature to locate all references to a particular topic (de-inking). Then use your copy-and-paste feature to collect information from a variety of sources and to create a new file, which you may want to consider a section of your paper. Keep track of each source number so that you can cite each chunk of information correctly.

If you discover new information on a subject, enter it into your main file and then copy it into the smaller file you have created for that sub-topic. If you decide to rename one of your smaller files, consider using the global search feature to find all references to your old heading in your data base (waste management) and then revise the heading (recycling and efficiency).

The purposes of this planning are to (1) create your own library of information on your subject and (2) construct your own subject heading index so that you can find the information you want once you begin drafting. Indeed, the subheadings in your index may well end up representing major sections of your paper.

Filling Gaps

Planning the research paper is like planning any other paper. As you evaluate your information, you discover that you need more or different kinds of material. As you conduct your research, you constantly refine and restrict your subject. By the time you finish taking notes on the sources you first discovered and the sources you have uncovered along the way, you know where the holes in your research are, what gaps you have to fill if you are to present a thorough and coherent argument.

The research process, like the writing process, is recursive. You must loop back to the beginning to devise additional subject headings and check specialized bibliographies and other references to find the sources to fill the gaps in your information. When you begin writing your paper, you may have to make yet another loop to discover information that forges missing connections. Because you have worked through the process once and know what you are looking for, however, these further efforts should be quick and to the point.

Writing Assignments

Narrate   **1.**   Freewrite in your journal about some special childhood experiences you had in your school or public library. Make a list of the sights and smells you remember, the books you read, the people you met. Then compose a narrative about how the library introduced you to new worlds.

Observe   **2.**   Review the speculation example in Chapter 2 (pages 30–33). Study the activity of the people in the reference room of your own library. Observe how various students and faculty consult the reference tools and reference librarians in the room. Then write an essay (perhaps a comic one) for your student newspaper on the various *styles* of research you observed.

Investigate **3.**   Interview the head reference librarian at your university library. Ask him or her to discuss how computer technology has changed library research in the last five years and to speculate on what new technologies will become available in the next five years. Then write a profile of the reference librarian for your university's alumni magazine, explaining to former graduates how things have changed since they thumbed their way through the card catalogue and the *Readers' Guide.*

Collaborate **4.**   Your writing group has been asked to update your university library's guide. Assign each member of the group to a specific area—circulation, reference, periodicals, special collections, and so on. Ask librarians how the area is supposed to function, and students about the problems they encounter when they try to work there. Then ask them both what improvements they would like to see implemented. Collect your evidence and then revise the guide.

Read   **5.**   Read selected passages from a book such as Robert D. Altick's *The Scholar Adventurers* (New York: Macmillan, 1965). Then write an essay in which you comment on one of these adventurers or in which you discuss your own adventures tracking down and interpreting some piece of evidence. Consider as your audience students about to begin their first research paper and as your purpose convincing them that research is *adventurous.*

Respond   **6.**   Read Robert Weber's speculations about the future of library research in "Library Without Walls." *Publisher's Weekly.* 8 June 1990: S20–22. Respond to his description of the computerized library from one of two positions: 1. as someone who is overwhelmed by the advances in technology, or 2. as someone who is excited by these new advances.

Analyze   **7.**   Consider the various sources you used in your research. What did you learn from interviewing people? What did you learn by reading books? Then write a letter to your writing teacher analyzing the benefits of *real-world* research as a strategy for enriching *library-based* research.

Evaluate   **8.**   Read the statements on plagiarism in your university's catalogue or student manual. Evaluate the degree to which these statements explain the conventions of citation and documentation you need to learn to write a successful research paper.

Argue **9.** Argue that your library needs to provide more systematic instruction on how to use its new computer technology. Acknowledge that such explanations seem abstract unless the researcher has a specific problem to solve. For that reason, argue that instruction in the library's computer technology should be linked in some official way with instruction in a basic writing course, where students are writing their first college research paper. Address your argument to the directors of the library and the freshman writing program.

Argue **10.** In a letter addressed to the chair of the English Department, argue that students should be required to complete two kinds of research assignments: (1) the library research paper (based on secondary sources), and (2) the field research paper (based on observations, interviews, questionnaires, and other kinds of primary sources). To support your argument, you may want to use both secondary sources (e.g., Robin W. Winks, ed., *The Historian as Detective: Essays on Evidence* [New York; Harper, 1968]) and primary sources (e.g., interviews with students, faculty, and future employers).

15 | Writing the Research Paper

For the research paper as for any writing project, eventually you must stop planning and start writing. The large stack of note cards or computer printout you have prepared points to two accomplishments: (1) you have learned a systematic procedure for gathering information (a procedure you can apply to other subjects), and (2) you have learned a great deal about the research that has already been published on your subject. But, as Barbara Tuchman suggests, most people are "overimpressed by research. People are always saying to me in awed tones, 'Think of all the *research* you must have done!' as if this were the hard part. It is not; writing, being a creative process, is much harder and takes twice as long" (Barbara Tuchman, "Problems in Writing the Biography of General Stilwell," *Practicing History*).

Your sources will guide you through the hard part of research—writing your paper. But they can also present two problems: (1) you have probably gathered more information than you can use in one paper, and (2) you have become so immersed in what other researchers have written about your subject that you may no longer know what *you* want to write about it. The most effective way to overcome these difficulties is to settle down and write a first draft.

This chapter will discuss the basic steps in writing that first draft. It will also show you some of Jill Taraskiewicz's initial difficulties with getting started on her first draft. And further, it will give you detailed advice about how to quote and document sources in the final draft. Read Jill's final draft and accompanying annotations in the readings at the end of the chapter to see how she resolved her difficulties and integrated her research into her writing.

The major topics discussed in this chapter are

▼ Organizing a preliminary outline
▼ Developing a thesis
▼ Writing the first draft
▼ Creating the introduction
▼ Quoting sources
▼ Documenting sources
▼ Listing sources
▼ Typing the final draft

ORGANIZING A PRELIMINARY OUTLINE

To organize a preliminary (or *scratch*) outline, read through your notes, collecting information that deals with specific subdivisions of your subject. If you have written subheadings at the top of your note cards, then you should be able to sort them into smaller stacks. If you are working with a computer, you can produce the same results by searching your data base for chunks of information to copy and paste into smaller files. If you discover that some divisions (1) focus on similar aspects of your subject, (2) do not contain enough information, or (3) deal with subject headings no longer appropriate to the emerging design of your paper, then relabel, combine, or eliminate these divisions so that they begin to form a logical and coherent sequence.

Before drafting your paper, try several preliminary outlines to determine the most effective pattern for presenting your information. After you have completed your first draft, use a *descriptive* outline (or *revision agenda*) to evaluate what you have written. Once you are ready to write the final draft of your research paper, prepare a *formal* outline to guide your composing process. (You may want to review the types, formats, and purposes of these strategies as they are described in Chapters 3 and 4). Your instructor may require you to submit your formal outline with your paper as a kind of table of contents.

Once you have established your categories, arrange them into various patterns to find the one that seems most effective. (You may wish to review the patterns in Chapter 5, "Common Methods of Development," or in Chapter 11.) Some of your subject headings may suggest a simple pattern (a *definition* of recycling); others may point to a more complicated pattern (a *causal analysis* of why people seem so fascinated with recycling). Jill's research, for example, led her to study the problems with recycling and the difficulties with alternative forms of waste management. Because she understood the pros and cons of this controversy, she considered organizing her paper as a *comparison and contrast* essay. But she was perplexed about how to arrange her material. Which side should she analyze first—prorecycling or antirecycling? What was her purpose in comparing the two positions? She sorted her notes again and discovered that she needed to be more precise about her purpose.

PRELIMINARY OUTLINE: The Recycling Controversy

1. Critics of recycling

    expensive

    inefficient

    cheaper alternatives

2. Defenders of recycling

    expensive because of established business practices

    inefficient because of poor public policy

    alternatives are dangerous

3. Environmental policy

why do we have to choose *one* solution?

why not reduce waste first rather than getting rid of it later?

what is an effective environmental policy?

A preliminary outline reveals at a glance the kind of paper your sources will allow you to write. As Jill looks at her outline, she sees that her planning has uncovered several interesting issues. Her reading has helped her to match up the points in the first two sections. Each side's arguments were convincing, but she is bothered by the either/or aspects of the controversy. Does she have to decide whether to be for or against recycling? That question prompts her to create a third section filled with a series of other questions. Jill suspects that if she uses these questions to review her research, she may have some insights that will help her revise her preliminary outline so that it demonstrates a thesis.

DEVELOPING A THESIS

Developing a thesis is the most difficult task in composing the research paper. Your notes, even when they are sorted and arranged in a compelling pattern, represent the voices of authority. It is easy to be intimidated by your own research, to let your sources speak for you. But remember your main aim is to advance your own argument—to discuss and analyze a topic from your own point of view. Like all other writing assignments, the research paper requires you to write with a purpose.

To find that purpose, review the comments you wrote about your notes. If you consistently commented on or posed questions about the ideas in your notes, then you have already established a degree of independence from your sources. As you reread your comments, look for common denominators in your thinking. What fascinated you about your subject? What connections did you see among the various sources you read?

Once you have identified some common themes, covert each into a hypothesis and try to match it with some point in your preliminary outline. Some of your hypotheses may match up easily, leading to assertions that explain each subdivision and pointing toward a thesis. Others may require you to revise the subdivisions or expand the range of categories you need to consider. Still others may suggest that you reorganize your outline completely. The thesis you try to advance in your first draft depends on a number of factors: your personal preference, your understanding of the information you have gathered, and your confidence in your ability to demonstrate what you propose to prove.

As Jill looked back through her comments, she discovered two ideas expressed by other writers that clarified what she wanted to prove in her own research: (1) Bruce Van Voorst convinced her that the technology for recycling was not cost-efficient; and (2) William L. Rathje and Cullen Murphy convinced her that most people did not know enough about the technology of recycling to understand what it could and could not accomplish.

Jill began to speculate that the questions she posed in the third section of her preliminary outline might place the recycling controversy in a larger context. She formulated three hypotheses that she hoped would help her escape the gridlock she had created in the first two sections of her preliminary outline.

1. Recent reports on recycling reveal that it is not working out as well as most environmentalists had hoped.
2. The arguments about the ineffectiveness of recycling have to be compared with the arguments about the dangers of alternative solutions.
3. The debate about the effectiveness of recycling has to be placed in the larger context of trying to understand how to manage all the waste in our environment.

Exercise ——— Discuss how each of Jill's hypotheses matches up with her preliminary outline (pages 436–437). In what ways will each hypothesis require her to change the major headings and subdivisions of her outline? What information will she have to add, eliminate, or relabel?

WRITING THE FIRST DRAFT

Writing the first draft of your research paper is like writing the first draft of any other paper—it is a discovery exercise. You have to discover whether your planning will enable you to communicate a subject to an audience for a purpose. Some of your discoveries will seem familiar because they are common in every writing situation: the information that seemed so complete in your notes now seems sketchy; and the overall purpose of your paper, so clear in your mind when you began, now strikes you as confused or inconsistent. Other discoveries may prove unsettling because they seem unique to the research paper: your first draft may follow your preliminary outline and support your thesis, but it may seem stiff, mechanical, and dull.

For most inexperienced writers, first-draft dullness derives from the inability to compose a simple, straightforward introduction that asserts a thesis and the inability to weave quoted material gracefully and naturally into the body of the paper. The following sections will illustrate and discuss some methods for solving these problems.

CREATING THE INTRODUCTION

Do not be surprised if you have to struggle with the introduction to your research paper. You have learned a great deal about your subject and are eager to display that learning in the body of your paper. But in order to do that you have to write an introduction that establishes the focus of your subject, attracts the attention of your readers, and asserts the purpose of your paper. Some writers cannot write such an introduction until they have discovered precisely what they are going to say in the body of the paper. For that reason, they prefer to write the introduction after they have drafted the rest of the paper—when they know exactly what they want to introduce. Other writers cannot develop the body of the paper until they have defined its exact direction. For that reason, they draft several versions of the introduction, hoping to learn what they want to introduce. Either method will require you to make a series of adjustments—some large, some small—to the introduction and to the body when you revise the final draft.

Jill is intrigued by her first hypothesis but suspects that it may simply trap her in the controversy she is trying to clarify. She decides to use it in some form to develop the antirecycling section of her paper. Her attempts to work out the implications of her other two hypotheses and to find a purpose for her paper produce two different introductions. Her revision agendas reveal her dissatisfaction with them because each fails to establish her subject and clarify her thesis. Here are both introductions and the revision agendas.

FIRST DRAFT: Introduction

Recycling products such as paper and plastic seems like a good way to protect the environment, save space in landfills, and reduce wastefulness in general. But according to recent studies, recycling may not be working out as well as environmentalists had hoped. But if recycling has proved too costly and complicated, its alternatives— landfills and incinerators—have proved too costly, complicated, and dangerous. According to William Rathje and Cullen Murphy, these technologies pose a "threat to public health" (180).

REVISION AGENDA

1. <u>What did I try to do in this draft?</u>
   I tried to establish the controversy about the effectiveness of recycling and then expand the debate by suggesting that the alternatives were also controversial.
2. <u>What are its strengths and weaknesses?</u>
   I focus on the controversy, although the reference to the hopes of environmentalists is vague. I criticize the popular side first—recycling is ineffective—then counter with criticism about alternatives. I don't really present any positive solutions. I just say that all solutions are not working. I don't like using quote for thesis. Besides it points away from subject—recycling.
3. <u>What revisions do I want to make in my next draft?</u>
   a. Present both sides fairly.
   b. Explain why recycling is good.
   c. Establish larger purpose for studying controversy.
   d. Compose my own thesis sentence.

SECOND DRAFT: Introduction

One of the most controversial issues facing American citizens is what to do with the garbage. For several years the solution seemed obvious—recycle. But recent studies have made recycling into a controversy. On the one hand, critics argue that recycling is expensive and inefficient. On the other side, advocates argue that recycling is essential to our environmental health. The problem with this controversy is that it poses a false dilemma—forcing America to reject or embrace recycling. Recycling may not do everything economists and environmentalists dreamed it would, but at least it helps to eliminate some of the garbage that threatens to overwhelm the environment.

REVISION AGENDA

1. <u>What did I try to do in this draft?</u>
   Establish two sides in the controversy—fairly—but suggest that choosing one side or the other won't solve the problem.
2. <u>What are its strengths and weaknesses?</u>
   I set up the two sides of the controversy. Suggest that it is a false dilemma. We need recycling, even if it isn't perfect, if we are to solve the garbage problem. Thesis is better. Still not sure it points to larger issue of an informed environmental policy.
3. <u>What revisions do I want to make in my next draft?</u>
   a. Clarify the arguments on both sides—add a few details.
   b. Make point that we need to understand both sides in the controversy.
   c. Suggest that the purpose for studying the controversy is to understand the place of recycling in the larger context of environmental policy.

When she finished her second revision agenda, Jill was confident that her third hypothesis had led to a thesis and purpose for her paper. She reworked the introduction and drafted the body of her paper, encountering and solving a number of tricky problems. She had to decide, for example, how to weave her source material into her text and how to prepare her list of works cited. You will see how Jill handled these problems when you read her paper and the annotations that accompany it on pages 462–475.

Exercise ———— Compare Jill's two draft introductions (pages 439–440) with the introduction she uses in her final paper (page 465). How do her revision agendas help her expand her introduction and sharpen her thesis? What specific decisions seem to produce the most important changes in her final draft?

Drawing by Bruce Eric Kaplan; © 1992 The New Yorker Magazine, Inc.

QUOTING SOURCES

The most persistent challenge posed by the research paper is deciding *when* and *where* to cite your sources to support your argument. For every division of your outline, you have notes that contain the words and ideas of other writers. If you use this material, you must acknowledge the sources of your information (see "Documenting Sources," pages 446–452, and "Listing Sources," pages 452–459). It's a common beginner's error, however, not just to use sources but to let the sources write the paper for you. Excessive quoting distorts the balance between your writing and the writing of others and makes your paper seem to be a scrapbook of other people's opinions. And it can disrupt the flow of your argument by introducing ideas and images that may not deal directly with your thesis.

To avoid these problems, you should be selective when you quote. Because each quotation creates a special effect, ask yourself these questions when you are deciding whether to quote a passage.

1. ***Will the substance of the passage make a significant contribution to my subject?*** Sometimes a passage may seem significant because it provides extensive evidence for its conclusions. But you may be able to make the same point more effectively by summarizing or paraphrasing rather than quoting the passage.

2. ***Will the phrasing of the passage seem memorable to my readers?*** You do not want to blur the effect of a quotation by quoting too much material.

Nor do you want to quote uninspired or unintelligible writing. You should quote only key sentences or phrases—those that convey the author's meaning in especially vivid language.

3. *Will the reputation of the author give credibility to my argument?* The mere mention of certain "experts" produces controversy or distorts your argument. If the authority of your sources is suspect, there is no point in quoting them.

When you determine that you want to use a particular quotation, you have to decide how to incorporate it into your own writing. There are several methods for quoting material; the one you choose depends on why you are quoting the passage and how much you intend to quote.

Introducing Quotations

All quotations must be placed within quotation marks or set off from your text. They must be documented with a parenthetical reference that includes the exact page numbers from which they were taken and, if necessary, the authors' names or other words or phrases that identify the sources. A lead-in phrase or sentence identifying the person you are quoting and the reason he or she is being quoted helps your readers follow your reasoning and prepares them for the special effect conveyed by a quotation. There are at least three ways to introduce a quotation. Here is the most common method:

In "Too Many Bottles Break the Bank," environmentalist Dan Charles points out that "every one of the 50 states in the US has now passed a law that either encourages or requires local governments to set up some kind of recycling program" (12).

The author to be quoted (Dan Charles), his occupation (environmentalist), and the source of the quotation ("Too Many Bottles Break the Bank") are all identified. But the purpose for which Charles is being quoted is not explained; presumably, this passage will appear in a paragraph in which the context or reason for the quotation has been established. Introductory phrases such as the one here help your readers see how your argument is advanced by an authority.

In the second form of introducing a quotation, the author being quoted and the reason he or she is being quoted are both identified in a sentence that concludes with a colon; the quotation then follows, as in this example:

Environmentalist Dan Charles, in "Too Many Bottles Break the Bank," explains the extent to which Americans have embraced recycling: "every one of the 50 states in the US has now passed a law that either encourages or requires local governments to set up some kind of recycling program" (12).

The third method of identifying a quotation relies on the assumption that you introduced the author's full name and credentials earlier in the paper.

"Every one of the 50 states in the US," Charles reports, "has now passed a law that either encourages or requires local governments to set up some kind of recycling program" (12).

Compare this with Jill's treatment of the Charles passage on page 469.

Length of Quotations

The length (and look) of your quotation will determine its effect. A brief, pointed quotation, generally worked into the syntax of your sentence, is often the best way to advance your argument. But on rare occasions (perhaps no more than two or three times in a ten-page research paper), you may want to quote a long passage that expresses the main ideas you are trying to present.

Long quotations (four or more lines of prose; three or more lines of poetry) are usually introduced by a colon or comma, set off from your text by triple-spacing above and below, and indented ten spaces from the left margin. This special placement identifies the passage as a quotation, so do not enclose it in quotation marks. In such block quotations, the final period goes *before* rather than *after* the parenthetical reference. Here is an example.

Consumer advocate Lynn Scarlett explains why recycling programs do not accomplish their purpose:

> Curbside recycling programs put more collection trucks—one set to pick up recyclables, another for remaining waste—on the road. This means more fuel consumption, which means more air pollution. And some recycling processes produce high volumes of water waste and are energy intensive. In short what saves landfill space may use more water or fuel. (17)

Short Quotations (less than four lines of prose, less than three lines of poetry) are usually run in with your text, unless they deserve special emphasis. You can introduce a short quotation by one of the three methods described earlier. Or, as in the example below, you can work brief phrases from your source into the syntax of your sentence, using quotation marks and identifying the source with a parenthetical reference. See how Jill uses this passage in her paper on page 466:

In her article, "Will Recycling Help the Environment?" consumer advocate Lynn Scarlett argues that because recycling programs require more collection trucks, they create "more fuel consumption, which means more air pollution" (17).

Integrating Quotations

Sometimes, to make a quoted passage fit smoothly into the flow of your sentences, you will have to use *ellipsis* and *brackets*. Use ellipsis points when you want to omit part of the quoted passage to make it conform to your sentence. Use three points (. . .) to indicate omission of material within the sentence. Use four points (. . . .) to indicate the omission of a whole sentence or more. Use brackets when you need to add your own words to a quotation to make the passage complete or grammatically correct or, on occasion, when you need to make an editorial comment. (See Sections 27 and 28, on brackets and ellipsis, respectively, in the "Handbook of Grammar and Usage.")

Here is a lengthy passage from Bruce Van Voorst's article "The Recycling Bottleneck":

> In large measure, the present disequilibrium in recycling is the result of policies that work at cross-purposes with the goals of one another. Environmentalists argue—correctly—that recycled materials suffer in the marketplace against virgin materials because of government subsidies. Newsprint producers, for instance, are indirectly subsidized through public-area logging and logging access roads. The oil depletion allowance for petroleum subsidizes producers of oil-based plastics.

Notice how Jill uses ellipses and brackets to incorporate Van Voorst's phrasing into one of the early drafts of her paper:

> The excessive costs of "recycled materials [are the result of] government subsidies. . . . for newsprint producers. . . . and producers of oil-based plastics (53).

See page 468 to see how Jill uses this passage to advance the argument in her paper.

Using Summary and Paraphrase

Often the most efficient way to work your sources into your own writing is to summarize or paraphrase them. As you remember from Chapter 14, a summary states the thesis or outlines the principal points of an author's argument; a paraphrase is a restatement of the author's ideas in *your own words* (see page 429). Because the words of a summary or paraphrase are yours, they do not have to be enclosed by quotation marks. But because the ideas come from someone else, you do need to cite the source in your text and document the passage with a parenthetical reference.

The following passage is from Dori Jones Yang, William C. Symonds, and Lisa Driscoll's article "Recycling Is Rewriting the Rules of Papermaking":

> With dumps overflowing, most cities started curbside pickup of used newspapers. To create a market for the stuff, seven states, including California and Connecticut, mandated last year that newspapers published in their jurisdic-

tion be partly printed on recycled newspapers. Publishers in 11 other states and all major newspaper chains have followed the trend.

Jill paraphrases this passage as follows.

Moreover, the demand for recycled paper is so depressed that some states have had to pass legislation forcing newspapers to print part of each new edition on recycled paper (Yang 100H).

See how she works this material into her paper on page 467.

Plagiarism

Plagiarism is the use of someone else's writing without giving proper credit— or perhaps without giving any credit at all—to the writer of the original. Whether plagiarism is intentional or unintentional, it is a serious offense that can be easily avoided by adhering scrupulously to the following advice. You should document your sources whenever you

▼ Use a direct quotation.

▼ Copy a table, chart, or other diagram.

▼ Construct a table from data provided by others.

▼ Summarize or paraphrase a passage in your own words.

▼ Present specific examples, figures, or factual information that are taken from a specific source and used to explain or support your judgments.

The following excerpt from John E. Young's *Discarding the Throwaway Society* and these three examples of students' use of it illustrate the problem.

Original Version

The relative worth of different types of recycling can be ranked: the most valuable is the manufacture of new products from similar, used items; the least valuable is the conversion of waste materials into entirely different products for which uses must be created. The key criterion is whether the recovered material is substituted for a virgin one in production, thus closing the loop.

Version A

The relative worth of different types of recycling can be ranked: the most valuable is the production of new goods from similar, used items; the least valuable is the conversion of waste materials into entirely new products for which uses must be created. The key criterion is whether the recovered material is substituted for a virgin one in production, thus closing the loop.

This is plagiarism in its worst form. Because the writer of Version A does not indicate in the text or in a parenthetical reference that the words and ideas belong to Young, his readers will believe that the words are his. He has stolen the words and attempted to cover the theft by changing or omitting an occasional word.

Version B

> John E. Young points out that the relative worth of different types of recycling can be ranked: the most valuable is the manufacture of new products from similar, used items; the least valuable is the conversion of waste materials into entirely different products for which uses must be created. The key criterion is whether the recovered material is substituted for a virgin one in production, thus closing the loop (27).

Version B is also plagiarism, even though the writer acknowledges his source and documents the passage with a parenthetical reference. Obviously the writer has copied the original word for word, yet he has supplied no quotation marks to indicate the extent of the borrowing. As written and documented, the passage masquerades as a paraphrase, when in fact it is a direct quotation.

Version C

> In his <u>Discarding the Throwaway Society</u>, John E. Young argues that the effectiveness of various types of recycling can be measured: "the most valuable is the manufacture of new products from similar, used items; the least valuable is the conversion of waste materials for which uses must be created" (27).

Version C represents one, although not the only, satisfactory way of handling this source material. The writer has identified his source at the beginning of the sentence, letting his readers know who is being quoted. He then uses an introductory phrase and a colon to characterize and set up the material he plans to quote. He marks the original passage in quotation marks. Finally, he provides the parenthetical reference. By following this procedure, he has made perfectly clear which words are his and which belong to Young. See how Jill uses this passage in her paper on pages 471 to 472.

DOCUMENTING SOURCES

The purpose of documenting each source with a parenthetical reference is twofold: (1) to avoid the appearance of representing somebody else's work as your own and (2) to refer your readers to your list of works cited, where they will find a complete citation on your source. Although there is general agreement about the purpose of documentation, different fields of learning, periodicals, and publishers prefer different styles.

The two most commonly used styles are those recommended by the Modern Language Association in its *MLA Handbook for Writers of Research Papers,*

Fourth Edition, and by the American Psychological Association in its *Publication Manual of the American Psychological Association, Fourth Edition.* The two styles differ:

MLA Style	**APA Style**
Sources are documented by parenthetical reference to author's last name and to page number. No punctuation separates these elements, and no abbreviation for *page* or *pages* is used.	Sources are documented by parenthetical reference to author's last name, publication date, and page number. Commas separate these elements, and the abbreviations *p.* and *pp.* are used.

Here is the same source documented according to each style:

MLA Style

Wellman, Inc., America's largest plastic recycler, "gobbled up most of the 1.5 billion liter bottles handed in for recycling" but could supply only half the demand for its product (Cahan 116–17).

WORKS CITED

Cahan, Vicky. "Waste Not, Want Not? Not Necessarily." <u>Business Week</u>. 17 July 1989: 116–17.

APA Style

Wellman, Inc., America's largest plastic recycler, "gobbled up most of the 1.5 billion liter bottles handed in for recycling" but could supply only half the demand for its product (Cahan, 1989, pp. 116–17).

WORKS CITED

Cahan, Vicky (1989, July 17). Waste not, want not? Not necessarily. <u>Business Week</u>. pp. 116–117.

Different departments in your college or university may require a particular style; your instructors will tell you which documentation style they require. If you are writing a research paper in the social sciences, your instructor is likely to require APA style. If you are writing a research paper in the humanities, your instructor is likely to require MLA style. Because this chapter is designed to help you write a research paper in a composition class, its examples, including Jill's research paper, follow MLA style.

Sample Citations

Frequently you will need to cite sources that are not as straightforward as the Cahan example, such as a book written by more than one author or several works by the same author. In these cases, follow the specific styles given here.

Each example of a citation is followed by the entry that would appear in the works cited list.

Citing One Work by an Author of Two or More Works

If you are citing two or more titles by the same author, place a coma after the author's last name, add a shortened version of the title of the work, and then supply the relevant page numbers. Another solution is to cite the author's last name and title in your sentence and then add the page numbers in a parenthetical reference.

Once society reaches a certain stage of industrial growth, it will shift its energies to the production of services (Toffler, Future 221).

Toffler argues in The Third Wave that society has gone through two eras (agricultural and industrial) and is now entering another—the information age (26).

WORKS CITED

Toffler, Alvin. Future Shock. New York: Random, 1970.

---. The Third Wave. New York: Morrow, 1980.

Citing One Work by an Author Who Has the Same Last Name as Another Author in Your List of Cited Works

When you are citing two or more authors with the same last name, avoid confusion by supplying each author's first name in the parenthetical reference or in your sentence. In the list of cited works, the two authors should be alphabetized by their first names.

Critics have often debated the usefulness of the psychological approach to literary interpretation (Frederick Hoffman 317).

Daniel Hoffman argues that folklore and myth provide valuable insights for the literary critic (9–15).

WORKS CITED

Hoffman, Daniel G. Form and Fable in American Fiction. New York: Oxford, 1961.

Hoffman, Frederick J. Freudianism and the Literary Mind. Baton Rouge: Louisiana State UP, 1945.

Citing a Work by More Than One Author

If you are citing a book by two authors, you have the option of naming them in your sentence or of putting their names in a parenthetical reference. If you are citing a book by three or more authors, you should probably place their names in a parenthetical reference to sustain the readability of your sentence. The authorship of a work by three or more authors can be given in a shortened form by using the first author's last name and "et al." (an abbreviation for the Latin phrase *et alia,* meaning "and others").

Boller and Story interpret the Declaration of Independence as Thomas Jefferson's attempt to list America's grievances against England (58).

Other historians view the Declaration of Independence as Jefferson's attempt to formulate the principles of America's political philosophy (Norton et al. 124).

WORKS CITED

Boller, Paul, and Ronald Story. <u>A More Perfect Union: Documents in U.S. History</u>. Boston: Houghton, 1984.

Norton, Mary Beth, et al. <u>A People and a Nation: A History of the United States</u>. Boston: Houghton, 1984.

Citing a Multivolume Work

If you are citing one volume from a multivolume work, indicate in your parenthetical reference the specific volume you used.

William Faulkner's initial reluctance to travel to Stockholm to receive the Nobel Prize produced considerable consternation in the American embassy (Blotner 2: 1347).

WORKS CITED

Blotner, Joseph. <u>Faulkner: A Biography</u>. 2 vols. New York: Random, 1974.

Citing a Work by Title

If you are citing a source for which no author is named, use an abbreviated version of the title—or the whole title, if it is short—in either the text citation or a parenthetical reference. If you abbreviate the title, be sure to begin with the work by which the source is alphabetized in the list of cited works.

The recent exhibit of nineteenth-century patent models at the Cooper-Hewitt Museum featured plans for such inventions as the Rotating Blast-Producing Chair, and Improved, Creeping Doll, and the Life Preserving Coffin: In Doubtful Cases of Actual Death ("Notes").

Notice that page numbers are omitted from the parenthetical reference when a one-page article is cited.

WORKS CITED

"Notes and Comments: The Talk of the Town." New Yorker. 16 July
    1984: 23.

Citing an Illustration   Place the illustrative material as close as possible to the part of the text it illustrates. The illustration—a photograph, advertisement, map, drawing, or graph—should be labeled "Figure" (often abbreviated "Fig."), assigned an Arabic number, and, if appropriate, given a caption and complete citation. In your text, use a parenthetical reference to guide the reader to the illustration: "(see Fig. 1)." Place all necessary information below the illustration:

Fig. 1. "Your Gateway to Tomorrow." Advertisement. Money Mar.
    1983: 1–2.

Citing Literary Works   Because some literary works—novels, plays, poems—are available in several editions, MLA recommends that you give more information than just a page number so that readers who are not using the same edition as you are can locate in their books the passage you are citing. After the page number, add a semicolon and other appropriate information, using lower-case abbreviations such as *pt., sec.,* and *ch.* (for *part, section,* and *chapter*).

Although Flaubert sees Madame Bovary for what she is—a silly,
romantic woman—he insists that "none of us can ever express the
exact measure of his needs or his thoughts or his sorrows" and that all
of us "long to make music that will melt the stars" (216; pt. 2, ch. 12).

WORKS CITED

Flaubert, Gustave. Madame Bovary: Patterns of Provincial Life. Trans.
    Francis Steegmuller. New York: Random-Modern Library, 1957.

When you cite classic verse plays and poems, omit all page numbers and document by division(s) and line(s), using periods to separate the various numbers. You can also use appropriate abbreviations to designate certain well-known words. For example, "*Od.* 8.326" refers to book 8, line 326, of Homer's *Odyssey.* Do not use the abbreviations "1" or "11" to designate lines because they can be confused with numbers. Once you have established in your text which numbers indicate lines, you may omit the words *line* and *lines* and simply use the numbers.

Also, as shown in the *Odyssey* citation just given, use Arabic numbers rather than Roman numerals for division and page numbers. Some teachers prefer Roman numerals for designating acts and scenes in plays (for example, "*Mac.* III.iv"), but if your instructor does not insist on them, use Arabic numbers: "*Mac.* 3.4."

Citing More than One Work in a Single Parenthetical Reference

If you need to mention two or more works in a single parenthetical reference, document each reference according to the normal pattern, but use semicolons to separate the citations.

(Oleson 59; Trimble 85; Hylton 63)

WORKS CITED

Hylton, Marion Willard. "On the Trail of Pollen: Momaday's <u>House Made of Dawn</u>." <u>Critique</u> 14.2 (1972): 60–69.

Oleson, Carole. "The Remembered Earth: Momaday's <u>House Made of Dawn</u>." <u>South Dakota Review</u> 2 (1973): 59–78.

Trimble, Martha Scott. <u>N. Scott Momaday</u>. Western Writers Series. Boise, ID: Boise State College, 1973.

Although the MLA style provides this procedure for documenting multiple citations within parenthetical references, that kind of documentation is often the result of "scholarly" padding and may be disruptive for readers. If multiple citations are absolutely necessary, MLA recommends that they be placed in a bibliographical endnote or footnote.

Using Notes with Parenthetical References

A *superscript numeral* (a number raised above the line) placed at an appropriate place in the text—usually at the end of a sentence—signals a note. The note itself, identified by a matching number, may appear at the end of the text (as an endnote) or at the bottom of the page on which its superscript appears (as a footnote).

In MLA style, notes (preferably endnotes) are reserved for two specific purposes.

Notes Containing Additional Commentary

Thurber's reputation continued to grow until the 1950s, when he was forced to give up drawing because of his blindness.[1]

[1]Thurber's older brother accidentally shot him in the eye with an arrow when they were children, causing the immediate loss of that

eye. He gradually lost the sight of the other eye because of complications from the accident and a cataract.

Notes Listing or Evaluating Sources or Referring to Additional Sources

The argument that American policy in Vietnam was on the whole morally justified has come under attack from many quarters.[2]

[2] For a useful sampling of opinion, see Buckley 20; Draper 32; Nardin and Slater 437.

Notice that the sources cited in note 2 are documented like parenthetical references. Complete citations would be given in the works cited list.

WORKS CITED

Buckley, Kevin. "Vietnam: The Defense Case." <u>New York Times</u> 7 Dec. 1978: 19–24.

Draper, Theodore. "Ghosts of Vietnam." <u>Dissent</u> 26 (1979): 30–41.

Nardin, Terry, and Jerome Slater. "Vietnam Revisited." <u>World Politics</u> 33 (1981): 436–48.

LISTING SOURCES: SAMPLE ENTRIES

In the MLA documentation style readers can locate complete information about your sources only in a list of cited works. The list goes at the end of your paper and, as its title, Works Cited, suggests, contains only the sources you have *cited* in your paper. Occasionally, your instructor may require a list of the works you *consulted*. Such a list would include not only the sources you cited in your paper but also the sources you consulted while conducting your research. (If you have questions about the kind of list you are to prepare, ask your instructor.)

Even though the list of cited works appears at the end of your paper, it must be compiled *before* you begin writing. The bibliographic information on your source cards will eventually constitute your works cited list. In order to create the list, you must alphabetize your source cards, being careful that each entry is complete according to the appropriate format. As you write, you may need to add or delete source cards. Be sure to identify your sources clearly and accurately in your text and to provide complete bibliographic information about each one in your list of cited works.

When you type your final list, follow the instructions given below. For an illustration of this format, see Jill's works cited list on pages 474 to 475.

1. Paginate the works cited list as a continuation of your text. If the conclusion of your paper appears on page 9, begin your list on page 10, unless there is an intervening page of endnotes.

2. List all entries in alphabetical order according to the last name of the author.

3. Double-space between successive lines of an entry and between entries.

4. After the first line of an entry, indent successive lines five spaces or one-half inch.

5. If you are listing more than one work by the same author, alphabetize the works according to title (excluding any initial articles—*a, an, the*). Instead of repeating the author's name with each citation, for the second and additional works, type three hyphens and a period, and then give the title:

Lanham, Richard A. <u>Literacy and the Survival of Humanism</u>. New
    Haven: Yale, 1983.

---. <u>Style: An Anti-Textbook</u>. New Haven: Yale, 1974.

The form of each entry in your works cited list will vary according to the type of source you are citing. The major variations are illustrated below. If you need additional information, consult *MLA Handbook for Writers of Research Papers, Fourth Edition.*

Books

Citations for books have three main parts—author, title, and facts of publication. Separate each part with a period followed by one space. (The first sample entry is described completely; significant variations in subsequent entries are noted in marginal annotations.)

A Book by a Single Author or Agency

Tuchman, Barbara W. <u>A Distant Mirror: The Calamitous 14th Century</u>.
    New York: Knopf, 1978.

▼   The author's last name comes before the given name or initial to facilitate alphabetizing. Use the name exactly as it appears on the title page of the sources.

▼   If the book is the work of an agency (committee, organization, or department) instead of an individual, the name of the agency takes the place of the author's name.

▼   If no author or agency is given, the citation begins with and is alphabetized by the title of the source.

▼   The title and subtitle of the book are underlined.

▼   The place of publication, the publisher, and the date of publication are named in that order and are punctuated and spaced as in the preceding Tuchman citation. A colon separates the place of publication from the name of the publishing company, and a comma separates the publisher's name from the date.

▼ If more than one place of publication is given on the title page, mention only the first.

▼ If the place of publication might be unfamiliar or unclear to your readers, add an abbreviation identifying the appropriate state or country: Cambridge, MA.

▼ Shorten the publisher's name, as long as the shortened form is easily identifiable: *Houghton Mifflin* can be *Houghton*; *Harvard University Press* can be *Harvard UP*.

▼ When you cannot locate one or more pieces of information concerning the facts of publication, use these abbreviations in the appropriate positions.

No place: n.p.
No publisher: n.p.
No date: n.d.

A Book by Two or Three Authors

Ashby, Eric, and Mary Anderson. <u>The Rise of the Student Estate in Britain</u>. Cambridge, MA: Harvard UP, 1970.

Lee, Lawrence, George Seddon, and Frances Stephens. <u>Stained Glass</u>. New York: Crown, 1976.

A Book by Three or More Authors

Sheridan, Marion C., et al. <u>The Motion Picture and the Teaching of English</u>. New York: Appleton, 1965.

A Book with an Editor

Kuhn, Thomas, ed. <u>The Essential Tension: Selected Studies in Scientific Tradition and Change</u>. Chicago: U of Chicago P, 1977.

A Book with an Author and an Editor

Emphasis on author

Ginsberg, Allen. <u>Journals: Early Fifties, Early Sixties</u>. Ed. Gordon Ball. New York: Grove, 1977.

Emphasis on editor

Ball, Gordon, ed. <u>Journals: Early Fifties, Early Sixties</u>. By Allen Ginsberg. New York: Grove, 1977.

Works in an Anthology

Citation of one work only

Tyler, Anne. "Still Just Writing." <u>The Writer on Her Work</u>. Ed. Janet Sternberg. New York: Norton, 1980, 3–16.

Basis for multiple citations

Sternberg, Janet, ed. <u>The Writer on Her Work</u>. New York: Norton, 1980.

Multiple citations   Walker, Alice. "<u>One</u> Child of One's Own: a Meaningful Digression Within the Works." Sternberg 121–40.

Walker, Margaret. "On Being Female, Black, and Free." Sternberg 95–106.

An Article in an Alphabetically Arranged Reference Book

"Graham, Martha." <u>Who's Who of American Women</u>. 13th ed. 1983–1984.

Frequently revised work   Hayward, Jane. "Stained Glass." <u>Encyclopedia Americana</u> 1983 ed.

A Multivolume Work

Citing all volumes   Blotner, Joseph. <u>Faulkner: A Biography</u>. 2 vols. New York: Random, 1974.

Citing one volume   Blotner, Joseph. <u>Faulkner: A Biography</u>. New York: Random, 1974. Vol. 2.

An Edition Other than the First

Bailey, Sydney. <u>British Parliamentary Research</u>. 3rd ed. Boston: Houghton, 1971.

An Introduction, Preface, Foreword, or Afterword

Bernstein, Carl. Afterword. <u>Poison Penmanship: The Gentle Art of Muckraking</u>. By Jessica Mitford. New York: Random, 1979. 275–77.

A Book in a Series

Longley, John L., Jr. <u>Robert Penn Warren</u>. Southern Writers Series 2. Austin, TX: Steck, 1969.

A Republished Book

Malamud, Bernard. <u>The Natural</u>. 1952. New York: Avon, 1980.

Published Proceedings of a Conference

Shusterman, Alan J., ed. <u>Capitalizing on Ideas: New Alliances for Business</u>. Proceedings from a Conference of Indiana Business Leaders. 10–11 April 1983. Indianapolis: Indiana Committee for the Humanities. 1983.

A Translation

Mâle, Émile. <u>Chartres</u>. Trans. Sara Wilson. New York: Harper, 1983.

A Book with a Title Usually Italicized in Its Title

Miller, James E., Jr. <u>A Critical Guide to</u> Leaves of Grass. Chicago: U of
   Chicago P, 1957.

Articles

Citations for articles in periodicals, like citations for books, contain three parts: author, title, and facts of publication. But articles include more complicated facts of publication such as the periodical title, the volume number, year of publication, and inclusive page numbers. You can usually find this information on the first page of the article and on the cover or title page of the periodical. The first entry is discussed completely; significant variations in subsequent entries are noted in marginal annotations.

Fulwiler, Toby. "How Well Does Writing Across the Curriculum Work?"
   <u>College English</u> 46 (1984): 112–25.

- ▼ Cite author (last name first).
- ▼ Place title of article within quotation marks.
- ▼ Underline title of periodical.
- ▼ Place volume number after title of periodical.
- ▼ Enclose year of publication within parentheses.
- ▼ Use colon to separate date of periodical from inclusive page numbers of article.
- ▼ If a periodical pages its issues continuously through an annual volume, as does *College English*, give only the volume number, not the issue number.

An Article in a Journal that Pages Each Issue Separately or Uses Only Issue Numbers

Bird, Harry. "Some Aspects of Prejudice in the Roman World."
   <u>University of Windsor Review</u> 10.1 (1975): 64–75.

An Article from a Monthly or Bimonthly Periodical

Jacobs, Jane. "The Dynamic of Decline." <u>Atlantic</u> April 1984: 98–114.

An Article from a Weekly or Biweekly Periodical

Arlen, Michael J. "Onward and Upward with the Arts: Thirty Seconds."
    New Yorker 15 Oct. 1979: 55–146.

Article from a Daily Newspaper

Article with byline

Whited, Charles. "The Priceless Treasure of the Marquesas." Miami
    Herald 15 July 1973: 1.

Separately paginated sections

"Culture Shock: Williamsburg and Disney World, Back to Back." New
    York Times 21 Sept. 1975: sec. 10:1.

Newspaper title that does not include city name

"Oliver North Faces Congress." Union Star [Schenectady, NY] 7 July
    1987: 1.

Editorial, Letter to Editor, Review

"From Good News to Bad." Editorial. Washington Post 16 July 1984: 10.

Coldwater, Charles F., MD. Letter. The Muncie Star 17 June 1987: 4.

DeCurtis, Anthony, "Bob Dylan's Blue Highways." Rev. of The Bootleg
    Series, Volumes 1–3 (Rare and Unreleased), 1961–1991, by Bob
    Dylan. Rolling Stone 4 April 1991: 53–55.

Griswold, Charles L., Jr. "Soul Food." Rev. of Statecraft as Soulcraft:
    What Government Does, by George F. Will. American Scholar 53
    (1984): 401–6.

An Article Whose Title Contains a Quotation or a Title Within Quotation Marks

Carpenter, Lynette. "The Daring Gift in Ellen Glasgow's 'Dare's Gift.'"
    Studies in Short Fiction 21 (1984): 95–102.

An Abstract from Dissertation Abstracts (DA) or Dissertation Abstracts International (DAI)

Creek, Mardena Bridges. "Myth, Wound, Accommodation: American
    Literary Response to the War in Vietnam." DAI 43 (1982): 3593A.
    Ball State U.

Other Sources

You may sometimes have to list sources other than books and articles. In fact,
MLA changed the name of its concluding list of sources from "Bibliography"
(literally "description of books") to "Works Cited" because of the variety of

nonbook sources that may be cited. The particular treatment of these other sources depends on what information is available and what information needs to be included to enable readers to locate the same material themselves. Here are some sample entries with brief annotations.

Government Document

United States. Cong. House Committee on the Judiciary. <u>Immigration and Nationality Act with Amendments and Notes on Related Laws</u>. 7th ed. Washington: GPO, 1980.

Computer Software

<u>Nota Bene</u>. Computer software. Dragonfly Software, 1988. IBM, 512k, PC-DOS 2.0, disk.

Films; Radio and Television Programs

<u>The Last Emperor</u>. Dir. Bernardo Bertolucci. With John Lone and Peter O'Toole. Columbia, 1987.

"If God Ever Listened: A Portrait of Alice Walker." <u>Horizons</u>. Prod. Jane Rosenthal. NPR. WBST, Muncie. 3 Mar. 1984.

"The Hero's Adventure." <u>Moyers: Joseph Campbell and the Power of Myth</u>. Prod. Catherine Tatge. PBS. WNET, New York. 23 May 1988.

Performances

<u>A Walk in the Woods</u>. By Lee Blessing. Dir. Des McAnuff. With Sam Waterston and Robert Prosky. Booth Theatre, New York. 17 May 1988.

Ozawa, Seiji, cond. Boston Symphony Orch. Concert. Symphony Hall, Boston. 30 Sept. 1988.

Recordings

Mozart, Wolfgang A. <u>Cosi Fan Tutte</u>. With Kiri Te Kanawa, Frederica von Stade, David Rendall, and Philippe Huttenlocher. Cond. Alain Lombard. Strasbourg Philharmonic Orch. RCA, SRL3–2629, 1978.

Simon, Paul. "Under African Skies." <u>Graceland</u>. Warner's 7599–25447–1, 1986.

Works of Art

Botticelli, Sandro. <u>Giuliano de' Medici</u>. Samuel H. Kress Collection.
    National Gallery of Art, Washington.

Rodin, Auguste. <u>The Gate of Hell</u>. Rodin Museum, Paris.

Maps and Charts

<u>Sonoma and Napa Counties</u>. Map. San Francisco: California State
    Automobile Assn., 1984.

Published and Unpublished Letters

Fitzgerald, F. Scott. "To Ernest Hemingway." 1 June 1934. <u>The Letters
    of F. Scott Fitzgerald</u>. Ed. Andrew Turnbull. New York: Scribner's,
    1963. 308–10.

Stowe, Harriet Beecher. Letter to George Eliot. 25 May 1869. Berg
    Collection. New York Public Library.

Published and Unpublished Interviews

Ellison, Ralph. "Indivisible Man." Interview. With James Alan
    McPherson. <u>Atlantic</u> Dec. 1970: 45–60.

McPhee, John. Personal interview. 4 November 1986.

TYPING THE FINAL DRAFT

When you type the final draft of your research paper, follow these general
specifications.

1. Use white, 20-pound bond, 8½" × 11" paper.

2. Use a pica typewriter or high-quality printer.

3. Double-space the text throughout—*including* quotations, notes, and works
   cited list.

4. Maintain margins of 1 inch at the top and the bottom and on both sides of
   each page.

5. Indent 5 spaces at the beginning of each paragraph.

6. Leave 2 spaces after periods and other terminal marks of punctuation.

7. Leave 1 space after commas and other internal marks of punctuation.

8. Do not supply a title page. Instead, type your name, your instructor's
   name, the course title, and the date on separate lines (double-spacing
   between lines) in the upper-left corner.

9. A formal outline, if required, should be attached to the front of the paper.
   Use topics or full sentences, and follow the outline formats discussed in

Chapter 3. Type the title of your paper at the top of the first page of the outline; then type your thesis, triple-spaced below the title. Do not list your introduction or conclusion in your outline.

10. Type your title at the top of the first page of your paper. Triple space to the first sentence of your paper.

11. Number the pages of your manuscript consecutively, typing your last name and the page number in the upper-right corner.

12. Label any illustrations. Position the caption 2 line-spaces below the figure, and align the caption with the left side of the figure. Mount each illustration on bond paper using rubber cement or dry-mount tissue.

When you have finished typing, proofread every page carefully—including the title page, the formal outline, captions, endnotes, and the works cited list. Make a photocopy of your paper. If your instructor has asked you to hand in your notes with your paper, arrange them in a logical order and place them in an envelope.

Writing Your Research Paper on Your Computer

Writing your research paper on your computer makes the whole task more efficient. Print out from your data base the subdivisions you have created. Arrange them in various patterns to create a preliminary outline. Then determine what each outline will allow you to prove. If you have difficulty constructing a thesis, read back through the notes in your data base to see if some of your comments and questions will point you toward a working hypothesis that you can use to start a draft.

Before you begin drafting, set up your format (margins, line-spacing, etc.) according to the guidelines listed above. Then begin working your way through your outline, drafting each division of your paper. Examine the sources you want to use to support your argument. Determine what method for integrating them into your text is most effective. Sometimes you may want to focus on the key information in a source and incorporate it into your text (paraphrase) so that it does not interrupt your readers' train of thought. Other times, you may want to dramatize your citation by setting if off (block quotation) so that your readers understand its significance. Try to vary these strategies so that your readers follow *your* argument.

Use the various features of your word-processing program to create an attractive and effective text. Some software systems have both MLA and APA systems installed. If yours doesn't, you can construct the system you need by working with the various field divisions of your sort system. Transfer your bibliographic entries from your data base into a works cited file; your sort feature can help you accomplish this task. Then use your spell-checking feature to proofread your paper for spelling errors. Also proofread your paper yourself to make sure that your program has not missed words or constructions it does not recognize. Then, save your paper: you may need additional copies for your class, or you may want to revise it for the writing portfolio you submit for graduation or employment. Finally, print your paper and place it in an appropriate binder.

The Recycling Controversy [Research Paper: Student Model] | Jill Taraskiewicz

Reading the final draft of Jill's research paper will teach you many valuable lessons. You will see that an informed writer can make any subject, however unfamiliar, significant and interesting. You will see how a carefully crafted essay evolves from the complex and often confusing attempts to discover a subject, audience, and purpose. And you will see how Jill uses the specific techniques of analyzing, paraphrasing, quoting, and documenting sources to advance her purpose. Consider, too, as you read, how Jill has positioned her argument in relation to the two sides in the controversy.

Taraskiewicz 1

Jill Taraskiewicz

Mr. Johnson

English 104, Section 3

4 November 1992

The Recycling Controversy

<u>Thesis</u>: By examining both sides in the controversy, we can understand how recycling fits into our environmental policy.

I. Critics contend that recycling has become expensive.

    A. Recycling plants are not cost efficient.

    B. Recycling collection strains budgets.

    C. Recycling technology does not repay investment.

II. Critics argue that recycling is inefficient.

    A. Some materials are in over supply.

    B. Other materials are in short supply.

III. Critics suggest abandoning recycling.

    A. Landfills cost less.

    B. Incinerators seem more efficient.

IV. Advocates offer alternative explanations.

    A. The high costs of recycling are a result of unexamined business practices.

    B. The inefficiency of recycling is the result of unfocused public planning.

V. Advocates encourage legislation to support recycling.

VI. Advocates argue that landfills and incinerators are ineffective alternatives.

Taraskiewicz 2

  A. Landfill space is limited.

  B. Landfills create health hazards.

  C. Incinerators are inefficient.

  D. Incinerators cause disease.

VII. Each side in the recycling controversy has legitimate claims.

  A. The critics are concerned that the public will see recycling as the only solution.

  B. The advocates are concerned that the public will give up on recycling before it is given a thorough test.

VIII. Recycling has a limited role in our environmental policy.

  A. Not all forms of recycling are equal.

  B. No single process such as recycling will solve our complex garbage problem.

  C. In addition to waste management, we need to practice waste reduction.

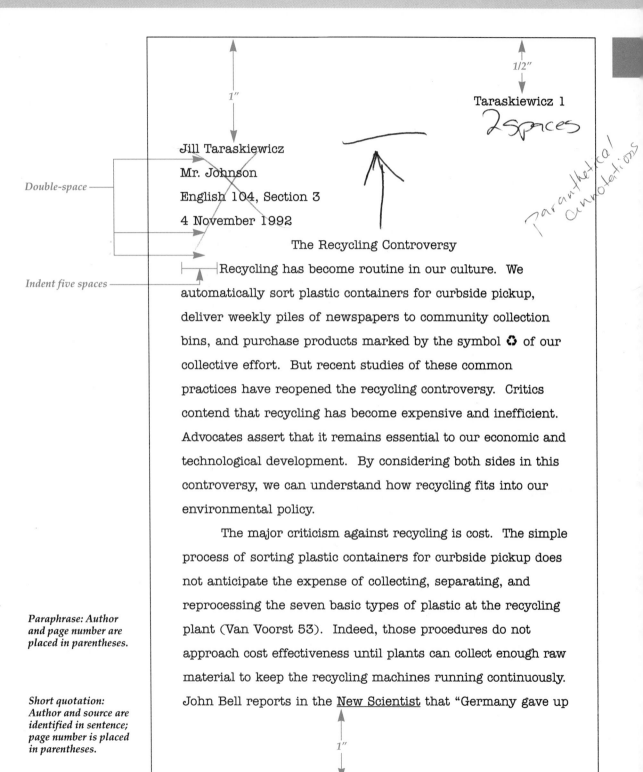

Taraskiewicz 1

1/2"

2 spaces

Parenthetical Annotations

Jill Taraskiewicz

Mr. Johnson

English 104, Section 3

4 November 1992

Double-space

Indent five spaces

The Recycling Controversy

Recycling has become routine in our culture. We automatically sort plastic containers for curbside pickup, deliver weekly piles of newspapers to community collection bins, and purchase products marked by the symbol ♻ of our collective effort. But recent studies of these common practices have reopened the recycling controversy. Critics contend that recycling has become expensive and inefficient. Advocates assert that it remains essential to our economic and technological development. By considering both sides in this controversy, we can understand how recycling fits into our environmental policy.

The major criticism against recycling is cost. The simple process of sorting plastic containers for curbside pickup does not anticipate the expense of collecting, separating, and reprocessing the seven basic types of plastic at the recycling plant (Van Voorst 53). Indeed, those procedures do not approach cost effectiveness until plants can collect enough raw material to keep the recycling machines running continuously. John Bell reports in the <u>New Scientist</u> that "Germany gave up

Paraphrase: Author and page number are placed in parentheses.

Short quotation: Author and source are identified in sentence; page number is placed in parentheses.

1"

Taraskiewicz 2

the idea of trying to run a recycling plant at Coburg because
it could not find 5 tons of waste plastic a day within 100
kilometers" (44). Even consumer advocate Lynn Scarlett
acknowledges that putting one set of trucks on the road "to
pick up recyclables, [and] another for remaining waste" not
only strains community budgets but also creates more fuel
consumption and air pollution.

 The cost of recycling is dramatically evident in the
elaborate "de-inking" technology required to convert old
newspapers into reusable paper. In his study, Dan Charles
describes some of the complicated steps in this expensive
procedure:

*Long quotation: A
quotation of more
than four typed lines
is set off from text and
is not placed in quota-
tion marks.*

> The process relies on turning old paper into pulp
> with water and chemicals, before spinning it in tubes
> to remove any heavy contaminants like staples or
> sand. . . . Ink particles attach themselves to air
> bubbles and rise to the surface, where they are
> scraped off. . . . [T]he paper fibers are bleached
> with hydrogen peroxide. . . . None of these processes
> do very well at removing or hiding laser print, glue
> or paper coatings. (13)

Because of the cost of such procedures--$50 million to build one
plant--many newsprint producers are reluctant to invest in
de-inking technology. Marcia Berss points out that recycling

Taraskiewicz 3

newspapers does not really save trees: "U.S. virgin newsprint is largely made from trees grown as a crop" (41). This agro-business has created such an "overcapacity of virgin newsprint" that newsprint producers see "no way to recoup the cost of capital outlays" for recycling plants (Berss 41).

Although recent studies of recycling discuss cost, they are more concerned about efficiency. The real issues, they contend, are the inequities in supply and demand. Old newspapers are in great supply. "New Jersey towns that just nine months ago pulled in $20 a ton for newsprint must now pay up to $10 a ton to ship it away" (Cahan 116). Indeed, Bruce Van Voorst reveals that over 100 million tons of newspaper collected in the United States never get recycled (52). Moreover, the demand for recycled paper is so depressed that some states have had to pass legislation forcing newspapers to print part of each new edition on recycled paper (Yang 100H). By contrast, plastic is in short supply. Bell reports

that although the world produces around 100 million tons of plastic a year, "not enough is reclaimed to enable the manufacturing industry to develop and market products made of recycled material" (44). Wellman, Inc., America's largest plastic recycler, "gobbled up most of the 1.5 billion two liter bottles handed in for recycling" but could supply only half of the demand for its product (Cahan 116-17).

Taraskiewicz 4

These studies have prompted some critics to conclude that we should abandon recycling. Landfills cost less. Berss points out that this year the citizens of San Jose, California, "will spend $160 a ton to recycle their waste, versus $93 a ton to dump it" (41). Incinerators seem more efficient. Bell explains why plastics are useful for the incineration of municipal waste: "If plastics are removed from waste along with other flammable solids such as paper, what is left is too wet to burn. But if the waste is burned with the plastics still there, potentially useful energy is generated" (44).

These same studies have prompted recycling advocates to generate alternative explanations for the problems of cost and efficiency. Much of what appears as excessive cost, they argue, is really the result of long-established and unexamined business practices. Van Voorst reports that the oil depletion allowance provides a significant subsidy for the producers of oil-based plastics (53). In an interview, environmentalist Pamela Popovich points out that American railroads charge more by the ton to haul recycled paper than they charge to ship virgin paper. "If these costs are taken into consideration," contends Allen Hershkowitz, senior scientist at the Natural Resources Defense Council, "recycling looks economically a lot more competitive" (Van Voorst 53).

The inefficiencies in recycling, say advocates, are the result of bad press, poor planning, and underdeveloped

Paraphrase: Author and source are identified at the beginning of the sentence to refer to the interview in the works cited list.

Taraskiewicz 5

technology. "Contrary to popular belief, recycled paper is as high-quality as the conventional stuff and competitively priced." (McAllister). Cahan indicates that when "state officials from Rhode Island, New York, and other Northeastern states met with the region's newspaper publishers and paper industry groups to push for the increased use of recycled paper," they seemed to get good results (117). Recyclers would get even better results with more effective technology. As Van Voorst suggests, "new processes . . . are needed to remove contaminants. Sorted solid wastes often include contaminants that gum up recycling systems, such as clear plastic tape on envelopes or sticky yellow Post-its on office paper" (54).

The most direct method for cutting costs and increasing efficiency is legislation. Charles reports that "every one of the 50 states in the U.S. has now passed a law that either encourages or requires local governments to set up some kind of recycling program" (12). Some laws require citizens to sort "each kind of rubbish in its own distinctive container" (Charles 12). Others mandate the minimum use of recycled materials in new products (Berss 41). Still others use tax incentives to encourage companies to develop new technologies (Van Voorst 52).

Recycling advocates are willing to support such extensive legislation because they are adamantly opposed to the

Short quotation: Ellipses are used in the middle of the quoted passage to shorten and focus material.

Documentation: Both quotation and para-phrase are documented by authors and page numbers within paren-theses.

Taraskiewicz 6

Summary: Lengthy arguments are summarized; authors and page numbers are placed in parentheses.

alternatives--landfills and incinerators. Landfills may be inexpensive and convenient, but space is limited and continues to decline (Glenn and Riggle 35). Where space is still available--in poor and sparsely populated areas--citizens are concerned about whether the deposit income justifies the dumping of garbage from rich communities out of state. Nobody wants to live next to a landfill, particularly when it can contaminate air, soil, and water (Gialanella and Luedtke SW/RR 18).

Documentation: Parenthetical reference reveals special page numbering in source.

Incinerators may cost less than recycling, but they are hardly efficient. Nancy Shute reports that "even if all [of New York's] five incinerators are up and running at full tilt, they could only burn 12,000 tons of garbage a day, less than half the amount the city now creates" (48). More important, incinerators create serious air pollution. In a letter to the New York Times, Elizabeth Holtzman indicates that "lead and mercury are emitted from garbage incinerators in large quantities, and can cause brain damage in children."

Quotation: Authors and source are identified in introductory phrase, and quotation is worked into the rest of the sentence.

And according to William L. Rathje and Cullen Murphy, authors of Rubbish! The Archaeology of Garbage, even "well run incinerators can release into the atmosphere small amounts of more than twenty-five metals . . . which have been implicated in birth defects and several kinds of cancer" (180).

Recycling is controversial because both sides present legitimate arguments. The critics are concerned that the

Taraskiewicz 7

public will see recycling as <u>the</u> solution to the complex problem of resource management. There is simply too much garbage and too little technology to justify this solution. Even in those instances where economies and technology may justify recycling, the critics are concerned that the procedures may create unacknowledged environmental problems such as high volumes of water waste and energy consumption (Scarlett).

Summary: Complex information is summarized in the writer's own words and documented with a parenthetical reference.

The advocates are concerned that the public will give up on recycling before improvements in education, technology, and public policy explore its potential as a solution to resource management. As Rathje and Murphy point out, "recycling is a fragile and complicated piece of economic and social machinery—a space shuttle rather than a tractor; it may frequently break down" (239). But advocates are willing to invest in the eventual success of recycling, particularly when they consider alternatives such as landfills and incinerators.

Although critics and advocates make legitimate claims, we need a larger perspective to understand the place of recycling in our environmental policy. First, we must realize that all types of recycling are not equal. John E. Young explains how to sort out the different types:

Long quotation: Major evidence to support the writer's thesis is highlighted by a block quotation.

> The most valuable is the manufacture of new products from similar, used items; the least valuable is the conversion of waste materials into entirely different products. The key criterion is whether the

Taraskiewicz 8

recovered material is substituted for the virgin one
in production, thus closing the loop. (27)
Some materials--such as glass, steel, and aluminum—rank high
in this scheme because they save virgin material from being
used. Some--such as plastic--rank low because virtually none is
"now being recycled back into original containers" (Young 27).
Still others--such as paper--fall somewhere in between because
"each time paper is recycled, the fibers it contains are
shortened by the process, making the new paper weaker"
(Young 27).

Second, we must become what Rathje and Murphy call
"garbage literate" because the label ♻ that identifies
products as recycled can be deceptive (242). In most cases,
manufacturers use the recycling symbol to indicate that their
products are environmentally friendly and responsible. But
these products are rarely made from materials that have
been turned in for recycling. Instead, they are made from
"pre-consumer" waste—that is, material left over from the
manufacturing process. Rathje and Murphy point out that
the "label one needs to look for is 'post-consumer recycled,'
and ideally the label will include a percentage, as in '30
percent post-consumer recycled.' Anything over 10 percent is
worthwhile" (243).

Third, we must acknowledge that our garbage problem
is so complex that no one process—such as recycling—will

Quotation: Quoted material is marked with quotation marks; quotations within the quotation are marked with single quotation marks.

Taraskiewicz 9

ever provide a single solution. Larry Schaper argues that the nation will continue to need landfills, and "as the industry gains more control over the types of materials going into municipal landfills and landfill designs become more reliable, the public may become more accepting of landfills" (65). Similarly, Gialanella and Luedtke argue that recent technological advances in the design of incinerators have improved "their ability to safeguard the environment and public health" (SW/RR 32). Rathje and Murphy contend that the goal is not to "bow" before one single approach but "to discern the varying roles each of these approaches should play locally in America's widely disparate communities and regions" (239).

> Finally, we need to develop other environmental policies such as waste reduction. Anne Magnuson reports that some communities encourage their citizens to precycle—that is, to buy products in bulk rather than in many small containers that require recycling. Other communities discourage the accumulation of waste by charging a flat fee for every trash bag. And some encourage citizens to use preprinted postcards to remove their names from junk mailing lists (30–37). Such policies discourage the introduction of more waste into the system. Unless we develop such waste reduction policies, all the recycling, landfills, and incinerators in the world will not save us from our own garbage.

Short quotation: Authors are identified in the writer's introductory clause; quotation is worked into writer's sentence.

Summary: Author is identified at the beginning of a series of assertions about waste reduction that contribute to the writer's conclusion. Documentation cites inclusive page numbers.

Taraskiewicz 10

Works Cited

Double-space

Bell, John. "Plastics: Waste Not, Want Not." <u>New Scientist</u> 1 Dec. 1990: 44–47.

Indent five spaces or one-half inch

Berss, Marcia. "Nobody Wants to Shoot Snow White." <u>Forbes</u> 14 Oct. 1991: 40–42.

Sample entry: An article in a weekly magazine.

Cahan, Vicky. "Waste Not, Want Not? Not Necessarily." <u>Business Week</u> 17 July 1989: 116–17.

Charles, Dan. "Too Many Bottles Break the Bank." <u>New Scientist</u> 18 (Apr. 1992): 12–13.

Gialanella, Mario, and Louis Luedtke. "Air Pollution Control and Waste Management." <u>American City and County</u> 106 (Jan. 1991): SW/RR 17–32.

Glenn, Jim, and David Riggle. "The State of Garbage in America." <u>Bio Cycle</u> 32 (Apr. 1991): 34–38.

Sample entry: The form for documenting a letter published in a newspaper divided into sections.

Holtzman, Elizabeth. Letter. <u>New York Times</u> 24 Jan. 1992: A28.

Magnuson, Anne. "What Has Happened to Waste Reduction?" <u>American City and County</u> 106 (Apr. 1991): 30–37.

McAllister, Celia. "Save the Trees—And You May Save a Bundle." <u>Business Week</u> 4 Sept. 1989: 118.

Popovich, Pamela. Personal interview. 12 Oct. 1992.

One space

Rathje, William L., and Cullen Murphy. <u>Rubbish! The Archaeology of Garbage.</u> New York: Harper, 1992.

Taraskiewicz 11

Scarlett, Lynn. "Will Recycling Help the Environment?"
Consumer Research 74 (Mar. 1991): 17.

Schaper, Larry. "Trends in Landfill Planning and Design."
Public Works 122 (Apr. 1991): 64–65.

Shute, Nancy. "The Mound Builder." Amicus Journal 12
(Summer 1990): 44–49.

Van Voorst, Bruce. "The Recycling Bottleneck." Time 14
Sept. 1992: 52–54.

Yang, Dori Jones, William C. Symonds, and Lisa Driscoll.
"Recycling Is Rewriting the Rules of Papermaking."
Business Week 22 Apr. 1991: 100H–100L.

Young, John E. Discarding the Throwaway Society.
Washington: Worldwatch, 1991.

Sample entry: An article by three authors.

Sample entry: A book by one author.

Writing Assignments

Narrate   1.   Select *one* core subject—such as history, literature, science, or math—that you have taken several times during your educational career. In what ways did the material seem different each time you studied it? What was the source of that difference—teacher, students, textbook, assignments? Focus on one experience that forced you to confront that difference. Then compose a narrative essay to dramatize the factors that made you see the subject differently.

Observe   2.   Attend a meeting where the town council is contemplating a new waste management strategy—new landfill, recycling centers, incinerators. Sort out who's on what side. How many sides are there? What factors make it difficult for the council to reach a decision? Write a column entitled "Bottleneck at City Hall" for your local newspaper.

Investigate   3.   Interview two people who have something at stake in a waste management controversy—an entrepreneur who wants to build a landfill, and a farmer who wants to protect land and water. Compose profiles of the opponents, looking for areas of common ground.

Collaborate   4.   Organize your writing group into a team of detectives to investigate how a particular university office creates and disposes of its waste. After completing your study, write a report recommending ways the office could manage its waste more effectively.

Read   5.   Read William L. Rathje and Cullen Murphy's "The Ten Commandments" in their *Rubbish! The Archaeology of Garbage* pages 234 to 245. In particular, make a list of the modest changes they think can make a big difference in waste management. Then write an article for your campus newspaper suggesting ways to reduce waste in a typical study lounge.

Respond   6.   Respond to Jill Taraskiewicz's argument by assuming an extremist's position on recycling. Argue that her final position diminishes the value of recycling, that if the system is going to work, people must dedicate themselves to adhering to the rules everyday.

Analyze   7.   Analyze John E. Young's criteria for effective recycling in discussing *The Throwaway Society,* especially pages 26 to 27. What kinds of evidence does he use to assess the value of recycling each kind of waste material? Why is "closing the loop" essential to his argument?" You may want to argue that such a position is *extreme,* making it difficult for any system to meet his criteria.

Evaluate   8.   Consider William L. Rathje and Cullen Murphy's distinction between "pre-consumer" and "post-consumer" waste. Examine the labels on the products you buy to determine which ones make such a distinction. Then write an essay for your local newspaper evaluating the truthfulness of package labels.

Argue   9.   Argue that new technology has made incinerators more effective than recycling. You may want to read Mario Gialanella and Louis Luedtke's "Air Pollution Control and Waste Management." *American City and County* 106 (Jan.

1991): SW/RR 17–32. Then decide whether your source will allow you to argue that burning garbage can be an effective method for converting waste into energy.

Argue ***10.*** Draft a letter to your town council recommending changes in the way various waste products are collected, sorted, and managed in your community. To collect information for your argument, follow the waste collectors from pickup to disposal.

Handbook of Grammar and Usage

The Evolution of English

The language that Americans speak and write is descended from the language spoken by the English, Scottish, and Irish immigrants who founded the British colonies in America. Their language, in turn, was descended from the languages of Germanic tribes who, during the fifth and sixth centuries, invaded Britain and settled there. One of these tribes, the Angles, later became known as the Englisc (English) and gave their name to a country and a language, both of which they shared with other peoples—the Saxons, the Jutes, and later, the Danes and the Normans.

The language that has come down to us from that Anglo-Saxon beginning has undergone great changes. Modern college students find Chaucer's fourteenth-century English something of a puzzle. And before Chaucer—well, judge for yourself. Here is the opening of the Lord's Prayer as it was written in the ninth, fourteenth, and seventeenth centuries, respectively:

Old English	*Middle English*	*Modern English*
Fæder ūre þū þe eart on heofonum, sī þīn nama gehālgod. Tōbecume þīn rīce, Gewurþe ðīn willa on eorðan swā swā on heofonum.	Oure fadir that art in heuenes, halwid be thi name; thi kyngdom cumme to; be thi wille don as in heuen and in erthe.	Our Father which art in heaven, Hallowed be thy name. Thy kingdom come. Thy will be done on earth as it is in heaven.

A contrast of these three versions offers a brief but revealing impression of the changes that occurred in the language during eight hundred years, and these differences would seem even greater if we could reproduce also the changes in sound that took place. For example, Old English ū and ī were pronounced like the *oo* in *boot* and the *e* in *me*, respectively, so that ūre was pronounced "oo′ruh" and sī, "see."

In grammar, the major change has been the simplification of grammatical forms. Old English (700–1100) was a highly *inflected* language, one that made grammatical distinctions by changes in the form of a word. For example, nouns were declined in five cases (nominative, genitive, dative, accusative and instrumental) as well as in singular and plural numbers. Adjectives and the definite article were declined to agree with the nouns they modified. Here is the declension, in the singular only, of "the good man," with the approximate pronunciation enclosed in quotation marks on the right:

Case	Declension	Pronunciation
N. (*man* as subject)	sē gōda mann	"say goada man"
G. ("of the good man" or "the good man's")	ðaes gōdan mannes	"thas goadan mannes"
D. ("to the good man")	ðǣm gōdan menn	"tham goadan men"
A. (*man* as object)	ðone gōdan mann	"thonna goadan man"
I. ("by the good man")	ðȳ gōdan menn	"thee goadan men"

In Modern English the article and the adjective are not declined at all. The noun retains the genitive case and has singular and plural forms. We distinguish between subject and object by word order, and we have replaced the dative and instrumental endings by the prepositions *to* and *by*. As a result, the whole declensional system has been greatly simplified. Verbs still show considerable inflection, though much less than in Old English.

Along with this simplification of grammatical forms went a great increase in vocabulary as new words were introduced through association with foreign cultures. During the eighth and ninth centuries, Scandinavian raiders settled along the coast of England and brought into the language some fourteen hundred place names and about one thousand common words. In 1066 the Normans conquered England, and for three hundred years their French language dominated the court and the affairs in which the nobility was most involved—government, army, law, church, art, architecture, fashions, and recreation. Between 1100 and 1500, over ten thousand French words were absorbed into the language. During the fourteenth, fifteenth, and sixteenth centuries, English writers borrowed heavily from Latin. Language historians estimate that more than half of the present English vocabulary came from Latin, either directly or through one of the Romance languages, especially French. And as the English-speaking countries grew in political, economic, and cultural importance, their language borrowed from all over the world the words it needed to name the things and ideas that Anglo-Americans were acquiring. Today the vocabulary of the English language is international in origin, as the following list illustrates:

algebra (Arabic)
amen (Hebrew)
bantam (Javanese)
boor (Dutch)
caravan (Persian)
cashew (Portuguese)
chorus (Greek)
coffee (Turkish)
dollar (German)

flannel (Welsh)
garage (French)
garbage (Italian)
inertia (Latin)
kimono (Japanese)
leprechaun (Old Irish)
polka (Polish)
polo (Tibetan)

silk (Chinese)
shampoo (Hindi)
ski (Norwegian)
tag (Swedish)
toboggan (American Indian)
vodka (Russian)
whiskey (Gaelic)

Understanding Sentence Elements

The ability to *compose* effective sentences does not depend on an ability to describe sentences grammatically or linguistically. Rather, most proficient writers use intuitive language skills, developed over a number of years, when they compose sentences. Yet when writers understand sentence elements and structure, they are better able to *revise* sentences to achieve a clear form and purpose. To help you in effective sentence revision, the following sections offer a brief overview of basic sentence elements.

1 RECOGNIZE THE BASIC ELEMENTS OF SENTENCES

Although many sentences are complicated word structures, all sentences, even the most complicated, are built from a few basic elements: *subjects* (S), *verbs* (V), *objects* (O), and *complements* (C). These elements work together to express a central idea that may be further developed or refined by other elements: *modifiers* (M) and *conjunctions* (Conj).

The verb with its objects, complements, and modifiers is known as the *predicate* of the sentence. The predicate describes the action performed by the subject or the state of being of the subject. Subject and predicate are the two main parts of a simple sentence.

    S   V
The lawyer wrote. [Subject + Verb.]

    S   V   O
The lawyer wrote the brief. [Subject + Verb + Object.]

      S   V   O CONJ
The trial lawyer hurriedly wrote the Hernandez brief but then carefully

  V   O
revised it.
[Subject + Verb + Object + Conjunction + Verb + Object. Modifiers used throughout.]

These examples show that a sentence composed of the basic elements can be made more specific and informative through expansion.

1a

Subjects **identify the people, places, things, ideas, qualities, or conditions that act, are acted upon, or are described in a sentence.**

Nouns and pronouns are the most common subjects, but phrases (groups of words without verbs) or clauses (groups of words with subjects and verbs) may also be subjects.

$$\overbrace{\text{To win}}^{S}\overset{V}{\text{ is }}\overset{C}{\text{her}}\text{ objective. [Subject }(phrase)\text{ + Verb + Complement.]}$$

What President Aquino wants most is political stability. [Subject (clause) + Verb + Complement.]

1b

Verbs **express action** *(select, walk)* **or a state of being** *(seem, is)***. Verbs consist of single words** *(develop)* **or groups of words** *(might have developed)***.**

A verb that requires an object to complete its meaning is a *transitive verb.* A verb that does not require an object to complete its meaning is an *intransitive verb.* Notice that some verbs can be either transitive or intransitive.

President Roosevelt **ordered** the evacuation.

After two years, Senator Harris **resigned.**

The building inspector **examined** the wiring.

Pandas **eat** voraciously.

A verb connecting a complement to a subject is a *linking verb.*

The child **seemed** frightened.

After years of study, Fred **became** an aerospace engineer.

1c

Objects **are nouns or pronouns that complete the ideas expressed by subjects and transitive verbs.**

Direct objects answer the questions *what?* or *whom?* *Indirect objects* answer the questions *to whom?* or *for whom?*

With great care, Dr. Rodriguez completed the **report.**
[*Report* is *what* Dr. Rodriguez completed.]

Dr. Rodriguez sent the **immunologist** the **report.**
[*Report* is *what* Dr. Rodriguez sent; *immunologist* is *to whom* he sent it.]

1d

Complements* are adjectives or nouns that complete the ideas in a sentence by modifying the subject *(predicate adjective)* or by renaming the subject *(predicate noun).

Complements are joined to the subjects of sentences by linking verbs, such as *am, are, is, was, were, become, get, feel, look,* and *seem.*

                               S   V   C
Throughout the competition, Warren remained **optimistic.**
[Predicate adjective modifies the subject *Warren.*]

                     S   V   C
In the end, Warren was first **runner-up.**
[Predicate noun renames the subject *Warren.*]

1e

***Modifiers* (typically adjectives, adverbs, and prepositional phrases) describe or limit subjects, verbs, objects, complements, or other modifiers.**

Modifiers alter the meanings of other words by answering one of these questions: *what kind? which one? how many? whose? how? when? where? how often?* or *to what extent?*

Long speeches are unacceptable. [What kind of speeches?]

Those four-wheelers are dangerous. [Which four-wheelers?]

We received **sixty-seven** applications. [How many applications?]

The subcommittee shared **its** findings. [Whose findings?]

The immigrant **slowly** completed the form. [How did he complete it?]

After the tennis match, we celebrated. [When did we celebrate?]

Leave the carton **in the mailroom.** [Where should it be left?]

Michael called his doctor **frequently.** [How often did he call?]

The glassblower **very** skillfully formed the stem. [What degree of skill did the glassblower use?]

1f

***Conjunctions* join and relate two or more words, phrases, or clauses in a sentence.**

Coordinating conjunctions (*and, but, for, nor, or, so,* and *yet*) link equivalent sentence elements.

John Kander **and** Fred Ebb collaborated on several major musicals. [Conjunction links two subjects.]

The burglars gained access to the vault **yet** left its contents intact. [Conjunction links two verbs.]

He fought unenthusiastically **but** skillfully. [Conjunction links two modifiers.]

I will not do it, **nor** will I recommend anyone else who might. [Conjunction links two clauses.]

Correlative conjunctions, such as *both . . . and, either . . . or, neither . . . nor,* and *not only . . . but also,* work in pairs and also link equivalent sentence elements.

Both Senator Robins **and** Representative Hershell received contributions from the tobacco industry. [Conjunction links two subjects.]

Marion will go **either** to Butler University to study pharmacology **or** to Indiana University to study dentistry. [Conjunction links two modifiers.]

Subordinating conjunctions, such as *after, although, because, even if, so that, until,* and *when,* join clauses but subordinate one clause to another. The subordinate clause, introduced by the subordinating conjunction, can be positioned at the beginning, in the middle, or at the end of a sentence.

Because she was outspoken on the subject of women writers, Virginia Woolf has become a central figure in feminist criticism. [Subordinate clause first.]

Virginia Woolf has become a central figure in feminist criticism **because she was outspoken on the subject of women writers.** [Subordinate clause last.]

Virginia Woolf, **because she was outspoken on the subject of women writers,** has become a central figure in feminist criticism. [Subordinate clause embedded.]

Exercise

Identify each of the underlined words or phrases as a subject (S), verb (V), object (O), complement (C), modifier (M), or conjunction (Conj). (Consider proper names as single elements but consider all other words separately.)

1. Although the 1981 baseball strike lasted seven weeks, the 1985 baseball strike lasted only three days.

2. Cadets at West Point are considered members of the regular Army.

3. Jason sent me an application for Duke University, in hopes that I too would apply for admission.

4. In 1967, a fire aboard Apollo 1 killed Virgil Grissom , Edward White, and Roger Chaffee.

5. General Washington commissioned seven ships to fight against the British Navy.

6. Universal Studios and 20th Century-Fox produced the five motion pictures with the highest revenues.

7. The Iliad and the Odyssey, composed by the Greek poet Homer, are mainstays of most humanities curricula.

8. Thomas à Becket was the archbishop of Canterbury during the reign of Henry II.

9. In spite of recent declines in sales, General Motors, Ford, and Chrysler are still among the fifteen largest corporations in the United States.

10. U. S. Grant was an effective general but an ineffectual president.

2   RECOGNIZE BASIC SENTENCE PATTERNS

There are four basic sentence patterns: simple, compound, complex, and compound-complex.

2a

A *simple sentence* contains one independent clause, that is, a subject and verb that can stand alone as a grammatically complete sentence.

The subject and verb of a simple sentence may appear in compound form. A simple sentence need not be simplistic, but it does present a single idea. In fact, simple sentences, because they present ideas clearly, are useful for creating emphasis.

>   S   V   C
> Hurricanes are frightening.

>   S   S   V   C
> Hurricanes and other tropical storms are both frightening and dangerous.
> [Though more complicated than the preceding example, this is a simple sentence because it has one (compound) subject and one predicate; the sentence also includes one compound complement.]

2b

A *compound sentence* contains two or more independent clauses joined by a comma and a coordinating conjunction *(and, but, for, nor, or, so,* and *yet)* or by a semicolon alone.

A compound sentence presents a balanced relationship between the clauses that are joined, thus emphasizing that the ideas in the sentence are of equal importance.

> We moved to the Gulf coast to escape the cold Ohio winters, but then we were terrified by tropical storms. [Two independent clauses joined by a conjunction.]
>
> We moved to Florida in 1978; we stayed only five years, however, and then returned to Ohio. [Two independent clauses joined by a semicolon and a conjunctive adverb.]

2c

A *complex sentence* contains at least two clauses: one independent and one or more subordinate clauses.

Subordinating conjunctions, such as *although, because, since, when,* and *while,* and relative pronouns, such as *that, what, which,* and *who,* join the clauses in a complex sentence. One clause, and thus the interrelationship of the ideas in the sentence, is emphasized over the others.

> S V   S V   C
> Although it rains in the midmornings, the afternoons are generally sunny. [Subordinate clause, then independent clause.]
>
> S V   O   S V   O
> We enjoyed our stay in Florida, even though we knew that we could not
>
> remain. [Independent clause, then subordinate clause.]

2d

A *compound-complex* sentence contains three or more clauses—at least two independent clauses and one subordinate clause.

A compound-complex sentence establishes a complicated relationship among a series of ideas.

> S V   S V   O
> While we lived in Florida, we survived four minor hurricanes without
>
> S   V   O
> injuries or property damage, but we never developed the nonchalance of native Floridians. [Subordinate clause, then independent clause, then another independent clause.]

Exercise

Identify the following sentences as simple, compound, complex or compound-complex.

1. Lightning is a discharge of electricity between two clouds or between a cloud and the earth.

2. Because of deaths during the war with the Soviet Union and because of massive emigration to Iran and Pakistan, Afghanistan's population has shrunk by one-third in the last decade.

3. According to some statistics, Northern Ireland has the highest unemployment rate in Europe.

4. The original purpose of the Crusades was to take Christianity to the non-Christian "infidels," but the holy wars also served to enrich trade and the arts in Europe.

5. Although the 1986 Tax Reform Act is supposed to be revenue neutral, it provides too may loopholes for selected businesses.

6. Mongolia is located in eastern Asia, between Siberia and China, and is slighter larger than Alaska.

7. After his notorious raid on Harpers Ferry in 1859, John Brown was captured and hanged; in the years that followed, his name became a symbol of ineffectual militant protest.

8. Although *bona fide* means "in good faith" in Latin, it is commonly used today to mean "genuine."

9. Because the costs of American materials and labor are high, sales of American-made shoes have plummeted, and sales of imports from Brazil and South Korea have risen.

10. Most Americans assume that the U.S. Navy is our oldest maritime service, yet the U.S. Coast Guard was established in 1790, eight years before the Navy.

3   EXPAND AND VARY SENTENCE PATTERNS

As writers move from drafting sentences to revising them, they make decisions about diction, about the placement of phrases and clauses, and about the structural patterns of sentences. The larger issue—sentence patterns—is important because sentence construction (and reconstruction) often determines how effectively writing communicates with readers.

3a   Use Coordination

When isolated, successive sentences present ideas that together establish an important, parallel relationship, those sentences can be effectively combined by coordination. *Coordination* is the joining of simple sentences to form compound sentences, and it is also the meshing or combining of related sentence elements through pairing or seriation.

> President Reagan initially denied that the United States had traded arms for
> *but t*
> hostages. ~~T~~he Tower commission subsequently revealed otherwise.
> [Two sentences effectively joined by a coordinating conjunction.]
>
> *and John Poindexter's*
> Oliver North's activities were largely unsupervised. ~~John Poindexter's activities were also unsupervised.~~
> [Combining the sentences—by using a compound subject—improves the emphasis.]

3b   Use Subordination

When isolated, successive sentences present related ideas, the sentences can be combined through subordination. *Subordination* is the joining of simple sentences to form complex or compound-complex sentences, but it is also the embedding of words, phrases, or clauses in the structure of the most important sentence.

> Marc Chagall ~~was~~ a native of Russia. ~~He~~ emigrated to France. ~~While in~~
> *where*
> ~~France~~ he produced vibrant and dreamlike paintings.
> [Three independent clauses compressed into one complex sentence.]
>
> *Because*
> Chagall's images are often childlike. ~~U~~ndiscerning observers sometimes find
> *but o*
> his work simplistic. ~~O~~bservant critics see an ingenious use of childhood perception in his work.

[Three independent clauses reworked into a compound-complex sentence that reveals a cause-and-effect relationship among the ideas.]

Subordination is a useful means of indicating emphasis and bringing variety to sentences. Consider subordination the groundwork of a mature and effective sentence style and work to use it to achieve your purpose.

Exercise

Use coordination and subordination to combine the following pairs of sentences.

1. Four men from the United States have won the Olympic figure-skating title. Only one, Dick Button, won the title twice.

2. *Amadeus* popularized the works of Mozart. The plot of the play and film is historically inaccurate.

3. Ten percent of home-study lawyers pass the California Bar Exam. Sixty percent of law school–trained lawyers pass.

4. Alfred Smith was the first Catholic to run for president. He lost by a wide margin to Herbert Hoover in 1928.

5. Trademarks are usually specialized symbols, products, or company names. They can also be individual words and letters.

Exercise

The following paragraph contains simple sentences only. Use coordination and subordination to combine sentences and produce an effective and varied paragraph.

The Beatles were the most successful pop group of all time. They began playing in Liverpool, England. The group had four members. They were John Lennon, Paul McCartney, George Harrison, and Ringo Starr. Their early music was characterized by a simple rhythm-and-blues style. It also had simple harmonies and lyrics. The Beatles' early hits included "She Loves You," "Please Please Me," and "I Want to Hold Your Hand." These simple songs attracted worldwide interest. John Lennon and Paul McCartney later wrote complicated songs. The lyrics became imaginative and philosophical. The music itself became varied. It was also complex. They experimented with new instruments and recording equipment. Their later work included the albums *Rubber Soul, The White Album,* and *Abbey Road.* The Beatles' most sophisticated work was the album *Sergeant Pepper's Lonely Hearts Club Band.* It contained some of the group's most memorable songs. Each member of the band developed separate interests. The group disbanded in 1970.

Understanding Sentence Elements: Review Exercises

In the following paragraph, label each of the underlined elements as a subject (S), verb (V), object (O), complement (C), modifier (M), or conjunction (Conj.).

Our Sun is a sphere of superheated gas. Hydrogen atoms at its core fuse, creating the atomic reactions that produce both light and energy. Scientists estimate that the temperature of the Sun's core is twenty million degrees centigrade, while the surface temperature is approximately six thousand degrees centigrade. The diameter of the Sun is roughly 850,000 miles. These figures suggest that our Sun is neither a hot nor a large star when compared with others in our solar system.

The following paragraph contains simple sentences only. Use coordination and subordination to combine sentences to make this paragraph effective. Then label sentences by type: simple (S), compound (C), complex (CX), and compound-complex (CCX).

The Black Death devastated Europe between 1348 and 1666. The disease was brought to Europe through Italy. Traders carried it from the Black Sea area. The epidemic of 1348 killed one-fourth of the population of Europe. The disease was carried by fleas. This was unknown in the fourteenth and seventeenth centuries. The fleas lived on rats. The disease raged, subsided, and reemerged for three hundred years. The worst epidemic in England occurred in 1665. Entire towns and villages were wiped out. London's population decreased by one-tenth. The population was approximately 450,000. People were terrified. They tried all kinds of cures. They didn't understand the nature of the disease. The cures failed. Samuel Pepys wrote about the Black Death in his *Diary*. Daniel Defoe wrote a fictional account titled *Journal of the Plague Year*.

Writing Logical and Effective Sentences

4   SENTENCE SENSE

Creating a uniform impression in your writing is important, especially at the sentence level, because readers need consistency to understand fully your ideas. Unnecessary shifts in point of view, tense, mood, and voice are distracting and may be confusing.

4a   Use a consistent point of view.

Point of view is the standpoint from which you present information. If you select the *first-person* point of view, then your subject *(I, we)* is the speaker. If you select the *second person,* then your subject *(you)* is being spoken to. If you select the *third person,* then your subject *(he, she, it, they)* is being spoken about. Selecting the appropriate point of view and maintaining it are important for clarity.

Swimming instructors must be patient if they work with children. ~~You~~ *They* must acknowledge that some children have never swum before, and ~~you~~ *they* must acclimate children to the water. Instructors must be willing to work slowly and teach skills gradually.

[Elimination of shift from third person *(swimming instructors)* to second person *(you)*.]

4b   Use verb tenses consistently.

Verb tenses signal chronological relationships among ideas. Unnecessary shifts in tense will confuse your readers.

After filling out a tentative class schedule, the student goes to see his or her advisor for approval. The advisor examine*s* the schedule to see that requirements ~~were~~ *are* met, and the student submits the signed computer form.

[The shifts from present tense *(goes)* to the past tense *(examined)* to the present tense *(submits)* make these sentences confusing. It is unclear whether they describe a typically repeated sequence, for which present tense would be appropriate, or a completed sequence, for which past tense would be suitable.]

4c

Use a consistent mood.

Three moods indicate how you view the actions or conditions you are describing in your sentences. The *indicative mood* is used to make statements of fact or opinion and ask questions. The *imperative mood* is used to express commands. The *subjunctive mood* is used to indicate doubt, conditional situations, statements contrary to fact, and wishes. In most writing, mood should remain consistent.

He suggested that peop[le]

Betting on a horse race, Mr. McMillan explained, can be risky. Bet only

they

money that ~~you~~ can afford to lose.
[Elimination of confusing shift from the indicative to the imperative. The first sentence *described*; the second *advised*.]

4d

Use a consistent voice.

Active voice and passive voice create different kinds of emphasis in sentences. They should not be mixed in successive sentences that describe the same subject. (See Section 5, "Active and Passive Sentences.")

The research assistants carefully compile the results of the questionnaire. First, they record the sex, age, race, and religion of each respondent. Then,

they record

profession, income, and education ~~were recorded~~. Next, the assistants note responses to individual interpretive questions. [Elimination of shift into the passive voice.]

---------------- *Exercise*

Revise each set of sentences so that it constitutes a paragraph that is consistent in mood, point of view, voice, and tense.

1. Department of Energy spokespersons have suggested that Americans save energy in small but important ways. They suggest walking rather than driving, coordinating short trips, and driving at slower speeds. Turn off lights when you are not in a room. Wash only full loads. Lower your thermostats.

2. The U.S. Fish and Wildlife Service now restricts waterfowl hunting in most areas. Hunters can no longer use lead shot, since it poisons birds that are wounded but not killed. You must also restrict hunting to specified seasons, and hunters must limit the number of birds they kill. Penalties are also severe if you are caught violating these protective laws.

3. The National Forest Service has made timberlands available to private logging companies. New logging roads are built, destroying the forest floor. Trees are removed, and fish and wildlife are threatened. Irreparable damage is being done.

4. In the last few years, industrial pollution of water has declined. The Clean Water Act has given government agencies the right to assign stiff fines to plants and foundries in violation of existing pollution standards. These companies then had to correct the problem or risk further fines. Most industries adapted to these procedures.

5. Spokespeople for these agencies and services address important issues at arranged press conferences. Facts are given, and violators are identified. The American people are given information by these spokespeople to help them understand these national concerns.

5   ## ACTIVE AND PASSIVE SENTENCES

Active sentences emphasize the people or things responsible for actions and conditions. *Passive* sentences focus on people or things that are acted upon. What would be the object in an active sentence is used as the subject in a passive sentence, and a form of the verb *to be* is used with the main verb. As a result, passive sentences are always slightly longer than active sentences. Although most readers and writers prefer active sentences, you should select the sentence pattern that most effectively conveys your purpose.

Active: Congress approved a multibillion-dollar highway improvement bill. [Congress is emphasized.]

Passive: The multibillion-dollar highway improvement bill was approved by Congress. [The highway improvement bill is emphasized.]

5a   Use Active Sentences Most of the Time

Use active sentences to indicate who takes responsibility for actions and events.

Dr. Taylor misdiagnosed and mistreated Jeremy's respiratory problem.

Use active sentences to create emphasis.

A tornado in Texas destroyed property worth over $50 million.

Use active sentences for economy of expression.

Active: Lionel Richie sang the national anthem at the opening game of the season. [13 words]

Passive: The national anthem was sung by Lionel Richie at the opening game of the season. [15 words.]

5b   Use Passive Sentences Selectively

Use passive sentences when the people who are responsible for actions are not known.

The superintendent's window was broken sometime over the weekend.

Use passive sentences to emphasize the receiver of the action instead of those responsible.

Van Gogh's *Sunflowers* was sold for $39.9 million.

Use passive sentences to emphasize actions that are more important than specific people who might be responsible.

Lasers are currently being used to treat medical problems as diverse as cancer, cataracts, and varicose veins.

―――――――――― *Exercise*

The following sentences are written in the passive voice. Rewrite those that would be more effective in the active voice.

1. Twenty people were killed when a car bomb exploded in Teheran.

2. Over $800 million had been deposited in personal Swiss bank accounts by Ferdinand Marcos, the ousted president of the Philippines.

3. Favorable trade conditions with China were supported by President Bush, despite controversy over the action.

4. Details of the nuclear accident at Chernobyl were withheld by Soviet officials for several days.

5. Franklin D. Roosevelt was elected to four terms as president.

6 MAINTAIN PARALLELISM AMONG SENTENCE ELEMENTS

Parallelism in a sentence requires that similar ideas be presented in similar form and that elements that are similar in function appear in similar grammatical form. Parallelism is an important principle of both grammar and style.

Grammatically, sentence elements linked by coordinating or correlative conjunctions should be similar in form: a clause should be followed by a clause, a phrase by a phrase, a noun by a noun, a verb by a verb of the same tense, and so on. (See Section 4b.)

Stylistically, parallelism creates balance and emphasis. It can, therefore, be used to create desired effects.

6a Maintain parallelism with coordinating conjunctions.

The evangelist ended the service with a hymn and ~~calling on~~ *with a call for* sinners to repent. [Two prepositional phrases separated by a coordinating conjunction.]

6b Maintain parallelism with correlative conjunctions.

The owners of VCRs can either tape films from network broadcasts or can rent films from video clubs.
[Correlative conjunctions followed by two verbs without auxiliaries.]

6c Repeat key words to clarify a parallel construction.

The commission has the power to investigate, *to* conciliate, *to* hold hearings, *to* subpoena witnesses, *to* issue cease-and-desist commands, *to* order reinstatements, and *to* direct hiring. [Parallelism emphasized by repeating *to*.]

——————————— *Exercise*

Revise the following sentences to eliminate faulty parallelism.

1. The narrator of *Invisible Man* was idealistic, intelligent, and tried to advance the cause of black people.

2. Holden Caufield, the main character of *Catcher in the Rye*, rejected hypocrisy in other people but was ignoring his own hypocrisy.

3. Thornton Wilder won Pulitzer Prizes not only for his plays *Our Town* and *The Skin of Our Teeth* but also he won for his novel *The Bridge of San Luis Rey*.

4. The stories of Flannery O'Connor allow readers to examine unusual characters, to explore psychological motivations, and consider macabre situations.

5. Willy Loman could neither understand his own problems nor could he accept the help of friends.

7   WORD ORDER

7a   Inversions

The common order of words in sentences can be briefly summarized as follows:

▼ Subjects precede verbs.

▼ Verbs precede objects or complements.

▼ Indirect objects precede direct objects.

▼ Adjectives precede the words they modify.

▼ Adverbs usually follow verbs they modify, but they precede adjectives or other adverbs.

▼ Prepositional phrases follow the words they modify.

▼ Independent clauses often precede subordinate clauses, although three variations are common: (1) clauses used as adjectives follow the words they modify, (2) clauses used as adverbs often precede the independent clause, and (3) clauses used as nouns occupy the subject or object positions.

▼ Closely related material is best kept as close together as possible.

Although these principles usually govern word order in sentences, any element of a sentence may be moved to create emphasis or interest. Variations of common word order, however, should produce neither awkward nor unidiomatic writing.

Common Order	*Inverted Order*
The chancellor **quickly and superficially** responded to the interviewer's questions.	**Quickly and superficially,** the chancellor responded to the interviewer's questions.

Common Order	*Inverted Order*
The team doesn't stand a chance **without Terry.**	**Without Terry,** the team doesn't stand a chance.
The computer terminals were installed **at last.**	**At last,** the computer terminals were installed.
The company will pay relocation expenses **if employees are transferred.**	**If employees are transferred,** the company will pay relocation expenses.
Jessica said, "I can only attend the Art Institute if I receive a scholarship."	"I can only attend the Art Institute," **Jessica said,** "if I receive a scholarship."

7b   Emphatic Order

To achieve a desired effect in a sentence, writers can vary the location of key information. In a typical sentence, information placed near the beginning or end will be emphasized. Placing important information in an independent clause, instead of in a subordinate clause or phrase, strengthens emphasis.

Place important information first or last; do not bury it in the middle.

Unemphatic: On April 14, 1865, **Abraham Lincoln was shot** at Ford's Theatre.
Emphatic: **Abraham Lincoln was shot** at Ford's Theatre on April 14, 1865.
Emphatic: At Ford's Theatre on April 14, 1865, **Abraham Lincoln was shot.**
Unemphatic: That novel, **as far as I know,** was my biggest commercial failure.
Emphatic: **As far as I know,** that novel was my biggest commercial failure.
Unemphatic: She is innocent, **in my opinion.**
Emphatic: **In my opinion,** she is innocent.

Place key information in independent clauses, not in subordinate clauses or phrases.

Unemphatic: He fell from the roof, **thus breaking his neck.**
Emphatic: He fell from the roof and **broke his neck.**

Exercise

Revise the following sentences to improve awkward or unemphatic word order.

1. The Supreme Court refused to consider the appeal, according to the late news last night.

2. The major evidence had been acquired during a search without a proper warrant, thus resulting in a dismissal of the case.

3. The evidence shows, the prosecuting attorney suggested, that Marshall Tireman is guilty of stealing industrial secrets.

4. The judge agreed to admit the videotape as evidence after the defense attorney made a special appeal.

5. The lawyers, even, had not expected such a large settlement in the case.

8 POSITION MODIFIERS CAREFULLY

A *modifier* must clearly relate to a word in a sentence and explain, describe, define, or limit the word to which it relates. When a modifier is not positioned properly, the modification can be both awkward and confusing.

8a Long modifiers should not separate a subject and verb or a verb and its complement.

Although modifiers may be placed between a subject and verb or between a verb and its complement, such positioning often makes a sentence difficult to read and interpret. Reposition the modifiers so that they do not break the flow of the sentence.

The renovation, because of fund-raising activities and because of competitive bidding by major contracting firms, was delayed.

The final bid was, even though it was thousands lower than the initial bids, still too high.

8b Avoid dangling modifiers.

Opening modifiers that do not modify the subject of a sentence are said to dangle—hence, the name *dangling modifier.* To correct such an error, either revise the independent clause so that the introductory phrase can logically modify the subject, or revise the introductory phrase to make it a subordinate clause.

To qualify for the award, ~~the committee requires that~~ candidates *must* have sixty class hours and a 3.50 GPA.

While waiting for my date in the lobby, two men in tuxedos got into a violent argument.

8c

Avoid squinting modifiers.

A *squinting modifier* seems to modify the word before it *and* the word after it. Reposition the modifier to clarify the meaning, or use *that* to eliminate confusion.

that
The reporter said before noon she would finish the article.

The reporter said before noon she would finish the article.

8d

Avoid split infinitives.

A *split infinitive* occurs when a modifier falls between *to* and the primary verb. Writers and readers disagree about whether split infinitives are grammatically or stylistically acceptable. To be on the safe side, reposition the modifier.

Darren began to furiously pack his luggage to try to make the nine o'clock flight.

─────────────── *Exercise*

Eliminate ambiguities in the following sentences by changing the position of misleading modifiers.

1. At one time his parents said he had been an engineering student.

2. The stage set, based on original paintings and engravings from the eighteenth century, was breathtaking.

3. The car was in the garage that he wrecked.

4. Marc promised on his way home to pick me up.

5. They talked about going on a second honeymoon but never did.

6. My brother hung the painting in the hallway that I gave him for his birthday.

7. The short story was, because of its convoluted sentences and obscure imagery, almost incomprehensible.

8. There is a panel discussion tonight about drug addiction in the student lounge.

9. I thought of writing often but never did.

10. Reading the personal letters of famous people is a way to usefully and completely understand their reactions to public situations.

9 COMPARISONS

When you include *comparisons* in your sentences, consider your diction carefully to ensure that the ideas are clear and complete.

9a **Include all the words needed to make a comparison clear and complete.**

Flying to Chicago is more convenient than a train. *(taking)*

Levi's are more popular than any jeans. *(other)*

9b **Do not write an implied comparison.**

An implied comparison presents only part of the necessary context. The words *better, less, more,* and *worse* and words formed with the suffix *-er* signal the need for fully stated comparisons; use *than* and explain the comparison completely.

The house on Elm Street is better suited to our needs. *(than the others we've seen)*

The orchestra's performance of Beethoven's Ninth Symphony was much worse. *(than expected)*

———————— *Exercise*

Revise the following sentences to make their comparisons logical and complete.

1. Once Carla began taking her medication regularly, she felt much better.

2. Having had a two-hour practice session, the students were no longer as confused.

3. Taking a taxi or riding the subway is certainly more convenient than a car.

4. Reeboks are more popular than any tennis shoe.

5. Revising a paper is much easier using a word processor.

10 CONCISENESS

Writing that is concise expresses ideas in as few words as possible; it is free of needless repetition and useless words. To make your writing concise, eliminate words, phrases, and clauses that do not further your purpose.

10a Do not repeat words needlessly.

The car we were looking for was a car for highway travel.
[12 words reduced to 9.]

10b Do not repeat ideas that are already understood.

The frown on Todd's face suggested that he was depressingly saddened by his interview. [14 words reduced to 10.]

10c Eliminate expletive constructions whenever possible.

Expletives, such as *it is, there is, there are, here is, here are,* and so on, add words to sentences without clarifying meaning.

There were three cars involved in the accident. [8 words reduced to 7.]

10d Write active sentences whenever possible. (See "Active and Passive Sentences," Section 5.)

My aunt Ruth made

The prize-winning quilt was made by my Aunt Ruth.
[9 words reduced to 7.]

10e Replace wordy phrases with brief expressions.

think

I am of the opinion that we should resubmit the insurance claim.
[12 words reduced to 9.]

10f Replace forms of the verb *to be* with stronger verbs.

must

Counselors are responsible for completing the transcript portion of the applications.
[11 words reduced to 9.]

10g

When possible, replace nonrestrictive clauses with appositives.

Nonrestrictive clauses, clauses that provide useful or interesting but inessential information, can often be replaced with *appositives*, simple words or phrases that provide definitions for other words or phrases in a sentence. (See also Section 20h.) To save words and tighten and clarify your writing, consider using appositives in place of nonrestrictive clauses.

Sandra Day O'Connor, ~~who was~~ the first woman appointed to the Supreme Court, assumed her duties in August 1981.
[19 words reduced to 17 through substitution of an appositive for a nonrestrictive clause.]

—————————— *Exercise*

Make the following wordy sentences concise. Note the number of words saved through revision.

1. There should be two waiters to serve every ten people at the banquet, or there will be unnecessary delays occurring. [20 words reduced to _____.]

2. After the violent eruption of Nevada de Ruiz, relief agencies joined together in their efforts to help the unfortunate victims. [20 words reduced to _____.]

3. Wynton Marsalis, who plays both classical and jazz trumpet, scorns pop music. [12 words reduced to _____.]

4. At this point in time, we should prepare for spring floods, in the event that the Wabash River will crest as it did last year. [25 words reduced to _____.]

5. Finalists in the oratory competition will be evaluated by seven judges. [11 words reduced to _____.]

6. The original prototype for the Ford Mustang is on display at the Ford Museum in Detroit, Michigan. [17 words reduced to _____.]

7. A house made of brick is more costly but more maintenance free than a house made of wood. [18 words reduced to _____.]

8. Secret Service agents are responsible for protecting the current president, past presidents, and their families. [16 words reduced to _____.]

9. In the humble opinion of this writer, Academy Awards present indications of popularity rather than quality. [16 words reduced to _____.]

10. The real truth is that there is no money available to support and maintain the scholarship. [16 words reduced to _____.]

Exercise

Revise the following paragraph to make it concise. Try a number of strategies and notice how much the paragraph improves when you eliminate unnecessary words and bloated phrases.

Prior to beginning the search for gainful employment, gather together necessary and essential information and materials. Assemble a list of your experiences in educational institutions and in the work place and be sure to include the months or years involved in each situation. Prepare a résumé that includes facts and information about yourself, personally, and about yourself, academically and professionally. Make sure that there are clear sections in the résumé to cover each of these important and crucial topics. Proofread the final copy of the résumé in order to be aware of and correct any errors or mistakes. Then photocopy the résumé so that you still have at your disposal a copy of the résumé for future reference.

Writing Logical and Effective Sentences: Review Exercises

Revise the following sets of sentences to create logical and effective sentences. Identify the kinds of problems that required correction.

1. Human figures were elongated and were rendered in sallow yellows and greens by the Spanish artist El Greco.

2. Cubism is, with its emphasis on presenting the surfaces of all objects—both living and inanimate—in abstract geometric forms, alien to many people's artistic sensibilities.

3. Although his work was not popular during his lifetime, van Gogh paints with bold colors and exaggerated forms. Modern collectors have valued his work since his death.

4. It is clear that there are only a few major pop art paintings of lasting aesthetic value. There are many others that are simply cultural curiosities.

5. When one sees the work of Rembrandt in a well-lighted gallery, you will be impressed by the rich texture of his work and the subtle variations in his gold and brown tones.

6. Neoclassical artists of the eighteenth century objected to the visual excesses of Baroque and Rococo art and imitate the symmetry and simple forms of Greek and Roman art.

7. Picasso's versatility as a sculptor is evident in his ability to skillfully and ingeniously use "junk" in his welded works.

8. Da Vinci, Raphael, David, Rembrandt, van Gogh, Monet, and Picasso would surely be included if one was to make a list of major European painters.

9. New York's Chrysler Building—with its use of zigzag forms, angular metal ornamentation, and strong vertical lines—is an exemplary model of Art Deco architecture.

10. Up until the middle of our current century, most prominent and important painters and sculptors from the United States of America trained and went to school in the countries of Europe.

11. Once, painters worked almost exclusively on wood panels or plaster walls. Then stretched canvas was used. Today, wood is being used again by many artists.

12. The Louvre in Paris houses more major works of art than any museum.

13. Prior to viewing a major exhibition, I would offer encouragement to inexperienced and untrained viewers to peruse or skim the catalogue prepared to accompany the exhibition.

14. To create what he described as an unconscious interpretation of reality, paint was splattered on canvas by Jackson Pollock.

15. Stressing the dreamlike, the unusual, and the bizarre, we found Surrealistic art unsettling.

Writing Grammatical Sentences

11   ELIMINATE SENTENCE FRAGMENTS

A *sentence fragment* is a group of words presented as if it were a complete sentence—with a capital letter at the beginning and a period at the end. A sentence fragment, however, lacks a subject or a verb or both and does not express a complete thought. Eliminate sentence fragments in one of four ways, depending on the type of fragment.

11a   Add a subject when necessary, or join the fragment to another sentence.

Charlie Chaplin was a multitalented man. ^He^ Wrote, directed, and starred in his own films.

Charlie Chaplin was a multitalented man, Wrote, directed, and starred in his own films.

11b   Add a verb when necessary, or join the fragment to another sentence.

Grigori Rasputin, a Russian monk in Czar Nicholas's court. He was assassinated in 1916.

11c   Omit the subordinating conjunction, or connect the fragment to an independent clause.

Mother Teresa
~~Because she~~ tirelessly helped the poor in Calcutta. *She* ~~Mother Teresa~~ was awarded the Nobel Peace Prize in 1979.

11d   Attach a phrase to a related sentence.

Leonard Bernstein received wide acclaim on Broadway, Notably for the score of *West Side Story.*

Eliminate each fragment by making it into a sentence or by combining it with a sentence.

1. The *Robert E. Lee,* a renovated river boat that now operates as a restaurant. It is an excellent place to eat.

2. We made our way up the mountain trail with much difficulty. Slipping on rocks and snagging our clothes in the underbrush.

3. Chad has only one ambition. To play the violin in a major symphony.

4. Many people dread one part of medical exams more than any other. Having a blood sample taken.

5. In a political speech, candidates should appeal to the entire audience. Not just to those who believe as they do.

6. Even though the cost of automobile insurance is high. Repairs on damaged cars are even more exorbitant.

7. Having come this far. We must see the matter through.

8. Whatever challenge the office presents. I believe our new member of Congress will meet it successfully.

9. When the chairperson stated, "I will not compromise on any issue on which I have taken a stand." I began to question her judgment.

10. Rita Moreno has won all major performance awards. An Oscar, an Emmy, a Grammy, and a Tony.

12 ELIMINATE FUSED SENTENCES AND COMMA SPLICES

A *fused sentence* (also called a *run-on sentence*) results when no punctuation or coordinating conjunction separates two or more independent clauses. A *comma splice* results when two or more independent clauses are joined with only a comma. Eliminate these sentence errors in one of four ways.

12a   **Use a period to separate independent clauses, forming two sentences.**

Lorraine Hansberry was the first black female playwright of importance,
she wrote *A Raisin in the Sun.*

12b   **Use a semicolon to separate independent clauses and form a compound sentence.**

Through flying, Charles Lindbergh gained his notoriety; Amelia Earhart lost
her life.

12c   **Insert a coordinating conjunction between independent clauses to form a compound sentence.**

Helen Keller was both blind and deaf, *but* she was a skillful author and lecturer.

12d   **Use a subordinating conjunction to put the less important idea in a subordinate clause and form a complex sentence.**

although Paul Revere is known to most people as a Revolutionary War patriot he is
known to collectors as a silversmith and engraver.

Be especially sensitive to the use of conjunctive adverbs, such as *consequently, however, moreover, nevertheless,* and *therefore.* They do not link clauses grammatically. Misinterpreting their function in sentences is a common cause of comma splices.

Oscar Wilde fancied himself a poet and critic, however, he is most remembered as a playwright and wit.

───────────── *Exercise*

Correct the following fused sentences and comma splices.

1. The comma splice can confuse readers, it is usually less troublesome, however, than the fused sentence.

2. Members of the Drama Guild have rehearsed carefully for tonight's show, the director feels certain it will be a success.

3. The war is over the fighting is not.

4. The air traffic controller made the best decision he could at the time, looking back, he saw what he should have done differently.

5. It is too late to sign up for the proficiency exam this term, however, students can sign up for next term's exam.

6. Pay attention to the instructions you must follow them exactly.

7. Much has been done the Civil Liberties Union believes that much more needs to be done.

8. Stockholders don't have to liquidate their assets this week, all they need to do is sign papers of intent.

9. Clean-up is scheduled for Monday, Tuesday, and Wednesday the plant closes on Friday.

10. No conclusive evidence has been uncovered, the commissioners will meet again tomorrow.

13 AGREEMENT

Agreement in grammar refers to the correspondence of key sentence elements in number, person, and gender. Two kinds of agreement are grammatically important in most sentences: subject-verb agreement and pronoun-antecedent agreement.

13a Subject-Verb Agreement

In simplest terms, a singular subject requires a singular verb, and a plural subject requires a plural verb. A number of troublesome constructions can cause confusion, however, and require consideration.

When subjects are joined by *and*, use a plural verb.

Although each of the subjects may be singular, the compounding makes a plural verb necessary.

O'Connor and Rehnquist **speak** articulately for the dissenters.
[Plural verb with compound subject.]

A fool and his money **are** soon parted.

When subjects are joined by *or, nor, but, either . . . or, neither . . . nor*, or *not only . . . but also*, use a verb that agrees with the subject that is nearer to the verb.

Either Weixlmann or Stein **is** my choice for president.
[Singular verb with two singular subjects.]

The coach or the co-captains **supervise** the practices each day.
[Plural verb agrees with *co-captains,* the nearer subject.]

Neither Lewis, his two partners, nor their lawyers **were** at the press conference.
[Plural verb agrees with *lawyers,* the nearer subject.]

Either Jean or you **are** to accept the award for the entire cast.
[Plural verb agrees with *you,* the nearer subject.]

When this rule produces an awkward though correct sentence, consider revising the sentence.

You ~~or he is~~ the leading contender. *two are*

When a subject is followed by a phrase containing a noun that differs in number or person from the subject, use a verb that agrees with the subject, not with the noun in the phrase.

The attitude of these men **is** decidedly hostile.
[Singular verb agrees with *attitude,* the singular subject.]

The ballots with her name **have** been recalled.
[Plural verb agrees with *ballots,* the plural subject.]

When an indefinite pronoun, such as *anybody, anyone, each, either, everybody, neither, nobody,* and *someone,* is used as a subject, use a singular verb.

Ultimately, someone **has** to accept responsibility.

Anybody who wants to **has** the right to attend the hearing.

Everyone **has** the same chance.

When a collective noun is used as a subject, use a singular verb *or* a plural verb to clarify the meaning.

When a collective noun emphasizes the unity of a group, use a singular verb. When a collective noun emphasizes group members as individuals, use a plural verb.

The clergy **is** grossly underpaid.
[Singular verb because whole group is meant.]

The clergy **are** using their pulpits to speak out against oppression.
[Plural verb because individual members are meant.]

When an expletive construction, such as *here is, here are, there is,* and *there are,* is used as both subject and verb, match the verb to the noun that follows.

Here **is** your receipt. [Singular verb with singular noun *receipt.*]

Here **are** the copies you requested. [Plural verb with plural noun *copies.*]

There **is** no excuse for such behavior. [Singular verb with singular noun *excuse.*]

There **are** several solutions to the city's problems.
[Plural verb with plural noun *solutions.*]

The verb in a relative clause introduced by *who, which,* or *that* agrees in number with the pronoun's antecedent.

> Jessica is one performer who **acts** with restraint.
> [Singular verb with singular antecedent *performer.*]
>
> Philip Roth writes books that **illustrate** the absurdities of modern life.
> [Plural verb with plural antecedent *books.*]

When a compound subject is preceded by *each* or *every,* use a singular verb.

> *Each* and *every* indicate that persons or things are being considered individually.

> Each boy and girl **takes** shop and home economics.
> Every basket of peaches and flat of strawberries **was** sold.

When a subject is followed by a predicate noun that differs in number from the subject, the verb agrees with the subject, not with the complement.

> Although predicate nouns restate the subject of the sentence, their word forms do not always agree in number; that is, the predicate noun and the subject may not be both singular or both plural. Use the subject, not the predicate noun, to determine the appropriate subject-verb agreement.

> Her chief source of enjoyment **is** books.
> [Singular verb with singular subject *source.*]
>
> Books **are** her chief source of enjoyment.
> [Plural verb with plural subject *books.*]

When a plural noun has a singular meaning, use a singular verb.

> Some subjects may initially appear to be plural, but they are singular. *Electronics, mathematics, semantics,* and *geriatrics* appear to be in plural form but are names of individual fields of study. Expressions such as *gin and tonic* and *ham and eggs* are also singular, because they name a single drink and a single dish.

> No news **is** good news.
> Scotch and soda **is** not as popular as it once was.

When fractions, measurements, money, time, weight, and volume are considered as single units, use singular verbs.

> Three days **is** too long to wait.
> Jerrid feels that 165 pounds **is** his ideal weight.
> Twenty-two percent **is** the accepted rate for credit-card financing.

With titles of individual works, even those containing plural words, use a singular verb.

> *All the King's Men* **is** an enlightening political novel.
> Dorothy Parker's "Good Souls" **is** about congenial, often exploited people.

Words used as words take a singular verb.

Amateur athletes is used to describe participants as varied as Little League pitchers and endorsement-rich track-and-field stars.

Pronoun-Antecedent Agreement

Pronouns must agree with their antecedents (the nouns or pronouns to which they refer) in number and person. A singular pronoun must be used with a singular antecedent; a plural pronoun must be used with a plural antecedent. (See also "Case," Section 14.)

The workers received **their** wages.
[Plural third-person pronoun with plural third-person antecedent *workers*.]
The DC 10 changed **its** course and landed at Cincinnati.
[Singular third-person pronoun with singular third-person antecedent *DC 10.*]

Singular pronouns must also agree in gender with their antecedents. A masculine pronoun must be used with a masculine antecedent; a feminine pronoun must be used with a feminine antecedent; and a neuter pronoun must be used with a neuter antecedent. (See also "Case," Section 14.)

Masculine:	he	him	his	himself
Feminine:	she	her	hers	herself
Neuter:	it	it	its	itself

The generic use of masculine pronouns is no longer universally acceptable. Use both masculine and feminine pronouns when an antecedent could be either male of female (*(he or she, his or hers)*. Alternatively, use plural, genderless antecedents and pronouns whenever possible.

Each teacher must submit **his or her** annual report by March 15.
[Singular masculine and feminine pronouns with male or female antecedent *teacher.*]
Teachers must submit **their** annual reports by March 15.
[Plural pronoun with plural antecedent *teachers.*]

These principles of pronoun-antecedent agreement apply consistently to all situations, but a number of troublesome constructions require special consideration.

When the antecedents *each, either, neither,* and *none* are followed by a phrase that contains a plural noun, use a singular pronoun.

Although the noun in the phrase may be plural, *each, either, neither* and *none* refer to elements individually. Consequently, the pronoun must be singular.

Neither of the boys would accept the responsibility for **his** actions.
[Singular pronoun with *neither* as antecedent.]
Either of these women may lose **her** position.
[Singular pronoun with *either* as antecedent.]

When *everybody, each, either, everyone, neither, nobody,* and *a person* are antecedents, use a singular pronoun.

Although in context these words may imply plurality, the word forms are singular and therefore singular pronouns are required. Do not use masculine pronouns generically to refer to these genderless singular antecedents. Use both masculine and feminine forms, or alternatively, substitute plural antecedents and pronouns for the singular forms.

Nobody had **his or her** work completed on time.
[Singular pronouns with singular antecedent *nobody*.]
The committee members had not completed **their** work on time.
[A plural pronoun with plural antecedent *members*.]

Collective nouns used as antecedents take singular or plural pronouns depending on the meaning of the sentence.

A collective noun that identifies the group as a single unit takes a singular pronoun. A collective noun that identifies the individual members of a group takes a plural pronoun.

The judge reprimanded the jury for **its** disregard of the evidence.
[Singular pronoun because reference is to group as a whole.]
At the request of the defense attorney, the jury were polled and **their** individual verdicts recorded.
[Plural pronoun because reference is to group members individually.]

When an antecedent is a person, use *who, whom,* or *that* to introduce qualifying phrases or clauses.

This is the architect **who** planned the civic center.
The interior designer **whom** we selected was unavailable.
The landscaper **that** worked on our property has moved.

When an antecedent is an object or concept, use *which* or *that* to introduce qualifying phrases or clauses.

Here is the package **that** she left behind.
The package, **which** she left behind, could not later be found.

When an antecedent is an animal, use *that* to introduce qualifying phrases or clauses.

Secretariat is the horse **that** you're speaking of.

Exercise

Circle the correct form in parentheses.

1. Neither she nor her sons (was, were) present at the reading of the will.

2. The jury (is, are) expected to reach a verdict before midnight.

3. Each of the children is expected to bring (his, her, his or her, their) own art supplies.

4. The horse (that, who) won the Kentucky Derby went on to win the Preakness and the Belmont.

5. The team lost (its, their) first game of the season, but (it, they) won the next five games.

6. Every one of the actors who auditioned (was, were) exceptionally talented.

7. There (is, are) both food and firewood in the cabin.

8. Students (which, who) maintain grade-point averages of 3.50 or better are eligible for alumni scholarships.

9. None of the applicants presented (himself, herself, himself or herself, themselves) well in the interview.

10. Thirty hours a week (is, are) a heavy work schedule, especially if you are taking two classes.

14   CASE

Case is the form or position of a noun or pronoun that indicates its relation to other words in a sentence. English has three cases: *subjective, objective,* and *possessive.* In general, a noun or pronoun is in the subjective case when it acts as a subject, in the objective case when it acts as an object, and in the possessive case when it modifies a noun, as in *"his* bicycle," "The *boy's* dog," *"their* future."

English nouns, pronouns, and adjectives once all showed case by changing their forms. In modern English, word order and idiomatic constructions have largely replaced case endings. Only pronouns—and chiefly the personal pronouns—still make any considerable use of case forms.

Personal pronouns change form dramatically to indicate case

		Subjective	Objective	Possessive
Singular	*1st person*	I	me	my, mine
	2nd person	you	you	your, yours
	3rd person	he, she, it	him, her, it	his, hers, its

		Subjective	Objective	Possessive
Plural	*1st person*	we	us	our, ours
	2nd person	you	you	your, yours
	3rd person	they	them	their, theirs

The indefinite or relative pronoun *who* also changes form to indicate case.

Subjective	Objective	Possessive
who	whom	whose
whoever	whomever	

The case of a pronoun is determined by the pronoun's function in its own clause. Pronouns used as subjects or predicate nouns, that is, nouns that follow linking verbs and restate the subject, are in the subjective case. Pronouns used as direct objects, as indirect objects, or as objects of prepositions are in the objective case. Pronouns that modify a noun or pronoun or that precede and modify a gerund are in the objective case. Use the following guidelines to select the appropriate case.

14a Uses of the Subjective Case of Personal Pronouns

▼ As the subject of a verb:

I think that **we** missed the flight.

▼ As the complement of the verb *to be:*

I'm sure it was **she.**

▼ As the appositive (restatement) of a subject or predicate noun:

The surveyors, Mr. James and **he,** plotted the acreage.

14b Uses of the Objective Case of Personal Pronouns

▼ As the direct object or indirect object of a verb:

Mother likes **her** best.
Todd gave **us** the concert tickets.

▼ As the object of a preposition:

Sara directed the salesman to **him** and **me.**

▼ As the appositive (restatement) of a direct or indirect object:

My sister and I gave them, Mrs. Lester and **her,** nothing but trouble.

▼ As the subject of an infinitive:

I want **them** to take my place.

▼ As the object of an infinitive:

Don't expect to see **her** or **me** at a classical music concert.

14c

Uses of the Possessive Case of Personal Pronouns

▼ As a modifier of a noun or pronoun:

These are **my** four children, and those are **his** three.

▼ As a modifier of a gerund:

Her skiing improved rapidly.
What's wrong with **my** buying new equipment?

14d

Distinguishing Between "We" and "Us" Used with a Noun in Apposition

The subjective case form is *we*; the objective case form is *us*. Select the pronoun that would be correct if the noun were omitted.

We tenants must file formal complaints against the management firm.
[Subjective case for subject of the sentence.]
Their inattentiveness has given **us** tenants little recourse.
[Objective case for indirect object.]

14e

Personal Pronouns with "Than" or "As"

The case of a pronoun following *than* or *as* in a comparison often causes difficulty. In an elliptical (incompletely expressed) construction, use the case that would be appropriate if all the words were expressed.

He is at least as capable as **she.**
[Subjective case because *she* is the subject of the unexpressed verb *is.*]
The crowd liked Navratilova better than **them.**
[Objective case because *them* would be the object of the verb if the comparison were expressed completely: *better than it liked them.*]

14f

Uses of the Subjective Case of the Relative Pronoun "Who"

▼ As the subject of a clause:

Ralph Nader is a consumer advocate **who** gets media attention easily.

▼ As the subject of a clause stated as a question:

Who donated the carpets?

14g

Uses of "Whom"—The Objective Case of the Relative Pronoun "Who"

▼ As the object of a verb:

Professor Frayne is a man **whom** we admire.

▼ As the object of a verb in a question:

Whom should we notify?

14h   **Distinguishing Between "Whoever" and "Whomever"**

The subjective case form is *whoever*; the objective case form is *whomever*. Be aware that even when a subordinate clause functions as an *object*, a pronoun that functions as the *subject* of the clause belongs in the subjective case.

> Invite **whoever** will come.
> [Subjective case because *whoever* is the subject of *will come.*]
> The committee will approve the appointment of **whomever** we select.
> [Objective case because *whomever* is the object of the preposition *of.*]

———————————— *Exercise*

Revise the following sentences to correct any errors in the use of case. Some of the sentences need no correction.

1. The police suspected Boris Kraykov's associates, but he is more likely to be responsible than them.

2. Jim, not me, must make the recommendation.

3. Us gun collectors must be aware of people's objecting to firearms.

4. Reverend Wehrenberg is the person to whom we will go for advice.

5. They gave the finalists, Sandi and he, an enthusiastic round of applause.

6. Whoever we appoint to the council must be willing to present our case with conviction.

7. There is really no excuse for him refusing to comment.

8. The comments were directed to we two, you and I.

9. Carol is at least three years older than him.

10. Sonia will have to train whoever accepts the job.

15   **VERB TENSES**

Verb tenses indicate the time of the action or state of being expressed. Most verbs in English have four principal parts and change in a predictable way to form the six basic tenses and the six progressive tenses.

Present-tense form: walk

Present participle: walking

Past-tense form: walked

Past participle: walked

Present tense: walk, walks

Past tense: walked

Future tense: will walk, shall walk

Present perfect tense: have walked, has walked

Past perfect tense: had walked

Future perfect tense: will have walked, shall have walked

Present progressive tense: am walking, are walking, is walking

Past progressive tense: was walking, were walking

Future progressive tense: will be walking, shall be walking

Present perfect progressive tense: have been walking, has been walking

Past perfect progressive tense: had been walking

Future perfect progressive tense: will have been walking, shall have been walking

Irregular verbs form their past tenses and their past participles through changes in spelling or word form that must be memorized. The following is a list of the principal parts of the most common or troublesome verbs.

Present tense	Present participle	Past tense	Past participle
am, is, are	being	was, were	been
bear	bearing	bore	borne
beat	beating	beat	beaten
begin	beginning	began	begun
bite	biting	bit	bitten
blow	blowing	blew	blown
break	breaking	broke	broken
bring	bringing	brought	brought
burst	bursting	burst	burst
cast	casting	cast	cast
choose	choosing	chose	chosen
come	coming	came	came
deal	dealing	dealt	dealt
do	doing	did	done
draw	drawing	drew	drawn

drink	drinking	drank	drunk
eat	eating	ate	eaten
fall	falling	fell	fallen
fly	flying	flew	flown
forbid	forbidding	forbade	forbidden
forsake	forsaking	forsook	forsaken
freeze	freezing	froze	frozen
give	giving	gave	given
go	going	went	gone
grow	growing	grew	grown
hang*	hanging	hung	hung
have	having	had	had
know	knowing	knew	known
lay	laying	laid	laid
lie	lying	lay	lain
ride	riding	rode	ridden
ring	ringing	rang	rung
rise	rising	rose	risen
run	running	ran	run
see	seeing	saw	seen
shake	shaking	shook	shaken
shoe	shoeing	shod	shod
shrink	shrinking	shrank (shrunk)	shrunk
sing	singing	sang (sung)	sung
sink	sinking	sank (sunk)	sunk
sit	sitting	sat	sat
slay	slaying	slew	slain
slink	slinking	slunk	slunk
speak	speaking	spoke	spoken
spin	spinning	spun	spun
spring	springing	sprang (sprung)	sprung
steal	stealing	stole	stolen
strive	striving	strove	striven
swear	swearing	swore	sworn

*The verb *to hang,* used in the sense of "to execute," is regular: *hang, hanged, hanged.*

swim	swimming	swam	swum
take	taking	took	taken
teach	teaching	taught	taught
tear	tearing	tore	torn
throw	throwing	threw	thrown
wear	wearing	wore	worn
weave	weaving	wove	woven
win	winning	won	won
write	writing	wrote	written

15a   **Use the present tense to describe habitual action or actions that occur or conditions that exist in the present.**

> Pamela **listens** to classical music when she writes papers.
> They **are** exhausted.

15b   **Use the present tense to express general truths and scientific principles.**

> The earth **tilts** slightly on its axis.

15c   **Use the present tense to describe or discuss artistic works, paintings, sculpture, etc., and literary works, novels, plays, poems, etc.**

> Polonius **offers** Laertes platitudes, not advice.
> The stark black and white in Picasso's large painting *Guernica* is the visual equivalent of the starkness of his message.

15d   **Use the past tense to describe completed actions or conditions that existed in the past.**

> Abolitionists openly **opposed** slavery, often at personal risk.
> They **were** exhausted.

15e   **Use the future tense to describe actions that will occur or conditions that will exist in the future.**

> The Congress **will reconvene** after a brief recess.

15f   **Use the present perfect tense to describe actions that started or conditions that existed at an unspecified time in the past and continue in the present.**

> For years, Mary Tyler Moore **has been** a spokesperson for the American Diabetes Association.

15g   **Use the past perfect tense to describe actions that started or conditions that existed before a specific time in the past.**

> In large part, Czar Nicholas **had ignored** the turmoil that preceded the Russian Revolution.

15h   **Use the future perfect tense to describe actions that will be completed or conditions that will exist before a specific time in the future.**

Natalie **will have submitted** her dissertation before the school year ends.

15i   **Use the progressive tenses to express ongoing actions that occur in the present, past, or future.**

I **am learning** to ski.
Sasha **had been planning** to attend the theater opening.
Rebecca **will be working** as a receptionist this summer.

15j   **Use present participles to express action that coincides with the action described by the main verb.**

Sensing that media coverage of the takeover would be negative, Albertson decided to cancel the press conference.

15k   **Use past participles and perfect participles to express actions that occurred, or to describe conditions that existed, before the action or condition described by the main verb.**

Shocked by the disparaging comments, Senator Robertson left the hearing.
Having completed her work, Sybil sat down to read.

15l   **Generally, use the past tense or past perfect tense in a subordinate clause when the verb in the independent clause is in the past or past perfect tense.**

This combination of past tenses is used to place one past action in a temporal or other relation with another past action.

Virginia Woolf **worked** in isolation because she **needed** quiet to concentrate well.
After he **had purchased** tickets for the World Series, Karl **was** unable to use them.

15m   **When the verb in the independent clause is in the present, future, present perfect, or future perfect tense, use any tense in the subordinate clause that will make the meaning of the sentence clear.**

In *Camelot*, Lancelot **thinks** that he **will succeed** at every venture.
Because twenty-four-carat gold **is** soft, detailed design work **will wear** away over time.

─────────────── *Exercise*

Select the appropriate verb tenses in the following sentences. Be ready to explain your choices.

1. Rain (is, was) water that (condenses, condensed) around dust particles and (falls, fell) to earth.

2. Normally the incidence of heart-worm disease (increases, increased) each year, but last year it (decreases, decreased).

3. On a bi-monthly basis, the Citizens' Action Coalition (sends, sent) a newsletter to its supporters.

4. Next fall, tuition at American universities (rises, will rise) to keep pace with inflation.

5. Becky Sharp (is, was) the main character of William Thackeray's *Vanity Fair*, an episodic novel published in 1847.

6. Isaac Singer (has written, had written) all of his stories in Yiddish, but they (are, were) immediately translated into English.

7. By the end of this season, we (will play, will have played) in thirty games and two tournaments.

8. (Serving, Having served) on the magazine's Board of Economic Advisors, the woman (is, was) a likely figure to head the Federal Reserve Board.

9. Because Da Vinci (experiments, experimented) with a variety of interesting pigments, many of his works (are, were) deteriorating.

10. (Opening, Having opened) the bomb casing with great care, the explosives expert (disconnects, disconnected) the timing mechanism.

16 ADJECTIVES AND ADVERBS

Adjectives and *adverbs* are both modifiers, but they serve separate purposes in sentences. Adjectives modify nouns and pronouns. Adverbs modify verbs, adjectives, and other adverbs; they may also modify phrases and clauses.

The *-ly* ending identifies many words as adverbs. It is not foolproof, however. Some adjectives end in *-ly (heavenly, lovely, leisurely)*, and many common adverbs *(very, then, always, here, now)* do not end in *-ly*. To avoid faulty modification, be certain to use adjectives only with nouns and pronouns and adverbs with verbs, adjectives, other adverbs, or whole phrases and clauses.

16a   **Use adjectives to modify nouns and pronouns.**

His **thoughtful** assessments are always **welcome.**

They are **dependable.**

16b   **Use adverbs to modify verbs, adjectives, and other adverbs.**

She **carefully** selected the flowers.

She was **especially** careful when she chose the roses.

She **very** carefully examined the buds and leaves on each stem.

16c   **Recognize the distinct uses of troublesome adjective and adverb pairs.**

The following two adjective/adverb pairs, and others you may have had trouble with in your writing, should be used carefully.

Bad/Badly: Use *bad,* the adjective form, to modify nouns and pronouns, even in conjunction with sensory verbs such as *appear, look, taste,* and so on. Use *badly,* the adverb form, only to modify a verb.

Lendl made a series of **bad** volleys during the third match.

His prospects may seem **bad,** but they really aren't.

Although Jimmy Stewart sang several great Cole Porter songs in films, he

acknowledged that he sang them **badly.**

Good/Well: The word *good,* an adjective, always modifies a noun or a pronoun. The word *well* can function as either an adverb or an adjective. As an adverb meaning "satisfactorily," *well* could modify a verb, an adjective, or another adverb. As an adjective meaning "healthy," *well* could only modify a noun or pronoun.

The lasagna smells *good.* [Adjective.]

Your point is *well* taken. [Adverb.]

Mrs. Biagi says that she feels *well* today. [Adjective.]

———————————— *Exercise*

Revise the following sentences to correct faulty modification.

1. If you move quiet and slow, you can sometimes see small wildlife in this
   area.

2. Miss Haversham, eccentric and oppressive, treated Pip bad.

3. Competitive cyclists must react calm and quick when they need to make repairs during tournaments.

4. Make sure that the knots are tied tight and secure, or the rocking of the waves may break the boat loose from the wharf.

5. When receiving chemotherapy treatments, most patients don't feel good.

Writing Grammatical Sentences: Review Exercise

Revise the following sentences to make them grammatical. Identify the problem in each sentence that made revision necessary.

1. Beginning in 1901, Nobel Prizes have been awarded to people who have made major contributions in the areas of peace, literature, physics, chemistry, and physiology or medicine, contributions in economics have been recognized since 1969.

2. A committee representing Yale University and the Bollingen Foundation presents their $5,000 award for poetry every two years.

3. The 1985 World Hunger Media Award was given to Bob Geldof, the rock musician who most people recognize as the organizer of the Live Aid concerts.

4. *Gödel, Escher, Bach: An Eternal Golden Braid*, Douglas R. Hofstadter's Pulitzer Prize–winning book, established philosophical and theoretical links between physics, art, and music.

5. Kennedy Center Honors have recognized the innovative work of a number of choreographers. George Balanchine, Martha Graham, Agnes de Mille, and Jerome Robbins, among others.

6. Although the musical *The Mystery of Edwin Drood* won five major Tony Awards in 1986, it has fared bad on overall ticket sales.

7. George W. Beadie and Edward L. Tatum, both of the United States, received Nobel Prizes in Physiology for their discovery that genes transmitted hereditary characteristics.

8. Each year, the Randolph Caldecott Medal, awarded by the American Library Association, recognizes whomever has produced the best illustrated book for children.

9. "We Are the World," the title cut from the album of the same name. Won Grammy Awards in 1985 for record of the year, song of the year, pop group of the year, and video-short form.

10. Henry Kissinger was Secretary of State from 1973 to 1977, under Nixon and Ford, he has received the Nobel Peace Prize (1973), the Presidential Medal of Freedom (1977), and the Medal of Liberty (n.d.).

11. Emory Holloway, Walter Jackson Bate, Justin Kaplan, Lawrence Thompson, Louis Sheaffer, and Richard W. B. Lewis have all won Pulitzer Prizes for biographies of major writers. In spite of the awards, however, their books are more recognized by name than them.

12. MacArthur Foundation Fellowships boast awards of $164,000 to $300,000, spread over five years, these fellowships free recipients to pursue their interests.

13. The Enrico Fermi Award is given to scientists who demonstrated an "exceptional and altogether outstanding" body of work in the field of atomic energy.

14. Milos Forman has won Academy Awards for directing two highly distinct films, *One Flew Over the Cuckoo's Nest,* a black comedy about a psychiatric ward, and *Amadeus,* a selectively retold biography of Mozart, also won Oscars as best film of the year.

15. The Columbia University Graduate School of Journalism won a George Foster Peabody Award for Broadcasting in 1985. Their collection *Seminars on Media and Society* were particularly acknowledged.

Choosing Effective Diction

Effective diction is the choice of words that best communicate your purpose to your audience. Your diction must be tailored to fit the specific context of your sentences and paragraphs and of your paper as a whole. Your choices of effective diction depend on your *subject*, *audience*, and *purpose*.

17 USE A DICTIONARY

No writer should work without a dictionary. Unabridged dictionaries, like the *Oxford English Dictionary*, usually found in the reference rooms of libraries, contain vast numbers of words and lengthy, thorough definitions. They are useful when you need to find highly detailed information like full word histories or to find the definition of an arcane word. Most of your needs, however, will be met by a standard desk-sized, collegiate dictionary such as

▼ *American Heritage Dictionary of the English Language*
▼ *Random House Dictionary of the English Language: College Edition*
▼ *Webster's New Collegiate Dictionary*
▼ *Webster's New World Dictionary of the American Language: College Edition*

Those dictionaries, and most other standard-sized collegiate dictionaries, provide a wide variety of general and useful information:

▼ A brief history of lexicography (the preparation and study of dictionaries)
▼ A brief history of the language
▼ An explanatory diagram of a sample word entry, with a key to the abbreviations that are used in the definitions
▼ Explanations and definitions of and guidance on matters of grammar and usage
▼ The dictionary of words (the main portion of the reference book)
▼ Lists of standard abbreviations
▼ Biographical entries (brief notes on important people)
▼ Geographical entries (brief notes on important places)
▼ Lists of foreign words and phrases

▼ Comparative tables of alphabets, calendars, and currencies

▼ Tables of measurements (both American and metric)

▼ Lists of signs and symbols in common use

▼ Maps and illustrations

▼ Pronunciation guides

▼ General guides to writing (business-letter forms, forms of address, manuscript preparation guidelines, and so on)

Dictionaries provide much more than definitions; they offer useful information about many subjects related to writing. Most often, however, you will turn to a dictionary to find information about specific words. To make your use of a dictionary efficient and productive, familiarize yourself with its general pattern of presenting information about words.

Spelling and Syllabication   Entries begin with the word spelled out and divided into syllables, usually marked with dots: con•tract. When a word has several acceptable spellings, each of them will be listed, but the most common spelling will be listed first. If alternative spellings are listed as *Am* (American) and *Brit* (British), use the American spelling in your writing.

Pronunciations   The pronunciation (usually enclosed in parentheses) follows, presented in a simplified phonetic transcription. The markings are matched to a pronunciation guide, which is usually printed at the bottom of

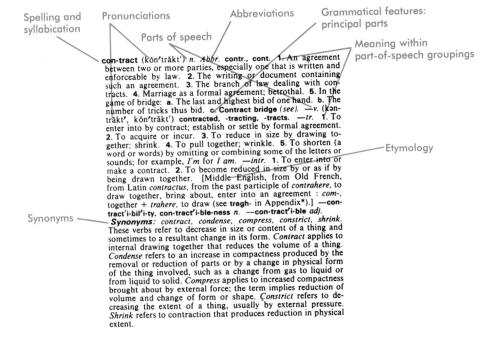

Spelling and syllabication

Pronunciations

Parts of speech

Abbreviations

Grammatical features: principal parts

Meaning within part-of-speech groupings

Etymology

Synonyms

con·tract (kŏn′trăkt′) n. *Abbr.* contr., cont. 1. An agreement between two or more parties, especially one that is written and enforceable by law. 2. The writing or document containing such an agreement. 3. The branch of law dealing with contracts. 4. Marriage as a formal agreement; betrothal. 5. In the game of bridge: a. The last and highest bid of one hand. b. The number of tricks thus bid. c. Contract bridge (*see*). —v. (kŏn-trăkt′, kŏn′trăkt′) contracted, -tracting, -tracts. —*tr.* 1. To enter into by contract; establish or settle by formal agreement. 2. To acquire or incur. 3. To reduce in size by drawing together; shrink. 4. To pull together; wrinkle. 5. To shorten (a word or words) by omitting or combining some of the letters or sounds; for example, *I'm* for *I am.* —*intr.* 1. To enter into or make a contract. 2. To become reduced in size by or as if by being drawn together. [Middle English, from Old French, from Latin *contractus,* from the past participle of *contrahere,* to draw together, bring about, enter into an agreement : com-, together + *trahere,* to draw (see **tragh-** in Appendix*).] —con·tract′i·bil′i·ty, con·tract′i·ble·ness *n.* —con·tract′i·ble *adj.*

Synonyms: *contract, condense, compress, constrict, shrink.* These verbs refer to decrease in size or content of a thing and sometimes to a resultant change in its form. *Contract* applies to internal drawing together that reduces the volume of a thing. *Condense* refers to an increase in compactness produced by the removal or reduction of parts or by a change in physical form of the thing involved, such as a change from gas to liquid or from liquid to solid. *Compress* applies to increased compactness brought about by external force; the term implies reduction of volume and change of form or shape. *Constrict* refers to decreasing the extent of a thing, usually by external pressure. *Shrink* refers to contraction that produces reduction in physical extent.

each page. When words have more than one syllable, accent marks (′ ′) indicate which syllables receive primary or secondary stress.

Parts of Speech   Abbreviations such as *n., v.,* and *adj.* indicate how a word can be used in a sentence. When a word can be used in various ways, the definitions are divided by parts of speech with, for instance, all meanings of the noun grouped together, followed by all meanings of the verb.

Abbreviations   If a word is commonly abbreviated, some dictionaries include the abbreviation in the entry; other dictionaries list abbreviations in a special section.

Grammatical Features   Distinctive grammatical features are noted in the entry. The principal parts of a verb are included, information that is especially helpful with irregular verbs—for example, *go, went, gone, going, goes.* Plural forms are provided for nouns that form plurals irregularly—for example, *mouse, mice.* When comparative and superlative degrees of adjectives and adverbs are formed by adding *-er* or *-est*—for example, *good, better, best* or *many, more, most*—dictionaries generally list them.

Meanings   Within part-of-speech groups, meanings are most commonly presented in order of their frequency of use. Some dictionaries, however, present definitions in historical order (from oldest to newest) or hierarchical order (from primary to secondary). Read the front matter of the dictionary you are using to see what pattern it follows.

Etymology   When word origins are known, they are provided, sometimes in abbreviated form (*Gk.* for Greek, *ME* for Middle English, and so on). Thus *contract* is one of a large class of words that came into English from Latin by way of Old French. It is made up of the prefix *con-* (from the Latin *com-,* meaning "together") and the root word *tract* (from the Latin *trahere,* meaning "to draw").

Labels   Labels are used to identify words according to a number of specific criteria: general level of usage (Nonstandard, Informal, Slang, Dial., and so on), regional usage (Brit., Southern), and usage within an area of specialization (Law, Med., Computer Sci.).

Synonyms and Antonyms   Many dictionaries include brief lists of synonyms for defined words (often introduced by the abbreviation *syns.*), to illustrate comparable word choices. Some dictionaries include antonyms as well (often introduced by the abbreviation *ant.*). Check the front matter of your dictionary to see whether these aids are used and where they are placed in the entries.

Exercise

Use the following questions to familiarize yourself with your own collegiate dictionary. You will have to use all parts of the dictionary to find your answers—the front matter, entries, and appended materials. Keep in mind that your responses may vary slightly from those of people using other dictionaries.

1. If you have to hyphenate *maleficence* at the end of a line, where could you appropriately place a hyphen before finishing the word on the next line?

2. How are the following words pronounced: *acclimate, banal, data, impotent, Wagnerian?*

3. Which is the preferred spelling, *aesthetics* or *esthetics?* Is the word listed under both spellings or only under one?

4. What synonyms does your dictionary list for *ghastly, lure, puzzle, single,* and *yield?*

5. What is the British meaning of the word *torch?* When *torch* is used as slang, what does it mean? What idiomatic expression uses the word *torch?*

6. What is a *schlemiel?* What is the origin of the word?

7. How many meanings are recorded for the word *vulgar?* By what pattern are the definitions arranged?

8. As what parts of speech can the word *square* be used? In what order do the parts of speech appear in the entry?

9. What are the plural forms of *alumna, fungus, graffito, hippopotamus,* and *medium?*

10. What do the abbreviations AAUW, EST, FNMA, MCAT, and VISTA stand for?

11. In what years were *Marian Anderson, D. W. Griffith, Marie Antoinette, Alfred Nobel, George H. Ruth,* and *Mary Cassatt* born?

12. In what countries are *Addis Ababa, Caracas, Kuala Lumpur, Mecca,* and *Sarajevo* located?

18 CONSIDER ISSUES OF DICTION

Standard English is the language of educated speakers and writers of English. American schools, government, businesses, and media have long used Standard English as the criterion by which speech and expository writing are judged; yet judgments about acceptable usage are sometimes hard to make because of the fluid nature of language and the effect of different writing situations. In a larger sense, word choices must be made in the context of a given piece of writing, depending on your subject, audience, and purpose. As a result, a word choice that is appropriate in one context may be inappropriate in another.

18a Changes and Variations in Language

Language is constantly evolving, and as a result standards of usage are also constantly changing. New words are introduced, old words assume new meanings, and some words are discarded. As a writer, you must be aware of such changes and keep your diction current. A newly coined word such as *houseperson* may at the present time be questionable usage, but another fairly recent word such as *chairperson* may generally be acceptable. You need to remain sensitive to such subtleties and make your word choices on the basis of what seems to be currently acceptable. A dictionary and your instructor can provide useful guidance.

Be aware as well that language varies from one region of the country to another. *Tag* may easily be understood in some areas, but in other regions the term *license plate* may be necessary to make your meaning clear. It is therefore important to familiarize yourself with regional word choices and to use or avoid using them, depending on your writing context.

18b The Writing Situation—Formal or Informal

Writers vary their diction and sentence structure to suit the writing context. A letter to the editor of the local newspaper in support of its position on a local issue, for example, AIDS education in the schools, would differ in many ways from a letter to a friend on the same subject. The difference is one of level of formality within Standard English. Formal usage—which typically uses an extensive vocabulary including learned words, no slang, few contractions and long, often complex sentences—may be appropriate for some topics and in some circumstances. Informal usage—generally characterized by the use of popular and colloquial words and some slang and contractions and short, simple sentences, often including fragments—may be appropriate for other topics and other circumstances. Whether a writer chooses a formal or informal style, or something in between, depends not on "correctness," for a broad range of styles is acceptable; rather, it depends on what is *appropriate* to the specific writing situation.

The following discussions address some key issues of diction, both formal and informal, and will help you choose your words selectively. (See Chapter 9, "Diction: The Choice of Words," for a fuller discussion.)

18c

Considering Denotation and Connotation

When you choose words, consider their *denotations* (the meaning in the dictionary) and their *connotations* (meaning derived from context). Look at these two sentences:

Nell Gwynn, a **famous** actress during the English Restoration, became the mistress of King Charles II.

Nell Gwynn, a **notorious** actress during the English Restoration, became the mistress of King Charles II.

Both of the words in bold type indicate that Nell Gwynn was well known; the denotations are similar. *Famous* and *notorious* have different connotations, however. *Famous* implies "celebrated," "renowned"; *notorious* implies "infamous," "widely but unfavorably known."

18d

Distinguishing Between Often-Confused Words

Some words are easily mistaken for each other because of similarities in spelling or pronunciation. When such confusion occurs, ideas become jumbled or unclear. Look at these two sentences:

In her closing remarks, the district attorney stated that the defendant had been **persecuted** because the evidence proved him guilty.

Darren received a summons for **wreckless** driving.

In the first, the verb *persecute* has been mistaken for *prosecute*; in the second, *wreckless* for *reckless*.

Commonly confused words include *advice* and *advise, cite, sight,* and *site, council* and *counsel, farther* and *further, loose* and *lose,* and *principal* and *principle.* Others are listed in "A Glossary of Contemporary Usage" (page 577).

18e

Avoiding Trite Language

Trite language is diction that is commonplace and unimaginative and consequently ineffective. Once-original expressions like *white as snow, in the final analysis,* and *rough and ready* have been used so often, in so many contexts, that they no longer offer new insight. Avoid using clichés and instead strive to communicate your meaning in your own language.

Ideally, aging
~~In an ideal world~~ boxers who are over the hill would retire before they ~~were~~ *lost their* *strength and agility.* ~~past their prime.~~

18f

Avoiding Jargon

Jargon, the specialized or technical language of a particular group, is sometimes appropriate when you are writing only to members of the group, but it is inappropriate when you are writing for a general audience. Keep your audience clearly in mind and use specific but common words instead.

By improving the quality and clarity of ~~horizontal transmittal correspondence,~~ *interdepartmental memos,* companies can ~~become more cost efficient.~~ *save money.*

Using Figurative Language

Figurative language imaginatively compares dissimilar things to present a significant insight. Figurative language can add interest to your writing, but you should be aware of some potential problems in its use.

▼ *Mixed metaphors* bring together images that clash because they establish incompatible impressions.

Shannon dove into her studies to reach the top of the class standings. [*Dove,* denoting downward movement, clashes with *reach the top,* connoting upward movement.]

▼ *Exaggerated personifications* result when inanimate objects or abstractions are given human or animal characteristics, thus creating images that are so far-fetched that readers find them strained—even laughable—rather than effective.

The craggy peak, covered with a few scraggly pines, brooded over the valley like a disapproving parent.

▼ *Unrecognizable allusions* are references to obscure historical or literary events or people. An allusion should illuminate a discussion, so use references that are likely to be recognized by a general audience.

Jeremy's letter to the editor, a condensed *Areopagitica,* railed against censorship. [The allusion to John Milton's tract on freedom of the press might be lost on many readers.]

Exercise

Revise the following sentences to eliminate problems with diction. Consult your dictionary, if necessary.

1. The sight for the new city counsel building has already been chosen.

2. We racked our brains for solutions to our financial problems, but solutions seemed few and far between.

3. The berserk parents shouted at the school's principle and refused to believe that Danny, their pride and joy, could have done anything wrong.

4. Purchasing a residence in a noncity environment was the Smiths' fondest wish.

5. Like a ship without a sail, Scott wandered threw the office building, looking for the lawyer's office.

6. The intelligence operative arranged for telephone surveillance of Dr. Russell's office.

7. For reasons too numerous to mention, Bradley Jennerman resigned.

8. One should always masticate one's food completely.

9. Like a scared monkey, the small child clung to his mother.

10. Researchers suggest that excessive involvement in the television-viewing process can effect the way a young person preforms in an educational institution.

───────────────── *Exercise*

Revise the following paragraphs to eliminate problems with diction.

In these troubled financial times, one is likely to find adults returning to their family domiciles to cohabitant with their parents. After attaining degrees from institutions of higher learning, many offspring return to their home areas to find gainful employment and save money by sharing the family dwelling. The money they save they often invest in automobiles, stereos, and haberdashery. Some save money to allow them to later invest in living quarters of their own or save money for a rainy day.

The psychological affects of adults returning to live with parents can be unfortunate. Offspring sometimes feel that they are not establishing their independence from Mom and Pop. Parents sometimes feel that their children, now grown, are imposing on their independence, and returning children create storm and strife when they return to the nest. But at this point in time, adults living with their parents is becoming more commonplace, and many people will have to learn to live with the situation.

Choosing Effective Diction: Review Exercise

Revise the following sentences to improve their diction.

1. An effective piece of transcribed discourse must be easily decipherable.

2. Like a sponge absorbs water, the dancer listened to and analyzed the comments of her choreographer.

3. In the final analysis, the institution of higher learning's operation was not cost effective.

4. The NSC's clandestine operations in Central America and the Middle East were less than effective.

5. The aggressive salesperson amassed a sizable commission.

6. It goes without saying that in this day and age oral communication is crucial for getting ahead in this dog-eat-dog world.

7. Sometime or other everyone will have difficulties with interpersonal relations.

8. The principal's principal objection was not to the principal the students presented but to their method of implementing it.

9. The Herculean task of planning the reunion fell on the shoulders of the two organizers.

10. The microscopic listening devices implanted in the concrete structural members of the U.S. Embassy in Moscow would make surreptitious monitoring of conversations possible.

Observing the Rules of Punctuation

Marks of punctuation serve specific purposes in sentences. They show where thoughts end, where ideas are separated, and where pauses occur. Punctuate sentences according to the principles noted here. Remember that using punctuation unnecessarily is as confusing as omitting it when it is required.

19 PERIODS, QUESTION MARKS, AND EXCLAMATION POINTS (./?/!)

Three marks of punctuation end sentences: the *period,* the *question mark,* and the *exclamation point.* They indicate that a thought is complete and perform— especially the period—other functions as well.

19a Accurate Use of Periods

Use a period to end a sentence that makes a statement.

Solar power is not yet a widely used energy source.

Use a period at the end of a question that is a courteously stated request or a command.

Will you please hand in your papers now.
Give your forms to the secretary when you've finished.

Use a period to end a sentence that contains an indirect question.

The landlord asked if we understood the terms of the lease.
[The sentence states that a question was asked; it does not directly pose the question.]

Use a period with most abbreviations.

Although a period in an abbreviation indicates that letters have been omitted, some standard abbreviations do not require periods. Consult a dictionary for guidance. (See also Section 35, "Abbreviations.")

With periods	Without periods
Mr.	FCC (government agency)
M.D.	IL (state)
Trans.	PBS (television network)

Use a period before a decimal point and with dollars and cents.

Production standards vary by only .14 millimeter.
Pi equals 3.14159.
The price was reduced to $39.95.

19b

Accurate Use of Question Marks

Use a question mark after a direct question.

The need for a question mark is usually indicated by inverted word order: part or all of the verb in the independent clause precedes the subject of the clause. In some instances, however, intent transforms a statement into a question.

Can we assume that the order has been shipped?
[*Can,* part of the verb, precedes the subject *we.*]
You mean he's ill?
[Intent, not word order, indicates that the sentence is a question; the question mark, though optional, confirms the writer's intent.]

Use a question mark in parentheses to indicate uncertainty about the accuracy of dates or numbers or other facts.

Modern scholars question whether Homer, a Greek poet of the ninth century (?) B.C., was the sole author of the famous epics attributed to him, the *Iliad* and the *Odyssey.*

It is not good usage to indicate possibly inaccurate words or to indicate irony by using a question mark in parentheses; changes in diction or sentence structure are more effective means of achieving these ends.

19c

Accurate Use of Exclamation Points

Use an exclamation point only to express strong emotion or to indicate unusual emphasis.

Be quiet!
Don't just stand there. Do something!

In most writing, exclamation points are not necessary or appropriate. Use them selectively.

20   COMMAS (,)

The *comma* is used to make the internal structure of a sentence clear. It does so in three general ways: (1) by separating elements that might otherwise be confused, (2) by setting off interrupting constructions, and (3) by marking words that are out of normal order.

20a   **Use commas to separate three or more coordinate items in a series.**

Using a comma before the conjunction (the word that joins the items in the series) is always correct and will avoid possible confusion.

> Her favorite novelists were Melville, Lawrence, and Faulkner.
> [Commas separating nouns.]
> We considered displaying the statue in three places: in the lobby, in the president's office, and in the reception room. [Commas separating phrases.]
> Jack designed the set, Ira did the flat painting, and Margo did the detailed painting.
> [Commas separating independent clauses.]

20b   **Use commas between coordinate adjectives or adverbs that are not joined by a conjunction but that modify the same word individually.**

When each of several adjectives modifies a noun individually, or when each of several adverbs modifies a verb, adjective, or adverb individually, commas should separate the modifiers. No comma separates the last modifier from the word it modifies. (See also Section 21d.)

> It was a dark, drizzly, depressing day. [Each adjective individually modifies *day.*]
> Rick slowly, methodically rechecked his documentation.
> [Each adverb individually modifies *rechecked.*]

20c   **In a compound sentence, use a comma before the coordinating conjunction that links the independent clauses.**

This usage prevents the subject of the second clause from being misread as an additional object in the first clause. When there is no danger of a confused reading, the comma may be omitted.

> Because of financial difficulties, the farmer sold his tractor and his plows, and his land remained uncultivated in the spring.
> [Without the comma, *land* could be misread as another direct object in a series with *tractor* and *plows.*]
> T. S. Eliot's poetry is highly regarded but his drama is not.
> [No comma necessary because no confusion is likely.]

20d   **Use one comma or a pair of commas to set off a conjunctive adverb.**

Conjunctive adverbs, such as *however, moreover, therefore, consequently,* and *nevertheless,* establish logical connections between sentences. Usually they provide a transition between two statements, and they come near or at the beginning of the second statement. If no confusion will result, the comma or commas may be omitted, but using commas in these cases will always be correct.

> The warehouse was severely damaged by fire. Subsequently, the property was sold at a loss.
>
> Recent advances in medical research have brought hope to victims of AIDS. Some medical experts, however, feel the optimism is premature.
>
> Streamlining corporate management helps companies operate more smoothly; moreover, it can save on operating costs.

20e **Use a comma after an introductory subordinate clause in a complex or compound-complex sentence.**

> Because OPEC's prices were high in the 1970s, American drivers began to conserve gasoline, showing that for once they were responsive to government recommendations.
>
> Although Middle English is somewhat difficult to read, the rewards of reading Chaucer make learning his language worth the effort.

Use a comma after an introductory infinitive or participial phrase.

> To prepare for her language proficiency exam, Pam skimmed five study guides.
>
> Moving cautiously through the rubble, the insurance agent made notes for the damage report.

20f **Use a comma after introductory elements that function as adjectives or adverbs unless the phrase is short and the meaning of the sentence is clear without the comma.**

A prepositional phrase at the beginning of a sentence that answers the questions *when, where,* or *under what conditions* is functioning like an adverb. Since such phrases modify the entire sentences of which they are a part, they should be followed by commas.

> After four weeks of intensive work, Jason finished the first draft of his master's thesis.
>
> After classes the five of us met to play basketball.
> [Short phrase does not require a comma.]

Use a comma to set off an introductory adverb that modifies an entire sentence.

> Finally, attending conferences and workshops is an important way to meet other professionals.

20g **Use one comma or a pair of commas to set off a nonrestrictive clause or phrase.**

A *nonrestrictive clause* or *phrase* does not limit a class to a particular group or individual but modifies the whole class. It supplies additional information but can be omitted from a sentence without substantially altering the sentence's meaning.

A *restrictive clause* or *phrase* specifies a particular member or members of a group. It supplies information that is necessary to the meaning of the sentence. Restrictive clauses or phrases are not set off by commas.

> The audio designer, **who creates sound effects for a play,** is an important member of a theater staff.
> [*Nonrestrictive clause* could be omitted without altering sentence meaning.]
>
> New recruits, **who may join after finishing high school** must make numerous adjustments before they are acclimated to military life.
> [*Nonrestrictive clause* could be omitted without altering sentence meaning.]
>
> The audio designer **who worked on** *Equus* should be fired.
> [*Restrictive clause* identifies a specific audio designer.]
>
> All soldiers **who complete basic training** will be assigned to duty within three weeks. [*Restrictive clause* identifies a specific group of soldiers.]

20h ## Use one comma or a pair of commas to set off nonrestrictive appositives.

An *appositive*—a word, phrase, or clause that renames a word or group of words in a sentence—can be nonrestrictive or restrictive. Nonrestrictive appositives provide inessential information and are set off by commas. Restrictive appositives provide essential information and are not set off by commas. Appositives are grammatically equivalent to the noun or pronoun they rename.

> PBS, **a nonprofit broadcasting network,** relies on corporate donations to cover most of its operating expenses.
> [*Nonrestrictive appositive* could be omitted without altering sentence meaning.]
>
> The superstation **TBS** broadcast the first colorized versions of many American film classics.
> [*Restrictive appositive* identifies a specific station.]

20i ## Use one or a pair of commas to set off contrasted elements.

> Young children react best to positive comments, not negative ones.
> South Korea, not Japan, has the highest literacy rate in Asia.

20j ## Use commas to set off the words *yes* and *no*, mild interjections (*well, okay,* and so on) that begin sentences, and words in direct address.

> Yes, James Joyce's *Ulysses* is a difficult novel to read.
> I suspect, my fellow Americans, that we are the victims of a hoax.
> Sarah, would you please share your interpretation of the poem?

20k ## Use commas to separate directly quoted material from explanatory expressions.

Expressions that signal direct quotations, such as "he said," "she replied," and so on, vary widely in form and position (they may be positioned at the beginning, in the middle, or at the end of a quotation). Wherever such expressions occur, they must be separated from the quotation, most often with commas.

Reverend Tobias said, "State lotteries are nothing but state-sanctioned gambling."

"Lotteries, however, provide revenues that can be used to support education," **Representative Fulwiller noted.**

"If we ignore the lottery as a way of increasing revenues," **he added,** "our state's finances will continue to suffer."

201 **Use commas with numbers containing four or more digits, dates, addresses, place names, and titles and academic degrees, according to the conventions shown below.**

▼ *Numbers:* Place a comma after every three digits, moving from right to left.

1,399   2,776,100

▼ *Dates:* In month-day-year order, a comma separates the day and year. If a date including month, day, and year appears in the middle of a sentence, a comma also follows the year.

No commas are required in the day-month-year order or when only the month and year are used.

George Washington was born on February 22, 1732.

On October 30, 1905, Tsar Nicholas issued the October Manifesto, guaranteeing individual liberties.

Sixty percent of Hiroshima was destroyed by the atomic bomb dropped on 6 August 1945.

Hitler annexed Austria in March 1938.

▼ *Addresses:* When an address is written in a sentence, separate each element with a comma. If the address appears in the middle of a sentence, a comma must follow the last element.

She moved to **719 Maple Avenue, Cleveland, Ohio,** shortly after the Thanksgiving holidays.

The Convention Center in **Landover, Maryland** was the site of the "Welcome Home" concert honoring Vietnam veterans.

The Olympics in **Munich, West Germany,** were plagued by terrorism.

▼ *Titles and academic degrees:* Use commas to set off these nonrestrictive elements.

At Honors Convocation, Rebecca Kingsley, **professor emerita,** presented the scholarship that bears her name.

William Leeds, **M.D.,** serves on the Marion County Health Board.

————————— *Exercise*

Supply periods, question marks, exclamation points, and commas in the following sentences. Make sure that a rule guides your placement of each punctuation mark.

1. CBS NBC and ABC America's largest networks are now advertising programs regularly on small independent cable networks

2. The novel originally priced at $2595 did not sell well but sales increased when the price was reduced to $1795

3. Address women as Ms unless you are certain that they prefer Mrs or Miss

4. Should we send our order to the Chicago Illinois distribution center or to the Atlanta Georgia center

5. Angered that her glares did not quiet the jabbering child the old woman finally shouted "Shut up"

6. The tour guide concerned that he adapt himself to the visitors' preferences asked if they wanted to spend more time in the chapel

7. The San Francisco earthquake of April 18 1906 measured 8.3 on the Richter scale but the March 2 1933 earthquake in Japan measured 8.9

8. Much to my surprise the word *calf* is used to describe young cattle elephants antelopes rhinoceroses hippopotamuses and whales

9. Even though he was working without State Department authorization Rev Jesse Jackson secured the release of Robert Goodman Jr from Syria

10. Did you know that the West Indian island Jamaica is smaller (4244 square miles) than Connecticut

11. Because she was aware of prejudice against women Amadine Aurore Dupin published her novels under the name George Sand

12. After four months of work the restorers gave up their attempts to salvage the Venetian fresco

13. Peonies irises roses and day lilies are among Americans' favorite perennial not annual flowers

14. To be competitive in a declining market American auto manufacturers slashed interest rates and offered special rebates

15. The Tyrannosaurus Rex with teeth that measured six inches long was the fiercest of the meat-eating dinosaurs

16. Passengers who need special assistance are always asked to board airplanes before other travelers

17. Ironically taking out a mortgage is considered more stressful than having a foreclosure on a mortgage

18. Many taxpayers choose to use the "short form"; however taxpayers who wish to itemize deductions must use the "long form"

19. The mineral calcium is needed to develop and maintain bones and teeth but it is lacking in many diets

20. The film *Gandhi* begins with the leader's assassination on January 30 1948 and then recounts his life in a long flashback

21   UNNECESSARY COMMAS

Too many commas in sentences can be as confusing as too few. To avoid excessive use of commas, observe the following rules.

21a   Do not use a comma before a coordinating conjunction that joins only two words, phrases, or dependent clauses.

Isak Dinesen married a Danish baron⁄and subsequently moved to Africa. [No comma with compound verb *married and moved*.]
I asked for advice first from my classmates⁄and then from Professor Bakerman. [No comma between two prepositional phrases joined by *and*.]

21b   Do not use a comma between subjects, verbs, and complements unless specific rules require that commas be used.

In the simplest sentences, no commas should break the subject-verb-complement pattern. When other information is added—appositives, nonrestrictive clauses, coordinate modifiers—commas may be necessary, but only as required by specific comma rules.

The angry soprano walked out of the rehearsal.
[No comma with subject-verb pattern.]
The angry soprano, **unhappy with the conductor,** walked out of the rehearsal.
[Nonrestrictive appositive set off by commas.]
Our university's pole vaulter was a strong contender for the title.
[No comma with verb-complement pattern.]
Our university's pole vaulter was, **by general agreement,** a strong contender for the title.
[Parenthetical comments, in this case a nonrestrictive prepositional phrase, require commas; see Section 20g.]

21c   Do not use a comma before the first or after the last item in a series.

Carla began attending exercise classes to build her stamina, to lose weight, and to tone her muscles.
[Comma would interrupt verb-complement pattern.]
Time, U.S. News and World Report, and *Newsweek* are the most popular weekly magazines in America.
[Comma would interrupt subject-verb pattern.]

21d   Do not use commas to separate adjectives or adverbs that cumulatively modify the same word.

When adjectives or adverbs work together to create meaning, they should *not* be separated by commas.

Four small red candles burned on the mantelpiece.
[No commas because *red* modifies *candles, small* modifies *red candles,* and *four* modifies *small red candles.*]

21e   Do not use a comma between an adjective or an adverb and the word it modifies.

An especially talented pianist opened the recital.
[No commas because the adverb *especially* modifies the adjective *talented,* which modifies the noun *pianist.*]

21f   Do not use commas to set off restrictive elements in sentences.

Barbra Streisand's song "Evergreen" won an Oscar in 1977.
[No commas because song title is necessary for sentence clarity. (Streisand had another Oscar-winning song in a different year.)]

21g   Do not use a comma before an expression in parentheses.

When a comma is necessary with a parenthetical expression, it should follow the closing parenthesis.

In hopes of graduating early, Brian took six English classes (English 307, 320, 337, 339, 412, and 445) but he could not manage the reading.

21h

Do not use a comma before either an indirect or a direct quotation introduced by *that*.

Marcos said, that he will someday return to the Philippines.

But: Marcos said, "I will someday return to the Philippines."

Wasn't it Winston Churchill who said that "an iron curtain has descended across the Continent"?

21i

Do not place a comma after either a question mark or an exclamation point in a direct quotation.

Question marks and exclamation points replace the commas that are frequently required with direct quotations.

"Will we never recover from the wounds created by the Vietnam War?," asked Representative Martin.

Exercise

Remove unnecessary commas from the following sentences. Be ready to explain why each comma you delete is not needed.

1. Sandy Koufax was named Most Valuable Player of the World Series in 1963, and in 1965.

2. Two American cities, (Chicago, and New York City) each employ more than ten thousand police officers.

3. Four, very, small cars can park in the spaces normally allotted to three full-sized cars.

4. The geriatrician said, the symptoms suggest that Uncle Rupert probably has Alzheimer's disease.

5. Chicago's O'Hare International Airport, is the busiest airport in the United States.

6. The aging movie theater, which was once the small city's pride, needed extensive, expensive, renovation.

7. The playwright, Sophocles, is known for perfecting the form, of classical Greek tragedy.

8. Since early 1982, the copper penny has been gradually replaced, by a copper-plated zinc coin.

9. "How can we expect students, who have never taken calculus, to perform well on this portion of the exam?," Professor Carino asked.

10. California, Pennsylvania, Illinois, Michigan, and Ohio, each distributes over $1.5 million annually in unemployment benefits.

22   SEMICOLONS (;)

The *semicolon* most often functions like a period, separating independent clauses. Though it can in some specialized instances replace a comma, the semicolon should not be used routinely as a substitute for a comma.

22a   Use a semicolon to join closely related independent clauses that are not connected by a coordinating conjunction.

In this usage, the semicolon most clearly functions like a period. As a result, make certain that each clause is, in fact, independent.

Take care of the children; let the adults take care of themselves.

22b   Use a semicolon to join independent clauses that are linked by a conjunctive adverb, or separate the clauses with a period.

The defense attorney's closing statements were brilliantly presented; however, the facts of the case favored the prosecution.

22c   Use a semicolon to separate three or more items in a series when one or more of the items contain internal commas.

In their essays, students commented on *The Fire Next Time,* an essay-novel by James Baldwin; *Soul on Ice,* a polemic by Eldridge Cleaver; and *Anger and Beyond,* a collection of critical essays edited by Herbert Hill.

22d   Do not use a semicolon in place of a comma with a subordinate clause.

Although revisions of the tax code will eliminate many deductions, most Americans will benefit from a reduction in their overall tax rate.

22e   Do not introduce a list or a clarifying phrase with a semicolon.

The colon (:) and the dash (—) are traditionally used to introduce a list or a clarification. The semicolon is not interchangeable with these marks of punctuation.

A number of long-distance services vied for consumer's business: AT&T, MCI, and Sprint.

23

COLONS (:)

The *colon* is a formal way to introduce a list or a clarification. The colon means "Note what follows." Use colons selectively to add clarity to your writing.

23a

Use a colon to introduce a list.

The items in the series should never be direct objects, predicate nouns, predicate adjectives, or objects of prepositions. An independent clause must precede the colon.

As suggested in Section 22e, a dash may be used in place of the colon.

American theater and film have produced a number of notable acting families: Barrymore, Bridges, Fairbanks, Fonda, and Sheen.

23b

Selectively use a colon between two independent clauses when the second explains the first.

The second clause may start with either a lower-case letter (as shown here) or with a capital letter.

Except for differences in the subject matter, the rules of grammar are like the laws of chemistry: they are generalizations describing accepted principles of operation.

23c

Use a colon to emphasize an appositive that comes at the end of a sentence.

Marlowe and Shakespeare introduced the dramatic use of blank verse: unrhymed iambic pentameter.

23d

Use a colon in place of a comma to introduce or emphasize a long quotation.

Churchill concluded an eloquent speech with this visionary statement: "Out of the depths of sorrow and sacrifice will be born again the glory of mankind."

23e

Use a colon between numerals designating hours and minutes, after formal salutations in formal or official correspondence, between titles and subtitles, between chapter and verse in Biblical citations, and between city and publisher in works-cited entries.

(See "Documenting Sources" in Chapter 14.)

The speaker was scheduled to arrive on a 9:40 A.M. flight from Los Angeles.

Dear Mr. Harper: Dear Professor Smithson:

Some Sort of Epic Grandeur: The Life of F. Scott Fitzgerald

Isaiah 12:2–4

Cambridge: Harvard UP

Boston: Houghton Mifflin

23f   **Do not use a colon between a verb and its complement or between a preposition and its object.**

Jerrid's favorite restaurants are⸜ Richard's Townhouse, The Broken Blossom, and Fernucchi's.

Exercise

Revise these sentences, using semicolons or colons.

1. Two lizards found in the southwestern United States and northern Mexico are venomous. They are the Gila monster and the Mexican bearded lizard.

2. The Democratic party considered five cities for its national convention. Those cities were Dallas, Texas, Chicago, Illinois, Atlanta, Georgia, Washington, D.C., and Los Angeles, California.

3. Mark Spitz was an outstanding Olympic competitor. However, he was only an adequate Olympic commentator.

4. Infertility counselor Roselle Shubin made this epigrammatic comment on parenthood, "There is more to being a mother than giving birth, and more to being a father than impregnating a woman."

5. Morocco, Algeria, Libya, Tunisia, and Egypt border the Mediterranean Sea. These are the only African countries that do.

24   **DASHES (—)**

A *dash* (made in typing with two hyphens with no space between or before or after them) serves a number of purposes in punctuating sentences. But it should be used with restraint because if overused the dash can become distracting and will lose its impact.

24a   **Use dashes to set off appositives in midsentence that contain commas.**

Five states—Indiana, Iowa, Kentucky, Missouri, and Wisconsin—share borders with Illinois.

24b   **Use a dash to set off a series that introduces or ends a sentence.**

Beaumont, Fletcher, Jonson, Kyd, Marlowe, and Webster—these dramatists were respected contemporaries of Shakespeare.

24c
Use dashes, singly or in pairs, to set off interpretations, evaluations, or interruptions.

> This answer—if we can call it an answer—is completely meaningless.
> This answer is completely meaningless—if we can call it an answer.

25
PARENTHESES (( ))

Parentheses, used in pairs to set off secondary information in sentences, can foster clarity. Use them selectively, however, because they break the flow of sentences and if overused make your writing seem choppy and fragmented.

25a
Use parentheses to enclose an explanation, qualification, or example that is not essential to the meaning of the sentence.

> Phnom Penh is the capital of Kampuchea (known to most Americans as Cambodia).

25b
Use parentheses around numbers or letters that identify a sequence within a sentence.

> Withdrawing money from an automatic-teller machine requires following seven simple steps: (1) insert your validated bank card; (2) type in your personal access code; (3) identify the account you want to take the money from; (4) indicate the amount of money you desire; (5) open the drawer and remove the money; (6) indicate that the transaction is complete; and (7) remove your bank card and the withdrawal slip.

———————————— *Exercise*

Using dashes and parentheses, revise these sentences.

1. In 1755, roughly 4,000 Acadians settlers in Nova Scotia, Canada, were forcibly relocated to Louisiana.

2. Sagamore Hill, Theodore Roosevelt's home at Oyster Bay, New York, became a national memorial in 1962.

3. Mali, Niger, and Nigeria these are the countries through which the river Niger flows.

4. Changing a tire requires following five relatively simple steps: 1. turn off the car's engine and engage the emergency brake, 2. jack up the car on the appropriate side, 3. remove the damaged tire, 4. put on the spare, and 5. lower the car and remove the jack.

5. Margaret Higgins Sanger 1883–1966 led the birth-control movement in America during the early years of the twentieth century.

26   QUOTATION MARKS ("/")

Quotation marks are most commonly used to enclose direct quotations (but see also "Quoting Sources" in Chapter 14). The most important issues with quotation marks are accuracy in recording other people's comments and accuracy in the placement of other punctuation marks.

26a   Place commas and periods *before* quotation marks.

My favorite story, "The Fall of the House of Usher," is by Poe.

26b   Place colons and semicolons *after* quotation marks.

Shelley creates a vivid image of a decayed civilization in his poem "Ozymandias": "Round the decay / Of that colossal wreck, boundless and bare / The lone and level sands stretch far away."

For the university newspaper, Rachel wrote "The Dilemma of Drug Testing"; the article won the school's journalism award in the spring.

26c   If a quotation is a question or an exclamation, place the question mark or exclamation point *before* the quotation marks.

If the whole sentence in which a quotation (or an exclamation) appears is a question (or an exclamation) but the quotation is not, place the question mark (or exclamation point) after the quotation marks.

I can't remember who wrote the ballad "What'll I Do?"

Were we supposed to read "What It Takes to Be a Leader"?

26d   Use single quotation marks ('/') around material that would be enclosed by full quotation marks if it were not already within a quotation.

Jeremy said, "Although 'Dover Beach' is one of Matthew Arnold's greatest poems, it is not one of my favorites."

27   BRACKETS ([/])

Brackets are used to enclose an editorial or a clarifying explanation or comment inserted into a direct quotation.

Richardson commented, "Using both systems [the U.S. Customary System and the International Metric System] has caused considerable confusion for American consumers and has put U.S. industries at a trade disadvantage."

28

ELLIPSES (. . .)

Ellipses, three spaced periods, are used to indicate the omission of one or more words from a quotation. The three periods, or points, that form the ellipsis are considered a unit. When the omission comes at the end of a sentence, a fourth point must be added as end punctuation. When a comma is required, it follows the ellipsis.

28a

Use ellipsis points to show where words have been omitted from a direct quotation.

Omit extraneous material—like parenthetical expressions or unnecessary clarifications—but do not leave out material if the omission changes the meaning of the original text.

Original Quotation	Elliptical Quotation
Lincoln's antislavery views, clarified in the Republican party platform of 1860, served to alienate not only the residents of southern states but also southern sympathizers in the North.	According to Walter Holtmire, "Lincoln's antislavery views . . . served to alienate not only the residents of southern states but also southern sympathizers in the North."

Use ellipsis points very selectively to indicate hesitation, a trailing off of thought, or an incomplete statement.

The deathbed scene in James Brooks's *Terms of Endearment* is . . . manipulative.

Observing the Rules of Punctuation: Review Exercise

Correct the punctuation errors in the following sentences. Be ready to identify the rules that guided your thinking.

1. The Internal Revenue Service IRS is responsible for administering the tax laws passed by Congress

2. From 1791 to 1862 the US government relied on tariffs to generate income in 1862 however Congress enacted the first income tax law to pay for the debts of the Civil War

3. Did you know that income taxes were not universally instituted until 1913

4. Following the 1986 tax law only a few major deductions will be allowed mortgage payments state and local taxes medical expenses and charitable contributions

5. Nevada South Dakota Texas Washington and Wyoming these states do not impose a corporate tax based on net income

6. The IRS operates from its various headquarters one national office in Washington seven regional offices sixty-three district offices and tax service centers and processes roughly 200 million returns annually

7. Beginning in 1943 taxes were withheld from wages a plan that increased the number of people who equitably paid taxes

8. According to new tax laws corporate rates will drop from 46 percent to 34 percent however a minimum tax will also be imposed to prevent major companies from paying no taxes

9. The nation's first sales taxes enacted in 1812 affected consumers of only four kinds of commodities gold silver jewelry and watches

10. Did you know that it was Benjamin Franklin who said But in this world nothing can be said to be certain except death and taxes

11. James Otis spoke the sentence that became a catch phrase of the American Revolution Taxation without representation is tyranny

12. In 1985 the IRS collected a total of $742,871,541,000 in taxes a figure so large it is hard to envision

13. Most Americans do not object to paying taxes many however object to how the tax money is spent

14. Various tables Schedule X Y or Z are used to compute the taxes of people with incomes of more than $50000

15. Taxpayers who wish to appeal a tax charge must follow four steps 1 discuss the charge with a local appeal's office 2 submit a written protest 3 wait for a judgment 4 pay the charge or file yet another appeal with the District Claims Court

Observing the Rules of Mechanics

Mechanical errors in the use of capitalization, italics, quotation marks, apostrophes, hyphenation, number style, abbreviations, and spelling distract readers from the content of your writing. Heeding certain rules as you prepare the final copy of a paper will help ensure that your reader's attention is focused not on preventable mechanical errors but on what you have to say.

29 CAPITALIZATION

29a Capitalize the first word of every sentence and of every line in conventional poetry.

Using a word processor saves time during revision.

Standardized tests present a major problem for minorities: they do not allow for cultural differences.

Whenas in silks my Julia goes
Then, then, methinks, how sweetly flows
That liquefaction of her clothes. . . .
> —Robert Herrick,
> "Upon Julia's Clothes"

29b Distinguish between *proper names*, which require capitalization, and *common names*, which do not.

I left the assignment in my professor's mailbox.
But: I left the assignment in Professor Sheldon's mailbox.
I worked in summer stock to gain experience.
But: I worked at the Summer Festival Theater to gain experience.

29c In titles, capitalize the first and last words and all important words.

As a general rule, capitalize all nouns, pronouns, verbs, adjectives, and adverbs. In addition, capitalize all prepositions and conjunctions of four or more letters. In words with two-part titles, the first word of the subtitle is also capitalized, regardless of the word's length.

Zora Neale Hurston's *Their Eyes Were Watching God*
Derrick Ashford's "Eighteenth-Century Comedy on the Modern Stage"
Marya Mannes's "TV Advertising: The Splitting Image"

29d   Capitalize the names of people, races, nationalities, languages, and places, whether used as nouns or as adjectives.

In American usage, the terms *black* and *white* are not capitalized. Native American, Hispanic, and Asian are capitalized.

Thomas Paine	Caucasian
Malaysia	Danish customs
Nairobi	Greek festival

29e   Capitalize the names of historical and cultural periods; historical, political, and cultural events; and documents.

the Age of Reason	the Emancipation Proclamation
the Romantic Movement	Elizabethan drama
the Battle of Hastings	Prohibition

29f   Capitalize the names of days, months, and secular and religious holidays.

Thursday	the Fourth of July
September	Hanukkah

29g   Capitalize the names of businesses and other organizations and government agencies and offices.

General Electric Company	National Rifle Association
Phi Delta Kappa	United States Senate

29h   Capitalize the names of schools, colleges, and universities; academic departments; specific sources; and degrees—but not general references.

Amherst College   [But *college classes*]
Thomas Jefferson High School   [But *high school teachers*]
Department of Education   [But *department meeting*]
Sociology 245   [But *sociology course*]
Bachelor of Arts [But *baccalaureate degree*]

29i   Capitalize the names of religions and their followers and religious terms for sacred persons, books, and events.

God	Islamic law
Buddha	Christian traditions
the Koran	the Immaculate Conception

556

29j

Capitalize titles that precede proper names.

> Doctor Erica Weinburg
> Secretary of State James Baker
> Professor Leon Edel

> Prime Minister Winston Churchill
> President Abraham Lincoln

A title used alone or following a proper name is not capitalized.

A college professor is the catalyst in a classroom.
Jimmy Carter, the former president, has contributed even in retirement to the benefit of the country.

29k

Capitalize nouns designating family relationships only when they are used as proper names or when they precede proper names.

After arthroscopic surgery, Mother's chances of leading a normal life improved.
I arrived at the apartment before Uncle Will got home from work.

Do not capitalize common nouns that name family relationships, even when the noun is preceded by a personal pronoun in the possessive case.

After arthroscopic surgery, my mother's life improved.
I arrived at the apartment before my uncle got home from work.
Never underestimate the influence of brothers and sisters.

29l

Capitalize *A.M.* and *P.M.* and *A.D.* and *B.C.*; capitalize the call letters of radio and television stations; capitalize abbreviated forms of business, organization, and document names. (Periods may or may not be required, according to convention; consult a dictionary.)

705 B.C.	ERA
A.D. 1066	WPFR radio
4:30 A.M.	KTVI television
4:30 P.M.	IBM

29m

Capitalize the first word of a direct quotation if the quotation is a complete sentence or an interjection that can stand alone.

Mr. Bennett remarked, "Though ornate by present standards, Baroque sculpture remains aesthetically pleasing."
Carla, surprised by the harsh criticism, responded, "Oh."

Exercise

Supply capitalization in the following sentences, noting the rule that guides each correction.

1. the elizabethan period, a cultural and aesthetic awakening in england,

   began roughly a century after the italian renaissance.

2. yom kippur, the holiest jewish holiday, was observed on thursday, september 15, this year.

3. although my mother and aunt beatrice are both normally critical television viewers, they both love *the young and the restless.*

4. an mba from harvard is an excellent passport to a lucrative job on wall street or with a fortune 500 firm.

5. students in french secondary schools are expected to learn english as well as one other foreign language.

6. james baker, the secretary of state, travels extensively in europe and the middle east for the department of state.

7. the reverend thomas r. fitzgerald serves as president of st. louis university, a catholic university enrolling over eleven thousand students.

8. who was it who said, "i cried all the way to the bank"?

9. the abbreviation ira could refer to the irish republican army or the international reading association.

10. dorothy parker once described katharine hepburn's performance in a play with this caustic sentence: "she ran the whole gamut of emotions from a to b."

30   ITALICS

In print, *italics,* slanted type, is used to give words distinction or emphasis. In handwritten or typed manuscript, the same effects are achieved using underlining.

30a   **Italicize the titles of books, periodicals, newspapers, pamphlets, plays, films, television series (but not individual programs), radio programs, long poems, long musical compositions, record albums, paintings, and sculpture.**

Marcel Proust's *Swann's Way* (book)
The *Washington Post* (newspaper)

NCTE's *Essentials of English* (pamphlet)
Oscar Wilde's *The Importance of Being Ernest* (play)
Sidney Pollack's *Out of Africa* (film)
Norman Lear's *All in the Family* (television program)
Casey Kasem's *Top-Twenty Count Down* (radio program)
Walt Whitman's *Leaves of Grass* (long poem)
Tchaikovsky's *The Nutcracker Suite* (long musical composition)
Paul Simon's *Graceland* (album)
Pablo Picasso's *Three Musicians* (painting)
George Segal's *Girl in Doorway* (sculpture)

30b   **Italicize the names of individual ships, trains, airplanes, and spacecraft.**

Jacques Cousteau's *Calypso* (ship)
the *Orient Express* (train)
Air Force One (airplane)
Voyager 1 (spacecraft)

30c   **Italicize foreign words and phrases.**

Confined to a hospital bed, Rachel had to vote *in absentia*.

Many foreign terms have been assimilated into standard usage and, as a result, do not require italics. Consult a dictionary for guidance.

30d   **Italicize words used as words, letters used as letters, numbers used as numbers, and symbols used as symbols.**

French contains two variations of *you*, one formal and one informal.
The letters *a* and *e* used to be printed *æ*.
Make sure that you distinguish your *1*s from your *7*s.
The ampersand, *&*, is unacceptable in formal prose.

30e   **Italicize words selectively for emphasis.**

In formal prose, this is not considered good usage.

Jason played the song *twenty-three* times in a row!

31   **QUOTATION MARKS ("/")**

Quotation marks are most commonly used to set off direct quotations, but they have a mechanical use as well.

31a   **Use quotation marks with the titles of brief works or parts of complete works.**

"Winning Hearts Through Minds" in *Time* (article)
Ernest Hemingway's "Old Man at the Bridge" (short story)
Gerard Manley Hopkins's "God's Grandeur" (poem)

Stephen Jay Gould's "Darwinism Defined: The Difference Between Fact and Theory" (essay)

Manhattan Transfer's "Tuxedo Junction" (song)

"The Spirit of Scholarship" in Richard Altick's *The Art of Literary Research* (chapter in a book)

"Captain Tuttle" from *M*A*S*H* (episode of television program)

Exercise

Insert italics (underlining) and quotation marks in the following sentences. Remember to place them accurately in relation to other punctuation.

1. Paul Conrad won Pulitzer Prizes for editorial cartooning when he worked for two different publications: the Denver Post and the Los Angeles Times.

2. Grammies for best song and best album went to Tina Turner for What's Love Got to Do With It? and Private Dancer, respectively.

3. To demonstrate aerodynamic possibilities, engineers developed the Gossamer Albatross, an airplane propelled by peddling.

4. Blattela germanica is an eloquent sounding term to use when you mean cockroach!

5. Stuart called here sixteen times while you were gone this weekend.

6. On your final charts, please write female and male rather than ♀ and ♂.

7. A View to a Death, a pivotal chapter in Golding's novel Lord of the Flies, offers a vision of primitive, ritualistic execution.

8. In an article titled A Man With Titanic Vision, Discover magazine honored Bob Ballard as its 1986 Scientist of the Year.

9. Many American musicals have plays as their source, among them Hello, Dolly (The Matchmaker), My Fair Lady (Pygmalion), and Cabaret (I Am a Camera).

10. Kurtz, a character in Conrad's novel The Heart of Darkness, has re-emerged in T. S. Eliot's Hollow Men, a brief poem, and Apocalypse Now, a long film.

32   APOSTROPHES (')

The *apostrophe* has three general uses: to indicate the possessive case of nouns and some pronouns, to indicate the omission of letters and numbers, and to indicate the plural of letters, numbers, and words used as words.

32a   **Use an apostrophe and an *s* to form the possessive of a singular noun or indefinite pronoun.**

Oprah Winfrey's guests
somebody's car
the men's dressing room
a month's rental fee
Harry Jones's first flight

32b   **Use only an apostrophe, without an *s*, when a noun is plural.**

scientists' projections
the Joneses' first flight

32c   **To show joint possession, add an apostrophe and an *s* to the last name in the group. To show individual possession, add an apostrophe and an *s* to each name in the group.**

Lerner and Loewe's musical reputation [Joint possession]
Shakespeare's and Marlowe's dramatic innovations [Individual possession]

32d   **Use an apostrophe to show the omission of letters and numbers.**

| couldn't | could not | there's | there is |
| I'll | I will (*or* I shall) | the '84 Olympics | the 1984 Olympics |

32e   **Use an *s* to form the plurals of numbers, letters, and words used as words.**

Kirsten received four *10*s during the final round of competition.
Her *s*'s look like *8*s.
His writing was cluttered with *very*s, *really*s, and *especially*s.

33   HYPHENATION (-)

Hyphens are used for two purposes: to divide a multisyllable word at the end of a line and to join two or more words of a compound.

33a   **Hyphenate a word that must continue on a new line**

Place hyphens between the syllables of words that must be divided (if necessary, consult a dictionary to see where a break may be made). Do not break one-syllable words or leave fewer than three letters at the end or beginning of any line. Do not hyphenate proper names.

The hurricane battered the coastline, damaging property in four cities.

33b **Hyphenate compound words according to convention; consult a dictionary.**

Some compound words are hyphenated; others are "closed up," written as one word; still others are written as two words.

Hyphenated	*Closed Up*	*Two Words*
sister-in-law	applesauce	wedding ring
razzle-dazzle	blackboard	living room
master-at-arms	landowner	free fall

33c **Hyphenate words that precede a noun and combine to modify it.**

heart-to-heart talk
off-the-cuff comments
never-ending problems
When the modifiers follow the noun, no hyphens are necessary.
The comments were off the cuff.
His problems were never ending.

33d **Hyphenate compound numbers ranging from twenty-one to ninety-nine; hyphenate fractions.**

a test score of sixty-seven
two-thirds of the voters

33e **Hyphenate words using the prefixes *all-*, *ex-*, and *self-*; hyphenate words using the suffix *-elect.***

all-consuming pride
ex-wife
self-motivated student
secretary-elect of the city council

33f **Hyphenate a compound consisting of a prefix and a proper noun.**

anti-Iranian
un-American
pre-Enlightenment
post-Modern

33g **Hyphenate words formed with a prefix if the unhyphenated form would be a homonym, a word with the same spelling but a different meaning.**

re-cover (to cover again)   recover (to regain)
re-lease (to lease again)   release (to let go)

34   NUMBERS

34a   **Spell out numbers that can be expressed in one or two words.**

thirty-two source cards   twenty-six thousand dollars
five million voters   fourteen hundred miles

34b   **Use digits for numbers that would require three or more words if spelled out.**

319 graduates (*not* three hundred and nineteen)
101 pages (*not* one hundred and one)

34c   **Spell out a number that begins a sentence, or revise the sentence so that it does not open with a number.**

Not: 412 art dealers attended the convention.
But: Four hundred and twelve art dealers attended the convention.
Or: There were 412 art dealers at the convention.

34d   **Use digits for addresses, dates, divisions of books and plays, dollars and cents, identification numbers, percentages, scores, and times.**

2300 North 12th Street (address)
11 January 1912 or January 11, 1912 (dates)
700 B.C., A.D. 700 (dates)
Chapter 17, Volume 2, Act 1, Scene 2 (divisions of books and plays)
$7.95, $1,230,000, $4.9 million (dollar amounts)
314-77-2248, UTC 41 69490 (identification numbers)
81 percent, 3 percent (percentages)
117 to 93 (scores)
6:10 A.M., 2:35 P.M. (times)

35   ABBREVIATIONS

Abbreviations, shortened forms of words, should be used sparingly. Any abbreviations you use should be familiar to your readers, and they must be appropriate to the writing context. To double-check conventional abbreviations, consult a dictionary.

35a   **Abbreviate titles that precede or follow people's names.**

Wiliam D. Grenville, Jr.   Judith Haverford, Ph.D.
Ms. Abigail Hample   Rebecca Blair, M.D.
Dr. Terence McDonald   the Rev. Stephen Pierson

35b

Use standard abbreviations and acronyms for names of organizations, corporations, and countries. Many of these abbreviations do not require periods.

Organizations: AFL-CIO, YMCA, FBI
Corporations: GTE, NBC, GM
Countries: USA, (*or* U.S.A.), USSR (*or* U.S.S.R.), UK (*or* U.K.)

35c

Before using an abbreviation that might be unfamiliar to some readers, spell out the complete name or term at its first appearance.

Idaho State University—located in Pocatello, Idaho—is a state-supported university serving over three thousand students. ISU offers especially strong programs in health-related professions.

35d

Use standard abbreviations with times, dates, and specific numbers. Use the dollar sign with specific amounts.

Note the placement of the abbreviations *A.M., P.M., B.C.,* and *A.D.*

$1,245.78	500 B.C.
11:20 A.M.	A.D. 496
4:15 P.M.	part no. 339 (*or* No.)

35e

Use standard abbreviations in works-cited entries.

(See "Documenting Sources" in Chapter 15.)

Abbreviation	Meaning
ed.	editor, edition
et al.	and others
rev.	revised
rpt.	reprint
trans.	translator, translated by
vol.	volume

35f

Use Latin abbreviations sparingly in prose.

Latin Abbreviation	English Equivalent
cf. (*confer*)	compare
e.g. (*exempli gratia*)	for example
et al. (*et alii*)	and others
etc. (*et cetera*)	and others, and so on
i.e. (*id est*)	that is
n.b. (*nota bene*)	note well

35g

In most writing, do not abbreviate business designations (unless the company does), units of measurement, days of the week, months, courses of instruction, divisions of books and plays, geographical names (except in addresses), or personal names.

Not	But
Co., Inc.	Company, Incorporated
lb, tbs.	pound, tablespoon
Fri., Oct.	Friday, October
psych., Eng.	psychology, English
chap., vol.	chapter, volume
L.A., VA	Los Angeles, Virginia
Wm., Robt.	William, Robert

Exercise

Insert necessary apostrophes and hyphens in the following sentences. In addition, correct the number style and forms of abbreviations.

1. 6 members of the committee returned the questionnaire, refusing to comment on MSUs drug testing program.

2. The suicide that ends Act four of *Hedda Gabler* shocked many narrow minded critics.

3. Doctor Connelly, a graduate of U. of TX at Austin, spoke to our faculty on Oct. 15, 1986.

4. To attract first rate teachers to our public schools, we will have to increase teachers salaries.

5. Stephen Sondheims *Sunday in the Park with George* presents a neo Impressionist view of human relations and art.

6. Karin was delighted to receive 2 *8*s and 2 *9*s on her performance until she realized that *15*s were possible.

7. The post Civil War period was a time of exploitation and manipulation in the South.

8. The Rams won the game thirty-six to seven, having passed for one hundred and fifty four yards and having made seventy four percent of the games interceptions.

9. My father in laws Social Security check ($24967) covers slightly over two thirds of his monthly expenses.

10. The president elect of the N.C.T.E. felt that her work would require working with a state of the art computer and printer, so she bought the pair.

Exercise

Revise the following paragraph so that it is mechanically correct and consistent with conventional usage. Errors in capitalization, italics, quotation marks, apostrophes, hyphenation, number style, and abbreviations are present in the paragraph.

1600 Pennsylvania Ave., Washington, District of Columbia, is perhaps the *most famous* address in the U.S. At that site is the "White House," the residence of the President and his family. The design for the Original house was selected by Pres. Washington and Pierre L'Enfant, the french born designer of the city, and the cornerstone was set on Oct. 13, 1792. In 1814, the building was razed during a Battle of the war of 1812, and in subsequent years the interior of the structure had to be rebuilt. But the original design was heavily modified. As Mrs. John N. Pearce notes in The White House: An Historic Guide Ever changing personalities and styles of living and building have inspired the continuing metamorphosis that has marked the history of the White House. Over the years, the "White House" has served as both the official and the private residence of the first family. The 1st floor's rooms are used for public functions like Receptions and State Dinners, and its expansive, public rooms are decorated with such famous artwork as Gilbert Stuarts portrait George Washington. The limited access rooms on the second and third floors are used by the presidents family and friends. In all, the "White House" has one hundred and thirty-two rooms.

36 SPELLING

Errors in spelling, like other mechanical errors, interfere with communication because readers notice and are distracted by them. To avoid such distractions in your writing, develop good spelling habits. If you are a naturally good speller, then you have only to refresh your memory of common spelling rules. If you are a weak speller, then you need to hone your spelling skills.

Do not worry about spelling while you are planning and working on early drafts of your papers. If you interrupt your writing to check the spelling of a word, you might lose a thought that you cannot recapture. Instead make a mark near the word in question—a checkmark in the margin, the abbreviation *sp.* above the word, or a circle around the word—and continue your writing. Then, when your final draft is complete, look up the spelling of the words you have marked. This approach—checking spelling during revision—will allow you to write with a sense of continuity and attend to potential problems before typing your final copy.

36a Review Spelling Rules

Form plurals according to the pattern of the singular word.

▼ When words end in a consonant plus *o*, add *-es*.

fresco	frescoes
motto	mottoes
tomato	tomatoes

Exceptions

auto	autos
dynamo	dynamos
piano	pianos

▼ When words end in a vowel plus *o*, add *-s*.

cameo	cameos
radio	radios
studio	studios

▼ When words end in a consonant plus *y*, change the *y* to *i* and add *-es*.

daisy	daisies
remedy	remedies
victory	victories

▼ When words end in a vowel plus *y*, add *-s*.

attorney	attorneys
key	keys
survey	surveys

▼ When words end in *s*, *ss*, *sh*, *ch*, *x*, or *z*, add *-es*.

bonus	bonuses	match	matches
overpass	overpasses	tax	taxes
wish	wishes	buzz	buzzes

▼ When words that are proper names end in *y*, add *-s*.

the Bellamys
the three Marys
two Germanys

Add prefixes, such as *dis-*, *mis-*, *non-*, *pre-*, *re-*, and *un-*, without altering the spelling of the root word.

similar	dissimilar
spell	misspell
restrictive	nonrestrictive
historic	prehistoric
capture	recapture
natural	unnatural

Add suffixes according to the spelling of both the root word and the suffix.

▼ When words end with a silent *e* and the suffix begins with a consonant, retain the *e*.

achieve	achievement
definite	definitely
refine	refinement

Exceptions

argue	argument
awe	awful
true	truly

▼ When words end with a silent *e* and the suffix begins with a vowel, drop the *e*.

accommodate	accommodating
grieve	grievance
size	sizable
tolerate	tolerating

▼ When words end with a silent *e* that is preceded by a "soft" *c* or *g* and the suffix begins with a vowel, retain the *e*.

notice	noticeable	singe	singeing
trace	traceable	outrage	outrageous
change	changeable		

▼ When a one-syllable word ends with a single consonant and contain[s]
one vowel and the suffix begins with a vowel, double the final conson[ant].

blot	blotted
clip	clipping
fit	fitting
skip	skipper
stop	stopping
trip	tripped

Distinguish between words spelled with *ie* and *ei*.

The order of the vowels *ie* and *ei* is explained in this familiar poem:

Write *i* before *e*
Except after *c*
Or when sounded like *ay*
As in *neighbor* and *weigh.*

These are some exceptions to this rule:

counterfeit	leisure
either	neither
foreign	seizure
forfeit	sovereign
height	weird

36b   Improving Your Spelling Skills

Use a full-sized dictionary to check meanings and spellings of words that are often mistaken for each other.

A standard dictionary provides definitions that will help you distinguish between *affect* and *effect, elicit* and *illicit,* and other confusing word pairs.

Use a spelling dictionary for easy reference when you know a word's meaning but are unsure of its spelling.

Spelling dictionaries contain lists of commonly used words with markings to indicate syllable breaks. These special dictionaries are helpful as quick references.

Concentrate on the most troublesome parts of easily misspelled words.

Give particular attention to the parts of words that lead to spelling errors—usually a single syllable or small cluster of letters.

acciden**tal**ly	des**pera**te
sep**ara**te	sec**re**tary
main**ten**ance	

569

Keep a record of words you have misspelled in your writing.

Most people have individual sets of words that they regularly use and regularly misspell. Use a note card, a sheet of paper, or a small notebook to record your personal list of troublesome words.

Carefully check the spelling of technical terms.

When your writing requires specialized language, verify the spelling of technical terms because their spelling is often tricky.

Use a spelling program if you are using a word-processing program.

If you use a word processor to prepare your papers, take advantage of software that can check spelling Although spelling programs are not without problems, they can be quite helpful.

Consult the following list of frequently misspelled words.

abbreviate	although	article
absence	always	artillery
absurd	amateur	ascend
accelerate	ambiguous	association
accidentally	ammunition	athlete
accommodate	among	athletics
accomplish	amount	attempt
according	analogous	attractive
accumulate	analysis	audible
accustom	analyze	audience
achievement	annual	authorities
acoustics	antecedent	automobile
acquaintance	anxiety	auxiliary
acquitted	apartment	awkward
across	apparatus	bachelor
address	apparent	balance
aggravate	appearance	balloon
aggression	appropriate	barbarous
airplane	arctic	barring
alleviate	argument	battalion
alley	arising	bearing
allotted	arithmetic	becoming
allowed	arouse	beggar
ally	arranging	beginning

believe
beneficial
benefited
biscuit
boundaries
breathe
brilliant
Britain
Britannica
bulletin
buoyant
bureau
buried
burying
business
busy
cafeteria
calendar
candidate
carburetor
carrying
casualties
causal
ceiling
celebrity
cemetery
certain
changeable
changing
characteristic
chauffeur
chief
choosing
chosen
clause

climbed
clothes
colloquial
colonel
column
coming
commission
commitment
committed
committee
companies
comparatively
compel
compelled
competent
competition
complaint
completely
compulsory
concede
conceivable
conceive
condemn
condescend
connoisseur
conqueror
conscience
conscientious
considered
consistent
contemptible
control
controlled
convenient
copies

corner
coroner
corps
corpse
costume
countries
courteous
courtesy
cries
criticism
criticize
cruelty
cruise
curiosity
curriculum
custom
cylinder
dealt
debater
deceitful
deceive
decide
decision
defendant
deferred
deficient
definite
definition
democracy
dependent
descendant
description
desirable
despair
desperate

Continued on the next page.

destruction
developed
development
diaphragm
diary
dictionary
dietitian
difference
digging
diphtheria
disappearance
disappoint
disastrous
discipline
discussion
disease
dissatisfied
dissipate
distribute
doesn't
dominant
don't
dormitories
dropped
drunkenness
echoes
ecstasy
efficiency
eighth
eligible
eliminate
embarrass
emphasize
employee
encouraging
encyclopedia
enthusiastic

environment
equipment
equipped
equivalent
erroneous
especially
eventually
exaggerate
exceed
excel
excellent
exceptional
excitement
exercise
exhaust
exhilaration
existence
experience
explanation
extensive
extracurricular
extremely
exuberance
fallacious
fallacy
familiar
fascinate
February
fiery
financial
financier
forehead
foreign
foremost
forfeit
forty
frantically

fraternities
friend
fulfill, fulfil
gaiety
generally
genius
genuine
glorious
government
grammar
grandeur
grievous
guarantee
guardian
guidance
handicapped
handkerchief
harass
hearse
height
heinous
heroes
hesitancy
hindrance
hoarse
hoping
horde
humorous
hurries
hygiene
hypocrisy
hysterical
illiterate
illogical
imaginary
imagination
imitative

immediately
implement
impromptu
inadequate
incidentally
incredible
indefinitely
independent
indicted
indispensable
inevitable
influential
innocent
inoculate
intellectual
intelligence
intentionally
intercede
interested
interpret
interrupt
irreligious
irresistible
irresponsible
itself
judicial
khaki
knowledge
laboratory
legitimate
leisure
library
lightning
literature
loneliness

losing
magazine
magnificent
maintain
maintenance
maneuver
manual
manufacture
mathematics
mattress
meant
medicine
medieval
messenger
millionaire
miniature
minute
mischievous
misspelled
modifies
modifying
momentous
mosquitoes
mottoes
mountainous
murmur
muscle
mysterious
necessary
necessity
neither
nervous
nevertheless
nickel
niece

ninety
ninth
noticeable
notorious
nowadays
obedience
obliged
obstacle
occasionally
occur
occurred
occurrence
official
omission
omit
omitted
opinion
opportunity
optimistic
organization
original
orthodox
outrageous
overrun
pamphlet
parallel
parliament
participle
particularly
pastime
peaceable
perceive
perform
permissible
perseverance

Continued on the next page.

persuade	questionnaire	schedule
phrase	quizzes	secretarial
physical	realize	secretary
physician	recede	seized
picnicked	receipt	sensible
piece	receive	sentence
playwright	receiving	sentinel
pleasant	recognize	separate
possess	recommend	sergeant
possessive	reference	severely
possible	referred	shining
potatoes	relevant	shriek
practice	religion	siege
prairie	religious	sieve
preceding	remembrance	similar
predominant	reminiscence	sincerely
preference	rendezvous	sincerity
preferred	repetition	skeptical
prejudice	replies	slight
preparation	representative	soliloquy
prevalent	reservoir	sophomore
primitive	resistance	source
privilege	restaurant	specifically
probably	rhetoric	specimen
professor	rheumatism	spontaneous
prominent	rhythmical	statement
pronounce	ridiculous	statue
pronunciation	sacrifice	stomach
propeller	sacrilegious	stopped
protein	safety	strength
psychology	salary	strenuously
pursue	sanctuary	stretched
pursuing	sandwich	struggle
putting	scarcely	studying
quantity	scene	subordinate
quarantine	scenic	subtle

succeed	traffic	vigilant
success	tragedy	vigorous
successful	transferred	village
suffrage	tremendous	villain
superintendent	tries	warrant
supersede	truly	warring
suppress	twelfth	weird
surprise	typical	welfare
swimming	tyranny	whole
syllable	unanimous	wholly
synonym	undoubtedly	wiry
synonymous	unnecessary	woman
tangible	until	women
tariff	usage	won't
tasting	useful	worried
technical	using	worrying
technique	usually	writing
temperament	vacancy	written
tenant	vacuum	yacht
tendency	valuable	your
thorough	vengeance	you're (you are)
thought	victorious	zoology
tournament	view	

Exercises

Use the following activities to help you eliminate any spelling problems that you happen to have. Keep in mind that your work will vary from that of other writers because individuals have individual difficulties with spelling.

1. Scan the list of frequently misspelled words (pages 570–575) and underline the words you know you have trouble spelling. Then write them on a 4" × 6" card for handy reference when you proofread your papers.

2. Review your graded papers from classes this term (or other recent samples of your writing) and make a list of the words you have misspelled. Include in this list any specialized terms that you frequently use.

3. Prepare a 4" × 6" card with a list of important names and terms used in your major and minor courses, especially those that present spelling problems. Include the names of writers, theorists, organizations, cities, titles, scientific terms, commonly used foreign phrases, and so on.

Observing the Rules of Mechanics: Review Exercise

Correct the mechanical errors in the following paragraph.

The civil war period in american history has had a tremendous impact on modern Culture, Science, Politics, and Economics—in fact, on almost all aspects of american life. Yet the real influences of the civil war are typically ignored because of the myths which americans prefer to perpetrate. Who has not created a fictionalized view of antebellum culture based on Historical Novels like Margaret Mitchells Gone With The Wind, Harriet Beecher Stowes Uncle Toms Cabin, or Margaret Walkers Jubilee? Who has not been influenced by the mini series The North and the South, The Blue and the Gray, or Roots? Modern Americans have seen president Lincoln portrayed by dozens of actors, have seen reenactments of the battle of Gettysburg, and have witnessed the sea battles of the Iron ships: The Monitor and others. Who has not seen dramatized versions of soldiers—both from the north and the south—heading to their homes, with The Battle Hymm of the Republic or Dixie as background music. We have stored images of generals Lee and Grant, as often as not based on the idealized statuary of the Franklin Mints Civil War Chess Set. Yet few of us have seen the civil war through the disturbing Psychological perspective of Stephen Cranes The Red Badge of Courage. Few have acknowledged in any real way that the reconstruction depressed the southern economy, gave rise to the ku klux klan, and failed to solve the ideological problems that continued to divide the country long after the deaths of six-hundred and fifty thousand soldiers.

A Glossary of Contemporary Usage

This glossary identifies words and constructions that sometimes require attention in composition classes. Some of the entries are pairs of words that are quite different in meaning yet similar enough in spelling to be confused (see **principal, principle**). Some, such as the use of *without* as a synonym for *unless*, are nonstandard usages that are not acceptable in college writing (see **without = unless**). Some are informal constructions that may be appropriate in some situations but not in others (see **guess**).

The judgments recorded here about usage are based on the Usage Notes contained in the *American Heritage Dictionary*, supplemented by other sources. Because these authorities do not always agree, it has sometimes been necessary for the author of this textbook to decide which judgments to accept. In coming to decisions, I have attempted to represent a consensus, but readers should be aware that on disputed items the judgments recorded in this glossary are finally mine.

Because dictionaries do not always distinguish among formal, informal, and colloquial usages, it has seemed useful to indicate whether a particular usage would be appropriate in college writing. The usefulness of this advice, however, depends on an understanding of its limitations. In any choice of usage, the decision depends less on what dictionaries or textbooks say than on what is consistent with the purpose and style of the writing. The student and instructor, who alone have the context of the paper before them, are in the best position to answer that question. All that the glossary can do is provide a background on which particular decisions can be based. The general assumption in the glossary is that the predominant style in college writing is moderate rather than formal or colloquial, so calling a usage informal in no way suggests that it is less desirable than a formal usage.

ad   *Ad* is the clipped form of *advertisement*. The full form is preferable in a formal style, especially in letters of application. The appropriateness of *ad* in college writing depends on the style of the paper.

adapt, adopt   *Adapt* means "to adjust to meet requirements": "The human body can adapt itself to all sorts of environments"; "It will take a skillful writer to adapt this novel for the movies." *Adopt* means "to take as one's own" ("He immediately adopted the idea") or—in parliamentary procedure—"to accept as law" ("The motion was adopted").

advice, advise   The first form is a noun, the second a verb: "I was advised to ignore his advice."

affect, effect Both words may be used as nouns, but *effect,* meaning "result," is usually the word wanted: "His speech had an unfortunate effect"; "The treatments had no effect on me." The noun *affect* is a technical term in psychology. Although both words may be used as verbs, *affect* is the more common. As a verb, *affect* means "impress" or "influence": "His advice affected my decision"; "Does music affect you that way?" As a verb, *effect* is rarely required in college writing but may be used to mean "carry out" or "accomplish": "The pilot effected his mission"; "The lawyer effected a settlement."

affective, effective See **affect, effect.** The common adjective is *effective* ("an effective argument"), meaning "having an effect." The use of *affective* is largely confined to technical discussions of psychology and semantics, in which it is roughly equivalent to "emotional." In this textbook, *affective* is used to describe a tone that is chiefly concerned with creating attitudes in the reader (see pages 254–256).

aggravate *Aggravate* may mean either "to make worse" ("His remarks aggravated the dispute") or "to annoy or exasperate" ("Her manners aggravate me"). Both are standard English, but there is still some objection to the second usage. If you mean *annoy, exasperate,* or *provoke,* it would be safer to use whichever of those words best expresses your meaning.

ain't Except to record nonstandard speech, the use of *ain't* is not acceptable in college writing.

all together, altogether Distinguish between the phrase ("They were all together at last") and the adverb ("He is altogether to blame"). *All together* means "all in one place"; *altogether* means "entirely" or "wholly."

allow When used to mean "permit" ("No smoking is allowed on the premises"), *allow* is acceptable. Its use for "think" ("He allowed it could be done") is nonstandard and is not acceptable in college writing.

allusion, illusion An *allusion* is a reference: "The poem contains several allusions to Greek mythology." An *illusion* is an erroneous mental image: "Rouge on pallid skin gives an illusion of health."

alright A common variant spelling of *all right,* but there is still considerable objection to it. *All right* is the preferred spelling.

among, between See **between, among.**

amount, number *Amount* suggests bulk or weight: "We collected a considerable amount of scrap iron." *Number* is used for items that can be counted: "He has a large number of friends"; "There are a number of letters to be answered."

an Variant of the indefinite article *a.* Used instead of *a* when the word that follows begins with a vowel sound: "an apple," "an easy victory," "an honest opinion," "an hour," "an unknown person." When the word that follows begins with a consonant, or with a *y* sound or a pronounced *h,* the article used should be *a:* "a yell," "a unit," "a history," "a house." Such constructions as "a apple," "a hour" are nonstandard. The use of *an* before *historical* is an older usage that is now dying out.

and/or   Many people object to *and/or* in college writing because the expression is associated with legal and commercial writing. Generally avoid it.

angle   The use of *angle* to mean "point of view" ("Let's look at it from a new angle") is acceptable. In the sense of personal interest ("What's your angle?"), it is slang.

anxious = eager   *Anxious* should not be used in college writing to mean "eager," as in "Gretel is anxious to see her gift." *Eager* is the preferred word in this context.

any = all   The use of *any* to mean "all," as in "He is the best qualified of any applicant," is not acceptable. Say "He is the best qualified of all the applicants," or simply "He is the best-qualified applicant."

any = any other   The use of *any* to mean "any other" ("The knife she bought cost more than any in the store") should be avoided in college writing. In this context, use *any other*.

anyone = all   The singular *anyone* should not be used in writing to mean "all." In "She is the most talented musician of anyone I have met here," omit "of anyone."

anywheres   A nonstandard variant of *anywhere*. It is not acceptable in college writing.

apt = likely   *Apt* is always appropriate when it means "quick to learn" ("He is an apt student") or "suited to its purpose" ("an apt comment"). It is also appropriate when a predictable characteristic is being spoken of ("When he becomes excited he is apt to tremble"). In other situations the use of *apt* to mean "likely" ("She is apt to leave you"; "He is apt to resent it") may be too colloquial for college writing.

as = because   *As* is less effective than *because* in showing causal relation between main and subordinate clauses. Since *as* has other meanings, it may in certain contexts be confusing. For example, in "As I was going home, I decided to telephone," *as* may mean "while" or "because." If there is any possibility of confusion, use either *because* or *while*—whichever is appropriate.

as = that   The use of *as* to introduce a noun clause ("I don't know as I would agree to that") is colloquial. In college writing, use *that* or *whether*.

as to, with respect to = about   Although *as to* and *with respect to* are standard usage, many writers avoid these phrases because they sound stilted: "I am not concerned as to your cousin's reaction." Here *about* would be more appropriate than either *as to* or *with respect to*: "I am not concerned about your cousin's reaction."

at   Avoid the redundant *at* in such sentences as "Where were you at?" and "Where do you live at?"

author   *Author* is not fully accepted as a verb. "To write a play" is preferable to "to author a play."

awful, awfully   The real objection to *awful* is that it is worked to death. Instead of being reserved for situations in which it means "awe inspiring," it is

579

used excessively as a utility word (see page 238). Use both *awful* and *awfully* sparingly.

bad = badly The ordinary uses of *bad* as an adjective cause no difficulty. As a predicate adjective ("An hour after dinner, I began to feel bad"), it is sometimes confused with the adverb *badly*. After the verbs *look, feel,* and *seem,* the adjective is preferred. Say: "It looks bad for our side," "I feel bad about the quarrel," "Our predicament seemed bad this morning." But do not use *bad* when an adverb is required, as in "He played badly," "a badly torn suit."

bank on = rely on In college writing *rely on* is generally preferred.

being as = because The use of *being as* for "because" or "since" in such sentences as "Being as I am an American, I believe in democracy" is nonstandard. Say "Because I am an American, I believe in democracy."

between, among In general, use *between* in constructions involving two people or objects and *among* in constructions involving more than two: "We had less than a dollar between the two of us"; "We had only a dollar among the three of us." The general distinction, however, should be modified when insistence on it would be unidiomatic. For example, *between* is the accepted form in the following examples:

> He is in the enviable position of having to choose between three equally attractive young women.
> A settlement was arranged between the four partners.
> Just between us girls . . . (when any number of "girls" is involved)

between you and I Both pronouns are objects of the preposition *between* and so should be in the objective case: "between you and me."

bi-, semi- *Bi-* means "two": "The budget for the biennium was adopted." *Semi-* means "half of": "semicircle." *Bi-* is sometimes used to mean "twice in." A bimonthly paper, for example, may be published twice a month, not once every two months, but this usage is ambiguous; *semimonthly* is preferred.

but that, but what In such a statement as "I don't doubt but that you are correct," *but* is unnecessary. Omit it. "I don't doubt but what . . ." is also unacceptable. Delete *but what* and write *that.*

can = may The distinction that *can* is used to indicate ability and *may* to indicate permission ("If I can do the work, may I have the job?") is not generally observed in informal usage. Either form is acceptable in college writing.

cannot help but In college writing, the form without *but* is preferred: "I cannot help being angry." (Not: "I cannot help but be angry.")

can't hardly A confusion between *cannot* and *can hardly.* The construction is unacceptable in college writing. Use *cannot, can't,* or *can hardly.*

capital, capitol Unless you are referring to a government building, use *capital.* The building in which the U.S. Congress meets is always capitalized ("the Capitol"). For the various meanings of *capital,* consult your dictionary.

censor, censure Both words come from a Latin verb meaning "to set a value on" or "judge." *Censor* is used to mean "appraise" in the sense of evaluating a book or a letter to see if it may be released ("All outgoing mail had to be censored") and is often used as a synonym for *delete* or *cut out* ("That part of the message was censored").

Censure as a verb means "to evaluate adversely" or "to find fault with"; as a noun, it means "disapproval," "rebuke": "The editorial writers censured the speech"; "Such an attitude will invoke public censure."

center around   "Center on" is the preferred form.

cite, sight, site   *Cite* means "to refer to": "He cited chapter and verse." *Sight* means "spectacle" or "view": "The garden was a beautiful sight." *Site* means "location": "This is the site of the new plant."

compare, contrast   *Compare* can imply either differences or similarities; *contrast* always implies differences. *Compare* can be followed by either *to* or *with*. The verb *contrast* is usually followed by *with*.

> Compared to her mother, she's a beauty.
> I hope my accomplishments can be compared with those of my predecessor.
> His grades this term contrast conspicuously with the ones he received last term.

complement, compliment   Both words can be used as nouns and verbs. *Complement* speaks of completion: "the complement of a verb"; "a full complement of soldiers to serve as an honor guard"; Susan's hat complements the rest of her outfit tastefully." *Compliment* is associated with praise: "The instructor complimented us for writing good papers."

***complement of* to be**   The choice between "It is I" and "It's me" is a choice not between standard and nonstandard usage but between formal and colloquial styles. This choice seldom has to be made in college writing, since the expression, in whatever form it is used, it essentially a spoken rather than a written sentence. Its use in writing occurs chiefly in dialogue, and then the form chosen should be appropriate to the speaker.

The use of the objective case with the third person ("That was her") is less common and should be avoided in college writing except when dialogue requires it.

continual, continuous   Both words refer to a continued action, but *continual* implies repeated action ("continual interruptions," "continual disagreements"), whereas *continuous* implies that the action never ceases ("continuous pain," "a continuous buzzing in the ears").

could of = could have   Although *could of* and *could have* often sound alike in speech, *of* is not acceptable for *have* in college writing. In writing, *could of, should of, would of, might of,* and *must of* are nonstandard.

council, counsel   *Council* is a noun meaning "a deliberative body": "a town council," "a student council." *Counsel* can be either a noun meaning "advice" or a verb meaning "to advise": "to seek a lawyer's counsel," "to counsel a person in trouble." A person who offers counsel is a *counselor*: "Because of his low grades Quint made an appointment with his academic counselor."

581

credible, creditable, credulous   All three words come from a Latin verb meaning "to believe," but they are not synonyms. *Credible* means "believable" ("his story is credible"); *creditable* means "commendable" ("John did a creditable job on the committee") or "acceptable for credit" ("The project is creditable toward the course requirements"); *credulous* means "gullible" ("Only a most credulous person could believe such an incredible story").

cute   A word used colloquially to indicate the general notion of "attractive" or "pleasing." Its overuse shows lack of discrimination. A more specific term is often preferable.

> His daughter is cute. [lovely? petite? pleasant? charming?]
> That is a cute trick. [clever? surprising?]
> He has a cute accent. [pleasant? refreshingly unusual?]
> She is a little too cute for me. [affected? juvenile? clever?]

data is   Because *data* is the Latin plural of *datum,* it logically requires a plural verb and always takes a plural verb in scientific writing: "These data have been double checked." In popular usage and in computer-related contexts, *datum* is almost never used and *data* is treated as a singular noun and given a singular subject: "The data has been double-checked." Either *data are* or *data is* may be used in popular writing, but only *data are* is acceptable in scientific writing.

debut   *Debut* is a noun meaning "first public appearance." It is not acceptable as a transitive verb ("The Little Theater will debut its new play tonight") or as an intransitive verb ("Cory Martin will debut in the new play").

decent, descent   A decent person is one who behaves well, without crudeness and perhaps with kindness and generosity. *Decent* can mean "satisfactory" ("a decent grade," "a decent living standard"). *Descent* means "a passage downward"; a descent may be either literal ("their descent into the canyon") or figurative ("hereditary descent of children from their parents," "descent of English from a hypothetical language called Indo-European").

desert, dessert   The noun *desert* means "an uncultivated and uninhabited area"; it may be dry and sandy. *Desert* can be an adjective: "a desert island." The verb *desert* means "to abandon." A *dessert* is a sweet food served as the last course at the noon or evening meal.

different from, different than   Although both *different from* and *different than* are common American usages, the preferred idiom is *different from.*

disinterested, uninterested   The distinction between these words is that *disinterested* means "unbiased" and *uninterested* means "apathetic" or "not interested." A disinterested critic is one who comes to a book with no prejudices or prior judgments of its worth; an uninterested critic is one who cannot get interested in the book. Dictionaries disagree about whether this distinction is still valid in contemporary usage and sometimes treat the words as synonyms. But in college writing the distinction is generally observed.

don't   *Don't* is a contraction of "do not," as *doesn't* is a contraction of "does not." It can be used in any college writing in which contractions are appropriate. But it cannot be used with a singular subject. "He don't" and "it don't" are nonstandard usages.

double negative   The use of two negative words within the same construction. In certain forms ("I am not unwilling to go") the double negative is educated usage for an affirmative statement; in other forms ("He hasn't got no money") the double negative is nonstandard usage. The observation that "two negatives make an affirmative" in English usage is a half-truth based on a false analogy with mathematics. "He hasn't got no money" is unacceptable in college writing, not because two negatives make an affirmative, but because it is nonstandard usage.

economic, economical   *Economic* refers to the science of economics or to business in general: "This is an economic law"; "Economic conditions are improving." *Economical* means "inexpensive" or "thrifty": "That is an economical purchase"; "He is economical to the point of miserliness."

effect, affect   See **affect, effect.**

effective, affective   See **affective, effective.**

either   Used to designate one of two things: "Both hats are becoming; I would be perfectly satisfied with either." The use of *either* when more than two things are involved ("There are three ways of working the problem; either way will give the right answer") is a disputed usage. When more than two things are involved, it is better to use *any* or *any one* instead of *either*: "There are three ways of working the problem; any one of them will give the right answer."

elicit, illicit   The first word means "to draw out" ("We could elicit no response from them"); the second means "not permitted" or "unlawful" ("an illicit sale of drugs").

emigrant, immigrant   An emigrant is a person who moves *out* of a country; an immigrant is one who moves *into* a country. Thus, refugees from Central America and elsewhere who settle in the United States are emigrants from their native countries and immigrants here. A similar distinction holds for the verbs *emigrate* and *immigrate.*

eminent, imminent   *Eminent* means "prominent, outstanding": "an eminent scientist." *Imminent* means "ready to happen" or "near in time": "War seems imminent."

enormity, enormous, enormousness   *Enormous* refers to unusual size or measure; synonyms are *huge, vast, immense:* "an enormous fish," "an enormous effort." *Enormousness* is a noun with the same connotations of size and can be applied to either good or bad effects: "The enormousness of their contribution is only beginning to be recognized"; "The enormousness of the lie almost made it believable." But *enormity* is used only for evil acts of great dimension: "The enormity of Hitler's crimes against the Jews shows what can happen when power, passion, and prejudice are all united in one human being."

enthused *Enthused* is colloquial for *enthusiastic*: "The probability of winning has caused them to be very enthused about the campaign." In college writing use *enthusiastic*.

equally as In such sentences as "He was equally as good as his brother," the *equally* is unnecessary. Simply write, "He was as good as his brother."

etc. An abbreviation for the Latin *et cetera*, which means "and others," "and so forth." It should be used only when the style justifies abbreviations and then only after several items in a series have been identified: "The data sheet required the usual personal information: age, height, weight, marital status, etc." An announcement of a painting contest that states, "Entries will be judged on the basis of use of color, etc.," does not tell contestants very much about the standards by which their work is to be judged. Avoid the redundant *and* before *etc.*

expect = suppose or suspect The use of *expect* for *suppose* or *suspect* is colloquial. In college writing use *suppose* or *suspect*: "I suppose you have written to him"; "I suspect that we have made a mistake."

fact Distinguish between facts and statements of fact. A fact is something that exists or existed. A fact is neither true nor false, it just *is*. A statement of fact, or a factual statement, may be true or false, depending on whether it does or does not report the facts accurately.

Avoid padding a sentence with "a fact that," as in "It is a fact that all the public opinion polls predicted Truman's defeat in the 1948 election." The first five words of that sentence add no meaning. Similarly, "His guilt is admitted" says all, in fewer words, that is said by "The fact of his guilt is admitted."

famous, notorious *Famous* is a complimentary and *notorious* an uncomplimentary adjective. Well-known people of good repute are famous; those of bad repute are notorious, or infamous.

farther, further The distinction that *farther* indicates distance and *further* degree is not unanimously supported by usage studies. But to mean "in addition," only *further* is used: "Further assistance will be required."

feature = imagine The use of *feature* to mean "give prominence to," as in "This issue of the magazine features an article on juvenile delinquency," is established standard usage and is appropriate in college writing. But this acceptance does not justify the slang use of *feature*, meaning "imagine," in such expressions as "Can you feature that?" "Feature me in a dress suit," "I can't feature him as a nurse."

fewer = less *Fewer* refers to quantities that can be counted individually: "fewer male than female employees." *Less* is used for collective quantities that are not counted individually ("less corn this year than last") and for abstract characteristics ("less determination than enthusiasm").

field *Field*, in the sense of "an area of study or endeavor," is an overused word that often creates redundance: "He is majoring in the field of physics"; "Her new job is in the field of public relations." Delete "the field of" in each of these sentences.

fine = very well   The colloquial use of *fine* to mean "very well" ("He is doing fine in his new position") is probably too informal for most college writing.

flaunt = flout   Using *flaunt* as a synonym for *flout* confuses two different words. *Flaunt* means "to show off": "She has a habit of flaunting her knowledge to intimidate her friends." *Flout* means "to scorn or show contempt for": "He is better at flouting opposing arguments than at understanding them." In the right context either word can be effective, but the two words are not synonyms and cannot be used interchangeably.

fortuitous, fortunate   *Fortuitous* means "by chance," "not planned": "Our meeting was fortuitous; we had never heard of each other before." Do not confuse *fortuitous* with *fortunate,* as the writer of this sentence has done: "My introduction to Professor Kraus was fortuitous for me; today she hired me as her student assistant." *Fortunate* would be the appropriate word here.

funny   Often used in conversation as a utility word that has no precise meaning but may be clear enough in its context. It is generally too vague for college writing. Decide in what sense the subject is "funny" and use a more precise term to convey that sense. (See the discussion of vagueness on pages 237–238).

get   A utility word. The *American Heritage Dictionary* lists thirty-six meanings for the individual word and more than sixty uses in idiomatic expressions. Most of these uses are acceptable in college writing. But unless the style is deliberately colloquial, avoid slang uses in which *get* means "to cause harm to" ("She'll get me for that"), "to cause a negative reaction to" ("His bad manners really get me"), "to gain the favor of" ("He tried to get in with his boss"), and "to become up to date" ("Get in the swing of things").

good   The use of *good* as an adverb ("He talks good"; "She played pretty good") is not acceptable. The accepted adverbial form is *well.* The use of *good* as a predicate adjective after verbs of hearing, feeling, seeing, smelling, tasting, and the like is standard. See **bad.**

good and   Used colloquially as an intensive in such expressions as "good and late," "good and ready," "good and tired." The more formal the style, the less appropriate these intensives are. In college writing use them sparingly, if at all.

guess   The use of *guess* to mean "believe," "suppose," or "think" ("I guess I can be there on time") is accepted by all studies on which this glossary is based. There is objection to its use in formal college writing, but it should be acceptable in an informal style.

had (hadn't) ought   Nonstandard for *ought* and *ought not.* Not acceptable in college writing.

hanged, hung   Alternative past participles of *hang.* For referring to an execution, *hanged* is preferred; in other senses, *hung* is preferred.

he or she, she or he   Traditionally the masculine form (*he, his, him*) of the personal pronoun has been used to refer to an individual who could be either male or female: "The writer should revise his draft until he achieves his purpose." Substituting pronouns that refer to both males and females in the group, such as *he or she*, or *she or he*, corrects the implicit sexism in the traditional usage but sometimes sounds awkward. An alternative is to use plural forms: "Writers should revise their drafts until they achieve their purpose."

hopefully   Opinion is divided about the acceptability of attaching this adverb loosely to a sentence and using it to mean "I hope": "Hopefully, the plane will arrive on schedule." This usage is gaining acceptance, but there is still strong objection to it. In college writing the safe decision is to avoid it.

idea   In addition to its formal meaning of "conception," *idea* has acquired so many supplementary meanings that it must be recognized as a utility word. Some of its meanings are illustrated in the following sentences:

> The idea (thesis) of the book is simple.
> The idea (proposal) she suggested is a radical one.
> I got the idea (impression) that he is unhappy.
> It is my idea (belief, opinion) that they are both wrong.
> My idea (intention) is to leave early.

The overuse of *idea*, like the overuse of any utility word, makes for vagueness. Whenever possible, use a more precise synonym.

illicit, elicit   See **elicit, illicit.**

illusion, allusion   See **allusion, illusion.**

immigrant, emigrant   See **emigrant, immigrant.**

imminent, eminent   See **eminent, imminent.**

imply, infer   The traditional difference between these two words is that *imply* refers to what a statement means, usually to a meaning not specifically stated but suggested in the original statement, whereas *infer* is used for a listener's or reader's judgment or inference based on the statement. For example: "I thought that the weather report implied that the day would be quite pretty and sunny, but Marlene inferred that it meant we'd better take umbrellas." The dictionaries are not unanimous in supporting this distinction, but in your writing it will be better not to use *imply* as a synonym for *infer*.

individual   Although the use of *individual* to mean "person" ("He is an energetic individual") is accepted by the dictionaries, college instructors frequently disapprove of this use, probably because it is overdone in college writing. There is no objection to the adjective *individual*, meaning "single," "separate" ("The instructor tries to give us individual attention").

inferior than   Possibly a confusion between "inferior to" and "worse than." Use *inferior to*: "Today's workmanship is inferior to that of a few years ago."

ingenious, ingenuous   *Ingenious* means "clever" in the sense of "original": "an ingenious solution." *Ingenuous* means "without sophistication," "innocent": "Her ingenuous confession disarmed those who had been suspicious of her motives."

inside of, outside of   *Inside of* and *outside of* generally should not be used as compound prepositions. In place of the compound prepositions in "The display is inside of the auditorium" and "The pickets were waiting outside of the gate," write "inside the auditorium" and "outside the gate."

Inside of is acceptable in most college writing when it means "in less than": "I'll be there inside of an hour." The more formal term is *within.*

Both *inside of* and *outside of* are appropriate when *inside* or *outside* is a noun followed by an *of* phrase: "The inside of the house is quite attractive"; "He painted the outside of his boat dark green."

in terms of   An imprecise and greatly overused expression. Instead of "In terms of philosophy, we are opposed to his position" and "In terms of our previous experience with the company, we refuse to purchase its products," write "Philosophically, we are opposed to his position" and "Because of our previous experience with the company, we refuse to purchase its products."

irregardless   A nonstandard variant of *regardless.* Do not use it.

irrelevant, irreverent   *Irrelevant* means "having no relation to" or "lacking pertinence": "That may be true, but it is quite irrelevant." *Irreverent* means "without reverence": "Such conduct in church is irreverent."

it's me   This construction is essentially a spoken one. Except in dialogue, it rarely occurs in writing. Its use in educated speech is thoroughly established. The formal expression is "It is I."

-ize   The suffix *-ize* is used to change nouns and adjectives into verbs: *civilize, criticize, sterilize.* This practice is often overused, particularly in government and business. Avoid such pretentious and unnecessary jargon as *finalize, prioritize,* and *theorize.*

judicial, judicious   Judicial decisions are related to the administering of justice, often by judges or juries. A judicious person is one who demonstrates good judgment: "A judicious person would not have allowed the young boys to shoot the rapids alone."

kind of, sort of   Use a singular noun and a singular verb with these phrases: "That kind of person is always troublesome"; "This sort of attitude is deplorable." If the sense of the sentence calls for the plural *kinds* or *sorts,* use a plural noun and a plural verb: "These kinds of services are essential." In questions introduced by *what* or *which,* the singular *kind* or *sort* can be followed by a plural noun and verb: "What kind of shells are these?"

The use of *a* or *an* after *kind of* ("That kind of a person is always troublesome") is usually not appropriate in college writing.

kind (sort) of = somewhat   This usage ("I feel kind of tired"; "He looked sort of foolish") is colloquial. The style of the writing will determine its appropriateness in a paper.

latter   *Latter* refers to the second of two. It should not be used to refer to the last of three or more nouns. Instead of *latter* in "Michigan, Alabama, and Notre Dame have had strong football teams for years, and yet the latter has only recently begun to accept invitations to play in bowl games," write *last* or *last-named* or simply repeat *Notre Dame.*

lay, lie   *Lay* is a transitive verb (principal parts: *lay, laid, laid*) that means "put" or "place"; it is nearly always followed by a direct object: "She lay the magazine on the table, hiding the mail I laid there this morning." *Lie* is an intransitive verb (principal parts: *lie, lay, lain*) that means "recline" or "be situated" and does not take an object: "I lay awake all night until I decided I had lain there long enough."

leave = let   The use of *leave* for the imperative verb *let* ("Leave us face it") is not acceptable in college writing. Write "Let us face it." But *let* and *leave* are interchangeable when a noun or pronoun and then *alone* follow: "Let me alone"; "Leave me alone."

less   See **fewer.**

liable = likely   Instructors sometimes object to the use of *liable* to mean "likely," as in "it is liable to rain," "He is liable to hit you." *Liable* is used more precisely to mean "subject to" or "exposed to" or "answerable for": "He is liable to arrest"; "You will be liable for damages."

like = as, as though   The use of *like* as a conjunction ("He talks like you do"; "It looks like it will be my turn next") is colloquial. It is not appropriate in a formal style, and many people object to it in an informal style. The safest procedure is to avoid using *like* as a conjunction in college writing.

literally, figuratively   *Literally* means "word for word," "following the letter," or "in the strict sense." *Figuratively* is its opposite and means "metaphorically." In informal speech, this distinction is often blurred when *literally* is used to mean *nearly:* "She literally blew her top." Avoid this usage by maintaining the word's true meaning: "To give employees a work vacation means literally to fire them."

loath, loathe   *Loath* is an adjective meaning "reluctant," "unwilling" ("I am loath to do that"; "He is loath to risk so great an investment") and is pronounced to rhyme with *both.* *Loathe* is a verb meaning "dislike strongly" ("I loathe teas"; "She loathes an unkempt man") and is pronounced to rhyme with *clothe.*

loose, lose   The confusion of these words frequently causes misspelling. *Loose* is most common as an adjective: "a loose button," "The dog is loose." *Lose* is always used as a verb: "You are going to lose your money."

luxuriant, luxurious   These words come from the same root but have quite different meanings. *Luxuriant* means "abundant" and is used principally to describe growing things: "luxuriant vegetation," "a luxuriant head of hair." *Luxurious* means "luxury-loving" or "characterized by luxury": "He finds it difficult to maintain so luxurious a lifestyle on so modest an income"; "The furnishings of the clubhouse were luxurious."

mad = angry or annoyed   Using *mad* to mean "angry" is colloquial: "My girl is mad at me"; "His insinuations make me mad." More precise terms—*angry, annoyed, irritated, provoked, vexed*—are generally more appropriate in college writing. *Mad* is, of course, appropriately used to mean "insane."

majority, plurality   Candidates are elected by a *majority* when they get more than half of the votes cast. A *plurality* is the margin of victory that the winning candidate has over the leading opponent, whether the winner has a majority or not.

mean = unkind, disagreeable, vicious   Using *mean* to convey the sense "unkind," "disagreeable," "vicious" ("It was mean of me to do that"; "He was in a mean mood"; "That dog looks mean") is a colloquial use. It is appropriate in most college writing, but since using *mean* loosely sometimes results in vagueness, consider using one of the suggested alternatives to provide a sharper statement.

medium, media, medias   *Medium,* not *media,* is the singular form: "The daily newspaper is still an important medium of communication." *Media* is plural: "Figuratively, the electronic media have created a smaller world." *Medias* is not an acceptable form for the plural of *medium.*

might of   See **could of**

mighty = very   *Mighty* is not appropriate in most college writing as a substitute for *very.* Avoid such constructions as "He gave a mighty good speech."

moral, morale   Roughly, *moral* refers to conduct and *morale* refers to state of mind. A moral man is one who conducts himself according to standards for goodness. People are said to have good morale when they are cheerful, cooperative, and not too much concerned with their own worries.

most = almost   The use of *most* as a synonym for *almost* ("I am most always hungry an hour before mealtime") is colloquial. In college writing *almost* would be preferred in such a sentence.

must (adj. and n.)   The use of *must* as an adjective ("This book is must reading for anyone who wants to understand Russia") and as a noun ("It is reported that the President will classify this proposal as a must") is accepted as established usage by the dictionaries.

must of   See **could of.**

myself = I, me   *Myself* should not be used for *I* or *me.* Avoid such constructions as "John and myself will go." *Myself* is acceptably used as an intensifier ("I saw it myself"; "I myself will go with you") and as a reflexive object ("I hate myself"; "I can't convince myself that he is right.")

nauseous = nauseated   *Nauseous* does not mean "experiencing nausea"; *nauseated* has that meaning: "The thought of making a speech caused her to feel nauseated." *Nauseous* means "causing nausea" or "repulsive": "nauseous odor," "nauseous television program."

nice   A utility word much overused in college writing. Avoid excessive use of *nice* and, whenever possible, choose a more precise synonym.

> That's a nice dress. [*attractive? becoming? fashionable? well-made?*]
> She a nice person. [*agreeable? charming? friendly? well-mannered?*]

not all that   The use of *not all that interested* to mean "not much interested" is generally not acceptable in college writing.

off, off of = from   Neither *off* nor *off of* should be used to mean "from." Write "Jack bought the old car from a stranger," not "off a stranger" or "off of a stranger."

OK, O.K.   Its use in business to mean "endorse" is generally accepted: "The manager OK'd the request." In college writing *OK* is a utility word and is subject to the general precaution concerning all such words: do not overuse it, especially in contexts in which a more specific term would give more efficient communication. For example, contrast the vagueness of *OK* in the first sentence with the discriminated meanings in the second and third sentences:

> The mechanic said the tires were OK.
> The mechanic said the tread on the tires was still good.
> The mechanic said the pressure in the tires was satisfactory.

one   See **you.**

only   The position of *only* in such sentences as "I only need three dollars" and "If only Mother would write!" is sometimes condemned on the grounds of possible ambiguity. In practice, the context usually rules out any but the intended interpretation, but a change in the word order would result in more appropriate emphasis: "I need only three dollars"; "If Mother would only write!"

on the part of   The phrase *on the part of* ("There will be some objection on the part of the students"; "On the part of business people, there will be some concern about taxes") often contributes to wordiness. Simply say "The students will object," "Business people will be concerned about taxes."

party = person   The use of *party* to mean "person" is appropriate in legal documents and the responses of telephone operators, but these are special uses. Generally avoid this use in college writing.

per, a   "You will be remunerated at the rate of forty dollars per diem" and "The troops advanced three miles per day through the heavy snow" show established use of *per* for *a*. But usually "forty dollars a day" and "three miles a day" would be more natural expressions in college writing.

percent, percentage   *Percent* (alternative form *per cent*) is used when a specific portion is named: "five percent of the expenses." *Percentage* is used when no number is given: "a small percentage of the expenses." When *percent* or *percentage* is part of a subject, the noun or pronoun of the *of* phrase that follows determines the number of the verb: "Forty percent of the wheat is his"; "A large percentage of her customers pay promptly."

personal, personnel   *Personal* means "of a person": "a personal opinion," "a personal matter." *Personnel* refers to the people in an organization, especially employees: "Administrative personnel will not be affected."

phenomenon, phenomena   *Phenomenon* is singular; *phenomena* is plural: "This is a striking phenomenon." "Many new phenomena have been discovered with the radio telescope."

plenty   The use of *plenty* as a noun ("There is plenty of room") is always acceptable. Its use as an adverb ("It was plenty good") is not appropriate in college writing.

practical, practicable   Avoid interchanging the two words. *Practical* means "useful, not theoretical," and *practicable* means "feasible, but not necessarily proved successful": "The designers are usually practical, but these new blueprints do not seem practicable."

première   *Première* is acceptable as a noun ("The première for the play was held in a small off-Broadway theater"), but do not use it as a verb. Instead of "The play premièred in a small off-Broadway theater," write "The play opened . . ."

preposition (ending sentence with)   A preposition should not appear at the end of a sentence if its presence there draws undue attention to it or creates an awkward construction, as in "They are the people whom we made the inquiries yesterday about." But there is nothing wrong with writing a preposition at the end of a sentence to achieve an idiomatic construction: "Isn't that the man you are looking for?"

principal, principle   The basic meaning of *principal* is "chief" or "most important." It is used in this sense both as a noun and as an adjective: "the principal of a school," "the principal point." It is also used to refer to a capital sum of money, as contrasted with interest on the money: "He can live on the interest without touching the principal." *Principle* is used only as a noun and means "rule," "law," or "controlling idea": "the principle of 'one man, one vote'"; "Cheating is against my principles."

proceed, precede   To *proceed* is to "go forward"; to *precede* means "to go ahead of": "The blockers preceded the runner as the football team proceeded toward the goal line."

prophecy, prophesy   *Prophecy* is always used as a noun ("The prophecy came true"); *prophesy* is always a verb ("He prophesied another war").

proved, proven   When used as past participles, both forms are standard English, but the preferred form is *proved:* "Having proved the first point, we moved to the second." *Proven* is preferred when the word is used primarily as an adjective: "She is a proven contender for the championship."

quote   The clipped form for *quotation* ("a quote from *Walden*") is not acceptable in most college writing. The verb *quote* ("to quote Thoreau") is acceptable in all styles.

raise, rise   *Raise* is a transitive verb, taking an object, meaning to cause something to move up; *rise* is an intransitive verb meaning to go up (on its own): "I raised the window in the kitchen while I waited for the bread dough to rise."

rarely ever, seldom ever   The *ever* is redundant. Instead of saying, "He is rarely ever late" and "She is seldom ever angry," write, "He is rarely late" and "She is seldom angry."

real = really (very)   The use of *real* to mean "really" or "very" ("It is a real difficult assignment") is a colloquial usage. It is acceptable only in a paper whose style is deliberately colloquial.

reason . . . because   The construction is redundant: "The reason he couldn't complete his essay is because he lost his note cards." Substitute *that* for *because:* "The reason he couldn't complete his essay is that he lost his note cards." Better yet, simply eliminate *the reason* and *is:* "He couldn't complete his essay because he lost his note cards."

refer back   A confusion between *look back* and *refer.* This usage is objected to in college writing on the ground that since the *re-* of *refer* means "back," *refer back* is redundant. *Refer back* is acceptable when it means "refer again" ("The bill was referred back to the committee"); otherwise, use *refer* ("Let me refer you to page 17").

regarding, in regard to, with regard to   These are overused and stuffy substitutes for the following simple terms: *on, about,* or *concerning:* "The attorney spoke to you about the testimony."

respectfully, respectively   *Respectfully* means "with respect": "respectfully submitted." *Respectively* means "each in turn": "These three papers were graded respectively A, C, and B."

right (adv.)   The use of *right* as an adverb is established in such sentences as "He went right home" and "It served her right." Its use to mean *very* ("I was right glad to meet him") is colloquial and should be used in college writing only when the style is colloquial.

right, rite   A *rite* is a ceremony or ritual. This word should not be confused with the various uses of *right.*

said (adj.)   The use of *said* as an adjective ("said documents," "said offense") is restricted to legal phraseology. Do not use it in college writing.

same as = just as   The preferred idiom is "just as": "He acted just as I thought he would."

same, such   Avoid using *same* or *such* as a substitute for *it, this, that, them.* Instead of "I am returning the book because I do not care for same" and "Most people are fond of athletics of all sorts, but I have no use for such," say "I am returning the book because I do not care for it" and "Unlike most people, I am not fond of athletics."

scarcely   In such sentences as "There wasn't scarcely enough" and "We haven't scarcely time," the use of *scarcely* with a negative creates an unacceptable double negative. Say "There was scarcely enough" and "We scarcely have time."

scarcely . . . than   The use of *scarcely . . . than* ("I had scarcely met her than she began to denounce her husband") is a confusion between "no sooner . . . than" and "scarcely . . . when." Say "I had no sooner met her than she began to denounce her husband" or "I had scarcely met her when she began to denounce her husband."

seasonable, seasonal *Seasonable* and its adverb form *seasonably* mean "appropriate(ly) to the season": "She was seasonably dressed for a late-fall football game"; "A seasonable frost convinced us that the persimmons were just right for eating." *Seasonal* means "caused by a season": "increased absenteeism because of seasonal influenza," "flooding caused by seasonal thaws."

-selfs The plural of *self* is *selves*. Such a usage as "They hurt themselfs" is nonstandard and is not acceptable in college writing.

semi- See **bi-, semi-.**

sensual, sensuous *Sensual* has unfavorable connotations and means "catering to the gratification of physical desires": "Always concerned with satisfying his sexual lust and his craving for drink and rich food, the old baron led a totally sensual existence." *Sensuous* has generally favorable connotations and refers to pleasures experienced through the senses: "The sensuous comfort of a warm bath," "the sensuous imagery of the poem."

set, sit These two verbs are commonly confused. *Set* meaning "to put or place" is a transitive verb and takes an object. *Sit* meaning "to be seated" is an intransitive verb. "You can set your books on the desk and then sit in that chair."

shall, will In American usage the dominant practice is to use *will* in the second and third persons to express either futurity or determination and to use either *will* or *shall* in the first person.

In addition, *shall* is used in statements of law ("Congress shall have the power to . . . "), in military commands ("The regiment shall proceed as directed"), and in formal directives ("All branch offices shall report weekly to the home office").

should, would These words are used as the past forms of *shall* and *will* respectively and follow the same pattern (see **shall, will**): "I would [should] be glad to see him tomorrow"; "He would welcome your ideas on the subject"; "We would [should] never consent to such an arrangement." They are also used to convert *shall* or *will* in direct discourse into indirect discourse:

Direct Discourse	**Indirect Discourse**
"Shall I try to arrange it?" he asked.	He asked if he should try to arrange it.
I said, "They will need money."	I said that they would need money.

should of See **could of.**

sight, site, cite See **cite, sight, site.**

so (conj.) The use of *so* as a connective ("The salesperson refused to exchange the merchandise, so we went to the manager") is thoroughly respectable, but its overuse in college writing is objectionable. There are other good transitional connectives—*accordingly, for that reason, on that account, therefore*—that could be used to relieve the monotony of a series of *so*'s. Occasional use of subordination ("When the salesperson refused to exchange the merchandise, we went to the manager") also brings variety to the style.

some   The use of *some* as an adjective of indeterminate number ("Some friends of yours were here") is acceptable at all levels of writing. Its use as an intensive ("That was some meal!") or as an adverb ("She cried some after you left"; "This draft is some better than the first one") should be avoided in college writing.

sort of   See **kind of.**

stationary, stationery   *Stationary* means "fixed" or "unchanging": "The battle front is now stationary." *Stationery* means "writing paper": "a box of stationery." To remember the distinction, associate the *e* in *stationery* with the *e*'s in *letter.*

suit, suite   The common word is *suit:* "A suit of clothes"; "Follow suit, play a diamond"; "Suit yourself." *Suite,* pronounced "sweet," means "retinue" ("The President and his suite have arrived") or "set" or "collection" ("a suite of rooms," "a suite of furniture"). When *suite* refers to furniture, an alternative pronunciation is "suit."

sure = certainly   Using *sure* in the sense of "certainly" ("I am sure annoyed"; "Sure, I will go with you") is colloquial. Unless the style justifies colloquial usage, use *certainly* or *surely.*

terrific   Used at a formal level to mean "terrifying" ("a terrific epidemic") and at a colloquial level as an intensive ("a terrific party," "a terrific pain"). Overuse of the word at the colloquial level has made it almost meaningless.

than, then   *Than* is a conjunction used in comparison; *then* is an adverb indicating time. Do not confuse the two: "I would rather write in the morning than in the afternoon. My thinking seems to be clearer then."

that, which, who   *That* refers to persons or things, *which* refers to things, and *who* refers to persons. *That* introduces a restrictive clause, and *which* usually introduces a nonrestrictive clause: "John argued that he was not prepared to take the exam, but the exam, which had been scheduled for some time, could not be changed"; "Anyone who was not ready would have to take the test anyway."

there, their, they're   Although these words are pronounced alike, they have different meanings. *There* indicates place: "Look at that dog over there." *Their* indicates possession: "I am sure it is their dog." *They're* is a contraction of "they are": "They're probably not home."

thusly   Not an acceptable variant of *thus.*

tough   The use of *tough* to mean "difficult" ("a tough assignment," "a tough decision") and "hard fought" ("a tough game") is accepted without qualification by reputable dictionaries. But its use to mean "unfortunate," "bad" ("The fifteen-yard penalty was a tough break for the team"; "That's tough") is colloquial and should be used only in a paper written in a colloquial style.

troop, troupe Both words come from the same root and share the original meaning, "herd." In modern usage *troop* can refer to soldiers and *troupe* to actors: "a troop of cavalry," "a troop of scouts," "a troupe of circus performers," "a troupe of entertainers."

try and *Try to* is the preferred idiom. Use "I will try to do it" instead of "I will try and do it."

type = type of *Type* is not acceptable as a variant form of *type of.* In "That type engine isn't being manufactured anymore," add *of* after *type.*

uninterested, disinterested See **disinterested.**

unique The formal meaning of *unique* is "sole" or "only" or "being the only one of its kind": "Adam was unique in being the only man who never had a mother." The use of *unique* to mean "rare" or "unusual" ("Americans watched their television sets anxiously as astronauts in the early moon landings had the unique experience of walking on the moon") has long been popular, but some people still object to this usage. The use of *unique* to mean merely "uncommon" ("a unique sweater") is generally frowned upon. *Unique* should not be modified by adverbs that express degree: *very, more, most, rather.*

up The adverb *up* is idiomatically used in many verb-adverb combinations that act as verbs—*break up, clean up, fill up, get up, tear up.* Avoid the unnecessary or awkward separation of *up* from the verb with which it is combined, since such a separation makes *up* look at first like an adverb modifying the verb rather than an adverb combining with the verb in an idiomatic expression. For example, "They held the cashier up" and "She made her face up" are awkward. Say "They held up the cashier," "She made up her face."

use to The *d* in *used to* is often not pronounced; it is elided before the *t* in *to.* The resulting pronunciation leads to the written expression *use to.* But the acceptable written phrase is *used to:* "I am used to the noise"; "He used to do all the grocery shopping."

very A common intensive, but avoid its overuse.

wait on *Wait on* means "serve": "A clerk will be here in a moment to wait on you." The use of *wait on* to mean "wait for" ("I'll wait on you if you won't be long") is a colloquialism to which there is some objection. Use *wait for:* "I'll wait for you if you won't be long."

want in, out, off The use of *want* followed by *in, out,* or *off* ("The dog wants in"; "I want out of here"; "I want off now") is colloquial. In college writing supply an infinitive after the verb: "The dog wants to come in."

want to = ought to, should Using *want to* as a synonym for *should* ("They want to be careful or they will be in trouble") is colloquial. *Ought to* or *should* is preferred in college writing.

where . . . at, to The use of *at* or *to* after *where* ("Where was he at?" "Where are you going to?") is redundant. Simply write "Where was he?" and "Where are you going?"

whose, who's   *Whose* is the possessive of *who; who's* is a contraction of *who is:* "In the play, John is the character whose son leaves town. Who's going to try out for that part?"

will, shall   See **shall, will.**

-wise   Avoid adding the suffix *-wise,* meaning "concerning," to nouns to form such combinations as *budgetwise, jobwise, tastewise.* Some combined forms with *-wise* are thoroughly established (*clockwise, otherwise, sidewise, weatherwise*), but the fad of coining new compounds with this suffix is generally best avoided.

without = unless   *Without* is not accepted as a conjunction meaning "unless." In "There will be no homecoming festivities without student government sponsors them," substitute *unless* for *without.*

with respect to   See **as to.**

worst way   When *in the worst way* means "very much" ("They wanted to go in the worst way"), it is too informal for college writing.

would, should   See **should, would.**

would of   See **could of.**

would have = had   *Would* is the past-tense form of *will,* but its overuse in student writing often results in awkwardness, especially, but not only, when it is used as a substitute for *had.* Contrast the following sentences:

Awkward	Revised
If they *would have done* that earlier, there *would have been* no trouble.	If they *had done* that earlier, there *would have been* no trouble.
	or:
	Had they *done* that earlier, there *would have been* no trouble.
We *would want* some assurance that they *would accept* before we *would make* such a proposal.	We *would want* some assurance of their acceptance before we *made* such a proposal.

In general, avoid the repetition of *would have* in the same sentence.

you = one   The use of *you* as an indefinite pronoun instead of the formal *one* is characteristic of an informal style. If you adopt *you* in an informal paper, be sure that this impersonal use will be recognized by your readers; otherwise, they are likely to interpret a general statement as a personal remark addressed specifically to them. Generally avoid shifting from *one* to *you* within a sentence (see page 493).

yourself   *Yourself* is appropriately used as an intensifier ("You yourself told me that") and as a reflexive object ("You are blaming yourself too much"). But usages such as the following are not acceptable: "Marian and yourself must shoulder the responsibility" and "The instructions were intended for Kate and yourself." In these two sentences, replace *yourself* with *you.* The plural form is *yourselves,* not *yourselfs.*

Index of Authors and Titles

Index

A BRIEF GUIDE TO THE HANDBOOK

(Continued)